Archaeology and Bible

Edited by

Israel Finkelstein (Tel Aviv) · Deirdre Fulton (Waco, TX)
Oded Lipschits (Tel Aviv) · Christophe Nihan (Lausanne)
Thomas Römer (Lausanne) · Konrad Schmid (Zürich)

6

Jordan Davis

The End of the Book of Numbers

On Pentateuchal Models and
Compositional Issues

Mohr Siebeck

Jordan Davis, born 1983; Master of Divinity (Whitley College – University of Divinity, Melbourne, Australia); Doktor der Theologie (Universität Zürich, Zürich, Switzerland).
orcid.org/0000-0002-6736-762X

Published with the support of the Swiss National Science Foundation.

ISSN 978-3-16-161856-7 / eISBN 978-3-16-161857-4
DOI 10.1628/978-3-16-161857-4
ISSN 2698-4520 / eISSN 2698-4539 (Archaeology and Bible)

The Deutsche Nationalbibliothek lists this publication in the Deutsche Nationalbibliographie; detailed bibliographic data are available at *http://dnb.dnb.de*.

© 2022 Mohr Siebeck Tübingen, Germany. www.mohrsiebeck.com

This book may not be reproduced, in whole or in part, in any form (beyond that permitted by copyright law) without the publisher's written permission.

The book was typeset by Martin Fischer in Tübingen, printed on non-aging paper by Laupp & Göbel in Gomaringen and bound by Buchbinderei Nädele in Nehren.

Printed in Germany.

For Joanna and Finn.

Preface

The following monograph grew out of a broader project entitled "The History of the Pentateuch: Combining Literary and Archaeological Approaches," funded by the Swiss National Science Foundation (Sinergia project CRSII1160785). The project – a joint venture of the universities of Zurich, Lausanne and Tel Aviv – was directed by Konrad Schmid (Zurich), Christophe Nihan and Thomas Römer (Lausanne), and Israel Finkelstein and Oded Lipschits (Tel Aviv). When I heard that I had been selected to take part in this prestigious project on the formation of the Pentateuch I was elated. However, I must confess that I found the idea of investigating "historical geography" rather daunting. Not only did I have very little exposure to archaeological matters from my previous studies, but I found the concept of looking at place names rather insipid. However, my ignorance proved to be greatly misguided, as it turned out historical geography not only opened the doors to new insights into the biblical text itself but also towards questions of those texts' place within the formation of the Pentateuch. Furthermore, the geographical findings are arguably the most interesting part of the argument … Mea culpa.

The resulting monograph features only a single name on the cover, however there were, of course, many supporting figures who undeniably helped it reach its final form.

Konrad Schmid, who not only made the decision to accept me as a doctoral student but who also suggested that I apply for the Sinergia project on the formation of the Pentateuch. Konrad not only helped me in his supervisory role but has continued to support me long after this official requirement ended. I feel lucky to have such a role model during this formative stage in my career.

Christian Frevel, for whom I worked as a research assistant during the writing of my dissertation. Christian's own work on the book of Numbers and the history of ancient Israel provided an enormous influence on my own thinking and I consider myself fortunate to have been in a position to engage with his work so closely. Christian also inspired me with his tireless work ethic and I am especially grateful for the detailed feedback he provided on the final draft of my dissertation.

Many other friends and colleagues contributed to my journey as well: Julia Rhyder, my fellow Aussie in Europe, with whom I had countless fruitful discussions and who continues to be an unending source of encouragement and in-

VIII   *Preface*

spiration. Jürg Hutzli, with whom I worked alongside as a co-editor as part of the Sinergia project and who provided welcome feedback on my dealings with the Priestly texts in Genesis. Katharina Pyschny, who shared her expertise on the book of Numbers and provided helpful critiques of my early ideas. Christophe Nihan, who invited me to present a workshop wherein I could discuss my ideas with the research team in Lausanne.

I would also like to thank the editors of ArchB – Israel Finkelstein, Deirdre Fulton, Oded Lipschits, Christophe Nihan, Thomas Römer, and Konrad Schmid – for accepting this monograph into the series and Mohr Siebeck for the publication – especially Elena Müller for her advice and help during the preparation and Markus Kirchner for his detailed feedback.

Finally, I wish to thank my family: My parents – Peter, Anne and Graeme – for their encouragement and support. My son Finn, who was born during the PhD and who provided countless hours of distraction and joy. And my wife, Jo, who left the good life in Melbourne to move to a country whose language we did not speak in pursuit of this crazy academic dream of mine.

Lastly, I would like to mention one study that I only became aware of too late in my own research: Dylan R. Johnson, *Sovereign Authority and the Elaboration of Law in the Bible and the Ancient Near East*. FAT II 122 (Tübingen: Mohr Siebeck, 2020). Dylan, a fellow researcher at UZH, also has extensive chapters on Num 27 (pp. 217–265) and Num 36 (pp. 266–295).

Zürich, 2022   Jordan Davis

Table of Contents

List of Figures XIII
List of Tables XIV

Chapter 1: Introduction 1

Chapter 2: Setting the Stage: Background for Understanding
the Book of Numbers 7

2.1 Pentateuchal Models and the Book of Numbers 7

2.1.1 The Documentary Hypothesis 7
    2.1.1.1 A Brief History of the Source Model 7
    2.1.1.2 The Problem of Deuteronomy 8
    2.1.1.3 The Documentary Hypothesis and the Book of Numbers 10
2.1.2 The Pentateuchal Crisis and the Introduction of New Models 17
    2.1.2.1 Farewell to the Yahwist 17
    2.1.2.2 The End of Pg and the Holiness Code 18
    2.1.2.3 The Bridge-Book Hypothesis 22
    2.1.2.4 Numbers as Part of a Pre-Priestly Narrative Composition 31
    2.1.2.5 Summary of Pentateuchal Models 40

2.2 Toward Certainty: Increasing the Size of the Data Pool 41

2.2.1 Empirical Evidence Regarding the Conflation of Sources 42
2.2.2 Extra-biblical Evidence and Historical Geography 46
2.2.3 The Samaritan Influence and the Formation of the Pentateuch 49

2.3 In Favour of an Exodus-Conquest Narrative 52

2.3.1 Jeroboam II and the Moses Story 53
2.3.2 Josiah and Early Joshua 56

2.4 The Structure of Numbers 68

Chapter 3: The Occupation of Transjordan 81

3.1 Old Layers and Historical Memories? 82

3.1.1 Reflecting on the Geography of Numbers 32:1 82
    3.1.1.1 Literary Geography 84

X   *Table of Contents*

3.1.1.2 Geographical Analysis 85
3.1.1.3 Historical Analysis 88
3.1.1.4 In Support of the Pre-Sihon Base Layer of Numbers 32 93
3.1.2 More Pre-Sihon Traditions 96
3.1.3 Tracing the Base Layer of Numbers 32 98
3.1.4 Reflections on the Non-Priestly Layer 107

3.2 The Sihon Tradition 109

3.2.1 Deuteronomy 2:24–3:18* and the Problem of Settlement
    in the Transjordan 110
3.2.2 Numbers 21:21–35* 125
3.2.3 Heshbon, Sihon's City 134
3.2.4 Sihon the Amorite? 137

3.3 Post-Sihon, Non-Priestly Updates in Numbers 32 139

3.3.1 Numbers 32:34–38 144
3.3.2 Numbers 32:39–42* and the Half-Tribe of Manasseh 148
3.3.3 Summary of the Non-Priestly, Post-Sihon Changes 153

3.4 Transjordan and the Priestly Material 153

3.4.1 Canaan and the Priestly Ideology of Land 154
3.4.2 The Priestly Elements in Numbers 32 159
3.4.3 Reflections on the Priestly Layer 164

3.5 Conquest of the Amorites 165

3.5.1 Deuteronomy Re-Imagines the Promised Land 166
3.5.2 Updating the Sihon Narrative in Numbers 21 169
3.5.3 Further Deuteronomistic Influences in Numbers 32 169

3.6 Joining Priestly and Deuteronomistic Texts 172

3.6.1 Completing the Sihon Narrative 172
3.6.2 Completing Numbers 32 176
    3.6.2.1 Leadership Harmonisation 178
    3.6.2.2 "City" Harmonisation 179
    3.6.2.3 Ideological Harmonisation 182
    3.6.2.4 Continuity Harmonisation 183

3.7 Conclusion 188

Chapter 4: Female Inheritance 191

4.1 The Legal Conundrum 193

4.2 The Universal Legislation for Heiresses: Num 27:8–11a 194

4.2.1 Property, Marriage and Inheritance in Ancient Israel 195

Table of Contents XI

4.2.2 Supplement or Replacement? Numbers 27:8–11a
and Deuteronomy 25:5–10 199
4.2.3 Summary 207

4.3 The Specific Case of Zelophehad's Daughters: Num 27:1–7a 208

4.4 Historical Connection to Zelophehad's Daughters? 218
4.4.1 The Wedge-shape Decorated Bowl 219
4.4.2 The Neo-Assyrian Two-way Deportation 223
4.4.3 On Pots and People 228
4.4.4 Other Biblical Support 229
4.4.4.1 Joshua 17:1–12 232
4.4.4.2 1 Kings 4:7–19 235
4.4.5 Summary 241

4.5 Numbers 36:1–12 in Detail 244

4.6 Conclusion 257

Chapter 5: Conclusion 261

5.1 Verifiable* Exegetical Tools 262
5.1.1 "Empirical" Studies on Conflation 262
5.1.2 Extra-biblical Evidence 263
5.1.3 Northern Traditions 263

5.2 Compositional Findings 264
5.2.1 Numbers 32 264
5.3.2 Zelophehad's Daughters 266

5.3 In Models We Trust 268

5.4 Clear Avenues for Further Research 270

Appendix: Comparison of Recent Models
vs the Documentary Hypothesis 273

Bibliography 277
Index of Ancient Sources 305
Index of Authors 308
Index of Subjects 311

List of Figures

Figure 1: Conquest according to Joshua 6–10* 58

Figure 2: Linear geographical structure of the exodus-conquest narrative 72

Figure 3: Generation change layered onto the exodus-conquest narrative 73

Figure 4: The Post-Priestly Pentateuch 74

Figure 5: Multiple structure of Numbers 75

Figure 6: Modified Gantt Chart of Numbers 26–36 with conceptual links 76

Figure 7: Reconstruction of Num 32:1 according to FINKELSTEIN et al. 87

Figure 8: Reconstruction of Num 32:1 according to the present analysis 91

Figure 9: Transjordan of Sihon and Og 113

Figure 10: "Heshbon and all its villages" and the King's Highway 131

Figure 11: Num 32:34–42 – Territories of Reuben, Gad and Half-Manasseh 145

Figure 12: Cities listed in Num 32:3 181

Figure 13: Map of "Zelophehad's daughters." 220

Figure 14: "Solomon's" districts 240

List of Tables

Table 1: Population changes between the first and second census 5

Table 2: Comparison of Num 22:1bβ; 26:3aγb; 36:13b 70

Table 3: Numbers 21:24 according to the MT and LXX 94

Table 4: Non-Priestly narrative of Numbers 32 99

Table 5: Tribal naming by verse 99

Table 6: Comparison of Sihon layers in Deuteronomy 112

Table 7: Comparison of Deut 2:24aβb and Deut 2:31 120

Table 8: Original Sihon Layer in Numbers 125

Table 9: Post-Sihon updates to the Non-Priestly narrative 139

Table 10: Side by side – Non-Priestly and Priestly narratives 161

Table 11: Comparison of the Sihon and Og narratives in Deuteronomy 167

Table 12: Numbers 32:1–42 177

Table 13: Comparison of Num 32:32 with Num 32:19b, 27 182

Table 14: Numbers 27:8–11a 194

Table 15: Numbers 27:1–7a 208

Table 16: Comparison of Num 27:7b and Num 27:8b 217

Table 17: Comparison of Num 27:4b and Num 27:7aβ 218

Table 18: Numbers 36:1–12 244

Table 19: Comparison of Num 27:1 and Num 36:1 245

Table 20: Comparison of Num 36:6b and Num 36:8aβ 256

Table 21: Comparison of Num 36:7 and Num 36:9 256

Chapter 1

Introduction

After the fire had extinguished atop the mountain and the embers had dulled, after the smoke had cleared to be remembered only by its lingering taint upon the clothes of all who had borne witness, after the ringing in the ears from the trumpet blast had faded, after the smell of blood from those slain by the Levites had been blown away, Israel departed the mountain.

It is in the aftermath of this most glorious and terrible scene that the book of Numbers begins. Yet even here, after all that had just transpired, the ineffability of the divine and the chosen nature of Moses still struggled to take root. Before leaving the shadow of the mountain Moses does not turn to Yhwh for guidance but to his Midianite brother-in-law, Hobab. We are told that they conversed and learn that Moses wants Hobab to join Israel on its journey; although there was likely some degree of familial duty involved, the real reason for the invitation is that Moses does not even know where to camp (Num 10:31). Israel's wilderness journey, then, appears to have been confusing not only for modern readers but for Moses also. As MacDonald observes, "For Israel and for the reader, the book of Numbers is an unwelcome detour on the way to destinations more interesting."[1]

Much of Numbers' unpopularity in earlier scholarship was due to three main reasons. First, it was devoid of most of the major themes of the Pentateuch (the history of origins, the patriarchal tradition, Israel's journey to the mountain of God) and so – perhaps justifiably – received less attention than the other Pentateuchal books. Second, of the five books in the Pentateuch, Numbers was the book in which the Documentary Hypothesis was the least effective.[2] Martin Noth, in particular, brought this observation into the limelight when he observed that had it been analysed in isolation, one would not conclude that Numbers was comprised of the three primary sources. However, the dominance of the Documentary Hypothesis and the lack of any viable alternatives at the time was also aptly demonstrated as Noth went on to conclude that because the source model was so effective at explaining the rest of the Pentateuch, one should also use it

---

[1] MacDonald, "Numbers," 113. Römer, "périphérie," 3, notes, "peu d'attention est accordée au livre des Nombres cependant" (*Little attention is given to the book of Numbers, however*).

[2] More accurately, the "New" Documentary Hypothesis, as developed particularly by Graf, *Bücher*; Kuenen, *Inquiry*; Wellhausen, *Composition*; Wellhausen, *Prolegomena*. For further discussion see, Baden, *Redaction*; Rogerson, "Protestant," 211; Römer, "Higher"; Smend, "Work." For a detailed exploration of nineteenth century scholarship on the Hebrew Bible/Old Testament, see Sæbø, HBOT 3.1.

to analyse the book of Numbers.[3] Lastly, the book's mixture of narratives, lists and legal materials was also deemed problematic, producing a work that was, at least to some degree, confusing. Binns, for example, observed in his 1927 commentary:

> As a piece of literature [the book of Numbers] falls short of the highest class owing to its lack of unity and proportion. At the same time it cannot be denied that it contains narratives of the greatest merit, strung like pearls on a string, but the underlying idea has been obscured by too great a profusion of detail, and the various authors and editors – even down to the unknown scribe who gave the book its final form – were not at one in their aims.[4]

Since the turn of the millennium things have begun to change for the book of Numbers, and it is now experiencing something of a renaissance in Pentateuchal scholarship.[5] This renaissance has resulted in new models being produced, which among other things seek to better explain the fourth book of the Pentateuch. These new models have only really been possible in light of the weakening of the Documentary Hypothesis, which no longer maintains its monopolistic position. The peculiar nature of Numbers and its contrarian relationship to the Documentary Hypothesis are the precise reasons that make it arguably the best testing ground for new hypotheses. The book of Numbers thus functions as the litmus test for the validity of new theories on the development of the Pentateuch.[6]

Despite being "freed" from the constraints of the Documentary Hypothesis, no new model has attained anywhere near the success of the source model. Indeed, the opposite rather seems to be the case, now more than ever is the field filled with dissenting voices. One major effort in the attempt to bring the wider field into closer alignment resulted in the volume entitled, *The Formation of the Pentateuch: Bridging the Academic Cultures of Europe, Israel, and North America.* In the volume's introduction the editors write:

---

[3] NOTH, *Numbers*, 4–5, writes, "If we were to take the book of Numbers on its own, then we would think not so much of 'continuous sources' as of an unsystematic collection of innumerable pieces of tradition of varied content, age and character ('Fragment Hypothesis'). But it would be contrary to the facts of the matter, as will already be clear from the contents of the book, to treat Numbers in isolation. From the first, the book has belonged, in the Old Testament canon, to the larger whole of the Pentateuch, and scholarly work on the book has consistently maintained that it must be seen in this wider context. It is therefore, justifiable to approach the book of Numbers with the results of Pentateuchal analysis achieved elsewhere and to expect the continuing Pentateuchal 'sources' here, too, even if, as we have said, the situation in Numbers, of itself, does not exactly lead us to these results."

[4] BINNS, *Numbers*, xiv.

[5] The title of RÖMER, "périphérie," rightly captures the idea that the study of Numbers has now moved from "de la périphérie au centre" (*from the periphery to the centre*). FREVEL, "Stücke," 271, likewise argues that the book of Numbers is now integral to discussions of literary history, the history of religion and theology. See the collected works by RÖMER, "Books;" FREVEL et al., *Torah.*

[6] This fact led ALBERTZ, "Numeri I," to begin his analysis with Numbers 20–21, two chapters of renowned redactional complexity.

1. Introduction

3

Recent decades have witnessed not simply a proliferation of intellectual models but, in many ways much more seriously, the fragmentation of discourse altogether as scholarly communities in the three main research centers of Israel, Europe and North America increasingly talk past one another ... scholars tend to operate from such different premises, employ such divergent methods, and reach such inconsistent results that meaningful progress has become impossible. The models continue to proliferate but the communication seems only to diminish.[7]

Although it must be admitted that it is not possible to analyse the Pentateuch without any model or without any presuppositions, it is possible to seek analytical methods that are less tightly correlated with a particular model. The present work, then, suggests some tools that can be used with any model in the hopes of engaging (at least as far as possible) in a text-to-model analysis rather than a model-to-text one. These tools are (1) the increased attention paid to "empirical" evidence for processes of literary production from both biblical and non-biblical literature, (2) non-biblical historical evidence, not least geographical references, and (3) the renewed attention paid to the "Northern Kingdom" (in both preexilic and postexilic periods) in the formation of the Pentateuch.[8] Why are these tools useful and why are they important?

Recent advances in the history of the ancient Levant have not only increased the reliability of data, but also significantly increased the amount of available data. This increase in data has caused dramatic shifts throughout the broader study of the ancient Near East, not least in Hebrew Bible studies. To provide one key example, the increased number of excavations performed in and around Jerusalem have helped bring the idea of a "Solomonic Golden Age" into serious doubt.[9] This in turn has given rise to the need for new explanations, not only for

---

[7] GERTZ et al., "Convergence," 2–3.

[8] Of course, the Northern Kingdom proper ended with the Assyrians, however a blanket term for Yahwists north of Judah/Judea/Yehud is lacking.

[9] SCHMID, *History*, 50, for example, argues, "viewed historically, we must now distance ourselves both from the political notion of a Davidic-Solomonic empire, projected by the Old Testament literature as a 'Golden Age,' and from the idea of a literary industry flowering in that period." FREVEL, *Geschichte*, 175, summarises: "Nimmt man die archäologischen und historischen Hinweise zusammen, ist die blühende vereinte Monarchie unter Salomo mehr Legende als Wirklichkeit. Die Evidenz reicht nicht aus, um verantwortet an der biblischen Darstellung festzuhalten. Die Legenden weisen zu weiten Teilen auf Zustände des 8. Jh.s v. Chr. Salomos Pracht war nicht Nichts, aber sie war sicher auch nicht groß. Für eine 'salomonische Aufklärung' (G. von Rad) jedenfalls fehlen ebenso die Voraussetzungen wie für umfassende Literaturproduktionen und Geschichtswerke. Vor dem Hintergrund der Entstehung der zwei Staaten Israel und Juda und der Erkenntnis, dass von einer vereinten Monarchie Abschied zu nehmen ist, muss die Frage gestellt werden, ob Salomo überhaupt eine historische Person gewesen ist. Die Frage lässt sich anders als bei David bisher nicht durch außerbiblische Zeugnisse positiv beantworten. Vieles lässt sich besser erklären, wenn die literarische Überlieferung zu Salomo in mehreren Schüben zusammen mit der Überzeichnung des Königs David, wie die Darstellung der Reichsteilung und die Darstellung der Frühphase der Königtümer Israel und Juda, als Brücke zwischen der älteren Davidüberlieferung und den Annalen der Omriden ge-

4 *I. Introduction*

the history of Israel and Judah in general, but also for the formation of the biblical traditions. Although scholars have always tried to link the biblical materials to history, it is not surprising that when one's view of history changes, one's understanding of the biblical traditions is also likely to change. One of the major goals of the present work, then, is to take a closer look at the topographical information contained in the biblical material and to see if new solutions can be found regarding the composition of those biblical texts in light of more up to date archaeological and historical results.

A further key insight used in the ensuing exegesis is the idea that one of the major drivers behind textual modification is ideological divergence. The present work takes this key insight gained from recent empirical investigations on textual conflation and editorial activity, which concludes that when ideological changes are minor, then the editing of the text is correspondingly minor, when a larger ideological shift is introduced, this introduces a much more overt change to the text.

With these tools in hand the question is: Which text(s) to analyse? Even among the newest Pentateuchal models the final chapters of Numbers remain somewhat mysterious. Thomas Römer, in a modified way, follows Noth's proposal that the final section of the book represents something of a "rolling corpus," in which disparate material was simply appended in the order in which it appeared. Reinhard Achenbach argues (with a few exceptions) that the entirety of Numbers 26–36 is the work of the three-part, post-Pentateuchal theocratic redactor (ThB I–III). Rainer Albertz goes even further and suggests that Num 25:19–36:13 is the work of a single redactor, PB5, whose major goal was to compensate for the loss of Joshua when the Hexateuch (Genesis – Joshua) was reduced to the Pentateuch (Genesis – Deuteronomy).[10] Thus, despite the hundreds of pages that have been

---

schaffen worden ist." (*If the archaeological and historical references are taken together, the flourishing United Monarchy under Solomon is more legend than reality. The evidence is not sufficient to maintain the biblical presentation in a responsible manner. The legend points to conditions of the 8th century* BCE. *Solomon's splendor was not nothing, but it certainly was not great either. For a 'Solomonic Enlightenment' [G. von Rad], at any rate, the prerequisites are lacking, as are comprehensive literary productions and historical works. Against the background of the emergence of the two states, Israel and Judah, and the realization that it is time to say goodbye to a United Monarchy, the question must be asked whether Solomon was a historical person at all. In contrast to David, this question cannot yet be answered positively by non-biblical testimonies. Much can be better explained if the literary tradition of Solomon was created in several phases together with the exaggeration of King David, such as the depiction of the division of the kingdom and the depiction of the early phase of the kingdoms of Israel and Judah, as a bridge between the older tradition of David and the annals of the Omrides.*) With regards to the biblical depiction of a Solomonic "Golden Age," KNAUF/GUILLAUME, *History*, 76, argue that the story of Solomon projects, "the glory of the Assyrian Empire onto a fabulous past to show how such an empire can only lead to ruin."

[10] This led ALBERTZ, "Redaction," 230, to propose that Numbers 25:19–36:13 was designed as a replacement of the book of Joshua by the editor responsible for shortening the Hexateuch into a Pentateuch. Speaking of the Transjordan conquest in Numbers 32 he writes, "This topic

1. Introduction   5

written on Numbers since its "return to glory," the issues pertaining to the final section of the book have remained largely unresolved.

The present work analyses two key traditions – one narrative, one legislative – that have a high chance of yielding positive results with regard to compositional questions. Although containing clearly disparate material, the final section of the book of Numbers can be summarised by the themes of conquest and settlement, both in its preparation and its enactment. The dense accumulation of topographic detail in the final section of the book of Numbers allow for recent archaeological advances to play a major role. Furthermore, the final section of Numbers features a curious emphasis on the tribe of Manasseh (cf. table 1), which at least *prima facie* provides a promising avenue for investigating the involvement of Northern scribes and traditions.

The narrative of Numbers 32 and the narrative-legislation of Numbers 27 and 36, then, represent a fortuitous intersection of redaction-critical difficulties, geographical details, and the tribe of Manasseh. Numbers 32 details the settlement of the Transjordan tribes, which includes the sudden and unexpected appearance of the half-tribe of Manasseh in the final verses. Numbers 27:1–11 and 36:1–12 are paired pericopes, united by the inheritance issues relating to the Manassite Zelophehad's daughters. Thus, these chapters represent fertile ground to make use of the three investigative tools identified above.

Via a detailed exegesis of these key chapters, it will be demonstrated that the compositional growth of the final section of the book of Numbers is neither the result of a disordered series of appendages, nor is it the product of a particularly limited number of late redactors.

Tribe	Population Change between Numbers 1 and Numbers 26	Tribe	Population Change between Numbers 1 and Numbers 26
Reuben	-2770	*Manasseh*	*+20500*
Simeon	-37100	Ephraim	-8000
Gad	-5150	Benjamin	+10200
Judah	+1900	Dan	+1700
Issachar	+9900	Asher	+11900
Zebulun	+3100	Naphtali	-8000

Table 1: Population changes between the first and second census

would well fit a redactor who was obliged to exclude the book of Joshua from Israel's founding document, on the one hand, but did not want to lose its important message within the Pentateuch, on the other hand."

Chapter 2

Setting the Stage: Background for Understanding the Book of Numbers

It is not possible to understand the current research on Numbers without a sufficient grounding in the underlying discussions on the formation of the Pentateuch. This chapter seeks to provide a general orientation regarding theories on the formation of the Pentateuch. This in turn will lead to a fuller discussion of the three key extra-biblical tools noted in the introduction. With these tools and the foregoing discussion on models, a broad proposal will be made regarding the origins of the Pentateuch. Finally, an overview of the structure of Numbers will be presented, with particular attention given to the final chapters of the book. All in all, this chapter functions as the foundation upon which the following exegetical chapters are built.

2.1 Pentateuchal Models and the Book of Numbers

It should come as no surprise that the resurgence in Numbers' popularity has a high degree of correlation with the recent shifts in Pentateuchal theory, or more precisely, with the models regarding the formation of the Pentateuch. Simply put, it was only after the Documentary Hypothesis lost its monopoly on Pentateuchal scholarship that the book of Numbers became a topic of interest. There are several factors relating to this that will be elaborated below.

2.1.1 The Documentary Hypothesis

2.1.1.1 A Brief History of the Source Model

As Otto remarks, it is rather ironic that source criticism first arose in order to defend the Mosaic authorship of the Pentateuch.[1] Astruc's[2] original conviction that Moses must have consulted various sources in order to write Genesis and the beginning of Exodus was continuously expanded by scholars such as de Wette[3]

---

[1] Otto, "Meaning," 29.

[2] Astruc only analysed Exodus up to chapter 2 because he believed the rest of the book to be genuinely Mosaic. See discussion in, e.g., Harvey Jr./Halpern, "Dissertatio," 51–52.

[3] De Wette, "Dissertatio." See discussion in Otto, "Truth."

8   *2. Setting the Stage*

and Hupfeld[4] to arrive at the idea that the entire Pentateuch was composed from various sources.

This trend in Pentateuchal criticism climaxed at the end of the nineteenth century with the so-called "New" Documentary Hypothesis, which is most famously connected with the names Graf,[5] Kuenen[6] and Wellhausen[7].[8] It was Wellhausen's *Prolegomena to the History of Israel* that largely settled the debates about the Documentary Hypothesis by concluding that the sources should be chronologically ordered with respect to the development of Israelite society and particularly in relation to cult centralisation – the Covenant Code, as the representative JE text, presented a decentralised cult (see esp. Exod 20:24), Deuteronomy (D) centralised the cult to one place (see esp. Deut 12:13–14), and P presupposed a centralised cult with its single sanctuary administered by a select priestly family – thus arriving at the well-known abbreviated sequence JEDP.[9] Such was the power of the Documentary Hypothesis as an explanatory framework that it held a virtual monopoly for almost a century, and even now, in the 21st century, it continues to play a significant role.[10]

2.1.1.2 The Problem of Deuteronomy

Having rearranged the chronological order of the four sources to JEDP, the New Documentary Hypothesis had difficulty explaining the book of Deuteronomy. The first difficulty was that Deuteronomy was the only source that functioned in a more or less standalone way. A more significant issue was that the Priestly source, although being the youngest, was largely absent in the book of Deuteronomy.[11] In contrast, de Wette's earlier model proposed that Deuteronomy was different to the other sources because it constituted the final layer of the Hexateuch/Pentateuch and thus the absence of P in Deuteronomy was not an issue.[12]

In 1943, Martin Noth proposed an answer to this problem that became the mainstay of Old Testament scholarship for the next half century.[13] Noting the

---

[4] See discussion in, e.g., VAN SETERS, *Edited*; BADEN, *Redaction*; RÖMER, "Higher."

[5] See discussion in ROGERSON, "Protestant," 211.

[6] KUENEN, *Inquiry*. See also SMEND, "Work."

[7] WELLHAUSEN, *Prolegomena*.

[8] See esp. overview in RÖMER, "Higher."

[9] WELLHAUSEN, *Prolegomena*, 27–169.

[10] As CARR, "Changes," 434, observes, "This basic four source theory for the formation of the Pentateuch … could be presupposed as given by most scholars writing on Pentateuchal topics for over a hundred years. It held sway over virtually all biblical scholarship, particularly in Euro-American contexts more or less linked to Protestant Christianity, from the rise of the Wellhausenian synthesis in the late nineteen hundreds to the later decades of the twentieth century."

[11] See esp. OTTO, "*Nachpriesterschriftlichen;*" OTTO, "Integration." This, of course, does not take into account recent discussions regarding the end of P. See below.

[12] See, e.g., OTTO, "Truth," 21.

[13] NOTH, *Studien*. See also RÖMER, "History."

many linguistic and stylistic links between the Former Prophets (Joshua – Kings) and Deuteronomy, Noth argued that these at one point constituted a self-contained epic of Israel's history. Noth proposed that in light of the fall of the kingdom of Judah, a scribe set out to interpret this catastrophe.[14] This explained why the Former Prophets (and Deuteronomy itself) could be seen to share a unified theology.[15] Noth called this composition the "Deuteronomistic History."[16]

The Deuteronomistic History introduced many benefits in understanding the structure and ideology of the Former Prophets and provided a simple explanation for the distinctive character of the book of Deuteronomy in the Pentateuch. However, it also meant that an explanation had to be provided for the Tetrateuch (Genesis – Numbers), which, devoid of the conquest and the death of Moses, was difficult to conceive as a complete standalone work.[17] Noth's solution to this problem was to suggest that the original ending of the Tetrateuch was lost or removed once the Pentateuch incorporated the book of Deuteronomy.[18]

The secondary literature on the Deuteronomistic History is immense, now spanning approximately 70 years of scholarship, and is still debated today.[19] Even for those in favour of a Deuteronomistic History, the model as originally proposed by Noth is rarely asserted.[20] Indeed, as Knauf succinctly observes, "In any case, Noth's Dtr has been abandoned by everyone."[21]

Efforts to retain the core idea of the Deuteronomistic History are achieved by modifying Noth's hypothesis with various expansions and alterations. Thus, Campbell likens the Deuteronomistic History to a house; its foundation and structure were built by Noth, but has become subject to numerous renovations, developments, and redecorations over time.[22]

---

[14] DE PURY/RÖMER, "Historiography," 51.

[15] RÖMER, "History," 648–649.

[16] For a detailed overview of the history of research, see DE PURY/RÖMER, "Historiography."

[17] ROSE, "Ideology," 426–427, for example, notes, "Noth's thesis actually destroys the unity of the Pentateuch (and the Torah) by excising Deuteronomy, which he makes the programmatic introduction of a great historiography." That said, it remains true that Deuteronomy is somehow separate. RÖMER, "Many," 39, for example, notes that of all the books in the Enneateuch (Genesis – 2 Kings) only Genesis, Deuteronomy, and 1 Samuel have "absolute beginnings," i.e., the remaining books open with joining introductions (e.g., "After the death of Moses ..." in Joshua 1:1). On the one hand this does speak to Deuteronomy being separate from the Tetrateuch, but the fact that 1 Samuel also contains an "absolute beginning" actually argues against the idea that Deuteronomy – 2 Kings were an originally stand-alone work.

[18] RÖMER, "Many," 27. Cf. OTTO, "Schlußstein."

[19] To name a few examples: MCKENZIE/GRAHAM, History; DE PURY et al., Israel; RÖMER, "Future;" GERTZ et al., Geschichtswerke.

[20] SCHMID, "Wellhausen," 20.

[21] KNAUF, "Historiography," 390.

[22] CAMPBELL, "History," 37. One of the most prominent "renovations" came from the Göttingen model, which asserted that there were three distinct layers of the Deuteronomistic History: a historical redaction (DtrH), a prophetic (DtrP), and a legislative (DtrN). For an overview of the Göttingen model, see, e.g., RÖMER, "History," 649–650.

10   2. Setting the Stage

Although much more could be said, it is sufficient to note that regarding the formation of the Pentateuch the concept of the Deuteronomistic History, in the most basic sense of a standalone work stretching from Deuteronomy – 2 Kings, is increasingly being understood to introduce more problems than it solves.[23] In light of this, it is becoming more common to speak of Deuteronomistic Histories in the plural, which represent editorial harmonisations in light of Deuteronomistic ideology rather than one single historical work.[24]

2.1.1.3 The Documentary Hypothesis and the Book of Numbers

It would be a mistake to suggest that all scholars follow the same concept of how the Documentary Hypothesis works. As Baden, for example, states, "from Wellhausen to Richard Elliott Friedman, virtually all adherents of the Documentary Hypothesis have posited three distinct redactions: J and E into 'JE,' by a redactor 'R^{JE}'; 'JE' and D into 'JED' by a redactor 'R^{JED}'; and JED and P into the canonical Pentateuch by the final reactor, 'R.'"[25] Yet Baden goes on to argue that this multiple compilation is not supported by the literary evidence and concludes, "There is, in short, no literary reason to assume more than one compiler for the canonical Pentateuch."[26]

However, for the purposes of the present discussion attention need not be given to these distinctions. Rather, the focus will rest upon the fundamental idea that, in all its variations, the Documentary Hypothesis assumes the Pentateuch is primarily composed from four originally standalone sources. Three of these sources – J, E and P – comprised narratives that spanned the whole pre-history of Israel, from creation until (at least) the death of Moses. The key point being

---

[23] To give only a sample of the criticisms now brought against the Deuteronomistic History. See, e.g., ALBERTZ, "Search;" FREVEL, "Geschichtswerk;" FREVEL, "Wiederkehr;" KNOPPERS, "Future;" KRATZ, "Ort;" SCHMID, "Emergence;" SCHMID, "Wellhausen;" VAN SETERS, *History*; VAN SETERS, "Redaction."

[24] As SCHMID, "Deuteronomy," 28, writes, "Regarding the thesis of a 'Deuteronomistic History,' it is clear in view of these considerations that this expression is only correct in the plural. There were various 'Deuteronomistic Histories' in the Enneateuch. One can discern an initial 'Deuteronomistic History' in Samuel – 2 Kings that was shaped not by Deut 12 but by the cult centralization in Jerusalem. Another 'Deuteronomistic History' is perceptible in Exodus – Joshua + Samuel – 2 Kings and is shaped by the first commandment, deriving its theological thrust through the literary arches of Exod 32 and 1 Kgs 12 as well as through the twofold theme of 'exodus from Egypt' and 'return to Egypt' in 2 Kgs 25:26 ('From Egypt to Egypt'). Finally, a third and, to my mind, post-Priestly 'Deuteronomistic History' is recognizable in Genesis – 2 Kings, which is already dominated by the notion of the 'Torah of Moses' that it applies to the story. Genesis – 2 Kings also coins the great literary inclusion stretching from Joseph in Egypt to King Jehoiachin at the table of the Babylonian king Amel-Marduk, thereby representing a diaspora theology for Israel." See also KNOPPERS, "Future;" FREVEL, "Geschichtswerk;" RÖMER, "History."

[25] BADEN, *Composition*, 218.

[26] BADEN, *Composition*, 221.

that issues with this model were observed well before the newer wave of criticism had taken root. Speaking of the Priestly material in Numbers Wellhausen had already observed that they "are in the style and colour of the Priestly Code, [but] have more and more the character of mere additions and editorial supplements to a connection which was already there and had a different origin."[27] This same difficulty was also clearly present in the analysis of Martin Noth noted above, who suggested that the source model as a whole was not really suitable for Numbers, but because of its effectiveness elsewhere in the Pentateuch applied it there anyway.[28]

As the following select survey will show, many commentaries using the Documentary Hypothesis recognised to a greater or lesser degree that the source theory was problematic for the contents of the book of Numbers, but for various reasons felt the need to continue to employ it as the foundation of their analysis.

A. Philip J. Budd

In his 1984 commentary, Budd observed that rather than being a relatively even mix of JE and P, the book of Numbers was primarily Priestly in nature. Even those chapters featuring non-Priestly materials were heavily reworked by Priestly hands.[29] Budd suggested that this points towards Numbers largely being a creation of the Babylonian golah and that it provided "both an apologia for this group of Jews, and also some programmatic proposals for restoration."[30]

Budd further identified several areas that are unique to the book of Numbers, which speak against its being purely composed of the same sources that run through Genesis – Leviticus. The first is the introduction of the Levitical order, which reinterprets the distinction made between Zadokites and Levites in Ezek 40–48 and makes the Levites subordinate to the Aaronites.[31] The second is the tent of meeting, which Budd contrasts to Moses's special tent in Exod 33:7–11. Lastly, Budd noted that the altar covering (Num 17:1–5 vs Exod 38:2), the waters of Meribah (Num 20:1–13 vs Exod 17:1–17), the expanded and more detailed Levitical genealogy (Num 26:57–60 vs Exod 6:16–25), and the use of money for cultic matters (Num 3:44–51; 18:14–18 vs Exod 13:13; 34:20) all point toward Numbers being developed somewhat independently from the other Pentateuchal books.[32]

---

[27] WELLHAUSEN, *Prolegomena*, 357.

[28] See note 3 on page 2.

[29] BUDD, *Numbers*, xviii–xix, argued that chs. 1–9, 15, 17–19, 26–31, 33–36 were Priestly creations; chs. 10, 13–14, 16, 20, 25, 32 had been heavily reworked by the Priestly scribes. The only chapters lacking such influence being 11–12, 21–24.

[30] BUDD, *Numbers*, xx.

[31] BUDD, *Numbers*, xx.

[32] BUDD, *Numbers*, xxi.

12   *2. Setting the Stage*

Budd still believes the non-Priestly material found in Numbers 10, 11–12, 13–14, 16, 20, 21–24 and 25–32 must belong to JE but that it is no longer possible to detangle the sources into their constituent parts.[33] Thus, Budd represents someone trying to escape the clutches of the source theory but could only do so to a limited degree.[34]

B. Jacob Milgrom

Jacob Milgrom published his commentary on Numbers in 1990. Although he continues to employ the traditional source labels, J, E and P, for Milgrom these do not function in a purely Wellhausenian way. For example, Milgrom emphasises the legislation in Numbers often presupposes or even borrows from the Holiness Code (Leviticus 17–26), which suggests that at least the final layers of Numbers were later than those in Leviticus.[35] He also points to the relationship between Numbers and Deuteronomy, such as with the Og narrative, where it is clear that Numbers represents the later version.[36] For Milgrom, then, the composition of the book of Numbers clearly cannot be explained by the idea of a "neutral" compiler whose sole goal was to join three pre-existing narratives together.

Thus, Milgrom is arguably not a true follower of the source theory. Although he maintains the traditional source labels, Milgrom's conclusions are more in line with the results of newer Pentateuchal models; he agrees that Numbers contains many late materials, but he also argues that Numbers influenced the material in other Pentateuchal books.[37]

---

[33] BUDD, *Numbers*, xxii, notes, "it is true that the meticulous division of verses or half verses into various documents has been widely abandoned, but general acceptance of where the earlier tradition is to be found in Numbers still exists."

[34] BUDD, *Numbers*, xxi writes, "There are other theories about the growth of the priestly literature which might explain the phenomena in question. On the other hand they do fit in with the view that the book has a degree of independence and integrity as a unit ... The view that the book had from the outset a degree of independence carries with it the assumption that 'authorship' is in some measure an appropriate idea."

[35] MILGROM, *Numbers*, xix.

[36] MILGROM, *Numbers*, xix, writes, "the victory over Og in Numbers 21:33–35 must be adjudged a copy of Deuteronomy 3:1–2, made for the purpose of conforming the Numbers narrative to the deuteronomic position that all of Transjordan was conquered at once."

[37] MILGROM, *Numbers*, xix, writes, "In sum, the pericopes of Numbers are not, in the main, unitary compositions but are composites of or contain insertions from other sources. Some of these sources are old poems, narratives in Exodus, and cultic material in Leviticus. Conversely, Numbers material can be shown to have influenced the composition of Exodus and Deuteronomy."

C. Eryl Davies

In discussing the source theory in his 1995 commentary, Eryl Davies begins with a several page long exposition of the seminal work of Rendtorff (to be discussed further in § 2.1.2.1). From this he concludes:

The work of Rendtorff, in many respects, carries the ideas of Noth to their logical conclusion. Rendtorff observed that most scholars since Noth had accepted the validity of both the standard source criticism of the Pentateuch (albeit in some modified form) and the traditio-historical approach; however, his own research led him to the conclusion that the two methods were fundamentally incompatible.[38]

Despite largely concurring with Rendtorff's findings and observing that his thesis raises many questions that the source theory is unable to answer, Davies concludes that the most prudent option is to still follow the source model.[39] Although commentaries, by their nature, are meant to be less progressive than other scholarly works, Davies' choice to continue with the source model, despite showing clear awareness of its weaknesses, represents a key example of how persuasive and dominant the Documentary Hypothesis is as an explanatory tool.

D. Baruch Levine

The last English example in this brief survey is Baruch Levine's Anchor Bible Commentary released in 1993 (Numbers 1–20) and 2000 (Numbers 21–36) respectively. Read in broad strokes, Levine is generally more positive about the value of the source theory insofar as he attributes the non-Priestly materials to a chronologically earlier source (JE) and the Priestly material, unsurprisingly, to P. Yet even Levine has some (albeit less dramatic) reservations:

There are additional considerations that recommend endorsement of the traditional alignment of the Torah sources in the order J, E, D, P, making the priestly source the latest in the literary chronology. By accepting this alignment one need not, however, accept the original basis for it. We need not endorse the same reconstruction of Israelite religion as had been proposed in the nineteenth century by Julius Wellhausen and others, who formulated the most widely accepted source-critical hypotheses.[40]

Furthermore, Levine also acknowledges that the Transjordan traditions are at least somewhat difficult to explain in terms of the basic four sources. Thus, he suggests that besides the Judean Jahwist (J) and the Northern Elohist (E), that

---

[38] Davies, *Numbers*, xlvi.

[39] Davies, *Numbers*, xlviii, writes, "Exigencies and space preclude a more detailed discussion of Rendtorff's contribution, but it is clear that his thesis raises questions which have yet to be answered satisfactorily. There are, admittedly, deficiencies and weaknesses in various aspects of the traditional source critical analysis of the Pentateuch, but it seems prudent, for the time being, to retain it as a working hypothesis, and to admit that, despite its limitations, it still provides the most plausible explanation for the way in which the Pentateuch developed into its present form."

[40] Levine, *Numbers 1–20*, 103.

14   2. Setting the Stage

there was most likely a Transjordan archive (T), which functions as a sub-source of the E tradition.[41]

As the preceding examples have already alluded, Levine also sees issues with the Priestly source that, although not insurmountable, require a more nuanced interpretation. First, he observes that in Numbers it is clear that the Priestly ideology has asserted itself over that of JE rather than simply being "compiled" with it. For example, Levine argues that JE's depiction of the spy mission has been obscured by Priestly reworking.[42] Second, like Milgrom, Levine also sees the Priestly legislation in Numbers as a further development of earlier Priestly materials and concludes that this points toward their being new creations that are not merely part of the Priestly source.[43]

E. Ludwig Schmidt

As the overview of Davies in particular demonstrated, commentaries on Numbers published in the 20th century struggled with viable alternative hypotheses to the source model. As will be discussed in more detail in § 2.1.2, although criticism of the Documentary Hypothesis had already begun in the 1970s, it was not really until the turn of the millennium that alternative models to the Documentary Hypothesis became the norm. The final two scholars (Ludwig Schmidt and Horst Seebass), in contrast to those listed above, stem from the German speaking world and are notable for the fact that they defend their use of the Documentary Hypothesis over against these newer models.

Ludwig Schmidt has written extensively on the book of Numbers, including a commentary, numerous articles, as well as summaries on recent research.[44] For Schmidt, the presence of doublets in the text are still best explained via the Documentary Hypothesis, and thus that is the model he continues to employ. While Schmidt is in many ways a purist when it comes to his use of the Documentary Hypothesis, he does utilize a number of important modifications to the traditional model that assist in avoiding some of the difficulties commonly associated with it.

---

[41] LEVINE, *Numbers 1–20*, 48.

[42] LEVINE, *Numbers 1–20*, 53, notes, "Num 13:26 is a pivotal verse but one that has been rewritten by P, so that its textual analysis becomes difficult."

[43] LEVINE, *Numbers 1–20*, 107, notes, "It would be accurate to state in summary that the priestly materials in Numbers 1–20 (as in Numbers as a whole) represent, by and large, the further development of priestly law and historiography well into the postexilic period. Such development was not merely a matter of redactional activity, but also involved new writings by the postexilic priesthood of Jerusalem and their associates."

[44] Commentary: SCHMIDT, *Numeri*. Articles: SCHMIDT, "Ansiedlung;" SCHMIDT, "Asylstädte;" SCHMIDT, "Kundschaftererzählung;" SCHMIDT, "Bileam;" SCHMIDT, "Sihon." Summaries: SCHMIDT, "Literatur;" SCHMIDT, "Neuere Literatur."

Somewhat idiosyncratically Schmidt argues that the Jehowist (i. e., JE or R^{JE}) was not only responsible for combining J and E, but that they also added unique contributions of their own.[45] He further argues that the Pentateuch redactor also added new material. Additionally, Schmidt concedes that some texts do not belong to any of the primary sources but were sourced from other traditions.[46] Whilst these unique deviations from the traditional model essentially allow Schmidt access to more layers to separate the text into, they also contradict his assertion about the unique suitability of the Documentary Hypothesis to explain the text. Schmidt even argues that the Pentateuch redactor was not the final editor of the text, rather he suggests that updates to the Pentateuch continued into the Hellenistic period: one striking example being his suggestion that the final Balaam oracle was written in light of the death of Alexander the Great in 323 BCE.[47]

The fact that Schmidt continues to utilise the Documentary Hypothesis does not mean he is ignorant of more recent models. One case in point being in his article on the spy narrative (Numbers 13–14) Schmidt devotes several paragraphs to arguing against Otto's exegesis of the same passage.[48] It is not my intention to adjudicate between these two views at this time, however it does demonstrate how one's presuppositions directly impact one's reading of a text. Schmidt's use of the Documentary Hypothesis predisposes him to see the earliest narrative layer in the non-Priestly text of Numbers 13–14, whereas Otto, who understands the book of Numbers as a whole to comprise late materials, understands these same non-Priestly materials to have been inserted at a post-Priestly stage.

Ultimately, even though Schmidt's modifications to the traditional Documentary Hypothesis are laudable for their innovation, they merely serve to highlight the fact that the Documentary Hypothesis itself is unable to adequately explain the textual problems found in the book of Numbers. Not only that, such modifications detract from one of the major selling points of the Documentary Hypothesis in the first place, its simplicity.

F. Horst Seebass

Horst Seebass – who has also written numerous articles as well as a three-book commentary on Numbers[49] – also departs from following the Documentary

---

[45] SCHMIDT, *Numeri*, 2–3.

[46] SCHMIDT, *Numeri*, 4, states, "Freilich stamen nicht alle Erzählungen aus einer drei Quellenschriften" (*Admittedly not all narratives come from the three source documents*).

[47] SCHMIDT, *Numeri*, 6.

[48] SCHMIDT, "Kundschaftererzählung," 45–50. Cf. OTTO, *Pentateuch und Hexateuch*, 26–62.

[49] Commentaries: SEEBASS, *Numeri 1;* SEEBASS, *Numeri 2;* SEEBASS, *Numeri 3.* Articles: SEEBASS, "Zu;" SEEBASS, "Hypothese;" SEEBASS, "Machir;" SEEBASS, "Vertrauenswürdige;" SEEBASS, "Gestalt;" SEEBASS, "Edom;" SEEBASS, "Erwägungen;" SEEBASS, "Holy;" SEEBASS, "Heutigen;" SEEBASS, "Fall;" SEEBASS, "Old;" SEEBASS, "Josua;" SEEBASS, "Komposition."

16   *2. Setting the Stage*

Hypothesis strictly and posits that a large portion of the book of Numbers should be attributed to a much later "Num-Komposition."[50] Seebass locates this special Numbers redactor around the end of the fourth century BCE and suggests that they were responsible for adding the lion's share of the material in Numbers: Num 1:20–46; 3:1–51*; 4:1–49*; 10:1–10; 15:1–31, 32–36, 37–41; 19:1–22; 25:19–26:65*; 27:1–11; 28:1–30:1; 30:2–17; 32:1–38; 33:1–49, 50–56; 34:1–15, 16–28; 35:1–34; 36:1–12*.[51]

Granting that Seebass attributes the majority of Numbers to the late Num-Komposition, this has ramifications for the parallels in the book of Joshua. As such he notes that if one wishes to speak of a Hexateuch, they must only do so as part of the very late Num-Komposition, as prior to this redaction layer there is no evidence for any connection between Joshua and Numbers.[52] Seebass also regards the Num-Komposition to presuppose that Deuteronomy had already been split from the Deuteronomistic History.[53]

As with Schmidt, Seebass's heavy use of a non-source-based redaction layer is at least somewhat contradictory with his view that the source model remains the best explanatory tool for the text. Thus, the two most recent commentaries on Numbers using the Documentary Hypothesis, actually only do so to a very limited degree. Both Seebass and Schmidt admit via their own modifications that the three sources, JEP, are inadequate to explain the book of Numbers.[54]

---

[50] SEEBASS, "Heutigen," 238.

[51] SEEBASS, "Heutigen," 238; SEEBASS, *Numeri 1*, 5.

[52] SEEBASS, "Heutigen," 246; SEEBASS, "Josua."

[53] SEEBASS, *Numeri 1*, 19.

[54] This conclusion is mirrored by ALBERTZ, "Numeri I," 172, who insightfully remarks, "Die beiden jüngsten deutschen Kommentare zum Numeribuch folgen zwar noch dem Paradigma der Quellentheorie, doch weisen sie erhebliche Anteile des Textes späten Redaktionsschichten zu, so L. Schmidt der Pentateuchredaktion, die er in die erste Hälfte des 4. Jh. v.Chr. datiert, aber noch bis in hellenistische Zeit mehrfach ergänzt sieht, und H. Seebass einer Numeri-Komposition, die er überhaupt erst an das Ende des 4. Jh. setzt. Seebass scheut sich nicht, mehr als die Hälfte der Texte im Numeribuch dieser späten Redaktion zuzuweisen. Dies bedeutet, dass bei ihm nur noch weniger als der halbe Textbestand des Buches mit Hilfe der Quellentheorie erklärt wird. Dabei wird in beiden Kommentaren, so gelehrt sie sind, eine strukturelle Schwäche der Quellentheorie unübersehbar ..." (*Although the two most recent German commentaries on the book of Numbers still follow the paradigm of the Source Theory, they assign substantial portions of the text to late redaction layers, L. Schmidt to the Pentateuch redaction, which he dates to the first half of the fourth century BCE, but sees further supplements through to the Hellenistic period, and H. Seebass to a Numbers-Composition, which he places at the end of the fourth century at the absolute earliest. Seebass is not afraid to assign more than half of the text in the book of Numbers to this late redaction. This means that for him, only as little as half the textual content of the book can be clarified with help of the Source Theory. Thereby both commentaries, as erudite as they are, make the weakness of the Source Theory obvious ...*).

2.1.2 The Pentateuchal Crisis and the Introduction of New Models

Although, as Schmid notes, the Documentary Hypothesis reached, "nearly a canonical status in Hebrew Bible scholarship in the twentieth century," the tables began to turn in its final decades.[55] Beginning in the 1970s, scholars began to seriously critique the seemingly assured result of the source theory. Carr calls this period the beginning of the "emerging crisis in Pentateuchal scholarship."[56] This crisis has continued to the time of writing. As Zenger notes, "Die Pentateuchforschung, einst Glanzstück der Bibelwissenschaft, ist ihr derzeit wohl schwierigstes und kontroversestes Feld" (*Pentateuchal research, once the centrepiece of Biblical Studies, is currently its most difficult and controversial field*).[57] For sake of this overview the collapse of the Documentary Hypothesis can be (perhaps overly) simplified as stemming from two main problems: The so-called "Farewell to the Yahwist" on the one hand, and the shortening of the Priestly source (i.e., Pg) on the other. These shall be briefly outlined before an overview of the models that stemmed from them are surveyed.

2.1.2.1 Farewell to the Yahwist

Although there were, of course, forerunners, it was Rendtorff's book that turned the tide against the long-held assumption that J, E and P constituted three separate accounts of Israel's history from creation to the death of Moses or even the conquest.[58] While it was already acknowledged that there were separate themes within the Pentateuch, it was Rendtorff who argued that these did not point back to pre-existing oral traditions from which J, E and P all compiled their works, but rather represented separate written traditions. Rendtorff began investigating the patriarchal narratives in Genesis and found that the theme of promise to the ancestors was nearly absent from the books of Exodus–Numbers.[59] From this Rendtorff concluded that the exodus and the patriarchs in fact represented two distinct and separate conceptions of Israel's founding.[60] Rendtorff's thesis further demonstrated that it was the Priestly source that first joined the patriarchal and the exodus narratives together.[61] Significantly, this meant that one could no longer speak of J or E as sources in the traditional sense of being self-con-

---

[55] SCHMID, "Yahwist," 29. For recent scholarly works on the formation of the Pentateuch see the collaborative works by DOZEMAN et al., *Pentateuch*; DOZEMAN et al., *The Pentateuch*; DIETRICH et al., *Entstehung*; GERTZ et al., *Formation*.

[56] CARR, "Changes," 438.

[57] ZENGER et al., *Einleitung*, 115.

[58] RENDTORFF, *Problem*. See synopsis in, e.g., RÖMER, "Yahwist," 18–19.

[59] See, e.g., DOZEMAN/SCHMID, "Introduction," 3.

[60] For more detailed arguments supporting this see especially SCHMID, "Yahwist;" SCHMID, *Genesis*.

[61] See, e.g., DE PURY, "Pg."

tained narratives spanning from creation to the conquest.[62] With this powerful observation, the idea that JE formed the skeleton upon which the rest of the Pentateuch was developed could no longer be held.

However, even before Rendtorff, there were already some signals that pointed in this same direction. To begin, it must be admitted that scholars had struggled to define precisely who the Yahwist was, and even Wellhausen and Kuenen had already dismissed the Elohist as a fully reconstructable source.[63] Ska outlines how J has adopted "a thousand faces" as different critical methods have been applied to the text, which should have already raised some warning flags to its being used as an interpretive cornerstone.[64]

Besides recent literary investigations that point to the problems of these sources, there are also more mundane reasons to doubt the existence of a self-contained grand narrative. Haran, for example, notes, "It is out of the question that works of an extent such as J or E, for example, could have been contained on one scroll – all the more so since their original scope was even larger than that which has come down to us."[65]

Significantly for the book of Numbers those texts that were traditionally categorized as J or E, now need to be re-examined. As already noted, Numbers did not readily lend itself to the four-source distinction of the Documentary Hypothesis, and so this "farewell" to the Yahwist represents an opportunity to look at the primary text without the baggage of former models.

2.1.2.2 The End of Pg and the Holiness Code

That Priestly texts can be distinguished from non-Priestly texts is considered one of the enduring bedrocks of Pentateuchal research.[66] It is somewhat strange

---

[62] Hence the titles of the following: GERTZ et al., *Abschied*; DOZEMAN/SCHMID, *Farewell*.

[63] KUENEN, *Inquiry*, 140, notes that the Elohist passages, "do not form a well connected whole; they are but fragments, and, moreover, in spite of all that they have in common, they do not always breathe the same spirit."; WELLHAUSEN, *Prolegomena*, 8, refers to the Elohist as being like a, "parasitic growth."

[64] SKA, "Yahwist."

[65] HARAN, "Beginning," 114. For further insights into scrolls and their limitations see also HARAN, "Israel."

[66] The thesis of NÖLDEKE, *Untersuchungen*, has stood the test of time and is still used as the basis for identifying P materials. NIHAN, "Covenant," 87, states, "that 'Priestly' texts can be distinguished from 'non-Priestly' texts on the basis of their language as well as their cosmology, anthropology, and theology probably remains the only result of pentateuchal criticism that, so far, has not been seriously called into question." SCHMID, "Distinguishing," 331–332, notes, "among the alleged sources [of the Pentateuch], there is one textual layer that is less controversial than others, which is P – the so-called 'Priestly Document'." CARR, *Formation*, 215, notes, "Biblical scholars can and will debate various details surrounding both the earlier and later formation of the Pentateuch, but the Priestly material in the Pentateuch is so distinctively different from the various forms of non-Priestly Pentateuchal material that scholars have reached a relative consensus, mentioned before, on the identification of 'P' material in the Torah on the

2.1 Pentateuchal Models and the Book of Numbers

then that no one seems able to agree precisely what P is (a source or a redaction), or where it ends.[67] This is, in part, because it has long been recognised that the Priestly material, although united in many aspects, was not written by a single author. Baden, for example, argues that one should not feel the need to detangle these various components of P but rather to understand that those responsible for creating the Priestly document used various materials in constructing the whole.[68] Römer conversely argues that this simply pushes the problem back a level rather than solves it.[69]

Traditionally it was believed that Deut 1:3, 32:48–52 and 34:1a,7–9 were part of the original Priestly source (i.e., the *Priestergrundschift*), these key verses rounded off the Pentateuchal story and therefore helped to explain why Deuteronomy was largely free of Priestly materials. In 1988 Lothar Perlitt published an article entitled, *Priesterschrift im Deuteronomium?*, which questioned this assumption and concluded that these Priestly passages in Deuteronomy could not be part of the earliest layer of the Priestly source (i.e., Pg) but were a Deuteronomistic-Priestly hybrid.[70] In the wake of Perlitt's article, numerous scholars sought a new ending for Pg. Unsurprisingly this resulted in as many solutions: some maintain that it spans the entire Pentateuch ending in Deuteronomy 34,[71] others that it was an originally Hexateuchal work, ending in Joshua 18 or 19,[72] but the majority of scholars, particularly in European circles, now see the ending of Pg at Sinai (be that Exodus 29;[73] 40;[74] Leviticus 8–9;[75] or 16[76]).[77] The core idea behind

---

one hand and 'non-P' material on the other." GUILLAUME, *Land*, 6, notes, "Pg is so peculiar that its identification is much more objective than is the case with other potential layers."

[67] See especially the collected works on the Priestly source in SHECTMAN/BADEN, *Strata*; HARTENSTEIN/SCHMID, *Abschied*. For the general contours of the Priestly source, see table in, JENSON, *Holiness*, 220 f. A fully reconstructed Pg spanning from Genesis–Joshua is suggested by GUILLAUME, *Land*, 13–30. DE PURY, "Pg," for example, argues that Pg was the original narrative upon which the non-P traditions in Genesis were based.

[68] BADEN, "Stratum."

[69] RÖMER, "Urkunden," 8.

[70] PERLITT, "Priesterschrift." Although Perlitt's general conclusion should still be regarded to be correct, it must be admitted that his reliance upon Numbers 27 as the assured P source is problematic.

[71] NOTH, *Studien*, 206; SCHMIDT, *Studien*, 271; WEIMAR, *Studien*, 17, argue that Pg ends in Deut 34:9. FREVEL, *Blick*, e.g., 380, alternatively argues for Deut 34:8.

[72] SEEBASS, "Pentateuch," 192; GUILLAUME, *Land*, 157–162; KNAUF, *Data*, 530–532.

[73] OTTO, "Forschungen," 35.

[74] POLA, *Priesterschrift*; BAUKS, "Signification;" KRATZ, *Composition*, e.g., 113.

[75] ZENGER, "Priesterschrift."

[76] KÖCKERT, *Leben*, 105–106; NIHAN, *Torah*, 379–382. RÖMER, "périphérie," 18, updated his earlier conclusion from 2002 noting, "Nonobstant, il est désormais devenu impossible d'exclure Lv 1–16 du débat sur l'origine des écrits sacerdotaux" (*Notwithstanding, it has now become impossible to exclude Lev 1–16 from the debate on the origin of Priestly writings*).

[77] There are, of course, other solutions, such as that of SKA, "sacerdotal," who argues that Pg ends in Numbers 27.

20 2. Setting the Stage

the ending at Sinai is that the Priestly ideology best represents that of the exiles in Babylon who had recently returned to Judea/Jerusalem (or were about to).

The Priestly narrative, then, depicts the father of Israel, Abra(ha)m, as leaving Ur of the Chaldeans (i.e., from the confines of Babylonia) and being sent by YHWH to the land of Canaan (Gen 11:31).[78] It was to Abraham and his descendants, Isaac and Jacob, that YHWH made a covenant to give them the land of Canaan. The problem, of course, was that in the Babylonian/Persian period, the land was not populated by Canaanites, rather it was those Judeans who were not sent into exile that remained in the land. These "people of the land" were logically resistant to the political machinations of the golah community and so were polemically branded Canaanites. Thus, it is only natural that the Priestly narrative did not end in a conquest, as dispossession by violence against the "Canaanites" was not the goal. Rather, the Priestly authors, especially via the figure of Abraham, depicted the ancestors living peacefully among the Canaanites as a מגור (*sojourners/resident aliens*).[79]

In this same light, the importance of the tent of meeting and the reception of laws outside that land takes on a new significance. Because it was the children of Israel, i.e., the golah community, who not only received the law and the movable sanctuary (the tent of meeting) outside the land, but it was also they who brought these institutions with them "from the wilderness" into the land of Canaan. Thus,

---

[78] See esp. WÖHRLE, *Fremdlinge*, 169–176.

[79] WÖHRLE, *Fremdlinge*, esp. 222, who writes, "In den priesterlichen Passagen der Vätergeschichte zeigt sich damit eine doch sehr spezifische, unter den Rückkehrern aus dem Exil vertretene Vorstellung vom Zusammenleben mit der während des Exils im Lande verbliebenen Bevölkerung. Die Rückkehrer verstehen sich zwar als das einzig wahre Gottesvolk und sprechen den im Lande Verbliebenen die Zugehörigkeit zu diesem Volk ab. Sie sehen sich unter der Verheißung, dass ihnen das Land nach ihrer Rückkehr wieder zum Besitz gegeben wird. Ja, sie fordern von denen, die nicht zur eigenen, als das wahre Volk Gottes verstandenen Gruppe gehören, dass sie sich auf getrennte Territorien zurückziehen. Doch erwarten sie nicht, dass dies gewaltsam durchgesetzt und die im Lande verbliebene Bevölkerung aus dem Land vertrieben oder gar ausgerottet wird. Sie sprechen sich lediglich gegen eheliche Verbindungen und so gegen die Vermischung mit den im Lande Verbliebenen aus. Nicht Gewalt, sondern Trennung, nicht Vertreib und oder Vernichtung, sondern ein Leben in friedlicher Koexistenz ist für sie die angebrachte Reaktion auf die Gegebenheiten nach ihrer Rückkehr aus dem Exil." (*In the Priestly passages of the patriarchal narrative, a very specific idea can be seen, in which those returning from the exile advocated the idea of living together with the population that remained in the land during the exile. The returnees understood themselves to be the only true people of God and disputed the membership of those who remained in the land to this people. They saw themselves under the promise that they would again be given possession of the land after their return. Indeed, they demand that those, who do not belong to those who understand themselves as the true people of God, withdraw themselves to separate territories. However, they do not expect, that this will be forcibly accomplished and those people who remained in the land will be driven out or even exterminated. They merely speak out against marital unions and so against mixed marriages with those who remained in the land. Not violence but separation, not expulsion or annihilation but a life in peaceful coexistence is the appropriate reaction from the conditions after their return from exile.*)

the Priestly source should not be understood as a history of origins, rather it is a mythical retelling of those origins.[80]

In light of this, it is not unreasonable to suppose that the standalone Priestly work completely reworked the traditions that were already known to both the golah community and to those who remained in the land with the express goal of promoting their own return.[81] Thus, Carr's suggestion that the Priestly narrative functions as a sort of counter-narrative to its non-Priestly equivalent has much to commend it.[82]

A further, related development in Pentateuchal scholarship concerns Leviticus 17–26, the so-called Holiness Code or H.[83] It has long been noted that this block of materials, whilst undoubtedly stemming from the Priestly milieux, is different to the materials in Leviticus 1–16.[84] Although Elliger had already proposed that the Holiness Code materials were later than the Priestly materials, it was arguably the work of Knohl that represented the major change in the scholarship of the Holiness Code.[85] Knohl's innovation was the concept of a "Holiness School," which was not only responsible for Leviticus 17–26 but also redacted other parts of the Pentateuch to align them with its "holiness" theology. In his own study, Knohl attributed the majority of Priestly materials in the book of Numbers to this Holiness School, and this explained why the Priestly materials in Numbers differed from those found particularly in Exodus.[86] Due to his reliance upon the source theory, Knohl equated the final redactor of the Pentateuch with his

---

[80] As NIHAN, *Torah*, 61, writes, "the entire Priestly narrative should be defined as a *myth of origins*. It follows a traditional pattern of creation myths, in particular as regards the close intertwining of creation, victory over mythical enemies, and the concluding building of a temple." (emphasis original)

[81] This conclusion explains why the promise of land and the death of Moses remains unresolved, contra FREVEL, "Ende;" FREVEL, "Formation," 6–15. That being said, it is true that the further back you push the end of Pg, the more redactional layers are required to explain the Priestly materials after it, as argued by NOORT, "Grenze," 104.

[82] CARR, *Formation*, 294, argues that the Priestly scribes clearly knew the non-Priestly materials but that they did not simply reproduce it, "Instead, they created a counter-composition covering the same narrative scope and many (though not all) of the same events as the non-P Hexateuch, one that originally stood separate from that work."

[83] The phrase, Heiligkeitgesetz (*Holiness Code*), was first coined by KLOSTERMANN, *Pentateuch*.

[84] NIHAN, *Torah*, 4, notes, "after Graf, the idea that the material gathered in Lev 17–26 originally formed an independent, pre-Priestly code, integrated only at a later stage into Leviticus by the priestly editors, rapidly became the scholarly *opinio communis*."

[85] KNOHL, *Sanctuary*; ELLIGER, *Leviticus*, 16. One notable exception being BLUM, "Issues," who argues against the idea that the Holiness Code stems from a separate redaction, stating that doing so, "means the collapse of 'Pg'." For recent studies on the Holiness Code see, e.g., ACHENBACH, "Heiligkeitgesetz;" GRÜNWALDT, *Heiligkeitsgesetz*; JOOSTEN, *People*; MILGROM, *Leviticus 1–16*; MILGROM, *Leviticus 17–22*; NIHAN, *Torah*; OTTO, "Code;" STACKERT, "Legislation;" STACKERT, *Rewriting*.

[86] KNOHL, *Sanctuary*, 71f.

Holiness School.[87] Otto, whose model differs significantly from Knohl's, also shares the assumption that the Holiness Code and related materials were added by the Pentateuch redactor.[88] Once again, however, the book of Numbers makes this suggestion dubious as the key features of H are often not present in the Priestly material in Numbers, in addition to a number of legislative text that even appear to belong to post-H developments.[89] Thus, whilst many of the materials in Numbers can be seen to postdate Pg, one cannot simply ascribe them to the Holiness School.[90]

2.1.2.3 The Bridge-Book Hypothesis

With the recognition that the non-Priestly material of the Pentateuch, especially those between the books of Genesis and Exodus, could no longer be regarded as a self-contained unit but rather belonging to various blocks of tradition, scholars could no longer fall back upon the idea of the preeminent historian known as the Yahwist. Similarly with the recognition that the earliest Priestly narrative ended at Sinai, the book of Numbers, above all, was left in limbo. For this book now contained none of the Documentary sources. This gave rise to the idea, put in very loose terms, that Numbers was designed to bridge the Priestly Creation-Sinai narrative with the Deuteronomistic narrative.[91] As the following survey will demonstrate, this has resulted in various proposals. One of the major points of debate being whether this Deuteronomistic narrative represents the so-called Deuteronomistic History (DtrH: Deuteronomy – 2 Kings) or a Deuteronomistic "Landnahmeerzählung" (*conquest narrative*) (DtrL: Deuteronomy – Joshua).

A. Thomas Römer

Thomas Römer was one of, if not the, first scholars to recognise what the repercussions of the farewell to the Yahwist and the shortening of Pg entailed for the book of Numbers. Most notably Römer argues that the book of Numbers functions as a bridge between a predominantly Priestly Tritoteuch (Genesis – Leviticus) and Deuteronomy, which had been split from the Deuteronomis-

---

[87] See, e.g., KNOHL, *Sanctuary*, 224.

[88] See, e.g., OTTO, "Code."

[89] NIHAN, "Code," 121, for example, notes, "H's influence in Numbers is manifestly less marked than in Exodus and Leviticus ..."

[90] Here the trap of circular reasoning is quite apparent. As SCHWARTZ, "Introduction," 9, notes, "if all redactional activity is automatically attributed to HS, the catalogue of features associated with HS will soon come to include a number of those having no connection with H whatsoever and whose only qualification for inclusion among the literary features of the Holiness School is that they appear in redactional passages in the Pentateuch ..." See a similar observation in, NIHAN, *Torah*, 564.

[91] See the analogy in MACDONALD, "Numbers," 121.

2.1 Pentateuchal Models and the Book of Numbers

tic History during the formation of the Pentateuch. Frevel thus rightly refers to Römer as the "'Vater' der modernen Brückenbuchthese" (*'father' of the modern bridge-book thesis*).[92]

Much of the content of Römer's articles on the topic of the book of Numbers detail the observations outlined in § 2.1.2.1 and § 2.1.2.2 above. Thus, Römer argues that a new ending for Pg must be sought given that it can no longer be regarded to end in Deuteronomy 34 or Joshua – the Priestly passages in these books being late Priestly/Deuteronomistic blends.[93] With this foundational observation Römer demonstrates that none of the Priestly texts in the book of Numbers provide a suitable ending for a story beginning in Genesis. This dictates that Pg must have ended at Sinai: either Exodus 40, with the conclusion of the sanctuary instructions, Leviticus 9, with the appointing of the priests, or, in light of more recent studies, Leviticus 16 with Aaron replacing Moses as the one to minister in the sanctuary.[94] Römer also emphasises that the non-Priestly texts in the Pentateuch can no longer be regarded to constitute a Pentateuchal skeleton, based on the evidence that Pg was the first source to combine the patriarchal narratives with the exodus narrative.[95] Thus, Römer argues that these observations logically lead to the conclusion that the book of Numbers was a late product that was designed to join or bridge the narrative of the Priestly Tritoteuch to that of Deuteronomy.[96] In other words, the book of Numbers only came into being during the formation of the Pentateuch.[97]

There are also some particularities in Römer's work that serve to differentiate this basic conception from the other contributors. First, Römer notes the strong parallels between the beginning and ending of the books of Numbers and Leviticus, and argues that this was a deliberate technique to both join but also distinguish the two books. In particular Römer argues that the beginning of Numbers clearly situates the book after the Sinai event – Num 1:1 explicitly sets the narrative במדבר סיני (*in the wilderness of Sinai*) – which serves to indicate that the legislation in Numbers is to be regarded as a supplement to the Priestly and Deuteronomistic laws.[98] This same conception is used to explain why the legislation in the book of Numbers is scattered throughout the book rather than collected into one place like in the other books: it is not presenting a new law code but updating or expanding existing law.

---

[92] FREVEL, "Stücke," 281.

[93] RÖMER, "Numeri," 216; RÖMER, "Sojourn," 423–427.

[94] RÖMER, "Sojourn," 425; RÖMER, "périphérie," 18.

[95] See, e.g., RÖMER, "Numeri," 218–220.

[96] RÖMER, "Numeri," 220–224; RÖMER, "Sojourn," 427. The corollary of this being that the Priestly materials in the book of Numbers must be later than Pg. See also RÖMER, "Numeri," 216–218.

[97] RÖMER, "Entstehungsphasen," 68. For Römer, the Hexateuch was a later development than the first Pentateuch, see RÖMER/BRETTLER, "Deuteronomy 34."

[98] RÖMER, "Sojourn," 428.

Römer further argues that because these supplements were added in a (new) separate work rather than being appended to the parent laws, that the books of Exodus, Leviticus and Deuteronomy were most likely already "closed" to further updates.[99] The idea that certain books were closed to updates represents a modification of Noth's suggestion that Numbers 26–36 represents a "rolling corpus" of continuous updates and supplements, by suggesting that the whole book can be viewed to function in similar way.[100] Lastly, Römer draws attention to the fact that the "murmuring stories," in which Israel complains against God and against Moses and Aaron, are deliberate but skewed parallels of the positive stories of God's provision in the desert found in Exodus.[101] From a compositional standpoint, these stories with their parallels in Exodus frame the Sinai revelation (cf. discussion in § 2.4).[102]

While Römer's arguments – taken in broad strokes – are very powerful, there are issues with the particulars.[103] The idea of "closing" of books, which resulted in disparate materials being lumped into Numbers, is particularly problematic. This argument can be countered with the example of the golden altar of incense, which is mentioned in Exodus 30, 35, and Leviticus 4. The ordeal of Numbers 16–17 clearly has no knowledge of an altar for incense, neither does Leviticus 10. Both of these narratives have the priests (and laity in Numbers 16) using censers to present incense and make no mention of a golden altar. Even Ezekiel's vision of the Temple does not feature a golden altar. The only references to the golden altar for incense are found in the books of Chronicles (1 Chr 6:49; 28:18; 2 Chr 26:16) and Maccabees (1 Macc 1:21; 4:49), which suggests that it should be understood to be a late innovation.[104] If the authors of the final Pentateuch were happy to insert passages like Exodus 30 and Leviticus 4, then why were the legal materials in the book of Numbers not given the same freedoms? This suggests that another explanation should be sought. In § 2.4 it will be suggested that the scattered laws are not in fact randomly placed, but function as part of a cycle of provision and rejection.

---

[99] Römer, "Nombres," 204; Römer, "périphérie," 24.

[100] Noth, *Numbers*, 10, wrote, "No proper sequence is maintained in this whole complex of later additions. We shall have to reckon with the fact that the individual units were simply added one after the other in the order in which they appeared." Cf. Römer, "périphérie," 23.

[101] Römer, "périphérie," 26–27.

[102] Römer, "Nostalgia," 84.

[103] For a more detailed critique see, esp., Frevel, "Stücke," 281–286.

[104] The golden altar that Solomon built in the book of Kings does not explicitly state that it is for incense, rather Solomon is also said to have built dishes for offering incense in, e.g., 1 Kgs 7:50. The incense altar in Exodus was also demonstrated to be late and have a complicated literary history by Christophe Nihan in a paper titled "Transposition in the Transmission of the Pentateuch: The Case of the Incense Altar" presented in Leuven in 2016. The paper has, at the time of writing, not been published.

B. Reinhard Achenbach

In 2003 Reinhard Achenbach published his *Die Vollendung der Tora*, which is arguably the most significant monograph on the book of Numbers to be published this millennium.[105] The undoubted importance of his work is tempered, however, by the fact that it is simultaneously the most praised and the most criticized work on Numbers in recent times.[106] It is praised for its comprehensive detail but it is criticized because of his reliance upon the Pentateuchal model of Eckart Otto, which in many cases seems to override other exegetical concerns.[107] One clear example of this can be found in his analysis of Numbers 32 (see Chapter 3), where Achenbach is forced to attribute disparate parts of the chapter to the same late editorial layer because his model precludes him from attributing any of the text to the Pentateuch redactor. The reason for this is because according to the model, one of the primary alterations made by the Pentateuch redactor was to shorten the Hexateuch by removing the book of Joshua, which is interpreted to mean that one of the goals of the PentRed was to downplay conquest themes.[108]

Similarly to Römer, Achenbach sees the book of Numbers as a late link between the Exodus, Sinai, the Book of the Covenant and Holiness Code traditions on the one side, and Deuteronomy and the Conquest traditions on the other side.[109] Unlike Römer, Achenbach follows Otto in understanding Deuteronomy and Joshua to have originally formed standalone "Landnahmeerzählung" (DtrL) rather than a Deuteronomistic History (DtrH).[110] One of the main distinctions between Achenbach's and Römer's understanding of the merger between the two major traditions is that for Achenbach the editorial bodies responsible for joining them were not developing a "compromise document," but rather were interested in creating a continuous narrative that included the disparate traditions.[111]

Regarding the composition of the book, Achenbach argues that there are three main issues that need to be solved, these are: 1) In what sense can one speak of

---

[105] Achenbach's exegesis of the spy narrative (Numbers 13–14) is not found in Achenbach, *Vollendung* but was published prior as an article: Achenbach, "Erzählung." Frevel, "Stücke," 275, notes, "Seine Arbeit darf als ein Meilenstein der jüngeren Numeriforschung bezeichnet werden …" (*His work can be described as a Milestone in recent Numbers research*).

[106] Cf., e. g., Frevel, "Vollendung;" Nihan, "Review."

[107] Römer, "périphérie," 29, for example, cautions that Achenbach's model has sometimes been applied too rigidly to its detriment, and suggests that it should be modified to leave more room for specific interventions and supplements that cannot be attributed to an editorial layer covering the whole book (i. e., HexRed or PentRed).

[108] Specifically, Achenbach, *Vollendung*, 388, states, "[Num 32] ist nicht auf den PentRed zurückzuführen, welcher an dem Landnahme-Thema kein Interesse zeigt" (*[Num 32] is not attributable to the PentRed, which shows no interest in the conquest theme*).

[109] Achenbach, *Vollendung*, 1–2.

[110] See, e. g., Otto, "Synchronical."

[111] Achenbach, "Grundlinien."

pre-Deuteronomistic sources within the book of Numbers? 2) How to categorise the Priestly materials: are they parts of its origin, parts of its own source, or editorial? 3) If the bridging function of the book of Numbers can be confirmed, how to describe the editorial process by which it was formed?[112] At the core of Achenbach's analysis is the assertion that the book comprises primarily of the work of a Hexateuch redaction (HexRed), Pentateuch redaction (PentRed) and what he names as "nachendredaktionellen" (*post-final redactional*) edits (ThB I–III).[113]

In undertaking his analysis, Achenbach suggests that chapters 16–18 most aptly demonstrate the various redactional hands at work in the book of Numbers.[114] To this end, the earliest layer is represented by the Dathan–Abiram layer, which is characterized by their denial to enter the promised land and their desire to return to Egypt. Achenbach sees these themes as characteristic of the HexRed, whose story is focused upon the conquest and division of land between the tribes of Israel.[115] To this layer was added the story of the 250 men, where the major theme revolves around the holiness of the people in relation to Moses and the priesthood. Achenbach sees these themes as corresponding to the aims of the Holiness Code, which asserts the need for the people to be holy, but at the same time promotes the hierarchical ideology of the priesthood with its tiered system of holiness. As with Knohl and Otto, Achenbach sees the authors responsible for the Holiness Code as the same authors responsible for the Pentateuch redaction.[116] Thus he attributes the 250-man story to the PentRed.[117] The final layer is the Korah layer, which promotes the Aaronites even above the other Levitical tribes. For this layer Achenbach notes the many parallels with Ezekiel (particularly ch. 44), wherein the Zadokites are given sole permission to minister before God and the remaining Levites are confined to a minor clerical role. This layer Achenbach calls a "Theokratischen Bearbeitung" (*theocratic revision*), which corresponds to the time when the priesthood fulfilled the role of Israel's true leaders.[118] For Achenbach this theocratic revision did not take place in a

---

[112] ACHENBACH, *Vollendung*, 11.

[113] ACHENBACH, *Vollendung*, 34.

[114] Achenbach calls these chapters the "Schlüsseltext" (*key text*). See ACHENBACH, *Vollendung*, 37–172. Prior to the publication of his monograph, ACHENBACH, "Erzählung," had already proposed that the spy narrative (Numbers 13–14) was also a Schlüsseltext.

[115] ACHENBACH, *Vollendung*, 43 f.

[116] Cf. KNOHL, *Sanctuary*, 100–103, 224, who writes, "HS's openness to popular creativity, combined with its profound knowledge of the Priestly heritage from which it originated, prepare it, in the course of time, for the gigantic task of editing the Pentateuch, which consisted primarily of combining Priestly and popular material." OTTO, "Code," 139, writes, "The dependence of H on P and D is what the Holiness Code has in common with the post-priestly and post-deuteronomistic formation of the Hexateuch and Pentateuch, such that fifteen years ago I had already come to the conclusion that H was part of the redaction of the Pentateuch."

[117] ACHENBACH, *Vollendung*, 54 f.

[118] ACHENBACH, *Vollendung*, 66 f.

single phase, rather he identifies three separate layers of theocratic editing (hence ThB I–III), who were responsible for the majority of Numbers 1–10 and Num 26–36. The first theocratic revision (ThB I) was primarily responsible for the re-depiction of Israel as a theocratic community. This layer introduced the concept of Israel being an *"ecclesia militans,"* via the introduction of the censuses as well as the structured camp; it introduced the tiered cultic organisation of the Priests and Levites, including the transferal of leadership to Joshua *and* Eleazar, which served to promote the "secular" leadership of the high priesthood. It also introduced the material dealing with the division of the land, including the allocation of Levitical cities. The second theocratic revision (ThB II) was responsible for the updated (post-Holiness Code) cultic practice and legislation: i.e., Numbers 5; 6; 15; 19; 28–29 and 30:2–17. Achenbach describes the final revision "Midrasch und Nachträge" (*Midrash and Supplements*), which is self-explanatory and includes Numbers 7; 8:1–4, 5–26; 9:1–14, 15–34; 10:1–10; 31 and 33:1–49.

To highlight one significant issue with this model: there are no Priestly texts in Achenbach's Hexateuch Redaction (including the pre-Deuteronomistic fragments that it incorporated), furthermore the HexRed – in almost all cases – aligns with the traditional JE (see table 23 in the Appendix). This observation is especially important because of the fundamental idea that the HexRed is a post-Priestly work designed to join the Priestly text to the Deuteronomistic text. Thus, even at the most basic level of engagement, one would expect the HexRed would clearly comprise a blend of Priestly and Deuteronomistic language. A clear example of this is Numbers 16 – Achenbach's "Schlüsseltext" – where the (non-Priestly) Dathan–Abiram layer shows no awareness of the (Priestly) 250-men layer and vice-versa, the only layer that contains a mixture of Priestly and non-Priestly language is found in the Korah layer. Thus, one is hard pressed to disagree with Baden's conclusion that, "what we have in Numbers 16 and 17, then, is not supplementation, but compilation: two independent texts brought together by a third hand."[119]

As noted above, Achenbach's work is undoubtedly significant, both in terms of its scale and the boundaries it pushes. It is fair to say that no scholar working on Numbers for the foreseeable future can afford to ignore this important work and the insights that it provides. Even if, ultimately, the underlying model is deemed unconvincing.

C. Rainer Albertz

Rainer Albertz has published several articles on the book of Numbers in light of his proposed Pentateuchal model, which in broad strokes amalgamates what he sees as the positive aspects of various other models. From Eckart Otto, Albertz

---

[119] BADEN, "Stratification," 245.

28   2. Setting the Stage

accepts the idea that during the exile there were two major pillars of tradition, approximating "der erweiterten Priesterschrift …(Gen 1–Lev 16)" (*the expanded Priestly writing* …[Gen 1–Lev 16]) on the one side and Deuteronomy on the other side.[120] Albertz acknowledges that Otto's double-constellation foundation provides a solid explanation for the unique nature and special character of Deuteronomy in the Pentateuch.[121] Albertz also highlights several points of weakness. First, he draws attention to the fact that Otto has difficulty in explaining why an originally standalone Priestly work later incorporated the non-Priestly material into Genesis–Leviticus. Second, he suggests that Otto's criteria for classifying between Hexateuchal and Pentateuchal materials are often unclear. He notes that texts that appear to be stylistically the same are differentiated between these two layers based on concepts that are not always clear to define (e.g., land vs law), which brings the results of the analysis into doubt.[122]

From Erhard Blum (see below), Albertz modifies the core concept of a KD and a KP.[123] Albertz begins by acknowledging that it is unfortunate that Blum's model has never been fully fleshed out, however he argues that as far as it goes, Blum's KD and KP often align to JE and P respectively.[124] Albertz does not follow Blum's idea that KD preceded the Priestly writings, rather he suggests that it came afterwards. Albertz also adopts Blum's idea of a Mal'ak redaction, which inserted the concept of messengers of Yhwh leading Israel through the wilderness.

Albertz suggests a multi-staged development model that corresponds to various timeframes: (1) in the preexilic era there existed various, unconnected traditions including Genesis 2–11*, some patriarchal traditions, some exodus traditions, etc. (2) In the exilic period these traditions began to coagulate resulting in the patriarchal narratives (Genesis 12–50*), an exodus composition (Exodus 1–34*) and Deuteronomy 5–29*. (3) At the end of the 6th century BCE the first Priestly redaction PB1 (Genesis 1–Leviticus 16) as well as the Deuteronomistic History (Deuteronomy 1–2 Kings 25) were developed.[125] In addition to this, the so-called "Urgeschichtsredaktor" (inspired by the work of Markus Witte)

---

[120] Albertz, *Pentateuchstudien*, 21–22. Cf., e.g., Otto, "nachpriesterschriftlichen;" Otto, "Synchronical;" Otto, "Code."

[121] Albertz, *Pentateuchstudien*, 24, suggests that Otto's model, "ermöglicht eine stichhaltige Erklärung warum dem Deuteronomium eine Sonderstellung innerhalb des Pentateuch zukommt" (*enables a valid explanation for why Deuteronomy has a special position within the Pentateuch*).

[122] Albertz, *Pentateuchstudien*, 24.

[123] Cf. Blum, *Studien*.

[124] Albertz, *Pentateuchstudien*, 21.

[125] Albertz, *Pentateuchstudien*, 28, writes, "Als etwa in der Mitte des 5. Jhs. v. Chr. führende Priester und Laien der nachexilischen judäischen Gemeinschaft planten, ein autoritatives Gründungsdokument zu schaffen, das auf die Zustimmung aller Gruppen rechnen konnte, entschieden sie, dass das Deuteronomium, das bereits seit dem 7. Jh. einige Autoriät erworben hatte, eingeschlossen werden müsse". (*From around the middle of the 5th century BCE leading priests and laity of the postexilic Judean community planned to make an authoritative foun-*

was the first and only editor in Albertz's opinion who did not incorporate old traditions into their own work but to incorporate them into a foreign work, namely PB1.[126] Thus, via this unique redaction, R[UG], the books of Genesis–Leviticus came to comprise both Priestly and non-Priestly traditions. (4) In the early 5th century, the editor responsible for the Holiness Code and the other H materials updated PB1, creating PB2 (Genesis 1–Leviticus 27). (5) In the middle of the 5th century Deuteronomy was separated from the Deuteronomistic History and joined to PB2 by a non-Priestly D redaction, creating the first "Pentateuch" (Genesis 1–Deuteronomy 34). Along with updates to Genesis, Exodus and Deuteronomy, the key addition was the bridging material in what later became the book of Numbers (Num 10:33–36; 11:1–35; 12:1–16; 13:17b–20, 22–24, 27–31; 14:4, 11–25, 39–45; 21:1–3[?], 4*, 5–13aα, 14–16, 19–20). (6) The D redaction was edited by Priestly circles shortly afterwards (PB3), which added more material to the Pentateuch, primarily in the developing book of Numbers. (7) In the late 5th century, the Mal'ak Redaction (inspired by Blum) added the concept of heavenly messengers leading Israel. (8) In the late 5th century, the book of Joshua was incorporated to form the Hexateuch (Genesis 1–Joshua 24). (9) Shortly afterward, the books of Exodus and Numbers received updated legal materials, particularly focussed on purity, PB4. (10) The book of Joshua's participation was short lived as in the early 4th century a further Priestly editor (PB5) once again formed a Pentateuch. Among other additions, he added – in compensation for the loss of Joshua – Numbers 25:19–36:13, which functioned to bring the themes of land distribution within the borders of the Pentateuch. PB5 also updated the book of Joshua itself to better align with the newly inserted material in Numbers. (11) The Pentateuch was finalised in the early 4th century with further minor updates, such as supplementary materials to better align with Chronicles (see table 23 in the Appendix).[127]

On the one hand, Albertz's model does succeed in removing the ambiguity from the Otto/Achenbach model via adding greater granularity (i.e., more layers). On the other hand, it is questionable if the solution he provides actually overcomes the very weaknesses he identifies in the models he amalgamates, not to mention the issue of cumulative uncertainty with so many layers.[128] As noted above, Albertz accused Otto of insufficiently explaining why and how the non-Priestly material in Genesis–Exodus was inserted into the Priestly Triteuch. Yet

---

dational document, that could be agreed upon by all groups; they decided that Deuteronomy, which already from the 7th century had some authority, had to be included).

[126] Cf. WITTE, *Urgeschichte*.

[127] See a more detailed breakdown in ALBERTZ, *Pentateuchstudien*, 471–485.

[128] KNAUF, "Archaeology," 275–276, notes that with an 80 % accuracy – which is already quite good for the humanities – that chances of detecting literary strata after four redaction layers is below 50 %, which means, "flipping coins would, from now on, lead to better results than argumentation."

30   *2. Setting the Stage*

Albertz's own solution is arguably just as confusing. First, he proposes a pre-history redactor (R^{UG}) to explain the Priestly/non-Priestly conflation of the Primeval history within Genesis 1–11. Second, he then suggests that P1 was responsible, not only for authoring the Priestly materials from Genesis 1–Leviticus 16 (i. e., essentially Pg), but also for conflating this semi-standalone Priestly work with the non-Priestly patriarchal narratives (VG^2, i. e., second edition of the "Vater Geschichte") as well as the non-Priestly Exodus Composition (K^{EX}).[129] However, if P1 was happy to conflate its own Priestly work with its non-Priestly counterpart, then why must Albertz propose a D redaction to explain the non-Priestly material in Numbers? Why couldn't Albertz's PB3 also have been responsible for the P/non-P conflation in the earliest layer of Numbers? Even the idea that there were various groups in the 5th century (at least one who wrote in non-Priestly style and one who wrote in Priestly style) that took turns in adding material to the Pentateuch seems unduly optimistic in light of power issues and authority, let alone recent analyses of known conflation processes (see § 2.2.1). Of course, we do not have records of the actual processes at work, and even though the Bible attests to various conflicting ideologies being given space within the scriptures, it still seems unlikely to me that these debates took place "in real time" in the text of the Pentateuch. Whilst this critique admittedly overlooks many of the nuances in Albertz's reconstruction, the fact remains that – besides the issues regarding Deuteronomy's place in the formation of the Pentateuch – the joining of Priestly and non-Priestly materials is the most difficult and important aspect of any Pentateuchal model, and although Albertz's model succeeds in explaining Deuteronomy's position and distinctiveness, his explanation of the conflation of Priestly and non-Priestly material is rather less compelling.[130]

D. Summary

It is undeniable that the farewell to the Yahwist and the shortening of Pg require the basic assumptions of the source model to be re-examined. That there is a Priestly source on the one hand and that Deuteronomy represents a distinctive, largely self-contained work on the other hand must be considered the two safest observations about the Pentateuch. Therefore, the bridge model rightly emphasises these two aspects as keys to the formation of the Pentateuch. That being said, the bridge model – regardless of the particular outworking – contains other presuppositions that are less convincing. These will be elaborated in the following sections but for now they are: (1) The reasons behind the joining of the standalone Priestly work to the non-Priestly material in Genesis–Exodus, (2) that the earliest strata in Joshua was originally attached to Deuteronomy, be it

---

[129] See, esp., ALBERTZ, *Pentateuchstudien*, 275–276.
[130] See also critique in FREVEL, "Stücke," 277–281.

2.1 Pentateuchal Models and the Book of Numbers

via the concept of a DtrL or a DtrH, and (3) that the bridge model still retains one of the major assumptions of the source model that it seeks to replace, namely that conflated materials can (for the most part) be fully separated and reconstructed.

2.1.2.4 Numbers as Part of a Pre-Priestly Narrative Composition

The final broad categorisation of Pentateuchal Models are those models that, in quite different ways, conceptualise the non-Priestly texts in the book of Numbers to have already belonged to some kind of larger composition. Because these models have been employed by various scholars, this overview will depart from the format established above and instead categorise in terms of model.

A. A Post-Deuteronomistic Composition

In his 1976 monograph, H. H. Schmid asked:

> Könnte es sein, dass zumindest ein Teil dieser Schwierigkeiten darauf zurückzuführen ist, dass unser Bild von der Entstehung des Pentateuchs vielleicht doch nicht ganz zutrifft? Sind uns unter der Hand unsere Quellentheorien nicht in einer Weise erstarrt, das sich – gegen methodisch besseres Wissen – der Text oft mehr nach unseren Hypothesen zu richten hat als unsere Hypothesen nach dem Text? (*Could it be that at least a part of these difficulties can be traced back to the fact that our picture for the development of the Pentateuch is perhaps not entirely correct? Are we not in a sense frozen beneath the hand of our source theory, that we – against better methodical sense – have more often judged the text according to our hypotheses than our hypotheses according to the text?*)[131]

Accordingly Schmid concluded, contrary to the prevailing view at the time, that the Yahwist could not have been developed in the Solomonic period, but rather already presumed the existence of preexilic prophecy and therefore likely developed "near" the depiction of traditions according to the work of the Deuteronomists.[132] As such Schmid suggested that it is no longer possible to determine whether the Yahwist was developed before, after, or concurrently with the Deuteronomistic work, rather it is only possible to suggest that the Yahwist presented the relationship between prophecy and history in a different way.[133] This conclusion spoke, in particular, to the much closer relationship between the non-Priestly texts in the Tetrateuch to those in Deuteronomy.

Schmid's conservative conclusions were used as a foundation by John Van Seters who argued that the non-Priestly texts in the Tetrateuch were post-Deuteronomistic. Van Seters developed the theory that the Yahwist was a post-Deuteronomistic "historian" who took up diverse traditions (including both myth and legend via both written and oral transmission) about Israel's pre-his-

---

[131] Schmid, *Jahwist*, 12.
[132] Schmid, *Jahwist*, 167.
[133] Schmid, *Jahwist*, 169.

tory and used them to create a history of Israel's origins.[134] This history of Israel's origins was, from its inception, one that "could take the presentation of Israel's history from the conquest to the end of the monarchy for granted."[135] Thus, for Van Seters "the non-P (J) work was composed as a prologue to the national history of DtrH and never existed as a separate corpus."[136]

As such, for Van Seters the shared traditions in Numbers and Deuteronomy 1–3 do not provide the difficulty that they do for other scholars using alternative models. Because the Tetrateuch functioned as the post-Deuteronomistic prologue, all non-Priestly materials from Genesis–Numbers could draw upon Deuteronomy as a source. This same foundational understanding led Van Seters to conclude that Num 21:21–35, as a whole, was a late composite, a conclusion that will be questioned in Chapter 3 below. That being said, Van Seters wants to make clear, in line with Schmid, that the Yahwist is not merely an extension of Deuteronomy, e.g., a "D-Komposition," rather it exhibits a distinct theology and has its own emphases.[137]

In referring to a "D-Komposition," Van Seters primarily intends the work of Erhard Blum, who did in fact suggest that the non-Priestly Tetrateuch should be understood as a Deuteronomy-inspired "D-Komposition." Blum began with the observation that the narrative structure of the non-Priestly Pentateuch best belonged to a social context in which there was a great need to demonstrate that the tragedy of the destroyed temple and the experience of exile was not the end of Israel. With this, the idea that YHWH's relationship with Israel and their connection to their homeland was linked to promises given to the patriarchs brought hope. Likewise, the idea that Israel had to spend a generation in the wilderness but that the following generation would return to (i.e., conquer) the land also belongs neatly to this context.[138] Thus, for Blum, the non-Priestly texts belong to a context after the Deuteronomistic History had already been developed. Blum also used this post-DtrH setting to explain those passages in the Tetrateuch that either presupposed or were foreshadowed by Deuteronomy and thus argued that the non-Priestly texts belonged to this Deuteronomistic Composition (KD).

Despite his initial work being focussed on Genesis, Blum later altered his position in agreement with the theory of, e.g., K. Schmid and J. Gertz, that

---

[134] VAN SETERS, *Prologue*, 20–22.

[135] VAN SETERS, *Prologue*, 19.

[136] VAN SETERS, "Redaction," 302–303.

[137] VAN SETERS, *Life*, 467, writes that the Yahwist, "Should not be regarded as one of a series of Dtr redactions or a 'D-Komposition,' because the Yahwist takes a fundamentally different attitude to the Deuteronomic law and covenant ... The promises of land and blessing are not conditioned by a set of stipulations as in Deuteronomy. Instead, they have been transferred from the exodus generation to the patriarchs and are guaranteed to their descendants by the faith and obedience of Abraham."

[138] See, e.g., BLUM, *Studien*, 189–193.

2.1 Pentateuchal Models and the Book of Numbers

33

the Priestly writer was the first to join the patriarchs to the exodus narrative.[139] In particular, Blum agreed that there was little to connect the non-Priestly patriarchal and exodus traditions.[140]

Despite their differences, the scholars highlighted in this section forwarded the idea that non-Priestly texts need not be pre-Deuteronomistic. This important shift should not be overlooked. That said, to my knowledge, there is no scholar today working on Numbers that adheres to Van Seters' model, and Blum's idea of a KD has only rarely been taken up.[141]

Besides using popularity as an indicator, the key criticisms of these models pertain to their use of the Deuteronomistic History and to so-called "Deuteronomisms." As already discussed in § 2.1.1.2, the idea that there was a single Deuteronomistic History is now heavily questioned. Furthermore, the idea that the non-Priestly material of the Tetrateuch largely in its entirety can be brought under the umbrella of a single Deuteronomistic redactor is problematic.[142] Limiting the evidence to the shared traditions between Numbers and Deuteronomy 1–3, it is hard to explain why they differ in several key respects if the author of Numbers aimed at developing a harmonious introduction (Van Seters) or that they were developed with the same Deuteronomistic ideology in the background (Blum).[143] Rather, as will be argued in chapter 3, the differences are much more convincingly explained if a back and forth between the shared traditions is assumed.

---

[139] Cf. BLUM, *Komposition*.

[140] BLUM, "Verbindung," 151–152, notes, "Unsere kritische Durchsicht einschlägiger nichtpriesterlicher Überlieferungen in den Anfangskapiteln des Exodusbuches (Ex 3 f.; 12; 14; 18), in der Vätergeschichte (Gen 15 etc.) und der Texte an der Nahtstelle von Gen und Ex führte zumindest auf einige konvergierende Befunde und Koordinaten. Dazu gehört nicht zuletzt der 'negative' Befund, wonach auf vorpriesterlicher Ebene eine literarische Verknüpfung zwischen Gen und Ex bzw. Vätergeschichte und Exodusgeschichte nicht nachzuweisen ist. (*Our critical inspection of the pertinent non-Priestly traditions in the opening chapters of the book of Exodus [Exod 3 f.; 12; 14; 18], in the patriarchal narrative [Gen 15, etc.] and the texts at the interface between Gen and Exod led to at least some converging finds and coordinations. To these belong, not least, the 'negative' find, whereby at the pre-Priestly level a connection between Gen and Exod, or between the patriarchal and the exodus narratives cannot be proven.*)

[141] David Carr being one clear exception. However, in the case of Carr he prefers the original idea that KD included the non-Priestly Genesis texts. See, e.g., CARR, *Formation*, 255–282.

[142] According to RÖMER, "Entstehungsphasen," 53, those passages in Numbers that exhibit Deuteronomistic similarities can hardly be considered to be part of a either an "introduction" to the Deuteronomic History, nor do they seem to share sufficient links to constitute part of a pre-Priestly Deuteronomistic corpus.

[143] RÖMER, "Nombres 11–12," 483, argues that these scholars are inconsistent both with regard to which texts they attribute to being Deuteronomistic as well as in their description of the ideology of this pre-Priestly Deuteronomistic work.

34   *2. Setting the Stage*

B. A Pre-Deuteronomistic Composition

The final option comprises those models that see the bulk of the non-Priestly materials in the Pentateuch deriving from pre-Priestly and pre-Deuteronomistic sources. Within this larger category there are a variety of divergent reconstructions, but they all begin with the basic idea that preexilic traditions slowly coalesced into larger narrative structures. In the broadest possible terms, these models can be subdivided into those that see the non-Priestly material spanning from creation to conquest and those that see a sharp separation between "Genesis and the Moses story."[144]

Following the farewell to the Yahwist, the non-Priestly narratives in Genesis were no longer considered to be originally connected to Exodus, but rather represented a separate story of origins. This led to the question of where the narrative beginning in Exodus ended. As Schmid notes:

> There is reason to believe that the pre-Priestly Moses story, starting with the exodus, did not end at the Mountain of God but included – given the push of the narrative flow towards this goal – an account of the conquest of the land ... at this time, however, it is not possible to present a sufficiently well-founded hypothesis of the assignment of specific texts to particular sources for such a pre-Priestly account that includes both the exodus from Egypt and the conquest of the land."[145]

Although a number of scholars have forwarded the likelihood of an exodus-conquest narrative, many have done so at a more theoretical level.[146] As far as I am aware only two scholars have undertaken to precisely define what this earliest narrative layer comprised. In the year 2000, Reinhard Kratz released his *Die*

---

[144] To use the title of Schmid, *Genesis*.

[145] Schmid, "Exodus," 45–46. Germany, *Exodus-Conquest*, 1, begins his monograph with this quote and seeks to fill this lacuna.

[146] For a larger overview of the forerunners see esp. Germany, "Hexateuch," 139–142. Bieberstein, *Josua*, 336–341, for example, emphasised the intertextual links between Joshua 3, the beginning of the conquest and the books of Exodus and Numbers. In particular he saw parallels between Exod 3:20; 34:10 and Josh 3:5c; Exod 7:17 and Josh 3:10b; Exod 17:7 and Josh 3:10c; Num 11:18 and Josh 3:5b; Num 25:1 and Josh 3:1b. Berner, *Exoduserzählung*, 430–431, writes, "Der Itinerarbefund [in Exodus] zeigt eindeutig, daß die Exoduserzählung bereits in ihrem ältesten Bestand auf einen Erzählzusammenhang angelegt ist, der über den Moment des Auszugs hinausreicht, wobei sich im Anschluß an Kratz die Annahme nahelegt, daß sie ihr Ziel mit dem Bericht über die Landnahme im Josuabuch fand (Jos 2–12*)" (*The itinerary [in Exodus] clearly shows that the Exodus narrative already in its oldest form was created in a narrative context that extends beyond the exodus moment, whereby, following Kratz, the assumption suggests itself that it found its goal in the report of the conquest in the book of Joshua (Josh 2–12*)*). Knauf, *Josua*, 17, argues the earliest layer of Joshua belongs to an Exodus-Joshua narrative. Nihan, "Relationship," 108, writes, "At the very least, it seems logical to assume that when the first draft of the conquest account in Josh 6–10* was composed in the seventh century (presumably under the reign of Josiah;...), it was attached to this 'Moses-Exodus' story, thus forming a comprehensive narrative of the exodus and the conquest." Cf. Schmid, *Genesis*, 148, who suggests the narrative arc *Exod 2–2 Kings.

Komposition der erzählenden Bücher des Alten Testaments (2005 for the English version), which sought to analyse the two major narrative histories of the people of Israel (i.e., Genesis–2 Kings and Chronicles, Ezra and Nehemiah).[147] This, naturally, included an analysis of the Pentateuch.

Using a "Subtraktionsverfahren" (*subtraction procedure*) Kratz began with the extant text and then successively stripped away layers in order to reach the most fundamental material. This methodology has not gone without criticism and causes issues as will be discussed below.[148]

The result of this process led Kratz to propose that the non-Priestly material of the Hexateuch (Genesis–Joshua) should be divided into two major narrative units, which he confusingly labels J and E. Kratz's J represents the non-Priestly redactor responsible for joining disparate narrative units together to form the "Yahwistic primal history and patriarchal history."[149] This conflated narrative encompasses Gen 2:4b–35:21 and ends with Jacob burying Rachel and pitching his tent "beyond Migdol-eder/the tower of Eder."[150] Accordingly, the Joseph narrative represents a later "post-Yahwistic appendage," which was not originally intended to be a literary bridge to the exodus narrative, rather its purpose was to provide a counter-story to Exodus, showing that "Israel survived even in Egypt and gained great respect."[151] Kratz's E is an abbreviation of "exodus" rather than "Elohist" and as the name suggests represents the non-Priestly exodus-conquest narrative. In broad strokes this narrative spans Exod 2:1–Josh 12:24 (minus all of Deuteronomy except 34:5–6) and narrates Israel's leaving Egypt, their journey through the wilderness and their conquest of the land.[152]

In 2017 Stephen Germany published a monograph that sought to analyse the exodus-conquest narrative in light of recent Pentateuchal theory.[153] Although in many ways this work follows in Kratz's footsteps, Germany emphasises that his work overcomes the issue that, "Kratz does not always differentiate between pre-priestly and post-priestly material in the later additions to the *Grundschrift*, raising the question of the precise extent of further pre-priestly narrative material in Exodus through Joshua."[154]

In terms of results, Kratz and Germany reach similar (though diverging in several key instances) conclusions, which on the one hand should be viewed positively in light of reproducible results, but on the other hand both their

---

[147] KRATZ, *Komposition*; KRATZ, *Composition*.

[148] See, e.g., SCHMID, "Zurück." Cf. KRATZ, "Pentateuch," who emphasises that there is much more commonality between various analyses of the Pentateuch than there are points of disagreement.

[149] KRATZ, *Composition*, 273.

[150] See table KRATZ, *Composition*, 274.

[151] KRATZ, *Composition*, 278 and 279 respectively.

[152] KRATZ, *Composition*, 294.

[153] GERMANY, *Exodus-Conquest*.

[154] GERMANY, *Exodus-Conquest*, 4–5.

36   *2. Setting the Stage*

solutions create a narrative that is devoid of some important narrative drivers (in particular the resulting narrative contains no compelling explanation for Israel's journey into the plains of Moab). That being said, the solutions of both Kratz and Germany avoid the critique of the bridge-book proponents who argue that the end of Exodus does not flow into the story of Hobab in Num 10:29 f. in that they both allocate this non-Priestly text to a later layer.[155] However, both Kratz and Germany also remove the spy narrative because the non-Priestly text does not function without the Priestly material it is conflated with.[156] There is little question that the non-Priestly spy components do not form a complete narrative as they are preserved and Deuteronomy at least hints at a more positive wilderness experience (e. g., Deut 1:25; 2:7; 8:2; 29:5),[157] however Israel's extended journey via Edom and Moab requires an explanation else one is left wondering why they did not enter the land from the south.[158]

As Germany's study is focussed upon the non-Priestly strata, he does not enter a detailed discussion on the formation and development of the Priestly and post-Priestly elements. Kratz, on the other hand, outlines a full developmental model for the Pentateuch: (1) The two preexilic traditions J and E were expanded and further developed. (2) "Not long before and soon after 587 BC, the law was implanted in the exodus narrative, which was still independent in the framework of the Hexateuch," – by which Kratz means Exodus–Numbers–Joshua. (3) This three-book Hexateuch was joined with Deuteronomy and the Deuteronomistically-styled work, Samuel–Kings, via the addition of the bridge-book Judges to form an "Enneateuch" (which, again, is more correctly a septateuch; that is, minus Genesis and Leviticus). (4) The seven-book Enneateuch underwent fur-

---

[155] See esp. ALBERTZ, "Noncontinuous," 614–615; ALBERTZ, *Pentateuchstudien*, 354n72. Cf. BADEN, *Composition*, 78–79, who sees no issue with discontinuity. For his part KRATZ, *Composition*, 294, suggests that the narrative jumps from Exod 24:18b (Moses was at the mountain forty days and forty nights) to either Num 10:12a (The Israelites set out by stages from the wilderness of Sinai), 10:33a (They set out from the mountain of YHWH and journeyed three days) or 20:1aβb (and the people dwelt in Kadesh, Miriam died there and was buried there). GERMANY, *Exodus-Conquest*, 448–449, on the other hand omits the mountain event entirely jumping from Exod 19:2aα (they set out from Rephidim) to Num 20:1aβ (and the people dwelt in Kadesh).

[156] See discussion in GERMANY, *Exodus-Conquest*, 207–213.

[157] For further support of a positive wilderness journey, see FRANKEL, *Murmuring*; GARTON, *Mirages*.

[158] A further criticism is made by BLUM, "Pentateuch," 55, who suggests that the dependence upon Shittim as a literary bridge (Num 25:1; Josh 2:1; 3:1) is misguided. He notes, "The exact delimitation of this connection, however, proves to be difficult upon close inspection: For one thing, the current version of the Rahab story in Josh 2, with Rahab's confession of YHWH in 2:10–11, clearly belongs to a later- or post-Deuteronomistic context. Kratz solves this problem by means of a hefty literary-critical reduction of the narrative. The postulated base layer of Josh 2:1–7, 15–16, 22–23 is purely a profane text that is devoid of any theological theme, presenting itself as a sort of narrative facade, to the extent that one must ask oneself in the end why the piece really should have been narrated."

ther Deuteronomistic harmonisations in order to bring the full narrative into a more uniform alignment. (5) Within a similar timeframe, the Priestly writing (for Kratz Gen 1–Exod 40) was developed and existed alongside the seven-book Enneateuch.[159] (5) Possibly in light of the Priestly narrative's joining of Genesis with the exodus-conquest narrative, the non-Priestly J narrative, in an "initially quite loose" way was connected to the seven-book Enneateuch.[160] (6) A redactor (R[PJE]) worked the Priestly narrative into the now eight-book Enneateuch to create the complete nine-book Enneateuch spanning Genesis–2 Kings. (7) Following further post-conflational developments, the Enneateuch was split into the Torah (Genesis–Deuteronomy) and the Former Prophets (Joshua–2 Kings).[161]

Besides proposing an exodus-conquest skeleton that is missing key explanations for Israel's journey, Kratz also proposes some further puzzling developments. On the one hand, Kratz argues that the Deuteronomistic History robs the Tetrateuch of its natural conclusion,[162] on the other hand he later argues that, "It was the Priestly Writing that first reduced the Pentateuch, which had become the Enneateuch, to the Tetrateuch."[163] Thus, one is left wondering why this Priestly Tetrateuch is deemed to contain a satisfactory conclusion while the non-Priestly one was not. In conjunction with this, he also argues that the Enneateuch was originally split into a Tetrateuch and a Deuteronomistic History just prior to being re-split into the Torah and the Former Prophets but it remains unclear what prompted Deuteronomy to "switch sides" in this penultimate stage of development.[164]

The alternative model to the exodus-conquest model is that of an early creation–conquest narrative. The most famous and developed version of this being the so-called "Münsteraner Pentateuchmodell" (MP), which was initially conceived by Peter Weimar and Erich Zenger, and has since been adopted and adapted by several other scholars including Frank-Lothar Hossfeld, Christoph Dohmen, Michael Konkel and Christian Frevel.[165] This model posits that during the monarchic period there were various traditions, such as family-based ancestral narratives (i.e., a Jacob narrative from the North and an Abraham narrative from the South), a Northern Moses-Exodus narrative as well as other originally standalone traditions (Joseph novella, Balaam, destruction of Ai and Jericho, etc.).[166] These at first formed two separate origins stories: the family history traditions merged to create a united patriarchal narrative that promoted

---

[159] KRATZ, *Composition*, 245.
[160] KRATZ, *Composition*, 307.
[161] KRATZ, *Composition*, 306–307.
[162] KRATZ, *Composition*, 216.
[163] KRATZ, *Composition*, 220.
[164] KRATZ, *Composition*, 221.
[165] See ZENGER, *Einleitung*, 124.
[166] ZENGER, *Einleitung*, 124–125.

the neighbourly relations between the two kingdoms via the concept of shared origins, while the Moses-Sinai-Balaam-Joshua traditions were compiled into an exodus-conquest narrative that – in light of the Assyrian oppression – emphasised Yhwh as one who saves and frees from bondage and concludes with Israel – through the conquest – claiming the land as their own.[167] At this stage of the reconstruction, and at this macro-scale, the MP and Kratz's model are more similar than they are different. The major differentiator being that according to the MP the non-Priestly Genesis narratives were joined to the exodus-conquest narrative prior to Deuteronomy and the Priestly texts.

According to the MP, it was still during the Assyrian dominance and particularly after the fall of the North (likely during the reign of Josiah), that these two separate origin stories were joined together with the express goal of creating a normative history and a religious and political program of reform.[168] This newly formed tradition was created under the three-pronged influence of priests, administrative and prophetic circles.[169] This all-Israel narrative, spanning *Gen 2:4b–Joshua 24, is thus labelled the "Jerusalem historical work" (*Jerusalemer Geschichtswerk* – JG) or "Jehovist" (in so far as it more or less corresponds to Wellhausen's JE).[170]

The MP is a self-confessed "middle position" model in that it takes Wellhausen's JE as its base but explains it via more recent scholarly proposals using a combination of fragment, source and conflation hypotheses. After this foundational layer, however, it departs more strongly from the source theory and explains the growth of the Pentateuch more in line with post-Documentary models.[171]

Accordingly, the MP does not assume that Deuteronomy was originally part of a Deuteronomistic History, rather it assumes that Deuteronomy – particularly via the figure of Moses and the narrative frame of chapters *1–3 and 34* – was intended to be integrated into a Hexateuchal context.[172] The books of Samuel – Kings, then, represented a separate, self-contained tradition. It was only in via the postexilic book of Judges that an Enneateuch was formed.

Regarding the Priestly material, the MP also sees a strong connection to the returning golah community and the restoration of the second temple.[173] One important aspect of the reconstruction is the idea that Pg was subject to further Priestly expansions *prior* to being joined with the Deuteronomistically updated

---

[167] Zenger, *Einleitung*, 126–127.

[168] Zenger, *Einleitung*, 127–130.

[169] Zenger, *Einleitung*, 128.

[170] Zenger, *Einleitung*, 129–130. That being said, the earlier study of Weimar, Untersuchungen, suggested the Jahwist originally ended in Numbers 14:8 (cf. p. 163).

[171] Zenger, *Einleitung*, 124.

[172] Zenger, *Einleitung*, 132.

[173] Zenger, *Einleitung*, 133.

2.1 Pentateuchal Models and the Book of Numbers

JE narrative. On the one hand this allows for different conceptions of Pg to function within the same superstructure (e. g., Zenger argues that Pg ends in Lev 9:24 whereas Frevel argues for Deut 34:8),[174] on the other hand it is capable of explaining Priestly materials that are clearly divergent to Pg but that are not yet clearly conflated with non-Priestly texts. Support for this understanding of the Priestly material will be argued further in § 3.4. One example of this was already briefly argued in § 2.1.2.3.B, where it was suggested that bridge-book analyses of Numbers 16 had difficulty explaining why the Priestly styled 250-man layer makes no reference to and shows no awareness of the non-Priestly Dathan-Abiram layer (and vice versa). There it was suggested that the only layer that made sense as comprising a Priestly and non-Priestly blend was the Korah layer.

The final stage of the MP model is the combination of the Priestly and non-Priestly works, which is dated after 450 BCE.[175] However, even here the process is not simply one of pure conflation. Rather, the MP sees the Torah become ever increasingly self-referential (inner-biblical exegesis) as its position as the authoritative revelation of Yhwh through the arch-prophet Moses became more influential. This final stage is thus more an umbrella for numerous adjustments, reflections and emendations that likely took place over a longer period of time rather than during a single "redactional layer." In light of this growing authority, the Enneateuch became increasingly separated into the "Torah of Moses" and the "Former Prophets."[176]

Most strongly in its favour is the MP's firm rooting in the historical background of the kingdoms of Israel and Judah, wherein the first "narrative fragments" were developed. It also explains their conflation in light of the political situation of the Assyrian, and then Babylonian and Persian empires.[177] The avoidance of the Deuteronomistic History and the corresponding understanding of Deuteronomy 1–3 as a means of integration into the non-Priestly narrative also aligns with the arguments presented above. Lastly, the development of a stand-alone Priestly work beyond Pg and the laws of Leviticus 1–16 will be shown in § 3.4 to be the most logical conclusion.

The key questionable aspect is the beginning with JE and the understanding that more or less all non-Priestly texts from Genesis to Joshua formed the original narrative arc. As discussed above, the major outcome of Rendtorff's work was the understanding that the patriarchs and the exodus narrative were originally two separate histories of origins. This was emphasised by the fact that the non-

---

[174] ZENGER, *Einleitung*, 125.

[175] ZENGER, *Einleitung*, 134.

[176] ZENGER, *Einleitung*, 134–135.

[177] The historical reconstruction of Frevel, has been particularly impactful for the present author. See, e.g., FREVEL, *Geschichte*; FREVEL, "Jacob." As ALBERTZ, "Search," 1, argues, "I want to emphasize the old-fashioned opinion that a literary hypothesis can only be regarded as proved if it is possible to supply it with a plausible basis in real history."

40   *2. Setting the Stage*

Priestly exodus-conquest narrative appears to be ignorant of Israel's origins from Abraham, Isaac and Jacob; a development that was first introduced by the Priestly source.

2.1.2.5 Summary of Pentateuchal Models

This section began by noting that the long-dominant Documentary Hypothesis had particular difficulties with Numbers. Via a series of short examples, it was demonstrated that both before and after alternate models had become popular Numbers scholars recognised that the book contained unique features that did not accord well with the idea that the Tetrateuch was primarily a conflation of three sources.

Following this, the background for the key proposal that Numbers was a post-Priestly bridge-book was surveyed. This model took the two key findings that led to the decline of the Documentary Hypothesis – the farewell to the Yahwist and the shortening of Pg to Sinai – as its foundation. It was argued that although these two major advancements had much to commend them, the idea that these demanded that Numbers be considered a post-Priestly work was problematic. In particular, it was noted that there was little explanation for why the earliest materials in Numbers continued to comprise only non-Priestly texts despite their supposed post-Priestly origins. As shown in the Appendix, the earliest strata in Numbers according to both Achenbach and Albertz aligns very closely to the traditional JE. It was also briefly suggested that the bridge-models also struggled to explain how and why Priestly and non-Priestly narratives existed that appeared to show no awareness of each other, if the book developed primarily via Fortschreibung rather than conflation of originally separate sources.

Lastly a number of models were surveyed that treated the non-Priestly material as primarily pre-Priestly but each differed in the way that it was shaped and with its relationship to Deuteronomy. Although it was also suggested here that there was no model without some debatable aspects, it was suggested that the pre-Deuteronomistic models from § 2.1.2.4.B came the closest to a satisfactory conclusion. Interestingly, most of the issues identified in Kratz's model (K) were not present in the Münsteraner Pentateuchmodell (MP) and vice versa, thus suggesting some combination of the two would result in something even stronger. Hence, a model with the following ingredients recommends itself:

I. The origins of Deuteronomy in the context of a Deuteronomistic History was suggested to cause more issues than it solved. Rather it was suggested that if one wished to continue to speak of a Deuteronomistic History, that they should do so in light of the view that such a construct was the result of several Deuteronomistic harmonisations of originally separate traditions. Both K and MP suggest that Deuteronomy was first inserted into the non-Priestly narrative as a self-contained unit rather than belonging to a larger work. This only makes the most sense if one supposes there already existed a connection between Joshua and Numbers.

II. That a connection already existed between Joshua and Numbers is supported by both K and MP. However, it was the nature of this connection that represents one of the key divergences between the two models. Both agree that various traditions from the Monarchic period coalesced to form approximately a non-Priestly Genesis narrative on the one hand and a non-Priestly exodus-conquest narrative on the other. For its part, the MP supposes that these two traditions were joined prior to the incorporation of Deuteronomy and prior to the Priestly writing. It was argued above that this idea stood in conflict with the idea that Pg was the first to link the patriarchs to the exodus-conquest narrative. Thus, Kratz's suggestion that Deuteronomy was inserted into the exodus-conquest narrative prior to its being joined to the non-Priestly Genesis materials suggests itself. However, this should be divorced from K's thesis that this joining corresponded with the creation of the first "Enneateuch" (i.e., Exodus – 2 Kings), which is less compelling.

III. The final key ingredient is the idea that the Priestly source underwent its own separate process of growth and expansion prior to its being joined with the non-Priestly work. K, for his part, suggests that P+Ps reached only as far as Leviticus before it was combined with the non-Priestly "Enneateuch."[178] This then runs into the same criticism levelled at the bridge-book models in that it does not provide an adequate explanation for those narratives in Numbers that are best explained as comprising a conflation of Priestly and non-Priestly materials. The MP, on the other hand, suggests that the Priestly work was expanded as a standalone work to include material in Numbers. This expanded Priestly work is much better able to explain why the Priestly material in Numbers is both post-Pg in nature but also still represents an alternate depiction of the same (or similar) events as found in the non-Priestly text. Further arguments in support of this will be offered in § 3.4.

2.2 Toward Certainty: Increasing the Size of the Data Pool

Viewed in the abstract, the entire field of biblical studies faces a serious problem of limited data. The biblical text, despite there being different instances (MT, LXX, etc.), has more or less remained unchanged for over two millennia. This means the fundamental data pool of the discipline is extremely limited and essentially unchanging. The fixed nature of the biblical text means that the only thing that can change is the models applied to interpret it. Seen from this per-

---

[178] KRATZ, *Composition*, 307.

spective, it is little wonder that the discovery at the Dead Sea was so important: it significantly increased the available data.

However, scholars cannot sit around waiting for more Qumran-type events, which means that other avenues must be sought by which to verify and control the variety of options presented. One of the major problems facing biblical studies as a field is that in many cases hypotheses can neither be proved or disproved absolutely. As Blum notes,

> Without exaggerating one can say that the most essential disputes among Old Testament scholars are over the definitions of their texts. To put it somewhat pointedly, these disputes are over which interpretations deal with real literary works, and which deal with literary units that exist only in the exegetical imagination.[179]

Only the naive would claim to be innocent of this, so where to from here? Despite interpretation always being subject to some degree of uncertainty, it remains possible to differentiate between more probable and less probable options. However, such differentiation requires that some external controls are available. This section will briefly outline the three promising avenues, noted in the Introduction, that have either not always been available, or at least not used to their full potential to help provide further weight to an exegetical solution.

2.2.1 Empirical Evidence Regarding the Conflation of Sources

In the same article just quoted Blum argues "In order to understand a text, one should know where it begins and where it ends."[180] Although *prima facie* this statement is very simple, it deceptively difficult once redactional activity becomes involved. Furthermore, this section will argue that the undertaking is only really possible for the latest layers of a text with earlier layers being increasingly difficult, if not impossible.

Within much of biblical scholarship, there persists the idea that older texts were kept and that revisions were primarily enacted via the adding of new materials. Roskop expresses this basic underlying assumption as follows: "[Scribes] tended not to excise passages from the text when they revised, no matter how much they conflicted with what they were trying to write, but worked their revisions into the *traditum* as they copied it."[181] However, as Pakkala argues, the validity of this foundational assumption has never been proven. Even more pointedly, he argues that Deuteronomy 13:1 – "Every word that I have commanded you, observe and do it; you must not add to it or reduce it" – implies the

---

[179] BLUM, "Penateuch," 43.
[180] BLUM, "Pentateuch," 43.
[181] ROSKOP, *Itineraries*, 214.

2.2 Toward Certainty

exact opposite, for there would be no need to prohibit someone from reducing the text had such a process not been practiced![182]

Because of this basic presupposition, the bridge-book hypothesis argued that an early non-Priestly Exodus–Numbers narrative was unconvincing due to the fact that the non-Priestly material at the end of Exodus did not neatly flow into the non-Priestly material in Numbers.[183] But the bridge-book theories are hardly the only victims of this line of thinking. In the introduction to his monograph, Germany writes, "in order to evaluate the hypothesis of a pre-priestly and pre-Deuteronomistic exodus-conquest narrative, it is necessary to identify the pre-priestly and pre-Deuteronomistic narrative material in the books of Exodus through Joshua and then to evaluate whether this narrative material *is coherent and complete.*"[184] The idea that even the earliest traditions must be completely preserved was also one of the key insights that led Kratz to reject the thesis of the Deuteronomistic History – it required that the original ending of the Tetrateuch be omitted.[185]

That this expectation is false has been confirmed in several recent investigations of materials where the conflated sources are known. After surveying many traceable examples of redaction and conflation, Ziemer concludes in no uncertain terms, "in keinem einzigen Fall war die Vorlage vollständig und unverändert in einer redaktionellen Neuverschriftung enthalten" (*in not a single case was the Vorlage included complete and unchanged in the new redactional writing*).[186] A very similar conclusion is reached by Carr, who argues:

... ancient scribes rarely appropriated earlier compositions in their entirety. In particular, they often eliminated their beginning and/or end in the process of strategically redirecting them. In many cases, they chose not to reproduce material in the middle as well ... On the one hand, scribes seem to have shown their reverence for and mastery over earlier chunks of tradition by reproducing them whole and even expanding them. On the other

---

[182] PAKKALA, *Word*, 11–13. Referring to Deut 13:1, Pakkala further notes, "The existence of such a prohibition implies that in the author's context changes to the text – additions and omissions – were regarded as a possibility or were perhaps even commonplace." (p. 11)

[183] ALBERTZ, *Pentateuchstudien*, 220, for example, writes, "Noch mehr Probleme machen diejenigen nicht-priesterlicher Sinai-Texte von Num 10,29 an auftauchen. Sie stellen keine wirkliche Fortsetzung von Ex 34 dar." (*Still more problems appear from those non-Priestly Sinai texts from Num 10:29 on. They do not really present a continuation from Exod 34.*). Cf. BADEN, *Composition*, 79, who sees no issue with the Hobab episode following directly on from Exodus 34.

[184] GERMANY, *Exodus-Conquest*, 6, emphasis added.

[185] KRATZ, *Composition*, 216, writes, "It robs the Tetrateuch, the narrative work about the exodus from Egypt with the promised land as its destination, of its natural end. The hypothesis necessitates the additional assumption that the end of the Tetrateuch (Pentateuch) was lost when the 'Deuteronomistic history' was worked together. That is not only unsatisfactory but improbable, given that there is an old narrative of the settlement in Joshua which continues the narrative of Genesis–Numbers seamlessly."

[186] ZIEMER, *Wachstumsmodells*, 697.

44 *2. Setting the Stage*

hand, they do not seem to have shown the same regard for compositions as discrete literary wholes with their own integrity. Where contemporary literary critics and/or biblical scholars might focus on compositions as literary wholes, ancient scribes often seem to have felt free to appropriate fragments, chunks, and blocks of earlier material.[187]

According to Carr, the best traceable example of conflation is the Gilgamesh epic: "Here scribes appear to have built the classic Akkadian epic through appropriation and transformation of Sumerian tales about Gilgamesh that were current in the earlier scribal tradition."[188] This early work did not only remain in its original form but was often expanded to create new stories from the old core, such as via the addition of the Atrahasis flood story.[189]

But this process of modification did not continue endlessly. Carr also notes the range of available modifications as well as the severity of the modification gradually reduced as a text became more established.[190] This final point is particularly important for Carr's own view on the formation of the Pentateuch, which largely follows Blum's idea of a "post-D Hexateuch" that was later joined to the Priestly work.[191] Although Carr rightly emphasises that the joining of P and non-P material represents one of the most significant moments in the formation of the Pentateuch, it is does not follow that the formation of the Pentateuch should be reduced to two major redactions. To this latter point Pakkala provides a counter argument by highlighting that the festival legislation appears in the Covenant Code, Deuteronomy, the Holiness Code, Numbers 28–29 and lastly in the Temple Scroll, meaning that there are five *traceable* updates to the one tradition.[192] To Carr's idea of a fluid beginning slowly becoming more fixed, Pakkala also argues that this does not really differ from traditional German *Lit-*

---

[187] CARR, *Formation*, 99–100.

[188] CARR, *Tablet*, 35.

[189] CARR, *Tablet*, 39, writes, "For example, after the creation of the first edition of the Gilgamesh epic in the first millennium, someone inserted the Atrahasis flood story into it. This kind of recombination both honors the traditions being combined and modifies them through their juxtaposition."

[190] CARR, *Tablet*, 39, writes, "such texts often reached a point where only certain types of modification were permitted, if any."

[191] CARR, *Formation*, 137, writes, "Nevertheless, most arguments for the post-Priestly character of biblical texts are far weaker, involving isolated words without specific links to Priestly texts (and/or without a non-Priestly counterpart) and/or the sorts of isolated links to Priestly materials easily added in the process of scribal harmonization/coordination. As a result, the case for the post-Priestly character of a broad spectrum of texts, such as Genesis 14 (in the past) or Josh 24:1–32 (more recently), should not be considered successful." See also CARR, "Processes," 70–75.

[192] PAKKALA, *Word*, 71–72. RÖMER, "Write," for example, also takes issue with Carr's idea that many of the so-called post-Priestly texts of the Pentateuch should be understood as being triggered by the process of conflation rather than as post-conflational editorial activity. The legal materials in Numbers in particular do not make sense as belonging to a standalone Priestly work that also included Leviticus (i.e., chapters 1–27), as the laws in Numbers can in most cases be seen as later reworks/supplements of the Leviticus laws.

2.2 Toward Certainty   45

erarkritik.[193] Pakkala rather suggests that the evidence of textual transmission oscillates between more conservative alterations and radical ones. More specifically he suggests that when the ideology of the original and the updated text were very similar, the nature of the update was more conservative, when the ideology was markedly different, the update was correspondingly more radical.[194] Within the Pentateuch Pakkala uses the example of the Passover as an example: (1) The text of Exod 23:15, 18 was radically edited in the creation of the original layer of Deut 16:1–8*. (2) This in turn was conservatively edited in the extant version of Deut 16:1–8. (3) The Passover legislation in Lev 23:5–8 further radically revised the prior two laws. (4) The Passover legislation in Num 28:16–25, as ideologically near to the Holiness Code, represents a more conservative edit. (5) The Temple Scroll also represents a further radical edit.[195] However, although changes between legal materials are great for examples, it should not be understood that similar processes did not occur to narrative material also. In fact, the book of Numbers in particular is now regarded to contain a high density of texts that represent alterations or evolutions of pre-existing traditions.[196]

One final important observation in this overview is the idea of textual omissions. To begin, it must be admitted that in most cases it is impossible to determine that an omission has been made unless what has been omitted is known from somewhere else; even in those cases where a narrative lapse is observed can it only be postulated that an omission was made. Pakkala draws attention to 2 Chr 21:20 and notes that if we did not have 2 Kgs 8:24 to compare to, scholars (not least redaction critics) would never suspect that the Chronicler had used Kings as a source.[197] That being said, Pakkala goes on to argue that in traceable examples, that editors often seemed unwilling to completely remove a text, more often they would maintain its basic shape but depict it via their new ideology. He writes, "A replacement can more easily be regarded as an alternative explanation to the older account, while a sheer omission is a blatant challenge to the older text."[198]

The following analysis, then, will adopt several key takeaways from these findings.

---

[193] PAKKALA, *Word,* 70.

[194] PAKKALA, *Word,* 362.

[195] PAKKALA, *Word,* 361.

[196] As FREVEL, "Introduction," 210, observes, "Processes of textual supplementation, amendment, adaptation, alteration, and transformation have been identified as the trigger of literary production. The most intriguing insight in Pentateuchal studies is that processes of adaptive interpretation do not only comprise legal material, but also in various ways narrative texts. And this very feature has become a characteristic of the book of Numbers. Many of the narrative and legal materials can be characterized as interpretation of other texts."

[197] PAKKALA, *Word,* 40.

[198] PAKKALA, *Word,* 368.

46   *2. Setting the Stage*

I. Redaction criticism needs to be more flexible when reconstructing earlier strata. In light of the conclusion that complete sources are not retained through the process of conflation, it follows that one should avoid the expectation of narrative completeness as a criterion for establishing a redactional layer.

II. The observation that the basic shape of a source was commonly maintained even in cases where material was omitted – often due to ideological revision – allows a scholar to have a higher likelihood of discerning the basic shape of an earlier stratum despite probable omissions.

III. The idea that radical alterations were made due to ideological differences also allows the scholar to more confidently identify triggers of change and therefore redactional layers.

The power of these proposals will be presupposed in the exegesis of chapters 3 and 4.

2.2.2 Extra-biblical Evidence and Historical Geography

Even in the face of the unlikelihood of discovering more ancient texts such as those of the Dead Sea, extra-biblical evidence still represents the most promising avenue to increase the data pool. This statement may appear self-evident even to the point of being superfluous. However, it is important to remember that the fundamental goal of exegesis is to discover what a text meant during the time in which it was written. Yet the Bible's self-depiction lends itself not only to a huge variety of possible times but also suggests various events were historical that more likely were not. For example, the presentation of the United Monarchy and especially Solomon's advancements suggest that Israel was already highly developed and internationally relevant during the 10th century BCE. Yet the archaeological picture is radically different. As Frevel summarises, "Territorialstaatliche Perspektiven sind vor dem 9. Jh. v. Chr. nicht zu erkennen und entwickeln sich tendenziell eher aus dem Ausbau und dem Zusammenwachsen von existierenden Herrschaftsclustern" (*Territorial state perspectives before the 9th century BCE are not discernible and tended to develop from the expansion and merging of existing ruling clusters*).[199]

Thus, in dating the biblical texts one must have a time of production already in mind. However, as Na'aman notes, biblical texts face the difficulty of being "written hundreds of years after many of the events it describes," and even then are often obscured by "its literary nature, its marked ideological and theological nature, and the central part played by God in the events described."[200] But even accepting these difficulties, one cannot escape the use of the Bible as a key to discovering the timeframe of its own production. So, is this simply an endless loop,

---

[199] FREVEL, *Geschichte*, 129.
[200] NA'AMAN, "Archaeology," 166.

2.2 Toward Certainty

an unsolvable interdependence? Although there is undeniably some circularity to the process, it should not be viewed as a snake eating its own tail. Rather, as Lonergan argues, "It is a self-correcting process of learning that spirals into the meaning of the whole by using each new part to fill out and qualify and correct the understanding reached in reading the earlier parts."[201]

It is undeniable that archaeology and other historical sources from the ancient Near East provide the biblical scholar with an immense resource for further analysis. That being said, it should not be assumed that this is a simple process of correlating the biblical text to readily available external evidence. Archaeology in particular should not be considered an exact science.[202]

One significant example of where a comparative approach has yielded invaluable results is in understanding the laws of Deuteronomy in light of Assyrian vassal treaties.[203] At the other end of the spectrum, there are many cases where the evidence either remains unclear or even leads to a conflict of authority. To provide one clear example, one need only look to Bethel. Viewed purely from the biblical material, it is undeniable that Bethel played a major role in the history of Israel, first as a major cult site of the Northern Kingdom and then later as part of Judah.[204] As Knauf notes, "Bethel is, after Jerusalem, the place

---

[201] LONERGAN, *Method*, 159.

[202] See esp. NA'AMAN, "Archaeology," 166.

[203] OTTO, *Politische*. On the value of this contribution, see, e.g., RÖMER, "Contributions," 2.

[204] If the report in 2 Chr 13:19 is to be believed, Bethel changed ownership several times throughout its preexilic history (cf. BLENKINSOPP, "Priesthood," 31). By the time of Josiah, it seems that Bethel, alongside the land of Benjamin, belonged to Judah (e.g., 2 Kgs 23:4). KNAUF, "Bethel," 297, suggests that the transfer of Benjamin and Bethel from Samaria to Judah during the seventh century was, "dictated by demographic and economic factors." This is because of the wide-ranging loss of population (approx. 90 %) from Jerusalem, the Judean Desert, Jordan Valley, the Shephelah and the region west of the Dead Sea (cf. LIPSCHITS, "Rural," 102), which left the most fertile and populated area being the tribal area of Benjamin. LIPSCHITS, "Rural," 104, notes, "in the region of Benjamin, there were four important, central cities that were not destroyed by the Babylonians and that even flourished during the sixth century B.C.E.: Mizpah (Tell en-Nasbeh), Gibeah (Tell el-Fûl), Bethel (identified with the village of Beitin), and Gibeon (identified in the village of el-Jib)." According to 2 Kgs 23:15, Josiah dismantled the Bethel temple built by Jeroboam I, however there are concerns about the historicity of this action of reform (cf. BLENKINSOPP, "Bethel," 95). One argument suggesting against this is the selection of Mizpah as the location for the Babylonian governor, Gedaliah (2 Kgs 25:22–23). As KNAUF, "Bethel," 296, notes, the selection of Mizpah implies the site was strategically located with respect to the region under Gedeliah's control, meaning that the territory of Benjamin had already been incorporated into Judah. Furthermore, with the destruction of the Jerusalem temple and the relocation of the centre of power to Mizpah, it follows that Bethel became the premier cultic site in the region. Further evidence for the continued cultic function of Bethel is inferred from the strange tale in Jer 41:5, which reports that following the murder of Gedaliah, "eighty men arrived from Shechem, Shiloh and Samaria, with shaved beards, torn clothes and cuts, with offerings and incense in their hands to present to the temple of YHWH." As BLENKINSOPP, "Priesthood," 27 f., notes, it is unlikely that these eighty northerners would be travelling to the ruined temple in Jerusalem to present offerings, much more likely they were intercepted near

most frequently mentioned in the Bible."[205] The problem comes when one turns to the archaeological record. This record, largely comes from the results of the excavations undertaken by Albright in 1934 and Kelso in 1954, 1957 and 1960.[206] After re-examining the published data Finkelstein and Singer-Avitz conclude, "the idea that Bethel served as a prominent cult place in the Babylonian period is contradicted by the archaeological evidence," and further, "significant scribal activity at Bethel in this time span is not a viable option."[207]

Yet in this case the clear contradiction between the importance of the place according to the Bible and the seeming unimportance according to the archaeological record has raised some eyebrows. Lipschits, for example, presents a detailed critique of Finkelstein and Singer-Avitz, three points being of particular importance. First, he notes that the methodology of the Albright era was far less rigorous than it is today, such that archaeologists would often only keep the most interesting pottery and not bother with damaged or mundane pieces, thus the fact that surviving pottery from Albright and Kelso's excavations contained little to no Persian period pottery may in fact only indicate that the pottery from that period was largely damaged and/or deemed uninteresting.[208] Second, he draws attention to the fact that the excavation avoided the area of the present day village, focussing instead on the unoccupied (in many cases uncultivated) areas, Kelso even noted that the area that most likely contained the Persian period village was not excavated due to the area being occupied by the present-day village.[209] Third, the fact that remains of a temple were never found in Beitin/Bethel does not conclusively prove that there was no temple, rather there is a good chance that the temple was located outside the village (such as E. P. 914, located east of Bethel); Gen 12:8 even suggests that Abram's altar was built "east of Bethel."[210]

Na'aman also critiques this "proven" archaeological conclusion noting:

Upon returning to the results of the excavations at Bethel, first we should recall that unlike at many other Judahite sites, where clear destruction layers were exposed in the excavations, at Iron Age Bethel no destruction layers were detected. This indicates that the process of desertion and abandonment was gradual and took place over a long period of time. Second, the location of the temple remains unknown, so the sixth century settlement and cult place may be located in other parts of the mound. Third, Bethel is located in the highlands, where the bedrock is high and later construction and levelling works in the

---

Mizpah because that is where they were travelling to, with the logical extrapolation pointing to the nearby temple of Bethel.

[205] KNAUF, "Bethel," 291.

[206] See introduction in FINKELSTEIN/SINGER-AVITZ, "Bethel."

[207] FINKELSTEIN/SINGER-AVITZ, "Bethel," 45. See also FREVEL, *Geschichte*, 184.

[208] LIPSCHITS, "Bethel," 240.

[209] LIPSCHITS, "Bethel," 239.

[210] LIPSCHITS, "Bethel," 243. For the excavation of E. P. 914, see TAVGER, "East."

Hellenistic to the Byzantine periods might have removed the remains of older buildings and scattered the pottery away from its original location.[211]

On the one hand, the absence of material evidence should give pause to an overly positivistic view of the biblical presentation. On the other hand, one must be realistic about the limits of archaeology, especially when it is known that key areas could not be investigated or when there are good reasons to question the location of the dig. If nothing else, the example of Bethel is a reminder that one must be cautious with the conversion of data into meaning.

The present work will attempt to incorporate as much extra-biblical data as possible in order to better understand its two major case studies. In particular it will argue that a historical connection can be derived from the geographical indicators in the text. The underlying principle here is that immersion into a narrative world, especially one that is intended to depict a reality, is only successful so long as that world is capable of being believable. This believability is achieved not by a suspension of disbelief but rather by what Tolkien referred to as Secondary Belief:

> What really happens is that the story-maker proves a successful 'sub-creator'. He makes a Secondary World which your mind can enter. Inside it, what he relates is 'true': it accords with the laws of that world. You therefore believe it, while you are, as it were, inside. The moment disbelief arises, the spell is broken; the magic, or rather art, has failed. You are then out in the Primary World again, looking at the little abortive Secondary World from outside. If you are obliged, by kindliness or circumstance, to stay, then disbelief must be suspended (or stifled), otherwise listening and looking would become intolerable. But this suspension of disbelief is a substitute for the genuine thing, a subterfuge we use when condescending to games or make-believe, or when trying (more or less willingly) to find what virtue we can in the work of an art that has for us failed.[212]

The idea of David's great kingdom, for example, is not pure fantasy, rather it was rooted in a believable and even verifiable reality. As Sergi notes, "The literary shape of the story of Absalom and Sheba's revolts presupposes the power, extent and geo-political settings of the kingdom of Israel under the reign of Jeroboam II in the first half of the 8th century B.C.E., but ascribes it to David's rule."[213]

2.2.3 The Samaritan Influence and the Formation of the Pentateuch

One further new advancement in Pentateuchal research is the growing acceptance that the Samaritans played a far greater role in its production than previously acknowledged.[214] Recent research on the Samaritans can be seen to

---

[211] NA'AMAN, "Archaeology," 180.

[212] TOLKIEN, "Fairy-stories," 52.

[213] SERGI, "Monarchy," 352.

[214] Recent monographs include KARTVEIT, Origins; DUŠEK, Inscriptions; KNOPPERS, Jews; HENSEL, Juda; PUMMER, Samaritans.

50   *2. Setting the Stage*

have undergone two major changes that correlate directly with the increased knowledge afforded by extra-biblical discoveries. The first major change came as a result of the discovery and study of the Dead Sea Scrolls (and particularly the so-called proto-Samaritan texts) in the middle of the twentieth century. The second change, found only in the most recent studies, has largely come about following the publications of the extensive excavations of Mount Gerizim undertaken by Magen and his team since the 1980s.[215]

Prior to the discovery of the Dead Sea Scrolls the presence of pro-Judean materials in the Bible stemming from the Persian period suggested that the "schism" between Samaritans and Judeans occurred around this period.[216] This understanding was supported by the idea that the Samaritan Pentateuch was a relatively old document and could be dated prior to the two groups parting ways.[217] De Wette, for example, argued that it was after Sanballat undertook the construction of the temple on Mount Gerizim that, "there was hatred, deep and deadly hatred, between the two nations."[218]

Following the discoveries at Qumran, scholars were led to date the Samaritan Pentateuch much later, with the majority seeing it as the product of the mid-second century BCE.[219] This new dating was based on the SP's similarity with other materials found at Qumran that could be dated to that period more precisely. Cross notes that the Samaritan Pentateuch's textual type, orthographic style, Palaeo-Hebrew script, and linguistic usage, all point to it being written in the Maccabean and early Hasmonean periods.[220] This change in the dating of the Samaritan Pentateuch meant that Sanballat's temple construction could no longer be regarded as the "point of no return" between the two communities. Frey, for example, argues, "methodologically, we should not presuppose an immediate connection between the building of the temple [on Mount Gerizim] and the emerging schism."[221]

That being said, Hensel argues that many scholars (wrongly) still see the Gerizim temple as the beginning of tensions between Samaritans and Jews and thus represents the first stage in what he calls the "three-phase conflict model":

---

[215] Importantly see MAGEN et al., *Gerizim I*; MAGEN, *Gerizim II*. See also discussion in, e.g., DUŠEK, *Inscriptions*.

[216] As HENSEL, "Relationship," 1, notes, the term "schism" is problematic due to the fact that it, "presupposes an orthodox central group – which is believed to be the Judean or Jerusalem group – from which the Samaritans split off as a sect."

[217] See, e.g., KNOPPERS, "Revisiting," 255 f., for a rebuttal of these ideas. Knoppers further argues that even the claim of a polemic against the Samaritans by the Chronicler is misguided.

[218] DE WETTE, *Introduction*, 332.

[219] See, e.g., ANDERSON/GILES, *Penateuch*, 15 f. (esp. 22); SCHORCH, "Formation," esp. 9f; SCHORCH, "Samaritanische," 19.

[220] CROSS, "Aspects," 210, notes, "From whatever side we examine the Samaritan Pentateuch, by whatever typological development we measure it, we are forced to the Hasmonean period at [sic] earliest for the origins of the Samaritan recension of the Pentateuch."

[221] FREY, "Temple," 180.

the earliest phase of the conflict began with Sanballat's construction of a "rival" temple on Mount Gerizim, the second phase represented a period of growing tensions, and finally a complete break occurred when the Mount Gerizim temple was destroyed.[222]

In contrast Hensel argues that the Samaritans and Jews represented two distinct Yahwistic communities, that remained in contact and were co-developers of a shared Pentateuch. Importantly he argues that the extant Pentateuch still contains a suspicious amount of pro-Northern material, which directly speaks against the idea that it was primarily a Judean product, and that the North was considered an aberrant sect of the "official" Yahwism practiced in Jerusalem. In particular he notes that the Joseph narrative, if it indeed reflects postexilic period Yahwism, demonstrates that even here the North had a special standing over against the other sons of Israel (including Judah).[223] The understanding of

---

[222] HENSEL, "Relationship." For a more detailed discussion see HENSEL, *Juda*, 7–24.

[223] HENSEL, *Juda*, 408–409, writes, "Man kann daraus folgern, dass die Garizim-Gemeinde ein entscheidender und zumindest ebenbürtiger Gesprächspartner der Jerusalemer Eliten gewesen ist; beide konnten Kontakte auf Augenhöhe führen. Nimmt man allerdings das Schwergewicht an (vermutungsweise) originären Nordreichs-Traditionen im "Gemeinsamen Pentateuch" hinzu, kann man sich des Eindruckes nicht erwehren, dass – entgegen der einschlägigen Geschichtsdarstellungen und entgegen der Ausblendung der samarischen Kultur in der biblischen (judäischen) Geschichtsdarstellung, die mit dem Untergang des Nordreichs 722 v.Chr. begründet wird – der Einfluss jenes samarischen "Israels" in nach-exilischer Zeit immerhin so dominant gewesen sein muss, dass solche Konzessionen von judäischer Seite aus eingeräumt werden *mussten*. Sollte es zutreffen, dass die Joseph-Juda-Erzählung Gen 37–50 tatsächlich über die samarisch-judäischen Beziehungen in nach-exilischer Zeit Auskunft gibt, so wird die *kulturelle Dominanz Samarias* über die besondere Bedeutung des Nordreich-Eponyms Joseph ausgedrückt. Immerhin hängt an der Joseph-Figur, dem Erstgeborenen, der Segen ganz Israels. Die Dominanz des samarischen Jahwismus scheint auch der Grund dafür zu sein, dass die judäische Variante des JHWH-Glaubens mit diversen literarischen Strategien und Polemiken in einer solchen Vehemenz die samarische Geschwisterreligion in ihren nach-exilischen, biblischen Geschichtsnarrationen konsequent ausblendet und kultrechtlich entlegitimiert. (*One can conclude that the Gerizim community were a significant and at least equal interlocutor of the Jerusalem elites; neither party looked down upon the other. However, if one adds to that the emphasis on the (presumably) original Northern traditions in the "shared Pentateuch," one cannot avoid the impression that – contrary to the relevant historical presentation and contrary to the suppression of the Samarian culture in the biblical (Judean) historical account, which is founded upon the collapse of the Northern Kingdom in 722 BCE – the influence of that Samarian "Israel" must have been so dominant in the postexilic period that such concession had to be granted from the Judean side. If it is true that the Joseph-Judah narrative of Gen 37–50 actually discloses information regarding Samarian-Judean relations in the postexilic period, then Samaria's cultural dominance would be expressed in the special importance of the Northern eponym, Joseph. After all, the blessing of all Israel hangs on the Joseph figure, the firstborn. The dominance of Samarian Yahwism also seems to be the basis for why, in their postexilic biblical historical narration and in terms of cultic law, the Judean variant of YHWH belief consistently suppresses the Samarian sister religion with such vehemence via diverse literary strategies and polemics.*" (emphasis original). KNOPPERS, "Conceptions," 88, with a similar sentiment writes, "Moreover, when speaking of 'the place (מקום) at which I have caused my name to be remembered,' the SP alludes to the construction of an earlier altar. Within the literary context of the SP, the text is alluding to the 'place

52   *2. Setting the Stage*

the Samaritans being co-developers of the Pentateuch not only makes historical sense but importantly it solves the issue of why the Samaritans had a Pentateuch at all.[224] As Knoppers argues, the idea that the Samaritans were happy to adopt a purely Judean Torah would be, "unparalleled in the history of ancient religions – the wholesale borrowing of an entire set of scriptures by one people from another without the receptor group having any substantive role to play in the writing and redaction of the literature itself."[225]

Although it is admittedly difficult to detect Samaritan influence when it is not overt, it will be suggested in chapter 4 that the predicament of the Manassite (i. e., Samaritan) daughters of Zelophehad can be much more fully explained if it is assumed that it was written if not by, at least for, the Samaritans.

2.3 In Favour of an Exodus-Conquest Narrative

Although it was admitted that the models outlined in § 2.1.2.4.B were not beyond doubt, this section will outline some key clues that point towards the basic idea of a preexilic exodus-conquest being the most convincing starting point for the formation of the Pentateuch.

---

of Shechem' (מקום שכם) visited by Abram, following his arrival in the land of Canaan (Gen. 12:6–8). As scholars have long recognized, the SP suggests that Mt. Gerizim had been selected by the deity during ancestral times. Hence, in these SP texts, the authority and status of Mt. Gerizim are enhanced. There is, therefore, significant continuity in the SP from the ancestral era through the exodus and Sinaitic periods to the time of Israel's later encampment upon the Steppes of Moab. On these grounds, one may argue that the SP is more of a self-contained and internally coherent work than is the Jewish Pentateuch in that a single altar site is mentioned in a number of narrative and legal contexts. The divine favor extended toward a central sanctuary is hinted at or overtly declared at various passages in more than one book. Moreover, the fact that Yhwh has already chosen the site of the future sanctuary adds a sense of closure to the Pentateuch. Rather than the deity making his decision about which site should serve at some indefinite point in the future as the centre of a unified cult, the deity has already made his decision. It is simply a matter of Israelite corporate responsibility to exercise its divinely-given charge."

A further example is found in NODET, "Israelites," 121, who observes, "Besides the pious account in 2 Chron 3–6, neither Solomon's temple nor the one envisioned by Ezekiel nor the work of the returnees with Zerubbabel and Haggai match the rules stated by Moses."

Regarding the Judean polemics SCHORCH, "Samaritanische," 26, argues that it was during the reign of John Hyrcanus that the wording of Deut 27:4 was changed from Mt. Gerizim to Mt. Ebal in the Judean version. See also discussion in SCHORCH, "Origin," 28; SCHORCH, "Pentateuch," 27; HENSEL, "Relationship," 17. Cf. NIHAN, "The Torah," who rather sees the SP version of Deut 27:4 as an originally Judean concession, that was only later redacted with the anti-Samaritan "Mt. Ebal."

[224] As HJELM, "Perspectives," 193, argues, "New hypotheses about the production of the Pentateuch in the Persian and Hellenistic periods require new scenarios that present the Samaritans on Gerizim as (co-)authors, rather than receivers of a fully formed tradition." SCHMID, "Samaritaner," for example, argues that the pan-Israelite vision of Joshua 24 demonstrates a coordinated effort between Judea and Samaria.

[225] KNOPPERS, "Context," 164.

In so doing, it must be acknowledged that the following reconstruction is deliberately sweeping and lacking in important details. The intention is to provide a basic mental framework for the detailed exegetical analysis in chapters 3 and 4. With that, it is to be emphasised that a more rigorous scholarly proof of this thesis is still required and, like all scientific endeavours, is subject to revision and change.

2.3.1 Jeroboam II and the Moses Story

That the Pentateuch contains traditions that have a clear Northern origin was already recognised in the Elohist, which was in many ways considered to be the counterpart of the Judean's Jahwist.[226] In more recent times, there has been a growing appreciation for understanding Jeroboam II as being the most likely monarch to have at his disposal sufficient means of literary production and scribal acumen to have produced the first written versions of Israel's traditions.[227] As Finkelstein observes, "the archaeology-led analysis of alphabetic writing in the Levant during the Iron Age shows no infrastructure of compilation of literary texts before ca. 800 B.C.E."[228] Regarding the Northern origins of the exodus

---

[226] Wolff, "Fragments," 172, for example, states, "Many have noted that there are numerous indications that the material [of the Elohist] originated in the Northern Kingdom. It can be shown that the author was familiar with specific local traditions from the North." Cf. Jenks, "Elohist," 480; Gnuse, "Redefining," esp. 203. As Carr, Fractures, 146, notes, detangling the Elohist parts of a text, "tends to proceed in two steps: (1) presuppose that E 'must' be in a given section, and (2) use the fund of terminological indicators drawn from other texts to identify Elohistic fragments in the material that can be shaken loose from the Yahwistic context." Cf. Baden, Composition, 116 f. This general assumption of a Southern J and Northern E was not held by Kuenen, Inquiry, 248, who argued, "The yahwistic document (J) was composed in the north-Israelite kingdom within the ninth or quite at the beginning of the eighth century B.C. The elohistic document (E) was written, in the same kingdom, by an author who was acquainted with J, and who must have lived about 750 B.C. Both works were known and well received in Judah also. But they could not permanently satisfy the existing and gradually unfolding requirements of the latter kingdom. Accordingly, both alike were so expanded and recast that in the second half of the seventh century distinctively Judean editions of J and E had come into existence."

[227] On the textual production under Jeroboam II see, e.g., Finkelstein, Kingdom, 141–151; Knauf, "Jeroboam," 306; Frevel, Geschichte, 264–265. Finkelstein, "Corpus," 263, notes, "from the viewpoint of scribal activity, Israel provides evidence for bureaucratic writings (Samaria ostraca) and literary texts (Kuntillet 'Ajrud and Deir Alla) as early as the first half of the 8th century B.C.E., at least half a century but probably more than a century before Judah." That beings said, this scribal capacity should not be overstated. Kleiman, "System," 355, for example, writes, "clear archaeological evidence for a royal administrative system in the northern parts of the country is limited – even in the heyday of the kingdom, during the reign of Jeroboam II." On the idea of an 8th century BCE Northern Tradition, see also Blum, "Mose."

[228] Finkelstein, "Corpus," 262. Speaking of the origins of Hebrew literacy, Finkelstein/ Sass, "Inscriptions," 191–192, ask, "Does this signify that the Hebrew alphabet arose in Jerusalem and was transmitted thence to Samaria? Habitually the opposite is argued: it is the more developed Israel that is considered to have called the tune, with Jerusalem emulating Samaria." Frevel,

54   2. Setting the Stage

narrative, a number of scholars have noted that striking parallels between the story of Jeroboam I in 1 Kgs 11:26–12:25 and the beginning of Exodus.[229] Schmid summarizes this proposal as follows:

Like Moses (Exod 2:1–10), Jeroboam (1 Kgs 11:26) is of distinguished origin and revolts against the ruling power because of the burdensome forced labor (1 Kgs 11:26–28/ Exod 2:11–15). In both cases, the rebellion fails and Jeroboam, like Moses, must flee into foreign territory (1 Kgs 11:40/Exod 2:15). Both return after the death of the king (1 Kgs 12:2/Exod 2:23/4:19–20), an event that leads to negotiations about the forced labor (1 Kgs 12:3–15/ Exod 5:3–19). However, the negotiations do not resolve the problem but instead lead to the people's exodus in the one case and to the division of the kingdom in the other.[230]

In his earlier work, Albertz suggested that the narrative was historically rooted to the foundation of a new dynasty in light of the so-called division of the kingdom, thus functioning as a legitimation narrative of the newly crowned Jeroboam I.[231] More recent analyses suggest that the historical origins of Jeroboam I, as they are presented in Kings, are highly unlikely and that the deeds of Jeroboam I are more likely a negatively-skewed depiction of the achievements Jeroboam II put back in time to a founding figure.[232]

Geschichte, 265, more tentatively argues, "Von der Anzahl und Qualität der Schriftzeugnisse her beurteilt, bietet die wirtschaftliche Blütezeit Israels im 8. Jh. v. Chr. genügend Anhaltspunkte, um über die Entstehung der biblischen Überlieferung zu spekulieren, die besonders mit dem Norden verbunden ist. Dazu gehören, abgesehen von der Elischa-Überlieferung, die ältere Jakobüberlieferung, die Exodusüberlieferung und die älteren Traditionen eines "Retterbuches." (*Judged by the number and quality of the written records, the economic heyday of Israel in the 8th century BCE offers sufficient clues to speculate about the origin of the biblical tradition, which is particularly connected to the North. These include, apart from the Elisha tradition, the older Jacob tradition, the Exodus tradition and the older traditions in Judges, the so-called "Book of Saviors"*).

[229] Albertz, *Religionsgeschichte*, 72, 127. Although Van Der Toorn, *Family*, 300–301, incorrectly attributes this to a charter myth based on the Deuteronomistic account of Jeroboam, he correctly notes, "The story of the deliverance from Egypt had indeed all the potential for a national charter myth; it takes little imagination to see why it came to be used as such."

[230] Schmid, *Genesis*, 128.

[231] Speaking of Bethel and Dan, Albertz, *History*, 143, writes, "Thus we get the impression that after his successful fight for liberation from the house of David, Jeroboam, who had been guided by the Yahweh traditions from the time before the state, also wanted to develop an archaizing alternative to the state cult of Jerusalem, with all its innovations, which would strengthen continuity with conditions existing before the state."

[232] See esp. Römer, "Jeroboam II." Frevel, *Geschichte*, 193, writes, "Wahrscheinlich sind weder Jerobeam I. (927/26–907 v. Chr.) noch Rehabeam (926–910 v. Chr.) historische Figuren, sondern Konstruktionen, die von Jerobeam II. (787–747 v. Chr.) ihren Ausgang nehmen. Mit Jerobeam I. wird der Anfang des Nordstaates eponymenhaft verbunden worden sein als Israel unter Jerobeam II. eine außergewöhnliche Blütezeit erlebte. Diese wahrscheinlich mit Mose parallelisierte und heroenhaft gefärbte, fiktive Gründerfigur wurde von den judäischen Geschichtsschreibern in eine Gegenfigur umgewandelt. (*Probably neither Jeroboam I (927/26–907 BCE) nor Rehoboam (926–910 BCE) were historical figures, but constructions that originated from Jeroboam II (787–747 BCE). The beginning of the Northern Kingdom would have been connected eponymically with Jeroboam I when Israel experienced an extraordinary heyday under Jeroboam*

Further support for the Northern origins of the core Pentateuchal traditions is found in the province of Samaria. Hensel notes that the onomastic evidence from the Gerizim inscriptions reveals some interesting results. In particular, the names Joseph, Miriam, Eleazar and Phinehas appear commonly in these Northern inscriptions but "sind in keinem aramäischen oder hebräischen Text judäischer Provenienz belegt" (*are not referenced in any Aramaic or Hebrew text of Judean provenance*).[233] Although one must always be mindful of the maxim, the absence of evidence is not the evidence of absence, the general impression given by this evidence is that these characters have a stronger relationship to the North than they do to the South.

As will be argued in § 2.3.2, it seems most probable that this Northern monarchical Moses-exodus narrative was heavily reworked by Judean scribes, thus making the reconstruction of its precise contents very uncertain.[234] But this should not be seen as evidence against its existence rather it needs to be seen in light the discussion of § 2.2.1; in particular the idea that even when traditions were heavily reworked and repurposed, the general shape of a text was maintained.[235]

Whether or not Knauf is correct in suggesting that the original Northern Moses-exodus narrative ended in the land spanning from Bethel to Dan, the extant narrative has been so thoroughly reworked that one must at least expect

---

II. This fictitious founder figure, probably parallelized with Moses and heroically coloured, was transformed into a counter-figure by the Judean historians.)

[233] HENSEL, *Juda*, 150. MAGEN, *Gerizim I*, 61, writes that Miriam "was one of the most common women's names in the late Second Temple period," accounting for almost a quarter of the names of females discovered. KNOPPERS, *Judah*, 80–81, also writes, "when surveying the Mt. Gerizim onomasticon with the early Hellenistic period in view, one is struck by three things: 1) the number of common Yahwistic proper names; 2) the number of archaizing personal names, that is, names that recall the names of male and female figures associated with Israel's ancient past; and 3) the number of common Hebrew names."

[234] In his inimitable style, KNAUF, "Jeroboam," 306, states, "... the search for a pre-Sargonic version of the Moses-exodus story should look at Nimshide Samaria." This follows BLANCO WISSMANN, "Sargon," in particular, who suggests a 7th century setting by tradents of the Jehu Dynasty (and more likely during the prosperous time Jeroboam II) as the likely historical point of origin. For other support of the Northern origins of an exodus-conquest tradition, see, e.g., FINKELSTEIN/RÖMER, "Memories," 725; FINKELSTEIN, "Corpus," 263; FREVEL, *Geschichte*, 56. This is not to mention the supposed Northern origins of Deuteronomy, see discussion in, e.g., ALT, *Schriften*, 250–275; SCHORCH, "Origin" (cf. NIHAN, "The Torah," who argues that the references to Garizim should be understood to be a "concession made to the Yahwists residing in Samaria at the time of the redaction of the Torah" – p. 214). As NA'AMAN, "Rediscovering," 298, observes, "It is always difficult to demonstrate the existence of a lost work on the basis of inferences drawn from an existing literary work. This difficulty certainly emerges when dealing with a biblical text whose authors and redactors were directed by literary and theological motivation, made extensive alterations in the received texts, and frequently did not find it necessary to name their sources. Under such conditions, we can only present circumstantial evidence that, by cumulative force, might partly corroborate the existence of the presumed lost work."

[235] See further discussion in PAKKALA, *Word*, 40.

56 *2. Setting the Stage*

a Judean-Samarian amalgamation.[236] This is already suggested by the extant tradition concluding with the proto-Josianic Joshua (see below) conquering Josiah's Judah.[237]

The broad assumption of a written Moses tradition originating from the preexilic North will be decisive for the analysis in § 3.1.1, where it will be suggested that the Transjordan territory requested by the Reubenites and Gadites plausibly corresponds to that (re)taken during the reign of Jehoash or Jeroboam II. Not only does this Transjordan territory neatly correspond to Jeroboam's Israel but the very presence of Transjordan territory makes best sense in light of a Northern origin, where the Jordan was not historically conceived to be a political or theological boundary.[238]

2.3.2 Josiah and Early Joshua

Although the precise details of the Northern Moses-exodus narrative can no longer be determined, there is a better certainty that this narrative underwent some fairly significant changes when it was repurposed by the Judeans.[239] But this raises a fundamental question, why would the Judeans bother re-purposing Northern traditions at all? As Fleming states:

> This renders all the more striking the fact that Judah's origins are subordinated to those of Israel as the larger entity and that very little is said about Judah's particular role before the monarchy. This pattern appears to reflect the adoption by Judah of Israel's distinct traditions about origins, *which did not include Judah when they were created.*[240]

Although they have largely been removed from the extant Bible, there remain hints and traces that the original Moses-exodus story had Moses bring Israel

---

[236] KNAUF, *Josua*, 18, suggests, "Die Mose-Exodus-Überlieferung stammt aus dem Nordreich Israel, aber dort endete sie im Land zwischen Bet-El und Dan (vgl. 1 Kön 12,28–29; wahrscheinlich eine Tradition aus dem 8. Jh. v. Chr.)" (*The Moses-Exodus-Tradition stemmed from the Northern Kingdom of Israel, but there it ended in the land between Bet-El and Dan [cf. 1 Kgs 12:28–29; likely a tradition from the 8th century BCE]*).

[237] KNAUF, *Josua*, 16, argues that it was only during the Hexateuch redaction that Joshua was referred to as "son of Nun." The earliest Pentateuchal sources featuring Joshua are: Exod 17:9–10, 13–14; 24:13; Deut 3:21 and 28. All other Pentateuchal references to Joshua, particularly those in the book of Numbers (except Num 27:22, which is clearly a shorthand repetition of 27:18) refer to him as Joshua son of Nun. KRATZ, *Composition*, 112f., argues that the pre-Priestly Hexateuchal skeleton jumped from Num 25 to Josh 3:1 with shared reference to Shittim. Josh 3:1 also eschews the lineage, "son of Nun."

[238] KNAUF, "Jeroboam," 303, observes, "The concept of the Jordan river as Israel's eastern border could have developed at the end of the 7th century, when Judah reached the Jordan at Jericho, but not further east."

[239] KNAUF, *Josua*, 18. SCHMID, *Genesis*, 145, argues, "the Moses/Exodus story [underwent] a radical theological transformation ... the Northern Kingdom traditions were then transferred into the South, and there were reinterpreted mono-Yahwistically."

[240] FLEMING, *Legacy*, 28 (emphasis added).

2.3 In Favour of an Exodus-Conquest Narrative 57

into the land. Römer refers to these as "'censored' Moses Traditions."[241] Although many of these "censored" traditions likely arose much later, for example in light of Demotic literature, there remain some hints in the Hebrew Bible that potentially have much earlier origins.[242] 1 Samuel 12:8 in particular notes, "When Jacob came to Egypt and your ancestors cried out to YHWH, YHWH sent Moses and Aaron and they led your ancestors out of Egypt and settled them in this place." Taken at face value, this verse suggests that Moses not only led Israel out of Egypt but also brought them into the land, and it is not too much of a stretch to assume that that land was Jeroboam's Israel (and included the Transjordan cf. chapter 3).[243] As Fleming argues, devoid of a concluding conquest, "The exodus story by itself would be excruciatingly unsatisfying."[244]

This observation dovetails neatly with what is arguably one of the most peculiar features of the Hexateuchal narrative: that the prophet par excellence, the great leader Moses died outside the land. That this was not only a problem for modern readers can be inferred from the fact that even the various biblical editors could not agree on why exactly it was that Moses had to die: was he too old to lead a military campaign (Deut 31:2) or simply too old despite his good health (Deut 34:7), having reaching the natural maximum lifespan ordained by YHWH (Gen 6:3); was he punished as part of the generational punishment of the exodus generation (Deut 1:37; 3:26–27) or was he punished for his own disobedience (Num 27:12–14)?

The simplest explanation for this is that Moses had to die outside the land so that Joshua could lead the people into the land. Why? The thesis to be briefly proposed here is that the original Joshua narrative functioned as a major element in the Judean-based reworking of the Northern Moses-exodus narrative. This reworking can be seen, much like the Gilgamesh epic with the addition of the flood narrative, as an intentional taking up of known traditions and repurposing them into something new.[245]

The historical background for this Judean rework is based on the more recent histories of Israel (see below) in which the idea of the United Monarchy under David and Solomon must be seen as more legend than reality. In particular it relies on the idea that it was only after the fall of the North that Judah could be considered a "state" in its own right and that it could attain sufficient autonomy (due to its position as an Assyrian vassal, which only increased once Assyria's power in the region began to fade) to engage in territorial expansion.[246] This

---

[241] RÖMER, "Tracking."

[242] On the Demotic parallels, see RÖMER, "Tracking;" BÜHLER, "Demotic."

[243] Cf. note 236 on page 56.

[244] FLEMING, *Legacy*, 117.

[245] On the Gilgamesh modification, see CARR, *Tablet*, 39.

[246] Although one should not underestimate the importance that the weakening of Assyria had in contributing to Josiah's success, neither should it be overestimated. As FREVEL, *Geschichte,*

58 2. Setting the Stage

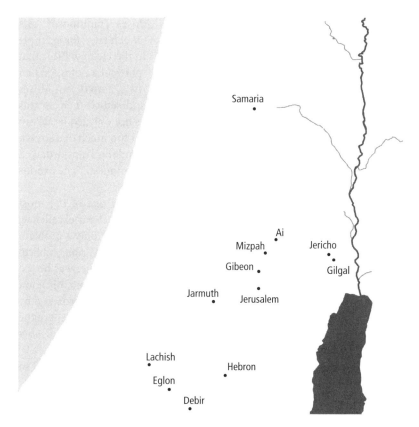

Figure 1: Conquest according to Joshua 6–10*[247]

increase in autonomy, and the favourable "international" political conditions made space for Josiah to expand the territory of Judah, first northward into the territory of Benjamin.[248]

---

306 remarks, "Der Abzug der Assyrer hinterlässt kein Machtvakuum" (*The withdrawal of the Assyrians left behind no power vacuum*), rather Judah more likely transferred from an Assyrian vassalage to an Egyptian one (under Psammetichus I).

[247] Map drawn by J. Davis. All location data from FREVEL, *Geschichte*, 444–449. Samaria is located at (1686.1870). Ai is located at et-Tell (1748.1471). Mizpah is located at Tell en-Nasbeh (1706.1436). Jericho is located at Tell el-Sultan (1921.1420), see also ANATI, "Trade." Gibeon is located at Al Jib (1676.1396). Gilgal is located at (1934.1425). Jarmuth is located at Khirbet el-Yarmûk (1470.1240). Jerusalem is located at (1724.1315). Lachish is located at Tell ed-Duweir (1357.1082). Hebron is located at (1598.1035). Eglon is located at (1425.0999). Debir is located at (1514.0934).

[248] NA'AMAN, "Josiah," 232, for example, notes that "Josiah enjoyed a protracted period of peace throughout his rule; following the Assyrian retreat, he took energetic action toward the stabilization of his kingdom, and perhaps also toward its northward expansion."

In light of this Josianic expansion of Judah's territory, the earliest conquest materials in Joshua take on new light. A growing number of scholars are recognising that the earliest narrative material in Joshua is found in chapters 6–10*, which narrate a conquest that begins in Benjamin and ends in southern Judah (see figure 1), and that this territory corresponds to Josiah's Judah.[249] Finkelstein and Silberman note, "The first two battles in the book of Joshua, at Jericho and Ai (that is, the area of Bethel), were fought in territories that were the first target of Josianic expansionism after the withdrawal of Assyria from the province of Samaria."[250] Seen in the context of a Josianic reappropriation of the Northern Moses-exodus narrative, this "new" ending can be seen to have rhetorical force.[251] In light of the locations actually described in the narrative, it is difficult to conceive of this narrative stemming from anywhere other than the South. One important aspect of this thesis is the idea that this narrative core ended in Josh 10:42[252] and that it did not originally arise as part of a Deuteronomistic corpus (DtrH or DtrL).[253] The idea that the original *Judean* exodus-conquest narrative

---

[249] See, e.g., KNAUF, *Data*, 347–355, esp. 347; ZENGER, *Einleitung*, 126. KRATZ, *Composition*, 294, suggests that Josh 6:1–3aα, 5, 12a, 14aα, 20b; 8:1–2a, 10a, 11a, 14, 19, were used as sources by E (i.e., Kratz's "Exodus redactor" not the Elohist!) and joined to Josh 10–11; 12:1a, 9–24. GERMANY, *Exodus-Conquest*, 448–449, suggests the earliest Joshua narrative comprised Josh 1:1–2*; 3:1a*, 14a, 16*; 4:(11a?), 19b; 6:1–3, 4aβ, 5*, 7a*, 11*, 14a*, 14b–16aα, 20*, 21, 24a; 8:1a*, 2b(?), 10*, 11aα*, 12*, 13aα*, 14a*, 19*, 21; 9:3, 6a, 8a, 15aα; 10:1aα, 1b, 3–4, 5–7*, 9a, 10aβb, 29–32*, 34–40*, 42(?).

[250] FINKELSTEIN/SILBERMAN, *Unearthed*, 93.

[251] Cf. NA'AMAN, "Rediscovering," who suggests Joshua was originally a Northern hero.

[252] KNAUF, "Buchschlüsse," 218–219; NIHAN, "Relationship," 105–109; GERMANY, *Exodus-Conquest*, 448–449. Cf. RÖMER, "Problem," 822–823, who argues in line with NELSON, *Joshua*, 138, that Josh 10:40–42* should rather be regarded as a "summation of southern conquests."

[253] Speaking of the evidence for an originally DtrH-compiled Joshua, VAN SETERS, *Redaction*, 304, observed, "Martin Noth's thesis of a DtrH rests heavily upon the view that the Book of Joshua contains a clearly identifiable deuteronomistic framework in 1,1–18 and 21,23–22,6 + 23,1–16 into which the conquest of the land narrative has been set." Although Joshua 23 does indeed contain a clear farewell speech, there has been a growing number of scholars who suggest that this was not the first conclusion to Joshua.
GERMANY, "Hexateuch," 133–135, highlights the fact that Noth's original preclusion of the Joshua narrative belonging to an early Pentateuchal narrative rested on only two "basic arguments …: (1) the P-like material in Josh. 13.1–21.42 had its own literary prehistory that is independent of both the other parts of Joshua and the Pentateuchal narratives; and (2) even in the other parts of the Joshua narrative, the literary evidence differs from that found in Genesis (the classsical case study for source-critical analyses)." (134).
FREVEL, "Wiederkehr," 20–25, highlights the problem of the interrelated contents of the end of Numbers and Joshua 13–22. Noth's solution to see Joshua 13–21, 22* as preceding the Numbers material faces multiple problems. First, because Josh 13:1 already anticipates Josh 23:2, he is forced to attribute this entire section to a different source that was worked into DtrG. Second, the high level of Priestly styled material in these same chapters is not explained, as in more recent analyses, as being evidence that Joshua 13–22 are post-Priestly. Rather, Noth must assert that these Priestly materials were dependent on the Deuteronomistically-edited Joshua 13–22 and worked in after Deuteronomy had been joined to the Pentateuch. To this Frevel notes, "Wichtig ist jedoch zu betonen, dass der kompositionelle Zusammenhang zwischen Josua und

60   *2. Setting the Stage*

ended in vv. 40a, 42 has much to commend it; this results in a narrative ending
as follows:

Joshua struck the whole land, the hill country, the Negeb, the lowlands, the slopes, and all
their kings [from Kadesh-barnea as far as Gibeon].[254] All these kings and their land Joshua
captured at one time, for YHWH, the God of Israel, fought for Israel.

Such a conclusion fits very well to the conquest described in Joshua 6–10*,
as Knauf writes, "Nach Jos 10,40–42 (wie nach dem Gebiet, das in Jos 6–10
tatsächlich erobert wird) ist das 'Verheissene Land' mit dem Königreich Juda
in den Grenzen unmittelbar vor 597 oder 586 v. Chr. identisch" (*According to
Josh 10:40–42 [like the area that was actually conquered according to Joshua
6–10] the 'promised land' is identical to the border of the kingdom of Judah
immediately before 597 or 586 BCE*).[255] That these verses comprise the original
ending of the Joshua narrative is debated. But this is hardly surprising given that
Knauf demonstrates that the book of Joshua contains no less than five separate
endings that function, "like rings on a tree," to indicate successive redactional
expansions:[256]

Numeri de facto einen nachpriestergrundschriftlichen Hexateuch bezeugt" (*It is important to
emphasise, however, that the compositional connection between Joshua and Numbers de facto
attests a post-Priestly Hexateuch*)(pp. 24–25). See further critiques in FREVEL, *Geschichtswerk*.

ALBERTZ, "Search," 2, highlights the quite simple yet damning observation that Noth's
suggestion that the Deuteronomist was "a single man" and "a relible historian who dissociated
himself from all other groups and was not obliged to anybody, cannot explain why he had such
influence on the literary history of the Bible." Further, Albertz concludes, "Noth's lack of interest
in situating the author in the Judean society of the exilic period means that Deuteronomism has
remained a historical riddle."

Regarding the idea that DtrH ended in Joshua 23, KNAUF, *Josua*, 188–190, labels Joshua 23
"ein Nicht-Schluss" (*a non-conclusion*), and instead argues that this chapter, together with
Joshua 24, functions as a Janus conclusion. Where Joshua 24 closes the Hexateuch, Joshua 23
links to the Former Prophets and continues in Judg 2:5, which reports an alternate account of
Joshua's death. Therefore Josh 23:2 contains exactly the same wording as Josh 24:1. BUTLER,
Joshua, 253, writes, "Joshua 23 thus plays a key role in the biblical story. It foreshadows the remainder of the history of Israel, placing that history under the dark shadow of curse from its
very inception." RÖMER, "Ende," in contrast argues that "Es ist jedoch auch möglich, dass ein
kürzerer Text von Jos 23 ursprünglich, wie 21,43–45 eine vollständig abgeschlossene Landnahme konstatierte und damit vielleicht eine Art 'DtrL' beendete" (*However, it is also possible
that a shorter text from Josh 23 originally, like 21:43–45, constituted a fully self-contained conquest
and thereby possibly ended a type of "DtrL"*).

[254] NIHAN, "Relationship," 105, includes 41a*.

[255] KNAUF, *Josua*, 14. See also FINKELSTEIN, "Corpus," 284.

[256] For the endings see KNAUF, "Buchschlüsse." For the tree-ring metaphor, see KNAUF, *Josua*,
178, where he writes, "Die Buchschlüsse in Jos dokumentieren dessen Wachstum so deutlich
wie die Jahresringe das eines Baumes" (*The book-endings in Joshua document its growth as
clearly as do the year-rings of a tree*). KRATZ, *Composition*, 294, adds a further possible ending
in Josh 12:24. In addition to these options are the idea that DtrL ended in Judg 2:2–9 (OTTO,
Pentateuch und Hexateuch, 4–5) or that it ended in Josh 22:1–6 (LOHFINK, "Kerygmata," 92–
93). Otto's model is further complicated by the fact that he posits that the editor responsible for

2.3 In Favour of an Exodus-Conquest Narrative

1. Joshua 10:42.
2. Joshua 11:15–23*.[257]
3. Joshua 18:1.[258]
4. Joshua 21:43–45.[259]
5. Joshua 24:1–33.[260]

DtrL incorporated and reframed a pre-existing "Landnahmeerzählung" that was not connected to the "Moses-Exodus-Erzählung." (p. 264)

[257] Although RÖMER, "Problem," 823, concedes, "[Josh 11:23] does indeed sound like a conclusion," he goes on to argue that it would be "a difficult, if not impossible, task" to reconstruct some kind of pre-Deuteronomistic story based on this ending. GROSS, *Richterbuch*, 184, writes, "Der Horizont von Jos 11,23 reicht nur bis in das Buch Dtn, nicht in das Buch Ex" (*The horizon of Josh 11:23 only reaches back to Deuteronomy, not back to the book of Exodus*). GERMANY, *Exodus-Conquest*, 437–438, observes, "In light of the complementary nature of Josh 10 and Josh 11, the former narrating the conquest of the south and the latter narrating the conquest of the north, several commentators have concluded that at least parts of these chapters are the product of a single author." However, Germany goes on to note that this idea is already stifled by several points. (1) Josh 10:40 already states that Joshua conquered the "whole land," suggesting that its author did not know of the continuation in Joshua 11; (2) the description of the land in Josh 11:1–3 and esp. v. 2 suggests that "the author of this verse was not very familiar with the actual geography of the North and instead used the geographical terms in 10:40 as a model; and (3) Joshua 11 includes southern regions, thus negating its function as the northern counterpart to Joshua 10.

[258] KNAUF, *Data*, 530–532, argues that Josh 18:1 represents the end of Pg, as this verse narrates the erection of the tent of meeting in the land and importantly links back to YHWH's command to humanity in the creation event via the rare lemma כבש (*to subdue*), which appears only in Gen 1:28; Num 32:22, 29 and Josh 18:1. Cf. GUILLAUME, *Land*, 158–162.

[259] After a detailed discussion NIHAN, "Relationship," 92, convincingly concludes: "This means that when Josh 21:43–45 was composed, the traditions about the conquest associated with the figure of Joshua were already in the process of being joined not just to Deuteronomy but to the traditions about the monarchy in Samuel–Kings as well. Within the sophisticated system of cross-references described above, Josh 21:43–45 thus marks the end of a distinct period – the conquest under Joshua – not of a discrete composition that would have been initially restricted to the narrative in Deuteronomy and Joshua. This period was followed by another one, extending from Israel's settlement inside the land until the building of the temple under Solomon, when the stipulation of Deut 12:8–12 was finally fulfilled, and this further era in the Dtr construction of Israel's history was framed by the joined reference in 1 Kgs 8:56 to Deut 12:9 and Josh 21:45."

[260] VON RAD, *Genesis*, 3, rightly labelled this chapter, "einen 'Hexateuch' in kleinster Form" (*a small scale 'Hexateuch'*). This is because it reviews the Hexateuchal narrative beginning with the patriarchs Abraham (24:2), Isaac (24:4) and Jacob (24:4); it connects to the Joseph narrative via the burying of his bones (24:32); the exodus is recalled (24:5–7a, 17) as is the promise of the צרעה (*Hornet*) that YHWH would send to drive out the inhabitants of the land (Exod 23:28; Deut 7:20: Josh 24:12); the wilderness wandering (Numbers 10–20; Josh 24:7b) and the events in the Transjordan are recalled (Numbers 21–24; Josh 24:8–10); finally the conquest of the land is recalled (Joshua 1–12; 24:11). For the proposal that Joshua 24 is a late text designed to bracket the Hexateuch see, e. g., RÖMER/BRETTLER, "Deuteronomy 34." FREVEL, "Wiederkehr," 27, agrees that in its extant form that Joshua 24 is nearly midrashic in character, however he suggests that a narrative about the character of Joshua logically ended with his death in its earliest form. Yet the idea that the original exodus-conquest narrative had to end with the death of Joshua must be questioned.

However, if one takes seriously the idea that the original layer of Joshua was pre-Deuteronomistic, then an ending in Josh 10:40–42* has much to commend it. Importantly, Germany observes that "There is no evidence that this narrative [i.e., one that ends in Josh 10:1aα, 1b, 3–4, 5–7*, 9a, 10aβb, 29–32*, 34–40, 42–43(?)] is aware of either the book of Deuteronomy or priestly literature."[261] Nihan similarly argues:

> Overall, therefore, there is something to be said for the view that the earliest form of the conquest account in Joshua (especially Josh 6–10*) was part of a broader narrative recounting the exodus, the sojourn in the wilderness, and the conquest of the land that ended in Josh 10:40–42*. This narrative was composed during the seventh century B.C.E., probably under the reign of Josiah. The composition of this document points to a stage when Judah was in the process of appropriating the title of "Israel" after the fall of Samaria and the end of the northern kingdom in 722 B.C.E. By identifying the territory conquered by Joshua at the end of the exodus with the territory controlled by Judah at the end of the seventh century, the authors of the Exodus–Joshua* narrative were able to claim that the state of Judah under Josiah's reign represented "Israel" and was the legitimate heir to the traditions associated with that name, such as, especially, the exodus and the conquest.[262]

Taken altogether, the cumulative power of these observations point toward an early Judean exodus-conquest narrative forming the original shape of what later became the Torah.

The rhetorical force of this proposal, and consequently the rhetorical force of a Judean rewriting of the Northern tradition only makes sense if one can reconstruct a suitable historical narrative that explains how and why Judah would have adopted Northern traditions in the first place. The first step towards verifying this proposal is to discuss the idea of how Northern traditions reached the South. Arguably the most common theory posits that the traditions reached the South after the fall of the North, as Northern refugees fled to Judah in the wake of the Assyrian aggression. Finkelstein, for example, summarises this as follows:

> The theory of migration of Israelites into Judah after the fall of the Northern Kingdom in 720 BCE emerged from biblical scholarship in an attempt to explain the impact of Israelite ideas on pivotal theological stances in the Hebrew Bible. It was then supported by archaeological work, which indicates dramatic demographic growth in Jerusalem and the various regions of Judah in the later part of the 8th century BCE.[263]

Finkelstein goes on to emphasise, "This Israelites-in-Judah premise is crucial for biblical exegesis – far beyond the fields of archaeology and historical reconstruction – because it has the potential to explain the incorporation of Northern texts, including those competitive to the Jerusalem temple (e.g., Jacob at Bethel)

---

[261] GERMANY, *Exodus-Conquest*, 423.
[262] NIHAN, "Relationship," 109.
[263] FINKELSTEIN, "Migration," 188.

2.3 In Favour of an Exodus-Conquest Narrative   63

and even hostile to the Davidic Dynasty, into Judahite literary works."[264] The core underlying principle of this theory lies in the fact that the migrating Northerners increased the population in Jerusalem to such an extent that the Southern literati *were obliged to include their traditions.* Again, Finkelstein argues, "The number of Israelites in Judah was probably *large enough to force* biblical authors to be mindful of their most important foundation myths and at least some of their royal traditions."[265] The most glaring question is: Does this theory even make sense? As Carr argues:

In the past, this mix of Northern and Southern traditions from the seventh century onward was explained with the idea of documents being brought South by refugees from the Northern kingdom that had been destroyed by the Assyrians. Yet it is hard to see how such documents merely appearing in Judah of the late eighth century would come to constitute the foundational center of the Judean literary corpus a couple of centuries later (the core of the 'Torah').[266]

Looking at this issue from a modern anecdotal angle, foreign cultures bring a noticeable impact on things like cuisine and business but have far less (typically no) impact on national stories, identity or ideology.[267] Thus, if modern society has any parallels with ancient ones, the theory that the appearance of a foreign element triggered a change of national stories appears to be fundamentally flawed. As Guillaume observes, "there are not many examples of governments of recipient countries willingly adopting the laws, customs and stories of incoming refugees."[268]

Besides these more general cultural observations, there are a number of factors that more specifically speak against a "flood" of Northern refugees into Judah. Arguably the decisive blow was already delivered by Na'aman when he observed:

The assumption that the Assyrians permitted thousands, possibly tens of thousands, of people to flee from the new province and settle in Judah, a vassal state that Assyria had not

---

[264] FINKELSTEIN, "Migration," 189.

[265] FINKELSTEIN, "Migration," 204 (emphasis added). FINKELSTEIN/SILBERMAN, *Unearthed*, 230, also write, "beginning with Israel's fall, suddenly altered the political and religious landscape. Judah's population swelled to unprecedented levels. Its capital city became a national religious center and a bustling metropolis for the first time. Intensive trade began with surrounding nations. Finally, a major religious reform movement – focused on the exclusive worship of YHWH in the Jerusalem Temple – started cultivating a revolutionary new understanding of the God of Israel."

[266] CARR, *Formation*, 486.

[267] In Germany, the Turkish Döner is arguably the most popular takeaway food, and the population of people of Turkish descent in Germany is also very high, yet the German national story has in no way incorporated Turkish myths. Other examples include the fact that England's national dish is Chicken Tikka Masala, yet has in no way incorporated Indian traditions into their national story. Or the fact that nearly 25 % of Melbourne's population is of Asian ancestry yet the "national story" of Australia is still firmly Euro-centric (data from the 2016 Australian census: https://guest.censusdata.abs.gov.au/webapi/jsf/login.xhtml).

[268] GUILLAUME, "Flood," 202.

64   *2. Setting the Stage*

annexed and had no wish to strengthen, contradicts everything known about the policy of the Assyrian Empire in the newly annexed territories. Accepting thousands of refugees from Israel into the territory of Judah would have amounted to an open provocation against the king of Assyria and a serious blow to the Assyrian efforts to establish and stabilize their new province. Hezekiah was unlikely to take such a risk.[269]

In addition to the argument on the validity of refugees in general,[270] other points of rebuttal include onomastics (which do not suggest any form of increase of Northern-style names),[271] the expansion of Jerusalem's fortifications (which cannot be connected to a sudden increase in population),[272] religious motivation (Knauf, for example, suggests that the continuing operation of the sanctuary at Bethel [cf. § 2.2.2] meant that Jerusalem was not de facto the only remaining centre for YHWH worship after the Assyrian invasion),[273] economics (although Judah's economic situation noticeably improved, other destinations would have still been economically more attractive),[274] and the demography of the Shephelah (although there is evidence of population growth in this area, the destruction of all settlements in the Shephelah in 701 BCE dictates that clearly Northern markers would be readily available in the remains but they are not).[275]

---

[269] NA'AMAN, "Jerusalem," 35.

[270] GUILLAUME, "Flood," in particular emphasises this point, he notes, "The flood-of-refugees hypothesis reflects modern anxieties more than ancient probabilities. The syndrome of the nation under the mortal danger of a flood of refugees resonates in modern Jerusalem as all parties nurture the refugee problem." (p. 207). KNAUF, "Crisis," 164, also notes that "Refugees were not migrants. They returned home as soon as the danger of marauding roughnecks was gone."

[271] NA'AMAN, "Myth," 4–5, draws attention to the (admittedly sparse) onomastic evidence from pottery and inscriptions noting that instead of a sudden increase in names featuring the Northern theophoric element *yw* in comparison to the Judean *yhw* in the late 8th–7th centuries, there is, if anything, a decline and certainly not a sudden explosion of *yw* names. See also KNAUF, "Bethel," 294; FREVEL, *Geschichte*, 280–281. FINKELSTEIN, "Migration," 194, counters that because the onomastic evidence is so meagre it "is not pertinent to this debate."

[272] KNAUF, "Bethel," 293, argues that the fortifications should be attributed to Manasseh rather than Hezekiah. GUILLAUME, "Flood," 198, argues, "there is no necessary correlation between the number of inhabitants of a city and that of its fortified area." NA'AMAN "Myth," 11–13, draws attention to the more modest estimated population of Jerusalem proposed by Geva, of around 8000 inhabitants, which in turn suggests that Jerusalem's population can be explained by natural growth. He further notes the recent investigations show that the settlement on the South-western Hill predate the fortifications and so cannot be attributed to a sudden influx of Northerners. See also KNAUF, "Crisis," 167. FINKELSTEIN, "Migration," 196, on the other hand convincingly argues that although it is technically true that fortifications are not directly correlated with the population size, the expense of fortifications demand that there be sufficient population to justify the cost.

[273] KNAUF, "Bethel," 293.

[274] KNAUF, "Bethel," 294, names Philistia and Egypt. To this FINKELSTEIN, "Migration," 189, curtly states, "I choose not to deal with speculations."

[275] NA'AMAN, "Myth," 8–9. Na'aman also asserts that the timeframe between 722 and 701 is too narrow for the Northerners to have developed such settlements. He notes that for a large number of refugees to settle in any area, they need to receive permission from the local author-

2.3 In Favour of an Exodus-Conquest Narrative

But perhaps the most damning argument of all is presented by Finkelstein himself, when he amended his earlier views and conceded that there was more likely a "continuous trickle" of Northern Israelites entering Jerusalem both before and after 701 BCE.[276] Thus, Knauf rightly observes that, "Finkelstein's article already includes most of the arguments against itself."[277]

Having demonstrated that the influx of Northerners into Judah in the wake of the Assyrian invasion cannot be the solution for how Northern traditions became incorporated into Southern literature, it is now time to suggest that a more compelling answer is to be found in the idea that Judah was – for most of the monarchic period – a branch kingdom of the North. The basic idea of this theory is that the first "statehood" was that created by Omri in the North and that a branch king was installed in Jerusalem who was answerable to the Omrides.[278] With the Nimshide takeover of the North, Judah did not gain independence, but rather simply became a Nimshide branch kingdom (cf. the fall of Athaliah in 2 Kgs 11:20). The arguments supporting this can be summarised as follows:[279]

I. The historical and archaeological data do not support the idea of a great United Monarchy under David and Solomon.[280]

II. Even the biblical data about David and Solomon is suspiciously vague. It is difficult to imagine that had Solomon been a great king with extensive learning that both he and David would be recorded with a round and symbolic forty-year reign.[281]

III. There are no archaeological traces that even refer to Solomon, and his depiction as a great builder with international renown and wisdom greater than any other fits better to an idealised figure. Knauf and Guillaume argue that the story of Solomon projects, "the glory of the Assyrian Empire onto a fabulous past to show how such an empire can only lead to ruin."[282]

---

ities, and this takes time. FINKELSTEIN, "Migration," 195–196, rebuts that there is good evidence to support the assertion that Israelite olive oil specialist brought their skills and technology to the Shephelah during this period, specifically he notes the presence of stone installations for olive oil processing that appear in Judah in the Iron IIB period, these same stone installations were already in use in Samaria from the Iron IIA suggesting that the Samarians familiar with their use brought them south.

[276] FINKELSTEIN, "Migration," 201.

[277] KNAUF, "Crisis," 159.

[278] See, esp. FREVEL, *Geschichte*, 98–99, 201–266.

[279] See, esp. FREVEL, *Geschichte*, 186–190.

[280] DAVIES, *Search*, xi–xii, writes, "evidence of a Saul, David, Solomon, Rehoboam or Jeroboam remains largely lacking. Already in 1992 it was becoming clear that the feasibility of a large Davidic empire was minimal, because of the relative demographic and economic poverty of the southern highlands compared with the northern, and the lack of sufficient appropriate architecture in Jerusalem."

[281] See, e.g., KNAUF, *Data*, 89–90.

[282] KNAUF/GUILLAUME, *History*, 76.

IV. The names Jeroboam and Rehoboam are suspicious, both because of their similar sounds but importantly because they are contrasting pairs, meaning "the people contend" and "enlarges the people" respectively. Furthermore, the fact that most of Jeroboam I's deeds are historically more plausible being attributed to Jeroboam II suggests that both Jeroboam I and Rehoboam are constructs.[283]

V. The depiction of the division of the kingdom is clearly written from a Judean perspective, yet this does not accord with the political dominance of the North over the South, which is not least indicated by the fact that the North received ten tribes to the South's two (1 Kgs 11:29–35).[284]

VI. The Judean bias is also indicated by the depiction of the Northern Kingdom as being especially unstable, marked by a continuous string of uprisings and hostile takeovers.

VII. Signs of an early developed kingdom in the south are lacking in both the archaeological as well as the epigraphic record.[285] Furthermore, Judah's expansion to the west presupposes the end of the Aramean dominance over the Philistines. This could only occur after Hazael's campaigns (approx. 840–830 BCE) as well as the subsequent weakening of the Arameans due to Assyrian pressure.

VIII. Arguably the biggest clue is found in the shared names of the monarchs operating in approximately the same timeframes: Ahaziah, Joram, Joash/Jehoash all appear in both Northern and Southern Kingdoms more or less in pairs. As Frevel argues, "Die Nähe der Namen und die Assoziationen sind so auffallend, dass die Annahme, das alles sei Zufall, an Grenzen der Plausibilität stößt" (*The proximity of the names and the associations are so conspicuous that the assumption that all this is coincidence reaches the limits of plausibility*).[286]

So far, the repercussions of the idea that Judah functioned as a branch kingdom have not been fully articulated with regard to the formation of the Judean exodus-conquest narrative. If Judah was – for most of its history – subject to the Northern kings, not least Jeroboam II, then it follows that a Northern Moses-exodus narrative would have already been known, if not employed propagan-

---

[283] On the Jeroboam I/Jeroboam II issue, see note 232 on page 54.

[284] KRATZ, *Israel*, 27, writes, "All in all, Judah at the time of the Omrides seems to have been the far inferior partner in league with the greater Israel – a dynamic that corresponded to the northern kingdom's opposition to Assyria and which proved to be beneficial for the southern kingdom."

[285] In speaking of the cities featuring six-chamber gates, which were originally understood to be Solomonic in origin, FINKELSTEIN/SILBERMAN, *Unearthed*, 189 190, note, "Archaeologically and historically, the redating of these cities from Solomon's era to the time of the Omrides has enormous implications. It removes the only archaeological evidence that there was ever a united monarchy based in Jerusalem and suggests that David and Solomon were, in political terms, little more than hill country chieftains, whose administrative reach remained on a fairly local level, restricted to the hill country."

[286] FREVEL, *Geschichte*, 189.

distically, by its branch-kings in Judah. This not only suggests that the Northern traditions reached Judah before the fall of the North, but it also provides ample basis for the Judeans to repurpose it. More specifically, such a reconstruction suggests that the replacement of Moses's conquest with Josiah-Joshua's conquest and the corresponding death of Moses outside the land functioned primarily as a Judean counter narrative.

In the wake of the fall of the North and Josiah's semi-independence after the weaking of Assyria, the propagandistic and/or subversive (re-)use of Northern traditions has much to offer. Not only did this new ending depict the promised land as being confined to Judah, it also depicted the character of Moses (who, as shown in § 2.3.1, shared many parallels with the Jeroboam tradition) as being punished to die outside the land, thus reflecting the loss of the North.

One further point in favour of this proposal is that such a reconstruction can readily explain Israel's wilderness journey. As discussed in § 2.1.2.4, one of the biggest weaknesses of the solutions proposed by Kratz and Germany was their removal of the narrative logic behind Israel's journey east of the Jordan and their entry into the land from the plains of Moab. Within the confines of the outline given above, these important narrative details make much more sense. A Northern Moses-exodus narrative would have had little regard for the territory of Judah and instead focussed upon the core territory of Israel in the Manasseh hill country and the Transjordan. It is possible that Exod 13:17 derives from this earliest version explaining why Israel did not travel up the coast but eastward.[287] In any case, it follows that after the Judeans reappropriated the Nimshide narrative they were faced with the issue of Israel's bypassing the core territory of Judah. In this context the spy narrative would represent a Judean modification that not only functioned to prepare the way for Moses's premature death outside the land (and Josiah-Joshua's taking up his mantle) but also to explain Israel's non-entry into Judah from the south. Although this must remain conjecture at this stage, the basic outlines of the above proposal provide some very compelling avenues for further investigation.

One final point to be addressed is the idea that preexilic Israel was not sufficiently "theological" to create a proto-Torah (or indeed a proto-proto-Torah). This is specifically related to the idea that the Judean exile has long been seen as the catalyst for the transition from a temple based, iconic ancient Near Eastern religion to a religion of the book.[288] Levin for example states:

---

[287] ALBERTZ, *Exodus, Band I*, 16, also allocates this verse to the earliest layer of Exodus.

[288] "Israel" here is used as a blanket term to describe the people of both North and South. One of the most telling indicators of this shift in focus is the pre-exilic existence of material culture depicting "YHWH and his Asherah" in both Samaria and Judah. See discussion in e.g., KEEL/ UEHLINGER, *Göttinen*; UEHLINGER, "Göttinen."

68   *2. Setting the Stage*

If we follow the Old Testament account, the Exile was the most important turning point in Israel's history. It is the watershed dividing the kingdoms of Israel and Judah from the Judaism of the Persian and Hellenistic eras.[289]

Knauf similarly argues:

Nach der neueren Forschung war das Exil, die "Babylonische Gefangenschaft der Kinder Israel," die Wiege des biblischen Israel als dem Volk der Tora. Das vorexilische Israel (10. Jh. v. Chr. bis 720) und Juda (10. Jh. bis 586/582) erweisen sich zunehmend als ganz "normale" vorderorientalische Mittel- und Kleinstaaten des Altertums. (*Following recent research, the exile, the "Babylonian captivity of the children of Israel", was the birthplace of biblical Israel as the people of the Torah. Preexilic Israel (10th Century B.C.E. until 720) and Judah (10th Century B.C.E. until 586/582) are increasingly proving to be completely "normal" middle- and lower ancient Near Eastern states.*)[290]

A thorough discussion of these important statements is beyond the scope of the present work, however a few remarks are in order. First, one must be mindful that the idea of a Josianic-coloured exodus-conquest narrative is not directly tied to the idea of the Torah. In fact, it seems highly plausible that a history of origins transitioned from more political origins, to become increasingly theological. Once again, if we take the arguments in § 2.2.1 seriously, processes of conflation during their early phases were not bound by the constraint of simply rephrasing or updating the general ideas that were already present, rather early traditions were honoured by their reappearance, even when they were put to use in markedly different metatexts. Thus, the idea that the exodus-conquest narrative was originally more politically than theologically motivated does not stand in contradiction to the experience and importance of the Babylonian exile.

2.4 The Structure of Numbers

Having laid the foundation for understanding the present state of Pentateuchal research with a particular emphasis on the book of Numbers, it is now time to briefly look at the book's structure. As already noted in the introduction, the structure of Numbers is a well-known difficulty. Dennis Olson observed, "One important obstacle in interpreting Numbers has been the failure to detect a meaningful structure for the book as a whole."[291] This issue has persisted even in light of the newer Pentateuchal models outlined above. Proposed solutions include two-part, three-part, five-part and even seven-part structures, yet all can be shown to have some level of weakness. This led MacDonald to ask, "Since the book of Numbers often has no clear sense of direction and contains such dis-

---

[289] Levin, "Introduction," 1.
[290] Knauf, *Data*, 499.
[291] Olson, *Numbers*, 3.

parate materials as lists, narratives, and law, is it meaningful to talk about these thirty-six chapters as a book at all?"[292]

Two-part structures commonly take one of two forms. The first divides the book genealogically, this structure most famously proposed by Dennis Olson focusses upon the transition between the first and second generations, capstoned by the first and second censuses in Numbers 1 and 26 respectively.[293] According to this breakdown, the first part of Numbers is characterised by decline and so describes the fall of the exodus generation while the second part is characterised by hope as demonstrated in the new life granted to those born in the wilderness. The issue with this suggestion is not that it is incorrect per se, rather that it is insufficient as the sole structuring indicator. As Frevel notes, "Although the transition from the generation of the fathers to the generation of those given the land is a very decisive moment in the structure in Numbers, the generational change does not prove successful as the only structuring device in the book."[294]

The other two-part structure is better understood as a super-structure rather than a structure in its entirety. The guiding idea behind this is that only the Sinai section of the book (Num 1:1–10:10) is distinctive and so is separated from "the rest" (Num 10:11–36:13).[295] Proponents of this structure admit that the book is more complex, but that further subdivisions cannot be performed in a clear and blanket fashion. Although scholars such as Milgrom, Pitkänen, Seebass and Wenham propose this super-structure, they reach their conclusion by arguing that Numbers is only given its sense within the context of the Pentateuch or Hexateuch.[296] Milgrom, for example, suggests the whole Hexateuch should be understood as a chiasm, with Lev 1–Num 10:10 forming a chiastic pair with Exodus 19–24 and Num 10:11–36:13 pairing with Exod 16–18.[297]

One attempt at adding complexity but keeping this basic observation was undertaken by Cocco. He proposes a nested structure such that Num 10:11–36:13 has a substructure of Num 10:11–21:20 and Num 21:21–36:13. The latter segment of this substructure is then further subdivided into Num 22:1–33:49 and Num 33:50–36:13.[298] Fistill also begins with the two-fold super-structure and subdivides the second segment into increasingly smaller subunits, however Fistill suggests that no single overarching structure can adequately explain Num 21:21–36:13.[299]

---

[292] MacDonald, "Numbers," 115.

[293] See esp. Olson, *Death*.

[294] Frevel, *Transformations*, 57. A similar point is made by MacDonald, "Numbers," 117.

[295] See, e. g., Lee, *Punishment*; Knierim/Coats, *Numbers*, 9.

[296] Wenham, *Numbers*, 15–16; Seebass, *Numeri 1*, 1.

[297] Milgrom, *Numbers*, xviii. Milgrom's proposal is affirmed by Pitkänen, *Numbers*, 16–17.

[298] Cocco, *Women*, 118–121.

[299] Fistill, *Ostjordanland*, 37–44.

70   *2. Setting the Stage*

Three-part structures typically divide the text based on geographical markers. The issue, as Davies notes, is that scholars are inconsistent with which geographical indicators are the important ones.[300] While scholars almost unanimously agree on Sinai representing the first division, the second division is less clear.[301] In his commentary Noth saw Kadesh as the key marker and so suggested a split between Num 11:1–20:13 and Num 20:14–36:13.[302] More commonly scholars see the three major divisions being Sinai/Wilderness/plains of Moab.[303] Schmidt, for example, argues that this division is supported by the geographical inclusio based on the plains of Moab between Num 22:1 and 36:13.[304] Somewhat amusingly, Schmidt criticises Olson's generational proposal because it ignores this inclusio, yet the wording of Num 36:13 actually matches to Num 26:3 – the beginning of the second census – and not to Num 22:1![305]

Num 22:1bβ	Num 26:3aγb	Num 36:13b
בערבות מואב מעבר לירדן ירחו	בערבת מואב על ירדן ירחו	בערבת מואב על ירדן ירחו
in the plains of Moab *across from* the Jordan at Jericho	in the plains of Moab *upon/ by* the Jordan at Jericho	in the plains of Moab *upon/ by* the Jordan at Jericho

Table 2: Comparison of Num 22:1bβ; 26:3aγb; 36:13b

If anything, the double "introduction" to Israel's arrival in the plains of Moab (i.e., Num 22:1; 26:3) suggests that a greater granularity is required than a three-part division allows. Forsling, for example, argues that even an expanded geographical sequence Sinai (Num 1:1–10:10), wilderness (Num 10:11–14:45), geographically undefined (Num 15:1–19:22), wilderness (Num 20:1–21:35), Moab (Num 22:1–36:13), remains inadequate, noting, "we are dealing with a fractured plot."[306]

Frevel argues for a five-part structure. It begins with the two-part generational division as its base and then further subdivides the text. In particular Frevel notes, "The stubbornness of the old generation is not a determining feature (especially in Num 1–10) until the scout narrative (in Num 13–14), nor is the blessing in the Balaam narrative (Num 22–24) limited entirely to the side of the exodus

---

[300] DAVIES, *Numbers*, lii.

[301] A unique division is proposed by BUDD, *Numbers*, xvii: "Constituting the community at Sinai" (Num 1:1–9:14); "The journey – its setbacks and successes" (Num 9:15–25:18); "Final preparations for settlement" (Num 26:1–35:34), with chapter 36 functioning as an appendix.

[302] NOTH, *Numeri*. LEVINE, *Numbers 1–20*, 48, also divides his commentary at Kadesh but also suggests that such a division was not the only option.

[303] This general division is followed by GRAY, *Numbers*, xxii; BINNS, *Numbers*, xxvi–xxxviii; GOLDBERG, *Numeri*, 13–14; SCHMIDT, *Numeri*, 1. ASHLEY, *Numbers*, 2, represents something of a middle positions and labels Num 10:11–19:22 "at or around Kadesh."

[304] SCHMIDT, *Numeri*, 1. See also ARTUS, *Études*, 15–40.

[305] The LXX versions also do not match. Cf. ZENGER/FREVEL, "Bücher," 50.

[306] FORSLING, *Artistry*, 135–136.

2.4 The Structure of Numbers 71

generation."[307] Therefore he proposes dividing the text into (I) Num 1:1–10:10; (II) 10:11–14:45; (III) 15:1–20:29; (IV) 21:1–25:18; (V) 26:1–36:13. However, even with this proposal Frevel admits, "One remaining problem with this division is that it does not match the spatial division provided by the itinerary notices in Part III and IV with the 'mental' boundaries."[308]

A seven-part division was famously proposed by Mary Douglas, who argued that Numbers was designed in a ring structure (i. e., a type of chiasm) that emphasised the alternation of narrative and law. Although Douglas should be commended for highlighting the issue of law and narrative, which many discussions of structure overlook, her division of passages is less convincing. One example is her pairing of Numbers 7–9 with Num 31:1–33:49 as type "story" under the heading of "offerings."[309] Neither is it clear how all these chapters can be categorised as story elements nor how they all relate to offerings.

Thus, there is currently no completely satisfactory structure to define every aspect of the book. Rather there seems to be space to understand Numbers to have overlapping structures that are not united in their goals. This idea was already flagged by Frevel, but not worked out in any detail.[310] A strange bedfellow in this regard is Harrison, who – despite his markedly conservative stance – suggested that, "The rather general nature of the chronological framework undergirding Numbers made it possible for Moses and the *šōṭĕrîm* to insert legislative and cultic materials during the compilatory processes at places that best suited the theological interests of the narrative."[311] Based upon the suggested major elements of growth proposed in § 2.1.2.5 above, it will here be proposed that the conflicting structural elements can best be explained by the major redactional moments in the formation of the Pentateuch.

The structure of the exodus-conquest narrative was a linear narrative of Israel's escape from Egypt, their journey through the wilderness, their arrival in the plains of Moab and then their crossing the Jordan and subsequent conquest of Judah (cf. § 2.3.2). The "Numbers part" (it was unlikely its own book/scroll at this point) of this narrative thus represented the spatial transition from the wilderness to the arrival in the plains of Moab as shown in figure 2.[312]

When Deuteronomy was joined to the exodus-conquest narrative (ignoring for the moment what might have been the driver behind such an endeavour),

---

[307] Frevel, *Transformations*, 57.

[308] Frevel, *Transformations*, 58.

[309] Douglas, *Wilderness*, 118.

[310] See discussion in Frevel, "Understanding" and esp. Frevel, *Transformations*, 23–50.

[311] Harrison, *Numbers*, 15–16 and 19–20 respectively. Harrison pits himself against the "liberal scholars" and suggests (based on Num 1:16–18) that Moses formed a guild of scholars (*šōṭĕrîm*) who "would commit to writing whatever judicial decisions were made and would also be responsible for recording the occurrence of important events during the wilderness period."

[312] Frevel, *Understanding*, 119, thus correctly notes that Numbers occupies the central portion of the sequence Egypt – Mountain – Desert – Moab – Canaan.

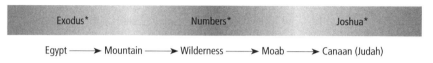

Figure 2: Linear geographical structure of the exodus-conquest narrative

there arose the issue of Deuteronomy and the Covenant Code being in the same document, given that both law-codes proport to convey what Yhwh revealed to Moses atop the mountain.

As Otto has convincingly argued, Deuteronomy began its narrative life as Moses's recitation of the laws immediately after the Horeb event.[313] This recitation, as made clear in Deut 5:2–4, was made to those who were alive during the exodus from Egypt. Thus, one might suggest that Deuteronomy was originally intended to function as the "Directors Cut" of the Covenant Code with "bonus footage and deleted scenes" included.[314]

In order to give due reverence to both traditions a new narrative device was needed so that both laws could appear in the same narrative construct without one being given undue priority over the other. Deuteronomy was thus reframed with what Otto labels the "Moab Redaction" that functioned to shift Moses's recitation of the Deuteronomic law to the end of Israel's wilderness journey in the plains of Moab. The Moab Redaction therefore depicts Moses expounding the law (Deut 1:5) anew, with the result that the so-called second law could not also be considered a second-tier law.[315]

The paired censuses in Numbers further emphasise this function of Deuteronomy by explaining that Moses's giving of the law a second time was due to the death of the exodus generation. Thus, in the extant Pentateuch, Deuteronomy

---

[313] Otto, *Deuteronomium 1,1–4,43*, 332, for example, highlights that the central theological theme of the Horeb Redaction is the covenant made at Horeb. Otto, *Deuteronomium 4,44–11,32*, 785, writes, "Die Horebredaktion hat das Sch^{e}ma' Israel, das ursprünglich als Einleitung des spätvorexilisch-deuteronomischen Deuteronomiums dient ..." (*The Horeb Redaction had the Sch^{e}ma' of Israel, which originally served as the introduction of the late preexilic deuteronomic-Deuteronomy*).

[314] See discussion in Otto, *Politische*. "Mit dem Deuteronomium ist der Glücksfall gegeben, daß wir im Bundesbuch die Vorlage zahlreicher Rechtssätze des Deuteronomiums erhalten haben und sich auch hier eine stringente Konzeption der Rechtsreform unter dem Gesichtspunkt der Kultzentralisierung in der Rezeption der Rechtssätze des Bundesbuches auf- weisen läßt. (*We have with Deuteronomy the fortunate case that numerous legal rules have the Covenant Code as Vorlage and also that here can be shown a stringent conception of legal reform from the point of view of cult centralisation in the reception of the legal rules of the Covenant Code.*)

[315] As Crawford, "Deuteronomy," 140, remarks, "Deuteronomy may be termed the 'second law' but clearly had attained first place in Second Temple Judaism."

represents Moses expounding the law to the wilderness generation who were not present at Sinai/Horeb. One complication with this structuring device is that the censuses are near unanimously attributed to Priestly hands, thus while the Moab redaction functioned to unite Deuteronomy to the exodus-conquest narrative, the census arrangement and the idea of the exodus generation dying in the wilderness must be considered a post-Priestly innovation.[316]

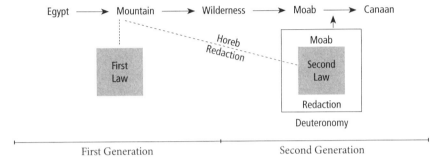

Figure 3: Generation change layered onto the exodus-conquest narrative

The precise means by which the Priestly narrative was incorporated into the non-Priestly work is beyond the scope of this overview. Whatever the processes were, the end result was a Pentateuch centred about Sinai and the book of Leviticus. With this, the events in the book of Exodus were granted "negative" counterparts in the book of Numbers, such as the waters of Meribah episode (Exodus 17; Numbers 20), which depicted Israel's journey in the wilderness as a repeating cycle of provision/blessing and disobedience/murmuring.[317] It is as part of this cyclical structure, that the seemingly scattered laws in Numbers can be interpreted as a means of blessing aimed at breaking Israel's spiral of decline. For example, after rejecting the land in Numbers 13–14, Numbers 15 contains laws that are introduced by the phrase "When you come into the land in which you shall dwell, which I am giving to you." (v. 2); After the punishment for questioning the cultic order in Numbers 16–17, provision is given in Numbers 18 so that no more Israelites shall die from cultic transgression; etc. Thus, unlike the common critique that the laws are randomly placed, they function as an integrated part of this cyclical structure.[318]

---

[316] On the (post-)Priestly nature of the censuses, see ACHENBACH, *Vollendung*, 443–479 (ThB I); BUDD, *Numbers*, xxii; DAVIES, *Numbers*, 3; GRAY, *Numbers*, xxvi–xxix; KNIERIM/COATS, *Numbers*, 12; LEVINE, *Numbers 1–20*, 129–142; MILGROM, *Numbers*, xvii; NOTH, *Numbers*, 13; PITKÄNEN, *Numbers*, 28; SEEBASS, *Numeri I*, 26–27 (Num-Komp).

[317] For a detailed study on the Meribah episode see GARTON, *Mirages*. On the parallelism between Exodus and Numbers, see, e.g., RÖMER, "périphérie," 26–27.

[318] A narrative-contextual placement of Numbers 15 is also argued by ACHENBACH, "Reading."

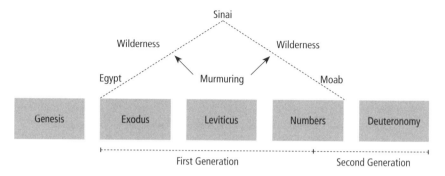

Figure 4: The Post-Priestly Pentateuch

Thus, the present form of the book of Numbers can be seen to contain traces of all three major redactional levels, which do not overlap precisely.

Even with this multi-tiered structure, the final chapters of the book present something of a mystery. Speaking of these final chapters of Numbers, Noth famously declared that:

> No proper sequence is maintained in this whole complex of later additions. We shall have to reckon with the fact that the individual units were simply added one after another in the order in which they appeared.[319]

Frevel observes, "[Noth's] impression gets as many things wrong as it gets right, but ultimately proves to be a great misjudgement."[320] Admittedly the collection of materials in this final section of the book have only a loose correlation to one another but they can be shown to contain a weak sequentiality. More importantly, they all share the overarching theme of preparing for life in the land.[321] In order to visualise the logic to the ordering of the various segments of this final section, they can better be seen when placed into a modified Gantt chart as shown in figure 6. Gantt charts are properly used in business planning to show the critical path, that is, which tasks cannot be started until one or more tasks have already been completed. In figure 6, the critical path is demonstrated via broad categorisation under which the individual chapters are arranged.

---

[319] Noth, *Numbers*, 10.
[320] Frevel, *Transformations*, 24.
[321] Milgrom, *Numbers*, xiii, similarly writes, "The final eleven chapters of Numbers (26–36) are motivated by a single theme, the immediate occupation of the promised land ..."

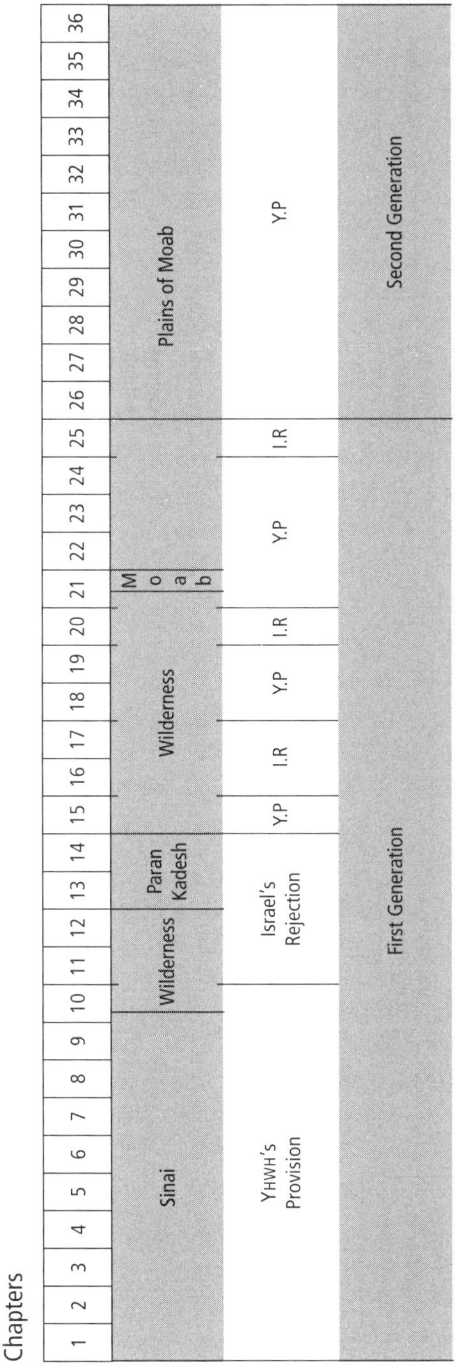

2.4 The Structure of Numbers

Figure 5: Multiple structure of Numbers

76　　　　　　　　　　　　　　　　2. Setting the Stage

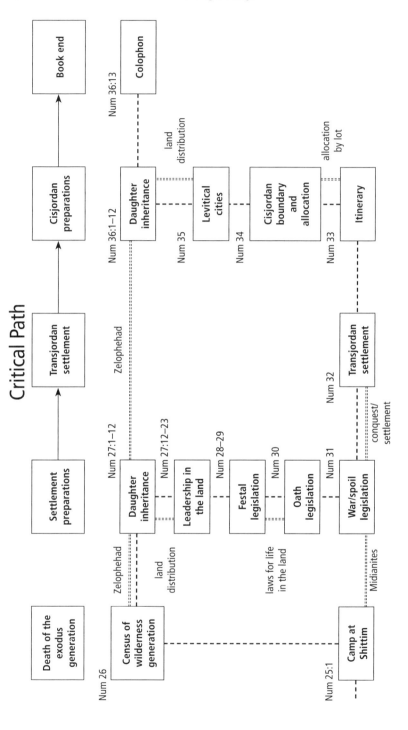

Figure 6: Modified Gantt Chart of Numbers 26–36 with conceptual links

As shown, the critical path can be summarised as follows: Death of the exodus generation → settlement preparations → settlement of Transjordan → Cisjordan conquest preparations → End of book.

The first major milestone aligns with the generational change, which is flagged by the second census and is further emphasised via the geographical bracketing of Num 26:3 and 36:13 – בערבת מואב על ירדן ירחו (*in the plains of Moab upon/by the Jordan at Jericho*).[322]

The category, settlement preparations, are covered in Numbers 27–31. According to the logic of the critical path, all five pericopes share a dependence level. However, it can clearly be observed that the individual units have little connection to one another, which is one of the key factors leading scholars to regard the end of Numbers as a random collection of materials. Despite this, there does appear to be some ordering principles that are highlighted by the double-dash lines in figure 6. These lines are intended to highlight texts that feature shared themes or a conceptual proximity. By this it is simply suggested that passages dealing with similar (but not sequentially dependent) themes or topics are placed side by side.

The placement of the daughters of Zelophehad ordeal (Num 27:1–11) immediately following the census is likely based on two complementary factors. First, the daughters make an unexpected appearance in the census of Num 26:33, which requires an explanation for why women are named in an otherwise male-only list. This shared feature links the daughters' pericope to the census.[323] Second, Num 36:1–12 is sequentially dependent upon Num 27:1–11 and thus must belong to a later link in the critical path. As shown visually in figure 6, these paired blocks now function as a second layer of bracketing, which further emphasises the final section of Numbers. Thus, of those pericopes falling under the broader category of pre-conquest preparations, Num 27:1–11 is most fittingly placed first.

The placement of Num 27:12–23, the commissioning of Eleazar and Joshua, in the second position is likely based on the idea of conceptual proximity. As one of the primary tasks of Joshua and Eleazar is the distribution of the land, the critical path dictates that this text must be placed prior to the settlement of Transjordan (cf. Num 32:28). Furthermore, the task of land distribution is of relevance to Num 27:1–11, but it is not of relevance to Numbers 28–31. Thus, the commissioning of Joshua and Eleazar is correspondingly located next to the Zelophehad's daughters text.

The placement of the war against the Midianites (Numbers 31) and the corresponding law regarding the spoils has several intersecting priorities. First, as

---

[322] There is admittedly some confusion and overlap of details due to the problems of Shittim in Num 25:1; Josh 2:1; 3:1. Cf. critique by Blum in note 158 on page 36.

[323] See, e.g., Budd, *Numbers*, 302; Knierim/Coats, *Numbers*, 273.

legislation regarding the spoils of war, this text must logically be given prior to the first conquest event, which occurs in Israel's battle in Transjordan. The problem with this is that in the extant book of Numbers, Israel's first "conquest" event was its victory against Sihon. Accordingly, the legislation regarding the spoil of war should actually occur before Numbers 21. However, the preamble to the legislation is Israel's attack against the Midianites, which is triggered by the Baal Peor event. The Baal Peor event is narrated in Numbers 25, some four chapters after the Sihon event, thus chapters 21–25 and 31 are constrained by competing chronological and geographical concepts.

In terms of the narrative sequence in the extant book of Numbers, Israel crosses the Arnon and first encounters Sihon the Amorite (Numbers 21:21–35), it is only after this that the events of the Balaam narrative (Numbers 22–24) occur. According to the extant Balaam narrative, the Moabite king Balak approaches the elders of Midian (Num 22:4) to join forces in cursing Israel. Following this Numbers 25 reports the sin of Baal Peor wherein the Midianites once again make an unexpected appearance alongside the Moabites.[324] This repeated and negative appearance of the Midianites reaches its conclusion in Numbers 31, where Israel is ordered to attack Midian due to their cooperation in the evil of Balaam.[325] The main issue is that the Balaam narrative has been edited to presuppose the Sihon narrative and so cannot be located before it. This in turn means that the attack on Midian cannot be located before the Sihon narrative. At the same time, as the attack on Midian is the climax of Numbers 22–24, 25, it must be located after those events. Lastly, the tradition in the book of Joshua seeks to make sense of the confusing mixture of Amorites, Moabites and Midianites by making the princes of Midian Sihon's generals (see esp. Josh 13:21). Thus, in the extant book of Numbers, the settlement of Transjordan is linked to Israel's defeat of both Amorites and Midianites.[326]

This leaves the two law codes (Numbers 28–29; 30 respectively), unaccounted for within the broader category of pre-settlement preparations. With Numbers 27:1–11 and 27:12–23 being linked and Numbers 31 and 32 being linked, the only place for these laws to fit was in between. The placing of the oath law after the festival laws may perhaps be further guided by the principle of importance, with the festival law having a greater significance than the latter.

Thus, even though Numbers 27–31 are not related in terms of narrative chronology or even in terms of content, the ordering does not appear to be random.

---

[324] FREVEL, *Transformations*, 209–222, suggests that the merging of Midianites and Moabites is a veiled reference to the influx of Arabian peoples in the Persian period.

[325] On the issues of construing Balaam as a villain, see FREVEL, *Transformations*, 155–187.

[326] Cf. MARQUIS, "Composition," 293.

Having received all the instructions from Moses regarding the upcoming settlement of greater Israel (i. e., the Israel that is not confined to Canaan), the next link on the critical path is the settlement in Transjordan (Numbers 32).

The critical path continues to the Cisjordan preparations. Numbers 33, which is dominated by Israel's exodus-wilderness itinerary thus seems to be misplaced. The basis for its placement in this section could be Numbers 33:50–56, which contain the instruction that the land must be distributed by lot. This commandment makes better sense being received after the Transjordan settlement, as the distribution of the Transjordan was not performed by lot.[327]

The instruction to distribute the land by lot in Numbers 33 reappears in Numbers 34 and so also follows the principle of conceptual proximity. Furthermore, the ordering of Numbers 34 after Numbers 33 might have a further conceptual ordering in that where Numbers 33 looks backwards to what has already passed, Numbers 34 looks forward to what is yet to occur.

Numbers 35, the regulations for the Levitical cities, makes sense as being placed next to the second regulations for the daughters of Zelophehad (Num 36:1–12), as both texts deal with more specific details of settlement.

Finally, the book's colophon (Num 36:13) can only appear at the very end.

It cannot be denied that the final section of Numbers contains disparate materials, but at the same time they appear to be ordered in such a way that depicts Israel moving toward the conquest. Thus, the findings of this section must echo Frevel's conclusion that although the structure of Numbers is complex, it does indeed have an intentional order and was designed with a deliberate and carefully arranged trajectory.[328]

---

[327] For a discussion on Num 33:50–56, see KNOPPERS, "Establishing."

[328] See, e. g., FREVEL, *Transformations*, 23–26.

Chapter 3

The Occupation of Transjordan

The settlement of Israelite tribes in Transjordan marks one of the most perplexing events in the Pentateuch, both from a narratological perspective as well as a theological one (but not, of course, from a historical one). The extant narrative of Numbers suggests that, had all gone to plan, Israel would have entered the promised land via the Negeb (Num 13:17b) from Kadesh (Num 13:26)/ the wilderness of Paran (Num 13:3) and so would have presumably dwelt exclusively in Cisjordan (perhaps even exclusively in Judah, cf. Num 13:17b; Josh 10:40–42*). However, the spies caused the people to rebel, and they refused to enter; as punishment they were forced to wander the desert until the entire exodus generation had passed away (Num 14:35). Read synchronically this entailed Israel travelling east around the ים המלח (*the Dead Sea*) and northwards until they reached the plains of Moab across the Jordan from Jericho, or more specifically, Shittim (Num 25:1). At Shittim a new census was made, those named being granted the right to inherit the land (Num 26:53). The introductory frame of Deuteronomy depicts the plains of Moab as the location of Moses's final speech (Deut 1:5), which he makes before all Israel prior to his death in Deuteronomy 34. The book of Joshua begins with Israel leaving Shittim (Josh 2:1; 3:1) and experiencing a second miraculous parting of water (this time the Jordan), which mirrors the beginning the exodus event in Exodus 14, thus forming an eisodus.[1]

With this synchronic bird's-eye view, the whole Hexateuchal story line appears to understand the promised land to be confined to Cisjordan. This is emphasised by the following examples: The eisodus motif only functions if Israel's entry into Cisjordan is equated with the entry into the promised land. The emphasis in Deut 34:4 is that Moses was not allowed to enter the land promised to Abraham, Isaac and Jacob, which only functions if the "plains of Moab" lay outside that. The Sihon narrative also presupposes that the Transjordan was not originally envisioned to be part of Israel's territory (see below) as aptly summarised by Schmidt: "Aber bereits die Bitte, durch das Land Sihons ziehen zu dürfen, setzt voraus, dass das Ostjordanland nicht zu dem verheißenen Land gehörte" (*But already the request to be allowed to pass through Sihon's land, requires that the*

---

[1] For the Eisodus motif see Krause, *Exodus* (esp. p. 259f). See also Dozeman, *Joshua 1–12*, 1f.

82 *3. The Occupation of Transjordan*

land east of the Jordan does not belong to the promised land).[2] All this raises some serious questions with regard to the idea that Israel conquered Transjordan territory and dwelt there.[3]

Granting all these indications that the extant shape of the Pentateuchal narrative were disrupted by a settlement in Transjordan, the narrative of Numbers 32 needs an explanation. As already noted in the introduction, Numbers 32 represents fertile ground upon which to engage in a textual analysis with a particular sensitivity towards topographical details and ideological shifts (e. g., changing land conceptions).

3.1 Old Layers and Historical Memories?

In his commentary on the book of Numbers Noth argued that Numbers 32 contains the, "last appearance in the book of Numbers [of the] old Pentateuchal sources," by which he meant J and E.[4] Although the present work does not operate under the Documentary Hypothesis, it agrees with Noth's suggestion that Numbers 32 contains "old" layers. In this regard the present section will argue that the earliest narrative layer in Numbers 32 supports the hypothesis of a Northern charter myth that plausibly dates to the reign of Jeroboam II (cf. § 2.3.1).[5]

3.1.1 Reflecting on the Geography of Numbers 32:1

There is little doubt that Numbers 32 is a composite text and that the various layers have been more smoothly worked into one another than is typically the case.[6] That being said, the chapter still features a number of internal con-

---

[2] SCHMIDT, "Sihon," 317.

[3] See, e. g., discussion in WEINFELD, *Deuteronomy*, 173–178.

[4] NOTH, *Numbers*, 235.

[5] For the relevance of Jeroboam II for the scribal origins of Northern traditions, see discussion in § 2.3.1.

[6] This difficulty can be seen in the numerous reconstructions. GRAY, *Numbers*, 426, for example, argues that "The presence of linguistic peculiarities and Deuteronomic characteristics, and the fact that some of the most marked peculiarities of P are embedded in sections that in other respects most closely resemble JE, render it more probable that the whole narrative has been recast than that is it the result of simple compilation from JE and P, such as is generally found elsewhere." LEVINE, *Numbers 21–36*, 478, agrees with Gray and argues that a source critical analysis "would be of dubious value." ACHENBACH, *Vollendung*, 388, sees the earliest materials in vv. 34–39, (41), 42, however he suggests that these verses were incorporated only in the final stage of the editing process (part of the post-redactional additions), the core narrative was developed by the HexRed, vv. 1, 2a, 5*, 6, 20*–22, 25–27, 33, 40, (41), this was further expanded by ThB, vv. 2b, 3–4, 7–15, 16–19, (20*), 23 f., 28–32. ARTUS, *Numbers 32*, 370–371, sees the text to contain two major layers. The first layer comprising vv. 1–2a, 5–6, 16–22, 25–27, 29–33,

3.1 Old Layers and Historical Memories?

traditions that point toward the idea that the present narrative was formed from some kind of doublet:[7]

1. The Reubenites and Gadites are granted the land in advance by Moses (v. 33) but they are also prohibited from settling there (vv. 28–29) until they join in the conquest of Cisjordan (vv. 20b–22*).

2. The Reubenites and Gadites wish to build cities (v. 16), but they also wish to occupy the cities that Israel had already conquered (v. 4).

---

40. This was updated (not necessarily all at once) with vv. 2b–3, 7–15, 20–22, 28, 34–39, 41–42. BAENTSCH, *E.L.N*, 660 f., separates the narrative into the four primary sources, as well as their redactions. J – 1*, 4*, 5*, 6, 20–22*, 23, 25–27, 33*, 39, 41–42; E – 3, 16–17, 24, 34–38; JE – 2*; P – 1*,2*, 4*, 18–19, 28, 29*, 30; Rp – 5*, 7–15, 22*, 29*, 31–32; Rd – 33*, 40. The next most common division separates v. 1 from vv. 2 f.. BUDD, *Numbers*, 342, for example divides the chapter into a pre-Yahwistic tradition (vv. 34–38, 39, 41–42), a Yahwistic story (vv. 1, 16–27), a Deuteronomistic adaptation (vv. 5–15, 40), and a Priestly adaptation (vv. 2–4, 28–33, with minor editing to vv. 11 and 12). DE VAULX, *Nombres*, 362–363, argues for a Yahwistic story (vv. 1–4, 5–6, 20–23, 25–27, 33), which included some pre-Yahwistic traditions (vv. 33b, 39–42), and a redactor with the style of D and P (vv. 7–15). FISTILL, *Ostjordanland*, 127 f., considers the core narrative to comprise vv. 1*, 5–32. Added to this were older traditions concerning Transjordan (vv. 39, 41–42), a redactor then aimed to further harmonise this narrative with the presentation in Deuteronomy (vv. 33, 40), as well as strengthen the introduction with vv. 2–4. Fistill is unsure of the origin of vv. 34–38, but concludes that it is unlikely to belong to the original Gad-Reuben narrative. GERMANY, *Cartography*, argues for a base narrative comprising vv. 2*, 4–6, 16–17, 20a, 22b, 24–25, 33*, 34–38. To this the remaining verses were added in one or more updates. MARQUIS, *Composition*, 423–425, divides the text into two standalone narratives (E – vv. 1, 2*, 4, 5*, 17*, 18, 19, 20*, 22*, 23, 24*, 33, 39–42; P – vv. 2, 3, 5*, 6, 16, 17*, 20*, 21, 22*, 24*, 25–32, 34–38) that were later conflated and supplemented by the Pentateuch redactor (vv. 7–15). MITTMANN, *Deuteronomium*, 104, attributes vv. 1, 16*, 17a, 34, 35, 37, 38 to one of the old Pentateuch sources, J or E. To this was added the extended conquest notice in vv. 39, 41 f. Finally the speech in vv. 16–17 generated several expansions, the first comprising vv. 2*, 4b, 6–11, 16*, 17b–18, 20aα, 24, 33a, 33b, 35, 36; the second vv. 5, 12–15, 20aβ–23; third vv. 19, 25–29; and lastly vv. 30–32 (This reconstruction is followed by DAVIES, *Numbers*, 330–331). SCHMIDT, "Ansiedlung," 501, sees the base narrative, which he attributes to E, to comprise vv. 1, 2a, bα, 4aβ, b, 5a, 6, 16, 17a, 20aα, 24, 33a*, b, 34, 35*, 36, 37, 38*. To this the Pentateuch Redactor added 4aα, 5a, b, 7–11, 13–15, 20aβ–23, 25–27, 33a*. A later editer contributed 17b–19, 28–32, 36b (12?) to connect the narrative more closely to the version in Deuteronomy. See also SCHMIDT, *Numeri*, 198. SCHORN, *Ruben*, 155 f., attributes vv. 1*, 2a, 4*, 5, 6, 16 f., 20*, 24, 25 f., 34–38* to the base layer, vv. 1 (the change of sequence Reuben-Gad, the Land of Jazer), 2b, 3, 4*, 18 f., 20, 21a, 22 f., 27, 28–32, 35 f. to Priestly additions, vv. 7–15 to an extension of the salvation history narrative, vv. 21b, 33, 35*, 39–42 to a third editorial addition. SEEBASS, "Erwägungen," allocates vv. 1, 2a, bα, 4aβ–6, 16–17a, 19b–20a, 22b–25, 34–38 to the original J narrative. He sees vv. 7–15 to be a secondary insertion and vv. 2b–4aα, 17b–19a, 20b–22a, 23, 26–33*, 36b to be the work of an editor, "im priesterlich-dtr Stil" (*in the priestly-deuteronomistic style*). See also SEEBASS, *Numeri 3*, 328 f.. STAUBLI, *Bücher*, 334 understands the chapter to have developed in four stages: vv. 1–6, 16–24, 25–27, 28–32, 33 comprise a pre-Priestly, core narrative, vv. 7–15 represents a "D Interpolation", finally two further attachments comprising vv. 34–38 and 39–42 respectively. VAN SETERS, *Life*, 436–439, attributes vv. 1, 2*, (3), 4–9, 13–27, 28, 29–42 to J, and the remainder to P. WÜST, *Untersuchungen*, 95–99, attributes vv. 1*, 16a, 16b, 17, 20aα, 34–38 to the base layer, vv. 20aβ, 22aβb, 23 to the first supplemental addition, vv. 2abα, 5*, 6, 25, 28 f. to the second supplement, and the remaining verses: 2b 3, 4, 5*, 7–11, 12–15, 18, 19a, 19b, 20b, 21, 22aα, 26 f., 27, 29–33, 39–42 to various editorial additions.

[7] These discrepancies are neatly laid out in MARQUIS, "Composition," 410–413.

84   *3. The Occupation of Transjordan*

3. The text also contains other stylistic differences, such as the presence of different terms for allotment, נחלה (*inheritance*) vs אחזה (*possession*), or the idea that the Reubenites and Gadites go to battle לפני בני ישראל (*before the sons of Israel*) vs לפני יהוה (*before YHWH*).

Yet even with these relatively clear markers, there is no consensus between scholars as to how Numbers 32 should be separated into various layers. For the present purposes of demonstrating the possibility of a pre-Priestly and pre-Deuteronomistic layer, simply finding the non-P elements is insufficient. The starting point for the investigation, then, will not be to simply propose yet another reconstruction based upon purely literary markers. Rather the analysis will proceed from geographical conceptions, which not only help to separate the material into redactional layers but also to order them with regard to their relative chronology.

3.1.1.1 Literary Geography

The major text for unlocking the various layers of Numbers 32 is found in v. 1, which, following the Hebrew word order, can be rendered:

Many livestock had the sons of Reuben and the sons of Gad: very many. And they saw the land of Jazer and the land of Gilead, and behold, the place was a place for livestock.

This text is unanimously allocated to the earliest layer because it forms the introduction to the subsequent narrative. Yet the geographical area described as "the land of Jazer and the land of Gilead" is peculiar for a number of reasons as will be illuminated below.

To begin with the land of Gilead. The term "Gilead" has a rather nebulous meaning in the Hebrew Bible – sometimes referring to a city (e.g., Hos 6:8), sometimes to the entirety of Israelite Transjordan from the Arnon to the Jarmuk (e.g., Josh 22:9), and most commonly to a more specific area of Israelite Transjordan. This means it is not always obvious which conception of Gilead is intended.

According to Deut 3:10, there are three distinct portions of Transjordan: the Mishor, the Gilead and the Bashan. According to Deut 3:16, the Reubenites and Gadites settled "from the Gilead until the Wadi Arnon, with the middle of the Wadi as a border, until the Jabbok, the Wadi being the border of the sons of Ammon." According to Deut 3:12, this area constitutes the Mishor and חצי הר־הגלעד (*half the hill country of the Gilead*). The half-tribe of Manasseh, according to Deut 3:13, received, "יתר הגלעד (*the rest of the Gilead*) and all the Bashan." This clearly suggests that the Gilead spans the Jabbok, reaching south to the Mishor and north to Bashan.

Like Deuteronomy, Joshua 13 divides the Transjordan into three portions, however here the territories are granted to the Transjordan tribes roughly according to this division. Reuben is approximately granted the Mishor (Josh 13:16–20), Gad is granted most of the Gilead (Josh 13:25–27), and the half-tribe of Manasseh is granted the north-eastern portion of the Gilead and Bashan (Josh 13:30–31).[8]

If Num 32:1 follows this same conception, then it raises the question: Is "the land of Jazer" an alternative designation for the Mishor? As has been widely observed, the ארץ יעזר (*land of Jazer*) plays no further part in the narrative of Numbers 32, nor does it appear anywhere else in the Bible.[9] In Num 32:3 and 35, Jazer is mentioned as a city and there is no indication that it is a city of any particular importance. Numbers 32:3, rather, is centred upon the city of Heshbon, which according to the Sihon narrative, is the capital city of the Amorite king (Num 21:26; Deut 1:4; 2:4, 26, 30; 3:2, 6; 4:46, etc.). This is significant because the following analysis will argue that the earliest layer of Numbers 32 does not know the Sihon narrative. In fact, besides v. 33, which logically represents a late harmonisation, Sihon is never mentioned in the narrative of Numbers 32.[10]

Outside of Numbers 32, what can be known about Jazer? Although Jazer does appear elsewhere in the Bible, such as the oracles of Isa 16:9 and Jer 48:32, the wider biblical tradition hardly acknowledges Jazer as a site of importance. Several manuscripts of 2 Sam 24:5, for example, do not even seem to recognize Jazer and so rendered אל־יעזר (*towards Jazer*) as אליעזר (*Eliezer*), including the LXX (Ελιεζερ). Importantly, Jazer is never mentioned in the parallel report in Deuteronomy 2–3.[11]

Thus, based solely on the biblical tradition, the territory envisioned by the land of Gilead and the land of Jazer remain unclear. Importantly, the rarity of Jazer in the broader biblical tradition speaks against the description in Num 32:1 as being a late harmonisation of other Transjordan traditions. However, it must be admitted from purely literary grounds the precise size and shape of "the land of Jazer and the land of Gilead" remains unclear.

3.1.1.2 Geographical Analysis

In the previous section it was suggested that the label, Gilead, had a rather nebulous meaning in the Hebrew Bible but that Deuteronomy 3 and Joshua 13

---

[8] For a map showing the distribution of Joshua 13, see Lissovsky/Na'aman, "System," 317; Hobson, "Israelites," 43.

[9] The issues of the land of Jazer have been widely discussed. See, e. g., Täubler, *Epoche*, 220–223; Wüst, *Untersuchungen*, 164–168; Schorn, *Ruben*, 154–155; Fistill, *Ostjordanland*, 116.

[10] Scholars such as Mittmann, *Deuteronomium*, 104; Budd, *Numbers*, 342; Schorn, *Ruben*, 155f; Seebass, "Erwägungen," 35; Schmidt, "Ansiedlung," 501 and Wüst, *Untersuchungen*, 95–99, allocate the Sihon and Og reference in Num 32:33 to a late update. One notable exception is Achenbach, *Vollendung*, 388, who allocates v. 33 – as a whole – to the HexRed (i. e., the base narrative).

[11] McCarter Jr., *II Samuel*, 510.

86   *3. The Occupation of Transjordan*

appeared to depict a fixed entity. This raises the question of where the historical Gilead might be?

The origin of the name, Gilead, likely derived from its being the mountainous region in northern Transjordan that stood in contrast to the neighbouring Bashan, whose name means fertile plain.[12] This description is also suggested by the Jacob narrative, which typically speaks of the הר הגלעד (*hill country of the Gilead* – Gen 31:21, 23, 25, etc.), which is described as lying between the Euphrates and the land of Canaan. This is further corroborated by the fact that it is those cities above the Jabbok that have the word "Gilead" appended to their name (e.g., Ramoth-gilead, Jabesh-gilead, etc.). Additionally, both Jair the Gileadite (Judg 10:3) and the prophet Elijah (of Tishbe Gilead – 1 Kgs 17:1) come from locations north of the Jabbok.[13]

In Deuteronomy, Gilead is divided into two halves, with the Jabbok representing the dividing line (cf. Deut 3:12). It is this lower half-Gilead that Finkelstein, Lipschits and Koch argue is the land described in Num 32:1. More specifically they note that the area north of the Mishor and south of the Jabbok can be divided into two separate regions, "a higher, plateau-like area in the south, with an altitude of 950–1000 m above sea level, and a lower, enclosed, plateau-like area in the north, ca. 500 m above sea level," and thus they suggest that "the land of Jazer" describes this higher, southern region and "the land of Gilead" corresponds to the northern, lower region.[14] This interpretation is supported by Levine, who argues that the construct, "XXX ארץ" should be understood in a technical sense to refer to the area surrounding a city, such that both Jazer and Gilead are to be understood as cities. The key evidence for this assertion is found in Josh 17:8, where the ארץ תפוח (*land of Tapuah*) belonged to Manasseh, while the town itself belonged to Ephraim.[15] Levine's system only works in this case because there is in fact a city of Gilead south of the Jabbok.

The city of Gilead is commonly associated with modern day Gal'ad, which is located in the lower-elevation region, just below the Jabbok.[16] The location of Jazer is more uncertain, with the two most popular options being Khirbet Ḡazzir or Khirbet eṣ-Ṣār.[17] Phonetically Ḡazzir is the more fitting option, however

---

[12] Lemaire, "Galaad," 46. On the meaning of Bashan, see also Speier, "Bemerkungen," 306.

[13] See, e.g., Frevel, "Gilead;" Finkelstein et al., "Gilead," 137. The villages of Jair primarily belong to the Bashan. 1 Kings 4:13 states that the official of Ramoth-gilead was responsible for the villages of Jair. Tishbe is commonly located 4km north-west of Ajlun at el-Istib/Listib.

[14] Finkelstein et al., "Gilead," 133–134.

[15] Levine, *Numbers 21–36*, 482.

[16] On the location of the town of Gilead, see esp. discussion in Finkelstein et al., "Gilead" and Frevel, *Geschichte*, 444–450.

[17] Gass, *Moabiter*, 173 and MacDonald, *Territory*, 34–35, argue for Jazer at Khirbet Ḡazzir (2198.1583), whereas Frevel, *Geschichte*, 446 and Finkelstein et al., "Gilead," 140, prefer Khirbet eṣ-Ṣār (2280.1500).

3.1 Old Layers and Historical Memories? 87

Figure 7: Reconstruction of Num 32:1 according to FINKELSTEIN et al.[18]

---

[18] Map drawn by J. Davis. Cf. FINKELSTEIN et al., "Gilead." The boundary of the Ammonites is historically difficult to determine. See, e.g., SIMONS, "Problems I;" SIMONS, "Problems II;"

88   *3. The Occupation of Transjordan*

Finkelstein, Koch and Lipschits argue that eṣ-Ṣār, "fits best the information in the Hebrew Bible."[19]

Figure 7 demonstrates the territory envisioned by Num 32:1, if Finkelstein, Lipschits and Koch are correct in correlating the "land of Gilead" with Deuteronomy's half-Gilead below the Jabbok.

3.1.1.3 Historical Analysis

There is little reason to doubt that "half the Gilead" as it appears in, e.g., Deut 3:12 corresponds to the upper plateau area shown in figure 7. The issue with this solution is that such a territory has little correlation to Israel's historical occupation of Transjordan. Not to mention the fact that the extant biblical text clearly contains many traditions in which Israel dwells north of the Jabbok.

Although it is true that biblical narratives do not necessarily need to directly relate to "real" history, normally one would expect an invented history to be more glorious than reality (such as from Dan to Beersheba) rather than less so. It follows, then, that unless a clear literary or theological reason can be provided for why an author might alter reality (such as with the Sihon narrative, see below), there seems little reason to assume that the boundaries of the narrative Transjordan would not match the present, or "remembered," boundaries of Israelite Transjordan.[20] One further issue is that Deuteronomy and Joshua, wherein the concept of the two "halves" of Gilead is most clearly present, both operate under the assumption of the Sihon narrative, which must be considered a later innovation than Num 32:1 (again see below). Deuteronomy and Joshua also provide no reason to suppose that above the Mishor there was any "land of Jazer," they speak only of "half the Gilead."

Historically, the southern boundary suggested by "the land of Jazer" fits neatly to the situation after Mesha's campaign, when the southern portion of Transjordan, previously conquered by the Omrides, was (re-)claimed by Moab. The Mesha stele reports that Mesha expanded his dominion at least as far north

---

Gass, "Amalekiter;" Roskop Erisman, "Border." Gilead is located at Galʿad (2235.1695), see Gass, *Ortsnamen*, 673; Frevel, *Geschichte*, 446. Heshbon is located at Tell Ḥesbān (2265.1342), see MacDonald, *East*, 93; Gass, *Ortsnamen*, 674; Frevel, *Geschichte*, 446. Jazer is located at Khirbet eṣ-Ṣār (2280.1500), see MacDonald, *East*, 106–108, 112; Finkelstein et al., "Gilead," 140–141; Frevel, *Geschichte*, 446 (cf. MacDonald, *Territory*, 34–35). Mt. Nebo is located at Khirbet el-Muḥayyat (2206.1286), see MacDonald, *East*, 86–87; Gass, *Moabiter*, 172–188; Frevel, *Geschichte*, 446. Shittim is located at Tell el-Kefrēn (2118.1397), see Gass, *Moabiter*, 176; Frevel, *Geschichte*, 447 (cf. MacDonald, *East*, 89–90). Jahaz is located at Khirbet el-Mudēyine et-Temed (2362.1109), see MacDonald, *East*, 103–106; Frevel, *Geschichte*, 446 (cf. Gass, *Moabiter*, 187, who prefers Khirbet er-Rumēl).

[19] Finkelstein et al., "Gilead," 140.

[20] On the idea of "historical memories" see esp. Finkelstein/Römer, "Memories."

as Nebo, which aligns with the idea that the Wadi el-Kefren functioned as the borderline between Israel and Moab.[21]

Granting that the southern border defined by "the land of Jazer" appears to be historically grounded, it seems logical to suppose that the northern border defined by "the land of Gilead" is also historical, stemming from the same time period. But where and when might that be? As already suggested, the *terminus post quem* for the reality behind Num 32:1 must be after Mesha had expanded the territory of Moab northwards. According to Lemaire, the most likely historical period for when Mesha would have been able to do this was during the severe weakening of Israel due to Hazael's aggression in the north.[22] At the very least, this suggests that Num 32:1 depicts the situation after the Omride dynasty had been replaced by the Nimshides.

According to 2 Kgs 10:33, Hazael took control of the entirety of Israelite Trans-jordan, as well as conquering deep into Israelite Cisjordan territory. This expansion is supported archaeologically both by the presence of the inscription at Tell Deir ʿAlla as well as a series of expanding destruction layers in Cisjordan.[23] 2 Kings 13:25 reports that it was not until the reign of Jehoash that Israel began to reclaim some of its lost territory, likely on the back of the renewed pressure on Aram from Assyria.[24] 2 Kings 13:17 indicates that Jehoash was able to reclaim Israel's lost territory as far north as Aphek, which would suggest that Jehoash pushed Aram back at least to the Jarmuk.[25] Importantly Jehoash appears to have retaken only the western portion of Transjordan, and it was during the reign of

---

[21] On the Wadi el-Kefren as the border see Wüst, *Untersuchungen*, 94; Naʾaman, "Rezin," 113; Naʾaman, "Inscription," 176. Importantly Mesha does not mention that he took Heshbon, which can either be interpreted to mean that he did not expand so far north, or (more likely) that Heshbon was too insignificant to be worth mentioning. For further discussion on Mesha's campaign see, e.g., Naʾaman, "Mesha." Heshbon likely fell under Ammonite control in the Iron IIA-B period – see Daviau, "Border;" Bienkowski, "Transjordan," 421.

[22] Lemaire, "Mesha," 140. This position is also forwarded by Naʾaman, "Inscription," 156. Aharoni, *Land*, 307, alternatively argues that Mesha expanded during the reign of Ahab rather than of Joram.

[23] On the destruction layers likely attributable to Hazael see esp. Kleiman, "Subjugation." Knauf, "Jeroboam," 296, locates Tell Deir ʿAlla at biblical Penuel, however this is rejected by Finkelstein et al., "Gilead," 148–149. Other scholars alternatively propose the location to be biblical Succoth (see, e.g., Franken, "Evidence," 4). For an overview of the finds at Tell Deir ʿAlla see esp. Hoftijzer/Van Der Kooij, *Texts*. For an overview of recent scholarship on Tell Deir ʿAlla, see Burnett, "Prophecy," 142–149. If Blum, "Wandinschriften," 36–40, is correct in supposing that the building site that housed the inscription was in fact a scribal school, then it further speaks against this site being located in a contested area. Rather it suggests that during the height of Hazael's kingdom, the Aramean occupation extended both south and west of Tell Deir ʿAlla.

[24] See, e.g., Aharoni, *Land*, 311.

[25] The precise location of Aphek is still contested, however the options are all located in the region near the Sea of Galilee. See, e.g., Finkelstein, *Kingdom*, 121; Bosserman, "Aphek." Arie, "Reconsidering," proposes that it was Jehoash who was able to expand Israel's border all the way up to Dan for the first time.

90   *3. The Occupation of Transjordan*

his son, Jeroboam II, that Israel was further expanded from Lo-debar (=Lidbir) to Karnaim (most likely representing Bashan).[26] This historical reality matches quite accurately to the allotment of Gad found in Josh 13:25–26, which is described as extending from Jazer to the border of Lidbir and עד־קצה ים־כנרת (*until the end of the sea of Chinnereth* = sea of Galilee).[27] It therefore seems plausible that Num 32:1 and Josh 13:25–26 represent two alternative descriptions of the same area, shown in figure 8.[28]

One possible alternative is that the "land of Jazer" and the "land of Gilead" represent the names of the Assyrian provinces of central and northern Transjordan respectively, however this is difficult to prove and in any case is more than a little unlikely. It is not clear how long after Jeroboam II that Israel was able to hold on to its expanded territory from Jazer to Bashan. According to the inscriptions of Tiglath-pileser III, when Assyria took the Transjordan, the entire region north of Moab belonged to Aram, not Israel.[29] If accurate, Tiglath-pileser's

---

[26] See Amos 6:13. For further discussion see, e.g., FINKELSTEIN, "Stages," 240.

[27] For a visual representation see Map 2 in LISSOVSKY/NA'AMAN, "System," 317. See also HOBSON, "Israelites," 42–43.

[28] One possible explanation for the alternate rendering in Joshua 13 is that those ex-Israelite cities belonging to the now-expanded Moab were allocated to the (extinct?) tribe of Reuben, whilst the territory remaining under Israelite control was allocated to the (still existing?) tribe of Gad. This is based upon the idea that the tribe of Reuben had died out, or come to irrelevance, in the pre-Monarchic era. CROSS, "Reuben," 53, for example argues that, "Reuben's place in the genealogy presumes that Reuben once played a major role in Israelite society, even a dominant one, whether political or religious." KNAUF/GUILLAUME, *History*, 47, suggest that, historically, the tribe of Reuben cannot be detected after the 10th century BCE. (See also KNAUF, *Josua*, 129).

The bible itself alludes to the idea that Reuben died out: The fable that he slept with his father's concubine and therefore became cursed (Gen 35:22; 49:4), functions to explain how the firstborn was no longer a prominent tribe. The tribal "blessing" in Deut 33:6 suggests that Reuben was dwindling tribe, if not already gone. The missing verse of 1 Samuel 10 found in 4Q51 (10a6–9) further suggests that prior to Saul becoming king, Nahash the Ammonite oppressed Reuben and Gad such that only 7000 men were left to escape to Jabesh-gilead. On the reliability of this insert see discussion in Tov, *TCHB*, 342–344. 1 Samuel 13:7 also suggests that during the time of Saul the Transjordan was populated by Gadites and Gileadites, with the Reubenites remaining unmentioned. Historically the presence or absence of Reuben is hard to verify. It is true that the Mesha Inscription makes no mention of a tribe of Reuben, however one must be careful in drawing any firm conclusions from this silence. Cf. SCHORN, *Ruben*, 285, who claims to have refuted the commonly held position that Reuben either died out or never existed in the first place.

One potential avenue to explain the strange background to the tribe of Reuben is to see Reuben from the perspective of the Josianic subversion of the Nimshide charter myth (see § 2.3). From this viewpoint, Reuben would be a veiled reference to the Nimshides who "lost their firstborn rights" when the Assyrians took the kingdom. Another option is to see the Reubenites as referring to the Omrides, who lost their place to the Nimshides. At this point in time, however, these can only remain conjecture.

[29] Inscriptions (III R 10.2 and ND 4301+) celebrate Assyria's dominance over Bit Haza'ili (the house of Hazael). See TADMOR, "Aram," 114; TADMOR/YAMADA, *Inscriptions*, 105. More contentious is A-bi-il-[...], which is said to be situated "on the borderland of the house of Omri," i.e., Israel.

3.1 Old Layers and Historical Memories?

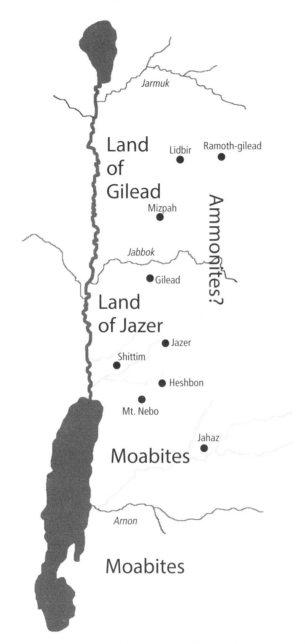

Figure 8: Reconstruction of Num 32:1 according to the present analysis[30]

---

[30] Map drawn by J. Davis. On the trouble of the Ammonite territory as well as the topographic details, see notes for figure 7.

inscription directly contradicts the biblical account in 2 Kgs 15:29, which indicates that the Gilead belonged to Israel when it was captured.[31] Aside from assuming that Tiglath-pileser's inscription was mistaken, Galil has argued, based upon other Assyrian royal inscriptions, that even when one kingdom is referred to in the opening line, that the subsequent listing can include other kingdoms. This would mean that the direct naming of Aram does not necessitate that all territory named after this must be Aramean.[32] In any case what is important is how one understands the four toponyms mentioned in Tiglath-pileser III's report.[33] Tadmor suggests that these toponyms divide up the territory of southern Aram into the Assyrian provinces of Dimašqa (Damasucs), Haurīna (Hauran), Qarnini (Qarnaim), Magiddu (Megiddo) and Gal'aza (Gilead), however Tadmor's reconstruction relies (1) on the original thesis of Emil Forrer (1920)[34] and (2) the contentious reconstruction of A-bi-il-[...] to refer to Abel-Beth-Maacah.[35] Although Forrer's study has long been regarded as the standard, "whose scope has not been superseded and whose methodology and conclusions are still largely accepted today," most recent research suggests that Forrer's understanding that there existed a correlation between the places listed on Assyrian cuneiform tablets and Assyrian provincial centres is increasingly doubtful.[36] Recently Bienkowski has provided a strong criticism against the earlier accepted hypothesis of a clear Assyrian presence in the Transjordan region. First, he demonstrates that not only is Ga-al-'a-z[..] commonly *mis*translated to mean Gilead, but that "it is therefore now certain that Gilead does not appear in any known Assyrian administrative list of provinces."[37] Second, Bienkowski points to the fact that neither Ammon, Moab nor Edom became Assyrian provinces, but rather retained their own kings who were forced to pay tribute.[38] This is further corroborated by the fact that

---

[31] GALIL, "Boundaries," 40, in particular argues, "In light of the special and close relations between Rezin and Peqah and in light of the Transjordanian origins of Peqah, it is unreasonable to suppose that Damascus, in its final years, controlled the Gilead."

[32] GALIL, "Look," 513.

[33] Inscription III R 10.2 mentions four cities in the following order: [...]áš-pu-ú-na, [...]-ni-te, Ga-al-'a-z[..], and A-bi-il-[...]. Of these, scholars are broadly agreed that [...]áš-pu-ú-na and Ga-al-'a-z[..], refer to Kashpunah and Gilead respectively, with the meaning of [...]-ni-te and A-bi-il-[...] being uncertain at best. Given that the other references are names of cities, Ga-al-'a-z[..] probably refers to Ramoth-Gilead rather than the region of the Gilead. (See, e.g., TADMOR, "Aram," 114; GALIL, "Look," 513; GALIL, "Boundaries," 41; TADMOR/YAMADA, "Inscriptions," 105).

[34] FORRER, *Provinzeinteilung*.

[35] TADMOR, "Aram," 118. More convincing is the suggestion (from, e.g., NA'AMAN, "Rezin," 105; GALIL, "Boundaries," 41; WEIPPERT, *Textbuch*, 294) that A-bi-il-[...] refers to Abel-Shittim, which results in a clear north-south progression of conquest: Beginning from Kashpunah ([...] áš-pu-ú-na) in north-eastern Aram, via an unknown [...]-ni-te, all the way through northern Transjordan (Ga-al-'a-z[..]), to Abel-Shittim (A-bi-il-[...]) in central Transjordan.

[36] BIENKOWSKI, "Transjordan," 46.

[37] BIENKOWSKI, "Transjordan," 46.

[38] BIENKOWSKI, "Transjordan," 48.

"there is a striking absence of identifiable Ammonite, Moabite, and Edomite names in Assyria ... which suggests that the Assyrians had not deported peoples from there in any number, if at all (and therefore presumably had not resettled the areas)."[39]

Thus, while it remains possible that the land of Jazer and the land of Gilead refer to Assyrian or even Babylonian provinces, there is little historical data to support such a theory. The most secure solution, then, is to suppose that Num 32:1 reflects the period and setting of the reign of Jeroboam II. The connection with Jeroboam II also provides an important foundation for explaining the question posed at the beginning of this chapter, that is, How can one explain the Transjordan tradition when it seems to cause nothing but problems within the wider exodus-eisodus paradigm, with the idea that the land of Canaan was what YHWH promised and with the idea that Moses was not allowed to step foot in the land that YHWH was giving Israel? As suggested in § 2.3.2, the Jordan as a hard border seems to have originally been guided by the Judean vision of the land and has little to do with the Omride and Nimshide areas of influence. If the proposed "Josianic" repurposing of the Northern traditions suggested in § 2.3.2 is correct, it is not difficult to suppose that the settlement of Transjordan was inherited tradition that needed to be justified in light of the new ideological framework of the exodus-conquest narrative. To this end, it will be argued that the Sihon tradition was one of the means by which the later Judean authors tried to solve the problems caused by the "Nimshide" Transjordan settlement tradition.

3.1.1.4 In Support of the Pre-Sihon Base Layer of Numbers 32

In a recent article Frevel has convincingly demonstrated that the Pentateuch contains two different conceptualisations of Moab, and that the Sihon narrative represents a later, fictional update that pushed the traditional boundary of Moab southward to the Arnon. The earlier view understood that Moab extended north of the Arnon such that the "plains of Moab" actually belonged to the Moabites (see figure 8).[40] Given this expanded (i.e., Mesha's) Moab, it is not difficult to suppose the "land of Jazer" was understood as that territory located north of the plains of Moab and south of Gilead.

The precise location of the city of Jazer is disputed, however the common options are located in the region of the Amman plateau, which fits neatly to the idea that the area above the plains of Moab, was described by the "land of

---

[39] BIENKOWSKI, "Transjordan," 51. He goes on to note, "The paucity of Transjordan names contrasts with at least forty-seven probable Israelite names in Neo-Assyrian sources (excluding royal inscriptions) of the eighth and seventh centuries BCE."

[40] See esp. FREVEL, "Shapes." Roskop Erisman further argues that alongside a shift in Moab's borders, the Sihon narrative also disrupted or relocated the Ammonite border (see ROSKOP, *Itineraries*, 204–215; ROSKOP ERISMAN, "Transjordan," 775; ROSKOP ERISMAN, "Border").

Jazer." This in turn supports the theory that the narrative beginning in Num 32:1 did not know of the Sihon narrative, whose capital city of Heshbon is geographically proximate to Jazer but remains unmentioned.[41] Indeed, if the narrative of Numbers 32 was intended to align with the Sihon narrative's idea that the Amorites controlled central Transjordan all the way to the Arnon, then one is left wondering why the Reubenites and Gadites did not observe the land of Sihon, the land of Heshbon, or even the plains of Moab alongside the land of Gilead. By referring to "the land of Jazer" the authors of Num 32:1 seem to be emphasising that the land in question was the land north of "the plains of Moab" (cf., Num 22:1; 26:3, 63; 31:12; etc.).

But it is not only Num 32:1 that leads to this conclusion. The Sihon narrative itself suggests that Jazer was problematic for the changed conception of the Transjordan after Moab had been (narratively) pushed back to the Arnon. First, one must explain the appearance of Jazer in the LXX rendering of Num 21:24, but its alteration in the MT.

ויכהו ישראל לפי־חרב ויירש את־ארצו מארנן עד־יבק עד־בני עמון כי עז גבול בני עמון	and Israel put him to the sword and dispossessed his land from the Arnon to the Jabbok, as far as the sons of Ammon, because the border of the sons of Ammon was strong.
Καὶ ἐπάταξεν αὐτὸν Ισραηλ φόνῳ μαχαίρης καὶ κατεκθρίευσαν τῆς γῆς αὐτοῦ ἀπὸ Αρνων ἕως Ιαβοκ ἕως υἱῶν Αμμαν ὅτι Ιαζηρ ὅρια υἱῶν Αμμων ἐστίν	and Israel put him to death by the sword and possessed his land from the Arnon to the Jabbok, as far as the sons of Ammon, because Jazer is the border of the sons of Ammon.

Table 3: Numbers 21:24 according to the MT and LXX

Following the general scholarly opinion that the LXX represents the more original version, this raises the question: Why would a scribe alter/remove the reference to Jazer from the text?[42] The answer to this seems to be found in the prohibition against Israel from taking any land from the Ammonites (Num 21:24; Deut 2:19; 2:37; 3:16). By claiming that the border of the Ammonites was Jazer, it could be understood that Jazer was an Ammonite city rather than an Amorite one. Thus, it follows that the reference to Jazer being the border of the Ammonites was altered in order to remove the implication that Israel took Ammonite land (cf. Judg 11:13).

This same concern likely explains Num 21:32, which clearly stands outside of the Sihon narrative proper (cf. it is absent in Deuteronomy) and states, "Moses sent [men] to spy out Jazer, and they captured its villages and dispossessed the Amorites that were there." Once again, this notice makes it explicit that (1) the conquest of Jazer was undertaken at Moses's command and (2) that it was

---

[41] Isaiah 15:4; 16:8–9 and Jer 48:2, 34 and 45 also attest to Heshbon belonging to Moab rather than Israel.

[42] See, e.g., GERMANY, *Exodus-Conquest*, 242.

occupied by Amorites, not Ammonites. This strange verse is difficult to explain if it does not presuppose the mention of Jazer in Num 32:1 already existed.[43] That the editors responsible for inserting the Sihon narrative into the book of Numbers appear to have gone to some effort regarding (the otherwise seemingly unimportant) Jazer suggests that the narrative of Numbers 32 was already present and was deemed to be problematic for the Sihon tradition. This required strategies to ameliorate the tension between these two related narratives.[44]

Further support for this conclusion is found in Num 32:16, where the Reubenites and Gadites wished to build cities for their livestock and families. Such an endeavour makes far more sense within a narrative construct in which Israel has not engaged in any battles in Transjordan. It makes less sense following the Sihon narrative, where the entire region from the Arnon to the Jabbok – including its fortified cities (cf. Num 21:25; Deut 2:34 and esp. Deut 2:36) – had been cleansed of enemies (cf. Num 21:25, 30, 31 and esp. Num 21:35).

One further point in support of the theory of a pre-Sihon narrative is the seemingly unimportant role played by Heshbon. If the narrative of Numbers 32 does indeed trace its origins back to the charter myth of Jeroboam II, then it reflects an accurate view of Heshbon during that time. Archaeological findings suggest that during the Iron II, Heshbon was little more than a small, un-walled village.[45]

In sum: whilst it is not impossible to understand Num 32:1 according to figure 7, the idea that the Jabbok was the northern border of the land requested by the Reubenites and Gadites appears to more suitably derive from the Sihon narrative, which it was argued cannot be in the background of Num 32:1.[46] Thus, the most plausible reconstruction of Num 32:1 is that the Jabbok functions as the dividing

---

[43] Num 21:32 is commonly understood to be a late, harmonising verse. See, e.g., ACHENBACH, *Vollendung*, 366; SEEBASS, *Numeri 2*, 363; SCHMIDT, *Numeri*, 112. Cf. MITTMANN, *Deuteronomium*, 95.

[44] ACHENBACH, *Vollendung*, 363, also notes that the land of Sihon expands the area conquered by the Israelites into that historically owned by Ammonites.

[45] LaBIANCA/WALKER, "Tall Hisban," 112. See also KNAUF, "Heshbon," 137–138; MacDONALD, "Territory," 36–39; MacDONALD, *East*, 92–93; STORDALEN, "Heshbon," 251.

[46] The idea that the Jabbok was considered a border since the Bronze Age seems quite likely. LEMAIRE, "Galaad," 45, notes, "il est *a priori* assez vraisemblable que le Yabboq constituait déjà la frontière sud du territoire primitifde Galaad" (*it is* a priori *quite probable that the Jabbok already constituted the southern border of the primitive territory of Gilead* – italics original). One alternative suggestion is offered by SERGI, "Gilead," 336, who argues that the Jabbok likely marked the border between Aram-Damascus and Israel during the Omride regency and that most of northern Transjordan functioned in some way as a shared space. See also FREVEL, *Geschichte*, 116–119.

96   *3. The Occupation of Transjordan*

line between the land of Jazer and the land of Gilead, i.e., between central and northern Transjordan as shown in figure 8.[47]

3.1.2 More Pre-Sihon Traditions[48]

Having suggested that the land desired by the Reubenites and Gadites was the Transjordan territory above "the plains of Moab," are there other narratives in the book of Numbers that also support such a reading? In particular, are there other narratives that also suggest the Sihon narrative was added at a later stage of redaction into the book of Numbers?

Working backwards from Numbers 32, the next relevant narrative is found in Numbers 25, where Israel is said to be camped[49] at Shittim (=Abel-shittim), which is situated opposite Jericho. Here we are told that ויחל העם לזנות אל־בנות מואב (*the people began to have* [improper] *intercourse with the daughters of Moab*). This gives rise to two possibilities, either Shittim stood near (or even within) the Moabite border or the men of Israel were so desirable that the women of Moab were willing to cross the Arnon and walk some thirty kilometres north in order to seduce them. Granting that option 1 is far more plausible it can be concluded that Numbers 25 also presupposes that the border of Moab was north of the Arnon.

Moving further back is the story of Balaam (Numbers 22–24), which has regularly been considered to comprise a standalone piece of tradition grafted into the book of Numbers.[50] This narrative is redactionally complex, and it is beyond the scope of the present investigation to treat it in any detail.[51] However among the many locations that Balak takes Balaam to curse Israel is to the top of Pisgah (Num 23:14), which again presupposes that Balak's Moab, like Mesha's,

---

[47] The idea that the area describes the territory inherited by Jeroboam II is reinforced by the discussion in § 2.3.1. See esp. note 227 on page 53.

[48] This section is largely repeated in DAVIS, "Redaction."

[49] The wording of Num 25:1 is actually ישב וישב ישראל בשטים (*and Israel was dwelling in Shittim*), departing from the typical itinerary formula, which uses the word חנה (*to camp*). If "dwelling" is taken literally, then it follows that Num 25:1 and Num 32:1 cannot belong to the same narrative thread and that the ordeal at Baal Peor is a fragment inserted into the narrative. However, Deuteronomy uses ישב (*to dwell*) to suggest a longer-term, but still temporary stay (e.g., Deut 1:6, 46). This same usage appears to be present in Num 20:1, which reports that the people ישב in Kadesh, which is likely borrowed from Deut 1:46.

[50] On the Balaam narrative originally comprising a stand-alone narrative see, e.g., OTTO, *Deuteronomium 1,1–4,43*, 256, who dates it to the exilic period, and ZENGER, *Einleitung*, 125, who dates it to the 8th century at the latest (Lit.: vor/um 700). LEVINE, *Numbers 21–36*, 137, argues that, "internal analysis shows little direct interaction between Numbers 22–24 and what precedes and follows these chapters."

[51] The Balaam narrative has received a broad scholarly treatment. To name some examples: BICKERT, "Israel;" BÜHRER, "Bileams;" BURNETT, "Prophecy;" ROBKER, *Balaam*; SCHMIDT, "Bileam;" SEEBASS, "Gestalt;" WITTE, "Bileams."

extended at least as far north as Nebo (cf. Mesha Stele ln 14 – "Go, take Nebo from Israel!" [COS 2.138]).[52]

The final stage of the current investigation is to see if the itinerary prior to the Sihon narrative is conducive to the idea that there existed a narrative thread that linked Israel's journey from Kadesh to Shittim (Numbers 25), where the Reubenites and Gadites could see the land of Jazer and the land of Gilead in Num 32:1.

Following the disastrous results of the spy event (Numbers 13–14), which occurred after Moses sent out spies from Kadesh (Num 13:26), the key movements of the people of Israel are reported in Num 20:1, 22; 21:4a, and 10–20. As has been widely observed, the journey described in Num 21:10–20 contains different itinerary styles and so results in a nonsensical, "hodgepodge" journey.[53] Although various reconstructions exist, it will be argued below that Num 21:12, 13aα and 20* contain the more original itinerary.[54]

Although the precise breakdown of the itinerary of Numbers 21 is admittedly complex, it can broadly be characterised by two competing ideas. The first itinerary, comprising at least Num 21:12, 13aα and 20* suggests that Israel travelled peacefully through the land of Moab, via Nebo before arriving at Shittim. The second itinerary reports that Israel did not enter the territories of Edom or Moab on their journey north, and rather travelled via the wilderness to the east of these nations. As Davies argues, "Previous attempts to interpret Num 21:12–20* have started from the presumption that it describes a route passing through the desert to the east of Moab. But the phrases on which this presumption is based are probably redactional additions to an older nucleus, which may have referred to a route further west."[55]

The priority of the western itinerary is indicated by several cumulative factors. First, when one compares the itinerary in Deuteronomy, it is those toponyms found in Num 21:12, 13aα and 20* that most closely align to the itinerary of Deuteronomy, namely the Wadi Zered (Num 21:12; Deut 2:13) and the Arnon (Num 21:13; [Deut 2:18]; Deut 2:24).[56] These two rivers constitute two clear checkpoints of Israel's journey north and are curiously absent from the eastern

---

[52] On the association of Pisgah with Nebo, see esp. Deut 34:1.

[53] MILLER, "Journey," 587, for example, concludes, "The result of this, of course, is a geographical hodgepodge totally incomprehensible in terms of the geographical realities of southern Transjordan." For discussion on the breakdown of these verses see, e.g., ACHENBACH, *Vollendung*, 352f; BADEN, "Narratives;" DAVIES, "Itineraries;" DAVIES, *Way*, 93; GERMANY, *Exodus-Conquest*, 277–288; FREVEL, "Understanding," 131–134 (=FREVEL, *Transformations*, 138–141); ROSKOP, *Itineraries*, 204–215.

[54] ROSKOP, *Itineraries*, 204–215, argues that Num 21:12–13a, 18b–20 function as a post-Priestly update used to incorporate the Balaam narrative.

[55] DAVIES, *Way*, 93.

[56] In this specific instance the direction of dependence is not relevant, as it follows that the earliest layer forms the foundation for the other.

itinerary.[57] Second, it is more logical to suppose that the itinerary describing Israel's journey through Moab predates the Sihon narrative rather than postdates it. This can be seen most clearly in the juxtaposition of v. 20 and v. 21. Numbers 21:20 concludes Israel's journey בשדה מואב ראש הפסגה ונשקפה על־פני הישימן (*in the field/region of Moab at the top of Pisgah and looks upon Jeshimon/the wasteland*), however this notice makes no sense transitioning into the beginning of the Sihon narrative, which reports that Sihon battled Israel at Jahaz (Num 21:23), far east of Pisgah/Nebo (cf. figure 10). Conversely the idea that Sihon battled Israel at Jahaz follows much more logically from verse 13aβ, where Israel is said to be במדבה היצא מגבול האמרי (*in the wilderness extending from the border of the Amorites*). Verse 13aβ in turn follows naturally on from Num 21:11, where Israel is said to be במדבה אשר על־פני מואב ממזרח השמש (*in the wilderness which faces Moab from the east*). From this location, east of the inhabited settlements of the Transjordan, it makes perfect sense for Moses to send a message to Sihon requesting passage westward towards Canaan (Num 21:21). In addition to this, it is difficult to explain why a later redactor would feel the need to insert a contradictory journey through Moab if the itinerary explaining Israel's journey around Moab already existed.

In sum, there is good reason to see a pre-Sihon layer that at least includes the itinerary notices in Num 21:12, 13aα and 20*, parts of the Balaam narrative (Num 22–24*), the non-Priestly fragments of the Baal Peor incident (including, at least, Num 25:1a)[58] and the base layer of Numbers 32.[59] These all share the idea that Israel travelled into a central Transjordan in which the plains of Moab still belonged to Moab (at least as far north as Nebo), rather than the later conception that limited Moab's upper border to the Arnon.

3.1.3 Tracing the Base Layer of Numbers 32

Given the above evidence, the following analysis will argue the narrative beginning in Num 32:1 was an originally non-Priestly narrative comprising:

[Num 32:1]Many livestock had [the sons of Reuben {and the sons of Gad, very many.}] And they saw the land of Jazer and the land of Gilead and behold, the place (מקום) was a place for livestock.

…

[Num 32:5b*][and they said,] "do not make us cross over the Jordan."

---

[57] Oboth (Num 21:10b) is not mentioned in Deuteronomy at all, and the ערבות מואב (*plains of Moab* – Num 22:1b) only appears in Deut 34:1 (a post-Priestly verse), Deuteronomy rather speaks of the ארץ מואב (*land of Moab* – Deut 1:5; 29:1; 32:49, 34:5, 6).

[58] FREVEL, *Transformations*, 159–160, suggests that "roughly" Num 25:1a, 3, 5 are Yehowistic and vv. 1b, 2, 4 are Deuteronomistic, the remainder belonging to one or more Priestly stratum. See also SCHMIDT, *Numeri*, 146.

[59] That Num 32:1 predated the Sihon narrative was already argued by NOTH, *Numbers*, 237: "From the point of view of the history of traditions, the basic form of 32:1ff. is certainly older than that of 21:21ff."

Num 32:6*and Moses said, "[...] you sit here?"

Num 32:16*and they said, "we will build walls for our sheep here and cities for our children

Num 32:17awe will equip ourselves and hasten before the sons of Israel until we have brought them to their place (מקום)

Num 32:20aand Moses said to them, "If you do what you have said,

Num 32:22aβafterwards you can return and be clear from Yhwh and from Israel

Num 32:24build cities for your children and walls for your sheep and do what came from your mouths."

Table 4: Non-Priestly narrative of Numbers 32

The foregoing analysis has argued that Num 32:1b provides the key to unlocking the non-Priestly base narrative. There are also several points of interest in v. 1a that should be discussed. First, v. 1a comprises the only instance in Num 32, where the sons of Reuben are named before the sons of Gad, in all other cases (vv. 2, 6, 25, 29, 31, [34 and 37]) Gad is named first. However, this is only the case for the MT as the following table shows:

	MT	SP	LXX	4Q27
Num 32:1	Reuben-Gad	Reuben-Gad-Manasseh	Reuben-Gad	Reuben-Gad-Manasseh
Num 32:2	Gad-Reuben	Gad-Reuben-Manasseh	Reuben-Gad-Manasseh	Gad-Reuben-[Manasseh][60]
Num 32:6	Gad-Reuben	Reuben-Gad-Manasseh	Gad-Reuben	Reuben-Gad-Manasseh
Num 32:25	Gad-Reuben	Reuben-Gad-Manasseh	Reuben-Gad	Reuben-Gad-Manasseh
Num 32:29	Gad-Reuben	Reuben-Gad-Manasseh	Reuben-Gad	Reuben-Gad-Manasseh
Num 32:31	Gad-Reuben	Reuben-Gad-Manasseh	Reuben-Gad	...
Num 32:34–42*	Gad-Reuben-Manasseh	Gad-Reuben-Manasseh	Gad-Reuben-Manasseh	Gad-Reuben-Manasseh

Table 5: Tribal naming by verse[61]

The simplest solution to this anomaly is that the MT represents the original ordering whereas the other versions represent various attempts to "fix" the perceived problems with the changing order and the sudden appearance of the half-tribe of Manasseh in vv. 39–42.

---

[60] The text of v. 2 is incomplete but 4Q27 appears to otherwise follow the SP.

[61] The anomalies of v. 6 in the LXX and v. 2 in the SP and 4Q27 are less clear, but it is interesting that these two verses in particular will be argued to have been more heavily reworked when the Priestly version was conflated with the non-Priestly version.

100 *3. The Occupation of Transjordan*

Returning to the MT wording, although the phenomenon is typically explained by other means it will be argued below there seems to be some validity to allocating the different name orders to different redactional layers.[62] The order Gad-Reuben appears to be a signature of the Priestly text (vv. 2, 25, 29, 31), whereas the verses allocated to the non-Priestly narrative seem to prefer the designators they/them (vv. 5*, 16, 20), the only verses that speak against this trend are vv. 6, 33, both of which will be argued to feature signs of later editing.[63]

The second point of interest is that v. 1a features awkward wording, such that the half-verse ends with, עצום מאד (Lit: *very mighty*), which Wüst describes as "unangenehm nachhinkenden" (*unpleasantly lagging*).[64]

Schmidt suggests a literary solution to this anomaly, proposing that the reason why Gad is placed before Reuben (besides verse 1) is because where the sons of Reuben had "many" livestock, the sons of Gad had "very many" and thus constituted the greater tribe.[65] While the idea that Gad grew to become a more significant tribe finds support both within and without the Bible, Schmidt's explanation remains unconvincing.[66]

Schorn suggests that Num 32:1 originally presented the more common ordering Gad-Reuben, but that it spoke only of the land of Gilead.[67] The verse was later updated as a result of Priestly editing such that the ordering of the tribes was reversed to the more familiar Reuben-Gad, and the land of Jazer was inserted so that Gilead could describe the Reubenite area, whilst Jazer (based upon Num 32:25) could describe the Gadite area.[68] However, one wonders why the Priestly editors chose to update v. 1 with their preferred tribal sequencing but left the remainder of the narrative unchanged. Additionally, Schorn does not adequately explain why these Priestly editors chose Jazer from among the many other cities belonging to the Gadites in vv. 34–35. Thus, this suggestion is also unconvincing.

Wüst proposes that the story was originally concerned only with the tribe of Reuben and their settlement in the land of Jazer.[69] First, he notes that in the song of Deborah it was the tribe of Reuben who ישבת בין המשפתים (*dwelt amidst the dung heaps*) to hear the piping of their sheep (Judg 5:16a). This report in Judges 5 aligns with Num 32:16 (which, according to Wüst, followed v. 1 in the original narrative) where the Reubenites and Gadites propose to build cities for their children and walls for their sheep.[70] Second, he proposes that the awkward ending

---

[62] NOTH, *Numbers*, 239, suggests that the ordering Gad-Reuben is "surely on the basis of an old source-tradition."

[63] See, e.g., ACHENBACH, *Vollendung*, 369–374.

[64] WÜST, *Untersuchungen*, 115 See also NOTH, *Numeri*, 205.

[65] SCHMIDT, "Ansiedlung," 498.

[66] See note 28 on page 90.

[67] SCHORN, *Ruben*, 144 f..

[68] SCHORN, *Ruben*, 156.

[69] WÜST, *Untersuchungen*, 91 f..

[70] WÜST, *Untersuchungen*, 95.

of v. 1a, was intended to make the verse function as a chiasm when the tribe of Gad was added alongside Reuben. Thus the logic of the verse proceeds, (A) רב (*many*) livestock had (B) the sons of Reuben (B') and the sons of Gad (A') עצום מאד (*very many*).[71] Finally, Wüst argues that the land of Gilead was added into v. 1 when the core narrative was altered from a report about the how the Reubenites inherited the Transjordan, to a narrative demonstrating that the Transjordan was inherited as a result of the faithfulness of Reubenites and Gadites in assisting the conquest of the land of Canaan.[72]

Wüst's suggestion that v. 1a conforms to a chiastic structure is convincing. Furthermore, the idea that the Gadites were not originally part of the narrative finds support if the historical Gadites are considered. First, the tribe of Gad clearly lived in "Moabite" territory, below the area described by the "land of Jazer."[73] This is made clear in the Mesha stele – "And the men of Gad lived in the land of Ataroth from ancient times" (COS 2.137) – where the Gadites are reported to live far south of the area possibly covered by "the land of Jazer" (cf. figure 11).[74] Numbers 33:45–46 also support this assertion as there Dibon is alternatively named Dibon-gad suggesting that Dibon was a Gadite town.[75] In light of the historical link to Jeroboam II argued above, it seems plausible to suspect that the narrative originally related to the Nimshide expansion, and that this was later altered in light of the fable of the twelve tribes of Israel that dictated that the Gadites be located in Transjordan (see § 3.3).

Outside of verse 1, there are no clues that the Gadites are a secondary insertion, thus for sake of simplicity the following analysis will continue to speak of both tribes, even if, as just argued, the 12-tribe conception most likely only came into being somewhat later.

A further point of interest in v. 1 is the use of the word מקום (*place*) for the territory under discussion, which functions to link to v. 17a, wherein the Reubenites and Gadites vow, "we will equip ourselves and hasten before the sons of Is-

---

[71] WÜST, *Untersuchungen*, 115 f..

[72] WÜST, *Untersuchungen*, 113, suggests that the land of Gilead normally contains the article (as in Num 32:29) but this was removed in v. 1 to so that it matched Jazer, which already existed without the article in the original form of v. 1.

[73] The label "Moabite" is here used imprecisely. As DEARMAN, "Border," 206, highlights, one should not mistake political identity with cultural identity. It is therefore more appropriate to conceive the people of Gad (under the leadership of Mesha) to have aligned themselves with the political entity of Moab, in contradistinction with those who argue that Gad was a "Moabite" tribe.

[74] For an alternative English translation of the Mesha Inscription see PRITCHARD, ANET, 320. For the dating of the inscription see, e.g., BIENKOWSKI, "Beginning," 1; LEMAIRE, "Mesha;" NA'AMAN, "Inscription."

[75] KNAUF, *Midian*, 162, highlights that, "there can be little doubt that Mesha of Dibon himself stemmed from the tribe of Gad." See also KNAUF, *Data*, 94n46.

102   *3. The Occupation of Transjordan*

rael until we have brought them to their מקום."[76] The Reubenites' and Gadites' promise to go to war לפני בני ישראל (*before the sons of Israel*) links with the same phrase in Deut 3:18 and must be seen in contrast with Moses's suggestion that they should go to battle לפני יהוה (*before YHWH*), which will be discussed in more detail below.[77]

The vow of v. 17a naturally connects to v. 16 where the Reubenites and Gadites propose that they, "build sheep pens for our livestock here and cities for our children."[78] The major issue with v. 16 is the opening verb, נגש (*approach*), which Schorn notes is, "nur ohne vorherigen Dialog denkbar sei" (*only conceivable without prior dialogue*).[79] One notable solution to this issue, famously proposed by Wüst, is that v. 1 was originally followed by v. 16a.[80] This has the advantage that there is no prior dialog (so Schorn) but it also explains who the "they" are due to following directly on from v. 1. Yet this same verb, נגש (*to approach*), is also the cause of the biggest difficulty in connecting v. 16 directly to v. 1, as without a forgoing narrative it is unclear who the "him" they approach is. If v. 16 was originally connected to v. 1 then it is logical to suppose that v. 16 would specifically report that the Reubenites and Gadites approached Moses.

The more convincing explanation, then, as several scholars have observed, is that the verb נגש need not only be understood as indicating a physical change of location, rather it can also be used to indicate a change in tone or mood. Milgrom, for example, argues that when this verb is used in the middle of a conversation it is to be interpreted as indicating a more intimate/personal manner is being

---

[76] As observed by, e.g., SCHORN, *Ruben*, 149. MILGROM, *Numbers*, 270, suggests that the Transjordan tribes offered to function as "shock troops" due to the fact that they would not be encumbered by their families and possessions unlike the 9.5 tribes. Milgrom highlights this reading by noting that Joshua 4:13 reports approximately 40,000 men from Transjordan crossed over, yet Num 26 notes that the two-and-a-half tribes comprised some 110,580 fighting men. Milgrom interprets this small force to represent the elite fighting troops of the Transjordan tribes, the remainder presumably remained in Transjordan to complete the fortifications and defend them. See also discussion in SEEBASS, *Numeri 3*, 355.

[77] MARQUIS, "Composition," 412, understands the phrases לפני יהוה (*before YHWH*) and לפני בני ישראל (*before the sons of Israel*) in light of the camp arrangement of Numbers 2. However, the idea that לפני יהוה should be interpreted to mean literally in front of YHWH (i.e., the tabernacle – Num 2:17) is particularly unconvincing. Marquis' argument that לפני בני ישראל should be read negatively, such that Reuben and Gad were trying to go above their allotted station of second position (Num 2:16), is also unconvincing given that this same phrase appears in Deut 3:18 as part of Moses's command. That it should not be understood negatively is further underscored in Josh 4:12–13, which harmonises the two different presentations: "the sons of Reuben and the sons of Gad and half the tribe of Manasseh crossed over armed לפני בני ישראל just as Moses had told them. About 40000 equipped for war crossed over לפני יהוה to battle towards the plains of Jericho." See also discussion in SEEBASS, *Numeri 3*, 355.

[78] This aligns with most commentators, see note 6 on page 82.

[79] SCHORN, *Ruben*, 148.

[80] WÜST, *Untersuchungen*, 97–99. See also MITTMANN, *Deuteronomium*, 97; BUDD, *Numbers*, 342.

adopted for the request, as in Gen 44:18 and Gen 45:4.[81] Several points suggest that this emphatic understanding of נגש makes the best sense in v. 16. First, it most readily explains why the object of the verb is "him" and not "Moses" – Moses had just finished speaking in v. 15 (or more likely v. 6, see below). Second, it explains why נגש was selected as opposed to בא (*come*) as in v. 2. Third, it means that the verb נגש can logically be present in v. 16 with prior conversation already taking place. That being said, it seems more plausible that ויגשו אליו (*and they approached him*) was added by the same redactor responsible for inserting vv. 7–15 and that v. 16 originally simply began, ויאמרו (*and they said*). This is because the emphatic approach of the Reubenites and Gadites is best understood as relating to Moses's critique in vv. 7–15 so that the Reubenites' and Gadites' response in v. 16 begins by emphasising that the two tribes were immediately willing to assuage any misgivings Moses might have.

Another issue with v. 16 is the word order, where וערים לטפנו (*and cities for our children*) comes after the word "here" and so appears to be misplaced, leading some scholars to suggest that the second clause was a later addition.[82] However, the strange ordering can be explained to flag a low-key critique of the Reubenites and Gadites. As Milgrom notes, this ordering is highlighted in rabbinic literature because Moses uses the reverse ordering (family-sheep) in v. 24 and so is understood as a rebuke.[83] Bamidbar Rabbah 22:9 states:

... 'A wise man's heart is to his right,' that is Moshe; 'but a fool's heart is to his left,' that is the Children of Reuven and the Children of Gad, who made the essential, secondary, and the secondary, essential. Why? Because they loved their possessions more than the [human] souls. As they said to Moshe (Numbers 32:16), 'We will build here sheepfolds for our flocks, and towns for our children.' Moshe said to them, 'This is nothing; rather make the essential, essential. First "build towns for your children," and afterwards "sheepfolds for your flocks"' (Numbers 32:24).[84]

The theory that v. 16 and 24 function as a rebuke of the Reubenites and Gadites finds support in the critique of Reuben in Judg 5:15–16, where the tribe of Reuben ישבת בין המשפתים (*dwelt amidst the dung heaps*) to hear the piping of their sheep.

Within the context of the geographical investigation above, the idea that the Reubenites and Gadites needed to build cities makes sense in a narrative predating the Sihon layer where the land being viewed was the non-Moabite, non-Ammonite land of Jazer and the land of Gilead. Although one might question the validity of an empty land in historical terms, if the goal of the original Numbers 32 was to demonstrate that the land above the sons of Lot (Moab and Ammon)

---

[81] MILGROM, *Numbers*, 270. See also MITTMANN, *Deuteronomium*, 97.
[82] See, e. g., GERMANY, "Cartography."
[83] MILGROM, *Numbers*, 270.
[84] Translation from https://bit.ly/3cVI3NJ

104   *3. The Occupation of Transjordan*

and below the Arameans was "Israelite" from the ancient past, then it could not possibly have belonged to anyone else.

The addition of v. 17b with its mention of ערי המבצר (*fortified cities*) does not follow naturally after v. 16 where simply ערים (*cities*) are mentioned and can be understood as a later attempt to remove this empty land idea by suggesting there were other (unspecified) occupants in the land (see more below).

Working backwards, verse 16 connects to Moses's question in verse 6 via the word, פה (*here*), whereby the Reubenites and Gadites note that they will not remain "here" as Moses accused, rather they will only leave their family and possessions "here." Besides the presence of the shared word the main argument for seeing v. 6 as belonging to the non-Priestly layer is that, narratively speaking, the Reubenites' and Gadites' speech in v. 16 logically requires some kind of precursor that would instigate their promise to cross the Jordan before their brothers. As Schmidt notes, "Ohne v. 6 ist nicht einsichtig, warum die beiden Stämme in v. 17a betonen, daß sie die Israeliten militärisch unterstützen werden" (*Without v. 6 it is not clear why the two tribes emphasise in v. 17a that they will support the Israelites militarily*).[85] However, there are several factors that speak against the extant v. 6 being completely original. First, it must be questioned if Moses's rhetorical question in v. 6 alone is sufficient to generate the response in vv. 16–17a. Ignoring vv. 7–15, which set the Reubenites' and Gadites' request within the framework of Israel's unwillingness to enter Canaan in the spy narrative, the implied meaning of Moses's question in v. 6 is difficult to discern. Second, unlike the other non-Priestly passages, v. 6 eschews using the generic "they/them" (vv. 5*, 16, 20a) and rather uses the name order, Gad-Reuben, which contrasts the Reuben-Gad ordering in v. 1. Third, the paired terms בוא (*go*) and מלחמה (*war*) are uncommon in the Hebrew Bible and within the book of Numbers are only used in Priestly texts (Num 10:9; 31:21). Furthermore, the prefixed term, למלחמה (*to war*), is otherwise used in the Priestly verses of Numbers 32 (vv. 20b, 27, 29) and is used elsewhere in the book of Numbers to refer to battles that have been completed (Num 21:33; 31:21). In light of this evidence, it seems best to conclude that the extant v. 6 has been worked over by the Priestly narrative and only contains traces of its original form. Thus, the v. 6 reflected in table 4 only keeps the sub-clause containing the important פה.[86]

Just as the Reubenites' and Gadites' response in v. 16 required a trigger by Moses, so too does Moses's question in v. 6 require a trigger. It is no surprise, then, that most scholars also allocate v. 5 to the base narrative.[87] However, this too is not without issues. First, the speech introduction of v. 5 simply begins

---

[85] Schmidt, "Ansiedlung," 499.

[86] This argument only works if one accepts the idea that during the process of conflation, parts of the sources were omitted. Refer to discussion in § 2.2.1.

[87] See note 6 on page 82.

3.1 Old Layers and Historical Memories?

with "and they said" without specifying who the Reubenites and Gadites are speaking to. Most scholars solve this issue by supposing that a truncated v. 2 also belongs to the non-Priestly base layer, so that the character of Moses is introduced there.[88] The issue with this solution is that it makes the repeated speech introduction of v. 5 difficult to explain; the resulting text of vv. 2*, 5 being: "²*the sons of Gad and the sons of Reuben came and they said (ויאמרו) to Moses ⁵and they said (ויאמרו), 'if we have found favour ...'"[89] In order to get around this issue, scholars also attribute part or all of v. 4 to the base narrative so that the ויאמרו in v. 5 functions to separate the Reubenites' and Gadites' legal request from their description of the land.[90] A repeated speech introduction by the same speaker without an intervening reply appears to be a peculiarity of Biblical Hebrew and so this explanation is certainly possible.[91] However, without the need to explain this strange speech introduction there is no need to include v. 4 into the base narrative. Rather, as will be argued below, v. 4 is much better understood as the introduction to a parallel narrative source (i.e., the Priestly layer). A further problem with v. 2 is that it immediately names the tribes in the reverse order to that found in v. 1 (i.e., Gad-Reuben), which, again, points to it belonging to a different layer.[92] A better solution is, once again, to suppose that v. 5 originally followed some introduction of Moses that has now been replaced by the Priestly v. 2. The speech introduction of verse 5, then, belongs to the non-Priestly narrative and presupposes narrative material that is now lost.

A second issue with v. 5 is that it contains elements that do not fit to a non-Priestly, pre-Sihon narrative. It is commonly observed that v. 5 includes the priestly word, אחזה (*possession*), which is typically understood to be a late insertion into an otherwise non-Priestly text so that the Reubenites and Gadites originally requested, "grant this land to your servants," rather than, "grant this land to your servants as a possession."[93] Such single word insertions are

---

[88] See note 6 on page 82.

[89] See a similar critique in, e.g., Wüst, *Untersuchungen*, 99.

[90] For this argument see, e.g., Achenbach, *Vollendung*, 381; Seebass, *Numeri 3*, 330.

[91] Schmidt, "Ansiedlung," 501, notes Gen 20:10; 43:29; 47:4; Exod 3:14. Marquis, "Composition," 417, mentions Gen 17:3, 9, 15 as an example. Milgrom, *Numbers*, 268, alternatively suggests that the verb needed to be repeated, "because of the lengthy remark beginning in verse 2," but this seems to stretch the meaning of "lengthy" beyond common understanding.

[92] As already discussed for v. 1 above, the idea that later Priestly scribes felt the need to correct the ordering in v. 1 but not elsewhere throughout Numbers 32 is unconvincing, rather it seems preferable to suppose that the ordering should be used to assist in identifying separate layers.

[93] Although Achenbach, *Vollendung*, 380–381, rightly highlights that אחזה does not belong to the early narrative layer (in his case the HexRed), his arguments concerning which redactional layer each part belongs to are troublesome. Achenbach argues that the term אחזה largely appears in the Holiness Code, and therefore points to the word being a hallmark of the PentRed. However, Achenbach goes on to state, "[Num 32] ist nicht auf den PentRed zurückzuführen, welcher an dem Landnahme-Thema kein Interesse zeigt" (*[Num 32] is not attributable to the PentRed, which shows no interest in the conquest theme* – p. 388). In other words,

certainly possible, Carr in particular has drawn attention to what he describes as a "Priestly wash," whereby non-Priestly materials are increasingly reshaped by Priestly interests.[94] However, the word אחזה does not merely grant v. 5 a Priestly hue, it also reinforces the intertextual link to v. 22. Verse 5aβ states, יתן את־הארץ הזאת לעבדיך לאחזה (*give this land to your servants as a possession*), to which Moses responds in v. 22b, והיתה הארץ הזאת לכם לאחזה לפני יהוה (*this land will be your possession before YHWH*). Whilst the אחזה in v. 5 can be easily removed without damaging the overall flow and content of the verse, the same cannot be said of its parallel in v. 22. Granting that the parallelism between these two passages was intentional, it logically follows that אחזה in v. 5 was not a secondary insertion, but rather was a deliberate part of the overall construction. Yet should all of v. 5, then, be considered Priestly? Marquis suggests that v. 5 can be split into three separate clauses.[95] Following this, the final clause (v. 5b) can be allocated to the non-Priestly narrative, whilst the remaining clauses (vv. 5aα*–β) belong to the Priestly layer. This results in the Reubenites and Gadites simply requesting, "do not make us cross over the Jordan" in the non-Priestly narrative.

Having now found a core narrative comprising a request by the Reubenites and Gadites (v. 5b), Moses's query (v. 6*) and the Reubenites' and Gadites' response (vv. 16–17a), the final step is to discover Moses's answer. Returning to v. 17a, this verse links to v. 20a via the lexeme, חלץ (*equip*), which appears in the book of Numbers (in niphal) only in Num 31:3; 32:17, 20.[96] Allocating all of vv. 20–24 to a single unit is difficult because v. 21b contains the Deuteronomistic(?) word ירש (*to possess/dispossess*) whilst v. 22 contains the Priestly terms כבש (*subdue*) and אחזה (*possession*).[97] It is therefore no surprise that scholars are divided both on

---

because Achenbach's model dictates that the PentRed cannot contain conquest themes, the presence of אחזה in v. 5 must therefore be the work of the (post-PentRed) theocratic redactor. SEEBASS, *Numeri 3*, 352 also highlights that אחזה is a priestly term which does not belong to the otherwise non-priestly (in his case J) v. 5.

[94] CARR, "Data," 94–97.

[95] MARQUIS, "Composition," 414.

[96] ACHENBACH, *Vollendung*, 385, argues that חלץ (*equip*) in the niphal form (Num 32:17, 20) represents a later linguistic usage than this same verb in the qal passive participle (Num 32:21, 27, 29, 30, 32; Deut 3:18), and therefore suggests this is evidence for multiple redaction layers. However, the different verb forms make sense purely from their different functions within the conversation: the niphal representing a reflexive action can be translated in long-hand as, "we will equip ourselves," whilst the qal passive participle is rendered, "those of us equipped." This understanding is already given in the NRSV translation, which translates vv. 20–21 as follows: [20]"So Moses said to them, "If you do this – if you take up arms (niphal) to go before the Lord for the war, [21]and all those of you who bear arms (qal passive participle) cross the Jordan before the Lord, until he has driven out his enemies from before him ..."

[97] The term כבש (*subdue*) in particular is exceptionally rare, appearing only four times in the Hexateuch (Gen 1:28; Num 32:22, 29; Josh 18:1). KNAUF, *Josua*, 20, argues that this term is the key to Pg, and that Josh 18:1 represents the conclusion to YHWH's command in Gen 1:28. See also KNAUF, *Data*, 530–532. Although ירש (*to possess/dispossess*) does appear in Priestly texts, these are arguably Priestly texts that have already been influenced by conquest themes. See also

how to precisely detangle these verses as well as how to order them diachronically. Achenbach, for example, allocates vv. 20*–22 to the HexRed, which for him constitutes the base narrative, whilst Schmidt argues that vv. 20aβ–23 belong to the Pentateuch redactor and thus are secondary.[98] However, using the observations noted in § 3.1 above, it can be suggested that Moses's speech in vv. 20–24 contains two separate concepts regarding the feasibility of the Reubenites and Gadites being granted the Transjordan. The first concept consists of vv. 20a, 22aβ and 24, which follows neatly on from the Reubenites' and Gadites' offer to build cities for their families and pens for their livestock (vv. 16–17a). This narrative depicts Moses agreeing to their terms (v. 24) with the proviso that so long as they do what they promised (v. 20a) they will be clear (of obligation) before their fellow Israelites and Yнwн (v. 22aβ).[99] The second concept alternatively depicts Moses offering a compromise; if the Reubenites and Gadites take up arms and cross over the Jordan before Yнwн for war (v. 20b–21a) and the Cisjordan is כבש (v. 22aα), then will the Transjordan be granted as an אחזה (v. 22b).

After v. 24 the only other verse that might conceivably be allocated to the base narrative is a pre-redactional version of v. 33. However even after removing the references to Manasseh, Sihon and Og, the verse reports that Moses gave both land and cities, which contradicts v. 16's report that the Reubenites and Gadites needed to build cities. Verse 33, then, must be considered a later addition. Scholars often allocate vv. 34–38 to the base layer, however it will be argued in § 3.3 that these verses actually conflict with both the land description of Num 32:1 as well as the earliest Sihon narrative and so must also be a later addition.[100]

Thus, an original narrative thread can be found in vv. 1, 5b*, 6*, 16*, 17a, 20a, 22aβ, 24. Importantly, this narrative has not been completely retained, rather elements have been overwritten during the process of conflation. Despite this, the basic shape of the original narrative has remained and so demonstrates what Carr referred to as honouring the tradition being combined.[101]

3.1.4 Reflections on the Non-Priestly Layer

Several bold proposals were made regarding this earliest narrative layer that require further reflection. This chapter began with the observation that the

---

discussion in, e.g., Hutzli, *Origins*, 178. Thus, if anything, the presence of כבש might better be seen as indication of the conquest-inspired expansion of Pg argued for in § 3.4.

[98] Schmidt, *Ansiedlung*, 501; Achenbach, *Vollendung*, 388. Mittmann, *Deuteronomium*, 104, suggests that vv. 20aβ–23 belong to the second stage of the expansions generated by vv. 16–17. Wüst, *Untersuchungen*, 95–99 suggests that vv. 20aβ, 22aβb, 23 belong to the first supplemental addition to the base narrative.

[99] See note 6 on page 82.

[100] This conclusion goes against most commentators, who argue that vv. 34–38 are old. See note 6 on page 82.

[101] Carr, *Tablet*, 39.

Transjordan traditions were problematic for many of the key themes in the extant Pentateuch. The exodus-eisodus motif (cf. Josh 3:15–17) is at least weakened, if not outright disrupted. The idea that Moses should die outside the land is connected with his being forbidden to cross the Jordan (Deut 1:37; 3:27; 31:2; 34:4). The impact of this tragic end to Moses's life is at least lessened if Moses was able to participate in the beginning of the conquest. The land that was promised to the patriarchs is the land of Canaan, which does not include the Transjordan. This indisputable fact raises the question: Why were there Transjordan traditions at all? The simplest answer to this question is that the original Transjordan tradition existed prior to the above themes being introduced. This in turn suggests that the original tradition must trace back quite early indeed.

Beginning with an analysis of the historical geography in Num 32:1, it was posited that the prominence of the "land of Jazer" was peculiar and required a more convincing explanation. Two insights in particular suggested that this verse was the key to better understanding the narrative and the tradition it belonged to. The first insight was that the land of Jazer made little sense if Numbers 32 presupposed the Sihon narrative. The Sihon narrative revolves around a king of Heshbon, which makes the absence of Heshbon very puzzling. The second insight was that Jazer plays almost no role in the remaining Bible, and the phrase "the land of Jazer" appears only in Num 32:1. Thus, the simplest conclusion is that Numbers 32:1 derived from a different geographical background to these other biblical traditions (i. e., it came from the Northern Kingdom) and that this tradition did not know of Sihon.

A more detailed study of the possible meanings of "the land of Jazer" suggested that this designation functioned on the assumption that the "plains of Moab" were unavailable to Israel because they belonged to Moab. This insight was further supported by various traditions between Numbers 21–26, all of which contained clues that pointed to Moab extending north of the Arnon into central Transjordan. In historical terms it was argued that this fit neatly to the reign of Jeroboam II, which it was argued in § 2.3.1 likely represented the beginning of the textualization of Israel's traditions.

The idea of a preexilic origins of Numbers 32 was also supported by the fact that – at this stage in the tradition – the Transjordan settlement was not viewed in light of a conquest event. However, Moses's question in v. 6* as well as the promise to cross over to the Jordan in vv. 16*–17a, suggest that the dwelling in Transjordan was – even at this stage – conceived as being somehow against the original plan. These details point to the idea that this preexilic layer was already influenced by Judean interests. This aligns with the arguments made in § 2.3.2, that the exodus-conquest narrative – which spanned from Exodus to Josh 10:42* – was a Judean subversion of an originally Nimshide tradition.[102] As

---

[102] I would further emphasise that this reconstruction is superior to the idea that Numbers 32

Fleming aptly notes, "the finished Judahite version of Numbers 32 treats [the conquest of Transjordan] as something of an embarrassment."[103]

3.2 The Sihon Tradition

As has long been observed, an analysis of the Sihon narratives in Numbers and Deuteronomy must eventually deal with the issue of direction of dependence. In this regard there are three possible options (1) Deuteronomy used Numbers as a source, (2) Numbers used Deuteronomy as a source, or (3) both Numbers and Deuteronomy used a common, independent tradition. Commonly, option (1) has been the most popular due to the "theological expansion" of the Deuteronomistic version over its Numbers counterpart (to be discussed below). However, one must not overlook the fact that option (1) also conforms most naturally to the Documentary Hypothesis and so confirmation bias could also be at play. Option (2) has most famously been championed by Van Seters, whose underlying Pentateuchal model presupposes that the books of Genesis–Numbers were written as an extended introduction to the Deuteronomistic History.[104] As such it is of little surprise that Van Seters argues that Numbers represents a conflation of Deuteronomy's Sihon narrative and Jephthah's retelling in Judg 11:19–22. Option (3) is a relatively recent innovation popularised by Otto and adopted by Achenbach.[105] However, once again this option must be seen in the context of these scholars' Pentateuchal model, which seeks to demonstrate that the earliest layer in Numbers belongs to a post-Deuteronomistic Hexateuch Redactor. In order to justify option (3), a somewhat convoluted argument is employed that suggests the post-Deuteronomistic Hexateuch Redaction in Numbers more closely followed the source material of the pre-Deuteronomistic, standalone Edom-Sihon tradition than did Deuteronomy.

---

represents a late reservoir of historical "memories." FINKELSTEIN/RÖMER, "Memories," 717, are correct in noting that "there was no moment in history when Israel dominated such a territory as described in the above-mentioned texts: in the two expansionist periods of the Northern Kingdom, the Omrides did not rule north of the Yarmuk, and Jeroboam II did not dominate the mishor of Moab." However, they do not take into account that the expansion into the mishor of Moab only appears with the list of Gadite cities and the corresponding Sihon-the-Amorite narrative. This will be argued in the following sections.

[103] FLEMING, *Legacy*, 117.

[104] VAN SETERS, *Life*, 457. VAN SETERS, "Conquest," 186, writes, "it is quite remarkable that on each of the points where Judges departs from Deuteronomy, Numbers also differs from Deuteronomy *in the same way*." (emphasis original). Against Van Seters' article in particular, see BARTLETT, "Conquest." Cf. VAN SETERS, "Again," for his rebuttal.

[105] ACHENBACH, *Vollendung*, 358, states, "Bei der nun folgenden Analyse der Erzählungen über das Ostjordanland kann wiederum auf die redaktionsgeschichtlichen Ergebnisse von E. Otto zurückgegriffen werden" (*In the following analysis of the narratives about the Transjordan, one can fall back on the redaction-historical results of E. Otto*). Referring to OTTO, *Pentateuch und Hexateuch*, 129–138.

The present work also begins with a biased presupposition, namely that the base layer of Numbers 32 shows no awareness of even the earliest Sihon narrative and therefore the introduction of the Sihon narrative likely represents an ideological shift. This ideological shift reveals itself in two key alterations: (1) The Sihon narrative takes issue with the idea that Israel could dwell in land it did not ירש (*possess*), and therefore had not been divinely granted.[106] (2) the Sihon narrative functions to explain how the Reubenites and Gadites settled outside of the good land that YHWH swore to give to Israel's ancestors (cf. Deut 1:35), and therefore represents a reinforcement of the ideology that understands the Jordan as a boundary (cf. Numbers 34; Deut 1:34–37; 3:23–27; 34:4; etc.).

In light of this, it will be argued in the following sections that the Sihon narrative in Deuteronomy is in fact the earliest version, which was later retro-fitted into the narrative of Numbers. The major justification of this is that the key ideological drivers for the change are much more firmly rooted in Deuteronomistic thought and therefore most plausibly originated from there. Textual analysis will also point to this same conclusion as shown below.

3.2.1 Deuteronomy 2:24–3:18* and the Problem of Settlement in the Transjordan

Narrative A	Narrative B[107]
Deut 2:24aα [YHWH said …] "… arise, set out and cross over the nahal Arnon."	Deut 2:24Arise, set out and cross over the nahal Arnon. *Behold, I give into your hand Sihon, king of the Heshbon the Amorite and his land. Begin to possess by provoking him to battle.*
	Deut 2:25*This day I begin to put the dread of you and the fear of you upon the people under all the heavens. When they hear report of you, they will tremble and writhe before you*
Deut 2:26So I sent messengers from the wilderness of Kedemoth to Sihon, king of Heshbon, with words of peace saying,	Deut 2:26So I sent messengers from the wilderness of Kedemoth to Sihon, king of Heshbon, with words of peace saying,

---

[106] On the overwhelming concentration of this term in Deuteronomic/Deuteronomistic texts see esp. LOHFINK, יָרַשׁ, 370–371, who explains the underlying ideology as follows: "By right of conquest one people or nation succeeds another in ruling over a territory. This right of conquest is undergirded by divine providence and action, which can be expressed in a play on words using the hiphil of yrš (Dt. 9:1; 11:23; 18:14; Jgs. 11:23 f.)." I do not wish to enter into the complex discussions regarding the potential origins of Deuteronomy in the North (cf. SCHORSCH, "Origin"). Important for the present argument is the idea that the Jordan as a fixed border is best explained from a Judean perspective.

[107] Text of Narrative A shown in regular font, while later layers are shown in italics. It must be emphasized that no distinction is made between the various layers after the first. It is not the argument of the above presentation that Narrative B comprises a single update, see note 108 on page 112.

3.2 The Sihon Tradition

Narrative A	Narrative B
Deut 2:27"Let me pass through your land. I will walk only along the road, I will not turn aside to the right or to the left	Deut 2:27"Let me pass through your land. I will walk only along the road, I will not turn aside to the right or to the left
	Deut 2:28*I will eat food bought with silver and give me water for silver that I will drink. Only let me pass over on foot.*
Deut 2:29bα[β?]until I pass over the Jordan [to the land that Yhwh our god is giving to us]."	Deut 2:29*Just as the sons of Esau, who dwell in Seir, did for me and the Moabites, who dwell in Ar.* Until I pass over the Jordan to the land that Yhwh our god is giving to us.
Deut 2:30aBut Sihon, king of Heshbon, was not willing to let us pass over	Deut 2:30But Sihon, king of Heshbon, was not willing to let us pass over *because Yhwh your god had hardened his spirit and strengthened his heart in order to give him into your hand, as it is this day.*
	Deut 2:31*Yhwh said to me, "See I have begun to give before you, Sihon and his land. Begin to possess his dispossessed land."*
Deut 2:32Sihon came out to meet us, he and all his people for battle at Jahaz	Deut 2:32Sihon came out to meet us, he and all his people for battle at Jahaz.
Deut 2:33a[b?]and Yhwh our god gave him unto us [*and we struck him and his sons and all his people*]	Deut 2:33Yhwh our god gave him unto us, and we struck him and his sons and all his people
	Deut 2:34*At that time we captured all his cities and devoted all the men of the city and women and children, no survivor remained*
	Deut 2:35*We only we took the livestock as plunder and the spoil of the cities we captured,*
	Deut 2:36*from Aroer, which is upon the edge of Nahal Arnon and the city which is on the Nahal as far as the Gilead, there was no fortified city (קריה) that was too high for us. All this, Yhwh our god gave unto us.*
	Deut 2:37*only you did not come near the land of the sons of Ammon, all the banks of the Nahal Jabbok and the cities of the hill country, all that was forbidden by Yhwh our god.*
	Deut 3:1*We turned and went up the Bashan road. Og, king of Bashan, went out to meet us, he and all his people for battle at Edrei.*
	Deut 3:2 *Yhwh said to me, "Do not fear him because I have given into your hand, him and all his people and all his land. Do to him just like you did to Sihon, king of the Amorites, who dwelt in Heshbon.*

Narrative A	Narrative B
	Deut 3:3YHWH *our God gave into our hand Og, king of Bashan, and all his people and we struck him down until no survivor remained.*
	Deut 3:4*At that time we took all his cities, there was no fortified city (קריה) that we did not take from them. Sixty cities, all the region of Argob, the kingdom of Og in Bashan.*
	Deut 3:5*All these cities were fortified with high wall and gates and bars. Besides the very many unfortified cities.*
	Deut 3:6*We devoted (נחרם) them, just like we did to Sihon, king of Heshbon. Devoting all of the city: men, women and children.*
	Deut 3:7*We plundered all the livestock and spoil of the cities.*
	Deut 3:8*At that time we took the land from the hands of the two kings of the Amorites, who are beyond the Jordan. From the Wadi Arnon until Mt. Hermon.*
	Deut 3:9*The Sidonians call Hermon Sirion, while the Amorites call it Senir.[108]*
	Deut 3:10*All the cities of the Mishor and all the Gilead and all the Bashan, as far as Salecah and Edrei – cities from the kingdom of Og in Bashan.*
	Deut 3:11*Now only Og, king of Bashan, remained from the last of the Rephaim. Behold, his bed was a bed of iron; is it not in Rabbah of the Ammonites? Nine cubits long and four cubits wide by the common cubit.*
Deut 3:12bβand his cities I gave to the Reubenites and the Gadites.	Deut 3:12*This land that we took possession of at that time, from Aroer which is above the Nahal Arnon and half the hill country of the Gilead,* and his cities I gave to the Reubenites and Gadites.

Table 6: Comparison of Sihon layers in Deuteronomy

The Sihon narrative in the book of Deuteronomy is located within the narrative frame that Otto labels the "Moab Redaction" (cf. figure 3), which functions to re-frame the giving of the Deuteronomic laws into the narrative setting of Moses's

---

[108] One clear example that Narrative B should not be understood as a single redaction is the so-called "antiquarian notices," which a number of scholars see as their own redactional insertion. See, e.g., GERMANY, *Exodus-Conquest*, 256; OTTO, *Deuteronomium 1,1–4,43*, 452; SCHMIDT, "Sihon," 320.

3.2 The Sihon Tradition

Figure 9: Transjordan of Sihon and Og[109]

---

[109] Map drawn by J. Davis. Details of the toponyms can be found in figure 7 above.

114   *3. The Occupation of Transjordan*

farewell speech "beyond the Jordan" (Deut 1:1).[110] The Moab Redaction understands Moses's recitation of the law to take place *just before* Israel enters into the land. Deuteronomy 4:5, for example, states, "See, I teach you statutes and ordinances, just as YHWH my god commanded me, to do in the land you are about to cross into to possess." Similarly, the death of Moses tradition also presupposes that Moses died outside of the land, in Deut 1:37 Moses states, "YHWH was also angry with me because of you, saying, 'You too shall not enter there.'" Deuteronomy 34:4 makes this point particularly clear, "YHWH said to [Moses], 'this is the land I swore to Abraham, Isaac and Jacob, saying, "To your seed I will give it." I have let you see it with your eyes, but you shall not cross over there.'" Granting this important feature of the Moab Redaction, the idea that some Israelite tribes had already settled in Transjordan was surely problematic.

In broad strokes, the Moab Redaction consists of Moses summarising how Israel came to be "beyond the Jordan in the land of Moab" (Deut 1:5) after they left Horeb (Deut 1:6). In terms of tracing this journey, there is no need for the Deuteronomists to add a narrative of Israel's battle in Transjordan, rather the key events needed are (1) Israel's failure at Kadesh(-barnea) (Numbers 13–14; Deut 1:19–45*) after Israel refused to enter the land from the south in light of the spies' report (cf. § 2.3.2);[111] (2) Israel's expanded wilderness journey, crossing over the Zered (Num 21:12; Deut 2:13) and the Arnon (Num 21:13*; Deut 2:24aα), possibly including details of their journey through/around Edom and Moab (cf. § 3.1.2); (3) the death of the exodus generation (Numbers 26*; Deut 2:16) so that Moses would need to repeat the law to the new generation (cf. figure 3);[112] and (4) Israel's arrival in the plains of Moab across the Jordan (Num 22:1; 26:3, 63; 31:12; 33:48, 50; 35:1; 36:13; Deut 1:5; 29:1; 34:5, 6, 8).

However, if the analysis of § 3.1 is correct in suggesting that there already existed a tradition in which the Reubenites and Gadites negotiated to have their מקם (*place*) in Transjordan rather than having their מקם in Cisjordan alongside their brother tribes (Num 32:17), then it follows that the Deuteronomists would need to explain that event. Importantly the narrative of Numbers 32 needed to be brought into theological alignment with the Deuteronomistic concepts of ירשׁ (*possession/dispossession*) and particularly the idea that it was only that land across the Jordan that belonged to Israel's נחלה (*inheritance*). As the following analysis will demonstrate the Sihon (and Og) narrative in Deuteronomy 2:24–

---

[110] On the idea that the law of Deuteronomy first underwent a Horeb redaction beginning in Deut 4:45, and then later underwent a Moab redaction, see esp. OTTO, *Pentateuch und Hexateuch*, 110–129, 129–136 respectively.

[111] OTTO, *Pentateuch und Hexateuch*, 132.

[112] There are several text-critical issues associated with the census in Numbers 26, not least v. 4, which suggests that population counted in the census comprised "the children of Israel who went out from the land of Egypt" rather than the second generation. However, these will not be discussed here.

3:18 actually contains two different solutions to this problem. The first solution (henceforth Narrative A) depicts Israel's battle with Sihon in light of the laws in Deut 20:10–15 as a battle with city that is הרחקת ממך מאד (*very far from you –* Deut 20:15), and so represents an acquisition of territory that lies outside the borders of the nations that YHWH had designated for destruction (cf. Deut 7:1; 20:17) and that will comprise Israel's נחלה. The second solution (Narrative B) reframes the entire concept of the promised land so that it is not Israel's crossing of the Jordan but rather Israel's crossing of the Arnon that represents the beginning of the conquest (see esp. Deut 2:24–25). Thus, the Sihon narrative of Narrative A was updated in Narrative B with the additional detail that "Sihon, the king of Heshbon" was an Amorite (Deut 1:4; 2:24; 3:2, 8; 4:46, 47) and so belonged to those nations singled out for total annihilation (חרם) in Deut 7:1 and 20:17. King Og was also made into an Amorite (Deut 3:8; 4:47), and so the conquest of territory that far exceeded that needed for Israel to reach the Jordan river was justified.[113] These ideological shifts can be clearly observed in table 6 above.

It was suggested above that Deut 2:24aα logically belongs to the base narrative of Deuteronomy 1–3 because the crossing of the two major Transjordan rivers mark the most important waypoints on Israel's journey from Kadesh-barnea to the plains of Moab.[114] Thus, it follows that this verse belongs to Narrative A.

Verses 24aβ–25 are quintessentially Narrative B. As a number of scholars have observed, this can be quickly demonstrated due to the fact that YHWH's command in Deuteronomy 2:24aα is presented in 2mp form, whereas vv. 24aβ–25 use 2ms verbs and so it follows that these belong to a separate layer.[115] This is further corroborated by the fact that v. 24 is only one of two verses in Deut 2:24–3:11 (the other being 3:2) that introduce the idea that Sihon was an Amorite king, and so belonged to those nations marked for destruction (cf. Deut 7:1; 20:17). Verse 24 introduces this detail via the title סיהן מלך-חשבון האמרי (*Sihon, king of the Amorites, who dwelt in Heshbon*), elsewhere he is either called סיחן מלך חשבון (Deut 2:30; 3:6; 29:7) or simply סיחן (Deut 2:31, 32).[116] That Deuteronomy refers to Sihon as "king of Heshbon" rather than "king of the Amorites" as he is called in Numbers 21 (vv. 21, 26, [29*]) is an important detail both for the idea that in Narrative A the Deuteronomists wanted to portray Sihon as a city-king (see below) but also for the idea that the Numbers 21 version is secondary.

---

[113] Google Maps estimates a 23hr journey by foot for the most direct path from Mount Nebo to Irbid. This would naturally take an army with women, children, elderly, cattle, etc. significantly longer, let alone the exaggerated army of 600,000 men.

[114] Contra, e.g., MITTMANN, *Deuteronomium*, 71; GERMANY, *Exodus-Conquest*, 258.

[115] See, e.g., MITTMANN, *Deuteronomium*, 79; OTTO, *Deuteronomium 1,1–4,43*, 450; SCHMIDT, "Sihon," 315; GERMANY, *Exodus-Conquest*, 252.

[116] SCHMIDT, "Sihon," 319. On the relocation of the Ammonite/Moabite border in light of the Sihon narrative see, e.g., ROSKOP ERISMAN, "Transjordan;" FREVEL, "Shapes."

116   *3. The Occupation of Transjordan*

Verse 26 is placed jarringly next to vv. 24aβ–25. In Deut 2:24aβ–25 Yhwh commands Moses to cross the Arnon and take possession of Sihon's land, but then immediately in v. 26 Moses sends messengers requesting peaceful passage through Sihon's territory. Thus, Gesundheit argues, "God's command in v. 24... seems to be completely ignored by Moses. More than this: Moses does exactly the opposite!"[117] This heavy-handed juxtaposition only makes sense in light of a changing conception of the land between Narrative A and Narrative B. As the quote from Schmidt at the beginning of this chapter argued, the request for safe passage through Sihon's territory presupposes that none of the Transjordan was originally conceived to belong to the promised land, which suggests that v. 26 squarely belongs in Narrative A.[118]

Deuteronomy 2:26 is also programmatic for understanding the subsequent narrative as Moses's request for passage is accompanied by דברי שלום (*words of peace*)." This small addition is instrumental in linking Sihon Narrative A to Deut 20:10, which states, "when you come near a city to fight against it, proclaim peace to it." Thus, despite Gesundheit's protests, Narrative A presupposes an ensuing battle will occur.[119]

Verses 27–29 contain the contents of Moses's message wherein he assures Sihon that he and the Israelites will travel only along the road and that they will pay for any food or water that they consume while inside Sihon's land, just as they had done with the Edomites and Moabites beforehand. The problem with these verses is that they do not fit directly into either the law for an enemy "very far from you" (Narrative A) or for enemies designated for destruction (Narrative B). However, it must be noted that the scenario envisioned in the law of Deut 20:10 assumes that Israel is deliberately besieging a foreign city with the intention of a hostile takeover. In the Sihon narrative Moses's intention was not battle but peaceful passage. In this light, it is only appropriate that Moses send a message requesting travel rights, the "words of peace," then, function as a frame of reference for interpreting the ensuing battle rather than flagging Moses's secret agenda. Granting this, at least Deut 2:27aα and 29bα plausibly belong to Narrative A (i.e., let me pass through your land ... until I cross over the Jordan ...). The question is: Are the other elements of vv. 27–29 secondary?

---

[117] The early rabbis already saw this tension. See discussion in Gesundheit, "Midrash-Exegesis." Germany, *Exodus-Conquest*, 252, also notes, "the most significant break ... lies not between 2:19 and 2:24 but instead between 2:25 and 2:26."

[118] See note 2 on page 82.

[119] This same conclusion is reached by Otto, *Deuteronomium 1,1–4,43*, 457, who writes, "Die deuteronomistische Erzählung zeichnet Mose mit dem Friedensangebot als einen Gesetzestreuen, der dem Kriegsgesetz in Dtn 20 folgt ... Dtn 20,10 sieht ein Angebot zur Vermeidung der Erstürmung einer belagerten Stadt vor" (*With the offer of peace, the Deuteronomistic narrative depicts Moses as a law-abiding citizen following the law for war in Deut 20... Deut 20:10 intends the offer [of peace] to avoid the storming of a besieged city*).

3.2 The Sihon Tradition

The major issue with these verses is their relationship to the Edom narrative. Verse 28 is reminiscent of Deut 2:6 and v. 29 directly refers to the "sons of Esau, who dwell in Seir." More specifically, the Edom-Esau connection that governs Israel's treatment of Edom logically has its roots in Genesis. This raises the issue of when such Genesis traditions might have influenced the authors of Deuteronomy.[120] Otto proposes that the Edom narrative in Num 20:14*, 17*, 20b, 21a represents a preexilic kernel and that the Edom-Esau equivalence should be understood as a postexilic Fortschreibung of the earlier tradition.[121] But there are difficulties with this view:

I. The first difficulty is that the Edom narrative in Deuteronomy is so wildly different, both from the Sihon narrative in Deuteronomy but also to the Edom narrative found in Numbers. In contrast the Sihon narratives in both Numbers and Deuteronomy share several key similarities and the Edom narrative in Numbers is remarkably similar to the Sihon narrative in Numbers. Without exploring the Edom texts in detail, the basic shapes of the four narratives suggest that Numbers' Edom narrative is the youngest version rather than the oldest.

II. A post-Priestly setting for Numbers' Edom narrative is already suggested by the reference to Kadesh in Num 20:14a. As Kadesh is typically used in Priestly texts (see esp. the Priestly spy narrative Num 13:26), while Kadesh-barnea more commonly appears in non-Priestly texts (e.g., Deut 1:2, 19; 2:14; 9:23; Josh 14:6, 7; 15:3).[122]

III. The mention of fields and vineyards (Num 20:17) does not make much sense if Edom is to be located (most logically) near the Arabah Valley and the "Edomite plateau," rather fields and vineyards belong much more naturally to Sihon's territory about the Madaba Plain or the agricultural zones in the Negev (suggesting an expanded conception of Edom).[123]

IV. Even the idea that there existed an early "kingdom" of Edom is problematic. Knauf notes, "the massive increase of agricultural settlements on the Edomite plateau, which is attested for the 7th century – on a plateau where agriculture was not feasible without heavy investment in the organization and maintenance of water storage and water distribution facilities – presupposes a massive influx of capital into Edom, which was provided by the Assyrian-dominated world economy. If there ever was an Edomite state, it existed in the 7th and early 6th

---

[120] This is not an issue for those following the Münsteraner Pentateuchmodell, for this connection is already present in JG/JE. For other models, the joining of Genesis to the exodus-conquest narrative only occurred with Pg. See, e.g., RENDTORFF, *Problem*; DE PURY, "Pg;" SCHMID, "Genesis."

[121] See, e.g., OTTO, *Deuteronomium 1,1–4,43*, 420. See also ACHENBACH, *Vollendung*, 335–344, who similarly argues for a "re-integrated" pre-Deuteronomistic narrative by the HexRed.

[122] See, e.g., OSWALD, "Revision," 221.

[123] See, e.g., GERMANY, *Exodus-Conquest*, 266; FREVEL, "Esau," 338.

centuries BC."[124] Thus the fact that Deuteronomy makes no reference to a "king" of Edom (cf. Num 20:14) but only to the territory of Israel's kindred arguably has an earlier historical conception in the background.

V. The promise to only use the King's Highway (in Numbers) within Edomite territory is problematic for Israel's journey from Kadesh, as it suggests that Israel circumnavigated the entire Edomite plateau. As Frevel argues, "Die Wendung nach Süden, die Überquerung des Araba-Grabens und der Königsweg bis an das Nordende des Toten Meeres bis zur Überquerung des Jordan biete die einzige Möglichkeit, Idumäa ganz zu umgehen ... Die Erzählung von Num 20,14–21 hat ihren historischen Kontext im 4. Jh. v.Chr nach der Gründung der Provinz Idumäa" (*The turn towards the south, the crossing over the Arabah Valley and the King's Road until the north end of the Dead Sea and onto the crossing of the Jordan offers a single possibility, to completely bypass Idumea ... The narrative from Num 20:14–21 has its historical context in the 4th cent. BCE after the establishment of the province of Idumea*).[125] Like with the mention of the king of Edom, the use of the King's Highway envisages a later development of the people groups occupying the "territory of Esau" as a state entity.

VI. The promise not to turn to the right or the left only appears in Num 20:17 and Deut 2:27 and does not appear in Num 21:22. Not only does this speak against a parallelism between a supposed Edom-Sihon narrative in Num 20:17 and Num 21:22 but Germany also notes that the wording of Num 20:17 is best understood as combining the phrasing of Num 21:22 and Deut 2:27, and thus representing the latest of the three.[126]

VII. Although a peaceful stance towards Edom, Moab and Ammon can be developed from Deuteronomistic legislation alone: none of these nations are listed in Deut 7:1 or 20:17[127] and so logically belong to category of "not-חרם" nations. The fact that Deuteronomy specifically refers to Esau rather than Edom (Deut 2:4, 5, 8, 29. Cf. Num 20:14, 18, 20, 21 which exclusively mention Edom!) cannot so easily be explained away. The repeated reference to Esau only makes sense if Deuteronomy's Edom narrative already presupposes knowledge of the Genesis narrative. The later laws of kinship in Deuteronomy 23 also presuppose the Genesis narratives whereby Edomites are permitted into the assembly of YHWH (Deut 23:7) but the Moabites and Ammonites are not (Deut 23:3), which has the relationship between Abraham and Lot, and the closer relationship between Jacob and Esau in the background.[128]

---

[124] KNAUF, *Data*, 106. Also see the discussion in FREVEL, *Geschichte*, 125–127.

[125] FREVEL, "Esau," 339.

[126] GERMANY, *Exodus-Conquest*, 267–268.

[127] The roots of the Deuteronomistic list are found in the idea that the local populations will lead Israel astray in worshipping other gods. NIDITCH, *War*, 62–68, labels this expression of חרם as "The Ban as God's Justice", which is made particularly clearly in Exod 23:23–25; Deut 20:17–18. Also see discussion in ACHENBACH, "Warfare," 16–21.

[128] OSWALD, "Revision."

3.2 The Sihon Tradition 119

In short, it seems safer to assume that the Edom-Esau relation is a later development. Thus, at least Deut 2:28–29a should be considered a secondary expansion that aimed to contrast Israel's treatment by Edom and Israel's treatment by Sihon under the same circumstances.[129]

Deuteronomy 2:27aβb contains Moses's assurance that Israel will only travel along the road and that they will neither turn to the right or the left. In contrast to Deuteronomy's wording that Israel will travel בדרך בדרך (*only on the road*), in Num 21:22 the Israelites assure Sihon that they will only travel בדרך המלך (*on the King's Highway*). Achenbach suggests that the Deuteronomistic removal of the reference to the well-known (since the time of the Assyrians) King's Highway, "… könnte theologisch motiviert sein und dem Namen eine doppelte Bedeutung zumessen: der Weg, den Israel beschreitet, ist nicht der, welchen der König vorgegeben hat, sondern der, welchen Jahwe ihm gebietet (vgl. Dtn 1,19; 2,1; 5,33 u. ö.), und von dem abzuweichen ihm im ethischen wie im praktischen Sinne verboten ist" (*… could be theologically motivated such that the name has a double meaning: The road that Israel walks along is not that which was set by the king, rather that which YHWH commanded (cf. Dtn 1:19; 2:1; 5:33; etc.) and thus to deviate from this is ethically and practically forbidden.*).[130] That being said, Deut 2:8 already suggests that Israel did not use King's Highway but rather travelled north via the דרך מדבר מואב (*road of the wilderness of Moab*), hence it is questionable if a theologically motivated explanation is necessary. The use of this more easterly road is further supported by the location of Jahaz as the place where Sihon meets the Israelites in battle (see § 3.2.1.2). Thus, the more likely solution is that the Deut 2:27 represents the more original form.

Verse 29bα – "until I pass over the Jordan" – on the other hand, logically forms the conclusion to Moses's request begun in v. 27. Significantly for the broader context of land conceptions, Otto notes, "Dtn 2,29b zeigt, dass für die Autoren der deuteronomistischen Moabredaktion die Landnahme erst mit dem Überschreiten des Jordan beginnt …" (*Deut 2:29b shows that, for the authors of the Deuteronomistic Moab redaction, the conquest first begins with the crossing of the Jordan*), thus again pointing to the idea that Sihon's territory was originally conceived as being "far away."[131] This land conception logically belongs to Narrative A. Furthermore, v. 29bβ emphasises the Deuteronomistic concern that land is granted by divine providence, which, it is being argued, is the driving force behind the insertion of the Sihon narrative in Deuteronomy in the first place.[132] Thus, in terms of conception v. 29bβ could belong to Narrative A. The argument

---

[129] This conclusion is also reached by, e. g., GERMANY, *Exodus-Conquest*, 254. On the parallelism between the Edom and Sihon narratives see, e. g., OTTO, *Deuteronomium 1,1–4,43*, 424. See also discussion in MITTMANN, *Deuteronomium*, 80; SCHMIDT, "Sihon," 317.

[130] ACHENBACH, *Vollendung*, 361.

[131] OTTO, *Deuteronomium 1,1–4,43*, 458.

[132] On the idea of a divine giving of the land, see, e. g., LOHFINK, יָרַשׁ.

against seeing this part verse as part of Narrative A is the shift in person from 1cs in v. 29bα (אעבר) to 1cp (אלהינו נתן לנו) in v. 29bβ.[133] Conceptually, then, Deut 2:29b is united, but linguistically it is not.

There is a broad consensus that v. 30 can be split into a base-layer v. 30a and a secondarily inserted v. 30b. Verse 30a reports the unwillingness of Sihon to allow Israel to pass through his land and logically belongs to Narrative A. Verse 30b, however, explains Sihon's recalcitrance via the motif of divine intervention (cf. Pharaoh in Exod 7:3, etc.). Deuteronomy 2:30b shares the same 2ms suffixes as vv. 2:24aβ–25 and also shares the theme that Israel's crossing of the Arnon marks the beginning of Israel's conquest.[134] As suggested above, this reframing of the Sihon narrative functioned to bring the Transjordan territory under the umbrella of the Amorites, which in turn functions to bring the Transjordan territory under that designated for destruction and so belonging to Israel's promised land (again cf. Deut 7:1; 20:17). Thus, it follows that v. 30a belongs to Narrative A and v. 30b belongs to Narrative B.

Verse 31 repeats the notion that the defeat of Sihon was achieved via the providence of YHWH. As has been widely observed, the wording of this verse is very similar to v. 2:24aβb suggesting that it too belongs to Narrative B:

Deut 2:24aβ,b	Deut 2:31
ראה	ראה
נתתי בידך	החלתי תת לפניך
את־סיחן מלך־השבון	את־סיחן
האמרי	ואת־ארצו
ואת־ארצו	החל רש
החל רש	לרשת את־ארצו
והתגר בו מלחמה	

Table 7: Comparison of Deut 2:24aβb and Deut 2:31

That being said the parallel isn't exact and the use of the shorter "Sihon" in v. 31 compared to "Sihon, king of Heshbon of the Amorites" suggests that v. 31 is older than the more harmonistic v. 2:24aβb.[135] Plöger, for example, argues based on the "Ich-Stil," that Deut 2:26–29, 31; 3:2 all belong to the same hand.[136] On the other hand Germany notes that the placement of v. 31 is awkward and "stands in tension with the course of events that immediately follow, in which it is *Sihon* who initiates the battle against Israel (2:32) and not vice versa," and thus suggests

---

[133] MITTMANN, *Deuteronomium*, 80; SCHMIDT, "Sihon," 317.

[134] MITTMANN, *Deuteronomium*, 80; OTTO, *Deuteronomium 1,1–4,43*, 459–461.

[135] So MITTMANN, *Deuteronomium*, 79–80; SCHMIDT, "Sihon," 316. Contra GESUNDHEIT, "Midrash-Exegesis," 77; GERMANY, *Exodus-Conquest*, 253. OTTO, *Pentateuch und Hexateuch*, 129–138. Esp. 136, originally allocated v. 31 to the base layer, but later in OTTO, *Deuteronomium 1,1–4,43*, 450, argued that Deut 2:25, 30b and 31 belong to a postexilic Fortschreibung designed to insert the idea that the promised land was located on both sides of the Jordan.

[136] PLÖGER, *Untersuchungen*, 27.

that it represents a later duplication of v. 2:24αβb.[137] Given this narrative interruption, as well as the overarching goal of Narrative A to depict the defeat of
Sihon, not as the acquisition of Israel's inheritance but rather the taking of land
that lies outside of that promised to the ancestors, Germany's conclusion can be
considered the correct one.[138] The shift in wording, therefore, is perhaps best
explained in light of Pakkala's observation that when the ideological change is
minor, it is very difficult to detect the where editing begins and where it ends.[139]

There is a broad consensus that vv. 32–35 in their entirety, which narrate
Sihon's aggression at Jahaz and his subsequent defeat, belong to base Sihon
narrative.[140] However, Germany, for example, has recently argued for seeing vv.
34αβ–35 as a later insertion.[141] These verses introduce the application of the ban
(חרם) in v. 34αβb and the particular details regarding the taking of spoil in v. 35.
As has been argued above, the חרם ideology belongs squarely to Narrative B with
its depiction of Sihon as an Amorite. Verse 34αβb makes it unmistakable that חרם
was enacted upon all the city, including the women and children, until there was
לא השארנו שריר (*no remaining survivor*). Deuteronomy 2:35 also appears to share
the חרם ideology of v. 34αβb with the report that only the livestock and spoil was
taken as plunder.[142] Without entering into a more detailed investigation on חרם,
Germany's suggestion that Deut 2:34αβ–35 are secondary is convincing.

The assignment of vv. 36 and 37 are heavily dependent upon how one recon-
structs the final shape of Narrative A.[143] For the purposes of the present reconstruction vv. 36–37 are important for the transition to the Og narrative, in that
they delineate the extent of Sihon's territory so that the subsequent battle against
Og makes geographical sense both narratively and militarily. Returning to the
discussion at the beginning of this section, the expanded frame of Deuteronomy

---

[137] GERMANY, *Exodus-Conquest*, 253–254, emphasis original.

[138] This conclusion is contrary to that suggested by SCHMIDT, "Sihon," 320 and OTTO,
Pentateuch und Hexateuch, 133.

[139] PAKKALA, *Word*, 362–369.

[140] So MITTMANN, *Deuteronomium*, 79–80; OTTO, *Pentateuch und Hexateuch*, 133; SCHMIDT,
"Sihon," 316. Depending upon how one interprets the כל־עמו (*all his people*), Deut 2:33 can be
understood to report only the killing of those in Sihon's army, rather than as the application of
חרם as is suggested by vv. 34–35.

[141] GERMANY, *Exodus-Conquest*, 256.

[142] The חרם ideology is somewhat nebulous in this regard and the taking of livestock is controversial. Deuteronomy 13:16, for instance, specifically states, ואת־בהמתה לפי־חרב (*even the livestock [are to be put] to the edge of the sword*). Joshua 6:21 agrees with this stricter application and
reports that at Jericho even the oxen, sheep and donkeys were put to the sword. On the other
hand, in Josh 8:2 YHWH commands Joshua to "do to Ai and its king just as you did to Jericho
and its king. *Only the spoil and the livestock may you take as plunder.*" For a more detailed discussion on חרם see, e.g., LOHFINK, הֶרֶם/הָרַם.

[143] GERMANY, *Exodus-Conquest*, 256, for example, argues, "the transition from the חרם
references in 2:34αβ–35 to the geographical references in 2:36 is not very smooth: The listing
of conquered areas in 2:36 connects much better to 2:34αα, providing further details regarding
the extent of Sihon's territory."

depicts Moses giving of the law in the plains of Moab in the vicinity of Mt. Nebo (cf. Deut 34:1), i. e., just north of the Dead Sea. This location makes perfect sense if Israel is understood as having fought Sihon at Jahaz and then travelled more or less directly north-west towards the Jordan (see figure 9). Within this narrative setting, the Og narrative *in its entirety* makes little sense.[144] There is no reason for Israel to cross the Jabbok into northern Transjordan let alone travel all the way north to Bashan. Rather the Og narrative only makes sense as part of Narrative B, which depicts the *conquest* of the *Amorites* so that the Transjordan belongs to the promised land. Simply put, the entire Og narrative only makes sense as part of Narrative B.

It is curious, then, that many commentators include elements of the Og narrative in the earliest layers of Deuteronomy 1–3. Schmidt, for instance, claims, "Nun geht es aber bereits in dem Abschnitt über Sihon um den Landbesitz Israels im Ostjordanland, zu dem auch der Baschan gehörte. Das spricht dafür, dass schon im Grundbestand von Dtn 1–3 auch von seiner Eroberung berichtet wurde" (*Now, [the theme of] Israel's conquest in Transjordan is already in the section about Sihon, to which the Bashan also belongs. That speaks therefore, for [Bashan's] conquest also belonging to the base narrative of Dtn 1–3*).[145] One exception is Mittmann who argues that the Og narrative should be considered secondary noting: (1) The journey report of Deut 3:1a differs from all other journey reports in Deuteronomy 1–3 in that the journey is not ordered by Yhwh; (2) although Deut 2:32 and Deut 3:1b are more or less verbatim parallels, Deut 2:33 and Deut 3:3 differ significantly, in particular Deut 3:3 appears to already incorporate elements from Deut 2:34, which it was argued above belongs to Narrative B. Thus Mittman concludes, "Die aufgezeigten Differenzen dürften zur Genüge J. G. Plögers leider nicht verifizierte Vermutung sichern, daß 'der Og-Bericht dem Sihon-Bericht höchstwahrscheinlich sekundär parallel nachgestaltet worden' ist" (*The demonstrated differences should be sufficient to reinforce J. G. Plöger's unfortunately unverified presumption that 'the Og-report has most likely been secondarily modelled to parallel the Sihon report'*").[146] This means that if one omits the Og narrative from Narrative A, there is less need to delimit the territory of Sihon *of Heshbon*. Thus, all of Deut 2:36–3:11 can be allocated to Narrative B.[147]

Jumping over the Og narrative leaves Deut 3:12–22 remaining, which contain the report of the distribution of territory. This section of text is widely regarded to comprise several disparate materials. As Otto summarises:

---

[144] See also Weippert, "Conquest," 16, who states, "At this point, one would have expected the Israelites to move straight on to the Jordan in order to reach the land of Canaan west of the river."

[145] Schmidt, "Sihon," 318.

[146] Mittmann, *Deuteronomium*, 82, quoting Plöger, *Untersuchungen*, 17.

[147] The exclusion of the Og narrative will be further supported in the discussion below, and particularly in § 3.3.2.

Dtn 3,12–22 gilt vielen Exegeten ... als ein ungeordneter Text von extremer Uneinheitlichkeit und Formlosigkeit, als 'eine Sammlung von Themen und Motiven', die anderswo einen passenderen Ort haben sollen. Dieser Eindruck entsteht, da Dtn 3,12–22 keine in sich abgeschlossene literarische Einheit innerhalb des Buches Deuteronomium ist, sondern in buchübergreifenden Perspektiven in Verbindung mit Josuabuch und dem Buch Numeri aufgeht. (*Many exegetes hold Dtn 3:12–22... to be a disordered text of extreme inconsistency and formlessness, as 'a collection of themes and motifs' that should have a more suitable place elsewhere. This impression arises because Dtn 3:12–22 is not, of itself, a closed literary unit within the book of Deuteronomy, rather opens up cross-book perspectives with the book of Joshua and the book of Numbers.*)[148]

There are multiple issues with Deut 3:12–22 that warrant a more extensive discussion, however for the purposes of the present investigation, the only pertinent issue is finding which verses, if any, belong to Narrative A.

Deut 3:16–17 can immediately be disregarded due to being a more precise elaboration of vv. 12b, 13.[149]

Deuteronomy 3:15 is more or less verbatim to Num 32:40, and so raises the question of direction of dependence. As the theme of Moses "giving" land belongs much more naturally to Deuteronomy (cf. Deut 3:12, 13, 15, 16, 19, 20) than it does to Numbers (Num 32:33, 40), it seems likely that Num 32:40 was inserted to harmonise with Deut 3:15.[150]

Deuteronomy 3:14 is unique within the land distribution report in Deut 3:12–17 in that it is the only item that is not covered by the verb נתתי (*I gave*) with Moses as subject. The reason for this will be elaborated in § 3.3.2, but to foreshadow the more extensive discussion there: The addition of the half-tribe of Manasseh in Numbers 32, which primarily involved only the tribes of Reuben and Gad, is best explained as being in response to the addition of the Sihon narrative, which shifted the Reubenites' and Gadites' territory from that envisioned in Num 32:1 (cf. figure 8) to the area of central Transjordan only (cf. § 3.2.3 and figure 12). Half-Manasseh, then, was added to the Transjordan tribes to occupy the territory of northern Transjordan (i. e., Gilead), after this territory was no longer "available" for the Reubenites and Gadites. Deuteronomy 3:14 also contains the idea that Jair acted independently from the rest of the Israelite army and took Havvoth-Jair for himself, which suggests that it too belongs to a pre-Og layer of tradition.

Verses 12–13* are typically allocated to the base narrative, yet allocating these verses in their entirety is problematic.[151] First, the repeated phrase בעת ההוא (*at*

---

[148] OTTO, *Deuteronomium 1,1–4,43*, 477.

[149] MITTMANN, *Deuteronomium*, 84–85. OTTO, *Deuteronomium 1,1–4,43*, 479, argues that these verses contribute to a chiastic structure centered around Deut 3:14.

[150] OTTO, *Deuteronomium 1,1–4,43*, 478.

[151] NELSON, *Deuteronomy*, 53, for example, concisely states, "the original text is vv. 12–13a." See also OTTO, *Pentateuch und Hexateuch*, 129–138. Esp. 136; ACHENBACH, *Vollendung*, 358.

124   *3. The Occupation of Transjordan*

that time), links the Sihon, Og and distribution narratives together, suggesting that v. 12a already presupposes the presence of the Og layer (Deut 3:4, 8).[152] It is, of course, conceivable that this phrase was later incorporated into the Og narrative to join it more seamlessly into the pre-existing narrative, however the more natural explanation is that v. 12a was added alongside the Og narrative. Second, for the same reason as v. 12a, v. 13 must also presuppose the Og narrative as he is directly mentioned in v. 13a. Verse 13b inserts the additional information that the Argob region belonged to the Rephaim, which Germany notes belongs to a series of notices (Deut 2:10–11, [12?], 20–21, [22–23?]; 3:11) establishing "a pattern whereby Israel and its neighbors Moab and Ammon all received their divinely apportioned land after defeating giants who previously inhabited the land."[153] This likely forms a parallel to the spy narrative, wherein the Israelites bring back the report that the בני ענקים (*sons of the Annakim*) dwelt in the land and so were too afraid to enter from Kadesh-barnea (Deut 1:28).

Having demonstrated that most of vv. 12–13 presuppose the Og narrative, v. 12bβ contains the statement ועריו נתתי לראובני ולגדי (*and his cities I gave to the Reubenites and the Gadites*). This small phrase has often been overlooked in analyses due to the general idea that the base narrative of Deuteronomy already included the campaign against Og. Yet the masculine suffix "*his* cities" does not naturally follow the feminine noun ארץ (*land*), indeed when the land's cities are clearly intended the feminine suffix is used (cf. Num 32:33). However, if one omits the Og narrative and its dependencies, then Deut 3:12bβ follows quite logically after Deut 2:33*: ועריו נתתי לראובני ולגדי... ויתנהו יהוה אלהינו לפנינו (*YHWH our god gave him before us … and his cities I gave to the Reubenites and the Gadites*). This reconstruction has the advantage of presupposing the existence of the base narrative of Numbers 32 (i. e., it explains how Reuben and Gad received their territory in Transjordan) and providing a Deuteronomistic reframing of that text. In other words, the Deuteronomistic Narrative A directly addresses, via the concept of Deut 20:10–15, how and why the Reubenites and Gadites received land that lay outside of Cisjordan.

Thus, Narrative A provides a Deuteronomistic-coloured background behind the request in Numbers 32. It uses the motif of attacking a city "very far from you" (Deut 20:15) and comprises Deut 2:24aα, 26, 27, 29bα(β?), 30a, 32, 33a(b?); 3:12bβ.[154] Thus, Moses begins by sending the offer of peace (Deut 2:26//Deut

---

[152] LOHFINK, "Darstellungskunst," 132.

[153] GERMANY, *Exodus-Conquest*, 259. See also OTTO, *Deuteronomium 1,1–4,43*, 488.

[154] This represents a rather radical departure from the more common allocations: GERMANY, *Exodus-Conquest*, 258 – Deut 2:26*, 27, 29b–30a, 32–34aα, 36; 3:1, 3a, 4a, 8a; OTTO, *Pentateuch und Hexateuch*, 129–138. Esp. 136 (also ACHENBACH, *Vollendung*, 358) – Deut 2:24aα, 26–30a, 31–35; 3:1–4a, 5–7, 8, 10a, 12, 13a, 21–22, 29; Otto later updated this in OTTO, *Deuteronomium 1,1–4,43*, 450 – Deut 2:24*, 25, 26*, 27, 28, 29b, 30a, 32–35; SCHMIDT, "Sihon," 320 – Deut 2:24aα, 26–28, 29bα(bβ?), 30a, 31–35; 3:1, 3, 4aα, 6–8a*, 8b, 10a*.

20:10), after Sihon refuses (Deut 2:30//Deut 20:12) the terms, Israel was free to possess his cities (Deut 3:12//Deut 20:13), but not to slay the women, children and livestock (cf. Deut 20:14 and Deut 2:34; 3:3//Deut 20:16). The granting of these cities to the Reubenites and Gadites incorporates the pre-existing base narrative of Numbers 32 into Deuteronomy but reframes it in light of Deuteronomistic ideals.

3.2.2 Numbers 21:21–35*

Num 21:21*Israel sent messengers to Sihon saying	Deut 2:26So I sent messengers from the wilderness of Kedemoth to Sihon, king of Heshbon with words of peace saying
Num 21:22*let me pass through your land ... until we pass over your border	Deut 2:27let me pass through your land. I will walk only along the road, I will not turn aside to the right or to the left
	Deut 2:29bα(β?)Until I pass over the Jordan [to the land that Yнwн our god is giving to us]
Num 21:23But Sihon would not give Israel passage in his border. Sihon gathered all his people and went out to the wilderness to meet Israel and he came to Jahaz and fought with Israel.	Deut 2:30aBut Sihon, king of Heshbon, was not willling to let us pass over
	Deut 2:32Sihon went out to meet us, he and all his people for battle at Jahaz
Num 21:24aIsrael put him to the sword	Deut 2:33a, (b?)and Yнwн our god gave him unto us [and we struck him and his sons and all his people]
Num 21:25bβin Heshbon and in all its villages.	
	Deut 3:12bβand his cities I gave to the Reubenites and the Gadites.

Table 8: Original Sihon layer in Numbers

If the above analysis is correct, then not only should the Sihon narrative in Numbers show clear dependence upon Deuteronomy's "Narrative A" delimited above, but the divergences should also be readily explainable. This section will work through Numbers' Sihon narrative and attempt an explanation for the discrepancies.

Arguably the biggest difficulty already appears in Numbers 21:21, where not Moses but Israel sends the request for passage to Sihon. This issue has most recently been raised by Schmidt who argues that it is difficult to conceive of why the editors of Numbers would remove references to both Moses and Yнwн had they had Deuteronomy's Sihon narrative before them, rather it is much more conceivable that the Deuteronomists altered the text of Numbers to conform to

126   *3. The Occupation of Transjordan*

a more theological profile.[155] The idea that the Deuteronomists "theologised" the previously more "secular" Numbers' Sihon narrative is widespread in scholarship. But the deliberate removal of these important figures is strongly suggested by Numbers' treatment of the Og narrative in Num 21:33–35, which otherwise follows the Deuteronomistic Og narrative verbatim. As Albertz notes, "Die Weise, wie mit der dtr. Og-Tradition in Num 21,33–35 umgegangen wird, legt die Einsicht nahe, dass Reduktion bzw. Ausblendung der theologischen Dimension in der Sihon- und übrigens auch in der Edom-Erzählung als ein bewusstes Stilmittel des hier tätigen Autors angesehen werden muss" (*The sense with which the Dtr Og tradition is bypassed, suggests the insight, that the reduction, or rather the fading-out, of the theological dimension in the Sihon and incidentally also the Edom narrative must be regarded as a conscious stylistic device of the author working here*).[156]

That Albertz's observation points in the right direction becomes clearer when one considers the underlying theological issues with the changed land conceptions introduced by the Sihon narrative. As it was argued in § 3.2.1 the original Sihon narrative in Deuteronomy (i. e., Narrative A) reframed Numbers 32's depiction of the reception of Transjordan land such that it conformed to the Deuteronomistic ideals of lawful acquisition following a battle with an enemy "very far from you." However, because the Deuteronomists depicted Moses sending "words of peace" (Deut 2:26), they inadvertently made him responsible for Israel's battle with Sihon (in light of Deut 20:10). By making Israel send the message, the Numbers narrative removes any hint of responsibility from YHWH's chosen leader.[157] This solution, unlike Van Seters' argument that "Israel" is drawn directly from Judges 11, does not rest purely on dubious scribal conflation rather it represents a theologically motivated alteration of the parent text.[158] Deuteronomy 3:12bβ further reports that Moses gave Sihon's territory to the Reubenites and Gadites again making their dwelling in Transjordan the result

---

[155] SCHMIDT, "Sihon," 321.

[156] ALBERTZ, "Numeri I," 179.

[157] The phrase ישראל appears 53 times in the book of Numbers without an accompanying בני, these are distributed with various qualifiers: ישראל (Num 3:13; 16:9, 34; 18:14; 19:13; 20:14, 21; 21:1, 2, 3, 6, 17, 21, 23, 25, 31; 23:7, 10, 21, 23; 24:1, 2, 5, 18; 25:1, 3, 4; 32:13, 14; 32:22), ראשי אלפי ישראל (Num 1:16; 10:4), נשיאי ישראל (Num 1:44; 4:46; 7:2, 84), רבבות אלפי ישראל(Num 10:36), זקני ישראל(Num 11:16, 30; 16:25), עדה ישראל (Num 16:9; 32:4), בית ישראל (Num 20:29), שפטי יש‍ ראל (Num 25:5), מטות ישראל (Num 31:4), אלפי ישראל (Num 31:5). Neither do all 30 occurrences stem from passages with similar stylistic features nor do they all exhibit an inherent "oldness," thus the use of ישראל instead of בני ישראל is difficult to explain. Perhaps its use simply relates to the presence of ישראל already in the other sections of Numbers 21.

[158] See VAN SETERS, "Conquest;" VAN SETERS, "Again." Against Van Seters' view, BARTLETT, "Conquest," 348, rightly observes, "If the Numbers editor of the Sihon story derived the use of 'Israel' from Judges 11, then he seems to have extended this use (on Van Seters' hypothesis) to a number of other stories between Num 20:14 and 25:6. It seems more likely, however, that Judges 11 drew on the wide range of materials available to him in Numbers than that Numbers

3.2 The Sihon Tradition 127

of Moses's actions and choices, however Numbers 32 depicts the Reubenites and Gadites requesting land that lay outside of the area designated by Yhwh for Israel. Taken altogether these shifts in Numbers appear to point toward the conclusion that the goal was to "save" Moses and his reputation. Furthermore, by removing Yhwh from the narrative the authors subtly point towards the conclusion that this event was not a divinely ordained victory and was not part of Yhwh's divine plan (as it becomes in Deuteronomy's Narrative B!).

A second issue is the fact that Sihon is already the "king of the Amorites" in Num 21:21. In § 3.2.1 it was argued that Sihon was only labelled an Amorite in Deuteronomy after the Transjordan was conceived to belong to the promised land, and so both Sihon and Og were brought under the umbrella of those nations designated for destruction (Deut 7:1; 20:17). If the reference to "Sihon the Amorite" is original, it would suggest that Numbers 21:21 f. is later than Deuteronomy's Narrative B. A more plausible alternative to this option is suggested by Schmidt, who argues that in the original Sihon narrative of Numbers, "wurden weder die Städte der Amoriter, noch Heschbon erwähnt. Sihon war nach ihr 'der König der Amoriter'" (*neither the Amorite cities nor Heshbon were mentioned. Sihon was [made] 'the king of the Amorites' after [the base layer]*).[159] Although it will be argued below that mention of Heshbon belongs to the original version of Num 21:21–35, Schmidt's suggestion that the Amorite connection is secondary will be further supported below.

Numbers 21:22 largely corresponds to Deut 2:28 but it also diverges in a number of ways. First, contrary to Deut 2:28 both Num 21:22 and Num 20:17 (Edom narrative) refer to fields and vineyards, which is one of the major pieces of evidence that Otto uses to support his theory of a pre-Deuteronomistic Edom-Sihon narrative. He writes, "das Motiv der vorgegebenen vordeuteronomistischen Quelle, man werde Felder und Weinberge nicht betreten und kein Brunnenwasser trinken (Num 20,17; 21,22), haben die deuteronomistischen Autoren in Dtn 2,6 um das Motiv der Bereitschaft, Nahrungsmittel und Wasser gegen Silber zu kaufen, erweitert" (*The Deuteronomistic authors in Dtn 2:6 have expanded the motif of the pre-existing pre-Deuteronomistic source, that one would not enter fields or vineyards and not drink well water [Num 20:17; 21:22], with the willingness to buy food and water with silver*).[160] Schmidt also argues that the motif of purchasing food and drink in Deuteronomy postdates the version in Numbers based on the idea that in Numbers the people of Israel are depicted as being self-sufficient, but in Deuteronomy they "sich nicht selbst versorgen konnten" (*could not take care of themselves*).[161] Schmidt justifies his conclusion

---

drew on Judges 11 and extended the use of 'Israel' in this way to other stories relating to this wilderness period."

[159] Schmidt, "Sihon," 321.
[160] Otto, *Deuteronomium 1,1–4,43*, 419.
[161] Schmidt, "Sihon," 322.

128   *3. The Occupation of Transjordan*

by suggesting that it is more difficult to explain Numbers' moving away from purchasing food and drink than it is to explain Deuteronomy's shift towards it.

It is admittedly difficult to draw any firm conclusions but there is some possibility to find clues in the words שדה (*field*) and כרם (*vineyard*) that suggest that Numbers' Sihon narrative is later than Deuteronomy's. Although neither of these words is particularly rare or distinct, it is interesting that the terms do not appear regularly as a pair in the Hebrew Bible, and in the Pentateuch the paired terms only appear in three narrative texts Num 16:14; 20:17; 21:22. As Numbers 20:17 can be considered dependent on 21:22, this leaves only Num 16:14 as a possible inspiration for Num 21:22. Numbers 16:14 comprises part of the Reubenites' (i.e., Dathan's and Abiram's) complaint against Moses that he took them out of Egypt and had not brought them to a land flowing with milk and honey and not נתני־לנו נחלת שדה וכרם (*given us a possession of fields and vineyards*).[162] It is possible, then, that the reference to fields and vineyards in Num 21:22 is yet another slur against the Reubenites, in that they request (in Num 32:5) the very first set of fields and vineyards they come across: Sihon's! This might also explain the general attribution of the southern-most land of central Transjordan to the Reubenites, again subtly suggesting the Reubenites took the very first land they were able.[163] Pushing the symbolism even further, this would also mean that Reuben did in fact receive the first allotment of land as dictated by his firstborn privilege, however that land lay outside of Canaan and so represents a negative twist.[164] Although one must remain cautious in stretching tenuous links beyond their breaking point, the reference to fields and vineyards in Num 20:17; 21:22 make a good deal of sense as a "thickening" of intertextual connections within the various narrative building blocks in the book of Numbers and the repeated motif of the decline of Reuben.[165]

Moving to v. 22, there are also clues that this verse presupposes Deuteronomy. As has been widely observed, v. 22 contains a numeruswechsel: Num 21:22aα uses the typical singular verb form used in vv. 21–24 – אעברה (*let me pass over*) – whereas the remainder of v. 22 uses plural verbs – נטה (*we will turn*), נשתה (*we*

---

[162] For נחלה (*possession*) belonging to a Deuteronomistic milieu see, e.g., KNAUF, *Data*, 521. For the term in the Dathan-Abiram narrative see, e.g., ACHENBACH, *Vollendung*, 45; PYSCHNY, *Führung*, 150.

[163] A similar solution is suggested by LEVINE, *Numbers 1–20*, 424–425, who argues that the Dathan-Abiram narrative originally served in JE to prepare for the narrative of Numbers 32, explaining why the firstborn Reuben ended up in Transjordan. See also discussion in SAMUEL, *Priestern*, 209n956.

[164] See discussion in note 28 on page 90.

[165] Several recent analyses utilising markedly different Pentateuchal models have concluded that the Dathan-Abiram layer is post-Priestly. See esp. ACHENBACH, *Vollendung*, 37–129; GERMANY, *Exodus-Conquest*, 224–233; PYSCHNY, *Führung*, esp. 285–290.

3.2 The Sihon Tradition

129

will drink), נלך (*we will go*) and נעבר (*we have passed over*).[166] Within the context of the people of Israel sending the message, the plural verbs make sense. It is no surprise then that v. 22aα exactly matches the wording of Deut 2:27aα, wherein Moses alone was speaking, suggesting that the scribe responsible for Num 21:22aα knew Deuteronomy.

As noted in § 3.2.1, a further key difference in Num 21:22 is Israel's assurance that they will only travel on the דרך המלך (typically translated as the *King's Highway*), which is geographically problematic. However, before discussing this issue directly Num 21:25 must first be discussed.

Verse 25bβ suggests that Sihon controlled a much more limited area than the entirety of central Transjordan, comprising only Heshbon and all its villages.[167] The Hebrew term בנתיה, which literally means "her daughters," is used to designate those smaller settlements surrounding a more established central place, Milgrom more specifically argues that it refers to the unwalled settlements surrounding a fortified city.[168] Thus, the polemical Judg 1:27 lists no fewer than five major cities with בנתיה within the allotment of the tribe of Manasseh that could not be dispossessed from the Canaanites dwelling there. Numbers 21:32 also refers to the בנתיה of Jazer, which not only supports the above interpretation but also shows that Jazer – which is geographically close to Heshbon – is implicitly excluded from Heshbon's בנת. These references point to the idea that that "Heshbon and all its villages" was intended to reflect Deuteronomy's depiction of Sihon as a city-king who dwelt "very far from you." Once again, the direction of dependence favours the idea that Deuteronomy was earlier than Numbers, as the idea of a king ruling over a city and its villages is a blind motif in Numbers, whereas it has a very clear purpose in Deuteronomy due to the phrase, "with words of peace" (Deut 2:26), connecting to Deut 20:10–15.

Granting this, it follows that the original Sihon narrative in Numbers jumped from v. 24a to v. 25bβ: "Israel put him to the sword … in Heshbon and in all its villages." Numbers 21:24b–25bα, then, represent a later update in light of Deuteronomy's Narrative B. This was achieved by adding the Amorite motif as well as expanding Sihon's territory "from the Arnon to the Jabbok." That these details were sandwiched between v. 24a and v. 25bβ can be seen as a deliberate obfuscation of the original narrative so that the idea that Sihon was an Amorite king ruling from the Arnon to the Jabbok took priority.[169]

The more limited territory of Sihon is important in the discussion of the King's Highway (Num 21:22), which was the major north-south trade route through

---

[166] See, e.g., GERMANY, *Exodus-Conquest*, 241. MITTMANN, *Deuteronomium*, 74, writes, "Der Text ist offensichtlich nicht aus einem Guß" (*The text is obviously not from a single source*).

[167] So, e.g., FREVEL, "Shapes," 280–281; GERMANY, *Exodus-Conquest*, 242; WÜST, *Untersuchungen*, 10–11.

[168] MILGROM, *Numbers*, 181; LEVINE, *Numbers 21–36*, 101.

[169] See also discussion in § 3.6.1.

Transjordan that connected Syria to the Gulf of Aqaba/Eilat (see figure 10).[170] As already briefly discussed in § 3.1.2, Israel's journey northwards is depicted in two contrasting routes (neither of which mention the King's Highway; a phrase that only appears in Num 20:17 and Num 21:22 in the entire Hebrew Bible). According to the western itinerary (approx. Num 21:12, 13a*, 20*), Israel travelled through Moab, crossed the Arnon and made their way north to "the valley which is in the field of Moab." Within this basic framework, Israel's use of the King's Highway is highly plausible.[171] The issue with this is the report in Num 21:23 stating that Sihon met Israel in battle at Jahaz, a city that makes much more sense if Israel travelled around Moab via the wilderness, i.e., the eastern itinerary.[172] For the western itinerary, it would make much more sense for Sihon to approach Israel at the corresponding fortification at Atroth-Shophan/Rujm 'Aṭarūz considering its closer proximity to the King's Highway (Knauf remarks that one can even see Dibon from this location).[173] Jahaz is often assumed to be a south-eastern border fortress erected by the Omrides, which MacDonald describes as occupying "the edge of the desert between Madaba and Dhiban."[174] In Deuteronomy's Sihon narrative, the report of a battle at Jahaz is perfectly logical considering that there is only a single itinerary; according to Deut 2:8 Israel travels northwards along the דרך מדבר מואב (*road of the wilderness of Moab* – see figure 10).[175] The mention of the King's Highway, then, is best explained as an attempt by the editors of Numbers to harmonise the (secondary) Sihon narrative with the pre-existing itinerary in Numbers 21, which understood Israel to travel peacefully *through* Moab, plausibly along the King's Highway. The confinement of Sihon to "Heshbon and all its villages," also fits into this same conceptual framework whereby the majority of central Transjordan could still be understood as belonging to the Moabites. It was only after reconfiguring Sihon's territory "from the Arnon to the Jabbok" that the eastern itinerary needed to be inserted into the Numbers narrative.

---

[170] See, e.g., AHARONI, *Land*, 44; FREVEL, *Geschichte*, 123, for maps. For the issues relating to the idea that the King's Highway was the ancient and traditional main route, see BIENKOWSKI, "Divide," 99–103.

[171] One possible alternative solution to this problem is proposed by NOTH, *Numbers*, 150, who suggests that the דרך המלך refers more generally to "a road which, in places where it was necessary, had been leveled off by means of 'embankments' to such a degree that one was able to drive wagons along it, especially chariots, so that even a king (with his retinue) could use it on official expeditions." The main objection to this line of argumentation is that it is more difficult to explain its removal in Deut 2:27, whereas Deuteronomy's use of the way of the wilderness of Moab (Deut 2:8) naturally precludes the use of the King's Highway.

[172] See already DEARMAN, "Cities," 56.

[173] KNAUF, *Midian*, 162n689. JI, *Tale*, remarks that Rujm 'Aṭarūz functioned to protect the large urban centre of Ataroth/Khirbat 'Aṭarūz. On Jahaz and Ataroth as a paired set of Omride fortifications see FINKELSTEIN/LIPSCHITS, "Architecture."

[174] MACDONALD, *East*, 105. See also FINKELSTEIN/LIPSCHITS, "Architecture."

[175] See AHARONI, *Land*, 44.

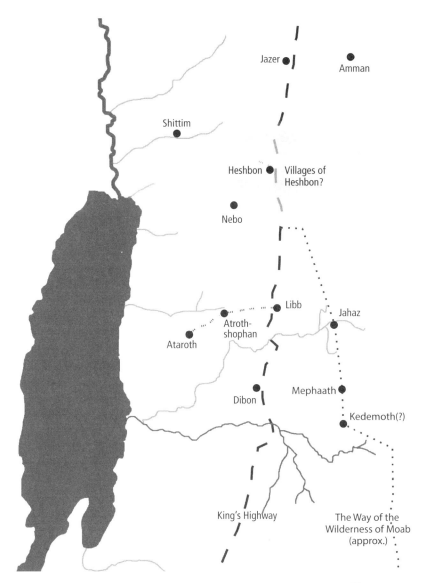

Figure 10: "Heshbon and all its villages" and the King's Highway[176]

---

[176] Map drawn by J. Davis. For the path of the King's Highway see, e. g., AHARONI, *Land*, 44; DEARMAN, "Cities," 62; FREVEL, "Shapes," 262. For the Way of the Wilderness of Moab see, e. g., AHARONI, *Land*, 44; DEARMAN, "Cities," 62. For the road connecting Libb – Atroth-Shophan – Ataroth, see DEARMAN, "Cities," 62; JI, "Tale," 218. Besides the toponym details that can be found in figure 7 and figure 11, Mephaath is located at Um er Raṣaṣ (2374.1010), see DEARMAN, "Cities," 63; GASS, *Ortsnamen*, 673. Kedemoth is tentatively located at Saliyah (2386.1096) see DEARMAN, "Cities," 63; FREVEL, "Shapes," 262.

132   3. The Occupation of Transjordan

Further support for the post-Deuteronomistic dating of Numbers' Sihon narrative is found in Num 21:22b, which refers to גבלך (*your border*) in contrast to Num 21:22aα, which refers to בארצך (*in your land*).[177] Albertz draws attention to the fact that not only is the emphasis on boundaries mirrored in the Edom narrative (Num 20:16, 17, 21) but it also appears in the subsequent death of Aaron narrative (Num 20:23), which takes place בהר ההר על־גבול ארץ־אדום (*on Mt. Hor upon the border of the land of Edom*), to which he suggests that all three references to borders "stammen sie wahrscheinlich von demselben Autor" (*they likely stem from the same author*).[178] If Albertz is correct then this would further suggest that the final form of Numbers' Sihon narrative is not only post-Deuteronomistic but that it belongs to a post-Priestly strata. This issue will be returned to in more detail below.

Verse 23 largely corresponds to Deut 2:30a and 32, with the major alteration being the insertion of המדברה (*towards the wilderness*). It is unclear if this addition was made to the original Sihon narrative or whether it was a later addition as it can be explained either way. Within the context of the restricted territory of Sihon, this note functions to explain why Sihon left the confines of "Heshbon and all its villages" and travelled to Jahaz. It further explains that Sihon aggressively came out against Israel even before they reached his territory. Within the Sihon the Amorite narrative (i.e., expanded territory), this same note functions to demonstrate that Jahaz still lay outside of Sihon's territory, and so explains why this city was not allocated to the Reubenites or Gadites. Achenbach suggests that the reference to the wilderness in v. 23 might form a link to the more specific מדבר קדמות (*wilderness of Kedemoth*) in Deut 2:26, but this connection already presupposes Israel's use of the דרך מדבר מואב (*road of the wilderness of Moab* – Deut 2:8) and so also assumes a journey that did not pass through Moab proper.[179] That the omission of the region in the vicinity of Jahaz from Israelite claims was at least somewhat problematic can be inferred from Josh 13:18 and Josh 21:37, where Kedemoth is mentioned alongside Mephaath as Reubenite territory, both of these locations are further south and further east of Jahaz (see figure 10).[180] Again, had these locations been included it would contradict the narrative logic as it would mean that Israel was already inside Sihon's territory when the request for safe passage was sent and that Israel travelled even further inside Sihon's territory – to Jahaz – before they were confronted in battle.

The double naming of Sihon in v. 23 is potentially also a sign of redaction, however Gaß argues that this is unnecessary as it is "ebenfalls erzähltechnisch motiviert, da nach der Ablehnung der Durchreise die Abwehrmaßnahmen

---

[177] Again see GERMANY, *Exodus-Conquest*, 241–242.

[178] ALBERTZ, "Numeri I," 176–177.

[179] ACHENBACH, *Vollendung*, 360.

[180] GASS, *Moabiter*, 188, locates Mephaath at *Umm er-Raṣāṣ* (2374.1010). See also MacDONALD, *East*, 135–137. Cf. KNAUF, *Midian*, 162, who suggests *Tell Ğāwā*.

3.2 The Sihon Tradition

Sihons geschildert werden und damit ein neues Thema eröffnet wird" (*likewise narrative-technically motivated, since after the refusal of passage Sihon's defensive measures are described and with that a new theme is opened*).[181]

Verse 24 contains several details that suggest it largely belongs to a secondary layer. As already discussed, the report that Israel "dispossessed his land from the Arnon to the Jabbok" stands in conflict with the idea that Sihon's territory only comprised Heshbon and all its villages and thus logically belongs to a different layer. The notice in v. 24bβ that Israel only possessed as far as the border of the Ammonites once again raises the issues regarding the Abraham-Lot relationship as well as the Ιαζηρ/עז issue discussed in § 3.1.1.1.[182] In short, both of these issues fit more neatly to the expanded territory of Sihon and thus to a later redactional layer.

Regarding the report in v. 24a that Israel put Sihon לפי־חרב (*to the sword*), Seebass observes, "völlig un-dtr ist hier keine Rede vom Vertreiben der Amoriter oder von der Vernichtung ihres Militärs, sondern nur vom Sieg über Sihon" (*completely un-Dtr is there here no talk of driving out the Amorites or of the destruction of their military, rather only the victory over Sihon*).[183] However, Seebass' argument supports the proposal being made here that the original Sihon narrative had nothing to do with Amorites or the enactment of חרם. Instead, the phrase לפי־חרב can be seen to relate to Deut 20:13 regarding the cities "very far from you," wherein all the males of those cities that do not submit peacefully are to be put לפי־חרב.

As already argued, v. 25 should be considered a composite. The reference to "all these cities" not to mention the report that "Israel dwelt in all the cities of the Amorites" only makes sense if Sihon's territory is much larger than "Heshbon and all its villages."[184]

Verse 26 can only belong to the updated Sihon narrative as it functions to explain how Sihon came to control the territory of Moab and to introduce the Song of Heshbon (vv. 27–30). These themes are only relevant once Sihon was no longer depicted as a city-king of Heshbon, but an Amorite king ruling over central Transjordan (cf. § 3.2.3).

---

[181] GASS, *Moabiter*, 191.

[182] GASS, *Moabiter*, 191, alternatively suggests that the shift from עז to Ιαζηρ "ist nicht notwendig" (*is not necessary*) and represents the LXX's attempt to make sense of the difficulties in the MT, "indem sie nach dem Kontext von Num 21,32 verbessert" (*in which they improved [the text] according to the context of Num 21:32*).

[183] SEEBASS, *Numeri 2*, 350.

[184] Thus, there is no need to entertain the arguments of VAN SETERS, *Conquest*, 189, that the sudden shift from "territory" in v. 24 to "these cities" in v. 25 is purely the result of conflation of Judges and Deuteronomy (Judg 11:22–23 and Deut 2:34 for vv. 24 and 25 respectively). As BARTLETT, "Conquest," 350, rightly observes, "if (ex hypothesi) Numbers was following Deuteronomy, why did the writer not simply copy Deuteronomy's 'all his cities' (Deut 2:34)?"

134   *3. The Occupation of Transjordan*

The Song of Heshbon, vv. 27–30, despite its apparent antiquity is also to be considered a later insertion designed to justify Israel's taking of the territory of Moab. Again, this is only an issue if Sihon is no longer considered to be a city-king of Heshon but an Amorite king of central Transjordan. This will be discussed further in § 3.2.3.

Verses 31–35 are all logically secondary as they presuppose the later development of Sihon as an Amorite and the expansion of the Amorite territory to include northern Transjordan, which was controlled by Og of Bashan.

Numbers 21:32 deserves some elaboration. As discussed in § 3.1.1, the special report about Israel's taking of Jazer is only necessary once Sihon's territory is conceived as encroaching upon Ammonite space. This encroachment is only possible in light of Num 21:24b, in which Sihon the Amorite ruled עד־בני עמון (*until the sons of Ammon*), which is secondary.

Thus, a plausible base Sihon narrative comprising Num 21:21*, 22*, 23, 24a, 25bβ can be identified. This narrative functions to harmonise the essential details of Deuteronomy's Sihon Narrative A with the pre-existing narrative in Numbers. Once again Sihon is depicted as a city-king who aggressively engages Israel in battle after they request peaceful passage through his realm.

3.2.3 Heshbon, Sihon's City

One of the linchpins of the present reconstruction is a convincing explanation for Heshbon being named as Sihon's capital. Indeed, as was already discussed in § 3.1.1.2, Heshbon shows little archaeological support as being a central place during the Iron II period and as will be discussed in § 3.2.4 below, the evidence also points against Sihon being a historical Amorite.

The most logical explanation for the development of Sihon as a ruler based in Heshbon is that it is rooted in an old tradition. Often this old tradition is assumed to be the so-called Song of Heshbon (Num 21:27aβ–30*). The key line is found in v. 28: כי־אש יצאה מחשבון להבה מקרית סיחן (*a fire has gone out from Heshbon, a flame from the city of Sihon*), which very clearly links Heshbon and the city of Sihon. Much of the same material is found in Jer 48:45bα, but this is generally considered to be later than the Numbers version due to its combination of elements from both Num 21:28 and 24:17.[185]

The precise origins of this song have long been disputed although there is a general agreement that at least its roots are older than its present context(s). A particularly conservative interpretation is offered by Hanson, who argues that the song "can most naturally be regarded as an Amorite Victory Song celebrating

---

[185] On the conflated nature of Jer 48:45 see, e.g., WEIPPERT, "Conquest," 20; HUWYLER, *Jeremia*, 191. VAN SETERS, "Conquest," 194, argues that both Num 21:27–30 and Jer 48:45 are better understood as deriving from a common *Vorlage*.

the victory of their hero Sihon over the Moabites," and thus dates back to the Bronze Age.[186] Besides its overtly maximalist position, Hanson's theory can also be rejected on the historical argument that the likelihood of Sihon being an Amorite king of Heshbon dating to the Bronze Age is extremely low (cf. § 3.2.4). Weippert understands the Song of Heshbon to be linked to the Book of the Wars of Yhwh mentioned in Num 21:14, which he states, "are unquestionably old."[187] Although it is likely that the roots of the song are older than its present context, it must also be acknowledged that there are several key factors in the extant Song of Heshbon that are most readily explained as being specifically designed for its use in the Sihon narrative, not least the idea that Sihon was an Amorite (cf. Num 21:29).[188] Schmitt summarises the five major options in past scholarship as (1) it originated during the time of the conquest (be that part of an Amorite victory over Moab, an Israelite victory over Sihon or an Israelite victory over Moab); (2) David's victory over Moab; (3) an Omride victory over Moab; 4) it dates to the late Monarchic period; or (5) to the exilic period.[189] Although some options are clearly less likely than others, no one option stands as the obvious winner. The best hypothesis therefore remains that the Song of Heshbon was developed for its present purpose and context from a *Vorlage* that can no longer be reconstructed.[190]

That the present oracle is written in Hebrew is also inconclusive, as Knauf notes:

Wegen *ʿīr* statt **qīr* (wie es im moabitischen Original der Aufforderung zur Gründung der Stadt geheißen haben müßte) Num 21,27b haben wir einen hebräischen Text vor uns, der fürs erste keine anderssprachige Vorlage zu erkennen gibt. Allenfalls die Aufnahme eines Textes, der sich als Sieges- oder besser Spottlied klassifizieren läßt, in eine das Paradigmatische und Überindividuelle betonende Sammlung von *məšālīm* läßt vermuten, daß die singenden Sieger nicht die sammelnden Hebräer waren. (*Due to Num 21,27b containing* ʿīr *rather than *qīr [like it must have been in the original Moabite invitation to found the city], we have a Hebrew text before us, which for the time being it is not possible to identify a* Vorlage *from another language. At best the reception of the text, which can be classified as a song of victory or, better, a taunt song, in a collection by* məšālīm *that em-*

---

[186] Hanson, "Song," 299.

[187] Weippert, "Conquest," 17. See also Wüst, *Untersuchungen*, 10.

[188] Germany, *Exodus-Conquest*, 244–245, more convincingly suggests, "In terms of its rhetoric, the Song of Heshbon serves to resolve a problem in Num 21:21–25, namely, that some readers may have regarded Heshbon as a Moabite city. Num 21:26 addresses this problem by insisting that Sihon, king of the Amorites, had taken all of the land of the king of Moab as far as the Arnon prior to the Israelites' defeat of Heshbon, thereby disavowing the Israelites of any involvement in taking Moabite land. This rhetorical function of the Song of Heshbon supports the conclusion that it was composed specifically for its present literary context."

[189] Schmitt, "Hesbonlied," 34.

[190] Stordalen, "Heshbon," 253, notes, there is evidence that oracles were taken up and redirected for new purposes (e.g., Ezek 31 applies an oracle against the king of Assyria to the king of Egypt) and it seems likely that the Song of Heshbon is another example of this.

phasises the paradigmatic and supra-individual, suggests that the singing victors were not the collecting Hebrews).[191]

Important for the present discussion is the original meaning of Sihon, which in its present context is clearly the name of the king of Heshbon. As Knauf demonstrates, if one assumes the original wording of the song was *byt syḥwn* (which can be inferred from Jer 48:45) then the range of possible etymologies for Sihon are still broad; it might represent the name of a clan or tribe (e.g., Hos 10:14 – Beth-arbel), a personal or family name (e.g., 1 Kgs 4:9 – Elon-beth-hanan), a geographical name (e.g., Num 33:49 – Beth-jeshimoth) or the name of a deity (Beth-baal-meon, Bethlehem, Beth-anat).[192] Perhaps the most convincing option (albeit still uncertain) is suggested by Schmitt, who notes that Sihon likely relates to the nearby Mount *Šīḥān*, located west of the King's Highway between Dibon and er–Rabba, and could refer to the name of a local deity.[193]

Although this issue cannot be resolved satisfactorily, it seems plausible to suppose that the authors of Deut 2:24–3:18* drew on this old tradition only so far as using the link between the deity(?) named Sihon and city of Heshbon. The Deuteronomists, who designed the Sihon narrative (i.e., Narrative A) to explain origins of the Reubenites' and Gadites' territory, used this connection to reframe "the land of Jazer and the land of Gilead" so that it described the territory between Heshbon and the Jabbok, i.e., that territory identified by Finkelstein, Lipschits and Koch in figure 7.[194]

The more pressing question is: When did the editors of Numbers insert the modified song into their text? As already argued, in its present context the Song of Heshbon functions to provide an "external" and "antiquated" justification for Israel's conquest of Moab's traditional territory. Yet what caused this shift in the depiction of Sihon? It is clear from the content of the song that when the song was inserted, Sihon was already conceived to be an Amorite (Num 21:29) who had conquered the land of Moab as far as Dibon (Num 21:28, 30). Thus, the song must presuppose the updated conception of Sihon the Amorite who ruled from the Arnon to the Jabbok.

In sum, the Song of Heshbon, even if it does indeed contain older material, cannot be seen as the catalyst for the reconfiguration of Sihon from city-king to Amorite overlord. This will be argued in more detail in § 3.3.

---

[191] KNAUF, "Heshbon," 137.
[192] KNAUF, "Heshbon," 139.
[193] SCHMITT, "Hesbonlied," 39n125.
[194] FINKELSTEIN et al., "Gilead."

3.2.4 Sihon the Amorite?

The reference to Sihon and his people as Amorites also warrants further consideration. It was argued that for Deuteronomy the label "Sihon king of Heshbon" was an intentional signal that the base narrative considered Heshbon to belong to those cities "very far from you" (Deut 20:15). The renaming of both Sihon and Og as "kings of the Amorites" (Deut 3:8) re-categorised Israel's victories in Transjordan to be conceived as belonging to the land promised by Yhwh, as the Amorites belong to the nations destined for destruction (Deut 7:1; 20:17). In the Sihon narrative of Numbers, Sihon is referred to as an Amorite from the beginning and he is only linked to the city of Heshbon in Num 21:26.[195]

The Amorites are currently a controversial topic in scholarship. The biblical term, Amorite, most likely represents a Hebrew equivalent of the Akkadian term, *Amurru*, which means "the West" and originally referred to those populations "west" of Mesopotamia.[196] But even here it is not always clear when an ethnicity is intended or merely a relative cartesian description. For example, Huffmon notes that in a letter found in the archives in Mari, an "amorite fig tree" is alluded to, which can only mean a western variety of fig tree.[197] In so-called maximalist positions, the spread of the nomadic Amorites into the Levant in the Early-Middle Bronze Age is a given. Mendenhall, for example, claims, "from the MB Age on there was no region of the Levant that had not been influenced by the Amorite language and culture in various ways and various degrees."[198] The minimalists, on the contrary, note that archaeological traces of the Amorites are problematic for the larger Amorite theories so popular in scholarship. Homsher and Cradic, for example, write:

> Even in a region considered to be the core "homeland" of presumed Amorite pastoral nomads, there exists no archaeological evidence to support an Amorite identity of the late-third- and early-second-millennia occupants of the region. If Amorites are invisible in the archaeology of their supposed homeland, then it is not possible to demonstrate their diffusion elsewhere on the basis of material culture.[199]

Taking seriously the minimalists' objections, one must be careful not to make too simple correlations between the Amorite expansion and the biblical traditions. However, it is not sufficient to conclude that all biblical mentions of the Amorites are merely inventions, the reference must have come from somewhere.

---

[195] See, e.g., Seebass, *Numeri 2*, 350.
[196] Mendenhall, "Amorites."
[197] Huffmon/Charpin, "Amorites," 1019.
[198] Mendenhall, "Amorites."
[199] Homsher/Cradic, "Amorites," 137. For a closer inspection of the difficulties of the pottery categorisation, see, e.g., Porter, "Potato." Mendenhall, "Amorites," on the contrary, states, "during the LB Age, the Amorites had evidently become thoroughly assimilated into local populations both in the E and the W, as well as in the NE Syrian homeland, so that after that is no longer possible to identify a specific Amorite cultural/linguistic population group."

138   *3. The Occupation of Transjordan*

One innovative proposal is offered by Fleming, who argues that the Bible operates on a system whereby the Amorites are identified with the highlands (pastoralists) and the Canaanites with the lowlands (sedentary farmers/city dwellers), "even if the logic of such naming was long forgotten."[200] If one ignores Sihon and Og, the Bible appears to follow Fleming's system by locating the Amorites in the *Judean* hill country. Genesis 14:13 depicts the Amorites in region of Mamre, Eshcol (cf. Num 13:23) and Aner, which are in the vicinity of Hebron. Deuteronomy 1:7 refers to the "hill country of the Amorites" alongside other toponyms that clearly belong to southern Judah – the Arabah, the Shephelah, and the Negeb.[201] Numbers 13:29, which most scholars allocate to a late addition, arguably represents the clearest demarcation of the various indigenous people groups: "The Amalekites dwell in the land of the Negeb, the Hittites, the Jebusites and the Amorites dwell in the hill country [of Judah?], and the Canaanites dwell by the sea and by the Jordan."[202] Lastly, 2 Kings 21:11 equates the regency of King Manasseh of Judah to be "more wicked than all that the Amorites, who were before him, did," which, once again, suggests that the Amorites were typically conceived as being located within the area of Judah. This suggests that the Amoriteness of Sihon and Og already stands in some conflict with the other biblical traditions.

Although some innovative solutions to resolve this issue have been suggested,[203] the most likely root of the label "Amorite" for Sihon and Og comes from

---

[200] FLEMING, "Amorites," 16–17.

[201] See JERICKE, "Bergland," 60, who writes, "Dass das 'Bergland der Amoriter' literarisch-topographisch über die von Juda beanspruchten Gebiete im Süden Palästinas zumindest andeutungsweise nach Osten ausgreift, gründet in der geschilderten zeitgenössischen Erfahrung der Verfasser von Dtn 1, dass bereits ab dem 7./6. Jh. v. Chr., verstärkt dann im 5./4. Jh. v. Chr. der Negeb und das südliche Ostjordanland in wirtschaftsgeographischer Hinsicht eine Einheit bildeten" (*That the 'hill country of the Amorites' literarily-topographically reaches out over the areas claimed by Judah in southern Palestine with a hint towards the east, is grounded in the portrayed contemporary experience of the authors of Dtn 1, that already from the 7th/6th century BCE, and reinforced in the 5th/4th century BCE the Negeb and the southern Transjordan, in an economic-geographical respect, formed a unit*).

[202] NOTH, *Numbers*, 107, states, "v. 29 hardly fits into the spies' report and is to be regarded as a later addition."

[203] BOLING, *Community*, 41, for example, suggests, "the kingdom of Sihon the Amorite in Transjordan was very likely a transplanted survival of a regime, possibly represented at Amarna by Abdi-Ashirta, after the destruction of Ugrit by the Sea Peoples." This solution has the advantage of originally locating Sihon closer to southern Judah rather than in Transjordan. But it must be ultimately admitted that this theory raises more problems than it solves. Arguably the biggest impediment to the historicity of Sihon and Og as Amorites comes from their names, both of which are not typically Amorite in style (see HUFFMON/CHARPIN, "Amorites," 1027). BOLING, *Community*, 43, suggests that, "the non-Semitic name of Og is now compared with Hittite and Luwian Ḫuḫḫa, and late Lycian *Kuga*." Extra-biblically, scholars often reference ln. 2 of a Phoenician sarcophagus inscription, Byblos 13, which RÖLLIG, "Inschrift," 2, interpreted to say: *h'g ytbqšn h-'dr* (*the mighty Og will avenge me*). This reading, however, was amended in the 5th edition of Kanaanäische und Aramäische Inschriften (KAI 280) to read העגזת בקשן האדר making the reference to Og contentious. See also discussion in

3.3 Post-Sihon, Non-Priestly Updates in Numbers 32

the biblical tradition itself. The Amorite nomenclature was chosen – over against the Hittites, Perizzites, Hivites, etc. – precisely because it was "the hill country of the Amorites" that Israel refused to enter in Deut 1:20–27. Thus, a parallel is made between the failed conquest of the Amorites from Kadesh-barnea and the successful conquest of the Amorites in Transjordan. In short, Sihon's and Og's Amorite ethnicity was chosen for stylistic reasons.

3.3 Post-Sihon, Non-Priestly Updates in Numbers 32

Num 32:1 Many livestock had *the sons of Reuben and the sons of Gad, very many.*[204] And they saw .was a place for livestock (מקום) the land of Jazer and the land of Gilead and behold, the place

...

Num 32:5b* [and they said,] "do not make us cross over the Jordan."

Num 32:6* and Moses said, "[...] you sit here?"

Num 32:16* and they said, "we will build walls for our sheep here and cities for our children

Num 32:17a we will equip ourselves and hasten before the sons of Israel until we have brought them to their place (מקום)

Num 32:20a and Moses said to them, "If you do what you have said,

Num 32:22aβ afterwards you can return and be clear from Yhwh and from Israel

Num 32:24 build cities for your children and walls for your sheep and do what came from your mouths."

Num 32:34 *and the sons of Gad built Dibon and Ataroth and Aroer*

Num 32:35 *and Ataroth Shophan and Jazer and Jogbehah*

Num 32:36a,(b?) *and Beth Nimrah and Beth Haran, (fortified cities and sheepfolds)*

Num 32:37 *and the sons of Reuben built Heshbon and Elealeh and Kiriathaim*

Num 32:38* *and Nebo and Baal Meon (the name has been changed) and Sibmah and they gave names to the cities which they built*

Num 32:39a *the sons of Machir, son of Manasseh, walked to Gilead and captured it*

Num 32:41 *and Jair, son of Manasseh, went and captured their villages and called them the villages of Jair* (הות יאיר)

Num 32:42 *and Nobah went and captured Kenath and its villages* (בנתיה) *and called them Nobah in his name*

Table 9: Post-Sihon updates to the Non-Priestly narrative

Cross, "Inscription;" Timm, *Moab*, 91n6. Knauf, "Heshbon," 135, for example, suggests that Og is an underworld figure related to the cult of the dead. This conclusion is supported by Og's giant bed (Deut 3:11) and his belonging to the last of the Rephaim (Josh 12:4), which connects to the mighty figure mentioned in KTU 1.108, who is said to have ruled in Ashteroth and Edrei, just like Og. This would suggest that the names of both Sihon and Og have their roots in foreign divine figures.

[204] On the Reuben/Gad issue in Num 32:1, see discussion in § 3.1.3 and further below.

Given that the Sihon narrative was initially designed to explain Numbers 32 through the lens of Deuteronomistic ideology, it follows that very little needed to change in Numbers 32 in response. That being said, there are non-Priestly materials that do not belong to the base layer of Numbers 32 and that cannot simply be attributed to a post-Sihon harmonisation.

The lists of cities in Num 32:34–38, which presume that the Reubenites and Gadites settled as far south as Dibon, are problematic as there appears to be no obvious catalyst for the expansion of Israel's territory into the plains of Moab. This list cannot be directly attributed to the Priestly scribes as the idea of building cities stands in conflict with the Priestly ideal that the Transjordan was granted only after the conquest of Cisjordan (cf. § 3.4). It was argued in § 3.2 that the original Sihon narrative in both Numbers and Deuteronomy understood Sihon to be a city-king who ruled a limited territory surrounding Heshbon. It does not follow, then, that the territory of Sihon, king of Heshbon, triggered the introduction of cities that clearly exceeded the boundaries of the pre-existing narrative(s). Both "the land of Jazer" (base layer of Numbers 32) and "Heshbon and all its villages" (base layer of the Sihon narrative) suggest the territory under discussion comprised the land north of the Mishor. Thus, the addition of the lists of cities in Num 32:34–38 requires another explanation.

The first possibility is that the Song of Heshbon was included during the process in which the base Sihon narrative was initially retrofitted into Numbers 21. This would mean that already in the original Sihon layer the claim that Israel took from Sihon the land "from Heshbon until Dibon" (Num 21:30). The issue with this proposal is that it is difficult to explain why the authors of Numbers clearly went to some efforts to preserve the major shape of the Deuteronomistic Sihon narrative (especially the idea of Sihon as a city-king) if they also chose to insert a poem that immediately contradicted key details. As already argued, it seems much more plausible to understand that the Song of Heshbon was added in response to the idea that Israel took "Moabite" territory rather than that it was the catalyst. In this way, the Song of Heshbon justified Israel's Moabite occupation in light of Israel's "international" relations with Moab (cf. Deut 2:9).

The second possibility relates back to the discussion of Num 32:1 undertaken in § 3.1.3, where several scholars argued that either the Reubenites or the Gadites were secondary to the original narrative. To very briefly recap, it was argued that Num 32:1a was phrased peculiarly, which suggested that the original narrative did not feature both tribes. This idea was somewhat reinforced by the observation that after Num 32:1 tribal names were no longer used in the non-Priestly base narrative; the Reubenites and Gadites were simply referred to by 3mp verbs and suffixes ("they said," "Moses said to them," etc.).

In historical terms, the Gadites lived in the vicinity of the Arnon, which largely matches to the list of Gadite cities in Num 32:34–36. As briefly discussed in § 3.1, the Mesha stele reports that "the men of Gad lived in the land of Ataroth

3.3 Post-Sihon, Non-Priestly Updates in Numbers 32   141

from ancient times" (COS 2.137) and Num 33:45–46 refers to the city of Dibon as Dibon-gad. Thus, it is hardly a stretch to understand Dibon, Ataroth, Aroer and Atroth-shophan listed as Gadite cities to be historically accurate. While the presence of the Gadites in biblical Transjordan narratives are undoubtedly fitting, Gadite territorial claims do not align with the historical development proposed above. The Gadite territory inferred from the Mesha stele contradicts the territory described in Num 32:1 and it also contradicts the reconstructed Sihon tradition, wherein Sihon is a city-king ruling in Heshbon. These difficulties point towards the conclusion that the Gadites were added secondarily, and that during the insertion of the tribe of Gad, the list of cities in Num 32:34–38 was also added.

To foreshadow the discussion in the following sections, this Gadite update introduced inconsistencies into the resulting narrative that resulted in a series of further updates, not least the depiction of Sihon as an Amorite king who ruled from the Arnon to the Jabbok (see § 3.5). The question is, then: What triggered this Gadite update?

The most plausible answer is that the Gadites were inserted as part of the creation of the ideological "pan-Israel," which is perhaps most prominent in the Jacob narrative.[205] Although the Jacob narrative is now broadly understood to have originally been separate Jacob-Laban and Jacob-Esau narratives, scholars such as Blum and Wöhrle have demonstrated that the extant Jacob narrative cannot simply be understood as the result of a mechanical joining of the two narratives, rather the resulting narrative reframes, corrects and alters the original intention of both narratives.[206] In light of this it is more meaningful to speak of

---

[205] GUNKEL, *Genesis*, 290, had already argued in 1901 that the Jacob narrative comprised four "sagas" that had been used by both J and E and then artfully interwoven into a narrative whole (JE). These sagas were a Jacob-Esau narrative, a Jacob-Laban narrative, a saga of cult places founded by Jacob and the narrative of Jacob's children (their birth and their later fates). Although Gunkel's allocation of the non-Priestly narrative to JE is no longer (broadly) accepted, the core insight that the Jacob narrative is a literary compilation of an originally standalone Northern Jacob-Laban narrative and a Southern Jacob-Esau narrative is still influential today. For an overview of scholarship on this see, e.g., NEUMANN, "Jacob," 36n4. Rather, in light of more recent research the Jacob narrative is increasingly being understood as an originally self-contained tradition of origins. See, e.g., SCHMID, "Theologies," 13, who argues, "The relative literary independence of the Jacob cycle is one of the most important insights of recent research on the Pentateuch, but there is another, often neglected element that is nearly as important: The Jacob cycle is not just one story among others, but a legend of Israel's origins." See also SCHMID, "Jakob," 48.

[206] BLUM, "Jacob," 182, notes that "We have reason, therefore, to speak not merely of a 'cycle of tales,' but of a major integrated story with themes of its own." WÖHRLE, "Koexistenz," 314, writes, "Die Verbindung und Erweiterung der älteren Jakob-Esau- und Jakob-Laban-Erzählungen zu einer übergreifenden Jakoberzählung ist daher nicht nur, wie zumeist angenommen, als ein Vorgang der Sammlung, Zusammenstellung und Ergänzung ältere Überlieferungen vorzustellen. Es zeigt sich hier vielmehr ein Prozess massiver Umarbeitung, ja, Korrektur ältere Überlieferungen." (*The joining and expansion of the older Jacob-Esau and Jacob-Laban*

142 *3. The Occupation of Transjordan*

the setting and background of the combined Jacob-Esau-Laban narrative, which, however, is much more difficult to determine.[207] As Hensel rightly emphasises, the concept of Israel also develops throughout the process of literary growth of the Jacob narrative.[208]

The key question is: When did the concept of Jacob being a common, founding ancestor appear in the tradition?

On the one hand, there are several indications that this idea was introduced in the late preexilic period and as such can still be attributed to a pre-Priestly conceptualisation. Wöhrle, for example, argues that the logic behind the positive depiction of Edom is related to the report in 2 Kgs 24:2, in which Nebuchadnezzar of Babylon sent Chaldeans, Arameans, Moabites and Ammonites against Judah, leaving the Edomites as the only non-participating neighbours.[209] The laws in Deuteronomy 23 also appear to reflect this same understanding wherein the Edomites are named as kin (vv. 7–8), while "Ammonites and Moabites shall not come into the assembly of YHWH" (v. 3). Frevel dates the historical kernel even earlier, arguing that the positive Jacob-Esau relationship reflects the Judah's south-western expansion made possible under Assyrian policy. More specifically the tense but overall positive relationship between Jacob and Esau touches upon the region in the southern Negev that was shared between Judahites

---

narratives into an overarching Jacob narrative is therefore not, like most assume, introduced only as the process of collecting, compiling and supplementing older traditions. Here it appears to be much more a process of massive reworking, or even a correction, of older traditions.)

[207] The combined nature of the Jacob narrative has caused many scholars difficulties in dating. If one focusses on the Jacob-Laban narrative, then one is led to the relationship between Israel and Aram, which SERGI, "Jacob," 299, dates to the regency of Jeroboam II, and argues that such a narrative functioned to show that Israel first achieved independence from Aram in the area of the Jabbok outlet and that this independence expanded across the Jordan to create a "new" unified people in the lower Gilead and the Canaanite hill country (Shechem and Bethel). (Cf. BLUM, "Jacob," 210, who highlights the positive view of the Aramean Laban as evidence against seeing the Jacob-Laban narrative as the product of Jeroboam II, who engaged in battle against Aram.) If one focusses on the Edom narrative, like NAʾAMAN, "Jacob," 104, then Jacob's fear of Esau is best explained in light of Edomite expansion into Judahite territory, which occurred after the fall of Jerusalem in the 6th century BCE. (SCHMID, "Jakob," 46–47, notes that the reference to "YHWH of Samaria" found on the pithoi of Kuntillet ʿAjrud, could point to the original Edom narrative also being of Northern origin.) If one focusses on the establishment of cultic sites like BLUM, "Jacob," 208, then the emphasis on Bethel points to a time before the fall of the Northern Kingdom in 722 BCE. Further confusion arises from the peculiar mention of Haran, the western capital of the Assyrian empire. FINKELSTEIN/RÖMER, "Comments," 322, suggest that this location was inserted into the narrative, "in order to demonstrate to the audience how to deal cleverly with the Assyrians, who are portrayed as ʿArameans.'" KNAUF, "Bethel," 320, on the other hand suggests that Jacob's finding a wife (or two) and employment in the city whose namesake was the deity, Sin of Harran, was intended to demonstrate that Yahwists could prosper and enjoy YHWH's blessing even if they had good relations with the Assyrians. (See also SCHMID, "Theologies," 26).

[208] HENSEL, "Edom," 59.

[209] WÖHRLE, "Koexistenz," 323.

and Edomites.[210] Furthermore, Frevel goes on to argue that the joining of the Jacob-Laban and Jacob-Esau stories created a common ancestor that aimed at a collective identification as early as the 7th century BCE.[211] The tribal names themselves also point towards the idea that the tribal-configuration was a Northern invention. Knauf and Guillaume persuasively point out that the name Benjamin means "sons of the south," which only makes sense if the reference point was the Ephraim/Manasseh region.[212] In a similar way, the Song of Deborah also conceives of various tribes (not the twelve sons of Jacob!) coming together for common cause. Importantly, the Song of Deborah does not mention the tribe of Gad, which further lends support to the theory of a later "Gadite update."[213]

On the other hand, most scholars regard the idea of the twelve named sons as an even later innovation, as the concept mainly appears in Priestly or even post-Priestly texts.[214] One key example in this regard is the spy narrative, where Deuteronomy mentions twelve spies, which likely represents "completeness" and has no reference to tribes.[215] Rather, it is only the Priestly spy narrative in Numbers that directly connects each spy to a corresponding tribe.

---

[210] FREVEL, "Jacob," 174.

[211] FREVEL, "Jacob," 177.

[212] KNAUF/GUILLAUME, History, 48.

[213] See, e.g., KNAUF, "Language," 169. OSWALD, Staatstheorie, 155, notes that older conceptions of Israel spoke of Israel and Judah as the "two/both houses of Israel" (Is 8:14) and the Song of Deborah depicts inter-tribal relations united by a common general (or perhaps even a common god) but not a common ancestor.

[214] TOBOLOWSKY, Sons, 80, writes, "Overall, then, it is very difficult to demonstrate the existence of a southern tradition of articulating Israelite identity in terms of the tribes of Israel in any early material connected with the south. When we add this to the difficulty of proving that the twelve-tribe concept existed in early northern material, or in material pre-dating the Priestly source generally, we get the conclusion offered here: that the Priestly author was the first to adapt an early, northern vision of the tribes to express Panisraelite identity." See also LEVIN, Fortsehreibungen, 111–123; WEINGART, "Jakob," 54–55; HENSEL, "Edom," 98–99. FISCHER, "Rahel," 179, sees the insertion of the tribes as increasing the importance of Judah and decreasing that of the North (Joseph). She writes, "Durch die Einfügung Leas als erste Hauptfrau Jakobs und ihres Sohnes Juda konstituieren die so bearbeiteten Jakobserzählungen eine genealogische Verbindung zwischen den Eponymen on Nord- und Südreich. Die Welt, die in den [Erzeltern-Erzählungen] erzeugt wird, ist damit ganz offenkundig jene, wie sie nach dem Untergang des Nordreichs 722 v.Chr. und nach dem Begraben aller Hoffnung auf Restauration durch den Beinahe-Untergang des Südreichs nach 700 entstanden ist: Es wird kein Nordreich und damit keine getrennten Reiche mehr geben. Israel-Juda ist zu einer einzigen Ethnie geworden." (By inserting Leah as the first wife of Jacob and her son Judah, the so-edited Jacob narratives constitute a genealogical link between the eponyms of the Northern and Southern kingdoms. The world that is produced in the patriarchal narratives is thus quite obviously the one that emerged after the fall of the Northern Kingdom in 722 BCE and after the burial of all hope of restoration by the near fall of the Southern Kingdom after 700: there will be no more Northern Kingdom and thus no more separate kingdoms. Israel-Judah becomes a single ethnic group.). The emphasis on Judah in the tribal birth order is also highlighted by NAʾAMAN, "Jacob," 109.

[215] See, e.g., FREVEL, "Jacob," 162–163, who suggests that Moses selects twelve spies to depict a symbolic "complete" contingent. This idea of completeness has parallels with Greek covenantal

144   *3. The Occupation of Transjordan*

In sum, the addition of the Gadites represents a complex problem that cannot be resolved satisfactorily at this stage. The arguments noted above supporting a late preexilic origin for the combined Jacob-Laban-Esau narrative could also sufficiently support the origins of the tribal conception of pan-Israel (even if these did not yet number twelve). Thus, it is at least *plausible* that the addition of the Gadites into the tribal organisation of Israel occurred at a pre-Priestly stage. That being said, it is probably safer to conclude that the twelve-tribe conception, and thus the addition of the tribe of Gad, only occurred after the development of the Priestly source. If this latter option is true, then it would suggest that the non-Priestly Exodus-Numbers-Deuteronomy-Joshua narrative was updated in light of this Priestly innovation. In any case, it remains clear that the addition of Gadites caused a drastic alteration to the Transjordan territory controlled by (narrative) Israel and so triggered a whole new series of updates and harmonisations as will be unfolded below.

3.3.1 Numbers 32:34–38

The cities listed in vv. 34–38 clearly presuppose that Israel took territory well below that suggested by "the land of Jazer" of Num 32:1, which bordered the "plains of Moab." Past scholarship's allocation of vv. 34–38 into the redactional history of the chapter has produced various results. Noth states, "to what stage in the literary history of the chapter [vv. 34–38] belongs cannot now be decided."[216] Other scholars (e.g., Schmidt, Wüst) alternatively allocate vv. 34–38 to the base layer of the narrative.[217] Although it is true that the list conforms to the non-Priestly narrative and contains no overtly Priestly lexemes, as discussed in the introduction to § 3.3 above, it follows that this list was only inserted after a pan-Israel ideology was applied to the Pentateuch.

This conclusion is based on two key observations. First, that "the land of Jazer and the land of Gilead" was deliberately worded to suggest that Israel did not take the plains of Moab and second that the Sihon narrative in its earliest form also did not understand Sihon to be an Amorite king who ruled from the Arnon to the Jabbok, rather that he ruled the area in the vicinity of Heshbon.

---

conceptions dating to the 7th and 6th centuries BCE. If there are parallels to be found in the Bible, then Deuteronomy might have borrowed the concept.

[216] Noth, *Numbers*, 239.

[217] Wüst, *Untersuchungen*, 96; Schmidt, *Numeri*, 196. Seebass, *Numeri 3*, 334–335 suggests vv. 34–38 belong to the base layer but that it also contains two later additions. Mittmann, *Deuteronomium*, 104, offers a more complex reconstruction wherein verse 1 only referred to the land of Jazer and a pre-edited vv. 34–38* list only the towns of Reuben.

3.3 Post-Sihon, Non-Priestly Updates in Numbers 32

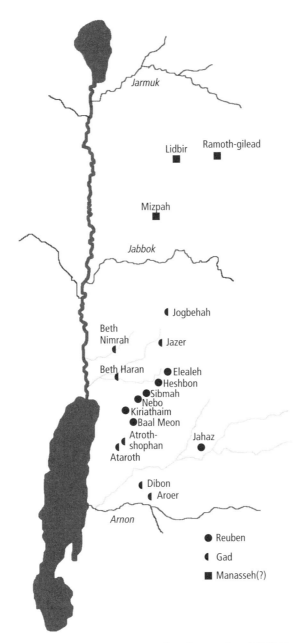

Figure 11: Num 32:34–42 – Territories of Reuben, Gad and Half-Manasseh[218]

---

[218] Map drawn by J. Davis. Besides the toponyms detailed in figure 7. Ramoth-gilead is located at er-Ramtha (2470.2120), see FINKELSTEIN et al., "Tell er-Rumeith;" FREVEL, *Geschichte*, 447;

146   *3. The Occupation of Transjordan*

One of the most peculiar features of vv. 34–38 is the precise allocation of territory between the tribes of Reuben and Gad. As figure 12 demonstrates, the territory of the Reubenites appears to be enclosed by the Gadite territory in a loosely concentric (crescent-moon) arrangement. Joshua 13 on the other hand has a much more logical distribution of territory with the Reubenites being allocated all the southern cities of central Transjordan and the Gadites the northern cities.[219] Against expectation, Heshbon does not occupy the central position of the Reubenites' territory, rather it lies near the northernmost point. This detail in particular suggests that the list of cities was not invented to support the Sihon narrative, rather that it was (at least in part) a pre-existing list that was later added into the text of Numbers 32. Despite this, the presence of the word בנה (*to build*) only really makes sense as a harmonisation with Num 32:16, 24 (pre-Sihon layer) wherein the Reubenites and Gadites promise to בנה sheep pens for their livestock and cities for their children. Thus, it does not follow that vv. 34–38 were simply "pasted" into position without being adapted to the present context.

The inclusion of Dibon is interesting because it is unlikely that it ever belonged to Israel in historical terms. In fact, Dibon appears to have been the hometown of Mesha and functioned as the launching point for his campaign against the Omrides.[220] Dibon (modern-day Tell Ḏībān) lies south of the Wadi Wala/Wadi eth-Themed, which Dearman argues functioned as the southern Omride border,

---

Lidbir is located at Tel el-Ḥiṣn (2330.2102), see FINKELSTEIN et al., "Gilead," 144; FREVEL, *Geschichte*, 447; Mizpah is located at Tell el-Maṣfā (2270.1930), see LEMAIRE, "Galaad," 44; FINKELSTEIN et al., "Gilead," 142; Jogbehah is located at el-Ǧubēha (2319.1594), see MACDONALD, *East*, 119–120; GASS, *Ortsnamen*, 674; Nimrah/Beth Nimrah is located at Tell Nimrîn (2098.1452), see GLUECK, "Towns," 11; MACDONALD, *East*, 114; GASS, *Moabiter*, 184; Beth Haran is located at Tell Iktanû (2135.1363), see GLUECK, "Towns," 20–23; MACDONALD, *East*, 120–122; Elealeh is located at Khirbet el-ʿĀl (2285.1365), see MACDONALD, *East*, 115–116; GASS, *Moabiter*, 186; Sebam/Sibmah is located at KhirbetʿUyūn Mūsā (2202.1318), see MACDONALD, *East*, 116–117; GASS, *Moabiter*, 188; FREVEL, *Geschichte*, 448; Kiriathaim is located at Khirbet el-Qurēye (2160.1242), see GASS, *Moabiter*, 187; FREVEL, *Geschichte*, 447 (cf. MACDONALD, *East*, 122–123); Beon/Baal Meon is located at Khirbet Māʿīn (2197.1207), see GASS, *Moabiter*, 186; FREVEL, *Geschichte*, 445 (cf. MACDONALD, *East*, 117–118); Atroth-shophan is located at Rujm ʿAṭārūs (~2150.1150), see MACDONALD, *East*, 118–119; JERICKE, "Atroth-Shophan;" JI, "Tale," 213; Ataroth is located at KhirbetʿAṭārūs (2132.1094), see MACDONALD, *East*, 112–114; FINKELSTEIN/LIPSCHITS, "Architecture," 29–32; FREVEL, *Geschichte*, 446; Aroer is located at KhirbetʿArāʾir (2281.0981), see GASS, *Moabiter*, 185; FREVEL, *Geschichte*, 444 (cf. MACDONALD, *East*, 166–167); Dibon is located at Ḏībān (2240.1010), see MACDONALD, *East*, 84; GASS, *Moabiter*, 186; FREVEL, *Geschichte*, 445. Two key cities of Og are not named in Numbers 32, but appear in Deuteronomy and Joshua: Ashtaroth is located at Tell ʿAštara (2455.2460), see MACDONALD, *East*, 152; FREVEL, *Geschichte*, 445; Edrei is located at Darʿā (2537.2246), see MACDONALD, *East*, 108; FREVEL, *Geschichte*, 445.

[219] For comparative maps see esp. HOBSON, "Israelites," 42–43.

[220] This is of course assuming that Dibon here refers to a city and not to a geographical area, as there is some debate whether Mesha's home city should better be understood to be Karchoh/Qarḥo, mentioned in the Mesha Stele. So, e. g., FREVEL, *Geschichte*, 122. SMELIK, "Inscriptions," 137n5, alternatively suggests that Karchoh is possibly a new quarter of the city of Dibon.

3.3 Post-Sihon, Non-Priestly Updates in Numbers 32   147

meaning that even during the period in which Israel had penetrated furthest south of central Transjordan, Dibon was still outside of Israelite territory.[221] Within the Bible, Isaiah 15 and Jeremiah 48 attest Moabite control over Dibon. If Dibon was never historically Israelite, why was it included in the tradition of Numbers 32? Two main options present themselves. The first is that the reference to Dibon was contained in the original taunt song that was the source for the Song of Heshbon (Num 21:27–30). Accordingly, the source text reported a victory over Moab, "from Heshbon until Dibon," which was carried over and so dictated that Dibon must be included in the list of cities taken. The problem with this is that the rest of the Song of Heshbon has so clearly been modified to fit its present context that it is purely on the basis of convenience to suppose that this precise detail was original. The second option is that the historical memory of the Gadites, however it was sourced, knew that the traditional territory of the tribe of Gad extended further south than the Omrides were able to penetrate. As already noted above, there are reasons to suspect that Mesha himself was a Gadite.[222] This solution obviously has difficulty in explaining how these historical details were sourced, but at least it makes good sense of the toponyms.

A further point of curiosity is the absence of Jahaz. In the reconstruction of the Sihon tradition performed above, it was suggested that both Numbers and Deuteronomy contained the detail that Sihon met Israel in battle at Jahaz. Historically speaking, Jahaz was an appropriate site for a battle as it functioned as the western Omride border fortress.[223] Mesha himself attests to the fact that Omri built both Ataroth and Jahaz and claims to have captured both.[224] The presence of Ataroth in the list of cities only further underscores the absence of Jahaz (which, however, appears as part of Reuben's inheritance in Josh 13:18). This absence can be explained on inner-biblical grounds.

When the Sihon narrative was inserted into Numbers 21 it included the report that Israel and Sihon battled at Jahaz. As was argued in § 3.1.2 above, in order for the logic of the Sihon narrative to function it was also important that Israel was not already inside Amorite territory when Moses requested passage through. Thus, due to Sihon's coming out to Jahaz to meet Israel, Jahaz was implicitly depicted to be outside of Sihon's territory. This understanding was further emphasised in Num 21:23 via the editorial insert, המדברה (*towards the wilderness*), which further highlighted that Jahaz was situated "in the wilderness"

---

[221] Dearman, "Cities." Daviau, "Border," similarly argues that a difference in Iron Age pottery can be discerned above and below the Wadi eth-Themed, which she argues helps to distinguish between Moabite and Ammonite styles. The presence of Dibon in the list further underscores that one cannot fall back on the idea of "historical memories" to explain the tradition of Numbers 32, as argued by Finkelstein/Römer, "Memories."

[222] Cf. Note 21 on page 89.

[223] See discussion in Finkelstein/Lipschits, "Architecture."

[224] For details on the Mesha stele see note 74 on page 101.

(cf. Deut 2:32 and Num 21:23). This information does not, of itself, suggest that Israel could not occupy Jahaz. Rather its exclusion only makes sense in light of the Deuteronomistic idea of ירש (*possess/dispossess*)(see discussion in § 3.2.1). If Jahaz lay outside of Sihon's territory it could not rightfully be claimed by right of conquest. Thus, the exclusion of Jahaz appears to be informed by Deuteronomistic ideals.

As it stands, the key to understanding Reuben's territory is that it spans the Madaba Plain, with Heshbon situated in the north, Nebo the west, and Baal-Meon the south. The Gadites, in contrast, occupy the remainder of the area of central Transjordan, from the Arnon to the Jabbok.[225] As already argued, the southern Gadite cities at least have historical support from the Mesha Stele and most likely reflect the historical Gadite origins. Numbers 33:45–46 in particular hints in this direction with the naming of Dibon as Dibon-gad.[226]

Although Num 32:3 contains many of the same details as vv. 34–38, it follows that these derive from different hands. This is supported by the fact that several toponyms are rendered differently (Nimrah vs Beth Nimrah, Beon vs Baal Meon, Sebam vs Sibmah). Judging purely on the names alone, the list in v. 3 gives the impression of conforming to a later naming convention, one in which theologically problematic toponyms were censored (Beon vs. Baal Meon). As such, it will be argued that v. 3 is better understood as a late harmonisation designed to better incorporate the Priestly narrative into the non-Priestly narrative (see § 3.6.1).

Although a number of details remain unclear, the observation that the list in vv. 34–38 was not specifically designed to harmonise with the Sihon narrative is significant. It suggests that the impetus behind adding these details was not the Sihon event but something else. This something else, it was suggested, was the inclusion of the Gadites as part of a pan-Israel update to the post-Deuteronomistic, non-Priestly traditions.

3.3.2 Numbers 32:39–42* and the Half-Tribe of Manasseh

Although the Sihon narrative solved the political and theological issues from the Judean perspective as well as the inner-biblical issues pertaining to Israel's relationship to Ammon and Moab, at the same time it created new issues that were not present in the original narrative beginning in Num 32:1. Namely, by limiting the Reubenites' and Gadites' territory to Sihon's territory, Israelite Transjordan was confined below the Jabbok. This caused continuity issues with the

---

[225] This does not directly contradict e.g., SCHORN, *Ruben*, 153, who notes, "die Annahme liegt also nahe, daß redaktionelle Vorgänge für die ungewöhnliche Gebietsbeschreibung in v. 34–38 verantwortlich zu machen sind." (*The assumption is therefore obvious that editorial processes are responsible for the unusual territorial description in v. 34–38*).

[226] DEARMAN, "Cities," 276 (emphasis original). See also WÜST, *Untersuchungen*, 142–144.

3.3 Post-Sihon, Non-Priestly Updates in Numbers 32 149

base layer of Numbers 32, wherein "the land of Gilead" was no longer occupied by the Reubenites and Gadites. Not to mention the (synchronically) later biblical traditions that depict Israel dwelling in northern Transjordan.[227] In the extant biblical tradition, this northern Transjordan territory was occupied by Og of Bashan, and Israel's victory over this king explains its incorporation into Israel's territory. However, as will be demonstrated, there are good reasons to suspect that Num 32:39–42 predate the Og narrative.

The secondary character of Num 32:39–42 within the narrative context of chapter 32 is clear, not only due to the sudden addition of the half-tribe of Manasseh into a narrative that had thus far pertained only to the tribes of Reuben and Gad (ignoring v. 33), but also because the description of the territory is conspicuously different to that given in vv. 34–38. Where vv. 34–38 systematically describe the cities בנה (*built*) by the Reubenites and Gadites, vv. 39–42* speak of the various descendants of Manasseh לקד (*capturing*) their territory independently from the larger Israelite force. The language of לקד by the Manassites suggests that the Og narrative did not yet exist and rather suggests that Num 32:39–42* were originally intended to fulfil the same function as the Og narrative, in that they provide a narrative explanation for how Israel acquired the territory in northern Transjordan once the Sihon narrative limited the Reubenites' and Gadites' territory to central Transjordan. This is further corroborated by the fact that none of the markers of the Og narrative (Og, Bashan, Ashtaroth, Edrei, Salecah), which are explicitly mentioned in Deuteronomy and Joshua are present in Num 32:39–42.[228] Additionally, Num 32:39–42* differ from the Og narrative ideologically, as one of the main ideas promoted by the Og narrative is that the entire army of Israel travelled together to claim the territory of northern Transjordan and Bashan as part of the Deuteronomistic ירש (*possessing/dispossessing* – see discussion in § 3.2.1). A further inconsistency between vv. 39–42* and the preceding narrative is that Num 32:6 suggests that the idea of acting in the interest of one's own tribe at the expense of the wider community was looked down upon, yet half-Manasseh's actions are made without comment. Furthermore, not only did the Reubenites and Gadites immediately pledge to support their fellow Israelites in the conquest of Cisjordan (Num 32:16–17) but they also gave up their claim to any inheritance in Cisjordan (Num 32:19). Manasseh on the other hand appears to be under no such restrictions; first it acts

---

[227] ACHENBACH, *Vollendung*, 379, insightfully notes that one of the goals of the conquest-related updates to the book of Numbers was to ensure that all the territory of Israel was allocated, or organized, by Moses.

[228] Og is mentioned as king of Bashan in Num 21:33; 32:33*; Deut 1:4; 3:1, 3, 4, 10, 11, 13; 4:47; 29:7; 31:4; Josh 2:10; 9:10; 12:4; 13:12, 30, 31. Cities named as belonging to Og include Ashtaroth in Deut 1:4; 9:10 Josh 12:4; 13:12, 31; Edrei in Num 21:33; Deut 1:4; 3:1, 10; Salecah in Deut 3:10; Josh 12:5; 13:11.

150   *3. The Occupation of Transjordan*

independently from the wider Israelite community and second it settles in both Cis- and Transjordan with nary a word said on the subject.

Although vv. 39–42* appear to describe a series of separate mini-conquests, the logic of these verses better follows a two-tier system. In v. 39 it is told that the sons of Machir travelled to Gilead (without the definite article) and לקד (*captured*) it.[229] Although the verb לקד is almost always used in reference to the taking of cities rather than regions,[230] the reference to Gilead here is better understood as connecting to Num 32:1, explaining that northern Transjordan was still taken by the Israelites despite the Reubenites and Gadites only receiving central Transjordan. This is supported by the fact that the city of Gilead is located in central Transjordan (see figure 12), which contradicts the otherwise clear idea that half-Manasseh occupied northern Transjordan (cf. Deut 3:16 and Josh 13:30–31). Furthermore, the characters of Nobah and Jair are better understood as descendants of Machir rather than brothers, this is primarily supported by the genealogy in Num 26:29, which includes the detail that Machir הוליד (*begat*) Gilead, which in the biblical practice of blending genealogy and geography, means that the region of Gilead belonged to the Machirites.[231] Numbers 26:29–32 is worded in such a way that Machir is the sole son of Manasseh and Gilead the sole son of Machir.[232] But this is problematic as it makes the half-tribe division illogical. If Machir was the only son of Manasseh and was granted the Gilead by Moses, then who precisely belonged to the other half of the tribe of Manasseh that received their inheritance in Cisjordan? Joshua 17 appears to correct Numbers 26 in making Machir the firstborn son, who was granted the Transjordan allotment with his son Gilead; the Cisjordan allotment was then granted לבני מנשה הנותרים (*to the remaining sons of Manasseh*), i.e., Abiezer, Helek, Asriel, Shechem, Hepher and Shemida, who in Num 26:30–32 are listed as sons of Gilead (cf. § 4.4). Assuming that Machir is the patriarch, it is only logical that Jair and Nobah are descendants of Machir.

The Machirite/Gileadite connection immediately runs into problems when other biblical traditions, particularly those in the book of Judges, are involved.

---

[229] For a fuller discussion on Machir in Transjordan, see Seebass, "Machir."

[230] לכד (*to capture*) is used in reference to taking towns in Deut 2:34, 35; 3:4; Josh 6:20; 8:19, 21; 10:1, 28, 32, 35, 37, 39; 11:10; 15:16, 17; 19:47. The only potential case where לכד might refer to a region is found in Josh 10:42, but it is certainly not explicit.

[231] On the idea that genealogy and geography intersect in the Bible, see especially Wright, "Remapping."

[232] The typical genealogical formula in Numbers 26 is, e.g.,: בני בנימן למשפחתם לבלע מופ־ חת הבלעי לאשבל משפחת האשבלי (*The sons of Benjamin to their clans: To Bela the clan of the Belaites; to Ashbel, the clan of the Ashbelites …*). However, the tribe of Manasseh does not conform to this typical formula, instead Num 26:29 states: בני מנשה למשפחתם למכיר מופחת המכירי ומכיר הוליד את־גלעד לגלעד משפחת הגלעדי (*The sons of Manasseh to their clans: To Machir the clan of the Machirites, and Machir begat Gilead; to Gilead, the clan of the Gileadites …*). This deviation from the typical formula has led scholars to suggest that it is a scribal gloss, see e.g., Noth, *Numbers*, 206–207; Wüst, *Untersuchungen*, 64.

3.3 Post-Sihon, Non-Priestly Updates in Numbers 32   151

The Song of Deborah in Judges 5 suggests that Machir and Gilead are two separate tribes.[233] In Judg 5:14, Machir is listed alongside those other tribes who heeded the call for battle, whilst Gilead appears in Judg 5:17 in the list of tribes who failed to join. Knauf argues that the praised tribes are ordered geographically from south to north, which would imply that Machir stands in place of Manasseh (the marching sequence is ordered Benjamin, Ephraim then Machir; Manasseh is unmentioned, as is Judah).[234] In contrast, Gilead is said to have "remained undisturbed (שׁכן) beyond the Jordan," which demonstrates it was conceived to be a Transjordan tribe. From this he concludes, "from the geographical point of view Judges 5 represents pre-Omride Israel."[235] But such a solution requires a considerable period of oral transmission. Boling's solution to this problem is to suggest that Machir was a Cisjordan tribe that was granted jurisdiction of the district of Gilead (reflected in the tradition in Deut 3:15), and that this resulted in Machir being the "father of Gilead."[236] Lemaire argues against using the Song of Deborah as a reliable source,[237] instead he argues that Machir represents a separate Transjordan territory to Gilead.[238] More specifically Lemaire argues, based on 2 Sam 9:4, 5; 17:27, that Machir was originally connected with Lo-Debar and so occupied the south-western portion of northern Transjordan: "Bien plus, le contexte des deux autres territoires mentionnes en 2 S. xvii 27, Ammon et Galaad, invite a situer plus precisement Makir a l'ouest ou au sud-ouest de Mahanayim (Tulul ed-Dahab) puisque Galaad en occupe le nord et Ammon l'est et le sud-est" (*Much more, the context of the two other territories mentioned in 2 S. xvii 27, Ammon and Gilead, invites to locate Machir more precisely in the west or south-west of Mahanaim [Tulul ed-Dahab] since Gilead occupies the north and Ammon the east and south-east).[239]

---

[233] KNAUF, *Data*, 359, concludes that the song "was first committed to writing at the Omride court (875–850), and not composed before the emergence in the 10th century of 'Israel' according to Judges 5…" See also GUILLAUME, *Waiting*, 31–33. Cf. FROLOV, *Judges*, 137 f., and especially FROLOV, "Old," who argues that the song is "roughly contemporaneous with Dtr and broadly compatible with the Deuteronomic/Deuteronomistic worldview and agenda" (p. 184).

[234] KNAUF, *Data*, 679. SNAITH, "Daughters," 126, is certainly incorrect in suggesting that Manasseh, as a whole, was originally a Transjordan tribe. Machir and Gilead aside, the names of the other children of Manasseh all correspond to Cisjordan cities or territories.

[235] KNAUF, *Data*, 679.

[236] BOLING, *Joshua*, 347.

[237] LEMAIRE, "Galaad," 47–48, writes, "En fait, les noms geographiques mentionnes dans le cantique de Deborah ne suivent pas un ordre geographique tres strict" (*In fact, the geographic names mentioned in the Song of Deborah do not follow a very strict geographic order*).

[238] LEMAIRE, "Galaad," 47, who notes, "Une migration de Makir de la Cisjordanie vers la Transjordanie est une pure conjecture car nous n'en avons aucune trace dans les textes" (*A migration of Machir from Cisjordan to Transjordan is pure conjecture because we have no trace of it in the texts*).

[239] LEMAIRE, "Galaad," 50. Cf. FINKELSTEIN, "Gilead," 143–145.

152   3. The Occupation of Transjordan

If Lemaire's reconstruction is correct, then this has a certain nearness to the Jacob-Laban narrative. In Gen 31:48 Laban and Jacob make a covenant at a location called both גלעד (*Galeed* – NRSV. *Gilead*?) and מצפה (*Mizpah*). This Mizpah – not to be confused with the Mizpah (Tell en-Nasbeh) in Benjaminite territory – also marks a border in the story of Jephthah; according to Judg 10:17 the Ammonite army camps in Gilead and the Israelite army camps at Mizpah.[240] Following this Jacob meets the angels/messengers of Elohim and calls that place Mahanaim (Gen 32:2). Jacob's next stop, after the interruption of the meeting with Esau, is פניאל (Peniel; Penuel?), where he wrestles and receives the name "Israel" (Gen 32:30). Jacob's itinerary takes him next to Succoth and finally to Shechem in Cisjordan. It is possible, then, that the Jacob-Laban itinerary approximates the borders of Machir, and that it was only after the defeat of the Arameans under the Nimshides that the territory north of Machir, i.e., the original Gilead, came under Israelite control. In this way it is possible that when Moses states in Deut 3:15 "to Machir I gave the Gilead," it reflects the historical expansion of the "Israelite" inhabitants of the south-western area of northern Transjordan further north.

Numbers 32:41–42, then, can logically be understood as extrapolating who the sons of Machir, mentioned in v. 39, are. Thus, the land acquired by Jair and Nobah is to be understood as providing a more precise definition to the more general notice in v. 39. Jair, son of Manasseh, went and captured הותים (*their villages*), and named them Havvoth-Jair, and Nobah took Kenath and its villages.

The reticence of information in vv. 41–42 is peculiar. If Num 32:41 was the only information regarding Jair in the Hebrew Bible, then it would be all but impossible to determine where Havvoth-Jair was located. In light of this it must be assumed that either v. 41 was drawn from a more detailed account that is now lost, or else the reader is expected to be familiar with these characters (e.g., from Deut 3:14).[241] Nobah and his city of Kenath are all but unique in the Hebrew Bible. 1 Chronicles 2:23 mentions Havvoth-Jair and Kenath together, however this verse is most likely dependent upon Numbers 32 rather than other way around.

Verse 40, on the other hand, largely matches Deut 3:15 and contains the information that Moses נתן (*gave*) Gilead to Machir. The notion of Moses giving territory makes better sense as a later harmonisation that reduces the problems with half-Manasseh capturing territory independently of the wider Israelite army.

Although these verses remain somewhat vague, it can more securely be suggested that they demonstrate no awareness of the Og narrative. Not only does Og

---

[240] Interestingly Jacob swears by the "Fear of his father Isaac," where the word for fear is פחד, which LEMAIRE, *pahad*, sees as the origins of צלפחד (*Zelophehad*), a name that most likely means "protection from fear" or "under the shade of פחד" (cf. chapter 4), which could point to the Machirite origins of Zelophehad. See further discussion of the name Zelophehad in, e.g., SEEBASS, *Numeri 3*, 154–155; BECHMANN, "Zelofhad;" COCCO, *Women*, 128.

[241] Joshua 13:30 also clarifies that the villages of Jair are in Bashan.

and his territory go unmentioned, but the underlying premise of half-Manasseh acting by itself stands in conflict with the wider Sihon+Og tradition. Thus, it follows that vv. 39*, 41–42 were added prior to the invention of Og of Bashan. Given the idea of a pan-Israel insertion for vv. 34–38 argued above, the addition of the half-tribe of Manasseh in these few verses would logically fit into this same update.

3.3.3 Summary of the Non-Priestly, Post-Sihon Changes

To briefly summarise the findings of this section. Although the Sihon narrative undoubtedly redirected and reshaped the Transjordan traditions, the core details of Numbers 32 did not need to be updated because Sihon was originally depicted as a city-king of Heshbon, so that the taking of his territory conformed to the law for cities "very far from you" (Deut 20:10–15).

However, Numbers 32 was updated with lists of cities that far exceeded the territory described in Num 32:1 and also clashed with the depiction of Sihon as a city king. Given that the Sihon narrative itself contained no obvious catalyst for this addition, it was suggested that the idea of the twelve tribes was a plausible driver for an update to Numbers 32. First, a list of cities was added wherein the tribe of Gad was depicted as settling alongside the tribe of Reuben in central Transjordan (vv. 34–38). Second, the now unaccounted for northern Transjordan was shown to be captured by Manassites, who could plausibly be a nod to the originally Nimshide occupation of that region.

3.4 Transjordan and the Priestly Material

Having delimited the first expansion of the non-Priestly base narrative via the addition of the Sihon narrative and the updates to Numbers 32 in vv. 34–42*, a large number of verses remain unaccounted for. Many of these remaining verses can be demonstrated to have a clear Priestly influence. Furthermore, as the following analysis will argue, these verses – taken as a whole – give the impression of functioning as an alternative account of the Reubenites' and Gadites' negotiation with Moses, rather than a further supplement of the non-Priestly base layer. As such, the following section will argue that the Priestly material of Numbers 32, although not stemming from Pg, belongs to an originally stand-alone Priestly version of Numbers 32.[242]

---

[242] This section is a slightly altered reproduction of the argument in Davis, "Redaction."

3.4.1 Canaan and the Priestly Ideology of Land

It is curious to note that the word כנען does not actually appear that often in the books of Exodus–Joshua. In fact the term appears more in Genesis than the rest of the Hexateuch combined: forty-six times in Genesis, three in Exodus, three in Leviticus, twelve in Numbers, once in Deuteronomy, and eight in Joshua.[243] Although there is discussion regarding certain non-Priestly attestations in Genesis, the phrase "the land of Canaan" is characteristically a Priestly term.[244] This is particularly clear in the book of Deuteronomy, where the single mention of Canaan belongs to the Priestly-styled, death of Moses insertion (Deut 32:48–52).[245] In Deut 32:49, Yнwн allows Moses to view the "land of Canaan, which I am giving to the children of Israel as a possession (אחזה)." Elsewhere Deuteronomy refers simply to הארץ (*the land*), with various qualifiers, e. g., בארץ אשר תירשון (*in the land which you shall possess* – Deut 5:33).

The idea that the land of Canaan is Israel's אחזה has important theological connotations. Bauks argues that מורשה and אחזה are Priestly terms that belong to the land conception, common in the ancient Near East, whereby a person could not own land; rather, land was granted, or gifted, by the deity or king for use by their subjects.[246] Guillaume describes the logic of this system as follows: "private property was recognized for livestock, tents, personal equipment, gardens, terraces and homes. However arable land was not privatized ... Each village shared out the arable land it controlled between its families in proportion to the number of male members or of ploughing teams."[247] This theological view of the land, as belonging solely to God, arguably finds its greatest expression in Lev 25:23:[248] "the land shall not be sold irrevocably, because the land is mine, because you are

---

[243] Admittedly Genesis features the son of Noah named Canaan, so not all occurrences refer to the land.

[244] CARR, *Formation*, 135, notes, "The 'land of Canaan,' though occurring in a number of P contexts (e. g., Gen 13:12; 16:3; 17:8; 23:2; etc.), also occurs in contexts with no clear relation to P (e. g., Gen 42:5, 7, 13, 32; 44:8; 45:25)." See also ZOBEL, כְּנַעַן, 7:216–217.

[245] A more extensive review cannot be performed here. To name only a few key positions: NELSON, *Deuteronomy*, 378, for example, argues that Deut 32:48–52 was designed to, "resume the narrative of the Tetrateuch after the 'interruption' of Deuteronomy." ALBERTZ, "Numeri I;" ALBERTZ, "Numeri II," argues that Deut 32:48–52 belong to the post-Holiness Code, Priestly redactor PB3.

[246] BAUKS, "Begriffe."

[247] GUILLAUME, *Land*, 109.

[248] For this reason GUILLAUME, *Land*, 109–117, argues, against the scholarly consensus that parts of Leviticus 23 and 25 (including Lev 25:23) belong to Pg. BAUKS, "Begriffe," 185, does not go as far, but similarly states, "... die Pg-Ausgaben zur göttlichen Landgabe auf einer theologischen Linie mit Lev 25 liegen und dessen Spitzensätze inhaltlich vorbereiten" (*The Pg depictions of the divine grant of land are in theological alignment with Lev 25, and prepare the content of its key sentences*).

גרים (*legal foreigners*) and תושבים (*residents*)."[249] Although this idea was common throughout the ancient Near East, Köckert argues that for the Priestly understanding it was further inspired by the tent of meeting as God's chosen place of residence upon the earth (e.g., Exod 25:8). He argues:

> das Land Kanaan ist der einzige Bereich auf Erden, in dem unter allen Volkern allein Israel, als Gottesvolk um das Heiligtum geschart, der Gegenwart des Weltschöpfers gewürdigt wird. Eine ausdrückliche 'Landgabe' zeichnet deshalb nur Israel aus. (*the land of Canaan is the single area upon the earth, in which, from all people, Israel alone, as God's people gathered about the sanctuary, are honoured by the presence of the creator of the world. An explicit "gift of land" is awarded only to Israel*).[250]

A detailed survey of the Canaan passages in Genesis goes beyond the scope of the present work; however, the Canaan passages of Genesis are of immense importance for the overall understanding of Priestly ideology and especially their relation to the conquest of Canaan and Transjordan. Although Abram's journey towards Canaan technically begins in the Priestly Terah passages (Gen 11:31–32), Abram's connection with Canaan is also a key feature in the non-Pg introduction to the Abram narrative (i.e., Gen 12:1, 7). That being said, it is Pg who introduces the idea that Canaan was given to Abram/Abraham and his descendants as an אחזה עולם (*a possession forever*), which was ratified via a covenant (Gen 17:8).[251] Several points are worth noting: first, even in the covenant formula Canaan is labelled as the "land of Abram's sojourning," which signifies that he is not the sole occupant of the land (see more below). Second and relatedly,

---

[249] This translation of גר and תושב was inspired primarily by ACHENBACH, "gêr," 46–48. See also KELLERMANN, גור; ALBERTZ, "Aliens."

[250] KÖCKERT, "Land," 154. See also BLUM, *Studien*, 293–301; SCHMID, "Ecumenicity," 26.

[251] On the allocation of these texts to non-Pg and Pg respectively, see summaries in JENSON, *Holiness*, 222 and GUILLAUME, *Land*, 194, who collectively overview the positions of Martin Noth, Karl Elliger, Norbert Lohfink, Peter Weimar, Karl Holzinger, Thomas Pola, and Philippe Guillaume. A full discussion of Gen 17:8 is beyond the present scope, but its different character is not insignificant. In a departure from the normal view of Canaan, the land is here described as כל־ארץ כנען (*all the land of Canaan*) rather than the more typical ארץ כנען, which has led some scholars to see the Abrahamic covenant, including the land, to apply to all of Abraham's descendants. DE PURY, "Pg," 118, for example, argues, "these nations (among them foremost the Ishmaelites and the Edomites) share with the Israelites the right to live in Canaan as well as the connubium, i.e., the right to marry each other's daughters (Gen 28,8–9), they practice circumcision and venerate God under the name of 'El Shadday." (For issues regarding the connubium and circumcision see discussion in BRETT, "Dissemination"). Against this view, WÖHRLE, *Fremdlinge*, 202–207, argues that the ecumenical outlook of Gen 17:8, regarding Abraham's "other seed/s," must be seen in light of other Priestly passages, esp. Gen 13:6 and 36:7, where Canaan is demonstrated to be too small for all Abraham's offspring, such that both Lot and Esau willingly dwell in their own respective lands (see also BRETT, "Dissemination," 95–96). Thus, even Gen 17:8 can be understood to present Canaan as the exclusive אחזה of Israel, even if Abraham's other offspring do share a number of other benefits of the Abraham covenant. An alternative option is suggested by HUTZLI, *Origins*, 168–171, who argues that Gen 17:8 provides evidence for a "proto-Priestly Abraham narrative."

at no stage is Abram/Abraham commanded to drive out the Canaanites before him in order to receive his אחזה. Instead of violence, Abraham's offspring are simply discouraged from marrying the Canaanites (see, e. g., Gen 28:1).[252] Third, the land of Canaan is shown to be separated from the neighbouring regions not via the idea that it was the land conquered by Abraham and his descendants but rather via peaceful, kinship-based relations: Lot (Moabites/Ammonites) is the nephew of Abram/Abraham, Ishmael (proto-Nabateans) is the half-brother of Isaac and Esau (Edomites/Idumeans) is the brother of Jacob. According to Gen 13:6, 11b, 12*, because their belongings were too great, the land was not able to support both Lot and Abram, and therefore the former moved to Transjordan.[253] In a similar way, the Jacob/Esau narrative also emphasises that Canaan could not support both brothers, and so "Esau settled in the hill country of Seir ..." (Gen 36:8). The idea that YHWH made a place for everybody, eschewing any need for violence is typically linked to the so-called ecumenical ideology of P.[254] Yet this still raises the question of why Abraham was promised Canaan while the Canaanites were not relocated as Lot and Esau were. Wöhrle insightfully argues that the patriarchal narratives of Pg must be seen from the perspective of the exilic community, who saw themselves as "true Israel" and like Abram were leaving their home and relocating to the land of Canaan.[255] Seen in this light, the Canaanites in the patriarchal narratives become a cipher for those "Israelites" who remained in the land through the exilic period (see, e. g., 2 Kgs 24:14).[256] The significance of this observation cannot be overstated, as the concept of conquest does not appear to fit within the ideology of Pg.

Apart from the song of Moses in Exod 15:15 – which Albertz suggests is a post-Priestly text in non-Priestly style – the remaining five references to Canaan in Exodus and Leviticus belong to Priestly texts (be that Pg or later strata).[257] In each of these five cases, the land of Canaan is equated with the land being given to Israel:

---

[252] WÖHRLE, *Fremdlinge*, 190.

[253] See, e. g., GUILLAUME, *Land*, 193, for these passages belonging to Pg.

[254] See e. g., SCHMID, "Ecumenicity;" KNAUF, *Data*, 666.

[255] See esp. WÖHRLE, *Fremdlinge*, 169–176.

[256] WÖHRLE, *Fremdlinge*, 222: "Nach den priesterlichen Passagen leben die Väter und die im Lande wohnende Bevölkerung somit in friedlicher Koexistenz. Die Väter und die fremde Vorbevölkerung sind einander nicht wie die Väter und deren Nachbarn verwandschaftlich verbunden aber sie wohnen doch friedlich getrennt nebeneinander" (*After the Priestly passages, the patriarchs and the people living in the land thus live in peaceful coexistence. The patriarchs and the pre-existing, foreign population are not related to each other like the patriarchs and their neighbors, but they nevertheless live peacefully separate from each other*).

[257] According to the summaries in JENSON, *Holiness*, 222 and GUILLAUME, *Land*, 194. ALBERTZ, *Exodus, Band I*, allocates Exod 15:15 to the Hexateuch redactor (p. 228) and Exod 16:35b to the post-Holiness Code editor, PB3 (p. 259).

3.4 Transjordan and the Priestly Material   157

1. Exod 6:4 – I also established my covenant with them [i.e., Abraham, Isaac and Jacob], to give to them the land of Canaan, the land in which they dwelt as legal foreigners.[258]

2. Exod 16:35b – they ate the manna until they came to the edge of the land of Canaan.

3. Lev 14:34a – when you come to the land of Canaan, which I am giving to you as a possession (אחזה).

4. Lev 18:3 – you shall not do like they do in the land of Egypt, in which you dwelt; and you shall not do like they do in the land of Canaan, to which I am bringing you. You shall not follow their statutes.

5. Lev 25:38 – I, Yhwh, am your god, who brought you from the land of Egypt to give to you the land of Canaan, to be your god.

Although it is admittedly less clear than in Genesis, the above passages do not feature any overt conquest overtones. Leviticus 18:3 in particular can be understood to suggest the continuing presence of the Canaanites in the land. In any case, the land of Canaan here is clearly equated with the land of the Israelites.

As with the above passages, the Priestly texts in the book of Numbers demonstrate several markers of continuity. Most important for the present work, the land here too is linked with Canaan. In the Priestly spy narrative, the men are commanded to inspect "the land of Canaan" (Num 13:17a), in contrast to "the Negeb and the hill country" (Num 13:17b) in the non-Priestly narrative.[259] This distinction is further emphasised by the fact that in the non-Priestly version the spies only go as far north as Hebron, in southern Judah (Num 13:22), whereas the Priestly version has them spy out the whole land of Canaan – "from the wilderness of Zin until Rehob" – that is, from the southern edge of the Negeb up to northern Galilee (Num 13:21).[260] Numbers 34:1–12 describe the boundaries of Canaan and make it very clear that these boundaries are confined to Cisjordan.[261]

---

[258] On the translation of גר, see note 249 on page 155.

[259] For the broad consensus that Num 13:17a belongs to P and that Num 13:17b–20* belong an earlier non-P narrative see, e.g., ACHENBACH, "Erzählung," 83; BUDD, *Numbers*, 141–142; DAVIES, *Numbers*, 128–129; LEVINE, *Numbers 1–20*, 347; MITTMANN, *Deuteronomium*, 42–43; NOTH, *Numbers*, 101; SCHMIDT, "Kundschaftererzählung;" SCHMIDT, *Numeri*, 43. MILGROM, *Numbers*, 387–390, agrees that the spy narrative should be divided into two layers, one in which the spies reached only up to Hebron and one in which they surveyed the entire land of Canaan, however he does not follow the traditional source division. GERMANY, *Exodus-Conquest*, 211–215, argues that the non-P narrative depends upon the P narrative's introduction and therefore must postdate it, but as discussed in § 2.1.2.4.B and § 2.2.1, the idea that a complete non-P narrative must be expected is incorrect.

[260] On the location of Rehob, see PETERSON/ARAV, "Rehob." It is beyond the present scope to discuss the different northern borders in Numbers 13 and 34.

[261] In terms of dating Num 34:1–12, a number of scholars argue that the land of Canaan described in Numbers 34 is more or less derived from the province of Canaan of the New Kingdom of Egypt, which is mentioned in EA 36.15 (for translation see RAINEY, *El-Amarna*, 344–345), and thus must be old (see, e.g., AHARONI, *Land*, 67–77; MILGROM, *Numbers*, 501). However,

158   *3. The Occupation of Transjordan*

The eastern border of the land of Canaan is described as following the Jordan River between the Sea of Galilee (i.e., יָם־כִּנֶּרֶת – Num 34:11b) and the Dead Sea (Num 34:12), thus making it unmistakable that the territory of Transjordan is not included.[262] This is also the case in Num 33:51, which states, "speak to the Israelites and say to them, 'when you cross over the Jordan to the land of Canaan,'" which logically presumes a sharp separation between the Transjordan and the land of Canaan. This trend fits with the Priestly depiction of Lot, who occupied Transjordan, in contrast to Abram/Abraham who occupied Canaan.

That being said, the passages in Numbers also appear to diverge from Pg's ecumenical outlook.[263] In Num 14:29 the punishment stemming from the spies' negative report is enacted upon those counted in the census, but the census presumes that Israel will go to war (Num 1:3).[264] Likewise, Moses's request for someone to replace him in Num 27:17, which is typically considered to belong to

---

this view has been critiqued from various angles. ACHENBACH, *Vollendung*, 586, for instance, notes that this reconstruction "ist ganz ungewiß und eher unwahrscheinlich" (*is quite uncertain and rather unlikely*). More damning is HUTCHENS, "Boundaries," who points out that neither the Egyptian nor the Hittite copy of the treaty mentions any boundary details. He further argues, "So, for the boundaries of this province Mazar depends upon a combination of Numbers 34, Josh. l.4, Papyrus Anastasi III, and the identification of the Zedad of Num. 34.8 and Ezek. 47.15 with the village of Zaddad, located north of the Anti-Lebanon" (p. 217). If one does not follow the circular argumentation above, then the connection between Num 34:1–12; Josh 15:2–12; and Ezek 47:15–20 suggests a rather late dating. Even scholars who follow the Documentary Hypothesis date these verses to the Pentateuch redactor or later, e.g., NOTH, *Numbers*, 248; SCHMIDT, *Numeri*, 208–209. ACHENBACH, *Vollendung*, 582–593, argues that the area described represents the (legendary) Solomonic empire, which has been amalgamated with the Transeuphratene satrapy of the Persian period. He further argues that this depiction has been inserted throughout the Bible and therefore belongs to the work of the Theokratische Bearbeitung (p. 592). The main issue with this reconstruction is that the Transeuphratene satrapy included Ammonites, Moabites and Edomites and therefore included the Transjordan, areas that are explicitly excluded in Numbers 34. This can be clearly seen even in the biblical witness, where the representatives from these "nations" are said to have complained about Nehemiah (e.g., Neh 2:9 speaks of Tobiah the Ammonite and Geshem the Arab, who must logically be associated with Transjordan). On Transeuphratene see, e.g., PETIT, *Satrapes*, 197–198. HUTCHENS, "Boundaries," 225–228, argues that both Numbers 34 and Ezekiel belong to Priestly literature and are most interested in establishing "cultic boundaries," by which the Priestly tradents could distinguish "between the clean land of Israel and the surrounding unclean lands" (p. 226). SEEBASS, *Numeri 3*, 397, notes that Numbers 34 belongs to a Priestly context but is presented in a Deuteronomistic style. In sum, it is fairly safe to assume the post-Priestly setting of Num 34:1–12.

[262] As NOTH, *Numbers*, 105, argues, for P, "the 'land of Canaan' … was restricted to the west bank of the Jordan."

[263] HUTZLI, *Origins*, 178, argues that in Exod 6:8 one already finds a shift due to the presence of מוֹרָשָׁה (*possession*), whose root is the verb יָרַשׁ (*to possess/dispossess*), which is a repeated verb in Deuteronomistic passages and so presupposes a connection to the non-Priestly account of Israel's conquest of the land.

[264] Although there is some uncertainty regarding the entirety of Num 14:29 belonging to Pg, several scholars still include it in their reconstruction. Again, see summaries in JENSON, *Holiness*, 222 and GUILLAUME, *Land*, 194.

3.4 Transjordan and the Priestly Material 159

a Priestly strata, uses military terminology – יצא (*go out*) and בוא (*come in*) (cf. 2 Sam 5:2 and 1 Chr 11:2) – and so also suggests a violent conquest.[265] The Priestly material in Numbers 32, which is not generally attributed to Pg, also shares the view of the conquest of Canaan. This conquest-focussed Priestly material thus deviates from Pg and supports the growing consensus that Pg ends before the book of Numbers.[266]

Although much more could be said, the two major observations pertaining to Numbers 32 are that 1) according to the Priestly writings (of various strata), the land of Canaan is that which YHWH shall give to Israel and this does not include the Transjordan; and 2) the ecumenical outlook of Pg understands the Canaanites to represent those "Israelites" who were not taken into exile and therefore depicts the patriarchs dwelling in peace alongside them. As such, the idea of a violent conquest of Canaan stands in contrast to this view. There is little question, then, that the story of a Transjordan settlement, not to mention the necessity of the Reubenites' and Gadites' assistance in the conquest of Cisjordan (see below) stands in conflict with Pg's broader ideology. This raises the question: How did the (later) Priestly scribes handle this conflict?

3.4.2 The Priestly Elements in Numbers 32

As noted in § 3.1, beside the geographical issues there are three major areas of internal contradiction within Numbers 32 that can be used to distinguish different narrative layers. Following these distinguishing markers, it will be suggested that a standalone Priestly narrative comprising vv. 2, 4, 5*, 20b, 21a, 22aα, 22b, 25–30* can be discerned.[267] Placed side by side, the non-Priestly and Priestly narratives are as follows (texts in *italics* belong to later redactions), and once again it must be emphasized that based on the discussion above, it is here assumed that the pre-redactional form of verses (especially vv. 6 and 28) cannot be recovered.

---

[265] See, e.g., MILGROM, *Numbers*, 235; FREVEL, *Blick*, 278.

[266] The different nature of the Priestly passages in Numbers is argued from another angle in JEON, "Promise." He highlights that "the most innovative aspect of the pivotal P text in Exodus 6 is to combine the land-promises to the Patriarchs and to the exodus generation, providing a continuity from Genesis to Exodus. In the alleged P text in Numbers, however, the land-promise is always for the exodus generation; the Patriarchal promise is never mentioned" (p. 527).

[267] Numbers 32:22aβ – and after you may return and be clear from YHWH and from Israel – logically connects to vv. 20a and 24 to form Moses's response to the Reubenites' and Gadites' proposal to build cities before going to battle לפני בני ישראל (*before the sons of Israel*). These verses do not belong to the same layer as the Priestly verses just identified.

Num 32:1Many livestock had the sons of Reuben and the sons of Gad, very many. And they saw the land of Jazer and the land of Gilead and behold, the place (מקום) was a place for livestock.

Num 32:5b*[and they said,] "do not make us cross over the Jordan."

Num 32:6*and Moses said, "... you sit here?"

Num 32:16*and they said, "we will build walls for our sheep here and cities for our children

Num 32:17awe will equip ourselves and hasten before the sons of Israel until we have brought them to their place (מקום)

Num 32:20aand Moses said to them, "If you do what you have said,

Num 32:22aβafterwards you can return and be clear from Yhwh and from Israel

Num 32:24build cities for your children and walls for your sheep and do what came from your mouths."

Num 32:34and the sons of Gad built Dibon and Ataroth and Aroer

Num 32:35and Ataroth Shophan and Jazer and Jogbehah

Num 32:36a,(b?)and Beth Nimrah and Beth Haran, (*fortified cities and sheepfolds*)

Num 32:37and the sons of Reuben built Heshbon and Elealeh and Kiriathaim

Num 32:38*and Nebo and Baal Meon (*the name has been changed*) and Sibmah and they gave names to the cities which they built

Num 32:39athe sons of Machir, son of Manasseh, walked to Gilead and captured it

Num 32:2The sons of Gad and the sons of Reuben came and they spoke to Moses *and to Eleazar the priest and to the chiefs of the congregation* saying,

Num 32:4"The land which Yhwh struck before the congregation of Israel it is a land for livestock, and your servants have livestock.

Num 32:5aα*–βIf we have found favour in your eyes, give this land to your servants as a possession (אחזה)."

Num 32:6*and Moses said to the sons of Gad and to the sons of Reuben,

Num 32:20*"If you equip yourselves before Yhwh to go to war

Num 32:22aα,b and the land is subdued (נכבשה) before Yhwh, this land will be to you a possession (אחזה) before Yhwh."

Num 32:25and the sons of Gad and the sons of Reuben spoke to Moses saying, "your servants will do just as our lord commands

Num 32:26our children, our wives, our livestock and all our beasts will be there in the cities of the Gilead

Num 32:27and your servants will pass over, all those equipped for war before Yhwh, for battle, just as our lord said."

Num 32:28*and Moses ordered them to Eleazar the priest and Joshua son of Nun and to the heads of the fathers of the tribes of the sons of Israel*

Num 32:29and Moses said to them, "If the sons of Gad and the sons of Reuben cross over the Jordan with you, all armed for war before Yhwh and the land is subdued (נכבשה) before them, then give them the land of the Gilead as a possession (אחזה)

Num 32:30but if they do not pass over armed with you, they will possess (נאחזו) in your midst, in the land of Canaan."

^{Num 32:41}and Jair, son of Manasseh, went and
captured their villages and called them the
villages of Jair (הות יאיר)

^{Num 32:42}and Nobah went and captured
Kenath and its villages (בנתיה) and called
them Nobah in his name

Table 10: Side by Side – Non-Priestly and Priestly Narratives

Verses 2 and 4 can be understood as an alternative introduction parallel to v. 1, which both introduces the major actors and the concept that the land was good for livestock. Besides its repetition of the key story points – already suggesting a doublet – the attribution of vv. 2, 4 to the Priestly layer can also be ascertained from several clues. Linguistically, the extant verses contain clear Priestly markers: Eleazar the priest, עדה (*congregation*),[268] etc. However, these are typically understood to be later additions as the following narrative refers only to Moses.[269] After removing these late Priestly markers, there remains some clues to support the idea that these were the beginning of a parallel narrative. First, v. 4 contains the term, עבדיך (*your servants*),[270] which appears in vv. 4, 5, 25, 27, 31, i.e., the other verses argued to be Priestly above. The phrase – which is only addressed towards Moses six times in the Hebrew Bible (Num 31:49; 32:4, 5, 25, 27, 31) – likely has its roots in the late conception of the inimitability of Moses as the divinely ordained leader (e.g., Num 16:28), the prophet par excellence (e.g., Num 12:6–8; Deut 34:10), or even God to Aaron (Exod 4:15–16), who has no true successor (Num 27:20).[271] This interpretation is supported by Num 32:25 and 27, where Moses is addressed as אדני (*my lord*) by the Gadites and the Reubenites, who then refer to themselves as עבדיך (*your servants*). The phrase, אדני (*my lord*), when directed towards Moses, is also uncommon in the Pentateuch, appearing in Exod 32:22; Num 11:28; 12:11; 32:25, 27; 36:2. As highlighted by Gunneweg, Exod 32:22, Num 11:28 and 12:11 likely stem from the same ideological background in which Moses's special role as the arch-prophet, the one who speaks to Yhwh face to face, is a key motif (cf. Deut 34:10–12).[272] However, many of these passages identified by Gunneweg are characteristically non-Priestly in nature

---

[268] There is some debate regarding whether the LXX attests to an earlier form of v. 4 that used the word υἱῶν (*sons*) instead of עדה as it appears in the MT. See, e.g., Carr, *Formation*, 93.

[269] The combined leadership of Moses, Eleazar and the leaders of the congregation links to Num 31:13, where these also appear together. See, e.g., Ashley, *Numbers*, 608; Fistill, *Ostjordanland*, 117. On the trend to see these as late additions see, e.g., Mittmann, *Deuteronomium*, 95–96; Schorn, *Ruben*, 145; Schmidt, *Numeri*, 198–199; Seebass, *Numeri 3*, 350.

[270] The use of the 2ms suffix also adds weight to the argument that Moses alone was the original recipient of the speech.

[271] On the increasing convergence of the Torah and Moses, see esp. Frevel, *Transformations*, 401–424.

[272] Gunneweg, "Gesetz."

162   *3. The Occupation of Transjordan*

as emphasised particularly by the concept of the tent of meeting being located outside of the camp (Exod 33:7). Numbers 32:25 and 27, however, fit better to a Priestly context meaning that the labelling of Moses as "my lord" cannot be used independently to identify a redactional layer. If Num 32:25 and 27 share the same conception of Moses as lord as Numbers 36, then this would suggest that the title should be understood in light of the increasing equivalency between Moses and the Torah. As will be discussed in more detail in § 4.5, one of the standout features of Numbers 36 is that Moses no longer explicitly consults YHWH for a decision, rather Num 36:5 reports, "And Moses commanded the sons of Israel by the word of YHWH ..." As Frevel argues, "'Moses in his superior position becomes Torah in a sophisticated manner and is functionally analogue to Deut 1:6, where his teaching expounds the Torah."[273]

As already discussed in § 3.1.3, v. 5aα*–β and vv. 20b, 21a, 22aα, 22b can be allocated to the Priestly layer due to their different outlook on the issue of settling in the Transjordan.

Within the Priestly narrative, v. 22b continues into Num 32:25–30, which comprise the response of the Reubenites and Gadites as well as Moses's order to the Israelite leadership.

Verse 26 must be seen in contrast to vv. 16 and 24, which contain the paired terms טף (*children*) and צנה (*flocks*) to represent the entirety of the Reubenites' and Gadites' family and possessions, in v. 26 four terms are used, טף (*children*), אשה (*wives*), מקנה (*cattle*) and בהמה (*beasts*).[274] Although none of these four terms are uniquely Priestly, the contrast to vv. 16 and 24 suggest that v. 26 belongs to a different narrative complex. Significantly, v. 26 also states that during their campaign, the just mentioned dependants will יהיו־שם בערי הגלעד (*be there in the cities of the Gilead*). First, this notice reinforces the claim that v. 26 should be seen in opposition to v. 16, where the Reubenites and Gadites wish to build cities. Second, the label הגלעד (*the Gilead*) contrasts with v. 1 where the definite article is missing. Additionally, the idea that the entirety of the Transjordan belongs under the umbrella "the Gilead" (as opposed to the land of Jazer and the land of Gilead or otherwise cf. Deut 3:12–17) can be found elsewhere in the Hebrew Bible, Joshua 22:9 in particular depicts the Transjordan territory owned by all two and a half tribes as "the Gilead". Third, the idea that there is already "the land struck before YHWH" in v. 4, in which the cities in the Gilead (v. 26) are located, logically presupposes the Sihon narrative as there is otherwise no battle reported. Marquis' argument that the Priestly text instead presupposes Numbers 31 does not work, as she herself observes that in that narrative the cities are de-

---

[273] FREVEL, "Leadership," 92.

[274] The only other occurrence of all four terms is in Num 31:9, which is also "Priestly" styled. Cf. Gen 36:6, where even more terms are included.

stroyed with fire (Num 31:10).[275] Unless one wishes to assume some other conquest narrative that has now been lost, it is only logical to assume the Priestly narrative was aware of the incorporation of the Sihon narrative and thus some kind of Deuteronomistic redaction of the non-Priestly narrative. Additionally, this further supports the suggestion made earlier that the Priestly material in Numbers belongs to a Priestly composition that has already moved away from Pg's purely peaceful outlook and has instead incorporated the idea of conquest.

The Reubenites' and Gadites' speech continues in v. 27 – and your servants will pass over, all those equipped for war before Yhwh, for battle, just as our lord said – which recalls to Moses's speech in vv. 20b–22*.

Verse 28 is a problematic text, although *prima facie* the presence of Eleazar the priest likely indicates a Priestly setting, there are several clues that suggest this verse belongs to one of the latest strata of the Pentateuch. In its present form the wording more or less matches Josh 14:1 and so likely functions as a later harmonisation.[276] Naming Eleazar before Joshua and the tribal leaders must be seen in light of Num 27:21, where Eleazar is given priority over Joshua in the post-Moses leadership of Israel. Numbers 27:21, 22b represent a late update to the commissioning of Joshua (Num 27:12–23), which forwards the concept of a theocratic leadership of Israel.[277] Although the extant v. 28 must be considered late, it is difficult to suppose that the Priestly version of Numbers 32 did not include vv. 29–30 and therefore some pre-redactional version of v. 28 must be presumed.

Verse 29 picks up the wording of vv. 20b–22* and reiterates that the Reubenites and Gadites must cross over and assist in כבש the land, after which they shall receive ארץ הגלעד (*the land of the Gilead*) as an אחזה. Although the precise wording differs between v. 26 and v. 29 (cities vs land respectively), this can easily be explained contextually. The families live in cities (v. 26) whilst it is the land that is tenured (v. 29). More important is the use of the definite article with the Gilead, which should be seen in contrast to v. 1.

Lastly v. 30 includes the important failure-case, "but if they do not cross over armed with you, they will נאחזו (*have possessions*) in your midst, in the ארץ כנען (*land of Canaan*)." *Prima facie* the "punishment" for the Reubenites' and Gadites' failure to assist their fellow Israelites hardly seems to be a punishment at all, they receive an allotment without having to endanger themselves in battle. This of course is counter-intuitive; however, this verse must instead be understood in light of the Priestly logic of land tenure. As argued above, the idea of land tenure functions on the idea that it is Yhwh's land, which is distributed accordingly.[278] Following this logic, the "punishment" for failure is not that the

---

[275] Marquis, "Composition," 410.

[276] Schmidt, *Numeri*, 197.

[277] See, e.g., Frevel, *Leadership*, 102–105.

[278] As Guillaume, *Land*, 109–117, argues, the modern mindset understands this as a dilution of profit (more people = smaller share) however the ancient mindset was a dilution

164　　　　　　　　　　*3. The Occupation of Transjordan*

Reubenites and Gadites will be destitute, rather the punishment is that they will not receive the special dispensation to dwell outside of the land of Canaan as they had requested.

3.4.3 Reflections on the Priestly Layer

From this brief overview of the Priestly texts in Numbers 32 some conclusions can be drawn. First, the texts highlighted demonstrate a markedly different understanding of the Israel's settlement in Transjordan. Unlike the non-Priestly narrative where the land was granted by Moses in advance, the Priestly version suggests the land would only be granted after the Reubenites and Gadites proved their solidarity by assisting their Cisjordan brothers. These observations point towards the conclusion that the Priestly texts are designed to present an alternative, or even counter, story to the non-Priestly account, rather than representing a Priestly coloured update of that text (i.e., Fortschreibung).

Second, assuming the verses delimited above are more or less correct, it implies that the negative depiction of the Reubenites' and Gadites' request introduced in Num 32:7–15 do not belong to the Priestly layer. This seems somewhat surprising given the above-mentioned conflict between the concept of Canaan and the Transjordan traditions. The answer to this likely lies in the setting in which the Priestly materials developed. It is becoming widely accepted that the Priestly Document was developed in the Persian period and reflects (to a greater or lesser degree) Persian Imperial ideology.[279] This suggests a social setting in which most "Israelites" did not live in Canaan. As such, it follows that the Priestly scribes had to emphasise the importance of Canaan but had to do so in such a way as to not simply alienate the wider Yahwistic community, not least the Jews that remained in Babylon. In light of this, it is not surprising that the Priestly materials in Numbers 32 reinforce the idea that Canaan is Yhwh's tenured land, but that those who wished to dwell outside this space were also given the option to do so, so long as they continued to act in accordance with and to the benefit of "the motherland." This relationship is made clearer in Joshua 22, where the Cisjordan tribes say to the Transjordan tribes, "nevertheless, if the land you possess is unclean, cross over to the land of Yhwh's possession, in which the tabernacle of Yhwh dwells, and take a possession among us. But do not rebel against Yhwh and do not rebel against us by building yourselves an altar apart

---

of risk (more farming plots = higher chance of good crops). Knauf/Guillaume, *History*, 43, additionally argue that, "in the [Iron Age] Levant, the full supporting capacity of the land was never reached." Thus, the Reubenites and Gadites being forced to dwell in Cisjordan would not constitute a silent punishment to the other tribes.

[279] See, e.g., Nihan, *Torah*, e.g., 19; Schmid, "Ecumenicity." On the idea that the Priestly authors did not set out to write "history" but rather a "mythological history" see esp. Knauf, *Data*, 519–534.

from the altar of YHWH our god" (Josh 22:19).[280] As several scholars have argued, Joshua 22 changes the depiction of Israelites dwelling in Transjordan from a "historical" narrative to a cipher for Israelites living in the Persian Diaspora.[281] This cipher is particularly suggested by Josh 22:23, where the Transjordan tribes assert an Elephantine-like limitation to make no עולה (*burnt offerings*), מנחה (*grain offerings*) or זבחי שלמים (*sacrifices of wellbeing*). As Knauf writes, "Es fällt schwer, zwischen Jos 22 und der Elephantine-Korrespondenz *keinen* Zusammenhang herzustellen" (*it is difficult* not *to establish* any *connection between Josh 22 and the Elephantine Correspondance*).[282] In its present form, Joshua 22 clearly presupposes the final form of Numbers 32 and draws clear connections to that text.[283]

3.5 Conquest of the Amorites

The next major innovation in the Transjordan traditions is the labelling of Sihon and Og as Amorite kings. With the addition of Num 32:34–42*, the Sihon narrative was no longer appropriate in its depiction of Sihon of Heshbon as an aggressive city-king that Israel encountered along their way towards the Jordan. Especially within the context of the original Moab Redaction in Deuteronomy 1–3, the report that Israel לקד (*captured*) territory far north of any logical path towards the Jordan (i.e., in northern Transjordan) makes little sense belonging to Moses's recollection of how the nation of Israel had arrived "beyond the Jordan" where they were about to embark upon the final step to possess the land promised to the ancestors (e.g., Deut 2:3, 9, 13, 18, 24, etc.).

---

[280] On the "Priestly logic" underlying the narrative of Joshua 22, see, e.g., KLOPPENBORG, "Joshua 22," 370.

[281] See, e.g., KNAUF, *Josua*, 182; ARTUS, "Numbers 32," 375.

[282] KNAUF, *Josua*, 183 (emphasis original).

[283] That the narrative of Joshua 22 originally contained an earlier layer can be inferred by the fact that there remain some traces where the half-tribe of Manasseh is not included (vv. 25, 32, 33 and 34), however detangling this earlier layer from the later harmonisations is fraught with uncertainties. Regarding the chapter as a redactional work, KNAUF, *Josua*, 184, notes, "Jos 22 setzt innerhalb der Schlussredaktion die Hexateuchschicht fort, indem typisches D-Vokabular mit ebenso typischem P-Vokabular kombiniert wird" (*Josh 22 continues within the Hexateuch layer, in which typically D vocabulary with likewise typically P vocabulary are combined*). ASSIS, "Position," 531, notes, "It seems to be the case that Priestly elements coexist with Deuteronomistic elements in this story, and, due to the limited nature of the research tools at our disposal today, it is impossible to reconstruct its development, although many have tried to do so." Examples of such attempts can be seen in, e.g., YOO, "Witness." For an overview of previous scholarship, see esp. BALLHORN, *Israel*, 347–355.

166 *3. The Occupation of Transjordan*

3.5.1 Deuteronomy Re-Imagines the Promised Land

In § 3.2.1 it was suggested that at least two major conceptions of the land can be detected in Deuteronomy 2:24–3:18. Narrative A (Deut 2:24aα, 26, 27, 29b, 30a, 32, 33a(b?); 3:12bβ) depicted Israel's engagement with Sihon, the king of Heshbon, as an application of Deut 20:10–15, the law for war against cities that are "very far from you," and so understood to the Transjordan to still lay outside of the land promised to Israel's ancestors. Narrative B, alternatively understood the Transjordan territory under question to belong to Amorites, thereby making it belong to one of the nations designated for destruction (Deut 7:1; 20:17). This functioned to incorporate the Transjordan into that territory that Israel should ירש (*possess/dispossess*).[284] Having already argued this in some detail, the following section will only highlight a few key aspects rather than labour the point a second time.

Deuteronomy's Sihon Narrative A was thoroughly reconceptualised via the addition of several key verses: Deut 2:24aβ–25, 30b, 31 and 34–35. Furthermore, the idea that Israel only took Sihon's cities as they were passing through on their way towards the Jordan was dramatically altered by the addition of the Og narrative in Deut 3:1–11*, and the expanded allotment notices in Deut 3:12–20*.

Regarding the updated Sihon narrative, each addition highlights that Sihon is no longer to be conceived merely as a city-king that Israel encountered on their way to the Jordan, rather he now represents Israel's first enemy of the conquest. First, the command to cross the Arnon in Deut 2:24aα was supplemented with the command to ירש (*possess/dispossess*) the land of סיחן מלך־חשבון האמרי (*Sihon, king of Heshbon, the Amorite*), which was guaranteed by the divine promise that YHWH had "given" it into Moses's/Israel's hand. Second, v. 25 takes up the language of the divinely promised conquest from Deut 11:25 via the key terms פחד (*dread*) and יראה (*fear*).[285] Third, v. 30b reformulates Sihon's unwillingness to allow Israel passage through his territory by emphasising that his reticence was due to YHWH hardening his heart (just like YHWH hardened Pharaoh's heart in Egypt, e. g., Exod 7:3). Fourth, v. 31 reiterates the divine command to ירש Sihon's land. Finally, vv. 34–35 formulate Israel's victory with חרם language, just as Deut 20:17 commands. These additions may be few in number, but they are major in terms of an ideological shift. Sihon is now clearly depicted as האמרי (*the Amorite*) and so designated for destruction (חרם) according to Deut 7:1; 20:17. His aggression is no longer an example of inhospitality but rather a divinely manipulated trigger to begin the conquest. His cities are no longer simply taken but the women and children are killed as part of Israel's "purifying" actions.

---

[284] See again discussion in WEINFELD, *Deuteronomy*, 173–178.
[285] See, e. g., OTTO, *Deuteronomium 1,1–4,43*, 450.

In addition to these changes, the narrative was further expanded in light of the need to extend Israel's territory to match that depicted particularly by Num 32:39–42*. This was primarily achieved by adding the Og narrative (Deut 3:1–8a).

As it is often assumed that the Og narrative belongs to the base layer of the Moab Redaction, a few further comments are necessary. The language of the Og narrative largely mirrors Deuteronomy's Sihon narrative as has long been observed, however it must be noted that the theme of חרם is much better integrated into the Og narrative, which *prima facie* supports the theory that the entire Og narrative is secondary.[286] However, Germany has recently argued that the חרם language can be removed from the Og narrative thus revealing an earlier narrative layer (Deut 3:1, 3a, 4a, 8a).[287] The main issue with his reconstruction is that v. 8a already labels both Sihon and Og as Amorites, thus unless one wishes to argue that Deut 7:1 and 20:17 are both later than the Og narrative, the avoidance of חרם would have to be interpreted as disobedience to the law.

[Deut 2:32]Sihon came out to meet us, he and all his people for battle at Jahaz	[Deut 3:1b]Og, king of Bashan, came out to meet us, he and all his people for battle at Edrei
[Deut 2:33]Yhwh our god gave him unto us and we struck him and his sons and all his people [Deut 2:34b]no survivor remained	[Deut 3:3]Yhwh our God gave into our hand Og, king of Bashan, and all his people and we struck him down until no survivor remained.
[Deut 2:34aα]We captured all his cities at that time	[Deut 3:4aα]We captured all his cities at that time
[Deut 2:34aβ]We banned (נחרם) all of the city: men, women and children	[Deut 3:6]We banned (נחרם) them, just like we did to Sihon, king of Heshbon. Banning all of the city: men, women and children.
[Deut 2:35]only we took the livestock as plunder and the spoil of the cities we captured	[Deut 3:7]But all the livestock and the plunder of the cities we took as spoil

Table 11: Comparison of the Sihon and Og narratives in Deuteronomy

Deuteronomy 3:1 begins, "We turned and went up the road to Bashan and Og, king of Bashan, came out to meet us, he and all his people for battle at Edrei." As argued in § 3.2.1, the narrative of Israel travelling into northern Transjordan, let alone all the way up to Bashan, does not align with the broader fable of the Moab Redaction, which depicts the law of Deuteronomy as Moses's farewell speech "in the land of Moab" (Deut 1:5). Thus Israel's "travelling up the road" to Bashan only makes narrative sense if Deut 2:24aβb is presupposed, i.e., the Transjordan is understood to constitute the beginning of Israel's conquest. This is further supported by the observation that Israel's journey prior to Deut 3:1 was always

---

[286] See, e.g., Otto, *Deuteronomium 1,1–4,43*, 452.

[287] Germany, *Exodus-Conquest*, 256. In contrast Otto, *Deuteronomium 1,1–4,43*, 452, argues for Deut 3:1,2–4a,5–8a*. Schmidt, "Sihon," 320, for Deut 3:1, 3, 4aα, 6–8a*.

directed by YHWH (e. g., Deut 2:3, 9, 13, 18, 24, etc.), whereas in 3:1 no such command is given.[288]

Scholars such as Schmidt and Germany argue that Deut 3:2 is a later update of to the base Og narrative. Germany argues, "in light of the conclusion that the divine speeches to Moses in Deut 2:31 and 2:37 are both secondary to Moses's retrospective in 2:26–30, 32–36*, it seems likely that the divine speech to Moses in 3:2 is also secondary to the most basic narrative of the conquest of Og."[289] In Schmidt's case the problem with v. 2 is not the divine speech – for this is in line with Deut 2:31, which (contrary to Germany) Schmidt allocates to the base layer – rather it is the fact that Sihon is referred to as an Amorite, which Schmidt rightly argues is a later development to the original Sihon narrative.[290] The issue, then, is not that Deut 3:2 is secondary to the base Sihon layer, rather it is proving that the other parts of the Og narrative are *not* secondary to the original Sihon narrative.

The difficulty in understanding parts of the Og narrative to be early can also be seen in the treatment of v. 3. Verse 3b – we struck him down until no survivor remained – clearly alludes to the application of חרם even if the term itself is not used. For his part, Germany (admittedly tentatively) argues that this is secondary due to the חרם theme, however without v. 3bα, there is no corresponding report that matches Deut 2:33, detailing the actual defeat of Og.[291] On the other hand those scholars keeping all of v. 3 to the base layer cannot adequately explain the application of חרם if Og is not already an Amorite. Again, the law of Deuteronomy 20 stipulates that enemies "very far from you" are first to be offered terms of peace (Deut 20:10), which implies that, if possible, bloodshed is to be avoided. It is only those nations who dwell in the land that YHWH is giving Israel as a נחלה (*inheritance*) that are to be subject to חרם (Deut 20:16–17). In light of this, Deut 3:6–7 also belong to the same conceptualisation as these verses clearly relate to חרם.

There is, however, a legitimate argument to be made that Deut 3:4b–5 are secondary to the base Og narrative. As Schmidt notes, these verse break the sequence of defeating Og (v. 3), capturing his cities (v. 4a) and performing חרם on the residents (v. 6).[292] The reference to Israel taking 60 cities in the region of Argob (Deut 3:4b) likely stems from Josh 13:30, where the Havvoth-Jair is said to comprise 60 cities.[293] Regarding v. 5 Otto argues that the fortifications of the cities were emphasised in order to demonstrate the power of YHWH, while the

---

[288] So MITTMANN, *Deuteronomium*, 82.

[289] GERMANY, *Exodus-Conquest*, 255.

[290] SCHMIDT, "Sihon," 319.

[291] GERMANY, *Exodus-Conquest*, 256.

[292] SCHMIDT, "Sihon," 319.

[293] See, e.g., OTTO, *Deuteronomium 1,1–4,43*, 467. KNAUF, *Josua*, 134, dates this verse to the latest strata in Joshua 13.

inclusion of unwalled settlements emphasised the completeness of the conquest.[294] It is possible that v. 5 also relates to the spy narrative in Numbers via the shared term ערים בצרות (*fortified cities*), and demonstrates that Israel's unwillingness to engage this strong and fearsome peoples was unjustified. In any case Schmidt's argument is convincing that vv. 4b–5 break the expected narrative sequence and so likely represent a later update to the Og narrative.

Deuteronomy 3:8b–11 comprise the so-called "antiquarian notices" and link to the book of Joshua and so logically represent a later development.[295]

The attribution of territory in Deut 3:12–16 further aligns the Deuteronomistic narrative with Numbers 32, the allotment of central Transjordan to the Reubenites and Gadites and the allotment of northern Transjordan to half-Manasseh is not part of the Sihon narrative in either Numbers or Deuteronomy and so must logically stem from Numbers 32. However, Deut 3:12–16 do not further influence the narratives in Numbers and so will not be analysed in more detail in the present work.[296]

3.5.2 Updating the Sihon Narrative in Numbers 21

While the Deuteronomists were happy to re-imagine the promised land in order to bring the Transjordan under that umbrella, the book of Numbers – probably due to its much greater Priestly influence – resorted to other solutions. The so-called "secularised" treatment of the Sihon and Og narratives in Numbers 21 make better sense as reflecting Priestly concerns, and so will be discussed in more detail in § 3.6.1, even if it is not fully possible to exclude the idea that the Sihon narrative underwent some level of updating at this stage.

3.5.3 Further Deuteronomistic Influences in Numbers 32

Beside the lists of cities (see § 3.3), finding texts that clearly display Deuteronomistic influence in Numbers 32 is fairly difficult. In fact, the non-Priestly layer does not appear to have undergone significant alteration. In the following discussion it will be argued that Numbers 32 was further updated with vv. 18, 19, 33 and 40.

Verses 18 and 19 can be associated with a Deuteronomistic insert due to the repeated use of the term נחלה (*inheritance*), which is ideologically a Deuterono-

---

[294] OTTO, *Deuteronomium 1,1–4,43*, 466–467.

[295] This follows the general consensus that the Og narrative originally ended at v. 8a. See, e.g., OTTO, *Deuteronomium 1,1–4,43*, 452; SCHMIDT, "Sihon," 320; GERMANY, *Exodus-Conquest*, 256.

[296] For a fuller treatment see discussion in, e.g., OTTO, *Deuteronomium 1,1–4,43*, 474–491; DOZEMAN, "Interpretation."

mistic term.[297] These verses must be seen in contrast with vv. 1 and 17a, which both refer to the various tribes having their מקום (*place*). Scholars have traditionally seen Num 32:16–17a as belonging to a separate layer to vv.17b–18, and some even suggest that v. 19 belongs to a separate layer again.[298] Mittmann and Schmidt, for example, suggest that a later redactor made vv. 16–17a more precise by appending vv. 17b–18.[299] According to this line of reasoning, v. 17b addressed why it was that Reuben and Gad needed to build cities before assisting in the conquest, while v. 18 made it clear that the Reubenites and Gadites would not only bring Israel into the land, but also remain there until each tribe's inheritance had been allotted.

The difficulty of seeing v. 17b as belonging to the same layer as vv. 18–19 is that its meaning in a "Deuteronomistic" context is unclear. Here the Reubenites and Gadites argue that they must build fortified cities for their children because of the ישבי הארץ (*inhabitants of the land*). However, within a post-Sihon narrative context it is unclear who these inhabitants are. According to Numbers 21 Israel killed all the Amorites in the land of Gilead and Bashan, Num 21:35 even notes that, "there was no remaining survivor." In this context it is possible that v. 17b refers to the neighbouring sons of Lot (i.e., the Ammonites and Moabites), who are not described as אחינו (*our brothers* – Deut 2:8) like the Edomites are, but who, in any case, Israel is forbidden to engage in battle (Deut 2:9, 19). Some support for this interpretation comes from Deut 23:4, which says in no uncertain terms that, "Ammonites and Moabites shall not enter the assembly of Yнwн …", and even expands on the typical restriction – "until the tenth generation" – with an additional עד־עולם (*forever*). In this line of reasoning v. 17b could foreshadow the oppression of Israel by the Ammonites as depicted in Judges 10–11 and 1 Sam 10a:6–9 (4Q51).[300] The issue with this solution is that the phrase ישבי הארץ is never used in these passages to describe the Ammonites, nor does the term appear in Deuteronomy. In the book of Joshua ישבי הארץ is used for the inhabitants that Israel must drive out in order to possess their land (Josh 2:9, 24;

---

[297] Knauf, *Data*, 521, argues, "Bei D erhält Israel sein Land als נחלה 'Lehen' und kann es darum im Ungehorsams-Fall wieder verlieren. Bei P ist das Land אחזה 'Eigentum' (Gen 17,8a) und kann insofern von Gott nicht mehr zurückgenommen werden" (*With D, Israel receives its land as a נחלה 'fief' and can, in cases of disobedience, lose it. With P the land is אחזה 'property' (Gen 17:8a) and in this respect can no longer be taken back by God*).

[298] See, e.g., Mittmann, *Deuteronomium*, 104.

[299] Mittmann, *Deuteronomium*, 97; Schmidt, "Ansiedlung," 498. The difficulties of this explanation can be clearly seen in the discussion by Schorn, *Ruben*, 149, who agrees that v. 18 makes v. 17 more precise, but disagrees that v. 17b makes v. 16b more precise. Achenbach, *Vollendung*, 385–386, tries to argue for the best of both worlds by suggesting that a late redactor (ThB) inserted vv. 16–19 as a block, however that redactor incorporated older materials (i.e., vv. 16–17a) into his own work.

[300] On 4Q51 see note 28 on page 90.

3.5 Conquest of the Amorites

171

7:9; 9:24; etc.), yet again this interpretation does not fit well into either a pre- or post-Sihon context of Numbers 32.

A more tempered solution is to understand v. 17b as an attempt to remove the (historically unrealistic) implication that the land desired by the Reubenites and Gadites was terra nullius. Instead of the land of Jazer and the land of Gilead being free for the taking (finders-keepers!), v. 17b demonstrates that it was inhabited. In any case, given that a clear link to Deuteronomy or Deuteronomistic ideology is missing, it seems best to understand v. 17b as an even later harmonisation rather than part of a Deuteronomistic update.

Returning to vv. 18 and 19, although the idea that these verses make the base narrative (vv. 16–17a) more precise is correct in a broad sense, it more specifically reframes the idea of a somewhat generic מקום (Num 32:1, 17a) into the more theologically grounded נחלה. The addition of vv. 18 and 19 brings the present narrative into theological alignment with texts such as Deut 4:38; 15:4; 26:1; Josh 11:23; etc., wherein the land is depicted as that which has been given to Israel by Yhwh. More specifically, the giving of land in Deuteronomy is tied to the idea of ירש (*possessing/dispossessing*) and thus to the idea of conquest over those nations that Yhwh flagged for destruction (cf. Deut 7:1–2). Verse 18 links to Deut 3:20, where Moses commands that the Transjordan tribes are not to return from Cisjordan until their brothers have also received the land that Yhwh is giving to them. The significance of v. 19, then, is that the Reubenites and Gadites further highlight that the land ירש from the Amorites will be their נחלה, and not just any land taken across the Jordan (cf. discussion of Jahaz above). Thus, these two verses, despite their diminutive size, actually function to completely reframe the narrative of Numbers 32 in light of Deuteronomistic ideas (i.e., the idea of Narrative B – see § 3.5.1). These two verses demonstrate that the land of the Reubenites and Gadites belongs to the wider נחלה of Israel, and that that נחלה is located in Transjordan rather than Cisjordan.

The major clue supporting the assertion that v. 33 belongs to this Deuteronomistic update is the idea that Moses נתן (*gave*) the land to the Reubenites and Gadites.[301] That this verse originally predated the conflation with the Priestly narrative is suggested by the fact that the idea of Moses giving the land contradicts the clear message of the Priestly layer argued in § 3.4.2, whereby the land was only to be granted (by Joshua and Eleazar – cf. Num 32:28) as an אחזה *after* the Reubenites and Gadites assisted with the conquest of Cisjordan. Furthermore, the language of נתן aligns with the report in Deut 3:12, 13, 15, 16 where it is repeated several times that Moses gave the Transjordan land to the two and a half tribes. The inclusion of the half-tribe of Manasseh as well as the inclusion of Og further point to v. 33 belonging to a layer responding to Deuteronomy's Narrative B.

---

[301] So also Seebass, *Numeri 3*, 357.

172   *3. The Occupation of Transjordan*

Finally, verse 40 (minus "son of Manasseh") is more or less a direct parallel of Deut 3:15 and logically represents a parallel insertion to bring the two narratives into closer alignment. Achenbach similarly concludes, "Durch Num 32,33.40 hat HexRed das dtr. Fachwerk rezipiert" (*The HexRed, through Num 32:33, 40, received the Dtr framework*).[302]

3.6 Joining Priestly and Deuteronomistic Texts

Having argued that the Priestly material of Numbers 32 is best understood as originally belonging to a standalone Priestly work, it is only logical to suppose that there remains evidence for the joining of the Priestly and non-Priestly narratives together. The following section highlights these updates in a rather systematic fashion. Importantly, it must be emphasised that these updates need not all stem from the same hand but may have occurred in multiple stages. It should also be recalled – as Carr in particular has emphasised – that minor alignments of verses may rather be attributed to inadvertent harmonisations during the process of copying, rather than intentional "redactional" or "ideological" imposition by later scribes.[303]

3.6.1 Completing the Sihon Narrative

Returning to the issue of the "secularised" treatment of the Sihon and Og narratives in Numbers 21. To begin it is important to return to the observation of Albertz, "Die Weise, wie mit der dtr. Og-Tradition in Num 21,33–35 umgegangen wird, legt die Einsicht nahe, dass Reduktion bzw. Ausblendung der theologischen Dimension in der Sihon- und übrigens auch in der Edom-Erzählung als ein bewusstes Stilmittel des hier tätigen Autors angesehen werden muss" (*The sense with which the Dtr Og tradition is bypassed, suggests the insight, that the reduction, or rather the fading-out, of the theological dimension in the Sihon and incidentally also the Edom narrative must be regarded as a conscious stylistic device of the author working here*).[304]

In § 3.2.2 it was argued that the original Sihon layer of Numbers 21 comprised vv. 21*, 22, 23, 24a, 25bβ. In terms of narrative adjustments, Num 21:21–35 were updated with the idea that (1) Sihon was an Amorite, (2) that Israel took a much larger part of central Transjordan, (3) that Israel יֵשֶׁב (*dwelt*) in the territory of the Amorites, (4) that Moses sent an expedition to Jazer, (5) the Song of Heshbon was inserted and (6) that Israel defeated Og of Bashan, these will be discussed

---

[302] ACHENBACH, *Vollendung*, 372.
[303] See, e.g., CARR, *Formation*, 31; CARR, *Tablet*, 39.
[304] ALBERTZ, "Numeri I," 179.

3.6 Joining Priestly and Deuteronomistic Texts 173

in turn below. As already argued in § 3.5.2, it is important to emphasise that not every aspect discussed below *must* be post-Priestly, but for sake of clarity and to avoid needless fragmentation into ever more unreliable strata, all remaining changes to the Sihon narrative will be covered here.

I. The insertion of the Amorite origins of Sihon can clearly be seen in Num 21:21, 25, 26, 29, 31, 32. Unlike Deuteronomy, this information in and of itself does not appear to come with the same connotations. The theme of חרם (*the ban*) has not been incorporated into Numbers' Sihon narrative in a clear way (cf. Num 21:32). It seems, rather, that Sihon was labelled an Amorite purely to maintain continuity with Deuteronomy rather than that the ideological background was adopted. This is particularly important in light of the idea Deuteronomy reconceptualised the Transjordan as belonging to the promised land but Numbers does not.

II. As discussed in § 3.2.2, the original conception of Sihon's territory comprised "Heshbon and all its villages" (Num 21:25). In line with the updated narrative in Deuteronomy and the list of cities in Num 32:34–38, v. 24 was expanded with the report that Israel ירש (*dispossessed*) Sihon's land "from the Arnon to the Jabbok."[305] The problem was that this territorial realignment caused issues with the conception of the land of the Ammonites. In light of Num 21:32 (see discussion below), the resulting land acquired spanned from the Arnon to the Jabbok, however the editors of Numbers still assumed that the Ammonites were located atop the Amman plateau. Thus, as it was already discussed in § 3.1.1.1, Num 21:24b specifies that Israel did not take any Ammonite territory and that this began at Jazer: "because Jazer was the border of the sons of Ammon." This rather technical understanding appears to have caused some confusion during the processes of transmission: Deuteronomy 3:16, in contrast, specifies that the "the wadi [the Jabbok] was the border of the sons of Ammon"; similarly, Num 21:24b was updated in the MT with the report that the border of the Ammonites was עז (*strong*). Thus, Roskop Erisman rightly speaks of a shifting border of the Ammonites.[306]

III. The report in Num 21:25 and 31 that the Israelites ישׁב (*dwelt*. The NRSV translates it *settled*) in the land of the Amorites is also problematic as it makes no sense in light of the narrative of Numbers 32. This is often explained as a foreshadowing of Numbers 32; however, such an explanation fails (a) because the base narrative of Numbers 32 had to be modified in order to accommodate the Sihon narrative and (b) it was argued that Numbers 32 originally presupposed the Reubenites and Gadites were requesting land that did not require a conquest to acquire. Furthermore, it must be acknowledged that Num 21:25, 31 represent

---

[305] So Wüst, *Untersuchungen*, 10; Germany, *Exodus-Conquest*, 242.
[306] Roskop Erisman, "Border."

174 *3. The Occupation of Transjordan*

a problem that only becomes more difficult to explain the later one dates it.[307] As Van Seters notes, "the references to settling in Num 21:25, 31 are in conflict with the subsequent episodes, and it is hardly adequate to dismiss them as 'anticipatory' of some later statements about the settlement of Reuben and Gad."[308] The solution to this problem appears to be the Balaam Pericope (Numbers 22–24), which required that Israel had *already* settled next to Moab. King Balak of Moab says to Balaam in Num 22:5, "behold, a people have come out from Egypt and behold, they cover the face of the earth and they dwell (ישב) before me." It is not the place to analyse the Balaam Pericope in any detail, however the general assumption that it was an originally separate narrative that was incorporated into the context of the book of Numbers is supported by several general observations.[309] On the one hand, Balak's hostility makes no sense within the context of Israel's peaceful journey through Moab (cf. § 3.1.2), as such a hostile king would surely not have allowed Israel safe and peaceful passage through his land. This suggests that the Balaam episode was not originally part of the exodus–conquest narrative. On the other hand, the fact that Balak took Balaam to Pisgah, suggests that the original Balaam narrative still operated under the land conception whereby the plains of Moab belonged to Moab. This suggests that the Balaam narrative was not originally written with the "updated" Moabite border of the Sihon narrative in view. According to Robker, the original Balaam narrative comprised Num 22:3a*, 4b, 5*, 6a*, 7b–11aαb, 12a, 13–20a, 21aαb, 36–41; 23:2b–4a; 5–9*, 10b–20*, 21b, 24–28, 30b; 24:1aαγ*b, 2aαb, 3abα, 4bα, 5*, 7–9a, 10–14a, and 25.[310] Importantly, this basic narrative lacks the verses that function to connect the Balaam narrative to the Sihon narrative. The relation of the Balaam narrative to the surrounding narrative in Numbers is admittedly complex, however the best explanation for the strange report of Israel ישב in the land of the Amorites is that it functions to more smoothly transition into the Balaam narrative.

IV. Numbers 21:32 contains the report that "Moses sent [men] to spy out Jazer and they captured it and its villages and dispossessed the Amorites who dwelt there." This verse harmonises both with the Song of Heshbon and Numbers 32. The Song of Heshbon depicts Sihon's territory spanning from Heshbon to Dibon (Num 21:30) meaning the region above Heshbon (which was argued in § 3.1.1 to comprise the land of the Ammonites and the land of Jazer) remained unaccount-

---

[307] The major point of contention is the transition from v. 24 to v. 25. SEEBASS, *Numeri 2*, 357, argues that v. 25 is a later gloss designed to transition more smoothly into the Song of Heshbon (vv. 27–30). See also SCHMIDT, "Ansiedlung," 507. GERMANY, *Exodus-Conquest*, 245, argues that the base narrative jumps from v. 24a to v. 25b. See also GASS, *Moabiter*, 194.

[308] VAN SETERS, "Again," 117.

[309] LEVINE, *Numbers 21–36*, 137, for example, notes, "the Balaam Pericope stands apart from the progression of the JE historiography in Numbers." OTTO, *Deuteronomium 1,1–4,43*, 256, also argues that the Balaam narrative was a standalone tradition.

[310] ROBKER, *Text*, 180.

ed for.[311] This same concern also connects Israel's battles with the Amorites to the Reubenites' and Gadites' request in Numbers 32, particularly "the land of Jazer" in Num 32:1. Furthermore, by specifying that the occupants of Jazer were Amorites mitigates any potential confusion that Jazer – which Num 21:24 depicts as the border of the Ammonites – was "out of bounds" from Israelite occupation (cf. Deut 2:19).[312]

V. The Song of Heshbon was already discussed to some degree in § 3.2.3. As noted there, it is likely that the song has more ancient roots but that it was reframed and repurposed by the Hebrew scribes. The main clue to allocating the song to a later stratum is the fact that it depicts Sihon's territory as extending south to Dibon (Num 21:30), which stands in conflict with the idea that Sihon was a city-king who ruled in "Heshbon and all its villages" (Num 21:25). It is not possible to determine if the mention of Dibon in the song influenced the idea that Sihon took Moabite territory to the Arnon or if the song was used as an "antiquated" justification of the Deuteronomistic depiction of crossing the Arnon as the beginning of the conquest (cf. Deut 2:24).

VI. As has been widely observed, Num 21:33–34 are more or less verbatim to Deut 3:1–2, with the main divergence occurring in Num 21:35. Seebass argues that the additional report in v. 35 that "they dispossessed his land" – which does not appear in Deuteronomy – brings the Og narrative into alignment with Numbers' Sihon narrative, where in Num 21:24bα it is also reported that "they dispossessed his land."[313] The removal of the reference to Yhwh's involvment (i.e., Deut 3:3aα) was already explained above (§ 3.2.2) as being a deliberate ideological decision that functioned to suggest that Israel's settlement in Transjordan was due to their own choice to live outside the boundary of the promised land, rather than being the result of Moses's or Yhwh's actions.[314] The extant Sihon narrative in Numbers 21 thus skilfully walks a fine line. On the one hand it absolutely affords continuity with Deuteronomy with its conception of ירש (*possession/dispossession*) and the idea that Israel defeated two Amorite kings. On the other hand, by careful omission of Yhwh's involvement in any of the events in Transjordan, space is made so that Israel's Transjordan settlement can still be depicted as a deliberate dwelling *outside* the land of Canaan, which Yhwh had ordained to be Israel's rightful אחזה (*possession*).

---

[311] Seebass, *Numeri 2*, 362.

[312] Levine, *Numbers 21–36*, 109.

[313] Seebass, *Numeri 2*, 362.

[314] Thus, Schmidt, "Sihon," 327, is incorrect in suggesting, "Das war entgegen der Auffassung von Albertz nicht die Absicht des Vefassers. Die Auslassungen gehen vielmehr darauf zurück, dass er den Abschnitt über Og teilweise an die Sihon-Erzählung angleichen wollte, die keine Parallelen zu Dtn 3,3a und dem Bann der Städte enthält." (*Contrary to Albertz' opinion, that was not the intention of the author. Rather, the omissions go back to the fact that he wanted to partially align the section on Og with the Sihon narrative, which contained no parallel to Deut 3:3a and the banning of cities.*)

3.6.2 Completing Numbers 32

Whether all the remaining text of Numbers 32 was added by a single redactor or was introduced by a variety of hands over multiple updates cannot be determined with any certainty. The following analysis has been separated thematically, demonstrating the various harmonising strategies employed to create as unified and complete a narrative as possible. As will be discussed below, the remaining verses function to reshape the resulting (conflated) narrative and introduce theological expansions to bring the narrative into greater alignment with the wider book of Numbers or to reduce perceived issues within the chapter itself.

[1]Many livestock had the sons of Reuben and the sons of Gad: very many. And they saw the land of Jazer and the land of Gilead and behold, the place (מקום) was a place for livestock.

[2]The sons of Gad and the sons of Reuben came and they spoke to Moses, *Eleazar the priest and the chiefs of the congregation* saying,

[3]*Ataroth, Dibon, Jazer, Nimrah, Heshbon, Elealeh, Sebam, Nebo and Beon*

[4]The land which Yʜwʜ struck before the congregation of Israel it is a land for livestock, and your servants have livestock

[5]and they said, "If we have found favour in your eyes, grant this land to your servants as a possession (אחזה), let us not cross over the Jordan

[6]and Moses said to the sons of Gad and to the sons of Reuben, "your brothers go to war and you sit here?

[7]*Why do you discourage the hearts of the sons of Israel from going over to the land which Yʜwʜ gave to them?*

[8]*Thus your fathers did, when I sent them from Kadesh-barnea to see the land*

[9]*they went up as far as Nahal Eshcol and saw the land and discouraged the hearts of the sons of Israel to prevent them from going into the land which Yʜwʜ had given to them*

[10]*And Yʜwʜ burned with anger on that day and swore saying*

[11]*The men who went up from Egypt, twenty years old and upwards, shall not see the ground that I swore to Abraham, to Isaac and to Jacob, because they have not wholly followed me*

[12]*except Caleb son of Jephunneh the Kennizite and Joshua son of Nun because they fully followed Yʜwʜ*

[13]*And Yʜwʜ burned with anger against Israel and they wandered in the wilderness forty years until all the generation, who had done evil in the eyes of Yʜwʜ, was gone*

[14]*and behold, you stand in place of your fathers, a brood of sinful men, to further increase the burning anger of Yʜwʜ upon Israel*

[15]*because you turn away from following him, he will rest longer in the wilderness, and you will corrupt all these people."*

[16]and they *approached him and* said, "we will build sheep pens for our livestock here and cities for our children

[17]we will equip ourselves and hasten before the sons of Israel until we have brought them to their place (מקום), *and our children will live in fortified cities because of those who dwell in the land*

[18]we will not return to our homes until the sons of Israel each inherit (התנחל) their inheritance (נחלה)

3.6 Joining Priestly and Deuteronomistic Texts

^{19}therefore we will not inherit (ננחל) with them from across the Jordan and beyond, because our inheritance (נחלה) comes beyond the Jordan to the east

^{20}and Moses said to them, "If you do what you have said, if you equip yourselves before Yhwh to go to war

^{21}all those of you, who equipped yourselves, cross over the Jordan before Yhwh until he has dispossessed his enemies from before him

^{22}and the land is subdued (נכבשה) before Yhwh, afterwards you can return and be clear from Yhwh and from Israel and this land will be to you a possession (אחזה) before Yhwh

^{23}*but if you do not do so, behold you have sinned against YHWH and know your sin which will find you out*

^{24}build cities for your children and walls for your sheep and do what came from your mouths."

^{25}and the sons of Gad and the sons of Reuben spoke to Moses saying, "your servants will do just as our lord commands

^{26}our children, our wives, our livestock and all our beasts will be there in the cities of the Gilead

^{27}and your servants will pass over, all those equipped for war before Yhwh, for battle, just as our lord said

^{28}*and Moses ordered them to Eleazar the priest and Joshua son of Nun and to the heads of the fathers of the tribes of the sons of Israel*

^{29}and Moses said to them, "If the sons of Gad and the sons of Reuben cross over the Jordan with you, all armed for war before Yhwh and the land is subdued (נכבשה) before them, then give them the land of the Gilead as a possession (אחזה)

^{30}but if they do not pass over armed with you, they will possess (נאחזו) in your midst, in the land of Canaan

^{31}*and the sons of Gad and the sons of Reuben answered saying, "that which YHWH has spoken to your servants, thus we will do*

^{32}*we will pass over equipped before YHWH to the land of Canaan but our possessed inheritance* (אחזת נחלתנו) *is with us beyond the Jordan*

^{33}and Moses gave to the sons of Gad and the sons of Reuben and the half tribe of Manasseh son of Joseph the kingdom of Sihon king of the Amorites and the kingdom of Og king of Bashan, the land and its cities throughout

^{34}and the sons of Gad built Dibon and Ataroth and Aroer

^{35}and Ataroth Shophan and Jazer and Jogbehah

^{36}and Beth Nimrah and Beth Haran, *fortified cities and sheepfolds*

^{37}and the sons of Reuben built Heshbon and Elealeh and Kiriathaim

^{38}and Nebo and Baal Meon *(the name has been changed)* and Sibmah and they gave names to the cities which they built

^{39}*the sons of Machir, son of Manasseh, walked to Gilead and captured it, and dispossessed the Amorites who were there*

^{40}and Moses gave the Gilead to Machir son of Manasseh and he dwelt there

^{41}*and Jair, son of Manasseh, went and captured their villages and called them the villages of Jair* (הות יאיר)

^{42}*and Nobah went and captured Kenath and its villages* (בנתיה) *and called them Nobah in his name*

Table 12: Numbers 32:1–42

3.6.2.1 Leadership Harmonisation

The first category of expansions are found in vv. 2, 4(?) and 28, which were already discussed to some degree in § 3.4.2.

As noted, the LXX version of v. 4 contains a shift in wording such that it says υἱῶν Ἰσραηλ (*sons of Israel*) rather than עדת ישראל (*congregation of Israel*) as it appears in the MT. Considering that it was argued earlier that the "leaders of the congregation" found in v. 2 was secondary it has also been suggested, particularly in light of the LXX, that the word עדה (*congregation*) in v. 4 is also secondary.[315] However, the shift from υἱῶν to עדה in v. 4 is not so easy to explain ideologically, particularly given that עדה is generally understood to be a characteristically Priestly word.[316] Against seeing the LXX's use of υἱῶν as providing insight to an earlier version, Wevers notes, "In fact, Num never translated עדת ישראל by συναγωγη Ισραηλ ... When a reference to συναγωγη does occur, as e. g., 13:26 14:5,7 15:26,36 19:9, it modifies υἱῶν Ισραηλ, never Ισραηλ."[317] Thus it can be assumed that the wording of the MT in v. 4 belongs to the original Priestly layer and that the LXX wording represents the stylistic choice of the translator.

The inclusion of Eleazar and the leaders in vv. 2 and 28 on the other hand can be explained ideologically. Again, it was already argued that apart from vv. 2 and 28 the narrative is concerned with a dialogue between Moses and the two Transjordan tribes (ignoring vv. 39–42 of course), meaning the appearance of the other leaders did not fit neatly to the original narrative. The first issue to be discussed is the difference between these two verses. In v. 2 the Reubenites and Gadites approach Moses, Eleazar the priest and נשיאי העדה (*the leaders of the congregation*), whereas in v. 28 Moses instructs Eleazar the priest, Joshua son of Nun and ראשי אבות המטות לבני ישראל (*the heads of the ancestral tribes of the sons of Israel*). The group addressed in v. 2 conforms with the leadership of Israel introduced primarily in the book of Numbers (the נשיאי העדה appear twice in Exodus – 16:22; 34:31 – but otherwise in the Pentateuch only appear in the book of Numbers), when Israel is re-envisioned to be organised by military camp divisions about the sanctuary (e. g., Numbers 1). Within the narrative of Numbers, the leadership group comprising of Moses, the priest (originally Aaron and later Eleazar) and the leaders of the congregation play a role in community matters:

1. Num 1:16–18 – they take the census for the tribes of Israel.
2. Num 4:34 – they take the census for the Levites (cf. 4:46).
3. Num 27:2 – they hear the daughters of Zelophehad's request for an inheritance.
4. Num 31:13 – they oversee the booty brought back after the defeat of the Midianites.

---

[315] So CARR, *Formation*, 93.

[316] On the idea that עדה is typically Priestly, see, e. g., LEVY/MILGROM, עֵדָה; JOOSTEN, *People*, 36–42; RUDNIG, "Gemeinde."

[317] WEVERS, "Notes," 528.

In Num 32:2, then, it is logical that this same group is approached by the Reubenites and Gadites when they wished to receive a special allowance to dwell in Transjordan.

The ordering of characters in v. 28 conforms to the theocratic update introduced particularly in Num 27:21, where Eleazar is placed over Joshua as the true leader of Israel. This leadership ordering is also found in Josh 14:1, where the distribution of the Cisjordan land to the 9.5 tribes of Israel is detailed, and Josh 21:1, where the Levitical cities (cf. Numbers 35) are distributed from amongst the cities of the Israelites. Knauf argues that this leadership body represents the Judean leadership of the Persian province of Yehud, which, in light of the Priestly concept of land tenure discussed in § 3.4.1 above, perform the distribution of land as "ein sakraler Akt, nicht Politik oder deren Fortsetzung mit anderen Mitteln" (*a sacred act, not political or its continuation with other agents*).[318] The presence of this same leadership group in Num 32:28 brings the distribution of the Transjordan into harmony with these later distribution narratives in the book of Joshua. But beyond this, v. 28 also links to Numbers 34, where this same leadership group is appointed to apportion the Cisjordan by lot. Thus, by updating v. 28 the allocation of the Transjordan is brought into alignment with the traditions regarding the allocation of Cisjordan.

Although a lexical comparison of v. 2 and v. 28 suggest that these verses represent two related but divergent concepts of Israel's leadership, the differences are better explained contextually. The leadership group of v. 2 includes Moses and therefore belongs – narratively speaking – to a time prior to Israel's occupation of the land. Verse 28, alternatively, looks ahead to the time when the land is to be distributed and therefore pertains to a leadership group after Moses's death. Given that the Reubenites and Gadites make their request prior to Deuteronomy 34, (i. e., while Moses is still alive), it is only logical that they bring that request to Moses and his leadership team. Likewise, Moses's instruction in vv. 28–30 presume that in the meantime he will have died, and therefore the post-Moses leadership receives the instructions.

3.6.2.2 "City" Harmonisation

The next verses to be discussed are 3, 17b, 36b and 38*. These updates contain minor additions that appear to reduce the conflict between the idea that the Reubenites and Gadites wished to build cities with the later idea that they came into possession of Amorite cities via conquest.

The geographical issues associated with v. 3 are much the same as those discussed for vv. 34–38 in § 3.3.1 and so will not be repeated here. It was already suggested that vv. 34–38 was a product of a "pan-Israel" update to the tradition

---

[318] KNAUF, *Josua*, 136.

that importantly brought the tribe of Gad and the territory in southern-central Transjordan into the narrative. This was inserted into the existing narrative particularly via the verb בנה (*to build*), which linked to the existing stipulations that the Reubenites and Gadites would build cities for their family and sheepfolds for their flocks.

Verse 3, on the other hand, functions to bring the Priestly narrative into greater alignment with the Sihon narrative and the resulting conflated narrative of Numbers 32. Like Num 32:34–38, the territory envisioned in v. 3 clearly extends below what could conceivably be labelled the "land of Jazer" and so logically already presupposes the addition of the Gadites, which the Priestly narrative certainly does (see figure 11). Verse 3, furthermore, clearly presupposes the Sihon narrative as Heshbon now appears in the central position of the list of nine cities, suggesting some kind of chiastic emphasis.

The distribution of the shorter list of nine cities is curious for several reasons. First, despite Heshbon's central location in the list, the geographical distribution of cities about Heshbon does not follow the logic of Num 21:25b – "Heshbon and all its villages" – but rather accords much better with the territorial description from the Song of Heshbon. This supports the conclusion drawn here that Num 32:3 already knows the complete Sihon and Og narrative of Num 21:21–35. Second, the gap left above Jazer is also cause for reflection. This gap possibly functions to align with the depiction of the Transjordan in Deuteronomy and Joshua, which understands Gilead to cross the Jabbok (cf. discussion in § 3.1.1.1 and 3.1.1.2). If correct, this would limit Sihon's territory to the area of the Mishor and that area suggested to be the "land of Jazer" by Finkelstein, Lipschits and Koch in figure 7.

In any case, by inserting the list of cities in v. 3, the later editors harmonised the Priestly text, the Sihon and Og text and the non-Priestly text that included vv. 34–42. The Priestly Num 32:4 already stated that the Reubenites and Gadites were requesting the "land which YHWH struck before the congregation of Israel," which clearly assumes that the land of Transjordan was occupied and that there were cities captured. Likewise, Num 21:21–35 describe a sweeping victory of Israel over the two Amorite kings that included the taking of cities (cf. Num 21:25, 31, 32, 35). The only issue, then, is that the non-Priestly narrative assumed that the Reubenites and Gadites needed to build cities themselves (cf. Num 32:16, 24). However, the conflated Numbers 32, by placing v. 3–4 at the beginning, already created a lens through which the word בנה could be interpreted to mean "rebuild" as it is translated in, e. g., the NRSV.

Verses 17b and 36b likely provide a further elaboration for why the Reubenites and Gadites requested to build cities: they needed to fortify the cities that they had conquered from the Amorites. That being said, it is curious that the addition of these verses causes a number of continuity issues. First, as already discussed in § 3.4.5, the idea that there remained "inhabitants of the land" does not sit

3.6 Joining Priestly and Deuteronomistic Texts   181

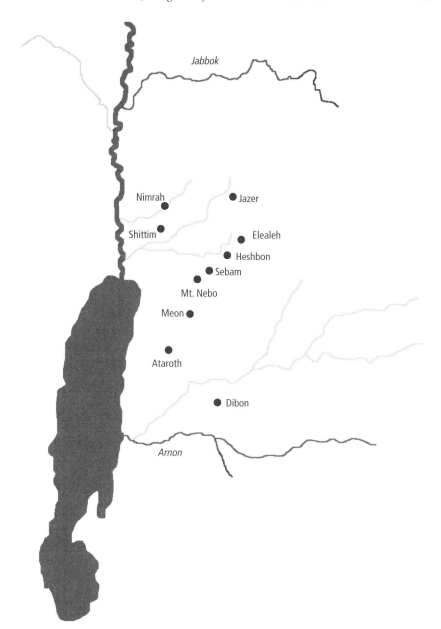

Figure 12: Cities Listed in Num 32:3[319]

---

[319] Map drawn by J. Davis. Toponyms detailed in figures 7 and 11 above,

182 *3. The Occupation of Transjordan*

comfortably with the idea that all the Amorites were destroyed. Second, the placement of the note in v. 36b is curious as it suggests that only the Gadites built fortifications whereas the Reubenites did not. Why this should be the case, however, belongs to the realm of supposition.[320]

Lastly, the additional information in v. 38, at least "the name has been changed" but perhaps also "and they gave names to the cities which they built," harmonises the alternate (later) list in v. 3, with the earlier vv. 34–38.

3.6.2.3 Ideological Harmonisation

Although this subsection only contains vv. 31–32, it is of great significance for supporting the above reconstruction and particularly the idea of a separate Priestly source. In these two short verses, not only can one find the important blending of the Deuteronomistic נחלה (*inheritance*) with the Priestly אחזה (*possession*) in the phrase אחזת נחלתנו (*our inherited possession*), but it functions as an important blending passage between the Priestly v. 30 and the Deuteronomistic v. 33, which are contradictory.[321] According the Priestly narrative, Moses commands the post-Moses leadership (v. 28) in vv. 29–30 to only allocated the Transjordan to the Reubenites and Gadites after they assist in the conquest of Cisjordan. Verse 33, on the contrary, explains that Moses gave the two and a half tribes the land and cities of Sihon and Og.

Verses 31–32 seek to harmonise these conflicting views by having the Reubenites and Gadites confirm to Moses, "that which YHWH has spoken to your servants, thus we will do. We will pass over equipped before YHWH to the land of Canaan but our possessed inheritance (אחזת נחלתנו) is with us beyond the Jordan."

First, as argued § 3.4.2, the self-designation עבדיך (*your servants*), functions within the later conception of Moses becoming analogous to the Torah. Second, v. 32 is an approximate amalgamation of the Deuteronomistic v. 19 and the Priestly v. 27, which further underscores its function as an ideological bridge.

Num 32:32we will pass over equipped before YHWH to the land of Canaan but our possessed inheritance (אחזת נחלתנו) is with us beyond the Jordan	Num 32:27and your servants will pass over, all those equipped for war before YHWH, for battle, just as our lord said Num 32:19bbecause our inheritance (נחלה) comes beyond the Jordan to the east

Table 13: Comparison of Num 32:32 with Num 32:19b, 27

---

[320] See, e.g., SCHMIDT, "Ansiedlung," 505.

[321] If later authors were simply content to replace נחלה with אחזה as, e.g., LEVINE, *Numbers 21–36*, 346, argues, then the combined phrase in v. 32 is difficult to explain.

Although it is not possible to completely remove the conflicting ideas, vv. 31–32 go some way to smooth out the passages by "meeting somewhere in the middle." On the one hand, the Priestly ideas of a "war before Yhwh" and אחזה are maintained, however they are tempered by the idea that Moses had already granted permission for the Reubenites and Gadites to build cities and sheepfolds in Num 32:24.

The overall idea that the land was granted in advance by Moses also carries into the book of Joshua in Josh 13:8. This same idea is also found in Josh 22:1–4, where Joshua confirms that the two and a half tribes (not only the Reubenites and Gadites) kept their promise and brought their kindred to a place of rest. In particular Joshua tells the two and a half tribes in Josh 22:4b, "now turn and go to your tents, to the land of your possession (אחזה), which was given to you by Moses the servant of Yhwh across the Jordan."

3.6.2.4 Continuity Harmonisation

The remaining verses (i. e., 7–15 and 23) bring the narrative into closer alignment with the broader, extant narrative of the book of Numbers.

Regardless of the underlying model, most scholars are agreed that verses 7–15 comprise a secondary insertion.[322] In many cases this was purely due to the idea that the base layer of Numbers 32 was traditionally attributed to J or E (or JE) and so the Deuteronomistic language present in vv. 7–15 logically belonged to a later insertion. This insertion, however, is of immense importance to the extant shape of Numbers 32, because it is only due to these verses that Moses is understood to react negatively to the Reubenites' and Gadites' request.[323] Where it was argued to be unclear how strongly one should understand Moses's opening question in v. 6 – your brothers go to war and you sit here? – vv. 7–15 are clearly accusatory.[324] Understanding vv. 7–15's place within the development of Numbers 32, then, is of special importance for understanding the underlying theology of the various redactional layers.

The extant form of vv. 7–15 can be seen to function chiastically, juxtaposing the faithfulness of Joshua and Caleb against the unfaithfulness of the Reubenites and Gadites.

A) vv. 7–9: R&G discourage Israel like their fathers
    B) vv. 10–11: Yhwh burned with anger and swore to punish Israel
        C) v. 12: Except Joshua and Caleb, who fully followed Yhwh
    B') v. 13: Yhwh burned with anger and punished Israel
A') vv. 14–15: R&G are behaving like their fathers

---

[322] See note 6 on page 82, and esp. overview of past scholarship in Budd, *Numbers*, 337 f..

[323] Artus, *Numbers 32*, 368, argues, "Verses 7–15 are not necessary for making sense of the narrative."

[324] Cf. discussion in § 3.1.3.

184   *3. The Occupation of Transjordan*

However, a number scholars have noted that within this structure, two distinct layers can be discerned.[325] This distinction is primarily based upon the alternation of the nomenclature בני ישראל (*sons of Israel* – vv. 7, 9, 10, 11) vs ישראל (*Israel* – v. 13, 14).[326] This raises the possibility that Num 32:13–15 were added concurrently with the Sihon narrative in the book of Numbers. Several aspects speak against this theory:

I. Significantly, v. 13 refers to Israel wandering in the desert forty years, which stems from the Priestly version of the spy narrative (Num 14:34 cf. Deut 2:14) and so logically belongs to a post-Priestly layer.[327]

II. Num 32:14 refers to the חרון אף־יהוה (*fierce anger of YHWH*), which only appears twice in the Pentateuch (Num 25:4; 32:14) and primarily in the prophets (Jer 4:8; 12:13; 25:37; 30:24; 51:45; Zeph 2:2; 2 Chr 28:11) and so also speaks against the idea that the singular ישראל represents a clue for an early layer. Verse 14 also contains the term תרבות (*brood*), which is a hapax legomenon in the Hebrew Bible. Although the theory that Moses's original response comprised vv. 6, 8, 13*, 14* remains plausible, it seems more likely that the use of ישראל without a qualifier functions to better link Numbers 32 with the Sihon narrative, where that same designator is prominent.

Taken as a whole, then, Num 32:7–15 comprise a single, late editorial layer that contains a mixture of non-Priestly, Deuteronomistic and Priestly references. As Marquis summarises,

> The conflation of phrases and ideas from J, P, D, and Joshua indicates an author cognizant only of the combined narrative in Numbers 13–14 and aware of details present in Deuteronomy and Joshua. The author of these verses combines the details readily and almost thoughtlessly; he does not know the individual stories, but rather the canonical account.[328]

Although one might take issue with the particulars of Marquis' statement, the core idea that the redactor responsible for composing vv. 7–15 presupposed some kind of combined, post-Priestly "Hexateuch" is compelling.

I. Verses 7 and 9 contain the rare combination of נוא (*discourage*) and לב (*heart*), which appear only in these verses and which Albertz identifies as a clue for the late providence of Num 25–36.[329]

II. The reference to Kadesh-barnea (as opposed to simply Kadesh) in v. 8 is not typically used in Numbers (only 32:8; 34:4), and elsewhere appears in Deuteronomy (i.e., 1:2, 19; 2:14, 9:23) and Joshua (i.e., 10:41; 14:6, 7; 15:3). The

---

[325] See esp. Mittmann, *Deuteronomium*, 97; Schmidt, "Ansiedlung," 500, and Wüst, *Untersuchungen*, 103–104.

[326] See note 157 on page 126.

[327] Further links can be seen in the use of the terms רב (*evil*) and תמם (*be finished*), which point to Num 14:35.

[328] Marquis, "Composition," 429–430.

[329] Albertz, "Redaction," 225n19.

3.6 Joining Priestly and Deuteronomistic Texts 185

use of the word, לראות (*to see*), also only appears in the non-Priestly spy narrative in Numbers.[330]

III. The reference to Wadi Eshcol in v. 9, stems from the non-Priestly version of the spy narrative (Num 13:23–24; Deut 1:24).[331]

IV. Verse 11 presupposes the joining of Genesis with the Moses story by mentioning the promise made to Abraham, Isaac and Jacob as well as the census regulation stipulating the counting of those twenty years old and upwards (Exod 30:14; 38:26; Num 1:3, 18, etc.). The combination of the land promised by oath and the patriarchs is rare in the Pentateuch (appearing in Gen 50:24; Ex 6:8; [Ex 32:12]; Ex 33:1; [Lev 26:42]; Num 32:11; and Deut 34:4), and is typically seen as the hallmark of the Pentateuch redaction, with Gen 50:24 and Deut 34:4 functioning as framing brackets.[332] However unlike the other verses mentioned above, Num 32:11 refers to the land as האדמה as opposed to הארץ, which suggests that it stems from a different layer than, e.g., Genesis 50 and Deuteronomy 34. The word, האדמה (*the land/ground*), is itself rare when used in reference to the promised land in the Tetrateuch (appearing only in Num 11:12 and Num 32:11), however it appears regularly in the book of Deuteronomy in variations of the formula: "the land Yhwh swore to your ancestors" (Deut 7:13; 11:9, 21; {26:15}; 28:11; 30:20; 31:20). Granting the overarching idea that vv. 7–15 belong to a post-compositional redactor, the use of the lexeme האדמה in Num 32:11 can be seen as an example whereby the late editors of the book of Numbers reframed the pre-existing material in Deuteronomy. In this case, by connecting האדמה promised on oath to the patriarchs, the editors of Numbers reformulate the Deuteronomistic presentation such that the Deuteronomistic אבת (*ancestors/fathers*) become equated with the patriarchs Abraham, Isaac and Jacob. This connection is more apparent in Num 11:12, which due to its position prior to the spy event cannot mean the first exodus generation as it does in Deuteronomy. The only logical ancestors that Numbers 11 could be referring to are the patriarchs. Thus

---

[330] This link was also noticed by, e.g., Noth, *Numbers*, 104. Whilst arguments for intertextual connections based upon the use of single (and commonly used!) words must always be viewed skeptically, within the context of spying, the word, ראה (*see*), is used rarely. In Deut 1:22, the people propose to send men to חגר (*explore*) the land and bring back a report, whilst in Joshua 14 Caleb recalls that he was sent to הגל (*go about/spy*) the land. Numbers 13 typically speaks of תור (*spying*) out the land, however this verb belongs to the Priestly elements of Numbers 13. In Num 13:18 Moses tells the people to ראה (*see*) what the land is like, which belongs to the non-Priestly portion of that narrative (see, e.g., Noth, *Numbers*, 104; Levine, *Numbers 1–20*, 347; Schmidt, "Kundschaftererzählung," 41n3; Baden, *Composition*, 143, who attribute Num 13:17b–20 to J (or JE)).

[331] Contrary to most reconstructions, Guillaume, *Land*, 195, attributes Num 13:23 to Pg.

[332] See, e.g., Clines, *Theme*, (esp. p. 29); Römer, *Väter*, (esp. pp. 561f.); Schmid, "Pentateuchredaktor," 185f.

186   *3. The Occupation of Transjordan*

Numbers 11 accomplishes implicitly what Numbers 32 accomplishes explicitly: the harmonisation of the (full) Pentateuchal traditions.[333]

V. Verse 12 refers to Caleb as "the Kennizite," which Knauf convincingly argues stems from a late, post-Priestly redaction and functions to demonstrate that Hebron did not belong to Persian period Yehud but rather was part of Idumea.[334]

VI. As already noted, the reference to the forty years wandering in the wilderness in v. 13 stems from the Priestly spy narrative, however the precise formulation of v. 13 is not replicated elsewhere.[335]

That vv. 7–15 are primarily focussed on the spy narrative is clear. The question is: Why was that particular story deemed important for the present context? One of the key characteristics of the book of Numbers, particularly in the central chapters (defined by the so-called "murmuring narratives"), is the intensification of required obedience.[336] The failure of the Israelites to show obedience reached its zenith (or is that nadir?) during the spy narrative, wherein their refusal to enter the land of Canaan (Num 13:2, 17) resulted in the entire exodus generation condemned to die in the wilderness.[337] In light of this watershed event, the idea that the Reubenites and Gadites even dared request land that lay outside Canaan was insufficiently explored in Moses's question in v. 6 alone. However, as with the Priestly version of the narrative (§ 3.4.2), the authors were careful to ensure that the Diaspora Yahwists were not implicitly targeted by Moses's rebuke. To this end the central clause of the chiasm (i.e., v. 12) addressed this concern.

As was noted above, Caleb is given the label, הקנזי (*the Kennizite*),[338] which emphasised that in the Persian period, Hebron – Caleb's city – no longer belonged to "Israel" (i.e., Yehud), but rather belonged to Idumea (i.e., Edom). Caleb's link to the Edomites/Idumea is made more firmly within the biblical material in

---

[333] This conclusion sits in contrast to Boorer, *Promise*, 114n216, who concludes that, "there is, then, no discernible pattern in the use of אדמה and ארץ in the oath of the land texts."

[334] Knauf, *Josua*, 138, labels this redaction the "Hexateuch" redaction, although Knauf's version of this differs from the more common Achenbach/Albertz/Otto version. Knauf further notes that during the Persian period many Judeans lived alongside Edomites and Arabs in Idumea. Gross, *Richter*, 130, also argues that Caleb likely belonged to the autochthonous residents in the Negev. Cf. Jericke, *Mamre*, 32–33, who observes that there are very few archeological finds in Hebron during the Persian period and it is not until the Hellenistic period that there are clear signs of settlement.

[335] No other spy narrative uses the verb, נוא (*wander*), however this verb appears in several prophetic texts (e.g., Jer 14:10; Am 8:12). Similarly, the phrase, כל־הדור (*all the generation*), does not appear in the other spy narratives, but does appear in Deut 2:14. Joshua 5:6 alternatively uses כל־הגוי (*all the nation*), in relation to the death of the first generation. Furthermore, the phrase, הרע בעיני יהוה (*evil in the sight of YHWH*) also does not appear in the spy narratives, however it does appear in Deut 31:29, where Moses foretells that Israel will do what is evil after he dies, and Judg 2:11, where Israel begins to act wickedly after the death of Joshua.

[336] See, e.g., Frankel, *Murmuring*.

[337] See, e.g., Frevel, *Transformations*, 65.

[338] As Artus, "Josué 13–14," 244, notes, "L'histoire littéraire des traditions concernant Caleb est complexe …" (*The literary history of the traditions concerning Caleb are complex …*).

several places: (1) In Gen 15:18–19, Abraham is promised that his descendants will inherit, among others, the land of the Kenites and Kennizites, (2) Gen 36:11, 15 and 42 report that Kenaz (the Kennizite patriarch) was a son of Eliphaz, son of Esau, whose descendants are said in Deut 23:8 to be allowed admittance into the assembly of Yhwh,[339] and (3) Knauf notes that the story of Caleb's daughter uses Aramaic word forms (e.g., the spelling of the word for 'melted' is המסו in Deut 1:28, whereas it is המסיו in Josh 14:8), which was the lingua franca of Idumea.[340] In the context of Numbers 32, there is no reason to suppose the authors were concerned with the allocation of Hebron, nor does it make sense to see this nomenclature as a derogation of the Judean hero in favour of his Northern counterpart, Joshua.[341] Caleb is here depicted, alongside Joshua, as a role model of faithful, Yahwistic behaviour. Therefore, the most logical explanation is that Caleb's Kennizite label functions to signify that both those within (Joshua) and without (Caleb) the land of "Israel" can be exemplary Yahwists, and that the issue being raised against the Reubenites and Gadites is the appearance that their request (1) arose from a lack of trust in the promises of Yhwh to bring them safely into the land of Canaan, just like the Israelites in the spy narrative and (2) the seeming disregard for the fate of their brother Israelites.

Moses's additional rebuke in vv. 7–15 is answered neatly by the following verses. In vv. 16–19, the Reubenites and Gadites prove that their request was neither motivated by fear of entering Canaan nor due to their lack of concern for their brother Israelites, for in these verses they propose not only to go before their fellow Israelites into battle but also to remain in Canaan until every tribe had obtained their land.

It seems likely that the authors of vv. 7–15 also updated v. 16 with "and they approached him" in order to further emphasise the Reubenites' and Gadites' humble response (cf. § 3.1.3). Furthermore, v. 23 – but if you do not do so, behold you have sinned against Yhwh and know your sin (חטאת) will find you – likely also belongs to this same update, so that Moses's acceptance of the Reubenites' and Gadites' proposal is more closely linked back to vv. 7–15 via the word חטאת, which appears in v. 14.

---

[339] See also discussion in Artus, "Josué 13–14," 245.

[340] Knauf, *Josua*, 139.

[341] On the association of Caleb and Joshua with Yehud and Samaria respectively, see also, Artus, "Numbers 32," 381.

3.7 Conclusion

This chapter began with the observation that the Transjordan occupation was so disruptive to the depiction of the promised land being confined to Cisjordan that it required a significant explanation.

This explanation was discovered via a detailed geographical investigation of Num 32:1, wherein "the land of Jazer" was shown to be a conspicuous detail that only made sense if one did not presuppose the Sihon tradition. It was argued that the extant Sihon narrative had pushed the Moabite border to the Arnon, with the result that "the plains of Moab" no longer belonged to the Moabites. Ignoring the Sihon tradition, it was suggested that the land envisioned in Num 32:1 most likely had historical roots and described the Transjordan territory controlled by the Nimshides. In this period, the Moabites did indeed occupy the "plains of Moab" with Israel occupying most of the rest of Transjordan.

Granting the arguments made in § 2.3.1, it was suggested that the reason why the Transjordan tradition was so disruptive was because it plausibly had its roots in the charter myth of Jeroboam II, possibly as part of a Moses-exodus narrative. In such a narrative, the idea of Israel dwelling in Transjordan would have not caused any theological issues, as the Jordan was simply a geographical separator within the territory of Israel.

The base narrative of Numbers 32 was argued to comprise Num 32:1*, 5b*, 6*, 16*, 17a, 20a, 22aβ, 24. This non-Priestly narrative, however, already contained details that suggested that this base layer could not be directly linked to a Northern charter myth. The very fact that the Reubenites' and Gadites' request was questioned by Moses (Num 32:6) and that measures had to be agreed upon for the request to be granted, rather point to the idea that the Jordan was already considered to border the promised land. In light of the fuller discussion in § 2.3.2, it was suggested that this early layer of the narrative is better understood to belong to a Judean re-interpretation, wherein the promised land described Josiah's Judah (cf. Josh 10:40–42*) and so making the Transjordan lay outside of that.

As the Pentateuchal traditions developed, this fundamental tradition was gradually brought into theological alignment with those traditions. It was argued in § 3.2 that the Sihon narrative was a theologically motivated response to Numbers 32, which instead aimed to explain the occupation of Transjordan via the Deuteronomistic ideal of ירש (possession/dispossession). Particularly with the key phrase דברי שלום (with words of peace) in Deut 2:26, the original Deuteronomistic Sihon narrative adopted the language of Deut 20:10–15 and depicted Sihon of Heshbon as a city-king, who dwelt outside the area that Yhwh had promised to give Israel as a נחלה (inheritance). This allowed the Transjordan to remain outside of the promised land but also provided a theologically grounded reason for why Israel occupied territory in Transjordan. In introducing the Sihon event into Moses's introductory speech in Deuteronomy, the Sihon event also needed to be narrated in Numbers. The analysis of Num 21:21–25* demonstrated that this narrative was not simply "pasted" into Numbers, but was rather carefully edited and adapted to better fit into the narrative context of the pre-existing Numbers narrative.

In § 3.3, it was observed that the list of cities in Num 32:34–38 and 39–42, did not align geographically with the idea of Sihon as a city-king and so did not belong to the same hand as the Sihon tradition. Rather it was suggested that the list of cities arose from the inclusion of the tribe of Gad into the conception of Israel, whose historical roots lay in southern Transjordan. The addition of Gad, it was argued, likely belonged to part of a "pan-Israel" update, whose initial aim was to bring the North and the South under a single Yahwistic umbrella via the shared ancestor of Jacob. That being said, the precise dating and location of this update represents the most uncertain step in the present reconstruction. More specifically, it remains unclear if this idea was already nascent in the preexilic period or if it only arose with the arrival of the Priestly source, which much more strongly conceived of the twelve tribes of Israel. Further research is required to resolve this uncertainty.

In § 3.4 it was argued that the Priestly material in Numbers 32 was better conceived as a parallel account to the non-Priestly narrative rather than as a supplement or Fortschreibung built atop the non-Priestly base text. This insight was solidified in the demonstration that a Priestly narrative – featuring an introduction, middle and conclusion – could be seen to sit alongside the non-Priestly narrative. The Priestly text, furthermore, demonstrated a different concept of the Transjordan that was not built upon Deuteronomy's idea of ירש. Despite introducing the land as the result of Yhwh's victory (v. 4), the text never equated this with any subsequent rights to dwell there. Rather the Reubenites and Gadites still needed to request special permission to dwell in that land. It was further suggested that one of the aims of this retelling was to reflect upon the Diaspora, in doing so the narrative granted the rights to dwell outside of Canaan but at the same time reinforced the special position of Canaan as God's land.

The pan-Israel expansion succeeded in bringing in the historical land of the Gadites into the biblical Transjordan tradition, however this also introduced the issue that the land of Sihon, king of Heshbon, could no longer logically describe the area claimed by Israel in Num 32:34–42. In order to maintain Deuteronomy's core theological stance of land inheritance, a new strategy was needed to explain Israel's Transjordan occupation. In § 3.5 it was argued that Sihon was subsequently made an Amorite king of central Transjordan and the character of Og was introduced, who was an Amorite king of northern Transjordan and Bashan. Israel's victory over these two kings was then used to explain Israel's right of ירש for the entirety of Transjordan, from the Arnon to Bashan. The key detail was the introduction of their Amorite heritage, which made these two Transjordan kings belong to those nations that Yhwh had designated for destruction. Particularly via the addition of Deut 2:24aβ–25, Sihon was shown to be the first enemy of Israel's conquest.

However, this same conception was not brought into the book of Numbers, which was perhaps due to the greater Priestly influence in that book. This is perhaps also supported by the so-called "secular" nature of Numbers' Sihon and Og narrative in contrast to Deuteronomy's.

Having argued that the Priestly material of Numbers 32 originally belonged to a stand-alone narrative, it followed that there would be evidence of conflation between the Priestly and non-Priestly material. Ranging from minor wording adjustments to the significant addition of vv. 7–15, it was shown in § 3.6 that most of the remaining verses demonstrated a very clear mixture of Priestly and Deuteronomistic language. Via these updates, tensions between the two originally separate versions were at least reduced, if not removed.

It was not the intention of the present investigation to develop a new Pentateuchal model, and although the major changes to the tradition identified above can likely correlate to redactional layers, it is methodologically unsound to propose a model for the growth of the whole Pentateuch based upon the investigation of so few chapters. What can more safely be concluded is the major changes identified above are best explained via the idea of texts responding to other texts; the development of the textual network was commonly guided far more by ideological/theological concerns brought about by the reaction between various texts than it was with historical concerns.

Perhaps unsurprisingly, most of the major ideological changes match to the three major building blocks already identified by scholars for at least the past 100 years (Priestly, Deuteronomistic, not-P-not-D). However, it was also suggested, particularly via the idea of a pan-Israel and the introduction of the Gadites, that there was at least one other major ideological change. Furthermore, it was also suggested that there was a clear idea of reciprocity to any given update. Numbers was updated in light of Deuteronomy, but Deuteronomy was also updated in light of Numbers. Even the idea of a standalone "Priestly Hexateuch" required that the peaceful ideals of Pg needed to be relaxed in order to accommodate the idea of Israel's conquest.

Chapter 4

Female Inheritance

The paired legislation concerning Zelophehad's daughters found in Num 27:1–11 and 36:1–12, almost regardless of model, are attributed to some of the latest materials in the Pentateuch. Once again, Noth wrote of Numbers 26–36:

No proper sequence is maintained in this whole complex of later additions. We shall have to reckon with the fact that the individual units were simply added one after the other in the order in which they appeared.[1]

Thus, according to Noth, the majority of chapters at the end of Numbers do not belong to a source and must be considered late. As shown in the Appendix, Campbell and O'Brien (who typically follow Noth) also suggest that neither of the Zelophehad's daughters pericopes belongs to a source, Achenbach attributes these materials to ThB I and III respectively and Albertz allocates both to his final redactor, PB5. Kratz suggests that both pericopes belong to late redactions that already presuppose the context of the Enneateuch (Genesis – 2 Kings) or even the Pentateuch (which for Kratz was a later development from the Enneateuch) and Seebass allocates both pericopes to his Num-Komposition.[2] Thus, it can be concluded that most scholars assume these legislative pericopes were composed after the Priestly writing had already been joined to the non-Priestly one.[3] As with Numbers 32, this chapter will seek to determine the compositional sequence of the two pericopes concerning Zelophehad's daughters in order to determine the veracity of these conclusions.

Within the book of Numbers, the legislation regarding Zelophehad's daughters belongs to the rare type of text that is both narrative and legislation. There are only four such legal-narratives in the Pentateuch: Lev 24:10–16; Num 9:6–10; Num 15:32–36 and Num 27:1–11, all of which share a common form and repeated linguistic markers. As Frevel summarises, "these texts ... are linked by the fact that Moses cannot settle the interpretation on his own on the basis of the extant law, but rather is dependent on a supplementary revelation from God."[4] Aaron labels these special legal-narratives "oracular scenes" whilst Chavel calls

---

[1] NOTH, *Numbers*, 10.

[2] KRATZ, *Composition*, 109; SEEBASS, *Numeri I*, 23.

[3] One important exception in this regard is SCHMIDT, *Numeri*, 9, who argues that Num 27:1–11 belongs to an expansion of the still independent P document.

[4] FREVEL, *Formation*, 24–25.

192   *4. Female Inheritance*

them "oracular novellas."[5] Oracular novellae are characterised by a situation in which the legal ruling is unclear.[6] Thus, the case is brought before Moses to receive a legal verdict, Moses in turn is unsure of the correct response and brings the case before the Lord. Yhwh responds to the specific case at hand with the proclamation of a new law for all Israel.[7]

In Num 27:1–11 the precise contours of the legal-narrative are as follows:

I. The legal conundrum (vv. 1–4): the five daughters of the Manassite Zelophehad come before the Israelite leadership and note that their father died without any male heirs. They petition for the right to receive their father's אחזה (*possession*) in his stead in order that his name not be removed from the clan.

---

[5] Aaron, "Ruse," 2, 4; Chavel, *Law*, 12. Fishbane, *Interpretation*, 98, simply refers to them as "*ad hoc* legal situations."

[6] Weingreen, "Zelophchad," 520, suggests that these instances should be regarded as, "indicative of the growth of case-law in ancient Israel."

[7] According to Chavel, *Law*, 6–7, oracular novellae follow a generalised form: (1) A narrative setting, e. g., "The children of Israel were in the wilderness" (Num 15:32a). (2) The legal conundrum, e. g., "they found a man gathering sticks on the day of the Sabbath" (Num 15:32b). (3) An inquiry is made to the legal authorities, e. g., "Those who found him gathering sticks brought him to Moses, Aaron, and the whole congregation." (Num 15:33). (4) The legal case is presented, e. g., In the case of Numbers 15, the case has already been detailed in the definition of the problem, in Num 9:7, for example, those Israelites who would miss the Passover ask, "Although we are unclean through touching a corpse, why must the opportunity to present Yhwh's offering at its appointed time among the children of Israel be withdrawn?" (5) An oracular inquiry is made, however this category is extremely inconsistent. The 'inquiry' is often implied rather than actually stated; thus Lev 24:12 states, "and they set him under watch, until they gained clarity by the word of Yhwh," and Num 15:34 states, "They put him in custody, because it was not clear what should be done to him," whilst Num 9:8 states, "Moses said to them, "Wait, so that I may hear what Yhwh commands concerning you," and Num 27:5 states, "Moses brought their case before Yhwh." (6) A ruling is given, e. g., "Bring the curser outside the camp, all who heard him shall lay hands upon his head and all the congregation shall stone him." (Lev 24:14). (7) A statutory law is given, e. g., "Speak to the children of Israel saying: Any man or his descendants, because he is unclean from a corpse or is far away on a journey, shall keep the Passover to Yhwh. In the second month on the fourteenth day, at twilight, they shall keep it ..." (Num 9:10–11). (8) The fulfilment is announced, "The whole congregation brought him outside the camp and stoned him to death, just as Yhwh had commanded Moses." (Num 15:36).

However, despite enumerating this detailed structure, none of the four oracular novellas contain all eight components. Indeed, in his concluding chapter, Chavel is unable to precisely define why these four oracles were presented in this peculiar way and others were not (p. 257 f.). Chavel suggests that the oracular novellas represent the crossover point between law and prophecy, by bringing further clarity to the roles of each with respect to each other (p. 15). He also argues that they represent the character and nature of the Priestly source, "stripped down to their essentials and crystallised in miniature form" (p. 18). This too is dubious considering that these four oracular scenes are generally considered to be very late texts.

Milgrom, *Numbers*, 230, suggests a 7-part form: "(1) identification/genealogy of the individual(s), (2) who 'comes forward' and (3) 'stands before' Moses and the assembly or priest and (4) states the case, after which (5) the case is brought before the Lord, who (6) gives a decision that is then (7) generalized through the formula, 'speak to the Israelite people' and (8) casts it in casuistic form, 'if a man ... if.'"

II. Seeking a solution (v. 5): Moses is unsure of the ruling and brings the case before YHWH.

III. A divine answer (vv. 6–7): YHWH gives a specific ruling for the daughters of Zelophehad, saying that they should indeed inherit in their father's stead.

IV. A universalised regulation (vv. 8–11): A more generalised ruling, including a hierarchy of claimants, is given for cases in which there is no direct male heir.

4.1 The Legal Conundrum

That Zelophehad's predicament was the source of a legal conundrum is itself a conundrum. This is because Israel already had a law that provided for the situation in which a man died without male heirs. This law is commonly referred to as the levirate marriage, which appears (in varied forms) in Genesis 38; Deut 25:5–10 and the book of Ruth. According to this custom, the widow of the deceased would marry her brother-in-law and the first son of that union would inherit the original husband's name and estate. It is somewhat curious then, that Zelophehad's wife is not once mentioned in the book of Numbers. One commonly provided explanation for why this is the case is that, for whatever reason, Zelophehad's wife was unable to produce an heir and thus the levirate marriage could not be fulfilled.[8] The solution of Zelophehad's daughters inheriting, under this understanding, therefore represents "Plan B." However, the present chapter will argue that the precise issues involved in the timing of Zelophehad's death mean that his (unmentioned) wife cannot be the solution to the problem.

In terms of its composition and structure, Num 27:1–11 represents a very interesting case. On the one hand, the text clearly contains materials stemming from two separate ideological backgrounds: The universal legislation of vv. 8–11a repeatedly uses the typically Deuteronomistic term נחלה (*inheritance*), the narrative introduction (vv. 1–4) uses the typically Priestly term אחזה (*possession*) and v. 7b functions as a harmonising transition featuring the rare combined term אחזת נחלה (*possession of inheritance*), which appears only in the final chapters of the book of Numbers (Num 32:39; Num 35:2 [inverted – נחלת אחזתם]).[9] Under a documentary perspective such linguistic markers are most naturally understood to represent different sources. However, as noted above, most scholars see this pericope as late, and so presuppose that it is already a post-Priestly construct, meaning that P and non-P had already been combined. However, the following analysis will demonstrate that there are several issues with seeing Num 27:1–11 comprising the work of a single redactor, even if he(/she) incorporated

---

[8] See, e.g., ACHENBACH, *Vollendung*, 568; LITKE, "Daughters," 213; MILGROM, *Numbers*, 233; NOTH, *Numbers*, 212; SCHMIDT, *Numeri*, 164; WENHAM, *Numbers*, 192–193.

[9] For a more detailed discussion of these terms see § 3.4.1.

194   *4. Female Inheritance*

earlier sources in developing his material. Once again, as Pakkala observed, when ideological differences were small, the nature of the editor's update was correspondingly minor, it is only in cases where an ideological leap was made, or when two separate sources where combined that such glaring fractures are easily discerned.[10]

4.2 The Universal Legislation for Heiresses: Num 27:8–11a

Num 27:8 Command the children of Israel saying, 'If a man dies without a son, then העברתם (*pass over/transfer*) נחלתו (*his inheritance*) to his daughter.

Num 27:9 if he has no daughter, then נתתם (*give*) נחלתו to his brothers.

Num 27:10 if he has no brothers, then give נחלתו to his father's brothers

Num 27:11a and if his father had no brothers, give נחלתו to the nearest kinsman from his clan and [the clan] shall possess it.'

Table 14: Numbers 27:8–11a

Although the generalised legislation contained in Num 27:8–11a result from the predicament of Zelophehad's daughters, there are a number of indications that this legislation was not initially designed as part of the oracular novella. As already observed, the language used in this legislation largely follows the Deuteronomistic style (esp. נחלה), whereas the narrative portion is Priestly styled (i.e., אחזה). More importantly, the generalised law does not actually match Yhwh's ruling concerning Zelophehad's daughters. Whereas all five of Zelophehad's daughters are given inheritance rights, the generalised law in verse 8 states that only one daughter shall be *transferred* the inheritance (see below).[11] Furthermore, the daughters' argument is rooted in the preservation of Zelophehad's name (Num 27:4) yet the generalised law does not once mention the perpetuation of the deceased's name, it is purely interested in where the property goes.

This raises the question of what precisely triggered the need to introduce this legislation. Particularly when the levirate law already seems to adequately solve the issues relating to death without a male heir. Knauf's claim – that the practice of daughter inheritance can be traced back to the practice of the Northern Kingdom from pre-biblical times (cf. Job 42:15) and was adopted by the Benjaminites who left for Elephantine in the 6th Century BCE and then introduced it into "Jewish" texts – is, of course, possible but it remains problematic; as the saying goes, "correlation does not imply causation."[12] Before dealing with this question directly, some broader observations on marriage and inheritance will be offered.

---

[10] Pakkala, *Word*, 362–369.

[11] This was also emphasised by Seebass, *Numeri 3*, 200.

[12] Knauf, *Josua*, 151–152.

4.2.1 Property, Marriage and Inheritance in Ancient Israel

The ancestral house, or household, (בית אב) was the fundamental social unit in ancient Near East.[13] Thus, as Ben-Barak argues, inheritance laws were designed to preserve two key components of the household: "1) the father's name and memory and 2) the patrimony that was its economic, social and legal basis, from generation to generation."[14] The household in ancient Israel, "was not only patriarchal, it was patrilocal," meaning that sons typically did not leave the house after they married, rather the newly-weds became incorporated into the בית אב of the son, and so fell under the authority of the son's father.[15] Correspondingly, when a man's daughters married they would leave their father's household and enter that of their husband (or their husband's father).

As Benjamin notes, "marriages in traditional cultures are always more a matter of economics than romance."[16] This is because, economically speaking, marriage typically comprised a two-way transaction: the groom would pay a bride price to the bride's household – either in direct monetary payments (e.g., Gen 24:53), by labour (e.g., Jacob worked for Laban in Gen 29:18), or even by completing a special task (e.g., Othniel seizing Kiriath-sepher – Judg 1:12–13; or David collecting 100 Philistine foreskins – 1 Sam 18:25–27) – and the wife in return provided the means for the husband to produce children who could later work the land (i.e., increase the family workforce) and continue the family line.[17]

One of the curious elements of Pentateuchal law is that no regulations for the מהר (*bride price*) are provided. That being said, Satlow convincingly argues the presence of the מהר in cases of seduction (Exod 22:15–17) suggests that it was practiced in standard marriages also.[18] A marriage document from the Miptahiah Archive,[19] found at Elephantine, records a *mohar* payment from the groom; TAD B2.6 states, "I [c]ame to your house (and asked you) to give me your daughter Mipta(h)iah for wifehood ... I gave you (as) *mohar* for your daughter: [silver], 5 shekels by the stone(-weight)s of [the] king. It came to you and your heart was satisfied herein."[20] In the case of TAD B3.3, which records Ananiah's marriage to the handmaid, Tamet, no *mohar* is mentioned, nor was it written

---

[13] Boer, *Economy*, 95, argues that the translation household is to be preferred over family or ancestral house because, "it is comprised of people, animals, the smells, sounds, tastes, and items of everyday life: tools, cooking pots, jugs, storage containers, clothes, pestles, lamps, and so forth ... households are eminently flexible, constantly reusing items for different purposes, and reconfiguring internal and external space in multiple ways, depending upon the needs of the moment."

[14] Ben-Barak, *Inheritance*, 3.

[15] Matthews/Benjamin, *World*, 16.

[16] Benjamin, "Rights," 5.

[17] Ben-Barak, *Inheritance*, 7.

[18] Satlow, *Marriage*, 200.

[19] Sometimes the name is rendered Mibtahiah.

[20] Translation from Porten et al., *Papyri*, 178.

196 *4. Female Inheritance*

that Meshullam, Tamet's master, was satisfied.[21] It is unclear how much the terms of Ananiah's and Tamet's marriage were influenced by economic factors (presumably it was a marriage between people at the poorer end of the spectrum), by the fact that Ananiah and Tamet already had a child together (Pilti), and/or how much it was influenced by the fact that Tamet was the handmaid of an Aramean, rather than of a fellow "servitor of YHH."[22] However, even in the relatively wealthy Miptahiah's marriage, the *mohar* amounted to a mere 5 shekels (which was hardly proportional to her dowry valued over 65 shekels), which could suggest that by the Persian period the *mohar* was more a formality and was no longer considered part of a two-way economic exchange.[23]

For her part, the bride would enter the marriage with a dowry, which functioned as financial security in cases of divorce or widowhood. Ben-Barak argues that the dowry, "belonged to [the wife], not to her husband, and she passed it on to her own children as she saw fit, regardless of her husband's children from other wives."[24] This function of the dowry can be well observed in the wedding documents from Elephantine. In the case of Miptahiah's marriage (TAD B2.6), it states that regardless of whether her husband wished to leave Miptahiah or whether she wished to leave her husband, "She shall [place upon] the balance-scale and weigh out to Eshor silver, 6[+1](=7) shekels, 2 q(uarters), and all that she brought in in her hand she shall take out, from straw to string, and go away wherever she desires, without suit or without process."[25] Even the handmaid, Tamet entered the marriage with a(n extremely modest) dowry (TAD

---

[21] See TAD B3.3 in PORTEN, *Papyri*, 208–211.

[22] Translation from PORTEN, *Papyri*, 208.

[23] SATLOW, *Marriage*, 206, suggests that already in the Persian period the *mohar* mainly functioned as a deterrent against hasty divorce.

[24] BEN-BARAK, *Inheritance*, 6.

[25] Translation from PORTEN, *Papyri*, 177–183. The entirety of lns. 7–15 of TAD B2.6 are as follows: "She brought into me in her hand: 1 new garment of wool, striped with dye doubly-well; it was (in) length 8 cubits by 5 (in width), worth (in) silver 2 karsh shekels by the stone(-weight)s of the king; 1 new [shawl?]; it was (in) length 8 cubits by 5 (in width), worth (in) silver 8 shekels by the stone(-weight)s of the king; another garment of wool, [finely-woven?]; it was (in) length 6 cubits by 4 (in width), worth (in) silver 7 shekels; 1 mirror of bronze, worth (in) silver 1 shekel, 2 q(uarters); h(ands); 2 cups of bronze, worth (in) silver 2 shekels; 1 jug of bronze, worth (in) silver 2 q(uarters). All the silver and the value of the goods: (in) silver 6 karsh, 5 shekel, 20 hallurs by the stone(-weight)s of the king, silver 2 q(uarters) to the 10." In lns. 22–26 it is noted, "Tomorrow o[r] (the) next day, should Miptahiah stand up in an assembly and say: 'I hated Eshor my husband,' silver of hatred is on her head. She shall [place upon] the balance-scale and weigh out to Eshor silver, 6[+1](=7) shekels, 2 q(uarters), and all that she brought in in her hand she shall take out, from straw to string, and go away wherever she desires, without suit or without process."

Regarding the problem that the practice at Elephantine was aberrant to that practiced in the "centres" Jerusalem and/or Samaria, ESKENAZI, "Shadows," 31–32, argues, "there was continuity during the Persian period between the practices of one Jewish community and another when both were under the same Persian imperial government, and communication was relatively easy and contacts were frequent."

4.2 *The Universal Legislation for Heiresses*

B3.3): "1 garment of wool, worth (in) silver 7 shekels; 1 mirror, worth (in) silver 7 (and a) half hallurs; 1 [pair?] of sandals; (ERASURE: 1 handful of) one-half handful of balsam oil; 6 handfuls of castor oil; 1 [tray?]; All the silver and the value of the goods: (in) silver {silver}, 7 shekels, 7 (and a) half hallurs."[26]

Satlow argues that traditionally the husband had access to the dowry and could use the funds as he saw fit during the term of the marriage, it was only in the case where the wife was no longer under the protection of her husband, such as in the case of divorce, or widowhood, that the husband's estate was legally obligated to return the full value of the dowry to the wife.[27] This meant there was always a risk that the husband would (illegally) squander the dowry and then be unable to repay it if the marriage dissolved.[28] This argument is supported by the deed of usufruct that Miptahiah's father granted his son-in-law, stating that Jezaniah (the son-in-law) was to "build up" the property but that it belonged solely to Miptahiah.[29] The key detail of this argument is that this property was not part of Miptahiah's dowry (cf. TAD B2.6) rather it was deeded separately and with precise limitations on the husband's control. Further support for the husband having control of the dowry is perhaps found outside of "Israelite"/"Jewish" circles in the Neo-Babylonian lawcode (LNB) from Sippar (~700 BCE). In § 13 it notes that if a woman remarries after her first husband died:

... she shall take (from her first husband's estate) the dowry that she brought from her father's house and anything that her husband awarded to her, and the husband she chooses shall marry her; as long as she lives, *they shall have the joint use of the properties.* If she should bear sons to her (second) husband, after her death the sons of the second and first (husbands) shall have equal shares in her dowry ...[30]

Thus, although the dowry remained an important part of marriages, even into the Roman period,[31] the Miptahiah archive already shows that the dowry was not necessarily all that a woman owned, and that property control was much more complex than the biblical evidence suggests. That being said, despite this very valuable evidence, it seems likely that life in the Egyptian colony, as it is reflected in the Miptahiah Archive, did not operate under the ideals of the biblical נחלה, and especially not the idea of an inalienable אחזה, thus one must remain cautious in attributing too much weight to the specific cases recorded

---

[26] The wording of TAD B2.4 reads, "But that house – you do not have right to sell it or to give (it) lovingly to others but it is your children from Miptahiah my daughter (who) have right to it after you (both)." Translation from PORTEN, *Papyri*, 209.

[27] SATLOW, *Marriage*, 204f.

[28] SATLOW, *Marriage*, 205.

[29] See PORTEN, *Papyri*, 172–175.

[30] Translation from ROTH, *Law*, 147–148 (emphasis added).

[31] On the discovery and general dating of the Babatha Archive, see, YADIN, "Expedition D," 235. For further discussion on the contents of the archive see, e.g., COTTON/GREENFIELD, "Property;" GOODMAN, "Story."

198 *4. Female Inheritance*

in Elephantine. As Satlow concludes, "it is safe to say that little in these texts is distinctly Jewish."[32]

Within ancient Israelite society a daughter was normally excluded from receiving an inheritance because her marriage to one outside the ancestral house would result in diminishing the family's patrimony, as anything belonging to the wife would be transferred to her husband (this issue is raised in Numbers 36, see § 4.5).[33] Satlow further argues that men generally wanted to avoid giving their women (both wives and daughters) direct access to property as it would grant the women independence. He further argues that the example of Miptahiah suggests that by keeping the deeded property separate from the dowry, a father could have more influence upon who his daughter married such that only in those cases where he approved of the husband would he then deed the property.[34]

According to Deut 21:15–17, when the head of an ancestral house died, the eldest son would receive a double portion of the inheritance and become the new head of that ancestral house.[35] This comprised the majority of cases and represents the standard practice. The patriarchal narratives emphasise this point in an inverted way, in that they depict the double portion being granted to Joseph, the firstborn of the favoured wife, Rachel, as an exceptional case in which the rightful firstborn, Reuben, son of the unloved Leah, is overlooked (cf. Gen 48:22).[36] In those rare cases where a man died with no male heir there arose a serious concern over who would inherit his property. The Bible testifies to two alternative resolutions to these rare cases. The first alternative is the so-called levirate marriage stipulated in Deut 25:5–10, while the second law is that found in Numbers 27:8–11a, whereby a hierarchy of claimants, beginning with the man's daughter, is provided.

---

[32] Satlow, *Marriage*, 206.

[33] Ben-Barak, *Inheritance*, 8–9.

[34] Satlow, *Marriage*, 205.

[35] The law in Deut 21:15–17 is similar to that found in the Neo-Babylonian laws (LNB) found in Sippar (~700 BCE). In § 15 it states, "A man who marries a wife who bears him sons, and whose wife fate carries away, and who marries a second wife who bears him sons, and later on the father goes to his fate – the sons of the first woman shall take two-thirds of the paternal estate, and the sons of the second shall take one-third...." Translation taken from Roth, *Law*, 148. See also discussion in Otto, *Deuteronomium 12,1–23,15*, 1653–1656.

[36] Giuntoli, "Ephraim," 228, persuasively argues, that the depiction of the sons of Joseph importantly function as a cypher for the returning exiles. He writes, "Like the returnees, Manasseh and Ephraim had been born outside the land, as Jacob himself underscores (cf. 48:5a) and, from a non-Israelite mother (cf. 41:50; 46:20a). However, by virtue of the patriarch Jacob's speech in 48:5–6, they become Israelites. Jacob declared them legitimate members of his family and, though they had never seen the land, they were made its owners. In fact by means of a subtle but key nuance, they were the only ones spoken of as having to fulfil the divine promises to become a קהל עמים, to inherit the land, to be fruitful and multiply there, and to perpetuate the names of Abraham, Isaac and Jacob."

4.2.2 Supplement or Replacement? Numbers 27:8–11a and Deuteronomy 25:5–10

Granting that the Bible contains two contrasting laws that deal with the same inheritance issue, the question naturally arises regarding how they interact. Many commentaries on Numbers argue that Num 27:8–11a presupposes, or at least acknowledges in some way, the levirate marriage law of Deut 25:5–10. Milgrom, for example, states, "The possibility of a man's wife surviving him and, where there are no children, marrying his brother (the levir: Deut 25:5–10) is not considered here, *but it must be assumed.*"[37] Budd even more strongly argues, "though the point is not stated explicitly it is surely to be assumed that Zelophehad's wife is dead ..."[38] Levine more specifically links the death of Zelophehad's wife to the fact that the daughters' request comes after the second census, and therefore, as part of the exodus generation, is implicitly dead.[39] Even if Levine is correct in his observation (it will be argued below that he is not), this does not explain why the generalised law in Num 27:8–11a conflicts with the levirate custom, as the generalised law cannot be connected to the wilderness setting of the narrative frame. Achenbach argues that the regulation in Numbers 27 implicitly presupposes that the levirate custom cannot be fulfilled, not only due to death, but also in cases whereby a wife may be unable to bear children (such as Naomi in Ruth, cf. 1:12).[40]

Although containing valuable observations, these solutions are not completely satisfying for several reasons. First, if the general law of Num 27:8–11a was indeed meant to come into effect only in cases where the levirate custom could not be enacted, then one must explain the significant issue that the levirate custom not only goes unmentioned in Numbers 27 but there are not even any shared lexemes to suggest that a scribal interaction between the two laws was intended. Second, the levirate law – in the specific case of Zelophehad's daughters – "is quite beside the point" as Litke correctly observes, as the issue being raised by Zelophehad's daughters is not about the *perpetuation* of Zelophehad's נחלה, the issue is rather that due to his lack of male heir, Zelophehad's household would have missed out on receiving a נחלה in the first place(!).[41] Within the narrative context of the Pentateuch the daughters make their request in the wilderness, before any tribe

---

[37] MILGROM, *Numbers*, 233 (emphasis added).

[38] BUDD, *Numbers*, 301. DAVIES, *Numbers*, 299, position is more complex but his conclusion is much the same as Budd's: "the most probable explanation for the lack of any reference to the levirate custom in the present narrative is that the narrator had assumed that the brother-in-law's obligation could not, in this particular instance, have been discharged, either because Zelophehad himself had no brother, or because Zelophehad's wife had also died, thus leaving no opportunity for her to be provided with male heirs."

[39] LEVINE, *Numbers 21–36*, 358.

[40] ACHENBACH, *Vollendung*, 568.

[41] LITKE, "Daughters," 213, also correctly points to the wilderness setting of Zelophehad's daughters' request as negating the levirate function.

200   *4. Female Inheritance*

or household had received their נחלה. Thus, Zelophehad's daughters' request must be understood as a request, not only to be heiresses, but more importantly, to be counted as the head(s) of a household *so that the household might receive its initial* נחלה alongside the other households of Manasseh (see more in § 4.2.3 below). Thus, the law of Num 27:8–11a should not be understood as "Plan B," nor should its interpretation hinge upon Zelophehad's wife, who also goes unmentioned in the other texts relating to Zelophehad's daughters (i.e., Num 26:33–34; 27:1–11; 36:1–12 and Josh 17:3–4).

Before proceeding with this question, it will be helpful to look at Num 27:8–11a on their own. Numbers 27:8 opens with a relatively rare formulation, ואל־בני ישראל תדבר לאמר (*and you shall speak to the sons of Israel saying*), which only appears elsewhere in Priestly texts (Exod 30:31; Lev 9:3; 24:15).[42] Similarly verse 11b concludes with a clearly Priestly, כאשר צוה יהוה את־משה (*as YHWH commanded Moses*), which only appears once in Deuteronomy (34:9 – typically attributed to P or post-P), but numerous times in Exodus and Leviticus. Verse 11 also contains the rare phrase חקת משפט (*statute of judgment*), which only appears in the present verse and Num 35:29.[43] This demonstrates that although the legal materials of vv. 8–11a use the Deuteronomistic word for inheritance (נחלה), the legal section as a whole has a Priestly frame.[44] This reinforces the conclusion that the generalised law of Num 27:8–11a was copied from a source and left largely unaltered by the Priestly editors.

In terms of form, each of the verses shares the same general shape: if [the man] has no X, then נתתם (*give*) נחלתו (*his inheritance*) to his Y.[45] With this general formula a cascading or rather ever widening circle of familial connections is stipulated: Daughter (sg) → brothers (pl) → uncles (pl) → nearest kinsman (sg). Although the cascading system is rather self-explanatory, it also raises some questions. First, as Wenham, for example, argues, the only innovation of law in Num 27:8–11a was the addition of daughters inheriting before the males, vv. 9–11a simply reiterate the traditional inheritance scheme (i.e., in cases where the levirate custom could not be enacted).[46] Furthermore, as Levine argues, with the amendment made in Numbers 36, "strict endogamy was imposed on daughters who inherited their father's land" meaning that daughters "ended up marrying into the same clan as would have inherited their father's land if there

---

[42] Cf. Cocco, *Women*, 157.

[43] The NRSV translates it as 'statute and ordinance', however the Hebrew text contains no particle for 'and'. See Litke, "Daughters," 217.

[44] Binns, *Numbers*, xxxvi–xxxviii, for example, allocates all of Num 27:1–11 as well as Num 36:1–12 to Ps. Achenbach, *Vollendung*, 557–573, allocates Num 27:1–11 to ThB I and Num 36:1–12 to ThB III.

[45] Verse 8 is the exception, but this will be discussed below.

[46] Wenham, *Numbers*, 192–193.

had been no dispensation to start with."[47] Thus, it is questionable what exactly the law in Num 27:8–11a achieves.

As § 4.2.1 discussed, there remained serious issues with women inheriting the patrimony, as the overarching system remained distinctly patriarchal. Even in the Elephantine documents, where daughter inheritance was clearly practiced even in cases where there were also male heirs, the tension between (female) inheritance and marriage is clearly present.[48] When Mahseiah deeds property to his daughter, Miptahiah, (TAD B2.3) the deed specifies, "I have no other son or daughter, brother or sister, or woman or man (who) has right to that land but you and your children."[49] Even though Miptahiah's children most likely took her husband's name and came under his authority, the legal document could still specify that the property belonged to Miptahiah and that it had to be passed on to her sons/children. Similarly in the right of usufruct granted to Miptahiah's husband, Jezeniah, the document (TAD B2.4) states that even in the case of divorce he could only claim half of the property as recompense for his work and even then, his half could only be passed on to his children from Miptahiah: "And furthermore, that half – it is your children from Miptahiah (who) have right to it after you."[50] But once again, one must remain cautious not to assume that the legal situation in Elephantine was universal.

Thus, the question remains as to why daughters were prioritised in the biblical text, especially because the additional ruling of Num 36:1–12, at the very least, significantly reduced their independence. Once again Levine's observation bears noting: "What complicates the present situation is the fact that the provisions of Numbers 27:1–11 are amended in Numbers 36, restricting their application … The daughters of Zelophehad ended up marrying into the same clan as would have inherited their father's land if there had been no dispensation to start with."[51] In light of this Chavel argues that the only potential difference introduced via the addition of heiresses was that the daughter was allowed to choose from a range of nearby relatives, rather than being forced to take the very nearest, but this seems a very pedestrian reason to introduce a new biblical law.[52] Seebass creatively suggests an interesting alternative explanation wherein the man who married a heiress chose to forego his own family rights and lineage, and instead continued the family line of the heiress's father. He further posits that such marriage terms would most likely be accepted by a third or fourth son, who would otherwise receive a very small inheritance from his own household and who, additionally,

---

[47] LEVINE, *Numbers 21–36*, 342.

[48] TAD B2.3 makes clear that Mahseiah also had sons (at least two, Gemariah and Jedaniah) as they appear as signatories on the deed of property to Miptahiah. See PORTEN, *Papyri*, 170.

[49] PORTEN, *Papyri*, 166.

[50] PORTEN, *Papyri*, 173.

[51] LEVINE, *Numbers 21–36*, 342.

[52] CHAVEL, *Law*, 247.

did not bear any real responsibility to perpetuate his own family line. Thus, the compensation for forgoing one's own family name by marrying an heiress was the benefits of a firstborn's portion of an inheritance.[53] In contrast to the levirate marriage law, which granted only burdens to the brother-in-law,[54] Seebass argues the introduction of daughter inheritance granted the accommodating male a financial benefit and therefore represents a major improvement.[55] Seebass supports his theory with reference to Neh 7:63 and Ezra 2:61–63, where it is reported that the priests, the sons of Habaiah, had married the daughters of Barzillai the Gileadite and were called by their name.[56] Whilst this theory is attractive, the idea of a husband taking on the heiresses name appears to be contradicted by the stipulations of Numbers 36 (see § 4.2.3), as if the husband did indeed take on the name of the deceased, the elders of Manasseh would have had no cause for complaint. Furthermore, it must be observed that whereas the levirate law of Deut 25:5–10 emphasised the preservation of the deceased's name (vv. 6, 7), in Num 27:8–11a the deceased's name is not once mentioned, rather it is only concerned with who receives the נחלה (also cf. Num 27:4).[57] Against this difficulty Davies argues that the word שם (*name*) in these cases is not to be taken literally, as neither Ruth nor Tamar actually name their children after their deceased husbands, rather he suggests that one's שם is connected with one's property.[58] This point will be continued below.

A completely different solution is offered by Kilchör, who, contrary to the vast weight of scholarly consensus, argues that the levirate marriage laws in Deut 25:5–10 were developed in light of the *older* legislation in Num 27:8–11a. Kilchör acknowledges that his reading is unconventional but argues that it makes better sense not only of the relevant texts but also of the, "natural reading position of the synchronic Pentateuch," by which he means that Deuteronomy's position as the final book in the Pentateuch means that it always has the final say.[59] More to the point, he argues that if one assumes that Deut 25:5–10 came first, then the law of Num 27:8–11a functions to overrule it, however if one assumes the opposite order, these laws are complementary.

Ultimately, however, the complete opposite of Kilchör's argument will be suggested here. In order to do so, Kilchör's argumentation will be outlined in some more detail as he correctly identifies the textual network that led to the devel-

---

[53] Seebass, *Numeri 3*, 201–202.

[54] In addition to producing an heir they had to support another wife, not to mention the potentially many daughters – both from the first husband as well as from his own "failed" attempts to produce a male heir – for which they received no compensation.

[55] Seebass, *Numeri 3*, 201.

[56] Seebass, *Numeri 3*, 201.

[57] See, e.g., Chavel, *Law*, 236.

[58] Davies, "Inheritance Rights 1," 141.

[59] Kilchör, "Marriage," 430.

4.2 The Universal Legislation for Heiresses

opment of the law of Num 27:8–11a. Kilchör correctly observes that neither Num 27:8–11a nor Deut 25:5–10 provide any clear textual links to indicate which one presupposes the other. It is true that the phrase בן אין לו (*a son was not [born] to him*) appears exclusively in these two passages (Num 27:8; Deut 25:5), but this alone cannot be used to suggest a direction of dependence. In light of this Kilchör argues that in a synchronic reading of the Pentateuch, one will encounter the law in Num 27:8–11a first and thus he proposes that when one encounters the law of Deut 25:5–10, they will already known the earlier law.[60] Such argumentation can be considered shaky at best, not least because the oracular novella style of Num 27:1–11 is broadly considered a late literary form and utilises a deliberate mixture of Priestly and Deuteronomistic language.[61] Thus, Kilchör's emphasis on the simplicity of a synchronic reading is unsatisfactory.

Kilchör's second major argument rests upon the intertextual link between Deut 25:5–10 and Lev 20:21. Leviticus 20:21 sits uneasily besides the levirate marriage law because it frowns upon a man taking his brother's wife in marriage. Because Kilchör suggests that the, "verbal coincidences between Lev 20:21 and Deut 25:5–10 are very vague", he once again argues that a synchronic reading makes better sense.[62] As such, Kilchör argues that Deut 25:5–10 represents a special case where Lev 20:21 does not apply (see below), as the son of such a union preserves the deceased brother's name.[63] Thus, a brief look at Lev 20:21 is necessary.

Leviticus 20:21 states, "if a man takes his brother's wife, it is impure. He has uncovered his brother's nakedness; they shall remain childless." This short prohibition contains two key markers that suggest that it was specifically designed to restrict the levirate practice. First, the word לקח (*to take*) in biblical parlance means "to marry," which is only possible if the man had died or had divorced his wife. If the taking was intended to only mean in sexual intercourse, this would rather be covered by the word שכב (*to lie*) and would fall under the law for adultery which resulted in execution rather than bareness (Lev 20:10). That the intention of the law is to remove the levirate responsibility (from a man whose brother had died), rather than to simply stop a man from marrying his brother's ex-wife is found in the second marker, which is that the penalty for failing to adhere to the law of Lev 20:21 is barrenness, an outcome that directly nullifies the entire purpose of the levirate marriage – to produce an heir.[64] However, al-

---

[60] KILCHÖR, "Marriage," 433.

[61] On the coordination of P and non-P materials see, e.g., CARR, "Method;" CARR, "Processes." On the late dating of the book of Numbers as a whole see esp. ACHENBACH, *Vollendung*; ALBERTZ, "Numeri I;" ALBERTZ, "Numeri II;" RÖMER, "Numeri;" RÖMER, "Sojourn;" RÖMER, "périphérie."

[62] KILCHÖR, "Marriage," 437.

[63] KILCHÖR, "Marriage," 437.

[64] NIHAN, *Torah*, 448–449, argues that the verb לקח is the same as that found in Deut 25:5, 7, 8, etc. and functions to link the two passages. See also MILGROM, *Leviticus 17–22*, 1758.

204   *4. Female Inheritance*

though the Holiness Code clearly frowned upon the practice of the levir, it did not forbid it outright. Schenker suggests that because of the presence of the levirate marriage law in Deuteronomy 25, the author of the Holiness Code could not completely forbid the practice, Nihan likewise calls Lev 20:21 a legal "compromise."[65] An additional point in favour of this conclusion is that the penalty of bareness stands in contrast to punishments of the other sexual laws, which range "he/they shall be put to death" (Lev 20:10, 11, 12, 13, 14, 15, 16) to "they shall be cut off in the sight of their people" (Lev 20:17, 18) to "he/they shall be subject to punishment" (e. g., Lev 20:19, 20).[66] The Holiness Code, then, legislated against the levirate custom, albeit not to the point of direct veto, but it provided no alternative in cases where a man died without a male heir.[67]

Granting that the Holiness Code speaks against the levirate custom, it follows that an alternative was needed. This alternative was logically provided for by the introduction of heiresses, which passed the responsibility of creating an heir for the deceased to the daughter rather than to a man's wife and his brother-in-law. This leads to one of the key details of the wording in Num 27:8, which suggest that the daughter was conceived to function as the means of producing an heir rather than a "true" inheritor in her own right. According to Num 27:8, the man's נחלה is to be עבר (*passed on/transferred*) to his daughter, whereas according to vv. 9–11a it is to be נתתם (*given*) to his male kin.[68] In fact vv. 7 and 8 are the only instances in the Bible where an inheritance is עבר, in all other cases an inheritance is either נתן or נחל (*inherited*).[69] By using the verb עבר, the authors draw attention to the different nature of the daughter's receiving of her father's נחלה and demonstrate that it is not the same process as that of the men. That a daughter was not "given" the property implies that she was intended to function as a temporary custodian rather than an owner in her own right, who

---

[65] SCHENKER, "Prohibitions," 172–173 and NIHAN, *Torah*, 448–449 respectively. See also MILGROM, *Leviticus 17–22*, 1758.

[66] Translations taken from NRSV.

[67] The Holiness Code's softer position was rewritten by the Temple Scroll via the use of the apodictic. In 11Q19 66:12b–13 it states, "A man shall not marry his brother's wife, so as to uncover his brother's skirt, whether it be his father's son or his mother's son, for this is impurity ..." Translation from WISE, *Study*, 40.

[68] This discrepancy was recognised by the SP, where the verb in v. 8 has been changed to נתן (*given*) in order to conform to the pattern provided by the other cases (vv. 9–11), however the SP did not replace עבר (*passed on*) in v. 7b, and so the transitional function of that verse is lost.

[69] Cf. COCCO, *Women*, 156, who, noting the verb change compared to vv. 9–11, argues, "by means of this literary stratagem – miniscule in size but of great significance in its effects – the author intends to emphasise that the transfer of the inheritance to the daughters constitutes something extraordinary from the legal point of view in that they are 'unqualified' to receive the paternal inheritance: they become its owners only through the direct intervention of YHWH who changes what up until that moment had been established practice."

4.2 The Universal Legislation for Heiresses   205

will similarly עבר the inheritance once a son is born to her.[70] Thus, the law for daughter inheritance functioned to pass the burden of producing a male heir from the wife to the daughter.

Not only does this solution solve the legal conundrum created by the Holiness Code, but it also alleviated society from what was clearly considered to be a burdensome practice. This is demonstrated not only in the narrative of Genesis 38, where Onan deliberately spilt his seed to avoid giving Tamar a child, but even the law in Deuteronomy 25 itself suggests the levirate custom was unpopular, as the majority of the law (vv. 7–10) is focussed upon what is to happen when the custom is refused.[71] This can also be seen in the story of Ruth (4:5, 10), where it was not the brother but a next of kin much further removed who fulfilled the role of the levir, and even then only in light of Ruth's wiles.

Despite this it must be admitted that by removing the levirate custom from standard practice, the law of Numbers 27 introduced new problems. First, as argued above daughter inheritance remained problematic due to the overarching patriarchal societal system. Second, without the levirate custom there was no longer a way to avoid "a sociological misfit, the young childless widow," because "the levirate not only continues the line of the deceased, it reaffirms the young widow's place in the home of her husband's family."[72] One must simply assume, as in the case of Naomi (Ruth 4:14–17), that the widow continued to be cared for by the estate.

Further support for the interpretation that the daughter functioned as a temporary custodian and that the intended recipient of the man's נחלה was his grandson can be found in later texts:

1. 1 Chronicles 2:34–35 narrates how Sheshan died without any sons and thus gave his daughter as a wife to his slave, however it was the son of this union, Attai, who ultimately carried on his name and lineage.

2. 1 Chronicles 23:22, reports that Eleazar died with only daughters and that they married the sons of his brother, Kish.[73]

3. The book of Tobit also suggests that late Israelite practice had transitioned from the principles of levirate marriage to that of heiresses marrying their cousins. Tobit 6:12 notes, "[Raphael] has no male heir and no daughter except Sarah only, and you, as next of kin to her, have before all other men a hereditary claim on her. Also, it is right for you to inherit her father's possessions ..." Here we can see that the daughter did indeed inherit her father's possessions, but this in no way meant that they did not ultimately belong to her husband.

---

[70] This understanding is also suggested by BEN-BARAK, *Inheritance*, 106; MILGROM, *Numbers*, 482.

[71] SCHMIDT, *Numeri*, 164, suggests that in the postexilic period difficult economic issues meant the levirate obligation was not always carried out.

[72] Kalmin, "Levirate," 297.

[73] See, e. g., BINNS, *Numbers*, 236; BUDD, *Numbers*, 389.

206 *4. Female Inheritance*

Although the above proposal solves most of the problems with daughter inheritance, the lack of clear intertextual links between Numbers 27 and Deuteronomy 25 still remains. To solve this problem a (brief) closer look at Deuteronomy 25 is required. The precise legal problem to be solved in Deuteronomy 25 is laid out in vv. 5–6:

> When brothers dwell together and one dies without a son, the wife of the deceased is not to marry a stranger, rather the husband's brother shall come and take her as a wife and perform the duty of a levir. The firstborn, which she bares shall rise up to take the name of the dead brother so as to not wipe out his name from Israel.

Although this law is often presumed to introduce the levirate law in its fundamental form, the law actually limits itself to cases in which, "brothers dwell together." Otto argues that, "Dtn 25,5–10 regelt nicht das Institut des Levirats im Grundsatz, sondern einen Grenzfall, den die gewohnheitsrechtlich funktionierende Institution des Levirats, d.h. die Verheiratung einer kinderlosen Witwe mit dem Schwager (*levir*) des Toten, nur schwer lösen kann" (*Deut 25:5–10 does not regulate the levirate institution in principle, rather a border case in which the customarily functioning institution of the levirate, i.e., the marriage of a childless widow with the deceased's brother-in-law* [levir]*, can only be solved with difficulty*).[74] Chavel similarly argues that, "the law in Deut 25:5–10... considers a case in which two brothers have deferred dividing their inheritance between them and live together; complication arises when one of the brothers, married but without children, dies; the remaining brother, rules the text, should marry the wife of the deceased, have a child, and so revive his dead brother's name."[75] Davies also argues that Deuteronomy 25 already represents an effort to tone down the pre-existing levirate custom, such as that found in Genesis 38, by limiting it to this specific situation.[76]

Several considerations support this interpretation. First, although it is true that the term אח (*brother*) need not only describe blood-related siblings, the additional condition in Deut 25:5 that the brothers must be "dwelling together," speaks against the idea that a more generalised communal "brotherhood" was envisioned and rather supports the idea that the law intends members of a single household.[77] Second, unless one wishes to presume that the story of Ruth contains a completely different conception of the *levir*, the levirate institution clearly contained a hierarchy of גאל (*redeemers/kinsmen*) that were not necessarily the

---

[74] Otto, *Deuteronomium 23,16–34,12*, 1850.

[75] Chavel, *Law*, 236. Lundbom, *Deuteronomy*, 706, likewise argues, "the levirate obligation as set forth here applies only when two brothers have been living together as joint heirs on the family estate."

[76] Davies, "Inheritance Rights 2," 266.

[77] Matthews/Benjamin, *World*, 8, for example, note, "'son'...'slave'... and 'brother'... in the Bible are often technical terms for covenant partners, people related to one another, not necessarily by blood, but by covenant."

deceased's אח (*brother*), and these remain completely unspecified in the law of Deuteronomy 25.[78] Ruth also employs the term מודע (*kinsman*) when it introduces Boaz in 2:1, which Campbell suggests is best understood as adding a "dimension of covenant responsibility to that of family responsibility."[79]

In short, there was no need for the editors of Numbers 27 to directly allude to (that is to say, combat/rebut) the law in Deuteronomy 25:5–10, as that law – strictly speaking – only covered an edge case in which the wife and the brother-in-law already shared the same living space. Because the basic levirate custom, which was presumably well known, was not actually legislated in the Pentateuchal laws, the introduction of the law for heiresses caused no conflict. The practice of heiresses could take priority over the (unwritten) levirate custom without having to contradict any pre-existing, authoritative Pentateuchal laws.

4.2.3 Summary

This section began by demonstrating that the generalised law contained in Num 27:8–11a, although undoubtedly joined to the narrative setting of Zelophehad's daughters, was in many ways completely separate from their precise situation. It was only via the Priestly framing verses 7b and 11b that vv. 8–11a were encapsulated into the narrative. Otherwise, the generalised law contained no evidence of being Priestly (it rather uses the Deuteronomistic נחלה whereas vv. 1–7 use אחזה) or for relating directly to the situation of Zelophehad's daughters. Furthermore, as will be discussed in § 4.3 Yhwh's ruling regarding Zelophehad's daughters in v. 7a was that all five daughters were to be נתן (*given*) their father's אחזה, but v. 8 rather commands that one daughter is to be עבר the father's נחלה. This in turn, led to the conclusion that the generalised law had to be analysed without recourse to the specific narrative situation that brought it forth.

It was also emphasised that the introduction of a law for heiresses stood in conflict with the levirate custom, which is alluded to in the legislation in Deut 25:5–10. This raised the question of how these laws were intended to interact, particularly because there exists no clear intertextual links joining the two passages.

---

[78] Campbell Jr., *Ruth*, 132, correctly observes, "if we judge from attested Israelite law as it is preserved in the casuistic law materials, those formulations of law which open with a statement of circumstances in an 'if such-and-such a thing happens' clause and concludes with a 'then ...' clause of consequence, we have nowhere else a connection drawn between marriage and redemption. If we trace redemption custom through the law codes, through narratives, and through the use of redemption language in speaking about God's care for his people, we appear to be in one circumscribed realm; if we do the same for the levirate custom, we are apparently in another. Only the Ruth story combines them."

[79] Campbell Jr., *Ruth*, 90.

208   *4. Female Inheritance*

That the levirate custom was broadly considered to be burdensome can not only be seen in the evidence of Onan and the unnamed גאל (*redeemers/kinsmen*) in Gen 38:9 and Ruth 4:6 respectively, it can also be seen in the prohibition of a man to marry his brother's wife (Lev 20:21). However, the Holiness Code itself did not detail an alternate solution for what was to happen when a man died without an heir. Thus, the introduction of an alternative legislation in Numbers 27:8–11a functioned to replace the broad practice of levirate marriage. The law given in Num 27:8–11a provides a hierarchy of potential claimants with the daughter being the first in line. Via the use of the special verb, עבר, the law in Num 27:8 suggests that the daughter is not conceived as a true owner, but rather she functions as a temporary custodian until a grandson can be produced to take over the role of a male head of the household. Interestingly, it was suggested that the introduction of this law caused no contradiction to the law of Deut 25:5–10, as that law already limited itself to the specific case in which brothers dwelt together.

That being said, replacing the levirate marriage custom with daughter inheritance created new problems, most notably that the deceased man's property was no longer guaranteed to remain within the greater clan/tribe. This issue is raised in Numbers 36 and will be discussed in more detail in § 4.4.5 below.

4.3 The Specific Case of Zelophehad's Daughters: Num 27:1–7a

Num 27:1The daughters of Zelophehad, son of Hepher, son of Gilead, son of Machir, son of Manasseh from the clans of Manasseh, son of Joseph came near, and these are their names his daughters, Mahlah, Noah and Hoglah and Milchah and Tirzah

Num 27:2and they stood before Moses and before Eleazar the priest and before the leaders and all the congregation at the entrance of the tent of meeting to say,

Num 27:3"Our father died in the wilderness and he was not in the midst of the congregation who met against Yhwh in the congregation of Korah, rather he died for his own sin and he has no sons

Num 27:4should our father's name be taken from the among his clan because he had no son? Give us a אחזה (*possession*) among our father's brothers"

Num 27:5Moses offered their case before Yhwh

Num 27:6and Yhwh spoke to Moses saying,

Num 27:7a"The daughters of Zelophehad have spoken rightly, you are permitted to give to them a אחזת נחלה (*possession of inheritance*) amongst their father's brothers.

Table 15: Numbers 27:1–7a

The basic outline of the argument to be elaborated below was already suggested in § 4.1.2. First, the specific narrative location of this oracular novella – after the second census, and thus the death of the entire first generation (sans Moses, Joshua and Caleb) but before any land had been allotted – logically plays an

4.3 The Specific Case of Zelophehad's Daughters

important role in how to interpret the request of Zelophehad's daughters. In this special and specific context, the granting of Zelophehad's אחזה to his daughters must be understood as the granting of the *initial* right of usufruct, such that Zelophehad's בית אב did not miss out when the land was first distributed after the conquest (cf. Josh 17:3–4). Second, in light of this, the absence of any links to the levirate custom or to Zelophehad's wife is readily explainable without having to "fill the gaps." Third, the literary features as well as the oracular novella genre itself all point towards Num 27:1–11, as a whole,[80] but vv. 1–7a in particular, belonging to one of the later redaction layers of the Pentateuch.[81]

In addition to this, one major, as yet unanswered question, is what prompted the creation of the narrative frame featuring five daughters of Manasseh? As discussed in § 4.1.2, besides the heiress connection, the generalised law of Num 27:8–11a has little in common with, or need of, the narrative introduction in vv. 1–7a. A hypothetical historical connection will thus be offered in § 4.3.4.

Verse 1 introduces the daughters of the Manassite Zelophehad, going back five generations including the ancestors, Gilead and Machir. These will be discussed further in § 4.4 (cf. § 3.3.2) so will not be detailed here.

Verse 2 reports that the daughters תעמדנה (*[they] stand*) before the Israelite leadership and all the congregation at the פתה אהל־מעד (*entrance of the tent of meeting*). This act of "standing" signals the presentation of a legal case, although the verb more generally applies to "drawing near" to the sanctuary (usually by a priest).[82] In the documents from Elephantine, the act of standing before העדה (*the congregation*) is performed in cases of divorce and presumably functions as a public declaration before the community (cf. TAD B2.6, B3.3, B3.8).[83] The Israelite leadership comprises of Moses (who represents the leader of the congregation), Eleazar (who functions "only" as a priest),[84] and the נשיאם (who most logically represent the heads of each of the tribes of Israel [cf. Num 1:16, 44; 2:3,

---

[80] See discussion on vv. 8–11a above.

[81] It will be argued in § 4.4.5 that Numbers 36 is later again. NOTH, *Numbers*, 211, for example, argued, "[Num 27:1–11] can scarcely belong to the original version [of P], but is certainly a later addition." BINNS, *Numbers*, xxxvi–xxxviii, likewise, allocates all of Num 27:1–11 as well as Num 36:1–12 to Ps. ACHENBACH, *Vollendung*, 557–573, allocates Num 27:1–11 to ThB I and Num 36:1–12 to ThB III. LEVY/MILGROM, עֵדָה, 471, also note that there has been a general consensus "that the *ʿēḏâ* was introduced only by a postexilic Priestly writing, and the presence of *ʿēḏâ* was a clear indication of late authorship or redaction."

[82] KNIERIM/COATS, *Numbers*, 273–274.

[83] The Elephantine Papyri indicate that the formal declaration of a divorce had to be given before an עדה (cf. TAD B2.6, B3.3, B3.8). See PORTEN, *Papyri*, 181–182, 209, 230 respectively. See also LEVY/MILGROM, עֵדָה.

[84] Because the initial case concerning Zelophehad's daughters occurs prior to Num 27:12–23, the eldest Aaronide son had not yet been invested with any "secular" authority. ACHENBACH, *Vollendung*, 567, argues that Num 27:1–11 and Joshua 17 have been deliberately linked together by ThB I in order to demonstrate that the Mosaic commandments of the Torah have been perpetuated by the Priestly cult (i.e., the priest Eleazar).

210   *4. Female Inheritance*

5, 7, 10; etc.][85] and perhaps, as Knauf argues, "repräsentieren den nachexilischen 'Hohen Rat', die Notablen- und Aristokratenversammlung, die seit Nehemia neben Gouverneur und Hohen Priester das Selbstverwaltungsorgan der Provinz Judäa bildete" [*represent the postexilic 'high council', the notable and aristocratic assembly, who from the time of Nehemiah, formed the administrative organ of the province of Judea alongside the governor and high priest*]).[86]

Besides the purely functional dynamics involved with this legal case, the social dynamics have in recent times become a common focus of feminist scholarship, whereby five women are seen to be critiquing the status quo of patriarchalism.[87] Seebass, for instance, writes, "so wird man zunächst kaum bemerken, wie kühn die fünf Frauen vorgehen, die dem höchsten denkbaren Gremium der Mosezeit eine Rechtssache vorlegten, ohne rechtlich einen nächstverwandten Mann einzuschalten" (*So one will initially hardly notice how bold the five women are, who proceeded to bring a case before the highest conceivable body in the Mosaic period, without the legal accompaniment of a closely related man*).[88] Such boldness must be placed both within the context of ancient Israelite society as well as the surrounding texts of the book of Numbers: the census of chapter 26 typically listed only males (which emphasises the strangeness of the inclusion of the five women in v. 33);[89] Numbers 30 stipulates that the oath of a woman can be nullified by her male "head" be that her father if she is unmarried, or her husband in the case that she is married; finally, Numbers 5 provides details for a ritual whereby the wife of a suspicious husband must drink a "cursed" concoction from the priest to prove her innocence, of course there is no reciprocal practice for males.[90] Later Jewish writings also attest to the merit of these women, Milgrom notes that the Midrash juxtaposes the daughters of Zelophehad's desire for

---

[85] See discussion in Pyschny, *Führung*, 193. One curiosity, as Samuel, *Priestern*, 163, 216, notes, is that even in those texts where the "leaders of the congregation" are present, they often play no role in the narrative.

[86] Knauf, *Josua*, 94.

[87] See, e.g., Sakenfeld, "Daughters;" Derby, "Daughters;" Ron, "Daughters;" Claassens, "Portion."

[88] Seebass, *Numeri 3*, 197. See also Ron, "Daughters," 261.

[89] Ron, "Daughters," 261, observes that in a complete reversal of tradition, the daughters of Zelophehad are named but not their husbands.

[90] That the social dynamics of marriage are primarily economic must also be kept in mind regarding the understanding of this ritual, although even that doesn't fully remove the bad taste it leaves in the mouth of the modern reader. As Frevel, *Transformations*, 305–310, has convincingly argued, adultery in the ancient world (economically speaking) could only affect men, as it was a husband's responsibility to support his wife and any children she might bare, regardless of whether they were from him or if they were the result of infidelity. Thus, (again economically speaking) the only party that could be injured in cases of adultery was the husband who was cheated on. As such, a ritual that effectively resulted in a divine abortion in cases of infidelity served both to protect the husband economically, but also to protect the wife from any ill-treatment from the ire of her husband (deserved or otherwise). See also the extended treatment in Cocco, *Women*, 7–116.

land in Canaan with the Israelite men's desire to return to Egypt (e.g., Numbers 14).[91] He further notes how the later rabbis took pains to compensate daughters in matters of inheritance (in light of the precedent set by Zelophehad's daughters), for example, by mandating that marriage contracts must contain the stipulation of support from the bride's father's estate.[92] Despite these positive and welcome ideologies, Aaron correctly notes that Numbers 27 and 36 inadvertently reinforce that Israelite society typically functioned without inheritance rights for women, for the story itself would be redundant if women were presupposed to already have such rights.[93] This must also be contrasted with other cultures in the ancient Near East where inheritance rights for women were much more common.[94] Milgrom notes:

Israelite practice contrasts sharply with that of its neighbours regarding a daughter's inheritance rights. It is clear that some other law codes expressly allow a daughter to inherit: Ancient Sumerian law ordains that an unmarried daughter may inherit when there are no sons, and so also do decrees of Gudea (ca. 2150 b.c.e), ruler of Lagash. Thus, the concession made by the Bible to Zelophehad's daughters was anticipated in Mesopotamia by a millennium.[95]

Egypt during the New Kingdom, for example, had especially favourable laws such that a wife would inherit a third of the estate with the remaining two-thirds being divided between the children (of both genders).[96] Thus, in the face of this evidence it must be concluded that the primary purpose of Num 27:1–11 and 36:1–12 has little to do with women's rights. Israelite society (at least biblical Israel) in general was far less "progressive" than its ancient Near Eastern neighbours. Yet despite this harsh reality, one also cannot avoid the observation that the story of Zelophehad's daughters portrays five women bringing a lawsuit against a patriarchal system and winning.[97]

The key to understanding the narrative portion of this oracular novella lies primarily in the daughters' petition. Verses 3 and 4 recount this petition, which contains some curious features. First, the daughters begin by noting that their father died in the wilderness, which is often taken to be self-evident, not only because of the content of the present pericope (which requires Zelophehad be dead) but rather because of the pericope's location after the census of Numbers 26, which presumes the exodus generation (sans Moses, Joshua and Caleb)

---

[91] Milgrom, *Numbers*, 230.
[92] For a fuller discussion see Milgrom, *Numbers*, 484; Satlow, *Marriage*.
[93] Aaron, "Ruse," 6.
[94] See, e.g., the survey of other ANE inheritance regulations in Ben-Barak, *Inheritance*, 111–200.
[95] Milgrom, *Numbers*, 482.
[96] Milgrom, *Numbers*, 482.
[97] Seebass, *Numeri 3*, 212.

212   *4. Female Inheritance*

had all died (cf. Num 26:53).[98] Second, the daughters state that their father was not בעדת־קרח (*in the congregation of Korah*) that came before Yʜwʜ, but that כי־בחטאו מת (*because of his own sin he died*). But what does this mean exactly?

The precise meaning behind the daughters' argument has often been the source of confusion. A number of scholars argue, based on texts such as 1 Kgs 21:8–16 (where Naboth's ancestral inheritance is taken by the state after he is convicted of committing treason – cf. Exod 22:27[28 NRSV]), Lev 27:20 (which states that if a field is not redeemed, it is no longer redeemable, and following the Jubilee it becomes "holy to Yʜwʜ" and an אחזה of the priests) and (indirectly) Ezra 10:7f. (whereby those who failed to attend the official gathering of exiles would forfeit [i.e., חרם] their property [i.e., רכוש {*goods*}]), that had Zelophehad been part of Korah's congregation he would have committed treason and therefore been prohibited from receiving an allotment.[99] Levine argues that the punishment enacted in the Korah event fell into the category of "*herem*, by which those condemned to death by the judicial process lost title to their estates, which would then be expropriated by the king or the temple."[100] A novel interpretation is offered by Fishbane who suggests that by bringing up the Korah event Zelophehad's daughters are subtly reminding Moses that Zelophehad was on his side during the rebellion and therefore it is time for Moses to return the favour.[101] How, then, should one interpret the reference to the congregation of Korah?

Numbers 16–17 comprises one of those stories where the non-P and P layers have been amalgamated but did not originally comprise parallel stories.[102] In broad terms, the character of Korah functions as the glue linking the Dathan-Abiram layer (who, as members of the exodus generation, complain to Moses about his failure to bring them to a land flowing with milk and honey or to grant them a נחלה – Num 16:7) to the 250-leaders layer (who contend that Moses and Aaron have wrongly set themselves apart from/above the congregation because all the congregation is holy [cf., e.g., Lev 19:2] and that Yʜwʜ dwells in the midst

---

[98] Cᴏᴄᴄᴏ, *Women*, 134–135, for example, argues, "The expression [our father died] includes a further element which is certainly not insignificant, the syntagma בַּמִּדְבָּר... the epilogue of the account of Num 14,1–35 leaves little doubt about the fact that the perishing of the whole generation of the Exodus is a direct consequence of lack of faith in YHWH by those who formed part of it. A lack of faith which – through divine intervention – is inexorably punished with their exclusion from entry into the land which God had sworn to give to the descendants of Abraham. That inevitably implies the death of them all בַּמִּדְבָּר הַזֶּה, 'in this desert.'"

[99] See e.g., Aꜱʜʟᴇʏ, *Numbers*, 545; Bᴇɴ-Bᴀʀᴀᴋ, *Inheritance*, 17; Kɴɪᴇʀɪᴍ/Cᴏᴀᴛꜱ, *Numbers*, 274; Mɪʟɢʀᴏᴍ, *Numbers*, 231; Sᴄʜᴍɪᴅᴛ, *Numeri*, 165; Sᴇᴇʙᴀꜱꜱ, *Numeri 3*, 207–208; Wᴇɪɴɢʀᴇᴇɴ, "Zelophchad," 521–522; Wᴇɴʜᴀᴍ, *Numbers*, 192.

[100] Lᴇᴠɪɴᴇ, *Numbers 21–36*, 345.

[101] Fɪꜱʜʙᴀɴᴇ, *Interpretation*, 98–99.

[102] For detailed treatments see esp. Aᴄʜᴇɴʙᴀᴄʜ, *Vollendung*, 37–129; Pʏꜱᴄʜɴʏ, *Führung*; Sᴀᴍᴜᴇʟ, *Priestern*, 202–235.

4.3 The Specific Case of Zelophehad's Daughters 213

of all and not just the elite [cf., e. g., Num 5:3; 35:34]).[103] The Korah layer, furthermore, adds a third level of contention, this time between the Aaronides and the other Levites (cf. Num 16:8–10).[104] So the first question is to identify which layer Zelophehad's daughters are referring to. First, as a Manassite, it seems highly improbable that Zelophehad's daughters are referring to the quarrel of the Levites, i. e., the Korah layer itself.[105] Second, Dathan and Abiram (and On? – cf. Num 16:1), were Reubenites not Manassites, which already suggests that this story should also be excluded. Ignoring this technicality, their punishment resulted in the earth swallowing אתם ואת־בתיהם (*them and their house* – Num 16:32), which, as v. 33 elaborates, meant that the punishment extended not only to Dathan and Abiram themselves but included כל־אשר להם (*all that [belonged] to them*), i. e., the women, children and animals. As such, had Zelophehad been included in the earth-swallowing event, there should not have been any daughters of Zelophehad to speak of. Thus, the only remaining possibility is that the daughters are arguing that Zelophehad was not one of the 250 leaders. According to Num 16:35, "fire came out from YHWH and consumed the two hundred and fifty men offering the incense." But even this layer contains no explicit references to the loss of inheritance rights. First, the punishment, in contrast to that of Dathan and Abiram, extended only to the leaders themselves, nowhere is it mentioned that the fire also consumed their households.[106] Second, even the children of Korah (who according to Num 16:32 should have been swallowed by the earth) did not suffer the fate of their father as Num 26:11 reports, "the sons of Korah did not die."[107] Thus, it would seem that none of the three strata of the Korah affair are directly applicable to Zelophehad.

First and most significantly, the nature of Zelophehad's death in the wilderness must be re-examined. As noted above, it is commonly assumed that Zelophehad was a member of the exodus generation, but is this correct? As has been

---

[103] As BADEN, "Stratification," 245, argues, "what we have in Numbers 16 and 17, then, is not supplementation, but compilation: two independent texts brought together by a third hand."

[104] ACHENBACH, *Vollendung*, 66. FRANKEL, *Murmuring*, 217, notes that there is almost no relation between the Dathan-Abiram layer and the Korah layer, and thus he suggests that the Korah layer was forced to include the Dathan-Abiram layer because it was already joined to the 250-man story.

[105] FREVEL, *Formation*, 25n94, correctly observes, "Korah himself wouldn't have any heredity title because he was a Levite."

[106] LEVINE, *Numbers 21–36*, 345, notes that the daughters' claim presupposes an ideology that does not recognise intergenerational punishment. This ideology is shared with Ezek 18:2–4 in particular, wherein the prophet hears a new word superseding the older model of generational punishment (cf. Ex 34:5–7). Such an ideology also corroborates the view, as suggested earlier, that the Zelophehad's daughter texts are late. Also, as noted above, the lateness of the texts are also suggested by the reference to Korah. See also MATHYS, "Numeri," 566–568.

[107] FREVEL, *Formation*, 25n94, correctly observes, "No consequences are mentioned regarding the offspring. Even in Num 16–17 there is no indication of any trans-generational condemnation."

widely observed, the census report in Numbers 26 typically only lists the משפחת (*clans*) for each tribe, however in the case of the tribes of Reuben and Manasseh the list extends beyond the משפחה to the בית אב.[108] Taking the listed Reubenites as a guide, it is reported that Dathan and Abiram belong to the third generation: Reuben → Pallu → Eliab → Dathan and Abiram (Num 26:5–9). This suggests that the third generation represents the generation that left Egypt as Dathan and Abiram complain that Moses took them out of a land flowing with milk and honey (i. e., Egypt) but did not bring them to their inheritance (Num 16:13–14). Looking, then, at the Manassites we find that Zelophehad is a fourth-generation descendant: Manasseh → Machir → Gilead → Hepher → Zelophehad → Mahlah, Noah, Hoglah, Milcah, Tirzah (Num 26:29–33).[109] Assuming an approximately synchronous system of generations leads to the conclusion that Gilead belongs to the same generation as Eliab, whilst Hepher belongs to the same generation as Dathan and Abiram.[110] As a result, this suggests that Zelophehad was born in the wilderness.

If it is correct to assume that Zelophehad was not part of the exodus generation, then it follows that Zelophehad did not die in the desert simply due to the sweeping condemnation of that entire generation (Numbers 13–14). Besides the spy event, the narrative of Numbers details three other "acts of god" that resulted in sweeping deaths in the wilderness. Working backwards from the second census the first act appears almost immediately. In the LXX the census in Numbers 26 begins with the linking phrase καὶ ἐγένετο μετὰ τὴν πληγήν (*and after the plague*), which relates to the events of Baal-Peor in Numbers 25.[111] The events of Baal-Peor, however, did not take place במדבר (*in the wilderness*), but already occurred in the plains of Moab, in Shittim (Num 25:1), thus this plague can also be excluded as an option. Continuing backwards the next divine death dealing takes place in Num 21:4–9, where "Yhwh sent fiery serpents (poisonous snakes – NRSV) among the people and they bit the people."[112] Here the text infers that those complaining belonged to the exodus generation as they complain, "why did you bring us from Egypt to die in the wilderness?" Thus, the serpent episode also appears to be a divine punishment against the complaining exodus generation. This means the only possible cause of death *explicitly narrated* in the book of Numbers that might apply to Zelophehad is that found in Numbers

---

[108] See definition of משפחה in Zobel, מִשְׁפָּחָה. In particular Zobel argues that the precise categorisation of the משפחה is demonstrated in Josh 7:14–18, where the casting of lots first selected by tribe (שבט), then by clan (משפחה), then by household (בית) and finally one by one (לגברים – to the man).

[109] Kislev, "Census," 243, argues that this additional detail in the genealogy "is thus anomalous", and further notes that the list goes beyond the clan level to the individual.

[110] For the inner consistency of genealogical generations see, e. g., Rendsburg, "Genealogies."

[111] This linking phrase is also absent from SP and 4Q27.

[112] The reference to fiery serpents has analogies in Demotic literature. See esp. Bühler, "Demotic."

4.3 The Specific Case of Zelophehad's Daughters 215

16–17. Numbers 16–17 is the only case in which those complaining do not necessarily derive from the exodus generation. Therefore, by mentioning the Korah episode, the daughters are highlighting that, although all deaths ultimately are controlled by God, Zelophehad's death was not caused by divine punishment against the people.

What seems to be at issue, then, is not some obscure or esoteric nuance within inheritance law, rather it simply questions the idea of the timing of Zelophehad's death.[113] Had Zelophehad "died for his own sins" after the second census was taken, then his name would have been recorded (cf. Num 26:1, 3) and so his household would have been automatically eligible to receive a נחלה as stipulated in Num 26:53 (the issue of Num 26:53 using the term נחלה will be discussed below). However, because he died "in the wilderness" he was not present during the second census and so his name would not have been recorded. It is important to note here that had Zelophehad's daughters not been successful, then there would have been no need for Zelophehad to be mentioned in Num 26:33; Zelophehad's name is only recorded because he functions as the bridge between Hepher and Mahlah, Noah, Hoglah, Milcah and Tirzah. Thus, what is essentially a philosophical question is at play: was Zelophehad's death before the census and before he had sons divinely ordained, or was it just "bad luck"? Had Zelophehad been punished for rebellion (such as in the congregation of Korah), then his early, heirless death might be construed as being his deserved fate, with the de facto punishment being that his name was not recorded in the second census, and thereby losing his right to a נחלה. This solution is supported by the foregoing arguments that suggested (1) Zelophehad did not belong to the exodus generation and (2) that he did not die as part of God's divine punishments against the "murmuring" people of Israel. The daughters' petition does not revolve around inheritance law but rather around the list of names in the second census being the indicator of who is eligible to receive a נחלה. Thus, their petition concludes, "should our father's name be taken from the among his clan because he had no son? Give us an אחזה (*possession*) among our father's brothers."

A further advantage of this solution is that the missing reference to a man's name in the generalised law of Num 27:8–11a is readily explainable (cf. § 4.1.2). The law of Num 27:8–11a pertains to inheritance whereas Zelophehad's daughters are not requesting inheritance rights in the basic sense of receiving Zelophehad's patrimony; rather their request is much more context specific: they are requesting to be counted as the head(s) of Zelophehad's בית, and therefore to be eligible to share in the אחזה. This is the most logical, narrative-sensitive solution

---

[113] MILGROM, *Numbers*, 231, for example notes regarding the idea that Zelophehad died for his own sins: "the meaning of this clause is unclear, for even if Zelophehad had been a member of Korah's faction, he still would have 'died for his own sin.'"

as at this point in the narrative Zelophehad did not yet own any land/land rights. As Litke argues, Numbers 27 is a challenge to the divine instructions regarding whom should be counted as belonging to the nation of Israel.[114] Without access to their father's שם, the daughters would have had no household to enter into after the conquest; they would be free-floating "homeless" women.[115] The daughters' solution to be given the right to bear their father's name not only granted them the protection of a household but gave them access to a household that would have otherwise been cut off in the wilderness.

Once again, this solution is not only narratively sensitive, but it also makes clear that the levirate custom was not an option even if Zelophehad's wife was still alive and well. Because Zelophehad died before the second census his name would not have been recorded and therefore his household would not have received an inheritance according to Num 26:53. Without an inheritance there was nothing to be preserved by the levir. With this context forming the background, then, Moses's actions and Yhwh's answer take on a whole different dimension of meaning. Not only that, but the inclusion of the law for heiresses in vv. 8–11a does not flow neatly on from the specific case raised by Zelophehad's daughters. However, as will be shown below, there is reason to suspect that these inheritance laws were added secondarily, and in so doing, completely altered the initial meaning of the narrative.

In vv. 5–7, Moses brings the case before Yhwh and receives an affirmative answer. The daughters are reported to be right in what they request and are to be given an allotment alongside Zelophehad's brothers. How this was practically meant to be enacted is not detailed, but a report is given in Josh 17:3–4 of the daughters receiving their promised inheritance along with the other Manassites. Verses 5–6 function to progress the narrative, however the real substance is found in v. 7. Several clues point to the conclusion that v. 7 should be divided into v. 7a and v. 7b, with each half performing a different duty.

The key term in v. 7b is the verb עבר, which mirrors that legislated in v. 8 and as argued in § 4.1.2 is best understood to have a technical meaning whereby the heiress functions as a temporary custodian until a grandson can be produced. Furthermore, like vv. 8–11a and unlike vv. 1–7a, v. 7b also refers to the father's נחלה. Thus, where v. 7a specifically states that all five daughters are to be נתן their father's אחזה, v. 7b states that his נחלה should be עבר to them. The differences between v. 7a and v. 7b, then, are not only ones of different terminology, they also have diverging understandings of what is meant for daughter inheritance. Thus, it follows v. 7b was designed to link the story of Zelophehad's daughters with the generalised law of verses 8–11a, but significantly it also suggests that the narrative of vv. 1–7a was not initially designed as an introduction to the leg-

---

[114] Litke, "Daughters," 209.
[115] A similar point is suggested by Ulrich, "Framing," 535.

islation.[116] Even if one wishes to propose that Priestly authors adopted older non-Priestly inheritance legislation and introduced it via an oracular novella form, one is confronted with the difficulty that without v. 7b, there is almost no continuity between the narrative and legislative portions of the text.

| 27:7b | העברת את־נחלת אביהן להן | transfer their father's possession to them |
| 27:8b | העברתם את־נחלתו לבתו | transfer his possession to his daughter |

Table 16: Comparison of Num 27:7b and Num 27:8b

If the context of the narrative portion was, from its inception, designed to introduce the laws of vv. 8–11a, then the question naturally arises: Why is the transition so opaque? That is: Why is it not more seamless?

Several further clues also suggest that v. 7b was added secondarily as a bridging verse. First, v. 7b also differs from v. 7a in the suffixes used. In the MT, v. 7a uses the masculine plural הם- whereas v. 7b uses the feminine הן-. That this was deemed problematic by later scribes can be inferred from the fact that in almost all versions besides the MT the text has been homogenised with the feminine plural throughout. Second, while the concept of transference applies to heiresses in the law of v. 8 and in the addition of v. 7b, this same concept is missing in v. 7a. Not only does this command share the same verb (נתן) that is only applied to the males in vv. 9–11a, but the lexeme is doubled – give a gift – so that further emphasis is placed on the daughters being the recipients rather than mere temporary guardians. Furthermore, what is gifted, using both the Deuteronomistic נחלה and the Priestly אחזה, is a place amongst the brothers of their father. The importance of this is the astonishing fact that Zelophehad's five daughters did not simply receive a subset of the territory of Hepher/Zelophehad, rather they each received a חבל (*portion*) in their own right. As Joshua 17:5 makes abundantly clear (see also figure 13), rather than six regions being allotted according to the six (Cisjordan) sons of Manasseh, ten regions are allotted. The logic of this relies on the idea that land was apportioned equally among each household (see discussion in § 3.4.1). For ten חבל to be allotted to the tribe of (Cis-)Manasseh, suggests that rather than the land being divided equally between Abiezer, Helek, Asriel, Shechem, Hepher, and Shemida (Josh 17:2), the land was rather divided *equally* between Abiezer, Helek, Asriel, Shechem, Mahlah, Noah, Hoglah, Milcah, Tirzah, and Shemida![117] Thus, so far as the author of Joshua 17 was concerned, each one of Zelophehad's daughters was a head of their own household. Once

---

[116] This point was also emphasised by SEEBASS, *Numeri 3*, 200.

[117] KNAUF, *Josua*, 151, similarly observes that the report of the ten-part division "widerspricht den Regelungen von 4 Mose 27 und 36, wonach sich die 'Töchter' mit je einem Fünftel des Sechstels hätten begnügen müsssen" (*contradicts the regulations of Numbers 27 and 36, according to which the 'daughters' each had to be content with one fifth of the sixth*).

218   *4. Female Inheritance*

again, one must be careful to not view such a distribution in light of the modern mindset of dilution of profits but rather of the distribution of risk (again see discussion in § 3.4.1). The final clue that suggests the original narrative of Zelophehad's daughters ended in v. 7a comes from the parallelism with Num 27:4:

27:4b	תנה־לנו אחזה בתוך אחי אבינו	give to us a possession amongst the brothers of our father
27:7aβ	נתן תתן להם אחזת נחלה בתוך אחי אביהם	give to them the gift of an inherited possession amongst the brothers of their father

Table 17: Comparison of Num 27:4b and Num 27:7aβ

Thus, it can confidently be concluded that Num 27:1–7a did not originally function as a narrative introduction to the generalised law, rather it was a legal-narrative in its own right that astonishingly ended with five women being granted an allotment alongside the other clan leaders of Manasseh. This raises the question: Why would such a narrative be produced?

4.4 Historical Connection to Zelophehad's Daughters?

In terms of dating the various chapters, the characters mentioned in the two scenes have commonly been paid little attention. This section will attempt to present a daring and hypothetical historical background for the origin of Zelophehad's daughters.

The first step in this regard is to demonstrate the geographical relationship to the names.

– Tirzah: the clearest and safest correlation is the daughter Tirzah with modern-day Tell el-Fārʿa (North).[118] Although the biblical account has Baasha (906–883* BCE)[119] be the first Northern king to dwell in Tirzah (cf. 1 Kgs 15:21, 33; 16:6; etc.), archaeological studies suggest that it was only occupied as an administrative centre approximately 100 years later as evidenced in Stratum VIId, when the site contained a palace, fortifications and "very large quantities of pottery characteristic of the eighth century BCE, including Samaria ware."[120]

– Noah: this name is attested in the Samaria Ostraca (No. 50, 52 and 64) and was identified by Lemaire as Khirbet ʿAnahum (1799.2009), Zertal has more

---

[118] See, e.g., DE VAUX, "Excavations;" FREVEL, *Geschichte*, 448; MANOR, "Tirzah;" NOTH, *Numbers*, 207.

[119] FREVEL, *Geschichte*, 423. Frevel emphasises that this dating is only approximate, being based on synchronisms rather than absolute data.

[120] CHAMBON, "Farʿah," 440. See also CHAMBON, *Tell El-Farʿah*, 12; HERZOG/SINGER-AVITZ, "Sub-Dividing," 176. In the earlier archaeological report of DE VAUX, "Excavations," 135, it was suggested that Tirzah was abandoned around 600 B.C.E., likely due to the presence of Malaria at the site.

4.4 Historical Connection to Zelophehad's Daughters?

recently argued that "this identification, however, 'stretches' the borders of the 'Land of Hepher' (I Kings 4:10), to which the Daughters of Zelophohad (*sic*) belong."[121] Zertal alternatively argues that the entirety of the Zebabdeh Valley functioned as a district referred to as No'ah.[122]

– Hoglah: based on the attestation of this name in the Samaria Ostraca (No. 45, 46, 47), Hoglah is understood by Aharoni to be a district north of Samaria, neighbouring No'ah.[123]

– Milcah: Zertal identifies Milcah with Khirbet Kheibar (1764.1954).[124]

– Mahlah: Zertal identifies Mahlah with Khirbet Mhallal (1939.1948).[125]

As figure 13 demonstrates, the "daughters of Zelophehad" are clustered in the territory to the north-east of Samaria. The question is, then: Does this clustered area have anything to do with inheritance issues, women or otherwise?

Before continuing it must be admitted that the following argument eschews heeding the warning that "correlation does not equal causation" and instead firmly grasps the impressive convergence between two phenomena. In figure 13 a shaded area is depicted in which the highest density of so-called wedge-shaped decorated bowls was found. As the following will elaborate, there is a growing consensus that these particular bowls are an archaeological marker for the presence of the foreign population imported by the Assyrians as part of their two-way deportation measures. Given this, the bold proposal is to see the granting of an אחזה to those without a proper patriarchal ancestry (i.e., the daughters of Zelophehad) as a cypher for the inclusion of the "non-Israelite" Samaritan Yahwists into the "people of Israel."

4.4.1 The Wedge-shape Decorated Bowl

In his 1989 paper, Adam Zertal began by noting that "during the Manasseh hill country survey, a previously unknown type of pottery decoration was found and isolated."[126] Here the emphasis should more squarely be placed on "isolated" rather than found, as samples of this pottery type had already been discovered, for example, in the Harvard expedition of 1908–1910.[127] Itach et al. describe these as "large, deep bowls with wedge-shaped impressions."[128]

---

[121] ZERTAL, *Hill Country 2*, 103, references to the Samaria Ostraca 52 and 64, as well as the reference to Lemaire's position also taken from Zertal. See also LEMAIRE, "Hepher." For Ostraca 50, see REISNER et al., *Samaria*, 237; AHARONI, *Land*, 321.

[122] ZERTAL, *Hill Country 2*, 103.

[123] AHARONI, *Land*, 318–327. See also TAYLOR, "Hoglah." For the Ostraca see REISNER, *Samaria*, 237; AHARONI, *Land*, 321.

[124] ZERTAL, *Hill Country 1*, 74, 241.

[125] ZERTAL, *Hill Country 1*, 261.

[126] ZERTAL, "Bowl," 77.

[127] REISNER, *Samaria*, 287, Fig. 162:14a. See more extensive list in ITACH et al., "Bowl," 81–82.

[128] ITACH et al., "Bowl," 77.

220   4. Female Inheritance

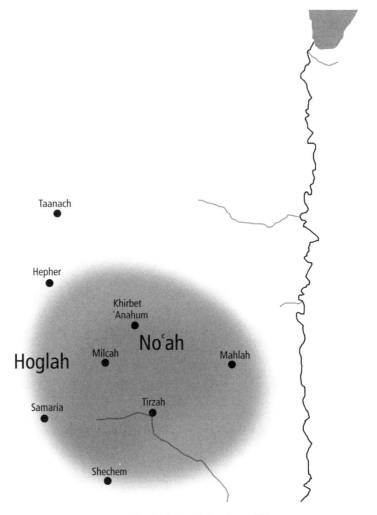

Figure 13: Map of "Zelophehad's daughters."[129]

---

[129] Map drawn by J. Davis. The grey shading approximates the area in which the so-called wedge-shape decorated bowls were most concentrated (see § 4.4.1). Taanach is located at Tell Taʻannek (1701.2142), see FREVEL, *Geschichte*, 448. ZERTAL, *Hill Country 1*, 71–71, 116, locates Hepher at Tell el-Muhaffar (1707.2054), but cf. NAʼAMAN, "District," 424. Noʻah is a district corresponding to the Zebabdeh Valley, whose northern border is marked by Khirbet ʻAnahum (1799.2009), see ZERTAL, *Hill Country 2*, 29–30. Hoglah is a district North of Samaria, AHARONI, *Land*, 318–327; BOLING, *Joshua*, 408; TAYLOR, "Hoglah." Milcah is located at Khirbet Kheibar (1764.1954), see ZERTAL, *Hill Country 1*, 74, 241. Mahlah is located Khirbet Mhallal (1939.1948), see ZERTAL, *Hill Country 2*, 109, 261. Tirzah is located at Tell el-Fārʻa (North) (1823.1882), see FREVEL, *Geschichte*, 448. For Samaria (1686.1870), see FREVEL, *Geschichte*, 447. Shechem is located at Tell Balāṭa (1768.1800), see FREVEL, *Geschichte*, 448. Regarding the grey shaded area, see esp. ZERTAL, "Bowl," 78–79. See an updated map in ITACH et al., "Bowl," 80.

4.4 Historical Connection to Zelophehad's Daughters?

In the same 1989 paper Zertal remarked:

The distribution of sites at which the decorated vessels were discovered is limited and well-defined, an elliptically-shaped region in the north-eastern hill country of Manasseh; it rarely appears outside that area. No examples are recorded in the Negev, Judaea, the Mediterranean coast, or the Galilee.[130]

Since that article was published, exemplars have been found in other locations, including Jerusalem.[131] Yet despite this new evidence it remains true that the overwhelming concentration of bowl specimens lies in the northern Samaria hill country. Itach et al. note that:

This unique distribution pattern might be said to arise from the meticulous nature of the Manasseh Hill Country Survey in northern Samaria over the last 40 years. But similar wide-ranging surveys were conducted by Zertal in other regions, such as the Jordan Valley where over 100 Iron II sites were surveyed, and very few such bowls were found.[132]

Thus, it is relatively safe to conclude that the wedge-shaped decorated bowl is a peculiar characteristic of this region.

What makes these bowls especially interesting is that their appearance is strongly correlated to the period following the fall of Samaria to the Assyrians. Zertal notes:

The wedge-shaped decoration is not found in the Iron II strata preceding the fall of Samaria, i.e., Shechem Stratum VIII; Samaria Periods V–VI; Tell el-Fār'a (North) VIId, etc.; nor does it exist in any stratum or site of the Persian period – Shechem Stratum V, Samaria Period VIII and Qadum. By elimination, therefore, the find is concentrated between 721/2 and 530 b.c.[133]

Even in the more recent study by Itach et al. it remains true that:

Based on sites where there is a reasonably clear date for the bowls, they appear in the late Iron Age, mostly after the Assyrian conquest. They are common from the late 8th to the 6th century, which corresponds to the Assyrian and Babylonian periods.[134]

Although Shechem and Hurvat 'Eres do contain Persian period examples, Itach et al. suggest that these "may be residual" because in "sites near Shechem where the Persian period is represented extensively, no wedge-impressed bowls were found."[135]

The wedge-shaped decoration has been interpreted to be Mesopotamian in style. Both Zertal and Itach et al. suggest that the earliest known example dates to the 3rd millennium BCE and was discovered at the Tell Hassuna excavation by

---

[130] ZERTAL, "Bowl," 77.
[131] BARKAY/ZWEIG, "Project," 22 Fig. 23.
[132] ITACH et al., "Bowl," 78.
[133] ZERTAL, "Bowl," 78.
[134] ITACH et al., "Bowl," 76.
[135] ITACH et al., "Bowl," 77.

Lloyd and Safar in 1943–1944.[136] More importantly for the present study, however, is the presence of similar pottery found in "southern Mesopotamia (Wadi Diyala and east of Kish), dating from the 6th to the 2nd centuries BCE."[137] As such, Itach et al. conclude that "this strongly suggests that at least in the first millennium, this ceramic tradition developed mainly in southern Mesopotamia."[138]

Interestingly, however, the bowls discovered in the Manasseh hill country, although Mesopotamian in style, were not Mesopotamian in origin. Itach et al. collected a sampling of fourteen wedge-shaped decorated bowls from various sites and subjected them to thin section petrographic analysis. From this study they conclude:

> [Regarding] the issue of provenance, it seems that the bowls incised with wedges from the Samaria Hills were mostly locally made, probably in the northern part of the region, although not all in the same production centre. Wedge bowls found in the territory of the Kingdom of Judah were made of different clay, derived from areas proximate to the find spots ... This means that a population living in northern Samaria chose to produce the type of bowls that others were producing in the Land of Israel, while adding a wedge impression similar to that found in Mesopotamia.[139]

This naturally gives rise to the question of what caused this peculiar pottery type to appear and in such an area. Zertal's argument, which will be expanded below, is that "the combination of the Mesopotamian elements with a local bowl may connect the appearance of the vessel in Samaria with the arrival of the populaces brought by the Assyrian kings from southern Mesopotamia, from Arabia, and from Elam."[140]

Against seeing the bowls as evidence of new people groups, London argued that the bowls' style was not decorative but functional; that is, the wedge impressions were used for grating food.[141] Against the Mesopotamian origin of these bowls, London cites similar grating bowls from Mexico that also date to the period 1500–1000 BCE. Thus, she argues that "it is problematic to use the graters in ancient Israel as dating evidence or to attach much significance to their presence or absence in major tells."[142] More pointedly she argues that the fact that such bowls were primarily found in the rural areas of the Manasseh hill country speak more to the focus of the archaeologist(s) and the nature of the location rather than being a marker of the residents:

---

[136] The ware is here referred to as a "husking tray." LLOYD/SAFAR, "Tell Hassuna," Fig. 3:8–10.
[137] ITACH et al., "Bowl," 85.
[138] ITACH et al., "Bowl," 85.
[139] ITACH et al., "Bowl," 88.
[140] ZERTAL, "Province," 397.
[141] LONDON, "Bowl," 89.
[142] LONDON, "Reply," 89.

One would expect to find food-processing equipment in villages and farms where food preparation is a regular activity. Such equipment is less likely to be found in tombs, temples, and public buildings of Samaria or other cities.[143]

Itach et al. tested London's theory of the wedges being a grinding tool and agreed that the impressions could indeed be used for grating. However, they also went on to say that, "the singular appearance of these wedges on bowls manufactured in the Samaria region in the late Iron II and Persian periods cannot easily be ascribed to sudden changes in methods of food preparation."[144] Hence they conclude "Zertal's suggestion to connect the bowls of this type found in the Samaria Hills to deportees brought by the Assyrians at the very end of the 8th century and in the 7th century remains the most probable explanation for their appearance."[145]

4.4.2 The Neo-Assyrian Two-way Deportation

According to 2 Kings 17 Yʜᴡʜ sent the Assyrian army to the Northern Kingdom as punishment for its sins. The story tells how the Assyrian king defeated Israel and deported the population to other parts of the empire (see esp. 2 Kgs 17:6). According to 2 Kgs 17:24, "The king of Assyria brought in people from Babylon, Cuthah, Avva, Hamath and Sepharvaim and placed them in the cities of Samaria instead of the sons of Israel, and they possessed Samaria and dwelled in its cities." Josephus likewise reports:

As of the Chūthaioi who were transported to Samaria – this is the name by which they have been called to this day because of having been brought over from the region called Chūtha, which is in Persia, as is a river by the same name – each of their tribes – there were five – brought along its own god, and, as they reverenced them in accordance with the custom of their country, they provoked the Most High God to anger and wrath. For He visited upon them a pestilence by which they were destroyed; and, as they could devise no remedy for their sufferings, they learned from an oracle that they should worship the Most High God, for this would bring the deliverance. And so they sent envoys to the king of Assyria, asking him to send them some priests from the captives he had taken in his war with the Israelites. Accordingly, he sent some priests, and they, after being instructed in the ordinances and religion of this God, worshipped Him with great zeal, and were at once freed of the pestilence. These same rites have continued in use even to this day among those who are called Chūthaioi (Cuthim) by the Greeks; but they alter their attitude according to circumstance and, when they see the Jews prospering, call them their kinsmen, on the ground that they are descended from Joseph and are related to them through their origin from him, but, when they see the Jews in trouble, they say that they have nothing whatever in common with them nor do these have any claim of friendship or race, and they declare themselves to be aliens of another race ... (Jos. Ant. IX:288–291)

---

[143] Lᴏɴᴅᴏɴ, "Reply," 89–90.
[144] Iᴛᴀᴄʜ et al., "Bowl," 89.
[145] Iᴛᴀᴄʜ et al., "Bowl," 93.

224   *4. Female Inheritance*

The picture given by these sources is that the Samaritan community was not only ethnically different from the golah community who returned to Jerusalem, but their worship of Yʜwʜ was somehow inferior. This supposed displacement of all the northern tribes led scholars to speak of the "ten lost tribes of Israel," and thus the Judean-biased story was often accepted uncritically.[146] The pendulum is now swinging the other way, however, with some scholars viewing the Judean story very critically. Hensel, for example, writes:

> The supposed multi-ethnic heritage of the Samaritans is very clearly a literary invention on the part of Judah regarding the Yahwism in the North. This phenomenon is well known in sociology as 'othering', and in the case of Judah has its roots in the Hellenistic period ...[147]

The first question, then, is: How accurate is this story?

Besides the accounts found in the biblical literature and Josephus, the Assyrian annals also report the conquest of the land of Israel. According to the reports found on large stone slabs at the palace of Tiglath-pileser III (744–727 BCE) in Kalḫu, Assyria's conquest included the annexation of "Gilead and *Abil-šiṭṭi*, which are the border of the land *Bīt-Ḫumri[a]*." (Kalḫu Annal No. 42, lines 5'b-8'a).[148] Concerning the land of Canaan the annals record, "(as for) the land of *Bīt-Ḫumria* (Israel), I brought [to] Assyria [..., its "au]xiliary [army"...] (and) all of its people, [...]." (Kalḫu Annal No. 42, lines 15'b-17'a // Summary Inscription 4, lines 1'–8'a).[149] The annals further note that eunuchs were installed as provincial governors (*piḫāti*) over these territories. Northern Israel was divided into three provinces, (Megiddo, Dor,[150] and Samaria), and across the Jordan river were situated three further provinces (Horan, Gilead, and Qarnaim).[151] The Nimrud Prism of Sargon II also reports:

> [The inhabitants of Sa]merina, who agreed [and plotted] with a king [hostile to] me, not to do service and not to bring tribute [to Aššur] and who did battle, I fought against them with the power of the great gods, my lords. I counted as spoil 27,280 people, together with their chariots, and gods, in which they trusted ... I settled the rest of them in the midst of Assyria. I repopulated Samerina more than before. I brought into it from countries conquered by my hands. I appointed my eunuch as governor over them. And I counted them as Assyrians.[152]

---

[146] See discussion in Knoppers, *Jews*, 5f., on the idea of the ten lost tribes.

[147] Hensel, "Relationship," 27.

[148] Tadmor/Yamada, *Inscriptions*, 105.

[149] Kalḫu Annal No. 42 found in Tadmor/Yamada, *Inscriptions*, 106. Summary Inscription 4 found in COS 2.117C.

[150] See arguments in Na'aman, *Dor,* for why Dor might not be the capital of an Assyrian province. See also Alt, "System," 236. Cf. Stern, *ALB*, 12, who writes, "a new list of Assyrian provinces in Syria-Palestine was published by F. M. Fales and J. N. Postgate. This list repeats again the names of Samaria and Megiddo, but it adds, for the first time, a third province in western Palestine, the province of Dor. Before the publication of this document, the problem of Dor as capital of a separate province was the topic of a long and intensive dispute."

[151] For more details see, e.g., Aharoni, *Land*, 368f; Zertal, "Province," 384.

[152] COS 2.118D. See also Pritchard, *ANET*, 284–285. Whilst there may at first appear to be

As with all such ancient reports, scholars have traditionally been divided on how accurate these are. The maximalist view takes the reports of sweeping deportations more or less at face value, whereas the minimalists suggest the deportations were confined to the elite (some going so far as to suggest only 3–4% were relocated).[153] Part of the ambiguity found in earlier scholarship was due to the limited archaeological data available concerning the Northern Kingdom/Samerina during the time of the Assyrian empire.[154] Following Zertal's survey of the Manasseh hill country, in which several previously unknown settlements enhanced the available data, the question of deportations can be more accurately addressed. Zertal estimates 8th century Israel likely comprised 60–70,000 people, Na'aman posits an even higher number suggesting as many as 100,000.[155] Thus even if one were to accept Sargon's figure of 27,280 deportees was not exaggerated, it still suggests that the population of Samerina remained primarily "Israelite." This speaks directly against the idea of the so-called "ten lost tribes of Israel."[156] That being said, it does not follow that the North was largely unaffected by these events. Zertal notes that 58% of the Persian period sites were either newly founded or re-founded after a gap of one period, suggesting that the new regime under the Persians brought a far greater freedom and opportunity for expansion and economic growth.[157] Regardless of the number of native Israelites remaining in the land, there is little doubt that the Assyrians did indeed import new populations into the former Northern Kingdom.

Following the Assyrian conquest Zertal reports a, "drastic decline" in the number of settlements in the Manasseh hill country area.[158] But it is too hasty to simply attribute this decline to sweeping destruction, not least because the aim of the Assyrian deportation policy was to make "die politische Kontrolle leichter, lässt aber zugleich die Wirtschaftskraft nicht zusammenbrochen" (*political control easier, but at the same time did not let economic power collapse*).[159] On the

---

a doubling up between the reports of Tiglath-Pileser III and Sargon II, Na'aman, "Changes," 105f., notes that that, "we may conclude that following the campaigns of 734–732, Tiglath-Pileser III annexed the northern areas of the Israelite kingdom but left the hill country of Samaria in the hands of Hosea, its last king." It was only later, following Sargon II's campaign (720 BCE), that Samaria was annexed as well. See further discussion in Frevel, *Geschichte*, 202–204, 274–275.

[153] See overview in Knoppers, *Jews*, 26f..

[154] Whilst not directly correlated with the situation in Samaria, the idea of an empty land in Judah has also become increasingly difficult to maintain. Several essays dealing with this topic can be found in both Lipschits/Blenkinsopp, *Judah* and Ben Zvi/Levin, *Concept*.

[155] See Zertal, "Province," 385 and Na'aman, "System," 231 respectively. For fuller treatment see especially Zertal, *Hill Country 1*; Zertal, *Hill Country 2*; Zertal/Mirkam, *Hill Country 3*.

[156] See overview in Knoppers, *Jews*, 5–8.

[157] See, e.g., Zertal, "Pahwah," 11.

[158] Zertal/Mirkam, *Hill Country 3*, 42.

[159] Frevel, *Geschichte*, 275. This should be contrasted with the large-scale destruction in Judah (a country who did not submit to Assyria) by Sennacherib – see, e.g., Na'aman, *Changes*,

226   *4. Female Inheritance*

one hand, Zertal suggests that most of the "Israelite" population abandoned their villages and moved to the, "richer and better defended Mediterranean zones."[160] On the other hand, the Assyrian practice in annexed lands was to remove the existing leadership and install new administrative centres and strategic fortifications. These administrative centres and fortifications would function as communication hubs as part of the greater imperial network. Liverani refers to the Assyrian model of imperial expansion as a "network empire," by which he argues that instead of imagining the expansion of the Assyrian empire like a spreading oil stain across the map, it is better to imagine it as a mesh that, through repeated imperial campaigns, thickens.[161] Parker similarly explains, "as the system of Assyrian strongholds became more contiguous across the landscape, the area came more firmly into the grip of the imperial administration and the stage was set for expansion further into the periphery or into the regions between these pockets of Assyrian control."[162] Thus, he suggests that "the construction of forts [was] a crucial step in the expansion of the Assyrian empire."[163] This meant that major centres like Megiddo and the city of Samaria would have contained a mixture of peoples. However, the smaller villages and farmsteads (such as those in the area of "Zelophehad's daughters") potentially formed cultural microcosms, somewhat similar to what sociologists call, "ethnic clusters," or more colloquially, ghetto communities.[164] Joshua 18:21–24 may provide biblical support for this assertion, Na'aman and Zadok argue that the Benjaminite town Avvim most likely refers to a town inhabited by those relocated from the area of Avva (mentioned in 2 Kgs 17:24) near Babylon.[165] As such, not only would these displaced communities likely find comfort in maintaining what was previously familiar, but they would also likely have been incapable of influencing the majority population of Israelites who remained in the land.

But even those who moved into places such as Samaria unlikely represented the alienating element that the Judean-biased reports suggest. On the contrary there is evidence to suggest that the foreign immigrants adopted the local culture and customs. A list of names was found at the Assyrian military and admin-

---

112 f.. KNOPPERS, "Revisiting," 268, notes, "The province of Samaria seems to have passed from the Neo-Assyrian and Neo-Babylonian Periods to the Persian Period without encountering any of the major destructions that its southern neighbor experienced. From an archaeological perspective, one finds in the territory of Samaria essentially one continuous period (Iron IIC or Iron III) from the late eighth century to the late fourth century."

[160] ZERTAL, *Hill Country 2*, 90.

[161] LIVERANI, "Growth."

[162] PARKER, "Garrisoning," 77.

[163] PARKER, "Garrisoning," 86. Two examples of Assyrian supported fortresses include Tell Qudadi (see, e.g., FANTALKIN/TAL, "Re-Discovering") on the coastal plain and Tell Jemmeh (NA'AMAN, "Changes," 108 f.), 10km south of Gaza.

[164] On the modern definition of ethnic clusters see e.g., PAMUK, "Geography," 291 f.

[165] NA'AMAN/ZADOK, "Deportations," 45.

istrative centre of Tell Jemmeh in which the first name in a row was Semitic in origin whilst the second name was non-Semitic. Na'aman and Zadok argue that this structure should be interpreted genealogically (i.e., X, son of Y), which demonstrates that the children of those imported by the Assyrians adopted Semitic names. They further note, "This pattern of name distribution is typical of immigrant communities: the parents, as newcomers, bear names of their motherland, but the second generation has local names, adapted to the new environment."[166] A similar idea of assimilation could be used to explain the mixed nature of the wedge-shaped decorated bowls; on the one hand they mimic local pottery style and materials, on the other hand they feature variants (wedges) based on the style used in the "motherland."

Taking a closer look at the area described by "Zelophehad's daughters," i.e., approximately the area that Zertal calls the Shechem Syncline, also reveals some interesting results. Zertal describes the period between 1000–721 BCE (which he calls the Iron II) as the period of peak settlement in the area, with the greatest growth occurring in the region of Samaria.[167] He attributes this to the growing prosperity and centralizing of power from the state, which enabled the wider population to benefit and flourish.[168] In contrast the period from 721–535 BCE (i.e., Zertal's Iron III) Zertal observes an almost 50% drop in inhabited sites (from 84 to 40), which he suggests probably relates to people movements caused by the Assyrian pressure, i.e., both internal relocations but also deportations. Additionally, Zertal notes that of the 40 inhabited settlements, 12 of them were newly established, 9 of which belong to the Sebastiyeh area (i.e., around Samaria and "Zelophehad's daughters").[169] The reason for this particular location for the new settlers appears to be due to the fact that this area was formerly king's land.[170]

Zertal notes that although none of the key sites has been excavated (the Manasseh Hill Country project consisted only of surveys) the suspected Cuthean sites "differ on several accounts from the 'regular' settlements of the area" in that (1) most of the pottery found dates to the Iron III, (2) the wedge-shaped decorated bowls are present "in large quantities" and (3) "in many settlements, where building plans can be delineated, the buildings are also 'Mesopotamian' in character."[171]

---

[166] NA'AMAN/ZADOK, "Deportations," 37.

[167] On the confusion of designations for the late Iron Age see, ZERTAL, "Province," 379–380; FREVEL, *Geschichte*, 34–37.

[168] ZERTAL, *Hill Country 1*, 56–57, writes, "the spread of settlement in the time of the Israelite monarchy attests to economic prosperity and political stability, which apparently depended on the power of centralized rule in the kingdom of Israel."

[169] ZERTAL, *Hill Country 1*, 57–58.

[170] ZERTAL, *Hill Country 2*, 63.

[171] ZERTAL, "Province," 404. Regarding point (3), Zertal cites sites 56, 142, 219, 224, 237–40 and 250 from ZERTAL, *Hill Country 1* and sites 12, 18, 82, 127, 132, 144, 197, 236 and 246 from ZERTAL, *Hill Country 2*.

228 *4. Female Inheritance*

Thus, from the evidence that is currently available, it would seem that Zertal's suggestion to associate the wedge-shaped decorated bowl with those imported by the Assyrians is, if not secure, at least highly plausible.

4.4.3 On Pots and People

So far, the discussion has avoided dealing with the well-known "Pots and People" debate. There is no doubt that the subject of ethnicity is one that has been rightly criticised in recent discussion.[172] Finkelstein, for example, notes that "pottery and architectural forms in Iron I sites on both sides of the Jordan reflect environmental, social, and economic traits of the settlers. They tell us nothing about ethnicity."[173] Particularly in the context of relating biblical data with archaeological findings, the "pots and people" issue often runs into problems of circularity; a classic example being the interpretation of the presence or absence of pig bones as an ethnic marker in light of the biblical taboo in Lev 11:7 and Deut 14:8.[174] Faust is more optimistic about the ability for archaeology to uncover evidence of ethnicity, but even still he notes:

We should be aware that ethnicity is not the only social dimension symbolized by material items. Economic status, prestige, religion, occupation, setting (urban versus rural) etc. should also be taken into account ... The difficult task is, therefore, to identify those aspects of material culture which are connected with ethnicity, and are not a result of ecology, wealth, status, setting (urban versus rural) etc."[175]

Thus, *prima facie* the arguments presented above appear to have fallen directly into this trap.

That being said, there are several counter arguments as to why the above reconstruction might be justified – in this case – in equating pots with people:

I. Bunimovitz and Yasur-Landau suggest that identifying a newly immigrated group is possible (1) providing that the immigrants originated in a "markedly different cultural milieu than the recipient culture," and (2) only at the initial stage of their immigration as "profound changes in the newcomers' material culture are likely to diminish its uniqueness and distinctiveness against the background of the indigenous material culture."[176]

1. The first condition is met in the case of the wedge-shape decorated bowls, which can – with a high degree of certainty – be dated to the period following the Assyrian invasion due to their distinctive style that was not found in Israel before this time. In addition, the wedge-shape bowl was found in the area in-

---

[172] See, e.g., Kletter, "Pots," 19; Davies, "Ethnicity."
[173] Finkelstein, "Pots," 226.
[174] See, e.g., discussion in Frevel, *Geschichte*, 81–85.
[175] Faust, "Complexity," 4.
[176] Bunimovitz/Yasur-Landau, "Pottery," 89.

4.4 Historical Connection to Zelophehad's Daughters? 229

habited by those imported by the Assyrians (i.e., it is described as being Meso-potamian in style).[177]

2. The second condition is also met via the fact that the presence of the wedge-shape decorated bowls largely disappears by the Persian period. Such an observation conforms directly to Bunimovitz and Yasur-Landau's point that clear indications of immigrants fade over time due to the processes of assimilation and integration. It seems likely that the disappearance of the bowls reflects the im-migrants adapting their diets and cooking techniques to the local environment. Importantly, this explanation is more plausible than that the bowls represented a short-lived fad in cooking methods that was invented and then abandoned by local inhabitants.

II. Unlike the arguments used to support the archaeological "proofs" of the conquest narrative, both Israelite (i.e., biblical) and Assyrian sources report of an Assyrian bi-directional deportation taking place in Samaria after the Assyrian conquest.[178] Granting that this double testimony has a higher degree of reliability, it follows that some level of evidence should be expected in the material culture. This is, once again, further reinforced by the fact that the bowls have strong similarities with Mesopotamian pottery, which is where the newcomers are said to have originated.

If it is accepted that the area of north-east Samaria formed the locus of where the Assyrians located the foreign groups, then one is faced with the remarkable fact that this area approximates that described by the daughters of Zelophehad.

Importantly, the short-lived nature of these vessels points towards the assimi-lation of these populations into the broader "Israelite" population in the Persian period and so to the foreign cultural practices (e.g., cooking) being eschewed for local ones.

4.4.4 Other Biblical Support

A further element to the present proposal is contained in the report from Jose-phus quoted above that the Χουθαῖοι (*Cutheans*) claimed that "they are descend-ed from Joseph and are related to [the Jews] through their origin from him." Al-though it is true that Josephus' claim is a clear case of "othering" (see Hensel's quote above), the core idea that some foreigners adopted Yahwism and were somehow consequently incorporated into the utopian depiction of "Israel" warrants further investigation.

2 Kings 17:24–27 reports that those brought in by the Assyrians came from Babylon, Cuthah, Avva, Hamath and Sepharvaim. The legend reports that be-cause these people did not worship YHWH, he sent lions to attack them, resulting

---

[177] Again see LLOYD/SAFAR, "Tell Hassuna," Fig. 3:8–10; ITACH et al., "Bowl," 85.
[178] On the "proofs" of the conquest see, e.g., FREVEL, *Geschichte*, 81–85.

230   *4. Female Inheritance*

in a priest of Yhwh being sent to teach them the משפט אלהי הארץ (*law of the god of the land*). Although scholars such as Tammuz see this narrative as "an impartial report about what happened in Samaria after the Jews were expelled," this report is more often viewed to feature a strong Judean bias.[179]

As noted above, the idea of an "empty land" that was filled by the Assyrians is not supported by the archaeological findings, rather these suggest that although there was a clear decline in the number and distribution of settlements, many remained unchanged from the transition to Assyrian occupation and consequently that the majority of inhabitants remained "Israelite."[180] Despite the biased nature of 2 Kings 17, there seems to be little reason to regard the listed peoples imported as being a complete fabrication. As already noted above, Na'aman and Zadok have proposed that Josh 18:3 likely alludes to the people from Avva dwelling in the area of Benjamin via the town of Avvim.[181] If this is true, it supports the assertion that the Bible contains traces of these various people groups becoming "Israelite" in one way or another. Thus, it does not seem unreasonable to suggest that Zelophehad's daughters are also a cypher for this process.

The genealogy of Manasseh is one fraught with inconsistencies.[182] Those texts dealing with Zelophehad's daughters in the extant book of Numbers all feature a consistent genealogy (i. e., Joseph → Manasseh → Machir → Gilead → Hepher → Zelophehad). However, even this single line has problems on closer inspection. According to Numbers 26 Machir was the sole son of Manasseh and Gilead was the sole son of Machir, thus, as Seebass observes, "nach dieser Gliederung ist die Sippe der Machiriten mit der Gileaditen identisch" (*according to this breakdown, the tribe of the Machirites is identical to the Gileadites*).[183]

Noth's solution to the problem of Manasseh's confusing genealogy was to modify the listing in Numbers 26 by omitting vv. 29aβ, 30aα, which function to subordinate Gilead under Machir. In light of this he argues that "Josh 17:1–3 has obviously made use of the Manasseh section of Num. 26 but in an original form in which the clans mentioned in vv. 30aβb, 31, 32 have been derived from the 'rest of the sons of Manasseh' (not grandchildren)."[184] Holzinger similarly argued, "Wenn v. 29αγ Glosse ist, so liegt hier ein Aufriss von Manasse vor, in dem Machir und Gilead zwei verschiedene Linien sind" (*If v. 29αγ is a gloss, then*

---

[179] Tammuz, "Ideology," 308. Tammuz goes on to state (p. 317) that the imported populations "had no knowledge of the risks that were involved in the life in their new home ... these newcomers were not aware of other dangers in their new home, such as lions and bears."

[180] The biblical depiction is also supported by Oded, *II Kings 17*, 40, who writes that the report in Ezra 4:2 and 10 "are unquestionably authentic."

[181] Na'aman/Zadok, "Deportations," 45.

[182] Speaking of the Manasseh section in Joshua 17 (see discussion below), Hawk, *Joshua*, 207, writes, "Manasseh is a mess – textually, socially, and geographically."

[183] Seebass, "Machir," 496.

[184] Noth, *Numbers*, 207.

here exists an outline of Manasseh in which Machir and Gilead are two separate lines).[185] Wüst argues that the Manasseh section of Numbers 26 contains materials from two separate origins, and concludes that Machir and Gilead were only ever joined at the literary level. Wüst draws attention to the fact that Num 26:30 opens with אלה בני גלעד (*these are the sons of Gilead*), which then goes on to list the משפחת (*clans*) of the Gileadites and that this stands in direct conflict with Num 26:29b, where Gilead itself is presented as a משפחה.[186] In support of Wüst's thesis, and what has often been overlooked in the scholarly discussion, is that the other Josephite line, the Ephraimites, feature this same nomenclature; verse 35 opens with אלה בני־אפרים (*these are the sons of Ephraim*), and then goes on the list the Ephraimite משפחת. This suggests that like Ephraim, Gilead was originally conceived to be a tribe in its own right (cf. Num 26:28, 37b) and was only later subordinated under the Manasseh-Machir connection in Num 26:29.[187] Wüst concludes, therefore, "daraus folgt, daß der in Num 26,29 f. genannte Gilead mit der gleichnamigen Landschaft östlich des Jordans nichts zu tun hat ..." (*from that it follows that the Gilead named in Num 26:29 f. had nothing to do with the region east of the Jordan with the same name ...*).[188] Although Wüst's solution does solve the issue, the assumption that – within a genealogical setting – a man named Gilead had nothing to do with the territory by the same name is dubious. As Briant notes:

The tribe is simultaneously a genealogical reality and a spatial reality: Maraphii and Pasargadae are both ethnonyms and toponyms. Each tribe and clan had a territory of its own ..."[189]

Wright similarly argues, "geography implodes into genealogy, and genealogy is expressed through geography."[190]

As the following discussion will elaborate, the problem with these solutions is that scholars continue to align the genealogies to the Monarchic period or even the pre-Monarchic period. Rather it will be argued that the solution to the strange geographical-genealogy of the Manassites is rather found in the exilic, or more likely the postexilic, reality of the province of Samaria. To this end, Josh 17:1–12 and 1 Kgs 4:7–19 will be briefly discussed to support this assertion.

---

[185] Holzinger, *Numeri*, 135.

[186] See discussion in Wüst, *Untersuchungen*, 63–71, esp. 69.

[187] This conclusion differs from Seebass, *Machir*, who argues that Num 26:30aα "ist kein traditionsgeschichtliches Urdatum, sondern aus Num. xxxvi 1, 11 abgeleitet" (*is no tradition-historical raw data, rather it is derived from Num 36:1, 11*). However, Seebass neglects the same formulation for Ephraim, which cannot be explained in light of Numbers 36. That both Gilead and Ephraim share the same structure speaks against these more convenient "literary" explanations.

[188] Wüst, *Untersuchungen*, 70.

[189] Briant, *Cyrus*, 18.

[190] Wright, "Remapping," 74.

232   *4. Female Inheritance*

4.4.4.1 Joshua 17:1–12

The geographical-genealogy of the Manassites is also detailed in Joshua 17, where the (Cisjordan) allotment to the tribe of Manasseh is detailed.[191]

In terms of genealogy, the same characters mentioned in Num 26:29–33 are mentioned in Josh 17:1–4. In both lists Machir is named the firstborn of Manasseh to whom were granted the lands of Gilead and Bashan. The first deviations occur in Joshua 17:2, where Abiezer, Helek, Asriel, Shechem, Hepher and Shemida, are listed as the "remaining sons of Manasseh," rather than as Machir's grandsons as they appear in the book of Numbers. The alterations made in Josh 17:1–3 function not only to remove the conflict between the two half-tribes of Manasseh but they also make better sense of those Manassite names relating to Cisjordan cities and regions.[192] Thus, although the precise reason underlying the alterations in Numbers 26 cannot be clarified, from a geographical-genealogical perspective Joshua 17 must be regarded as the more reliable reconstruction.

The distribution of territory to the Manassites also contains several other anomalies. First, the distribution to Manasseh falls under the larger umbrella of the "sons of Joseph" in Joshua 16–17. Although this fact in and of itself is not particularly remarkable, more curious is the fact that the allotment of the sons of Joseph is lacking a list of cities. In contrast Judah, Benjamin, Simeon, Zebulun, Issachar, Asher, Naphtali and Dan (Josh 15:21–62; 18:21–28; 19:2–8, 15*, 18–22, 25–31, 35–38 and 41–46 respectively) all contain lists of cities within their territory. A similar case occurs with the allocation of Transjordan where Reuben and Gad (Josh 13:17–21 and 25–27 respectively) receive a much more detailed treatment than half-Manasseh. Scholars have mused as to the reason behind this strange absence, such as the Judean author responsible for the text did not have sufficient data about the North to write a detailed town list, to which Knauf rightly asks, "aber woher hatten sie dann ihre recht guten Information über Galiläa?" (*but then where did they get their rather good information about Galilee?*).[193] Gaß notes that Josh 17:9 contains the phrase "these cities" and argues that this suggests that there was originally a city list that has been removed.[194] If Gaß is correct, then the argument that the list was removed as part of an anti-Samaritan bias has something to commend it. In any case, the omission is a curious anomaly even if an explanation is not immediately forthcoming.

---

[191] For a detailed discussion see GASS, *Landverteilung*, 180–213.

[192] LEVINE, *Numbers 21–36*, 322, argues that this forms the crux of the entire Zelophehad's daughters saga; the real intention was to demonstrate the right of the tribe of Manasseh to settle in the Transjordan region as well as Cisjordan.

[193] KNAUF, *Josua*, 149. See, e.g., BOLING, *Joshua*, 412, who writes, "for the listings of the northern tribes there was apparently no archival source comparable to that for Judah (and Benjamin) in the south."

[194] GASS, *Landverteilung*, 196.

One further point of interest is the absence of the lemma נחל, used either as a verb (*to inherit*) or a noun (*inheritance*), regarding the male Manassites.[195] All tribes contain the lemma at least once: Reuben (Josh 13:23), Gad (Josh 13:28), Judah (Josh 14:13, 14; 15:20), Benjamin (Josh 18:20, 28), Simeon (Josh 19:1, 2, 8, 9), Zebulun (Josh 19:10, 16), Issachar (Josh 19:23), Asher (Josh 19:31), Naphtali (Josh 19:39, 41), Dan (Josh 19:48). In the case of the Josephites the breakdown is as follows: Joseph (Josh 16:4; 17:14), Ephraim (Josh 16:5, 8) and Manasseh (Josh 17:4, 6 – both relate only to Zelophehad's daughters). In light of this Hawk observes:

Within the brief account, then, we are informed three times that the daughters received an 'inheritance' alongside 'brothers' and 'sons.' The repetition of this information strongly asserts the daughter's integration into a structure defined in male terms and in so doing challenges the strict social boundaries articulated by the listing of Manasseh's sons, the genealogical pedigree of Zelophehad, and the assembly of Israelite males.[196]

If one assumes that the emphasis lies not so much on the gender of Zelophehad's daughters but rather on their genealogical aberrance, then Hawk's observation aligns very well with the present argument that Zelophehad's daughters are to be understood symbolically and that their gender points towards them being somehow outside the normal patrilineal system.

Further curiosities are found in Josh 17:5–6. These verses detail that the Cisjordan territory of Manasseh was divided equally into ten portions. With the addition of Gilead and Bashan, this results in twelve portions granted to the Manassites and it is hardly a stretch to see this distribution symbolically. As Ballhorn observes, with this Manasseh reflects the whole people of Israel with 10 Cisjordan and 2 Transjordan tribes/portions.[197] More importantly, as noted in § 4.3 above, the ten portions in Cisjordan are divided equally between the five Cisjordan sons of Manasseh (sans Hepher) and the five daughters of Zelopehad, who in Josh 17:6 are rather labelled as the "daughters of Manasseh."[198] Hawk argues that this 5 son/5 daughter distribution results in a "structural equivalency" which "suggests a social equivalency."[199] This equivalency is also supported by the seemingly redundant note in Josh 17:2, which states, אלה בני מנשה בן־יוסף הזכרים למשפחתם (*these are the sons of Manasseh, son of Joseph, the males by their clans*).[200] The added emphasis on the "son"-ship of these Manassites also indirectly places emphasis on the non-"son"-ship of the daughters of Manasseh.

---

[195] HAWK, *Joshua*, 204.

[196] HAWK, *Joshua*, 208–209.

[197] BALLHORN, *Israel*, 278.

[198] As noted by GASS, *Landverteilung*, 198.

[199] HAWK, *Joshua*, 208.

[200] GASS, *Landverteilung*, 194, also argues that this note is a later addition and that it "kann daher wohl kaum zu einer alten Tradition gehören" (*can therefore hardly belong to an old tradition*).

234   *4. Female Inheritance*

Although it is possible to understand this in purely gender-based terms, it would then be, as Hawk notes, "explicit if seemingly redundant;" rather it makes more sense that this additional emphasis in Josh 17:2 is intended to highlight that the "daughters of Zelophehad" are not sons of Manasseh.[201]

Additionally, the distribution of Manasseh's Cisjordan territory into ten rather than six portions, of which one is subdivided between the daughters, speaks directly against the complaint of the Manassites in Numbers 36. There it is clearly presupposed that the daughters only received the portion of Zelophehad, who in turn only received his sub-portion from the land of Hepher. Numbers 36:2 states: "YHWH commanded my lord to give the land as an נחלה (*inheritance*) by lot to the sons of Israel. And my lord was commanded by YHWH to give our brother Zelophehad's נחלה to his daughters." Rather the ten-part division matches YHWH's proclamation in Num 27:7a, which it was argued in § 4.3 above formed the original ending of the Zelophehad's daughters episode.

If the daughters of Zelophehad are indeed intended to represent the imported people groups that adopted Yahwism, then this distribution depicts the [province of Samaria?] as being shared equally between both allochthonous and autochthonous "Israelites." In this light, Hawk's observation that, "Manasseh is further subdivided along kinship lines (17:1–2) and then according to gender (17:3–6), making it all the more difficult to fix a foundation for constructing tribal identity," might rather be interpreted as a coded reference to the Samaritans' mixed – but accepted by the wider Yahwistic community– composition.

Joshua 17:11–13 also report some puzzling information, which, in light of the present argument, provides yet a further clue. Verse 11 states, "And [belonging] to Manasseh in Issachar and in Asher was Beth Shean and its villages, Ibleam and its villages, the inhabitants of Dor and its villages, the inhabitants of En-dor and its villages, the inhabitants of Taanach and its villages and the inhabitants of Megiddo and its villages." The suggestion that Manasseh also took territory within the tribal boundaries of Issachar and Asher raises a number of issues. First, as Ballhorn correctly observes, the idea that Manasseh took territory inside the boundary of other tribes renders the whole point of describing boundaries moot, as their only purpose is to delineate who is in and who is out.[202] Second, it is prudent to take a look at these particular cities to see what significance they

---

[201] HAWK, *Joshua*, 207.

[202] BALLHORN, *Israel*, 278, writes, "Diese Feststellung, dass Städte des einen Stammes innerhalb des Gebietes eines anderen Stammes liegen, steht eigentlich im Widerspruch zur Gebietsbeschreibung durch Lose und Grenzen, denn deren Idee ist es ja gerade, durch die gezogene äußere Grenzlinie ein von diesen umschlossenes, nach innen homogenes Territorium zu kennzeichnen" (*This statement, that the cities of one tribe lay within the territory of another tribe, actually contradicts the specification of the area through lots and boundaries, whose idea is precisely that through the drawn outer borderline, an enclosed homogenous territory is indicated within*).

had with regards to particular historical settings. Knauf, for instance, argues that Josh 17:11 "zeigt Manasse als den staatstragenden Stamm Israels im (9. und) 8. Jh. v. Chr. Manasse besetzt bedeutende nicht-israelitische Städte, die im frühen 9. Jh. an Israel kamen und königliche Verwaltungszentren wurden: in der Jesreël-Ebene, der Bucht von Bet-Schean ('Issachar') oder im phönizisch besiedelten Küstenstreifen ('Asher') wie Dor" (*shows Manasseh as the state supporting tribe of Israel in the (9th and) 8th century BCE. Manasseh occupies important non-Israelite cities, which in the early 9th century became Israelite and became royal administrative centres: in the Jezreel Plain, the bay of Beth-shean ('Issachar') or on the Phonician-settled coastal strip ('Asher') like Dor*).[203] While this appears to be a plausible explanation in isolation, the subsequent report in vv. 12–13 – that these same cities remained in control of the Canaanites – makes such a proposal difficult, which is not satisfactorily solved by assuming this note was added purely in order to harmonise with Judg 1:27–28.[204]

Ignoring the issue of direction of dependence, the report that it was precisely these "extra" Manassite cities that Manasseh was unable to conquer makes no sense. Why specify that cities outside of Manasseh-proper were Manassite, if (1) they were located outside of the boundary of Manasseh, belonging within the boundaries of Issachar and Asher and (2) if the Manassites did not in fact conquer them but they remained in Canaanite possession? In light of this it seems preferable to understand this report as alluding to a historical reality. As such, the present proposal to understand the confusing nature of the Manassites as a cypher for the mixed peoples of the post-Assyrian situation, whilst still conjectural, is better able to explain these strange details.

Lastly, the Manassite cities listed as belonging to the areas outside Manasseh-proper also have an interesting relation to Solomon's districts listed in 1 Kgs 4:7–19, which in traditional interpretations were seen as the historical basis for Joshua's territorial divisions.[205]

4.4.4.2 1 Kings 4:7–19

The list of Solomon's districts has traditionally been understood to be historically reliable, dating to the time of the United Monarchy. Alt, for example, clearly proclaims the quintessential maximalist position:

---

[203] KNAUF, *Josua*, 152.

[204] GASS, *Landverteilung*, 208, for example, argues that this report takes up the failed conquest story from the beginning of Judges whereas KNAUF, *Richter*, 44, argues the opposite, that Judges borrowed from Joshua. CORTESE, *Josua 13–21*, 90, also argues that because Josh 17:11 f. is clearly secondary to the other Manasseh materials that they must have been taken from Judges.

[205] AHARONI, "Districts," 6, for example, states regarding Solomon's district list, "these lists were used by the editor of Joshua for the descriptions of the various tribal areas."

236 *4. Female Inheritance*

... in der Liste der Vögte und Gaue Salomos, 1. Kön. 4,7–19, eine Urkunde von hohem ge-schichtlichen Wert auf uns gekommen ist. Das Recht zu diesem Urteil kann kaum be-stritten werden; Form und Inhalt der Liste führen gleicherweise zu seiner Anerkennung. (*... in the list of bailiffs/governors and districts of Solomon, 1 Kgs 4:7–19, we have a document of great historical value. The correctness of this judgment can hardly be disputed; the form and content of the list also leads to its legitimation.*)[206]

As already discussed, in more recent studies the historicity of the United Monarchy in general, let alone a "Solomonic Golden Age," has become in-creasingly problematic (cf. § 2.3.1).[207] As Barton remarks, "thirty years ago it was all so simple ... For there had been a 'Solomonic Enlightenment', in which Is-rael had produced the first example of real history-writing in the ancient Near East, perhaps indeed the world."[208] Modern scholarship, in contrast, is far more sceptical.

The list itself is presented as the divisions introduced by Solomon to manage the finances of the United Monarchy. The twelve districts were overseen by twelve נצבים (the interpretation of which is uncertain, it is based on the lemma meaning "to stand" suggesting a translation along the lines of "representative," the NRSV uses the word "officials"), however as has long been observed these districts only cover northern and eastern Israel, the absence of Judah being so conspicuous that the LXX added it in v. 18b (v. 19b NRSV) with the clumsy word-ing καὶ νασιφ εἷς ἐν γῇ Ιουδα (*and one official in the land of Judah*).[209] Even at face value, then, there are already grounds to see the district list in 1 Kings 4 as more likely being a Northern system that was later attributed to Solomon, fur-ther arguments supporting this conclusion will be provided below.

---

[206] ALT, *Schriften*, 76. AHARONI, "Districts," 13, also proclaims, "nothing contradicts a Solo-monic date, and it even seems justified to fix a more precise date not before the middle of his reign."

[207] The literature on this is immense, to name a few examples: FINKELSTEIN/SILBERMAN, *Unearthed*, 243f; CARR, *Tablet*, 163f; SCHMID, *History*, 50. For an overview of the discussion, see FREVEL, *Geschichte*, Ch. 4.

[208] BARTON, "Dating," 95. A good example of this can be seen in WELLHAUSEN, *Prolegomena*, 9, who writes: "with regard to the Jehovistic document, all are happily agreed that, substantially at all events, in language, horizon, and other features, it dates from the golden age of Hebrew lit-erature, to which the finest parts of Judges, Samuel, and Kings, and the oldest extant prophetical writings also belong, – the period of the kings and prophets which preceded the dissolution of the two Israelite kingdoms by the Assyrians."

[209] For a discussion on the translation of נצבים and for a discussion of the reference to Judah, see, NAʾAMAN, "District," 420–421, 422–423 respectively. However, the present argument does not follow Naʾaman in assuming that a district of Judah originally existed. The suggestion of ALT, *Schriften*, 89 – that the absence of Judah is rooted in the Davidic system inherited by Solomon, whereby David's kingdom was originally confined to Judah and secondarily ex-panded to cover all Israel – is unconvincing if one follows the recent historical reconstructions that the first "kingdom" of Israel only arose during the reign of Omri – again see, FREVEL, *Ge-schichte*, 221–245.

Solomon's twelve districts are enumerated with a corresponding official as follows:[210]

I. The hill country of Ephraim.
II. Makaz, Shaalbim, Beth-shemesh and Elon-beth-hanan.
III. Arubboth (incl., Socoh and all the land of Hepher).
IV. Naphath-dor.
V. Taanach, Megiddo and all Beth Shean.
VI. Gilead and Bashan.
VII. Mahanaim.
VIII. Naphtali.
IX. Asher and Bealoth.
X. Issachar.
XI. Benjamin.
XII. Gilead (it seems the intent of this is to cover the territory of Sihon whereas the Gilead of District VI covers the "real" Gilead in northern Transjordan).

It is not the intention of the present discussion to analyse the list in detail, however already XII, with its labelling of central Transjordan as "Gilead," as well as the reference to Sihon and Og point to this twelve-district structure as a late construct (cf. Ch. 3).

Alt's original thesis was that:

Die Liste der salomonischen Gaue ist die letzte Urkunde, die den alten Dualismus zwischen Stämmen und Städten bezeugt. Es ist eine Aufgabe für sich, seine Geschichte zurückzuverfolgen von den Zeiten, da die Stämme und Städte in friedlichem Verein den königlichen Hofhalt Salomos bestreiten mußten, bis in jene dunklen Jahrhunderte, da sie den großen Kampf um ihr Dasein miteinander zu führen begannen." (*The list of Solomon's districts is the last document that testifies to the old dualism between tribes and cities. It is a task in itself to trace its history back from the times in which the tribes and cities, in peaceful union, must have financed the royal court of Solomon back to whichever dark century, in which they began to conduct the great battle of their existence with one another.*)[211]

However, being persuaded of the more recent, critical view of Israel's history, there was no such thing as a United Monarchy, and whilst there were undoubtedly tribal groups that first formed tribal unions, and were later ruled by kings (i.e., the Omrides), these were not limited to the twelve sons of Jacob (cf. § 3.3). In light of this, it must be asked where this district list originated and what it was originally intended to portray.

---

[210] For the sake of convenience, the names follow the spelling of the NRSV.

[211] ALT, *Schriften*, 89. AHARONI, "Districts," 5, states that this tribe/Canaanite city-state division functions as a "basic principle" for understanding the list.

238   *4. Female Inheritance*

Removing the districts that are "tribally" designated as well as the spurious District XII, leaves districts I–VII, which are shown in figure 14 below. Translating these districts into the terms of the Manassites reveals some very interesting results. In Transjordan the land of Machir is covered by District VII, while the land of Gilead (and Bashan) is covered by District VI (cf. discussion in § 3.3).[212] The land of the five "daughters of Manasseh" is squarely described by District III.[213] While the five "sons of Manasseh" as well as the remaining Josephites (i.e., the Ephraimites) belonged together in District I.[214] The allocation of the sons of Manasseh to District I is supported by the specific reference to "all the land of Hepher" in District III, which is the logical equivalent of "not the land of Abiezer, Helek, Asriel, Shechem and Shemida".[215] As to the "Canaanite" cities listed in Josh 17:11, Beth Shean, Taanach and Megiddo are listed by name in District V, whilst Dor logically belongs to District IV. District II falls outside any consideration of the tribe of Manasseh but makes sense in the context of a post-Assyrian historical setting for territory that was at some point "Israelite." Thus, apart

---

[212] This largely follows the arguments of LEMAIRE, "Galaad," who suggests that the name "Gilead" derives from the contrast with the neighbouring Bashan, which means "fertile plain." Lemaire further argues, based on texts such as 2 Sam 17:27, that "ainsi, bien que cette localisation reste approximative, Makîr était très vraisemblablement situé à l'est du Jourdain, à l'ouest et au sud-ouest de Maḥanayim, c'est à dire qu'il occupait la plaine du Ghor au débouché du Yabboq près de Deir 'Alla et pouvait aussi comporter le plateau assez fertile (Merj el-'Arḍe ou Arḍ el-'Arḍe) situé au sud-ouest du Yabboq et au nord-ouest du wadi Umm ed-Danânir." (*thus, although this location remains approximate, Machir was very likely located east of the Jordan, west and southwest of Mahanaim, i.e., he occupied the Ghor plain at the outlet of the Jabbok near Deir 'Alla and could also include the rather fertile plateau [Merj el-'Arḍe or Arḍ el-'Arḍe] located southwest of the Jabbok and northwest of Wadi Umm ed-Danânir.*)

[213] ZERTAL, "Arubboth," 476, argues that "from a geographic-historic viewpoint, it seems that the 3d Solomonic district coincided with the boundaries of Manasseh in the hill country (Josh 15:5–9; 17:7–13)." This third district is described in 1 Kgs 4:10: "Ben-hesed [was stationed] in Arubboth, to him [was] Socoh and all the land of Hepher." The location of Arubboth is difficult to identify given that 1 Kgs 4:10 is the only instance that it occurs in the Bible. The two most recent proposals are Khirbet el-Hamam (ZERTAL, "Arubboth." SMOAK, "Arubboth," 872, follows Zertal and suggests that Khirbet el-Hamam is currently the most convincing option.) and Rubutu/Tell el-Muḥafar (NA'AMAN, "Rubutu," 380; NA'AMAN, "District," 424). For the purposes of the present discussion, however, a decision is unnecessary as both options locate Arubboth in the Dothan Valley. More important is the region described by Socoh and all the land of Hepher. Genealogically and geographically speaking, "all the land of Hepher" logically describes the area occupied by Zelophehad's daughters as depicted in Figure 13 and Figure 14. Socoh is located at modern day Khirbet Shuweiket er-Ras on the fringe of the Sharon Valley (see ALT, *Schriften*, 78; AHARONI, "Districts," 5; NA'AMAN, "District," 424; ZERTAL/MIRKAM, *Hill Country 3*, 452).

[214] AHARONI, "Districts," 12, for example, understands this to mean the entirety of the Ephraimite mountains, reaching down to Mizpah, which forms the northern border of District XI.

[215] AHARONI, "Districts," 8–9, suggests that District III was on the coast so that District I covers the tribal boundaries of both Ephraim and Manasseh.

from District II, every non-tribal district contained Manassites; and it is difficult to assume that this is purely random or unintentional.

As Na'aman in particular has argued, the list of Solomon's districts has strong similarities to the provinces introduced following the Assyrian invasion.[216] Although there remains some important uncertainty, the old proposal of Forrer – that Assyria divided Aram and Israel into six distinct provinces – is still broadly accepted.[217] Importantly for the present discussion is the separation of the former Northern Kingdom into the provinces of Du'ru (Dor), Magidu (Megiddo) and Samerina (Samaria). These three districts more or less match the Manassite districts, with the only difficulty being that Samaria/Samerina is split into districts I and III. The Assyrian presence in all these areas, including District II, is supported archaeologically. For example, Barkay notes, "[Assyrian] ceramic coffins have been discovered at Megiddo, Tel Qataf in the Beth Shean Valley, Dothan, Tell el-Far'ah North, and Ammon,"[218] and Singer-Avitz notes that Assyrian-style carinated bowls were found at Samaria, Tirzah/Tell el-Fār'a (North), Shechem, Dothan, Khirbet Marjameh, Tel Rekhesh and Mizpah/Tell en-Naṣbeh.[219] In light of this, it is difficult not to see a correlation between the Manassite cities listed as remaining in Canaanite hands and those areas of the Northern Kingdom that belonged to the non-Samarian provinces.

The major difficulty with this is that "Samaria" is split into two districts and there is no firm evidence that this was ever the case historically speaking. Due to the paucity of evidence, it is generally assumed that the Assyrian province divisions were more or less maintained during the Babylonian as well as the Persian administrations. As Stern notes, "it appears that in Persian-period Palestine the administrative structure retained the basic divisions established during the Assyrian age, but in a more developed form."[220] However, if one assumes that this presentation of Samaria comprising two districts is not so much historically accurate in political terms but rather alludes to the mixed nature of the Samaritans (particularly taking the confluence of the area of Zelophehad's daughters with District III, which in turn describes the locus of the introduced peoples), then this division is yet another marker along the same lines as the separation of Manasseh into sons and daughters as it presented in Joshua 17.

---

[216] NA'AMAN, "District."
[217] FORRER, *Provinzeinteilung*; STERN, *ALB*, 10–13; NA'AMAN, "System," 223–225.
[218] BARKAY, "Iron," 353.
[219] SINGER-AVITZ, "Assyrian," 184.
[220] STERN, *ALB*, 372.

240   4. Female Inheritance

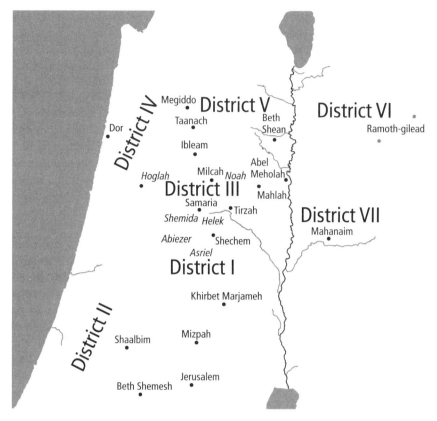

Figure 14: "Solomon's" districts[221]

---

[221] Map drawn by J. Davis. Besides the Toponyms identified in figure 13. Socoh is located at modern day Khirbet Shuweiket er-Ras (1534.1943), see ALT, *Schriften*, 78; AHARONI, "Districts," 5; NA'AMAN, "District," 424; ZERTAL/MIRKAM, *Hill Country 3*, 452. Beth Shean is located at Tell el-Husn (1972.2118), see, McGovern, "*Beth-Shan*;" FREVEL, *Geschichte*, 445. Megiddo is located at Tell el-Mutesellim (1676.2212), see FREVEL, *Geschichte*, 447. Dor is located at Tel Dor (1424.2247), see FREVEL, *Geschichte*, 445. Abel Meholah is located at Tall Abu Sus (2029.1978), see MACDONALD, *East*, 206; NA'AMAN, "District," 426; HERR, "Abel-Meholah." Mahanaim is located at Tall adh-Dhahab al-Garbiyya (2149.1771), see MACDONALD, *East*, 140–142; FINKELSTEIN et al, "Gilead," 146–148; FREVEL, *Geschichte*, 447. Ramoth-Gilead is located either at ar-Ramtha (2450.2186) or Tall al-Husn (2330.2102), see MACDONALD, *East*, 201–202; FINKELSTEIN, "Tell er-Rumeith," 22–23; FREVEL, *Geschichte*, 447. Ibleam is located at Khirbet Bel'ameh (1722.2058), see ZERTAL, *Hill Country 1*, 123–125; FREVEL, *Geschichte*, 446. For Beth Shemesh (1476.1286), see FREVEL, *Geschichte*, 445. Shaalbim is located at Salbit (1488.1418), also for the meaning of Makaz rather meaning מִקְצֵה (from+ end/extremity), i.e., "from the extremity of Shaalbim," see NA'AMAN, "District," 425. Mizpah is located at Tell en-Nasbe (1706.1436), see FREVEL, *Geschichte*, 448. For Khirbet Marjameh (1816.1554), see MAZAR, "Khirbet Marjameh." For the distribution of the regions Hoglah, Shemida, Helek, Abiezer and Asriel, see AHARONI, *Land*, 315–326. The location of Noah instead follows ZERTAL, *Hill Country 2*, 29–30.

4.4.5 Summary

This section began by emphasizing that the proposed historical background for the origin of Zelophehad's daughters was daring. However, as the discussion has demonstrated quite a number of clues converge to point toward the same conclusion.

The exegetical analysis of Numbers 27 argued that there was only a weak correlation between the specific case of Zelophehad's daughters (Num 27:1–7a) and the generalised legislation for daughter inheritance (Num 27:8–11a). These two loosely related text units were merged primarily via the bracketing verses 7b and 11b. In particular it was argued that – taken in isolation – Num 27:1–7a presented a narrative whereby all five daughters were granted inheritance rights and were construed as equal partners alongside the male Manassites. This result was rooted in the Priestly ideology of אחזה – the term used exclusively in vv. 1–7a – that operates with the idea of mutable allotments that grow and shrink based upon the number of members the land is being divided between (cf. § 3.4.1). This same understanding was the guiding principle in the narrative of Joshua 17, which more explicitly demonstrated that all five daughters of Manasseh received a portion that was equal to the remaining males of Manasseh. Joshua 17:5, thus reports that there were ten (not six) portions granted to the Manassites in Cisjordan.

In contrast the law for heiresses in Num 27:8–11a introduced a much more modest legislation whereby a single heiress merely functioned as a temporary guardian of the father's estate until a grandson could be produced. This was primarily flagged by the verb "transfer," which clearly differs from the rules for the male kin who are "given" the property. A further important point of divergence was that where vv. 1–7a operated on the principle of mutable land, the legislation of vv. 8–11a utilized the Deuteronomistic נחלה, and thus is better understood to imply that a man's property was fixed and immutable. Based on their disparate nature and their differing ideologies, it was suggested that vv. 1–7a must have originally fulfilled a different function than to simply be the narrative introduction to the general law.

Via an investigation of the geographical reality behind Zelophehad's daughters, it was noted that there was a striking correlation to the region in which the greatest concentration of the wedge-shape decorated bowls were found. In light of this and in light of the various allusions to the foreign nature of the Samaritan Yahwists, it was suggested that perhaps Zelophehad's daughters were not so much intended to depict women in a literal sense but rather to depict non-patrilineal inheritors and so to function as a cypher for the "foreign" elements of the Samaritan Yahwistic community. The fact that the narrative of Num 27:1–7a is written in the Priestly style, indirectly provides yet a further clue as such inclusivity fits much better to Priestly ideology.

242   *4. Female Inheritance*

This conjecture was then further strengthened in light of the various, and often disputed, peculiarities found in Joshua 17 and 1 Kings 4. In all three cases, various strategies were employed to depict the tribe of Manasseh, or more accurately the Samaritan area, as being populated by a curious mixture of inheritors: Numbers and Joshua used the fable of the sonless Zelophehad to introduce heiresses, while 1 Kings 4 depicted the province of Samaria as comprising two districts which so happened to match the division between the male descendants of Joseph (i.e., the sons of Manasseh and Ephraim) who were allocated to District I and the female descendants (the daughters of Manasseh/Zelophehad) who were allocated to District III.

If this interpretation is correct, then it would suggest that vv. 8–11a actually function as a means of obfuscation, shifting the focus away from "ethnicity" issues and moving it toward literal daughters and inheritance issues.

There remain some as yet undiscussed issues with this interpretation. Arguably the most glaring being that the presupposed historical setting is rooted in the 8th century, when the Assyrian deportees were concentrated to the area described by Zelophehad's daughters. Yet the Priestly style, let alone the oracular novella form, much more securely dates to the Persian, and likely even the late Persian period. Thus, one must explain the temporal gap.

Although the criticism of a large temporal gap deserves due consideration, the issue needs to be properly framed. The issue is not that after approximately two centuries that those with Mesopotamian roots would have forgotten those roots. Indeed, the apostle Paul remembers his Benjaminite roots many centuries after tribal associations had any meaningful political function (cf. Rom 11:1; Phil 3:5). Rather, the issue is why would the mixed heritage of the Samaritans be deemed important only two centuries later? As Hobson argues, the mixed culture and ethnicity of Yehud in the Persian period made "ethnicity" as the defining social binding force at least somewhat unsuitable. He instead suggests that "religious affiliation" is a much more suitable descriptor for describing social units.[222] In such a case, the Samaritan Yahwists naturally belonged to a single people group united by religious affiliation.

The most immediate option is that Num 27:1–7a was developed in response to those groups or factions operating in the Persian period for whom ethnicity in its most extreme form was significant. Ezra and Nehemiah in particular demonstrate that even those Yahwists who dwelt in Jerusalem, but who did not share the pro-Persian position of its leaders, were depicted as being less than "true Israel" and were deemed to belong to a sub-class of society.[223] However, as the discussion on the Samaritans in § 2.2.3 already suggested, scholars are now trending toward seeing the Persian period as a period of coexistence, with the Torah

---

[222] Hobson, "Israelites," 39.

[223] Brett, "Politics," for example, highlights how the patriarchal traditions represent a challenge to ethnocentrism and endogamy as espoused in Ezra and Nehemiah.

in particular being a jointly developed work from both Samaria and Judah.[224] Thus, although this solution is possible, the presuppositions behind it belong more securely under the old "Conflict Paradigm" than current interpretations.[225]

A second option comes from the fact that the Bible displays an increasing inclusivity towards outsiders. Achenbach for example aptly demonstrates that laws pertaining to the *gêr* follow a clear trajectory of growing inclusivity. The Covenant Code suggests that they be protected (e. g., Exod 22:20), Deuteronomy allows a limited participation in cultic events (e. g., Deut 16:11), the Holiness Code grants the *gêr* religious obligation (e. g., Lev 18:26) and finally late Priestly texts grant the *gêr* full religious integration (e. g., Num 15:15–16).[226] Hensel has recently argued that the Jacob narrative also shows an increasing inclusivity towards Edom, which eventually aimed at including Idumean Yahwists.[227] This solution, although heading in the right direction, is also unsatisfactory, as the major rhetorical thrust of Num 27:1–7a is that the "daughters" were still children of Manasseh, which does not accord with the idea that they were treated like *gêr*.

The more plausible solution, then, is to go back to basics. According to the fundamental Priestly tiered worldview, YHWH relates to the world in three major categories, each comprising an ever-increasing specificity. The first tier was defined via the giving of the Noahic covenant in Genesis 9, which secured YHWH's relationship to all creation. The second tier narrowed the circle to the descendants of Abraham, including Ishmael (Arabs) and Esau (Edom). Finally, the people of Israel, as the nation in which YHWH dwells in their midst, makes up the most exclusive tier. This Priestly system is typically described as Priestly ecumenicity.[228] The issue, then, is that were the Samaritan Yahwists of Mesopotamian heritage treated as *gêr*, they would belong to tier 2. The ruling of Num 27:1–7a functions to bring these Samaritan members into tier 1 via the strategy of non-partrilineal inheritance. This goal also aligns with the thesis presented in § 3.3, which suggested that the idea of twelve named tribes was most strongly present in Priestly and post-Priestly texts. Thus, the idea that the fable of Zelophehad's daughters was a Priestly innovation should not be deemed particularly surprising.

It seems unlikely that the Priestly authors responsible for Num 27:1–7a were scribes from the golah, i. e., those responsible for creating Pg. Rather, it seems far more likely that Northern scribes assimilated the Priestly ideology and mimicked the Priestly style. This further supports the theory that the Samaritans were co-authors of the extant Pentateuch.

---

[224] To name but one example, HENSEL, *Juda*, 299–302, argues that the anti-Samaritan polemic in Ezra 4 stems from the Hellenistic period and already stands in contrast to the temple building report in Ezra 5:1–6:15, where there is no resistance.

[225] The name of the model taken from HENSEL, "Relationship."

[226] ACHENBACH, "gêr," see figure 1. See also CHRISTIAN, "Openness."

[227] HENSEL, "Edom," 113–115.

[228] See, e. g., BRETT, "Dissemination;" SCHMID, "Ecumenicity."

244 *4. Female Inheritance*

Although this argument admittedly contains several tenuous links, I would argue that the resulting explanation makes far better sense of the peculiarities in the text than the prevailing scholarly solutions. In particular, those arguments that fall back on scribal error or confusion on the one hand, or those that presuppose the traditions are rooted in the Monarchic or even pre-Monarchic period on the other. Given the late dating of the narrative itself (i.e., late/post-Priestly), the idea that the underlying narrative reflects the issues prevalent in the postexilic Yahwistic community is a more logical connection.

4.5 Numbers 36:1–12 in Detail

Num 36:1The ancestral heads of the clan of the sons of Gilead, son of Machir, son of Manasseh, from the clans of the sons of Joseph came near and spoke before Moses and before the leaders, the ancestral heads of the sons of Israel.

Num 36:2They said, "Yhwh commanded my lord to give the land as an נחלה (*inheritance*) by lot to the sons of Israel. And my lord was commanded by Yhwh to give our brother Zelophehad's נחלה to his daughters.

Num 36:3But if they become the wife to one of the sons from the tribes of Israel, then their נחלה will be withdrawn from the נחלה of our ancestors and added to the נחלה of the tribe in which they are. Thus our allotted inheritance will be reduced.

Num 36:4and [even][229] if it is the Jubilee to the sons of Israel, their נחלה will again be added to the נחלה of the tribe in which they are, and from the נחלה of the tribe of our ancestors their נחלה will be withdrawn."

Num 36:5Moses commanded the sons of Israel, by the word of Yhwh, saying, "the tribe of the sons of Joseph speak rightly

Num 36:6This is the word which Yhwh commanded to the daughters of Zelophehad, "they are to be wives to who is good in their eyes, only let them be wives to those from the clan of their father's tribe.

Num 36:7no Israelite נחלה will go around from tribe to tribe, because the sons of Israel should each cling to the נחלה of the tribe of his ancestors.

Num 36:8every daughter who possesses a נחלה from the tribes of the sons of Israel are to marry one from a clan of the tribe of their father, in order that the sons of Israel each possess the inheritance of their ancestors.

Num 36:9no נחלה will go around from a tribe to another tribe, because each of the tribes of the sons of Israel shall cling to its inheritance.

Num 36:10just as Yhwh commanded to Moses, so the daughters of Zelophehad did

Num 36:11Mahlah, Tirzah, and Hoglah, and Milcah and Noah are the daughters of Zelophehad, they married the sons of their uncles.

Num 36:12they married from the clans of the sons of Manasseh, son of Joseph and their inheritance remained in the tribe of their father's clan.

Table 18: Numbers 36:1–12

---

[229] This word is missing from the text but its addition makes the point clearer. See discussion below.

The mere existence of Numbers 36:1–12 comes as something of a shock. After hearing Yʜᴡʜ pronounce that "the daughters of Zelophehad have spoken rightly" (Num 27:7) as well as the provision of a new inheritance law (Num 27:8–11a), one would think the matter was settled. However, Numbers 36 opens with the elders of Manasseh approaching Moses and the Israelite leadership with a complaint regarding these very same rulings. Thus, one wonders if Snaith is correct in suggesting that, "if Num. xxvii 1–11 had to do with the inheritance of family property, it was bad law, and had to be emended (Num. xxxvi 1–9)..."[230] Or perhaps Gevaryahu is correct in proposing that the law of Numbers 36 was only provided to the wilderness generation, because it would only be a matter of time before inter-tribal marriage took place.[231] Before such critiques can be answered, the content of the complaint as well as the subsequent amendment must be understood.

Verse 1 begins with an introductory formula that resembles Num 27:1 and so functions to link the present pericope to the earlier text:

Num 27:1a The daughters of Zelophehad, son of Hepher, son of Gilead, son of Machir, son of Manasseh from the clans of Manasseh, son of Joseph came near …

Num 36:1a The ancestral heads of the clan of the sons of Gilead, son of Machir, son of Manasseh, from the clans of the sons of Joseph came near …

Table 19: Comparison of Num 27:1 and Num 36:1

Despite their similarities, there are also a number of linguistic clues that point to the conclusion that Num 36:1–12 did not originate from the same hand as Num 27:1–11.[232] First, the leadership before whom the Manassites appear are simply labelled הנשיאם (*the leaders*) in Num 27:2, but appear with the much longer הנשיאם ראשי האבות לבני ישראל (*the leaders to the heads of the sons of Israel*) in Num 36:1. Second, the Manassite leaders themselves are labelled with the abbreviated form ראשי האבות (lit. *heads of the fathers*) – which is most likely a shortened form of ראשי בית־אבות (*heads of the ancestral houses*) as found in, e.g., Exod 6:14, or ראשי האבות למטות בני־ישראל (*heads of the ancestral tribes of the sons of Israel*) as found in, e.g., Josh 19:51 – which is found throughout the books of Ezra, Nehemiah and Chronicles, but rarely elsewhere, which suggests the present text should be dated to the late Persian period at the earliest.[233] Third, Eleazar is conspicuous by his absence (he is listed in the LXX and 4Q27). Seebass argues, "Eleasar hätte als

---

[230] Sɴᴀɪᴛʜ, "Daughters," 127.

[231] Gᴇᴠᴀʀʏᴀʜᴜ, "Root," 110.

[232] Most scholars see Num 36:1–12 as secondary. Aᴄʜᴇɴʙᴀᴄʜ, *Vollendung*, 571f; Asʜʟᴇʏ, *Numbers*, 658; Dᴇ Vᴀᴜʟx, *Nombres*, 405; Kɴɪᴇʀɪᴍ/Cᴏᴀᴛs, *Numbers*, 329; Lᴇᴠɪɴᴇ, *Numbers 21–36*, 575f; Mɪʟɢʀᴏᴍ, *Numbers*, 511f; Nᴏᴛʜ, *Numbers*, 257; Sᴀᴋᴇɴғᴇʟᴅ, "Daughters," 39; Sᴄʜᴍɪᴅᴛ, *Numeri*, 222; Sᴇᴇʙᴀss, *Numeri 3*, 452.

[233] See, e.g., Lᴇᴠɪɴᴇ, *Numbers 21–36*, 577; Sᴇᴇʙᴀss, *Numeri 3*, 458–459. For dating Ezra and Nehemiah to the Persian period see, e.g., Cᴀʀʀ, *Formation*, 123–124; Sᴄʜᴍɪᴅ, *History*, 162–163.

246   *4. Female Inheritance*

Priester hier sachlich keine Funktion" (*As priest, Eleazar had no relevant function here*), however this is only correct if some parallelism with Numbers 27 is not presupposed.[234] In Num 27:1–11 it was argued that Eleazar functioned purely in a priestly role as he had not yet been granted the leadership of the people alongside Joshua (Num 27:12–23). Despite already having been granted this position – chronologically speaking – by Numbers 36, Eleazar's absence can, on the one hand, be expected as Joshua is also absent, i.e., Moses is still the acting leader and so Joshua and Eleazar have not yet received that office. On the other hand, Eleazar's absence in his role as priest needs further clarification. Most plausibly the distinction is to be found in the fact that the daughters of Zelophehad stood before the entrance to the tent of meeting (Num 27:2), whereas the elders of Manasseh are said to simply appear before Moses and the leaders (Num 36:1). If this is correct, then Eleazar's presence in Num 27:1–11 is due to his position as the "manager" of the sanctuary. Although it is not entirely clear if the tent of meeting has been deliberately omitted, there are some clues in v. 5 (see below) that suggest that it was.

The basis of the complaint is provided in v. 2 and then further detailed in vv. 3–4. At issue is the interaction between the newly introduced daughter inheritance law and the property dynamics between husbands and wives, the details of which were already examined in § 4.2.1. This complaint contains several interesting details, which warrant closer inspection.

The introduction of the complaint, given in v. 2, is curious because the elders do not begin with the provision of an אחזה to each of the daughters of Zelophehad (as is stipulated in Num 27:7a), rather they first recall that the land is to be given as a נחלה בגורל (*inheritance by lot*) to the sons of Israel.[235] The allocation of the land via lot is not mentioned in Numbers 27:1–11, rather it is first found in Num 26:52–56, where it is the stipulated technique by which the land is to be allocated to those counted in the census (Num 26:1–51). The division by lot is also commanded in Num 33:54 and 34:13. Despite its repeated appearance, the concept of a division by lot is problematic and is generally understood to be a late innovation.[236]

---

[234] Seebass, *Numeri 3*, 459.

[235] Seebass, "Machir," 499, correctly notes, "... der Bezug zu xxvii 1–11 ist außerordentlich schwach. So beginnt die Fallbeschreibung v. 2 gar nicht mit dem Erbrecht der Töchter Zelofhads, sondern mit dem Programm der Landverteilung durch das Los." (*... the relation to [Num] xxvii:1–11 is extraordinarily weak. So the case description of v. 2 does not in any way begin with the inheritance of the daughters of Zelophehad, rather with the program of a division of the land through lot.*)

[236] This is clearly the case with Num 26:52–56. Numbers 26:53 begins with the command that the land is to be apportioned according to the number of names recorded in the census. Verse 54 adds that this distribution should be according to the size. The difficulty with v. 54 is that it does not specify which entity it is speaking about. The text literally translates, "to a large, his inheritance shall be abundant and to a small, his inheritance shall be few; each in proportion

4.5 Numbers 36   247

That the idea of a division by lot is a late innovation is broadly accepted, however this does not explain why such a system was deemed a necessary addition at all. According to Wüst, the concept is rooted in the narrative of Josh 18:1–10, where Joshua accuses the seven remaining tribes for failing to possess the land (in contrast to Reuben, Gad, Judah and Joseph [i. e., Ephraim and Manasseh], who all went and took their land), and so prescribes a system whereby the extent of the remaining land is to be documented and subsequently divided into seven portions that are allocated by lot.[237] But this explanation is not completely convincing as the use of lots in this instance is not only depicted negatively but also applies only to the unobliging tribes. Achenbach observes that the only appearance of the lot in the Pentateuch, outside the aforementioned verses, is found in the sin offering rite of Leviticus 16 – wherein Aaron casts lots to determine which goat is offered to YHWH and which is sent into the wilderness – and thus suggests that the practice itself must be Priestly at the earliest. More specifically Achenbach ties the practice, not to Joshua 18, but to its use evidenced in Babylonian and Persian period reports.[238] In this light, Achenbach finds further support in Neh 11:1, which states, "The leaders of the people dwelt in Jerusalem and the rest of the people cast lots to come, one from every ten, to dwell in Jerusalem the holy city and the other nine in the towns." Thus, he concludes:

Voraussetzung einer Zuteilung durch Lose ist natürlich die Bestimmung der Größe eines Distrikts bzw. eine Einteilung in feste Landeinheiten. Ohne sie macht eine Verlosung keinen Sinn. Gemeint ist also, daß den rund 600.000 Familien des Volkes ebenso viele Landanteile zustehen (26,51. 53), wobei die Annahme der legendär hohen Zahl vermutlich

---

to his number shall his inheritance be given." The NRSV, for example, fills in the lacuna with the word "tribe" resulting in "to a large tribe you shall give a large inheritance …" However, the word "tribe" is not immediately clear from the context of the census, as, unlike in Numbers 1, the list of names correspond to the משפחה (*clan*) level, thus the more logical reading of vv. 53–54 is that a large clan will receive a large inheritance, etc. Following this v. 55 inserts, for the first time, the command that the land is to be divided by lot לשמות מטות־אבתם (*according to the names of the ancestral tribes*). Which is then reinforced by v. 56 that stipulates that the lots shall apportioned according to their number, such that a larger tribe receives more than a smaller one. Thus, GERMANY, "Concepts," 315, for example, argues that v. 55 is a late insertion and that v. 56 should be understood to "reconcile the principle of proportionality from v. 54 with the division of the land by lot." Furthermore, as SCHMIDT, *Numeri*, 161–162, observes, the instruction to Moses as to how to divide up the land is surprising given that P had already clarified that Moses and Aaron were not allowed to bring the people into the land. Things are different in Num 33:54, where the division of the land is to be performed בגורל למשפחתיכם (*by lot according to your clans*). Numbers 34:13 is different again in that it suggests that the land is to be divided by lot and given to the nine and a half tribes.

In terms of redactional layers GERMANY, "Concepts," 320, suggests that introduction of the lot is at least five layers later than the original material of the book of Numbers (specifically he labels this addition Roman numeral, V+), whereas ACHENBACH, *Vollendung*, 573, allocates Num 26:52–56 to ThB I.

[237] WÜST, *Untersuchungen*, 201.
[238] ACHENBACH, *Vollendung*, 459–460.

248   *4. Female Inheritance*

der Vorstellung von der Größe der Satrapie Transeuphratene bzw. der legendären Ausdehnung des davidisch-salomonisch Reiches entspricht. (*The prerequisite for an allocation by lot is naturally the determination of the size of a district, or rather the division into fixed land units. Without which, the solution makes no sense. So what is meant is that the round 600,000 families of the people are entitled to equally many land units, whereby the assumption of the legendarily high number presumably corresponds to the conception of the size of the Transeuphratene Satrapy or the legendary extent of the Davidic-Solomonic empire.)*[239]

While Achenbach's suggestion that the lot system relates to the districts of Transeuphratene cannot be verified, the general idea that the lot system relates to fixed boundaries will also be argued below. More specifically it will be suggested that the shift to an allocation by lot directly relates to the idea of fixed tribal boundaries.

Given that Numbers 36 logically derives from a layer that post-dates Num 27:1–11, the use of the Deuteronomistic נחלה over against the Priestly אחזה deserves comment. Particularly when scholars point to the other language of this verse as being distinctively Priestly, particularly the צוה יהוה (*YHWH commanded …*) that is found throughout the Priestly corpus but seldom in Deuteronomy.[240] The argument to be unfolded in more detail below is that Numbers 36 appears to already combine Priestly and Deuteronomistic concepts into the same text and therefore most likely represents a text that was developed after the joining of Priestly and non-Priestly texts into the same work (i.e., a post-conflational addition). To briefly foreshadow the argument to be unfolded below, the use of נחלה over against אחזה is necessary due to the underlying ideology of the אחזה, which as discussed earlier conceives of the land as Yhwh's and that each member of the people of Yhwh is eligible to receive an equal portion. The key point of this ideology is that the size of that portion is mutable, growing and shrinking based on the number of members. When the idea of fixed tribal boundaries was introduced, the core premise of the אחזה – applying to the whole people – no longer made sense. Instead, the idea of tribal boundaries allocated by lot fit much more securely to the Deuteronomistic idea of the נחלה, which was an immutable possession that belonged to the tribe from generation to generation.[241] Therefore, the real issue of Numbers 36 is how these fixed, bounded tribal allotments interact when they come into contact with marriage law and property transfer of an heiress.[242]

Verses 3 and 4 recount the litigants' complaint, which importantly includes the idea that when a wife marries, her husband takes control of her property. This is

---

[239] ACHENBACH, *Vollendung*, 460.

[240] See, e.g., LEVINE, *Numbers 21–36*, 577; SEEBASS, *Numeri 3*, 459.

[241] Thus, providing further support to ACHENBACH, *Vollendung*, 460, suggestion that the behind the "allotted portion" lay the conception of districts. See also COCCO, *Women*, 163.

[242] Cf. BINNS, *Numbers*, 235; BUDD, *Numbers*, 388.

4.5 Numbers 36   249

expressly stated in v. 3, where the Manassites not only mention that the heiress's נחלה would be added to the husband's tribe, but also that this loss would מגרל נחלתנו יגרע (*reduce our allotted portion*). The inclusion of the root גרע (*lot*) here reinforces the concept of the lot in determining a tribally designated inheritance.[243] As discussed in § 4.2.1, the only logical understanding of the heiress law stipulated in Num 27:8–11a was that property transfer to a heiress did not function in the same way as to the male kinsmen, this was primarily flagged by the change in verb with the inheritance being עבר (*transferred*) to the daughter (Num 27:8) but נתן (*given*) to the male kinsmen (Num 27:9–11a). The complaint of the Manassite leadership also points in the same direction, this time by highlighting that marriage laws still take priority over inheritance.[244] But as Seebass notes, this interpretation must ignore the narrative portion of Numbers 27, particularly vv. 3 and 7, where the daughters of Zelophehad received the name of the father. Seebass further notes that the historical reality of Zelophehad's daughters also speaks against the ruling of Numbers 36 as the cities and regions still bear the name of the daughters and not their husbands, even accounting for the fact that after Num 36:11 those husbands were also Manassites.[245] This observation demonstrates that not only must Num 36:1–12 be considered secondary to Num 27:1–11 as most scholars tend to conclude but it also supports the arguments provided above that the narrative of Num 27:1–7a originally had different goals to the legislation of Num 27:8–11a. Thus, Numbers 36:1–12 makes more sense as a reaction to the law of Num 27:8 than it does to Yhwh's ruling in Num 27:7a.[246] That being said, the fact that the elders' complaint is directly linked to the daughters of Zelophehad demonstrates that the author of Num 36:1–11 did not know of a separate Num 27:8–11a but only to the full oracular novella.

After noting that marriage law takes precedence over inheritance rights for women in v. 3, the elders engage in a seemingly new line of argumentation in v. 4, stating ואם־יהיה היבל (*and if the Jubilee occurs …*).[247] This reference to the Jubilee has received mixed opinions.[248] Noth, for instance, notes, "The reference to the year of jubilee in v. 4 is, from both the literary and the factual point of view, out of place … V. 4 is an irrelevant addition."[249] The law for the Jubilee is

---

[243] Regarding the use of the term גרע, see discussion in Gevaryahu, "Root," 112.

[244] Thus, providing further support against the admittedly attractive suggestion of Seebass, *Numeri 3*, 201–202.

[245] Seebass, *Numeri 3*, 453.

[246] See, e.g., Davies, *Numbers*, 368.

[247] Levine, *Numbers 21–36*, 577, argues that this is atypical of how the verb היה (*to be*) is normally employed, and suggests that this more active, or forceful, usage is in keeping with late biblical texts such as found in Jonah 4:5, Qoh 6:12, 11:2, and Dan 8:19. Such late dating of the phrase is in keeping with the observations made elsewhere that Numbers 36 is a late text.

[248] Knierim/Coats, *Numbers*, 329, for example, observe that "Reference to the year of Jubilee in v. 4 is not clear, since in the Jubilee property should revert to its original owner."

[249] Noth, *Numbers*, 257. See also, Snaith, "Daughters," 127.

found in Lev 25:8–16 and supplemented in Lev 27:16–24, it covers (among other things) the return of ancestral property to the original owners at the end of 50 years.[250] Significantly, the Jubilee law functions with the underlying ideal of the Priestly אחזה, whereby the land is owned by Yhwh and correspondingly could not be bought in the true sense of the word but rather "sublet" for a period of time, with the maximum allowable lease period being until the next Jubilee year. Under this ideological construction the Jubilee represented a reset, land that was (most likely) sold to cover debt was redeemed and thus the rights of usufruct were returned to the original owner, who could then (ideally) profit from the land himself. But these matters are complicated by the fact that Num 36:1–12 employ the Deuteronomistic term נחלה on the one hand, and that the relation to the Jubilee law is stretched because it does not cover those cases when property is transferred due to marriage on the other. This latter point led scholars such as Aaron to propose that the Jubilee reference in Numbers 36 does not refer to the law found in the Holiness Code, but rather refers to an older, now lost tradition.[251] So how should one make sense of this reference to the Jubilee?

To begin, if one assumes the socio-cultural background of the original Priestly ideology was the returning exiles, then the claim that the land was Yhwh's and that all were to be granted an equal part of the usufruct very successfully bypassed any claims of ownership by those who had remained in the land.[252] With the whole land belonging to Yhwh, the returnees did not need to compete with the existing occupants over land claims, rather the usufruct system dictated that all people of Yhwh must subdivide the whole land equally regardless of whether their ancestors had been living there for generations or whether they had just returned from the Diaspora.[253] Stated plainly, the shift to a usufruct system directly benefitted the returning golah community and in equal measure took land away from those who were already there.[254] However, if it is correctly assumed that Numbers 36 was written quite some time after the golah community had returned, then those wielding the pen would no longer represent those outside finding legal-religious justification to come in, rather they would presumably be those finding legal-religious justification for keeping what they had (the example of Neh 11:1, noted above, is demonstration enough of the inherent inequalities of the system). If this hypothesis is correct, then it logically

---

[250] See discussion on the Jubilee laws of the Holiness Code in, e.g., Milgrom, *Leviticus 23–27*, 2162–2183, 2241–2270; Nihan, *Torah*, 520–535.

[251] Aaron, "Ruse," 15.

[252] For an overview of this position, see discussion in § 3.4.1.

[253] This is even if those who remained in the land were characterised as Canaanites as, e.g., Wöhrle, *Fremdlinge*, 169–176, argued.

[254] On the one hand, one must keep the argument of Guillaume, *Land*, 109–117, in mind that in most cases a division of land should be conceived as a reduction of risk rather than in terms of scarcity or a reduction of wealth. On the other hand, Neh 11:1 suggests the land was actually distributed according to class priority rather than according to the pure ideal of usufruct.

follows that the core idea of the אחזה needed to be limited, i.e., to be made *less* egalitarian. To this end it will be argued that the "land of Canaan" (i.e., the whole land belonging to Yʜwʜ) was no longer to be divided family by family via the concept of אחזה, rather the land was now divided into immutable tribal allotments (i.e., נחלה) and these were then subdivided equally between each tribal family (i.e., אחזה). Thus, Kislev correctly observes, "The author of Num 36,1–12 introduced an innovation according to which *tribal inheritance* must be preserved."[255]

Returning to v. 3, further evidence that the author of Numbers 36 represented someone working with the combined Priestly and non-Priestly work is provided by the use of both the Deuteronomistic שבט as well as the Priestly מטה for tribe. Importantly, the law in Num 27:11 details the transfer of an inheritance only up to the closest kinsman within one's משפחה (*clan*).[256] However, the command for the division of the land in Num 26:52–56, more specifically the additional stipulation for the division via lot in v. 55 specifies that the division is to be לשמות מטות־אבתם (*according to the names of their ancestral tribes*). Thus, it is not particularly surprising to find that v. 3 ends with the Manassites complaining ומגרל נחלתנו יגרע (*and the lot of our inheritance will be reduced*). The logic of an immutable tribal נחלה better reflected the reality of the late Persian period and even the early Hellenistic period. Perhaps this precise dynamic can be seen in passages like 1 Chr 2:21–23, where it is reported that the Judean Hezron married a daughter of Machir and that Jair the Gileadite was the product of this union, thus claiming Judean influence over this region.[257] Although Knoppers rightly cautions against taking a too monopolistic view from the ideology of Ezra-Nehemiah and observes that there is good evidence supporting Jewish-Samaritan intermarriage in both the Samaria papyri, Josephus (e.g., Ant. 11.297–312) and even in Ezra-Nehemiah themselves – there would be no need of reform had there not been intermarriage – the concept of patrilineal claim over another's traditional tribal boundary via marriage as shown in 1 Chr 2:21–23 was surely neither a neutral nor an unbiased political claim.[258] Under these considerations, the conception

---

[255] Kislev, "Innovation," 1, (emphasis original). See also Binns, *Numbers*, 235; Budd, *Numbers*, 388.

[256] Milgrom, *Numbers*, 512.

[257] Finkelstein, "Reality," 82, argues, "The genealogical lists [of 1 Chronicles 2–9] were probably intended to legitimize Jewish rule over this area, part of which was inhabited by a large Gentile population, by giving it an ancient Israelite tribal pedigree. This seems to be in line with several Hasmonean pseudepigraphic compositions … which looked to the Scriptures in order to explain and legitimize the gradual territorial expansion of Judea in the second century B.C.E." Japhet, *Chronicles*, 80, similarly writes, "[1 Chr 2:21–23's] main point is to claim a Judahite affiliation for large parts of Gilead, which was originally a Manassite and Machirite territory *par excellence*. For Jair, the son of Segub, the Judahite element takes precedence over the Machirite, as it is his father who comes from Judah and his mother from Machir." Cf. Oeming, "Rethinking."

[258] Knoppers, "Intermarriage," 30n77.

252   *4. Female Inheritance*

of an immutable tribal boundary was not only a logical but also a relevant socio-political innovation.

With the concept of an immutable tribal נחלה forming the background, the reference to Jubilee in v. 4 is not "irrelevant" as Noth suggested, but one of the major driving forces behind the entire chapter. To put it simply, the introduction of the heiress law of Num 27:8 opened a loophole in the Jubilee law whereby the heiress's estate could be transferred to another tribe with no means of return.[259] The Jubilee law covers those cases where an אחזה is temporarily "sublet" to an outside buyer or debt-redeemer and dictates that at the Jubilee the אחזה is returned to the original owner. In the case of an heiress, she *is* the original owner and when she marries this right of ownership transfers to her husband. The husband, therefore, is not equivalent to the man who buys the estate with temporary usage rights, rather he becomes the one to whom the estate returns.[260] Had the original Priestly ideology of the "land of Canaan" and the "people of Israel" continued to predominate, and the Yahwistic community continued to conceive itself as one unified whole, then the ideological foundation of the אחזה would not be violated by this principle; all the land is Yhwh's and all His people get to share in it equally. The issue is only introduced with the additional concept of immutable tribal boundaries. Only after that is it important that the heiress's property becomes her husband's, as only then could the heiress's land potentially be removed from her tribe. In those cases where the husband did come from a different tribe, the Jubilee would have no effect at the tribal level, the husband – and later the heiress's children – would have a higher claim to the land than any of the male kin from the heiress's original tribe/clan. Thus, it can be seen that the mention of the Jubilee here is not out of place but rather demonstrates that even the "great reset" enabled by the Jubilee would be insufficient to solve the issues introduced by daughter inheritance in light of inter-tribal marriage.

Having presented this legal conundrum, the standard form of oracular novellas dictates that Moses will be unsure of the solution and bring the case before Yhwh, who will provide a ruling. This form is readily observed in all other oracular novellas: Lev 24:12–13; Num 9:8–9; 15:34–35; 27:5–6. Verse 5, then, presents something of a surprise when it departs from this standard form and reports that "Moses commanded the Israelites according to the word of Yhwh, saying ..."[261] Chavel suggests that this is not especially significant:

---

[259] For the Jubilee not covering transfer via marriage see, e.g., Knierim/Coats, *Numbers*, 329; Levine, *Numbers 21–36*, 578; Schmidt, *Numeri*, 223–224.

[260] This is not the same as the Jubilee officially confirming the transfer of property as Pitkänen, *Numbers*, 210, suggests.

[261] That Moses is here presented exegeting the law along with the general revisionary character of the chapter led Achenbach, *Vollendung*, 572, to conclude that Num 36:1–12 belong to ThB III.

One should not draw any dramatic conclusions from this slight deviation [from the standard form], since the author has the narrator affirm unequivocally that Moses did not develop the verdict himself, but heard it directly from Yahweh (v. 5a), and the author has Moses introduce his ruling accordingly, זה הדבר אשר צוה יהוה לבנות צלפחד לאמר (v. 6a). The deviation, which shifts the focus from Yahweh the decider to Moses the promulgator, may work together with the emphasis laid on the petitioners' trust in Moses as divine intermediary.[262]

In contrast, Frevel understands this shift to be quite significant indeed:

This example of supplementing established law by *Fortschreibung* is based on the post-Sinaitic revelation and bound to Moses's mediation. The interplay of Num 27 and 36 with the explicit and positively approved need for amendment, expressed by the objection of the people, paradigmatically demonstrates characteristics of legal exegesis in general. Most remarkable is the change of an explicit plea of Moses (קרב לפני יהוה) in Num 27:5 to the tacit form in Num 36:5 (על־פי יהוה). This new formulation stresses the link between the supplementation of the law and the institution 'Moses', as the supplementation is given without an express order of God. This does not create an autonomous authority, but considerably increases Moses's competence in establishing law. That the decision of the supplementary legal case is not localized at the entrance of the tent of meeting, as it is the case in Num 27:2, is not an indication of a secondary nature but rather indicates a changed mode of legal decision. Thus, it is by no means by chance that the 'elaborative exegesis' – as Kislev calls the development of decision in Num 36 – forms the end of the book of Numbers. Now the principles are provided for any further adaptation, be it situational or necessary by conflicting objectives within the existing law. After this implementation of applied-oriented exegesis of the law, the book closes in v. 13. Moses starts to expound the Torah in Deut 1:6 anew.[263]

Support for Frevel's view is found in the wording of Num 36:2, where Moses is addressed as אדני (*my lord*), which was argued in § 3.4.2 to correspond with the increased equivalence between Moses and the Torah, or as Frevel put it, "the institution 'Moses.'" Within v. 5 itself the phrase, על־פי יהוה (lit.: *upon the mouth of YHWH*), also points towards an increased competence of Moses. As Seebass notes:

Mose vermochte also aus unmittelbarem Wissen des Wortes Gottes sofort Recht zu sprechen. Mose steht damit ganz nahe bei Gott, so daß er in Numeri ein letztes Mal legitim handeln konnte, ohne Gottes Gebot von Num 27,12 zu verletzten. (*That is, Moses is capable to immediately speak the law from a direct knowledge of the word of God. With that, Moses stands very near to God, so that he could act legitimately one last time in Numbers without violating God's command from Num 27:12.*)[264]

Occurrences of this phrase are highly concentrated in the book of Numbers (fifteen times in Numbers and only six times throughout the rest of the Bible) and often related to the "divinely ordained" movement of the people of Israel on

---

[262] CHAVEL, *Law*, 246.

[263] FREVEL, "Formation," 29–30.

[264] SEEBASS, *Numeri 3*, 460.

254   4. Female Inheritance

their journey (Exod 17:1; Num 9:18, 20, 23; 10:13; 13:3; 33:2, [38]).[265] The phrase can tentatively be paraphrased as "according to Yhwh's will," and besides the ordained movement is used in relation to instruction. Typically, however, this instruction is given *to* Moses (e.g., Num 3:16, 51), meaning that the report of Moses bringing forth the word of Yhwh in Num 36:5 is quite remarkable. Moses is depicted not so much as a mediator of the divine will, but he himself is able to bring forth the ruling of Yhwh.[266]

One further peculiarity with Num 36:5 that deserves some attention is that Moses addresses the Manassites as מטה בני־יוסף (*the tribe of the sons of Joseph*). This subtle alteration of those introduced in Num 36:1 as "the ancestral heads of the clan of the sons of Gilead" further highlights that the harm of the heiress law lay at the tribal level, as it is there that the fixed, allotted נחלה lay.[267]

Verses 6–9 comprise the ruling given by Moses concerning the case. The solution to the problem of heiresses on the one hand and immutable tribal allotments on the other is enforced endogamy.[268] Verses 6–7 pertain to the daughters of Zelophehad in particular, which is then expanded into a general ruling in vv. 8–9.

Verse 6a begins with what appears to be a Priestly formula, זה הדטר אשר צוה יהוה (*this is the word that YHWH commands*). This phrase, which only occurs eight times in the Bible (Exod 16:16; 16:32; 35:4; Lev 8:5; 9:6; 17:2; Num 30:2; 36:6) is typically used by Moses when relaying instructions to the people.[269] With this phrase the observations regarding Moses's competence in v. 5 are further supported. Moses, without explicit interaction with Yhwh, can in any case report what Yhwh commands.

Verse 6b provides the major details for the revision of the ruling given to Zelophehad's daughters. They are permitted to marry whoever they like, so long as whoever they like belongs to a משפחת מטה אביהם (*clan of the tribe of their father*).[270] This unique construct is not simply "a non-punctilious verbosity of diverse social

---

[265] For example, Exod 17:1a reads, "The whole congregation of Israel journeyed from the wilderness of Sin, their stages according to the word of Yhwh."

[266] Frevel, *Transformations*, 80, states it as follows, "Moses is alluding to Num 27:7, and Moses himself interprets the YHWH speech from Num 27. Thus, he corresponds to the revealed will. Moses is the means of interpretation and the normative frame of interpretation is the word of God given in the Torah."

[267] See also Kislev, "Innovation," 258.

[268] Cf. Davies, *Numbers*, 370, who, citing Josephus (Ant. IV.7.5), suggests "although it is not explicitly stated in the present text, it may be presumed that an heiress who married a man from another tribe would have lost all claims to her father's inheritance and that any property which had been bequeathed to her would have returned forthwith to her father's tribe."

[269] Levine, *Numbers 21–36*, 578; Seebass, *Numeri 3*, 461.

[270] The precise wording of "who they like" is לטוב בעיניהם (*who is good in their eyes*), a phrase that appears numerous times throughout the book of Genesis, and especially the books of 1 and 2 Samuel. As with Numbers 27, the suffix for "their" in this case is the masculine suffix rather than the feminine as it should be.

terminology" as Kislev suggests, rather it functions to link together the two ends upon which this whole legal case exists.[271] The first end, as already discussed, comes from the fact that Zelophehad's estate was awarded to his daughters at the clan level, this is made particularly clear by the ruling in Num 27:11 where the "last resort" case was to transfer the נחלה of a son-less, daughter-less, brother-less, uncle-less man to a שאר הקרב אליו ממשפחתו (*relative nearest to him from his clan*). The result of the inheritance ruling in Numbers 27, secured estates to the clan level.[272] The second end came from the complaint of the Manassite elders, where they observed that marriage laws still applied in those cases where a man's estate passed to his daughter. The issue with this was that the tribal allotments were at risk of changing shape/boundary due to the property interactions in marriage. Thus, the ruling in Numbers 36 states that the daughters were to marry someone belonging to *a* clan from their father's tribe.[273] Although *prima facie* this seems to be a superfluous detail considering that a clan is a subset of the tribe, the clue for understanding this is found in v. 5, where Moses addresses the claimants as "the tribe of Joseph." This same conception is found in Num 26:28 and Joshua 16–17, where Manasseh and Ephraim are specifically labelled משפחה rather than מטה. This likely relates to the historical background of the province of Samaria, which encompassed both sons of Joseph. Thus, the daughters must marry a Manassite, even if their marriage to an Ephraimite would not technically disturb the tribal boundary of Joseph. In contrast to this solution, Milgrom suggests that the heiresses are only allowed to marry Hepherite males, rather than simply any Manassite.[274] In support of his case, Milgrom cites the LXX wording of Num 36:6, which is missing the word φυλῆς (*tribe*) resulting in the construct τοῦ δήμου τοῦ πατρὸς αὐτῶν (*the family/clan of their father*). By itself this omission could support Milgrom's suggestion that the LXX contains the more original reading.[275] However, this is contradicted by the LXX wording of Num 36:12, which states ἐκ τοῦ δήμου τοῦ Μανασση υἱῶν Ιωσηφ ἐγένετο ἡ γυναῖκες (*from the family/ clan of Manasseh son of Joseph they were married/became wives*). The LXX wording of Num 36:12 supports the solution presented here, that the tribe was conceived to be the tribe of Joseph, and that the aim of the ruling was to limit the daughters' range of suitors to the Manassite clan, indeed there is no mention anywhere outside of Num 36:1, that the issue concerned the Gileadites (let alone the Hepherites) in particular.

Having been commanded to marry within their own clan, v. 7 defines the purpose of this ruling: inheritance should not be transferred from tribe to tribe, thus reinforcing the analysis already presented above. This is supported a second

---

[271] Kislev, "Innovation," 255.

[272] As also observed by Kislev, "Innovation," 253–254.

[273] The article is importantly missing from למשפחת.

[274] Milgrom, *Numbers*, 297.

[275] Milgrom, *Numbers*, 331.

256   *4. Female Inheritance*

time in v. 7b with the wording that each of the Israelites shall רבק (*hold on/ cling*) to the נחלה of their ancestral tribes. As already discussed, the use of the Deuteronomistic נחלה follows the logic of the tribal lands being determined by lot and being immutable. In this case the use of the Priestly אחזה would be inappropriate as that – per definition – is mutable land, growing and shrinking according to the number of families able to work the land.

Verses 8–9 transition from the specific ruling for Zelophehad's daughters to a generalised form. Unlike in Num 27:8 where the transition from the narrative ruling to the generalised law was signalled by the phrase, "You shall also say to the Israelites …", Num 36:8 features no such markers, it instead continues as part of the same speech of Moses. Not only that, but the language used in these verses is strongly reminiscent of vv. 6–7, making the generalised law seem somewhat superfluous.[276]

| 36:6b | אך למשפחת מטה אביהם תהיינה לנשים | Nevertheless, to the clan of their father's tribe shall they be married |
| 36:8aβ | לאחד ממשפחת מטה אביה תהיה לאשה | to one from the clan of her father's tribe shall she be married |

Table 20: Comparison of Num 36:6b and Num 36:8aβ

| 36:7 | ולא־תסב נחלה לבני ישראל ממטה אל־מטה כי איש בנחלת מטה אבתו ידבקו בני ישראל | and an inheritance of the sons of Israel shall not be transferred from tribe to tribe, so that the sons of Israel hold on to the inheritance of the tribe of their ancestors |
| 36:9 | ולא־תסב נחלה ממטה למטה אחר כי־איש בנחלתו ידבקו מטות בני ישראל | and an inheritance shall not be transferred from [one] tribe to another tribe, so that the tribes of the sons of Israel hold on to their inheritance |

Table 21: Comparison of Num 36:7 and Num 36:9

Despite the similarities of these verse pairs, they are different enough that it is possible that they did not arise from the same author.[277] This idea is at least partially supported by the fact that these verses break the sequence between the

---

[276] CHAVEL, *Law*, 246f, argues this generalised form functions to tie the addendum of Numbers 36 more tightly to the oracular scene of Num 27:1–11.

[277] The author of the SP also noticed these details and attempted to bring the narrative and generalised versions into closer alignment. These differences align well with what CARR, *Formation*, 31, identifies as "memory" based alterations which are typically minor discrepancies such as use of, "synonymous words, word order variation, presence or absence of conjunctions and minor modifiers, etc.". In the case above we can see 'minor changes' such as אל־מטה (*to tribe*) in v. 7 being changed to למטה in v. 9. The generalised form also seems to clarify or neaten the narrative version, either by adding 'minor modifiers' such as לאחד (*to one*) in v. 8, or אחר (*another*) in v. 9, or by removing terms that clutter the sentence, such as the "sons of Israel" appearing twice in v. 7 but only once in v. 9. See also CARR, *Tablet*, e.g., 39.

ruling of vv. 6–7 and the report of its fulfilment in vv. 10–12. Perhaps vv. 8–9 were added secondarily to better conform with the oracular novella form.

Verses 10–12 return to the Zelophehad's daughters and conclude by noting that they obeyed this legal addendum by marrying into the clans of the descendants of Manasseh. Milgrom correctly observes that the report that they married their cousins (lit.: the sons of their uncles), suggests that Zelophehad's daughters fulfilled the precise requirements of Num 27:8–11a, which ruled that the נחלה was to remain in the immediate clan. Furthermore, Milgrom also notes that by marrying these male kinsmen, "in effect, the daughters did not inherit. They merely transferred the property to those who, in any event, stood next in the line of succession – another indication that the original formulation of this law directed heiresses to marry within their clan, not the tribe."[278] As already discussed, the wording of v. 12 – that the clan level was actually Manasseh – suggests against this interpretation. That being said, Milgrom's observation supports the above interpretation that the verb עבר was used in a technical sense to signal that heiresses were conceived to be temporary custodians. This, furthermore, suggests that Num 36:1–12 has understood the ruling given in Num 27:8–11a to be binding rather than the specific result for Zelophehad's daughters given in Num 27:7a (and enacted in Josh 17:3–6).

4.6 Conclusion

To briefly restate the argument of this chapter:

I. A (post-)Priestly author created the fable of Zelophehad's daughters (Num 27:1–7a), which aimed at including the "non-Israelite" Samaritans into the Yahwistic community.[279] Although this does not *require* Samaritan authorship, such an origin would make a lot of sense. The Priestly rooting of this narrative was suggested to align very naturally with the tiered worldview of the Priestly ideology, wherein the "daughters of Zelophehad" were brought into Israel's exclusive tier.

II. While the precise motivation remains unclear, this narrative was then made into the introduction to a more literal work dealing with daughter inheritance. Via the Priestly-styled framing verses 7b and 11b, a generalized law for daughter inheritance was appended to the Zelophehad's daughters text (Num 27:8–11a). Significantly, this text actually legislated that heiresses could not become true heirs (as was the case with Zelophehad's daughters), rather via the use of the verb עבר it was suggested that daughters functioned as a more convenient (for

---

[278] MILGROM, *Numbers*, 298.

[279] Again, LITKE, "Daughters," 210–211, suggests that the term "daughters" may not be a literalism, and offers a number of suggestions.

258   4. Female Inheritance

males) replacement of the levir, functioning as temporary custodians of a man's property until a grandson could be produced for the deceased head of the household. This subtle but important shift away from the ruling given to the daughters of Zelophehad may have functioned as an obfuscation of the originally pro-Samaritan purpose of Num 27:1–7a. This conclusion also finds support in Num 36:1–12, where the specific ruling of Num 27:7a is ignored and Zelophehad's daughters are ordered to marry their cousins. This result not only contradicted the report in Josh 17:3–6, where the daughters are treated as full heirs with equivalent rights to the males, but it also contradicts the geographic-genealogic correspondence between the daughters of Zelophehad and the cities and regions by the same name.

III. With the legal introduction of heiresses, there arose a problem within the Torah concerning the divinely ordained tribal boundaries, as marriage laws still entailed a woman's property being transferred to her husband. Thus, the legal supplement of Num 36:1–12* was formulated to cover this issue. Importantly it was argued that the shift away from the Priestly אחזה to the Deuteronomistic נחלה was a clever means by which a tiered concept was introduced. Accordingly, the נחלה was conceived to operate at the tribal level as an immutable boundary. The concept of a tribal distribution via lot (e.g., Num 26:52–56) functioned to split Yhwh's land (i.e., Canaan) into immutable portions, which stood over the concept of a mutable אחזה, which now operated on a tribal rather than a "national" level.

IV. This supplement was likely further aligned with the oracular novella form via the addition of vv. 8–9.

In terms of Pentateuchal models and compositional issues, the analysis of these two chapters only allows for some tentative conclusions to be reached. First, where Num 27:1–7a are written using purely Priestly terminology and Num 27:8–11a are written using non-Priestly terminology, the bracketing verses 7b and 11b feature language that is clearly designed to harmonise these stylistic differences. In this instance, however, it does not automatically follow that the non-Priestly text is earlier. Although it is certainly plausible that the generalised law was an older text drawn from a now lost tradition, it is also quite plausible that Num 27:7b–11 were developed in light of the same ideology that guided the creation of Num 36:1–12. If correct, the apparent Deuteronomistic style of the text would not represent a marker for an earlier dating, rather it would mean that Num 27:7b–11 were post-Priestly material that deliberately eschewed using אחזה as it already presupposed the repurposing of נחלה from Num 36:1–12. Second, despite its purely Priestly style Num 27:1–7a also cannot blindly be allocated even to the expanded Priestly "Hexateuch" that was proposed for Numbers 32. Rather the reference to Korah in Num 27:3 demonstrates that this text must also be attributed to post-conflationary hands. To briefly recall, the character of Korah functions as a harmonising strategy to smooth the conflation between the non-Priestly Dathan-Abiram narrative and the Priestly 250-elders narrative in Numbers 16.

Numbers 36:1–12, on the other hand, is overtly post-conflationary both using very late conceptions of the land as well as using a seamless mixture of Priestly and non-Priestly terminology.

Chapter 5

Conclusion

The present study began by noting that the final section of Numbers was long treated as a black box. Indeed, little development has been made since 1985, when Dennis Olson highlighted the two censuses as the key structural indicator of the book.[1] A brief study of the various proposed structures of Numbers demonstrated that there was no single satisfactory model to explain the full shape of the text. However, the scholarly proposals generally coalesced into three major groupings: (1) geography, (2) census/generation change and (3) Pentateuchal/chiastic. Instead of adjudicating between these proposals, the present work suggested these structuring devices were better correlated to the major redactional changes in the Pentateuch. The geographical structure of the book accorded to the linear structure of the exodus-conquest narrative, wherein the book of Numbers contained Israel's journey from the mountain of God to the plains of Moab. The generational structuring, although post-Priestly in nature, further emphasised the purpose and place of Deuteronomy as the law given to the wilderness generation in the land of Moab (Deut 1:5). The final structure reinforced the centrality of the Sinai event by expanding the wilderness portion of the book with key parallels to events in Exodus.

It was further suggested that the alternation of narrative and law was not random, but rather cyclical, with the law representing a provision in light of the preceding failure of Israel (e.g., Numbers 18 responds to Numbers 16–17). However, even with these overlapping functions, the final section of Numbers remained an opaque structural unit. Using a modified Gantt chart, it was suggested that the final section of Numbers still contained a clear purpose and trajectory of moving Israel towards the land. This led to the conclusion that even this part of Numbers was intentionally arranged and followed a deliberate logic.

A closer inspection of two key traditions within this final section of the book, the Transjordan settlement and daughter inheritance, aimed at further demonstrating that Numbers 26–36 could not be treated as a single redactional unit. Rather that even this section of the book contained evidence of multiple layers of redaction. One of the issues highlighted in this task was that very often the underlying model employed by an exegete dictated the outcome at least to some degree. One of the goals of the present work, then, was to try – as far as pos-

---

[1] OLSON, *Death*.

262   *5. Conclusion*

sible – to avoid using an underlying model as a guiding voice, even if it was also admitted that a completely unbiased exegesis was impossible. However, in order to shift the focus away from a model-based approach, three key "tools" were proposed that could be used – at least in principle – as a more stable methodological foundation for analysis in the hopes of reaching less subjective results.

5.1 Verifiable* Exegetical Tools

It was noted that one of the major problems faced by the field of biblical studies in general was that the core data was essentially unchanging. The biblical text, although subject to some minor revision (e.g., BHS to BHQ), is an essentially fixed entity. This means that the only changing aspects are the models and the historical presuppositions that are applied to the text. One obvious problem with this is that when various presuppositions differ too widely, opposing views are more often ignored than engaged. This problem was emphasised in the recent collaborative volume on the formation of the Pentateuch, where the editors highlighted:

> In effect, three independent scholarly discourses have emerged. Each centers on the Pentateuch, each operates with its own set of working assumptions, and each is confident of its own claims.[2]

The present work had no illusions that it would be able to change this unfortunate situation.

That being said, it was proposed that some conclusions were more probable than others, even if they could not be verified to the point of certainty. To this end, it was suggested that three "tools" could be used to remove at least some uncertainty from an interpretation. The three "tools" were: (1) the observations resulting from "empirical" studies on the processes of literary production from both biblical and non-biblical literature, (2) non-biblical historical evidence, and (3) the renewed attention paid to the "Northern Kingdom" (in both preexilic and postexilic periods) in the formation of the Pentateuch.[3]

5.1.1 "Empirical" Studies on Conflation

The idea of "empirical" data relating to textual transmission has grown in popularity in recent periods. The outcomes of these investigations were not merely

---

[2] GERTZ et al., "Convergence," 4.

[3] Once again it is acknowledged that the term "Northern Kingdom," although technically inaccurate, represents the clearest blanket term for the Yahwistic community dwelling north of Judah/Yehûd/Judea.

an insipid attempt to make a humanities discipline appear more scientific, rather they resulted in several important and repeatable observations.

The first was that in all cases of conflation where the original sources were known, the resulting text never contained the entirety of any one source. Rather the evidence pointed toward later scribes selectively taking up the old traditions and purposefully using them to create a new work.

The second observation, particularly emphasised by Juha Pakkala, was that the nature of change from earlier texts to later texts was guided by mutations or shifts in ideology. The key insight in this regard was that the greater the ideological shift, the greater the earlier text was altered. Likewise, when a scribe adhered to essentially the same ideological foundations, the alterations within a text were correspondingly minor even to the point of being undetectable.

Besides being a clear word of caution about assuming one can explain every change down to the individual word, these empirical studies pointed towards the Pentateuch being the product of conflation rather than just pure growth. That is to say, the simplest and safest explanation for the presence of Priestly and non-Priestly material in the Pentateuch is that they represented two originally stand-alone traditions that had later been brought together into a single work.[4]

5.1.2 Extra-biblical Evidence

While the field of biblical studies has the problem of limited data, the fields of archaeology and other Levantine studies are continuously growing. The value of these related fields for biblical exegesis has long been appreciated, however the present-day biblical scholar has far more information to draw upon than ever before. The present work greatly benefitted from recent archaeological studies relating to the many toponyms mentioned in the final section of Numbers, which led to new and novel interpretations.

A further key influencing factor was recent reconstructions on the history of the Levant, and the history of Israel in particular, that were developed in light of the expanding archaeological picture. This included, but was not limited to, the archaeological evidence for state structures in the North and South, and not least the increasingly dubious idea of a United Monarchy.

5.1.3 Northern Traditions

The final "tool," a greater focus on northern traditions, is admittedly less broadly applicable than the previous two, however it was included in the present study

---

[4] Once again this concurs with CARR, *Formation*, 216: "our present Pentateuch is, in large part, a product of a Priestly-oriented conflation of the P and non-P documents along with late Priestly expansions of various non-P texts."

264   *5. Conclusion*

particularly in light of the curious increased focus on the tribe of Manasseh in the final section of the book of Numbers. Samaritan studies in particular have made great strides in recent years and have left their mark upon Pentateuchal studies also.

Yet the presence of a clue does not always correlate with the need of a tool. The mention of the half-tribe of Manasseh in Numbers 32, for example, was identified in advance as a likely indication of northern participation, but the resulting analysis was unable to make any real use of Samaritan studies or otherwise.

Although it must be admitted that the present study chose to analyse texts that were cherry picked for maximum effect, there is little reason to suppose that similarly novel results could not be achieved elsewhere.

5.2 Compositional Findings

5.2.1 Numbers 32

The analysis of Numbers 32 began by noting the curious reference to Jazer in Num 32:1 and suggested that that reference only made sense as belonging to the base narrative, because (1) Jazer played no role in the remaining Pentateuchal narrative and (2) the Jazer verses in the Sihon narrative were much better explained as reactions to Numbers 32 than the other way around.

Via a historical investigation of the territory described by Num 32:1, it was argued that this had a strong correlation to the territory retaken from Aram by Jehoash or Jeroboam II. Thus, it seemed logical to conclude that the origin of this narrative was the Northern Kingdom. This result aligned with the growing acceptance that Jeroboam II was most likely the first Israelite (including Judean) monarch to have been able to produce literary works, including a national charter myth. However, it was further noted that the non-Priestly narrative connected with Num 32:1 already presupposed that the Reubenites and Gadites were requesting something strange. The very fact that Moses questioned their request and that these two tribes had to promise to assist their brother tribes in the conquest pointed to the idea that even the earliest non-Priestly layer presupposed the Jordan was a boundary. In light of the discussion in § 2.3.2, this was argued to make perfect sense, as it was very likely that the narrative spanning Exodus–Numbers–Joshua (i.e., the exodus-conquest narrative) was a Judean work that subversively repurposed the Nimshide charter myth.

In § 3.4, a Priestly version of the same narrative was identified. This version followed the basic shape of the non-Priestly version but differed both in terms of the language used (with distinctive Priestly terms) and also in its view of the Transjordan settlement. Importantly, the Priestly version functioned on the premise that the Reubenites and Gadites were requesting הארץ אשר הכה יהוה לפני

עדת ישראל (*the land that* YHWH *struck before the sons of Israel* – Num 32:4), which logically suggested the Priestly version presupposed the Sihon narrative.

Granting particular attention towards the underlying ideology of the Sihon narratives (Num 21:21–25*; Deut 2:24–3:12*), it was argued that the first instance of this event occurred in Deuteronomy. This was because the earliest identifiable version of the Sihon narrative in Deuteronomy operated under the idea that Israel could only live in land that it had ירש (*possessed/dispossessed*) from enemies. The ideology of ירש was problematised by the concept that the Transjordan lay outside of the promised land. Thus, it was shown that the first Sihon narrative made deliberate allusions to the laws for war in Deut 20:10–15. Via the idea that Sihon was a city-king who dwelt "very far" from Israel, the Israelite settlement in Transjordan was brought under the concept of territorial expansion beyond the confines of the borders of the promised land.

The element with the greatest uncertainty in the analysis was the list of cities and the addition of the half-tribe of Manasseh found primarily in Num 32:34–42. It was proposed that the most likely explanation was that this addition arose in response to the introduction of a pan-Israel ideology. The major issue with this update was that it was not possible to determine with sufficient certainty when this ideology was introduced (tradition-historically speaking). Although there is support for the Jacob narrative already espousing the idea of a common ancestor in the preexilic period, most scholars ascribe the invention of the twelve tribes of Israel to Priestly or even post-Priestly scribes. If the pan-Israel updates to the Transjordan traditions in Numbers and Deuteronomy were indeed postexilic, this would dictate that the non-Priestly narrative was further updated after the Priestly materials were in circulation but not yet joined to the non-Priestly materials.

The pan-Israelite tradition not only increased Israel's share of central Transjordan but it also depicted the half-tribe of Manasseh acting independently to take northern Transjordan. Deuteronomy made several key changes to its version of the Sihon narrative in order to smooth out these problematic changes. First, in order to explain the ירש of northern Transjordan, the character of Og was introduced. Second, the city-king, Sihon, was transformed into an Amorite king who ruled the entirety of central Transjordan from the Arnon to the Jabbok. The Amorite "ethnicity" of these two kings was argued to be crucial because this functioned to bring the Transjordan under the umbrella of those nations YHWH had designated for destruction (Deut 7:1; 20:17). As Amorite territory, the Transjordan was now to be understood as belonging to the promised land. Because this Amorite update presupposed the changes introduced by the pan-Israel update, it must be dated even later. Thus, it remains uncertain how this update is to be interpreted in light of the Priestly material. That being said, if one assumes that even at this advanced stage, the non-Priestly material had not yet been conflated, then this adjustment to Deuteronomy would represent a radical attempt to harmonise the Transjordan traditions in the expanded non-Priestly text.

266   *5. Conclusion*

The biggest narrative-based/continuity issues appeared once the Priestly and non-Priestly texts were conflated. Although the late editors of Deuteronomy seem to have been willing to reimagine the boundary of the promised land, the Priestly authors were not. For their part, the promised land was the land of Canaan, which was squarely rooted in Cisjordan. Thus, the Transjordan traditions in the extant book of Numbers contain conflicting conceptions.

The final alterations to Numbers 32 contained a clear mixture of Priestly and non-Priestly elements and therefore were categorised as harmonisations. These harmonisations functioned to smooth the conflated narrative into a more unified whole. Although the harmonisations were interesting in their own right, it was remarkable that the tradition appeared to have developed through so many stages before the Priestly and non-Priestly works were conflated.

5.3.2 Zelophehad's Daughters

The legislative materials relating to Zelophehad's daughters also demonstrated several surprising outcomes when looked at through the lens of historical geography and ideological shifts.

The first major insight was that the generalised legislation in Num 27:8–11a was only weakly correlated to the narrative introduction relating to Zelophehad's daughters in Num 27:1–7a, rather these two sections were combined by the shared theme of inheritance and the blending verses Num 27:7b and 11b. This gave rise to an investigation of what each of these two segments aimed to achieve.

The generalised law for daughter inheritance, it was concluded, was a relatively straightforward law that was designed to shift the "burden" of producing an heir from the mother (via levirate marriage) to the daughter. This had the benefit of absolving the deceased's brother from any financial burden that would be incurred from supporting his widow and potential daughters. As the situation of Tamar and Ruth made clear, the role of the levir was typically accepted grudgingly and could even be abused. The law in Deut 25:5–10 also points in this direction as most of that law pertains to the case in which the male refuses to accept his responsibility. For its part, the Holiness Code, although not outright forbidding levirate marriage, essentially made the practice moot when it legislated that the punishment for a man taking his brother's wife in marriage was barrenness (Lev 20:21). The idea that the heiress was intended to function as a temporary guardian until a male heir (i.e., a grandson) could be born was flagged by the special use of the verb עבר (*transfer*), which stood in contrast to the verb נתן (*give*) that was applied to the man's male kinsmen in those cases when a man had neither sons nor daughters.

Given this major thrust to the generalised law, the ruling given by YHWH for the daughters of Zelophehad had several conflicting details. First, where v. 8 ruled that one daughter was to be *transferred* her father's נחלה (*property*), all five

5.2 Compositional Findings   267

daughters were *given* Zelophehad's אחזה (*possession*). Second, following Joshua 17, the five daughters of Zelophehad were not granted one sixth of the land (i. e., they did not divide up Zelophehad's portion) rather they each received an equal share alongside the other sons of Manasseh. Not only did this reinforce the ideal of the אחזה as mutable land that was divided equally, it also demonstrated that Zelophehad's daughters were each treated as the head of a בית אב (*household*), fundamentally conflicting with the idea that they merely represented temporary guardians. Thus, the differences were not simply the result of changes in terminology – from Priestly to Deuteronomistic – rather they represented markedly different ideologies.

Considering these stark contrasts, it was argued that it was illogical to conclude that Num 27:1–7a and Num 27:8–11a were the work of a single hand. This led to a closer investigation of the toponyms relating to Zelophehad's daughters in the hope of discovering some further clues. The region expressed via the "daughters of Zelophehad" was shown to have a strong correlation to the area in which the so-called wedge-shaped decorated bowls were discovered. These bowls were argued to be a marker of those populations imported by the Assyrians as part of their two-way deportation policy. Although admittedly provocative, it was argued that the depiction of "daughters" of Manasseh (cf. Josh 17:6) alongside "sons" of Manasseh was a deliberate means by which the Samaritan "foreign" Yahwists were depicted as belonging to the people of God. The use of Priestly terminology in Num 27:1–7a, in this case, further reinforced the connection to the paired Priestly ideologies of ecumenism and a tiered ordering of the world, with Israel comprising the highest tier. The fundamental tenets of the Priestly ideology were most conducive for supporting the Samaritans' mixed heritage. In light of this daring conclusion, it was tentatively suggested that Num 27:8–11a may even have been added in order to obfuscate the original intention of Num 27:1–7a. This was further supported by the fact that Num 36:1–12 only made sense as a reaction to Num 27:8 rather than to Num 27:7a.

Numbers 36:1–12 returned to Zelophehad's daughters a second time and raised the issue that marriage laws conflicted with the newly provided inheritance law. However, the arguments raised in Numbers 36 were shown to better be understood as a reaction to the general ruling in Num 27:8. More specifically the issue raised was the idea that property owned by females was in danger of altering the fixed tribal boundaries. One important detail in this case was the use of the Deuteronomistic נחלה, which it was argued was deliberately repurposed by the post-Priestly authors to sit over the mutable אחזה. More specifically, the idea of allotted immutable tribal boundaries could not be described with the Priestly ideology of אחזה, which operated on the idea of land usufruct meaning that one's portion grew or shrank based upon the number of families available to cultivate the land. The idea of allotted borders and fixed tribal boundaries, then, fit much better to the Deuteronomistic נחלה, which operated on the idea of fixed land units. This meant there was an ideological basis for Num 36:1–12 to use Deuteronomistic terminology despite it being undoubtedly post-Priestly in character.

5.3 In Models We Trust

Although the present work did not develop a Pentateuchal model (nor did it intend to), the findings from the detailed exegetical studies did serve to reinforce the conclusions drawn in Chapter 2.

There it was argued that the shift away from the Documentary Hypothesis was justified in light of two key insights: the shortening of Pg and the "farewell to the Yahwist."

With the growing consensus that Pg did not end in Deuteronomy 34, most scholars, although not in precise agreement, concluded that Pg must have ended at Sinai. This ending, it was argued, made a great deal of sense in light of Pg's emphasis on the ancestors, who were promised the land but who dwelt among the Canaanites in peace. It was suggested that this peaceful but separate coexistence was promoted by Pg since it represented the ideology of the returning golah community. As such, the Canaanites were not a people of a different ethnicity rather the Canaanites were those Judeans who had not been exiled and had remained in the land. Perhaps more importantly, they were labelled Canaanites because the returning golah community wished to depict themselves as the "true" Israel. The narrative of Pg was not an attempt to write history, rather it was an ideologically motivated retelling of Israel's pre-existing (non-Priestly) traditions, that is, it was from its inception understood to be a myth of origins. As such, Pg had no need of a conquest and had no need to "complete" Israel's journey into the land. What was important was the promise of land given to Abraham and his descendants and the giving of the sanctuary and the cultic laws outside of the land (so that they could be introduced into the land by the wilderness generation/the golah community).

Combined with this new understanding of the shape and nature of Pg was the shift in understanding of the non-Priestly material. This shift, given the catchy title, "farewell to the Yahwist," posited that there was no single non-Priestly text spanning from creation to conquest. For the non-Priestly traditions, the patriarchs and the exodus-conquest narrative represented two separate stories of Israel's origins.

One key outcome of these two insights was that Numbers no longer contained any of the traditional sources JEDP.

The Pentateuchal model that most strongly aligned itself with these two shifts was the so-called bridge-book model. This new model, despite having varied expressions, posited that Numbers was designed from its foundations as a late bridge between a Priestly shaped Genesis–Leviticus and a Deuteronomistic shaped work extending either to 2 Kings (DtrH) or to Joshua (DtrL). As a model that was at least in part, developed directly from the shortening of Pg and the farewell to the Yahwist, it *prima facie* appeared well positioned to explain the formation of the Pentateuch. Yet despite its promise, it was argued that the bridge-book model, regardless of which variation, fell short. One prime aspect being that these models understood the earliest bridging material to be the work of post-Priestly scribes, who rather inexplicably wrote in a purely non-Priestly style.

The other models discussed were of a more varied nature, but each was shown to have some degree of weakness. Those models that assumed the non-Priestly text of the Tetrateuch was post-Deuteronomistic operated on the fundamental idea that Deuteronomy was the beginning of the Deuteronomistic History. Yet it was briefly argued that a single literary work spanning from Deuteronomy to 2 Kings was problematic and so the models developed with this as the foundation were fundamentally flawed.

The second type of model understood there to be a pre-Deuteronomistic narrative spanning either from Genesis to Joshua (the Münsteraner Pentateuch-modell) or Exodus to Joshua (Kratz/Germany). These models were deemed preferable due to their better explanation of the non-Priestly materials, which were understood to have contained a complete narrative from the exodus to the conquest.[5] Both models understood Deuteronomy to have been inserted into this non-Priestly work in a more standalone fashion rather than belonging to a Deuteronomistic History from its inception. That being said, it was also argued that these models were not without faults, thus it was concluded that some "ingredients" from these final two models could be combined to produce a superior model. These ingredients were: (1) The first narrative arc was a non-Priestly exodus-conquest narrative developed in Judah; (2) although Deuteronomy had already been furnished with a narrative frame (the so-called Horeb redaction), it was given a new narrative frame (the Moab redaction) that allowed the Deuteronomic laws to be incorporated into the exodus-conquest narrative as Moses's expounding the law to the Israelites in the land of Moab (Deut 1:5); (3) the Priestly work, was the first to link the patriarchs to the Moses tradition, however this standalone work did not yet mimic the full exodus-conquest narrative rather it concluded at Sinai. That being said it was further argued that the Priestergrundschrift first underwent its own processes of expansion and development prior to being joined to the non-Priestly work.

Although admittedly limited, the evidence drawn from the present study supported all three:

---

[5] To clarify, these models do not argue that all non-Priestly texts belonged to this foundational layer.

I. The idea of an originally preexilic exodus-conquest narrative was supported by the earliest layer of the Transjordan traditions located in Numbers 32. The geographical details of Num 32:1 were best explained as being historically rooted in the Northern (Nimshide) Kingdom, but Num 32:5* and 17* were better understood as a Judean reformulation of the Transjordan settlement in light of the idea of the Jordan as a border. This idea was further supported by a brief survey of Numbers 21–25, which also shared the idea that Israel travelled peacefully through Moab, whose geographical reach extended into central Transjordan (i.e., the plains of Moab belonged to Moab).

II. The incorporation of Deuteronomy into the exodus-conquest narrative via the narrative frame of the so-called "Moab Redaction" was also supported by the investigation of the Sihon tradition. It was argued that this made the most sense as being a Deuteronomistic explanation for the Transjordan settlement described in Numbers 32. As such, the Sihon narrative functioned under the ideal of possession/dispossession and was best interpreted via the careful allusion to the laws for enemies "very far" from Israel (Deut 20:10–15).

III. In line with broader scholarship, it was argued that the Priestly material in Numbers did not belong to Pg. But the idea that the Priestly tradition first underwent its own process of expansion was supported by the Priestly narrative of Numbers 32, which was argued to form an independent parallel to the non-Priestly narrative. The Priestly version of Numbers 32 could not be considered a simple expansion of Pg because this later narrative operated under the idea of a violent conquest (cf. Num 32:4) and so represented a notable shift away from Pg's peaceful vision of coexistence among the Canaanites.

5.4 Clear Avenues for Further Research

In addition to these basic building blocks, several other key redactional moments were observed in the text. These moments require a more expansive study into other parts of the Pentateuch in order to verify as being "global" updates or at least gain a greater precision and certainty.

The most significant update concerns the pan-Israel perspective. In the present work it was argued that the introduction of the tribe of Gad caused a significant change in the pre-existing non-Priestly tradition of the Transjordan settlement. Numbers 32 received the introduction of the list of rebuilt cities in vv. 34–38 and the sudden introduction of the half-tribe of Manasseh in vv. 40–42*. The Sihon tradition in Deuteronomy and Numbers, in turn, received significant updates particularly via the character of Og.

These updates, it was argued, logically occurred on the still standalone non-Priestly text (i.e., the Deuteronomistically expanded exodus-conquest narrative joined with the first Moab Redaction of Deuteronomy). The complication, however, was that it is generally accepted that the idea of twelve tribes of Israel is a Priestly innovation. This would mean that these updates occurred at a post-Priestly stage, but without direct interaction (or conflation) with Priestly texts.[6]

The second key area requiring more research concerns those texts that arose after the conflation of Priestly and non-Priestly texts. Even within the limited investigation of the present work, it was demonstrated that there were at least two layers after the process of conflation occurred. It was shown that Num 27:1–7a presupposed the conflated version of Numbers 16–17 due to the reference to the character of Korah meaning that it must be dated as a parallel update at the earliest.

Demonstrably later than Num 27:1–7a were the texts of Num 27:8–11a and Num 36:1–12. Based on the Zelophehad's daughters texts alone, there are between two and four layers of tradition to be explored after the Priestly and non-Priestly texts were conflated.

The present work has (hopefully) succeeded in bringing clarity to a small part of the tapestry that is the Pentateuch. A few warps and wefts have been carefully traced, however there are many more requiring careful attention before the book of Numbers, let alone the whole of the Pentateuch, can be clarified. It my hope that some readers may be inspired to explore further in light of my own humble efforts.

---

[6] This would result in something similar to the suggestion in KRATZ, *Composition*, 278–279, who argues that the non-Priestly Joseph story is a "post-Yahwistic appendage."

Appendix

Comparison of Recent Models
vs the Documentary Hypothesis

Numbers	Campbell & O'Brien[1]	Achenbach[2]	Albertz[3]
1:1–2:34	P+Ps	ThB I	PB3
3:1–4	P+Ps	ThB I	PB5
3:5–10	P+Ps	ThB I	PB3
3:11–13	Ps	ThB III	PB4
3:14–39*	P	ThB I+	PB3
3:40–51	P+Ps	ThB III	PB4
4:1–49	P+Ps	ThB I	PB3
5:1–6:27	non-source	ThB II	PB4
7:1–88	Ps	ThB III	PB4
7:89	Ps	ThB III	PB5
8:1–4	non-source	ThB III	PB4
8:5–9:14	P+Ps	ThB III	PB4
9:15–23	P+Ps	ThB III	PB3
10:1–10	P+Ps	ThB III	PB4
10:11–28a	P+Ps	ThB I	PB3
10:28b	P+Ps	ThB I	HexR
10:29a	J	HexRed	HexR
10:29b	J	Pre-Deut.	HexR
10:30–32	J	Pre-Deut.	HexR
10:33abα	J	HexRed	D
10:33bβ	J	PentRed	D
10:34	J*	N/A	D
10:35–36	J	HexRed	D
11:1–3*	J	HexRed+Pre-Deut.	D
11:4–6*	J	HexRed+Pre-Deut.	D
11:7–9	J	N/A	D
11:10a	J	Pre-Deut.	D
11:10b*	J	HexRed	D
11:10bβ	J	PentRed	D
11:11–12	J	PentRed	D
11:13	J	Pre-Deut.	D
11:14–17	J	PentRed	D
11:18–20a	J	Pre-Deut.	D
11:21–23*	J	Pre-Deut. or HexRed	D

[1] CAMPBELL/O'BRIEN, *Sources*.

[2] ACHENBACH, *Vollendung*, 635–638.

[3] ALBERTZ, *Pentateuchstudien*, 471–485.

Numbers	Campbell & O'Brien	Achenbach	Albertz
11:24–30	J	PentRed	D
11:31–32*	J	Pre-Deut.	D
11:32–35	J	HexRed	D
12:1*	J	HexRed or PentRed	D
12:2a	J	PentRed	D
12:2b	J	HexRed	D
12:3–8	J	PentRed	D
12:9a	J	HexRed	D
12:9b	J	PentRed	D
12:10aα	J	PentRed	D
12:10aβ	J	HexRed	D
12:10b	J	PentRed	D
12:11–12	J	PentRed	D
12:13–16	J	HexRed	D
13:1–2a	P	PentRed	PB3
13:2b	P	ThB I	PB3
13:3a	P	PentRed	PB3
13:3b	Ps	ThB I	PB3
13:4–17a	Ps	ThB I	PB3
13:17b–20	J	Pre-Deut. + HexRed	D
13:21	P	PentRed	PB3
13:22–24	J	HexRed	D
13:25–26	P	PentRed	PB3
13:27–28	J*	Pre-Deut. + HexRed	D
13:29*	J*	ThB I	D
13:30–31	J	Pre-Deut. + HexRed	D
13:32–14:1a	P+Ps	PentRed	PB3
14:1b	J	HexRed	PB3
14:2–3	P	PentRed	PB3
14:4	J	PentRed	D
14:5	P	PentRed	PB3
14:6–10a	P	ThB I	PB3
14:10b–22	J*	PentRed	D
14:23–25	J*	Pre-Deut. + HexRed	D
14:26–29a*	P+Ps	PentRed	PB3
14:29b	Ps	ThB I	PB3
14:30a	Ps	PentRed	PB3
14:30b	Ps	ThB I	PB3
14:31–37	P+Ps	PentRed	PB3
14:38	P	ThB I	PB3
14:39	J	PentRed	D
14:40–45	J	HexRed	D
15:1–41	non-source	ThB II	PB4
16:1*	J+Ps	ThB I	PB3
16:2*	J	HexRed	PB3
16:2*–4	Ps	PentRed	PB3
16:5–11	Ps	ThB I	PB3
16:12–15	J	HexRed	PB3
16:16–18	Ps	PentRed	PB3
16:19–24	Ps	ThB I	PB3
19:25–26	J	HexRed	PB3

Comparison of Recent Models vs the Documentary Hypothesis

Numbers	Campbell & O'Brien	Achenbach	Albertz
16:27a	Ps	ThB I	PB3
16:27b–31	J	HexRed	PB3
16:32–33	J*	HexRed + ThB I	PB3
16:34	J	N/A	PB3
16:35	Ps	PentRed	PB3
17:1–18:32	Ps	ThB I	PB3
19:1–22	non-source	ThB I	PB4
20:1*–13	P+Ps	PentRed	PB3
20:1b	J	HexRed	PB3
20:14–18	E*	Pre-Deut. + HexRed + ThB I	HexR
20:19–20	J	Pre-Deut. + HexRed + ThB I	HexR
20:21	E	Pre-Deut.	HexR
20:22a	J	Pre-Deut. + HexRed + ThB I	PB3
20:22b–29	P+Ps	PentRed	PB3
21:1–3	J*	Pre-Deut.?	D?
21:4	J+P	N/A	D+PB3
21:5	J*	N/A	D
21:6–9	J*	Pre-Deut.	D
21:10–20	non-source	N/A	D+ HexR
21:21–31	E	Pre-Deut. + HexRed	HexR
21:32–35	E*		HexR
22:1b	P		PB3
22:1–3a	E*	HexRed	HexR
22:3b–4a	J	PentRed	HexR
22:4b–6	J	HexRed	Balaam Narrative
22:7a	J	PentRed	Balaam Narrative
22:7b–8	J	HexRed	Balaam Narrative
22:9–12	E	HexRed	Balaam Narrative
22:13–19	J	HexRed	Balaam Narrative
22:20	E	HexRed	Balaam Narrative
22:21–35	J	PentRed	Balaam Narrative
22:36–38a	J	HexRed	Balaam Narrative
22:38b–41	J+E	N/A	Balaam Narrative
23:1–4	E	HexRed	Balaam Narrative
23:5a	E	PentRed	Balaam Narrative
23:5b	E	HexRed	Balaam Narrative
23:6–16	E	N/A	Balaam Narrative
23:17–20	E	HexRed	Balaam Narrative
23:21–24	E	PentRed	Balaam Narrative
23:25–30	E*	HexRed	Balaam Narrative
24:1*–3a	J*	HexRed	Balaam Narrative
24:3b–4	J	PentRed	Balaam Narrative
24:5–7a	J	HexRed	Balaam Narrative
24:7b–9	J	PentRed	HexR*
24:10–14a	J*	HexRed	Balaam Narrative
24:14b–19	J*	ThB?	HexR
24:20–24	J*	ThB?	N/A
24:25	J	HexRed	Balaam Narrative
25:1–5	J*	HexRed	PB5
25:6–13	non-source	ThB I	PB5
25:14–18	non-source	ThB III	PB5

Numbers	Campbell & O'Brien	Achenbach	Albertz
25:19–27:11	non-source	ThB I	PB5
27:12–23	P	ThB I	PB5
28:1–30:1	non-source	ThB II	PB5
30:2–17	non-source	ThB III	PB5
31:1–54	Ps	ThB III	PB5
32:1	J	HexRed	PB5
32:2a	non-source	HexRed	PB5
32:2b–4	non-source	ThB I	PB5
32:5–6	non-source	HexRed	PB5
32:7–15	non-source	ThB I	PB5
32:16	J	ThB I	PB5
32:17–20*	non-source	ThB I	PB5
32:20*–22	non-source	HexRed	PB5
32:23–24	non-source	ThB I	PB5
32:25–27	non-source	HexRed	PB5
32:28–32	non-source	ThB I	PB5
32:33	non-source	HexRed	PB5
32:34–38	non-source	ThB I	PB5
32:39	J*	ThB I	PB5
32:40–41	J*	HexRed	PB5
32:42	J	ThB I	PB5
33:1–49	non-source	ThB III	PB5
33:50–56	non-source	ThB I	PB5
34:1–35:34	non-source	ThB I	PB5
36:1–12	non-source	ThB III	PB5
36:13	non-source	ThB I	PB5

Bibliography

AARON, DAVID H. "The Ruse of Zelophehad's Daughters." *HUCA* 80 (2009): 1–38.

ACHENBACH, REINHARD. "Die Erzählung von der gescheiterten Landnahme von Kadesch Barnea (Numeri 13–14) als Schlüsseltext der Redaktionsgeschichte des Pentateuchs." *ZABR* 9 (2003): 56–123.

–. *Die Vollendung der Tora: Studien zur Redaktionsgeschichte des Numeribuches im Kontext von Hexateuch und Pentateuch.* BZAR 3. Wiesbaden: Harrassowitz, 2003.

–. "Grundlinien redaktioneller Arbeit in der Sinai-Perikope." Pages 56–80 in *Das Deuteronomium zwischen Pentateuch und Deuteronomistischem Geschichtswerk.* FRLANT 206. Edited by Eckart Otto and Reinhard Achenbach. Göttingen: Vandenhoeck & Ruprecht, 2004.

–. "Das Heiligkeitgesetz und die sakralen Ordnungen des Numeribuches im Horizont der Pentateuchredaktion." Pages 145–175 in *The Books of Leviticus and Numbers.* BETL 215. Edited by Thomas Römer. Leuven: Uitgeveru Peeters, 2008.

–. "gêr – nåkhrî – tôshav – zâr: Legal and Sacral Distinctions Regarding Foreigners in the Pentateuch." Pages 29–51 in *The Foreigner and the Law: Perspectives from the Hebrew Bible and the Ancient Near East.* BZAR 16. Edited by Reinhard Achenbach et al. Wiesbaden: Harrassowitz, 2011.

–. "Divine Warfare and YHWH's Wars." Pages 1–26 in *The Ancient Near East in the 12th–10th Centuries BCE.* Edited by G. Galil et al. Münster: Ugarit-Verlag, 2012.

–. "Complementary Reading of the Torah in the Priestly Texts of Numbers 15." Pages 201–232 in *Torah and the Book of Numbers.* FAT II 62. Edited by Christian Frevel et al. Tübingen: Mohr Siebeck, 2013.

AHARONI, YOHANAN. *The Land of the Bible: A Historical Geography.* Translated by A. F. Rainey. London: Burns & Oates, 1967.

–. "The Solomonic Districts." *TA* 3.1 (1976): 5–15.

ALBERTZ, RAINER. *A History of Israelite Religion in the Old Testament Period: Volume I: From the Beginnings to the End of the Monarchy.* Translated by John Bowden. Louisville/Kentucky: John Knox Press, 1994.

–. *Religionsgeschichte Israels in alttestamentlicher Zeit: Von den Anfängen bis zum Ende der Königszeit.* GAT 8.1. Göttingen: Vandenhoeck & Ruprecht, 1996.

–. "In Search of the Deuteronomists: A First Solution to a Historical Riddle." Pages 1–17 in *The Future of the Deuteronomistic History.* BETL 147. Edited by Thomas Römer. Leuven: Leuven University Press, 2000.

–. "Das Buch Numeri jenseits der Quellentheorie. Eine Redaktionsgeschichte von Num 20–24 (Teil I)." *ZAW* 123 (2011): 171–183.

–. "Das Buch Numeri jenseits der Quellentheorie. Eine Redaktionsgeschichte von Num 20–24 (Teil II)." *ZAW* 123 (2011): 336–347.

–. "From Aliens to Proselytes: Non-Priestly and Priestly Legislation Concerning Strangers." Pages 53–69 in *The Foreigner and the Law: Perspectives from the Hebrew Bible and the Ancient Near East*. BZAR 16. Edited by Reinhard Achenbach et al. Wiesbaden: Harrassowitz, 2011.

–. *Exodus, Band I: Ex 1–18*. AT 2.1. Zürich: Theologischer Verlag, 2012.

–. "A Pentateuchal Redaction in the Book of Numbers? The Late Priestly Layers of Num 25–36." *ZAW* 125 (2013): 220–233.

–. "Noncontinuous Literary Sources Taken Up in the Book of Exodus." Pages 609–617 in *The Formation of the Pentateuch: Bridging the Academic Cultures of Europe, Israel and North America*. FAT 111. Edited by Jan C. Gertz et al. Tübingen: Mohr Siebeck, 2016.

–. *Pentateuchstudien*. Edited by Jakob Wöhrle. FAT 117. Tübingen: Mohr Siebeck, 2018.

ALT, ALBRECHT. "Das System der assyrischen Provinzen auf dem Boden des Reiches Israel." *ZDPV* 52.3 (1929): 220–242.

–. *Kleine Schriften zur Geschichte Israels*. Vol. 2. München: C. H. Beck, 1953.

ANATI, EMMANUEL. "Prehistoric Trade and the Puzzle of Jericho." *BASOR* 167 (1962): 25–31.

ANDERSON, ROBERT T. and TERRY GILES. *The Samaritan Pentateuch: An Introduction to Its Origin, History, and Significance for Biblical Studies*. RBS 72. Atlanta: Society of Biblical Literature, 2012.

ARIE, ERAN. "Reconsidering the Iron Age II Strata at Tel Dan: Archaeological and Historical Implications." *TA* 35 (2008): 6–64.

ARTUS, OLIVIER. *Études sur le livre des Nombres: Récit, Histoire et Loi en Nb 13,1–20,13*. OBO 157. Göttingen: Vandenhoeck und Ruprecht, 1997.

–. "Josué 13–14 et le livre des Nombres." Pages 233–247 in *The Book of Joshua*. Edited by Ed Noort. Leuven: Uitgeverij Peeters, 2012.

–. "Numbers 32: The Problem of the Two and a Half Transjordanian Tribes and the Final Composition of the Book of Numbers." Pages 367–382 in *Torah and the Book of Numbers*. FAT II 62. Edited by Christian Frevel et al. Tübingen: Mohr Siebeck, 2013.

ASHLEY, TIMOTHY R. *The Book of Numbers*. Grand Rapids: Eerdmans Publishing, 1993.

ASSIS, ELIE. "The Position and Function of Jos 22 in the Book of Joshua." *ZAW* 16.4 (2004): 528–541.

BADEN, JOEL S. "Identifying the Original Stratum of P: Theoretical and Practical Considerations." Pages 13–29 in *The Strata of the Priestly Writings: Contemporary Debate and Future Directions*. ATANT 95. Edited by Sarah Shectman and Joel S. Baden. Zürich: Theologischer Verlag, 2009.

–. *J, E, and the Redaction of the Pentateuch*. FAT 68. Tübingen: Mohr Siebeck, 2009.

–. *The Composition of the Pentateuch: Renewing the Documentary Hypothesis*. New Haven: Yale University Press, 2012.

–. "Source Stratification, Secondary Additions, and the Documentary Hypothesis in the Book of Numbers: The Case of Numbers 17." Pages 233–247 in *Torah and the Book of Numbers*. FAT II 62. Edited by Christian Frevel et al. Tübingen: Mohr Siebeck, 2013.

–. "The Narratives of Numbers 20–21." *CBQ* 76.4 (2014): 634–652.

BAENTSCH, BRUNO. *Exodus – Leviticus – Numeri*. HAT. Göttingen: Vandenhoeck und Ruprecht, 1903.

BALLHORN, EGBERT. *Israel am Jordan: Narrative Topographie im Buch Josua*. BBB 162. Göttingen: V&R Unipress, 2011.

BARKAY, GABRIEL. "The Iron Age II–III." Pages 302–373 in *The Archaeology of Ancient Israel*. Edited by Amnon Ben-Tor. New Haven/London: Yale University Press, 1992.

BARKAY, GABRIEL and ZACHI ZWEIG. "The Project of Sifting Soil from the Temple Mount – Preliminary Report (Hebrew)." Pages 213–238 in *New Studies on Jerusalem* 11. Edited by Eyal Baruch et al. Ramat Gan: The Ingeborg Renner Center for Jerusalem Studies, 2006.

BARTLETT, JOHN R. "The Conquest of Sihon's Kingdom: A Literary Re-Examination." *JBL* 97 (1978): 347–351.

BARTON, JOHN. "Dating the 'Succession Narrative'." Pages 95–106 in *In Search of Pre-exilic Israel: Proceedings of the Oxford Old Testament Seminar*. Edited by John Day. London: T&T Clark, 2004.

BAUKS, MICHAELA. "La Signification de l'Espace et du Temps dans 'l'Historiographie Sacerdotale'." Pages 29–45 in *The Future of the Deuteronomistic History*. BETL 147. Edited by Thomas Römer. Leuven: Leuven University Press, 2000.

–. "Die Begriffe מוֹרָשָׁה und אֲחֻזָּה in Pg: Überlegungen zur Landkonzeption der Priestergrundschrift." *ZAW* 116 (2004): 171–188.

BECHMANN, ULRIKE. "Zelofhad." (2011): https://www.bibelwissenschaft.de/stichwort/35298/.

BEN ZVI, EHUD and CHRISTOPH LEVIN, eds. *The Concept of Exile in Ancient Israel and Its Historical Contexts*. BZAW 404. Berlin: de Gruyter, 2010.

BEN-BARAK, ZAFRIRA. *Inheritance by Daughters in Israel and the Ancient Near East: A Social, Legal and Ideological Revolution*. Jaffa: Archaeological Center Publications, 2006.

BENJAMIN, DON C. "The Land Rights of Women in Deuteronomy: In Memory of John J. Pilch (1937–2016)." *BTB* 47.2 (2017): 3–15.

BERNER, CHRISTOPH. *Die Exoduserzählung: Das literarische Werden einer Ursprungslegende Israels*. FAT 73. Tübingen: Mohr Siebeck, 2010.

BICKERT, RAINER. "Israel im Lande Moab. Die Stellung der Bileamerzählung Num 22–24 in ihrem redaktionellen Kontext." *ZAW* 121 (2009): 189–210.

BIEBERSTEIN, KLAUS. *Josua – Jordan – Jericho: Archäologie, Geschichte und Theologie der Landnahmeerzählungen Josua 1–6*. OBO 143. Göttingen: Vandenhoeck & Ruprecht, 1995.

BIENKOWSKI, PIOTR. "Beginning of the Iron Age in Southern Jordan: A Framework." Pages 1–12 in *Early Edom and Moab: The Beginning of the Iron Age in Southern Jordan*. Sheffield Archaeological Monographs 7. Edited by Piotr Bienkowski. Sheffield: J. R. Collis, 1992.

–. "Transjordan and Assyria." Pages 44–58 in *The Archaeology of Jordan and Beyond: Essays in Honor of James A. Sauer*. Edited by Lawrence E. Stager et al. Winona Lake: Eisenbrauns, 2000.

–. "The North-South Divide in Ancient Jordan: Ceramics, Regionalism and Routes." Pages 93–107 in *Culture Through Objects: Ancient Near Eastern Studies in Honour of P. R. S. Moorey*. Edited by Timothy Potts et al. Michigan: Griffith Institute, 2003.

–. "Iron Age IIC: Transjordan." Pages 419–433 in *The Ancient Pottery of Israel and Its Neighbors: From the Iron Age through the Hellenistic Period. 1*. Edited by Seymour Gitin. Jerusalem: Israel Exploration Society, 2015.

BINNS, L. ELLIOTT. *The Book of Numbers*. London: Methuen & Co. Ltd., 1927.

BLANCO WIßMANN, FILIPE. "Sargon, Mose und die Gegner Salomos: Zur Frage vor-neuassyrischer Ursprünge der Mose-Erzählung." *BN* 110 (2001): 42–54.

BLENKINSOPP, JOSEPH. "A Jewish Sect of the Persian Period." *CBQ* 52.1 (1990): 5–20.

–. "The Judean Priesthood during the Neo-Babylonian and Achaemenid Periods: A Hypothetical Reconstruction." *CBQ* 60.1 (1998): 25–43.

–. "Bethel in the Neo-Babylonian Period." Pages 93–107 in *Judah and the Judeans in the Neo-Babylonian Period*. Edited by Oded Lipschits and Joseph Blenkinsopp. Winona Lake: Eisenbrauns, 2003.

BLUM, ERHARD. *Die Komposition der Vätergeschichte*. WMANT 57. Neukirchen-Vlyun: Neukirchener, 1984.

–. *Studien zur Komposition des Pentateuch*. BZAW 189. Berlin: De Gruyter, 1990.

–. "Die literarische Verbindung von Erzvätern und Exodus: Ein Gespräch mit neueren Endredaktionshypothesen." Pages 119–156 in *Abschied vom Jahwisten: Die Komposition des Hexateuch in der jüngsten Diskussion*. BZAW 315. Edited by Jan Christian Gertz et al. Berlin: De Gruyter, 2002.

–. "Issues and Problems in the Contemporary Debate Regarding the Priestly Writings." Pages 31–44 in *The Strata of the Priestly Writings: Contemporary Debate and Future Directions*. ATANT 95. Edited by Sarah Shectman and Joel S. Baden. Zürich: Theologischer Verlag, 2009.

–. "Pentateuch – Hexateuch – Enneateuch? Or: How Can One Recognize a Literary Work in the Hebrew Bible." Pages 43–71 in *Pentateuch, Hexateuch, or Enneateuch?* AIL 8. Edited by Thomas B. Dozeman et al. Atlanta: Society of Biblical Literature, 2011.

–. "Der historische Mose und die Frühgeschichte Israels." *HBAI* 1.1 (2012): 37–63.

–. "The Jacob Tradition." Pages 181–211 in *The Book of Genesis: Composition, Reception, and Interpretation*. Edited by Craig A. Evans et al. Leiden/Boston: Brill, 2012.

–. "Die altaramäischen Wandinschriften vom Tell Deir 'Alla und ihr institutioneller Kontext." Pages 21–52 in *Metatexte: Erzählungen von schrifttragenden Artefakten in der alttestamentlichen und mittelalterlichen Literatur*. Materiale Textkulturen 15. Edited by Friedrich-Emanuel Focken and Michael R. Ott. Berlin/Boston: De Gruyter, 2016.

BOER, ROLAND. *The Sacred Economy of Ancient Israel*. Louisville: Westminster John Knox Press, 2015.

BOLING, ROBERT G. *Joshua: A New Translation with Notes and Commentary*. TAB 6. Garden City: Doubleday & Company, 1982.

–. *The Early Biblical Community in Transjordan*. The Social World of Biblical Antiquity Series 6. Sheffield: The Almond Press, 1988.

BOORER, SUZANNE. *The Promise of the Land as Oath*. BZAW 205. Berlin: de Gruyter, 1992.

BOSSERMAN, CHRISTINA. "Aphek of Aram." *Lexham Bible Dictionary*, 2014.

BRETT, MARK G. "The Politics of Marriage in Genesis." Pages 49–59 in *Making a Difference: Essays on the Bible and Judaism in Honor of Tamara Cohn Eskenazi*. Edited by David J.A. Clines et al. Sheffield: Sheffield Phoenix Press, 2012.

–. "The Priestly Dissemination of Abraham." *HBAI* 3 (2014): 87–107.

BRIANT, PIERRE. *From Cyrus to Alexander: A History of the Persian Empire*. Translated by Peter T. Daniels. Winona Lake: Eisenbrauns, 2002.

BUDD, PHILIP J. *Numbers*. WBC 5. Waco: Word Books, 1984.

BÜHLER, AXEL. "The Demotic Literature and the Priestly Exodus: The Legend of Sesostris, the Inaros Stories and the Battles of Magicians Compared to the Priestly Exodus." in *The Historical Location of P*. ArchB. Edited by Jürg Hutzli and Jordan Davis. Tübingen: Mohr Siebeck, (forthcoming).

BÜHRER, WALTER. "Die zweifache Nachgeschichte Bileams." *ZAW* 128.4 (2016): 594–611.

BUNIMOVITZ, SHLOMO and ASAF YASUR-LANDAU. "Philistine and Israelite Pottery: A Comparative Approach to the Question of Pots and People." *TA* 23.1 (1996): 88–101.

BURNETT, JOEL S. "Prophecy in Transjordan: Balaam Son of Beor." Pages 135–204 in *Enemies and Friends of the State: Ancient Prophecy in Context*. Edited by Christopher A. Rollston. University Park: Eisenbrauns, 2018.

BUTLER, TRENT C. *Joshua*. WBC 7. Waco: Word Books, 1983.

CAMPBELL JR., EDWARD F. *Ruth: A New Translation with Introduction, Notes and Commentary*. TAB 7. New York: Doubleday, 1975.

CAMPBELL, ANTHONY F. "Martin Noth and the Deuteronomistic History." Pages 31–62 in *The History of Israel's Traditions*. JSOTSup 182. Edited by Steven L McKenzie and M. Patrick Graham. Sheffield: Sheffield Academic Press, 1994.

CAMPBELL, ANTHONY F. and MARK A. O'BRIEN. *Sources of the Pentateuch: Texts, Introductions, Annotations*. Minneapolis: Fortress Press, 1993.

CARR, DAVID M. *Reading the Fractures of Genesis: Historical and Literary Approaches*. Louisville: Westminster John Knox Press, 1996.

–. "Method in Determination of Direction of Dependence: An Empirical Test of Criteria Applied to Exodus 34,11–26 and Its Parallels." Pages 107–140 in *Gottes Volk am Sinai*. VWGT 18. Edited by Matthias Köckert and Erhard Blum. Gütersloher: Chr. Kaiser Gütersloher, 2001.

–. *Writing on the Tablet of the Heart: Origins of Scripture and Literature*. New York: Oxford University Press, 2005.

–. "Scribal Processes of Coordination/Harmonization and the Formation of the First Hexateuch(s)." Pages 63–83 in *The Pentatuech: International Perspectives on Current Research*. FAT 78. Edited by Thomas B. Dozeman et al. Tübingen: Mohr Siebeck, 2011.

–. *The Formation of the Hebrew Bible: A New Reconstruction*. New York: Oxford University Press, 2011.

–. "Changes in Pentateuchal Criticism." Pages 433–466 in *Hebrew Bible/Old Testament The History of Its Interpretation*. III/2. Edited by Magne Sæbø. Bristol: Vandenhoeck & Ruprecht, 2015.

–. "Data to Inform Ongoing Debates about the Formation of the Pentateuch: From Documented Cases of Transmission History to a Survey of Rabbinic Exegesis." Pages 87–106 in *The Formation of the Pentateuch: Bridging the Academic Cultures of Europe, Israel and North America*. FAT 111. Edited by Jan C. Gertz et al. Tübingen: Mohr Siebeck, 2016.

CHAMBON, ALAIN. *Tell El-Far'ah: L'Age du Fer*. Paris: Ed. Recherche sue les Civilisations, 1984.

–. "Far'ah, Tell el- (North): Neolithic Period to Middle Bronze Age." *NEAEHL* (1993): 2:438–440.

CHAVEL, SIMEON. *Oracular Law and Priestly Historiography in the Torah*. FAT II 71. Tübingen: Mohr Siebeck, 2014.

CHRISTIAN, MARK A. "Openness to the Other Inside and Outside of Numbers." Pages 579–608 in *The Books of Leviticus and Numbers*. BETL 215. Edited by Thomas Römer. Leuven: Uitgeveru Peeters, 2008.

CLAASSENS, J. "'Give us a portion among our father's brothers': The Daughters of Zelophehad, Land, and the Quest for Human Dignity." *JSOT* 37 (2013): 319–337.

CLINES, DAVID J.A. *The Theme of the Pentateuch*. JSOTSupS 10. Sheffield: JSOT, 1978.

COCCO, FRANCESCO. *Women in the Wilderness: The "Female Legislation" of the Book of Numbers (Num 5,11–31; 27,1–11; 30,2–17)*. FAT 138. Tübingen: Mohr Siebeck, 2020.

CORTESE, ENZO. *Josua 13–21: Ein priesterschriftlicher Abschnitt im deuteronomistischen Geschichtswerk*. OBO 94. Göttingen: Vandenhoeck & Ruprecht, 1990.

COTTON, HANNAH M. and JONAS C. GREENFIELD. "Babatha's Property and the Law of Succession in the Babatha Archive." *ZPE* 104 (1994): 211–224.

CRAWFORD, SIDNIE WHITE. "Reading Deuteronomy in the Second Temple Period." Pages 127–140 in *Reading the Present in the Qumran Library: The Perception of the Contemporary by Means of Scriptural Interpretations*. SymS 30. Edited by Kristin De Troyer and Armin Lange. Atlanta: SBL, 2005.

CROSS, FRANK MOORE. "Aspects of Samaritan and Jewish History in Late Persian and Hellenistic Times." *HTR* 59.3 (1966): 201–211.

–. "A Recently Published Phoenician Inscription of the Persian Period from Byblos." *IEJ* 29.1 (1979): 40–44.

–. "Reuben, the Firstborn of Jacob: Sacral Traditions and Early Israelite History." Pages 53–70 in *From Epic to Canon: History and Literature in Ancient Israel*. Baltimore/London: JHU Press, 2000.

DAVIAU, PAULETTE M. MICHÈLE. "Moab's Northern Border: Khirbat al-Mudayna on the Wadi ath-Thamad." *BA* 60.4 (1997): 222–228.

DAVIES, ERYL W. "Inheritance Rights and the Hebrew Levirate Marriage: Part 1." *VT* 31.2 (1981): 138–144.

–. "Inheritance Rights and the Hebrew Levirate Marriage: Part 2." *VT* 31.3 (1981): 257–268.

–. *Numbers*. The New Century Bible Commentary. London: Marshall Pickering, 1995.

DAVIES, G. I. "The Wilderness Itineraries and the Composition of the Pentateuch." *VT* 33,1 (1983): 1–13.

–. *The Way of the Wilderness: A Geographical Study of the Wilderness Itineraries in the Old Testament*. SOTS 5. Cambridge: Cambridge University Press, 2009.

DAVIES, PHILIP R. "Ethnicity." (2014): http://www.bibleinterp.com/opeds/2014/01/dav388016.shtml

–. *In Search of 'Ancient Israel': A Study in Biblical Origins*. New York/London: Bloomsbury, 2015.

DAVIS, JORDAN. "A Priestly Source in Numbers? Transjordan and the Priestly Ideology in Numbers 32." in *The Historical Location of P*. ArchB. Edited by Jürg Huztli and Jordan Davis. Mohr Siebeck, (forthcoming).

DE PURY, ALBERT. "Pg as the Absolute Beginning." Pages 99–128 in *Les dernières rédactions du Pentateuque, de l'Hexateuque et de l'Ennéateuque*. BETL 203. Edited by Thomas C. Römer and Konrad Schmid. Paris: Leuven University Press, 2007.

DE PURY, ALBERT and THOMAS RÖMER. "Deuteronomistic Historiography (DH): History of Research and Debated Issues." Pages 1–141 in *Israel Constructs Its History: Deuteronomistic Historiography in Recent Research*. JSOTSup 306. Edited by Albert De Pury et al. Sheffield: Sheffield Academic Press, 2000.

DE PURY, ALBERT ET AL., eds. *Israel Constructs Its History: Deuteronomistic Historiography in Recent Research*. JSOTSup 306. Sheffield: Sheffield Academic Press, 2000.

DE VAULX, J. *Les Nombres*. SBi Paris: Librarie Lecoffre, 1972.

DE VAUX, R. "The Excavations at Tell El-Far'ah and the Site of Ancient Tirzah." *PEQ* 88.2 (1956): 125–140.

DE WETTE, WILHELM MARTIN LEBERECHT. "Dissertatio Critica Qua Deuteronomium Diversum a Prioribus Pentateuchi Libris, Alius Cuiusdam Recentiori Auctoris Opus Esse Demonstrator." University of Jena, 1805.

–. *Critical and Historical Introduction to the Canonical Scriptures of the Old Testament*. Translated by Theodore Parker. Boston: Charles C. Little and James Brown, 1850.

DEARMAN, J. ANDREW. "The Levitical Cities of Reuben and Moabite Toponymy." *BASOR* 276 (1989): 55–66.

–. "The 'Border' Area Between Ammon, Moab and Israel in the Iron Age." *OTE* 9.2 (1996): 204–212.

DERBY, JOSIAH. "The Daughters of Zelophehad Revisited." *JBQ* 25 (1997): 169–171.

DIETRICH, WALTER ET AL. *Die Entstehung des Alten Testaments*. Stuttgart: Kohlhammer, 2014.

DOUGLAS, MARY. *In the Wilderness: The Doctrine of Defilement in the Book of Numbers*. JSOTSup 158. Sheffield: JSOT Press, 1993.

DOZEMAN, THOMAS B. *Commentary on Exodus*. Grand Rapids: Eerdmans Publishing, 2009.

–. *Joshua 1–12: A New Translation with Introduction and Commentary*. TAB 6b. New Haven: Yale University Press, 2015.

–. "Inner-biblical Interpretation of Gilead in the Wars against Sihon and Og and in the Tribal Territory East of the Jordan River*." Pages 163–178 in *Eigensinn und Entstehung der Hebräischen Bibel: Erhard Blum zum siebsigsten Geburtstag*. FAT 136. Edited by Joachim J. Krause et al. Tübingen: Mohr Siebeck, 2020.

DOZEMAN, THOMAS B. ET AL., eds. *Pentateuch, Hexateuch, or Enneateuch? Identifying Literary Works in Genesis through Kings*. AIL 8. Atlanta: Society of Biblical Literature, 2011.

DOZEMAN, THOMAS B. and KONRAD SCHMID, eds. *A Farewell to the Yahwist? The Composition of the Pentateuch in Recent European Interpretation*. SymS 34. Atlanta: Society of Biblical Literature, 2006.

–. "Introduction." Pages 1–7 in *A Farewell to the Yahwist? The Composition of the Pentateuch in Recent European Interpretations*. SymS 34. Edited by Thomas B. Dozeman and Konrad Schmid. Atlanta: Society of Biblical Literature, 2006.

DOZEMAN, THOMAS B. ET AL., eds. *The Penatateuch: International Perspectives on Current Research*. FAT 78. Tübingen: Mohr Siebeck, 2011.

DUŠEK, JAN. *Aramaic and Hebrew Inscriptions from Mt. Gerizim and Samaria between Antiochus III and Antiochus IV Epiphanes*. Boston: Leiden, 2012.

ELLIGER, KARL. *Leviticus*. HAT 1/4. Tübingen: Mohr Siebeck, 1966.

ESKENAZI, TAMARA C. "Out from the Shadows: Biblical Women in the Postexilic Era." *JSOT* 17.54 (1992): 25–43.

FANTALKIN, ALEXANDER and OREN TAL. "Re-Discovering the Iron Age Fortress at Tell Qudadi in the Context of Neo-Assyrian Imperialistic Policies." *PEQ* 141.3 (2013): 188–206.

FAUST, AVRAHAM. "Ethnic Complexity in Northern Israel During Iron Age II." *PEQ* 132 (2000): 2–27.

FINKELSTEIN, ISRAEL. "Pots and People Revisited: Ethnic Boundaries in the Iron Age I." Pages 216–237 in *The Archaeology of Israel: Constructing the Past, Interpreting the Present*. JSOTSup 237. Edited by Neil Asher Silberman and David B. Small. Sheffield: Sheffield Academic Press, 1997.

–. "Stages in the Territorial Expansion of the Northern Kingdom." *VT* 61 (2011): 227–242.

–. "The Historical Reality behind the Genealogical Lists in 1 Chronicles." *JBL* 131.1 (2012): 65–83.

–. *The Forgotten Kingdom: The Archaeology and History of Northern Israel*. Atlanta: Society of Biblical Literature, 2013.

–. "Migration of Israelites into Judah after 720 BCE: An Answer and an Update." *ZAW* 127.2 (2015): 188–206.

–. "A Corpus of North Israelite Texts in the Days of Jeroboam II." *HBAI* 6.3 (2017): 262–289.

FINKELSTEIN, ISRAEL ET AL. "The Biblical Gilead: Observations on Identifications, Geographic Divisions and Territorial History." *UF* 43 (2012): 131–159.

FINKELSTEIN, ISRAEL and ODED LIPSCHITS. "Omride Architecture in Moab: Jahaz and Ataroth." *ZDPV* 126.1 (2010): 29–42.

FINKELSTEIN, ISRAEL ET AL. "Tell er-Rumeith in Northern Jordan: Some Archaeological and Historical Observations." *Sem* 55 (2013): 7–23.

FINKELSTEIN, ISRAEL and THOMAS RÖMER. "Comments on the Historical Background of the Jacob Narrative in Genesis." *ZAW* 126.3 (2014): 317–338.

–. "Early North Israelite 'Memories' of Moab." Pages 711–727 in *The Formation of the Pentateuch: Bridging the Academic Cultures of Europe, Israel, and North America.* FAT 111. Edited by Jan C. Gertz et al. Tübingen: Mohr Siebeck, 2016.

FINKELSTEIN, ISRAEL and BENJAMIN SASS. "The West Semitic Alphabetic Inscriptions, Late Bronze II to Iron IIA: Archeological Context, Distribution and Chronology." *HBAI* 2 (2013): 149–220.

FINKELSTEIN, ISRAEL and NEIL ASHER SILBERMAN. *The Bible Unearthed: Archaeology's New Vision of Ancient Israel and the Origins of Its Sacred Texts.* New York: The Free Press, 2001.

FINKELSTEIN, ISRAEL and LILY SINGER-AVITZ. "Reevaluating Bethel." *ZDPV* 125.1 (2009): 33–48.

FISCHER, IRMTRAUD. "Rahel und Lea bauten ganz Israel auf – Rebekka ermöglichte eine gemeinsame Identität." Pages 167–183 in *The Politics of the Ancestors: Exegetical and Historical Perspectives on Genesis 12–36.* FAT 124. Edited by Mark G. Brett and Jakob Wöhrle. Tübingen: Mohr Siebeck, 2018.

FISHBANE, MICHAEL. *Biblical Interpretation in Ancient Israel.* Oxford: Clarendon Press, 1985.

FISTILL, ULRICH. *Israel und das Ostjordanland: Untersuchungen zur Komposition von Num 21,21–36,13 im Hinblick auf die Entstehung des Buches Numeri.* Frankfurt am Main: Peter Lang, 2007.

FLEMING, DANIEL E. *The Legacy of Israel in Judah's Bible: History, Politics, and the Reinscribing of Tradition.* Cambridge et al.: Cambridge University Press, 2012.

–. "The Amorites." Pages 1–30 in *The World around the Old Testament: The People and Places of the Ancient Near East.* Edited by Bill T. Arnold and Brent A. Strawn. Grand Rapids: Baker Academic, 2016.

FORRER, EMIL. *Die Provinzeinteilung des assyrischen Reiches.* Leipzig: Hinrichs, 1921.

FORSLING, JOSEF. *Composite Artistry in the Book of Numbers: A Study in Biblical Narrative Conventions.* Studia Theologica Holmiensia 22. Åbo: Åbo University Press, 2013.

FRANKEL, DAVID. *The Murmuring Stories of the Priestly School: A Retrieval of Ancient Sacerdotal Lore.* VTSup 84. Leiden: Brill, 2002.

FRANKEN, H. J. "Archaeological Evidence Relating to the Interpretation of the Text." Pages 3–16 in *Aramaic Texts from Deir 'Alla.* Edited by J. Hoftijzer and G. van der Kooij. Leiden: Brill, 1976.

FREVEL, CHRISTIAN. "Gilead." *LTK* 4 (1995): 651.

–. "Kein Ende in Sicht? Zur Priestergrundschrift im Buch Levitikus." Pages 85–123 in *Levitikus als Buch.* BBB 119. Edited by Heinz-Josef Fabry and Hans-Winfried Jüngling. Berlin: Bodenheim, 1999.

–. *Mit Blick auf das Land die Schöpfung erinnern: zum Ende der Priestergrundschrift.* HBS 23. Freiburg: Herder, 2000.

–. "Deuteronomistisches Geschichtswerk oder Geschichtswerke? Die These Martin Noths zwischen Tetrateuch, Hexateuch und Enneateuch." Pages 60–95 in *Martin Noth – aus der Sicht heutiger Forschung.* Edited by Udo Rüterswörden. Neukirchen-Vlyun: Neukirchener, 2004.

–. "Achenbach, Reinhard: Die Vollendung der Tora. Studien zur Redaktionsgeschichte des Numeribuches im Kontext von Hexateuch und Pentateuch." *OLZ* 100 (2005): 278–285.

–. "Understanding the Pentateuch by Structuring the Desert, Numbers 21 as a Compositional Joint." Pages 111–135 in *The Land of Israel in Bible, History and Theology: Studies in Honour Ed Noort.* Edited by Jacques van Ruiten and Cornelis de Vos. Leiden: Brill, 2009.

–. "Die Wiederkehr der Hexateuchperspektive." Pages 13–53 in *Das deuteronomistische Geschichtswerk.* ÖBS 39. Edited by Hermann-Josef Stipp. Berlin: Peter Lang, 2011.

–. "The Book of Numbers – Formation, Composition, and Interpretation of a Late Part of the Torah: Some Introductory Remarks." Pages 1–37 in *Torah and the Book of Numbers.* FAT II 62. Edited by Christian Frevel et al. Tübingen: Mohr Siebeck, 2013.

–. "Alte Stücke – späte Brücke? Zur Rolle des Buches Numeri in der jüngeren Pentateuchdiskussion." Pages 255–299 in *Congress Volume München.* VTSup 163. Edited by Christl M. Maier. Leiden: Brill, 2014.

–. "'Esau, der Vater Edoms' (Gen 36,9.43): Ein Vergleich der Edom-Überlieferungen in Genesis und Numeri vor dem Hintergrund der historischen Entwicklung." Pages 329–364 in *The Politics of the Ancestors: Exegetical and Historical Perspectives on Genesis 12–36.* FAT 124. Edited by Mark G. Brett and Jakob Wöhrle. Tübingen: Mohr Siebeck, 2018.

–. *Geschichte Israels.* KSB 2. Stuttgart: Kolhammer, 2018.

–. "Leadership and Conflict: Modelling the Charisma of Numbers." Pages 89–114 in *Debating Authority: Concepts of Leadership in the Pentateuch and the Former Prophets.* BZAW 507. Edited by Katharina Pyschny and Sarah Schulz. Berlin/Boston: de Gruyter, 2018.

–. "Editorial Introduction: The Importance of the Book of Numbers in Pentateuchal Research." *HBAI* 8.3 (2019): 203–212.

–. "The Various Shapes of Moab in the Book of Numbers: Relating Text and Archaeology." *HBAI* 8.3 (2019): 257–286.

–. *Desert Transformations: Studies in the Book of Numbers.* FAT 137. Tübingen: Mohr Siebeck, 2020.

–. "Jacob as Father of the Twelve Tribes: Literary and Historical Considerations." Pages 155–181 in *The History of the Jacob Cycle (Genesis 25–35): Recent Research on the Compilation, the Redaction and the Reception of the Biblical Narrative and Its Historical and Cultural Contexts.* ArchB 4. Edited by Benedikt Hensel. Tübingen: Mohr Siebeck, 2021.

FREVEL, CHRISTIAN ET AL., eds. *Torah and the Book of Numbers.* FAT II 62. Tübingen: Mohr Siebeck, 2013.

FREY, JÖRG. "Temple and Rival Temple: The Cases of Elephantine, Mt. Gerizim and Leontopolis." Pages 171–203 in *Gemeinde ohne Tempel: zur Substituierung und Transformation des Jerusalemer Tempels und seines Kults im Alten Testament, antiken Judentum und frühen Christentum.* WUNT 118. Edited by Beate Ego et al. Tübingen: Mohr Siebeck, 1999.

FROLOV, SERGE. "How Old is the Song of Deborah." *JSOT* 36.2 (2011): 163–184.

–. Judges. Grand Rapids: Eerdmans, 2013.

GALIL, GERSHOM. "A New Look at the Inscriptions of Tiglath-Pileser III." *Bib* 81.4 (2000): 511–520.

–. "The Boundaries of Aram-Damascus in the 9th-8th Centuries BCE." Pages 35–41 in *Studies in Historical Geography and Biblical Historiography: Presented to Zecharia Kallai*. VTSup 81. Edited by Gershom Galil and Moshe Weinfeld. Leiden: Brill, 2000.

GARTON, ROY E. *Mirages in the Desert: The Tradition-historical Developments of the Story of Massah-Meribah*. BZAW 492. Berlin: de Gruyter, 2017.

GASS, ERASMUS. *Die Ortsnamen des Richterbuchs in historischer und redaktioneller Perspektive*. ADPV 35. Wiesbaden: Harrassowitz, 2005.

–. *Die Moabiter – Geschichte und Kultur eines ortjordanischen Volkes im 1. Jahrtausend v.Chr.* ADPV 38. Wiesbaden: Harrassowitz, 2009.

–. "Die Amalekiter: Erbfeinde Israels." Pages 189–228 in *Studien zum Richterbuch und seinen Völkernamen*. SBA 54. Edited by Walter Groß and Erasmus Gaß. Stuttgart: Katholisches Bibelwerk, 2012.

–. *Die Landverteilung im Josuabuch: Eine literarhistorische Analyse von Josua 13–19*. FAT 132. Tübingen: Mohr Siebeck, 2019.

GERMANY, STEPHEN. *The Exodus-Conquest Narrative: The Composition of the Non-Priestly Narratives in Exodus–Joshua*. FAT 115. Tübingen: Mohr Siebeck, 2017.

–. "The Hexateuch Hypothesis: A History of Research and Current Approaches." *CurBR* 16.2 (2018): 131–156.

–. "Concepts of Land in Numbers and Joshua." *HBAI* 8.3 (2019): 313–331.

–. "Scribal Cartography in Numbers 32 and Related Texts." (forthcoming)

GERTZ, JAN CHRISTIAN ET AL. "Convergence and Divergence in Pentateuchal Theory: The Genesis and Goals of This Volume." Pages 1–7 in *The Formation of the Pentateuch: Bridging the Academic Cultures of Europe, Israel, and North America*. FAT 111. Edited by Jan Christian Gertz et al. Tübingen: Mohr Siebeck, 2016.

GERTZ, JAN CHRISTIAN ET AL., eds. *Abschied vom Jahwisten: Die Komposition des Hexateuch in der jüngsten Diskussion*. BZAW 315. Berlin: De Gruyter, 2002.

GERTZ, JAN CHRISTIAN ET AL., eds. *Die deuteronomistischen Geschichtswerke: Redaktions- und religionsgeschichtliche Perspektiven zur "Deuteronomismus" – Diskussion in Tora und Vorderen Propheten*. BZAW 365. Berlin: De Gruyter, 2006.

GERTZ, JAN CHRISTIAN ET AL., eds. *The Formation of the Pentateuch: Bridging the Academic Cultures of Europe, Israel, and North America*. FAT 111. Tübingen: Mohr Siebeck, 2016.

GESUNDHEIT, SHIMON. "Midrash-Exegesis in the Service of Literary Criticism." Pages 73–86 in *The Reception of Biblical War Legislation in Narrative Contexts: Proceedings of the EABS research group "Law and Narrative"*. BZAW 460. Edited by Christoph Berner and Harald Samuel. Berlin: de Gruyter, 2015.

GEVARYAHU, GILAD J. "The Root G-R-A in the Bible: The Case of the Daughters of Zelophehad and Beyond." *JBQ* 41.2 (2013): 107–112.

GIUNTOLI, FEDERICO. "Ephraim, Manasseh, and Post-Exilic Israel: A Study of the Redactional Expansions in Gen 48 Regarding Joseph's Sons." Pages 203–232 in *The Post-Priestly Pentateuch: New Perspectives on Its Redactional Development and Theological Profiles*. FAT 101. Edited by Federico Giuntoli and Konrad Schmid. Tübingen: Mohr Siebeck, 2015.

GLUECK, NELSON. "Some Ancient Towns in the Plains of Moab." *BASOR* 91 (1943): 7–26.

GNUSE, ROBERT K. "Redefining the Elohist." *JBL* 119.2 (2000): 201–220.

GOLDBERG, ARNOLD. *Das Buch Numeri*. Düsseldorf: Patmos, 1970.

GOODMAN, MARTIN. "Babatha's Story." *JRS* 81 (1991): 169–175.

GRAF, H. *Die geschichtlichen Bücher des Alten Testaments*. Leipsic: T.O. Weigel, 1866.

GRAY, GEORGE BUCHANAN. *A Critical and Exegetical Commentary on Numbers*. Edinburgh: T&T Clark, 1903.

GROSS, WALTER. *Richter*. HThKAT. Freiburg: Herder, 2009.

–. "Das Richterbuch zwischen deuteronomistischem Geschichtswerk und Enneateuch." Pages 177–205 in *Das deuteronomistische Geschichtswerk*. ÖBS 39. Edited by Hermann-Josef Stipp. Frankfurt am Main: Peter Lang, 2011.

GRÜNWALDT, KLAUS. *Das Heiligkeitsgesetz Leviticus 17–26: Ursprungliche Gestalt, Tradition und Theologie*. BZAW 271. Berlin/New York: Walter de Gruyter, 1999.

GUILLAUME, PHILIPPE. *Waiting for Josiah: The Judges*. London: T&T Clark, 2004.

–. "Jerusalem 720–705 BCE: No Flood of Israelite Refugees." *SJOT* 22.2 (2008): 195–211.

–. *Land and Calendar: The Priestly Document from Genesis 1 to Joshua 18*. LHBOTS 391. New York: T&T Clark, 2009.

GUNKEL, HERMANN. *Genesis*. Göttingen: Vandenhoeck & Ruprecht, 1964.

GUNNEWEG, A.H.J. "Das Gesetz und die Propheten: Eine Auslegung von Ex 33,7–11; Num 11,4–12,8; Dtn 31,14 f.; 34,10." *ZAW* 102 (1990): 169–180.

HANSON, PAUL D. "The Song of Heshbon and David's Nîr." *HTR* 61.3 (1968): 297–320.

HARAN, MENAHEM. "Book-Scrolls in Israel in Pre-Exilic Times." *JJS* 33 (1982): 161–173.

–. "Book-Scrolls at the Beginning of the Second Temple Period: The Transition from Papyrus to Skins." *HUCA* 54 (1983): 111–122.

HARRISON, R.K. *Numbers: An Exegetical Commentary*. Grand Rapids: Baker Book House, 1992.

HARTENSTEIN, FRIEDHEIM and KONRAD SCHMID, eds. *Abschied von der Priesterschrift?: Zum Stand der Pentateuchdebatte*. Leipzig: Evangelische Verlagsanstalt, 2015.

HARVEY JR., PAUL B. and BARUCH HALPERN. "W.M.L. de Wette's 'Dissertatio Critica': Context and Translation." *ZABR* 14 (2008): 47–85.

HAWK, L. DANIEL. *Joshua*. Berit Olam: Studies in Hebrew Narrative & Poetry. Collegeville: Liturgical Press, 2000.

HENSEL, BENEDIKT. *Juda und Samaria: Zum Verhältnis zweier nach-exilischer Jahwismen*. FAT 110. Tübingen: Mohr Siebeck, 2016.

–. "On the Relationship of Judah and Samaria in Post-Exilic Times: A Farewell to the Conflict Paradigm." *JSOT* 44.1 (2019): 19–42.

–. "Edom in the Jacob Cycle (Gen *25–35): New Insights on Its Positive Relations with Israel, the Literary-Historical Development of Its Role, and Its Historical Background(s)." Pages 57–133 in *The History of the Jacob Cycle (Genesis 25–35): Recent Research on the Compilation, the Redaction and the Reception of the Biblical Narrative and Its Historical and Cultural Contexts*. ArchB 4. Edited by Benedikt Hensel. Tübingen: Mohr Siebeck, 2021.

HERR, LARRY G. "Abel-Meholah." *EBR* (2009): 1:69–70.

HERZOG, ZE'EV and LILY SINGER-AVITZ. "Sub-Dividing the Iron Age IIA in Northern Israel: A Suggested Solution to the Chronological Debate." *TA* 33.2 (2006): 163–195.

HJELM, INGRID. "Northern Perspectives in Deuteronomy and Its Relation to the Samaritan Pentateuch." *HBAI* 4.2 (2015): 184–204.

HOBSON, RUSSELL. "Were Persian-Period 'Israelites' Bound by Ethnicity or Religious Affiliation? The Case of the Southern Transjordan." Pages 36–56 in *Religion in the*

288   Bibliography

Archaemenid Persian Empire: Emerging Judaisms and Trends. ORA 17. Edited by Diana Edelman et al. Tübingen: Mohr Siebeck, 2016.

HOFTIJZER, J. AND G. VAN DER KOOIJ, eds. *Aramaic Texts from Deir 'Alla*. Leiden: Brill, 1976.

HOLZINGER, HERMANN. *Numeri: Erklärt*. KHAT IV. Tübingen/Leipzig: J.C.B. Mohr, 1903.

HOMSHER, ROBERT S. and MELISSA S. CRADIC. "Rethinking Amorites." Pages 131–150 in *Rethinking Israel: Studies in the History and Archaeology of Ancient Israel in Honor of Israel Finkelstein*. Edited by Oded Lipschits et al. Winona Lake: Eisenbrauns, 2017.

HUFFMON, HERBERT B. and DOMINIQUE CHARPIN. "Amorites." *EBR* (2009): 1:1016–1028.

HUTCHENS, KENNETH D. "Defining Boundaries: A Cultic Interpretation of Numbers 34.1–12 and Ezekiel 47.13–48.1, 28." Pages 215–230 in *History and Interpretation: Essays in Honour of John H. Hayes*. JSOTSup 173. Edited by M. Patrick Graham et al. Sheffield: JSOT Press, 1993.

HUTZLI, JÜRG. *The Origins of P: Literary Profiles and Strata of the Priestly Texts in Genesis 1 – Exodus 40*. FAT. Tübingen: Mohr Siebeck, Forthcoming.

HUWYLER, BEAT. *Jeremia und die Völker: Untersuchungen zu den Völkersprüchen in Jeremia 46–49*. FAT 20. Tübingen: Mohr Siebeck, 1997.

ITACH, GILAD ET AL. "The Wedge-Impressed Bowl and the Assyrian Deportation." *TA* 44.1 (2017): 72–97.

JAPHET, SARA. *I & II Chronicles*. London: Westminster John Knox Press, 1993.

JENKS, ALAN W. "Elohist." *ABD* (1992): 2:478–482.

JENSON, PHILIP PETER. *Graded Holiness: A Key to the Priestly Conception of the World*. JSOTSup 106. Sheffield: JSOT Press, 1992.

JEON, JAEYOUNG. "The Promise of the Land and the Extent of P." *ZAW* 130.4 (2018): 513–528.

JERICKE, DETLEF. *Abraham in Mamre: Historische und exegetische Studien zur Region von Hebron und zu Genesis 11,27–19,38*. CHANE 17. Leiden: Koninklijke Brill, 2003.

–. "Das 'Bergland der Amoriter' in Deuteronomium 1." *ZDPV* 125 (2009): 49–63.

–. "Atroth-Shophan." *EBR* 3 (2011): 68.

JI, CHANG-HO C. "One Tale, Two 'Ataruz: Investigating Rujm 'Ataruz and Its Association with Khirbat 'Ataruz." *SHAJ* 12 (2016): 211–222.

JOOSTEN, JAN. *People & Land in the Holiness Code*. Leiden: Brill, 1996.

JOSEPHUS, FLAVIUS. *Josephus: Books IX-XI. Jewish antiquities. 6*. Translated by Ralph Marcus. LCL 326. London: William Heinemann LTD, 1958.

KALMIN, RICHARD. "Levirate Law." *ABD* (1992): 4:296–297.

KARTVEIT, MAGNAR. *The Origins of the Samaritans*. VTSup 128. Leiden: Brill, 2009.

KEEL, OTHMAR and CHRISTOPH UEHLINGER. *Göttinen, Götter und Göttessymbole: Neue Erkentnisse zur Religionsgeschichte Kanaans und Israels aufgrund bislang unerschlossener ikonographischer Quellen*. Freiburg: Academic Press, 2010.

KELLERMANN, D. "גור." *TDOT* (1999): II:439–449.

KILCHÖR, BENJAMIN. "Levirate Marriage in Deuteronomy 25:5–10 and Its Precursors in Leviticus and Numbers: A Test Case for the Relationship between P/H and D." *CBQ* 77 (2015): 429–440.

KISLEV, ITAMAR. "Numbers 36,1–12: Innovation and Interpretation." *ZAW* 122.2 (2010): 249–259.

–. "The Census of the Israelites on the Plains of Moab (Numbers 26): Sources and Redaction." *VT* 63 (2013): 236–260.

KLEIMAN, ASSAF. "The Damascene Subjugation of the Southern Levant as a Gradual Process (ca. 842–800 BCE)." Pages 57–76 in *In Search of Aram and Israel: Politics, Culture, and Identity*. ORA 20. Edited by Omer Sergi et al. Tübingen: Mohr Siebeck, 2016.

–. "A North Israelite Royal Administrative System and Its Impact on Late-Monarchic Judah." *HBAI* 6.3 (2017): 354–371.

KLETTER, RAZ. "Pots and Polities: Material Remains of Late Iron Age Judah in Relation to Its Political Borders." *BASOR* 314 (1999): 19–54.

KLOPPENBORG, JOHN S. "Joshua 22: The Priestly Editing of an Ancient Tradition." *Bib* 62.3 (1981): 347–371.

KLOSTERMANN, AUGUST. *Der Pentateuch: Beiträge zu einem Verständis und seiner Enstehungsgeschichte*. Leipzig: U. Deichert, 1893.

KNAUF, ERNST AXEL. *Midian: Untersuchungen zur Geschichte Palästinas und Nordarabiends am Ende des 2. Jahrtausends v. Chr*. Wiesbaden: Otto Harrassowitz, 1988.

–. "Heshbon, Sihons Stadt." *ZDPV* 106 (1990): 135–144.

–. "Does 'Deuteronomistic Historiography' (DtrH) Exist?" Pages 388–398 in *Israel Constructs Its History: Deuteronomistic Historiography in Recent Research*. JSOTSup 306. Edited by Albert de Pury et al. Sheffield: Sheffield Academic Press, 2000.

–. "Towards an Archaeology of the Hexateuch." Pages 275–294 in *Abschied vom Jahwisten: Die Komposition des Hexateuch in der jüngsten Diskussion*. BZAW 315. Edited by Jan Christian Gertz et al. Berlin: De Gruyter, 2002.

–. "Deborah's Language: Judges Ch. 5 in Its Hebrew and Semitic Context." Pages 167–182 in *Studia Semitica et Semitohamitica: Festschrift für Rainer Voigt anläßlich seines 60. Geburtstages am 17. Januar 2004*. AOAT 317. Edited by Bogdan Burtea, Josef Tropper and Helen Younansardaroud. Münster: Ugarit-Verlag, 2005.

–. "Bethel: The Israelite Impact on Judean Language and Literature." Pages 291–349 in *Judah and the Judeans in the Persian Period*. Edited by Oded Lipschits and Manfred Oeming. Winona Lake: Eisenbrauns, 2006.

–. "Buchschlüsse in Josua." Pages 217–224 in *Les dernières rédactions du Pentateuque, de l'Hexateuque et de l'Ennéateuque*. BETL 203. Edited by Thomas Römer and Konrad Schmid. Leuven: Leuven University Press, 2007.

–. *Josua*. AT 6. Zürich: Theologischer Verlag, 2008.

–. *Data and Debates: Essays in the History and Culture of Israel and Its Neighbors in Antiquity*. Edited by Hermann Michael Niemann et al. AOAT 407. Münster: Ugarit-Verlag, 2013.

–. *Richter*. AT 7. Zürich: Theologischer Verlag, 2016.

–. "Jeroboam ben Nimshi: The Biblical Evidence." *HBAI* 6.3 (2017): 290–307.

–. "Was There a Refugee Crisis in the 8th/7th Centuries BCE?" Pages 159–172 in *Rethinking Israel: Studies in the History and Archaeology of Ancient Israel in Honor of Israel Finkelstein*. Edited by Oded Lipschits et al. Winona Lake: Eisenbrauns, 2017.

KNAUF, ERNST AXEL and PHILIPPE GUILLAUME. *A History of Biblical Israel: The Fate of the Tribes and Kingdoms from Merenptah to Bar Kochba*. WANEM. Sheffield: Equinox, 2016.

KNIERIM, ROLF P. and GEORGE W. COATS. *Numbers*. TFOTL 4. Grand Rapids: Eerdmans Publishing, 2005.

KNOHL, ISRAEL. *The Sanctuary of Silence*. Winona Lake: Eisenbrauns, 2007.

KNOPPERS, GARY N. "Is There a Future for the Deuteronomistic History?" Pages 119–134 in *The Future of the Deuteronomistic History*. BETL 147. Edited by Thomas Römer. Leuven: Leuven University Press, 2000.

–. "Intermarriage, Social Complexity, and Ethnic Diversity in the Genealogy of Judah." *JBL* 120.1 (2001): 15–30.

–. "Establishing a Rule of Law? The Composition of Num 33,50–56 and the Relationships Among the Pentateuch, the Hexateuch, and the Deuteronomistic History." Pages 135–152 in *Das Deuteronomium zwischen Pentateuch und Deuteronomistischem Geschichtswerk*. FRLANT 206. Edited by Eckart Otto and Reinhard Achenbach. Göttingen: Vandenhoeck & Ruprecht, 2004.

–. "Revisiting the Samarian Question in the Persian Period." Pages 265–289 in *Judah and the Judeans in the Persian Period*. Edited by Oded Lipschits and Manfred Oeming. Winona Lake: Eisenbrauns, 2006.

–. "Samaritan Conceptions of Jewish Origins and Jewish Conceptions of Samaritan Origins: Any Common Ground?" Pages 81–118 in *The Samaritans and the Bible: Historical and Literary Interactions between Biblical and Samaritan Traditions*. SJ 70. Edited by Jörg Frey et al. Berlin: De Gruyter, 2012.

–. *Jews and Samaritans: The Origins and History of Their Early Relations*. New York: Oxford University Press, 2013.

–. "The Northern Context of the Law-Code in Deuteronomy." *HBAI* 4.2 (2015): 162–183.

–. *Judah and Samaria in Postmonarchic Times: Essays on Their Histories and Literatures*. FAT 129. Tübingen: Mohr Siebeck, 2019.

KÖCKERT, MATTHIAS. "Das Land in der priesterlichen Komposition des Pentateuch." Pages 147–162 in *Von Gott reden: Beiträge zur Theologie und Exegese des Alten Testaments: Festschrift für Siegfried Wagner zum 65. Geburtstag*. Edited by Dieter Vieweger and Ernst-Joachim Waschke. Neukirchen-Vlyun: Neukirchener, 1995.

–. *Leben in Gottes Gegenwart: Studien zum Verständnis des Gesetzes im Alten Testament*. FAT 43. Tübingen: Mohr Siebeck, 2004.

KRATZ, REINHARD G. "Der literarische Ort des Deuteronomiums." Pages 101–120 in *Liebe und Gebot: Studien zum Deuteronomium*. FRLANT 190. Edited by Reinhard G. Kratz and Hermann Spieckermann. Göttingen: Vandenhoeck & Ruprecht, 2000.

–. *Die Komposition der erzählenden Bücher des Alten Testaments: Grundwissen der Bibelkritik*. Göttingen: Vandenhoeck & Ruprecht, 2000.

–. *The Composition of the Narrative Books of the Old Testament*. Translated by John Bowden. London: T&T Clark, 2005.

–. "The Pentateuch in Current Research: Consensus and Debate." Pages 31–61 in *The Pentateuch: International Perspectives on Current Research*. FAT 78. Edited by Thomas B. Dozeman et al. Tübingen: Mohr Siebeck, 2011.

–. *Historical & Biblical Israel: The History, Tradition, and Archives of Israel and Judah*. Translated by Paul Michael Kurtz. Oxford: Oxford University Press, 2015.

KRAUSE, JOACHIM J. *Exodus und Eisodus: Komposition und Theologie von Josua 1–5*. VTSup 161. Leiden: Brill, 2014.

KUENEN, ABRAHAM. *An Historico-Critical Inquiry into the Origin and Composition of the Hexateuch: Pentateuch and Book of Joshua*. Translated by P. H. Wicksteed. London: MacMillan & Co., 1886.

LaBIANCA, Ø. S. and B. WALKER. "Tall Hisban: Palimpsest of Great and Little Traditions of Transjordan and the Ancient Near East." Pages 111–120 in *Crossing Jordan: North*

American Contributions to the Archaeology of Jordan. Edited by Thomas E. Levy et al. London/Oakville: Equinox, 2007.

LEE, WON W. *Punishment and Forgiveness in Israel's Migratory Campaign*. Grand Rapids: Eerdmanns, 2003.

LEMAIRE, ANDRÉ. "Le 'pays de Hepher'et les 'filles de Zelophehad'á la lumière des ostraca de Samarie." *Sem* 22 (1972): 13–20.

–. "Galaad et Makîr: Remarques sur la tribu de Manassé à l'est du Jourdain." *VT* 31.1 (1981): 39–61.

–. "A propos de paḥad dans l'onomastique ouest-sémitique." *VT* 35.4 (1985): 500–501.

–. "The Mesha Stele and the Omri Dynasty." Pages 135–144 in *Ahab Agonistes: The Rise and Fall of the Omri Dynasty*. LHBOTS 421. Edited by Lester L. Grabbe. London: T&T Clark, 2007.

LEVIN, CHRISTOPH. *Fortsehreibungen: Gesammelte Studien zum Alten Testament*. BZAW 316. Berlin/New York: Walter de Gruyter, 2003.

–. "Introduction." Pages 1–10 in *The Concept of Exile in Ancient Israel and its Historical Contexts*. BZAW 404. Edited by Ehud Ben Zvi and Christoph Levin. Berlin: de Gruyter, 2010.

LEVINE, BARUCH A. *Numbers 1–20: A New Translation with Introduction and Commentary*. TAB 4. New York: Doubleday, 1993.

–. *Numbers 21–36: A New Translation with Introduction and Commentary*. TAB 4a. New Haven: Yale University Press, 2000.

LEVY, DANIEL and JACOB MILGROM. "עֵדָה." *TDOT* (1995): X:468–480.

LIPSCHITS, ODED. "The Rural Settlement in Judah in the Sixth Century B.C.E.: A Rejoinder." *PEQ* 136.2 (2013): 99–107.

–. "Bethel Revisited." Pages 233–246 in *Rethinking Israel: Studies in the History and Archaeology of Ancient Israel in Honor of Israel Finkelstein*. Edited by Oded Lipschits et al. Winona Lake: Eisenbrauns, 2017.

LIPSCHITS, ODED and JOSEPH BLENKINSOPP, eds. *Judah and the Judeans in the Neo-Babylonian Period*. Winona Lake: Eisenbrauns, 2003.

LISSOVSKY, NURIT and NADAV NA'AMAN. "A New Outlook at the Boundary System of the Twelve Tribes." Pages 291–332 in *Ugarit-Forschungen: Internationales Jahrbuch für die Altertumskunde Syrien-Palästinas*. UF 35. Edited by Manfried Dietrich and Oswald Loretz. Münster: Ugarit-Verlag, 2003.

LITKE, JOHN D. "The Daughters of Zelophehad." *CurTM* 29.3 (2002): 207–218.

LIVERANI, MARIO. "The Growth of the Assyrian Empire in the Habur/Middle Euphrates Area: A New Paradigm." *SAAB* 2.2 (1988): 81–98.

LLOYD, SETON and FUAD SAFAR. "Tell Hassuna: Excavations by the Iraq Government Directorate General of Antiquities in 1943 and 1944." *JNES* 4.4 (1945): 255–289.

LOHFINK, NORBERT. "Darstellungskunst und Theologie in Dtn 1,6–3,29." *Bib* 41 (1960): 105–134.

–. "Kerygmata des Deuteronomistischen Geschichtswerk." Pages 87–100 in *Die Botschaft und die Boten: Festschrift für Hans Walter Wolff zum 70. Geburtstag*. Edited by Hans Walter Wolff et al. Neukirchen-Vlyun: Neukirchener, 1981.

–. "הֶרֶם/הָרַם." *TDOT* (1990): V:180–199.

–. "יָרַשׁ." *TDOT* (1990): VI:368–396.

LONDON, GLORIA. "Reply to A. Zertal's 'The Wedge-Shaped Bowl and the Origin of the Samaritans.'" *BASOR* 286 (1992): 89–90.

LONERGAN, BERNARD. *Method in Theology*. Toronto: University of Toronto Press, 2007.

292   *Bibliography*

LUNDBOM, JACK R. *Deuteronomy: A Commentary*. Grand Rapids: Eerdmans Publishing, 2013.

MACDONALD, BURTON. "Ammonite Territory and Sites." Pages 30–56 in *Ancient Ammon. Studies in the History and Culture of the Ancient Near East 17*. Edited by Burton MacDonald, and Randall W. Younker. Leiden: Brill, 1999.

–. *"East of the Jordan": Territories and Sites of the Hebrew Scriptures*. ASOR 6. Boston: American Schools of Oriental Research, 2000.

MACDONALD, NATHAN. "The Book of Numbers." Pages 113–144 in *A Theological Introduction to the Pentateuch: Interpreting the Torah as Christian Scripture*. Edited by Richard S. Briggs and Joel N. Lohr. Grand Rapids: Baker Academic, 2012.

MAGEN, YITZHAK. *Mount Gerizim Excavations Volume II: A Temple City*. JSP 8. Jerusalem: Judea & Samaria Publishing, 2008.

MAGEN, YITZHAK ET AL. *Mount Gerizim Excavations Volume I: The Aramaic, Hebrew and Samaritan Inscriptions*. JSP 2. Jerusalem: Judea & Samaria Publications, 2004.

MANOR, DALE W. "Tirzah (Place)." *ABD* (1992): 6:573–577.

MARQUIS (FELDMAN), LIANE M. "The Composition of Numbers 32: A New Proposal." *VT* 63.3 (2013): 408–432.

MATHYS, HANS-PETER. "Numeri und Chronik: Nahe Verwandte." Pages 555–578 in *The Books of Leviticus and Numbers*. BETL 215. Edited by Thomas Römer. Leuven: Uitgeveru Peeters, 2008.

MATTHEWS, VICTOR H. and DON C. BENJAMIN. *Social World of Ancient Israel, 1250–587 BCE*. Peabody: Hendrickson Publishers, 1993.

MAZAR, AMIHAI. "Excavations at the Israelite Town at Khirbet Marjameh in the Hills of Ephraim." *IEJ* 45.2/3 (1995): 85–117.

MCCARTER JR., P. KYLE. *II Samuel: A New Translation with Introduction and Commentary*. TAB 9. New York, et el.: Yale University Press, 1984.

MCGOVERN, PATRICK E. "Beth-Shan (Place)." *ABD* (1992): 1:693–696.

MCKENZIE, STEVEN L. and M. Patrick Graham, eds. *The History of Israel's Traditions: The Heritage of Martin Noth*. JSOTSup 182. Sheffield: Scheffield Academic Press, 1994.

MENDENHALL, GEORGE E. "Amorites." *ABD* (1992): 1:199–202.

MILGROM, JACOB. *Numbers*. The JPS Torah Commentary. Philedelphia: Jewish Publication Society of America, 1990.

–. *Leviticus 1–16: A New Translation with Introduction and Commentary*. AB 3. New York: Doubleday, 1991.

–. *Leviticus 17–22: A New Translation with Introduction and Commentary*. AB 3a. New York: Doubleday, 2000.

–. *Leviticus 23–27: A New Translation with Introduction and Commentary*. AB 3b. New York: Doubleday, 2001.

MILLER, J. MAXWELL. "The Israelite Journey Through (around) Moab and Moabite Toponymy." *JBL* 108.4 (1989): 577–595.

MITTMANN, SIEGFRIED. *Deuteronomium 1:1–6:3: literarkritisch und traditionsgeschichtlich untersucht*. BZAW 139. Berlin: Walter de Gruyter, 1975.

–. "Die Gebietsbeschreibung des Stammes Ruben in Josua 13,15–23." *ZDPV* 111 (1995): 1–27.

NA'AMAN, NADAV. "Population Changes in Palestine Following Assyrian Deportations." *TA* 20 (1993): 104–124.

–. "Rezin of Damascus and the Land of Gilead." *ZDPV* 111.2 (1995): 105–117.

–. "King Mesha and the Foundation of the Moabite Monarchy." *IEJ* 47 (1997): 83–92.

–. "Rubutu/Aruboth." *UF* 32 (2000): 373–383.

–. "Solomon's District List (1 Kings 4:7–19) and the Assyrian Province System in Palestine." *UF* 33 (2001): 419–436.

–. "Josiah and the Kingdom of Judah." Pages 189–247 in *Good Kings and Bad Kings*. Edited by Lester L. Grabbe. London: T&T Clark, 2005.

–. "Province System and Settlement Pattern in Southern Syria and Palestine in the Neo-Assyrian Period." Pages 220–237 in *Ancient Israel and Its Neighbors: Interaction and Counteraction: Collected Essays Volume 1*. Winona Lake: Eisenbrauns, 2005.

–. "Royal Inscription Versus Prophetic Story: Mesha's Rebellion According to Biblical and Moabite Historiography." Pages 145–183 in *Ahab Agonistes: The Rise and Fall of the Omri Dynasty*. LHBOTS 421. Edited by Lester L. Grabbe. London: T&T Clark, 2007.

–. "When and How Did Jerusalem Become a Great City? The Rise of Jerusalem as Judah's Premier City in the Eighth–Seventh Centuries B.C.E." *BASOR* 347 (2007): 21–56.

–. "Does Archaeology Really Deserve the Status of a 'High Court' in Biblical Historical Research?" Pages 165–183 in *Between Evidence and Ideology: Essays on the History of Ancient Israel Read at the Joint Meeting of the Society for Old Testament Study and the Oud Testamentisch Werkgezelschap Lincoln, July 2009*. OTS. Edited by Bob Becking and Lester L. Grabbe. Leiden: Brill, 2010.

–. "Was Dor the Capital of an Assyrian Province." *TA* 36.1 (2013): 95–109.

–. "Dismissing the Myth of a Flood of Israelite Refugees in the Late Eighth Century BCE." *Zeitschrift für die Alttestamentliche Wissenschaft* 126.1 (2014): 1–14.

–. "The Jacob Story and the Formation of Biblical Israel." *TA* 41.1 (2014): 95–125.

–. "Rediscovering a Lost North Israelite Conquest Story." Pages 287–302 in *Rethinking Israel: Studies in the History and Archaeology of Ancient Israel in Honor of Israel Finkelstein*. Edited by Oded Lipschits et al. Winona Lake: Eisenbrauns, 2017.

Na'aman, Nadav and Ran Zadok. "Sargon II's Deportations to Israel and Philistia (716–708 B.C.)." *JCS* 40.1 (1988): 36–46.

Nelson, Richard D. *Joshua: A Commentary*. OTL. Louisville: John Knox Press, 1997.

–. *Deuteronomy: A Commentary*. OTL. Louisville: Westminster John Knox Press, 2002.

Neumann, Friederike. "Jacob, Laban, and the Two Daughters: Insights into the Formation of the Jacob-Laban Story (Genesis 29–31)." Pages 35–55 in *The History of the Jacob Cycle (Genesis 25–35): Recent Research on the Compilation, the Redaction and the Reception of the Biblical Narrative and Its Historical and Cultural Contexts*. ArchB 4. Edited by Benedikt Hensel. Tübingen: Mohr Siebeck, 2021.

Niditch, Susan. *War in the Hebrew Bible: A Study in the Ethics of Violence*. New York: Oxford University Press, 1993.

Nihan, Christophe. "The Holiness Code between D and P: Some Comments on the Function and Significance of Leviticus 17–26 in the Composition of the Torah." Pages 81–122 in *Das Deuteronomium zwischen Pentateuch und Deuteronomistischem Geschichtswerk*. FRLANT 206. Edited by Eckart Otto and Reinhard Achenbach. Göttingen: Vandenhoeck & Ruprecht, 2004.

–. "Review of Achenbach, Reinhard, 'Die Vollendung der Tora: Studien zur Redaktionsgeschichte des Numeribuches im Kontext von Hexateuch und Pentateuch.'" *RBL* (2006): NP.

–. *From Priestly Torah to Pentateuch*. FAT II 25. Tübingen: Mohr Siebeck, 2007.

–. "The Torah between Samaria and Judah: Shechem and Gerizim in Deuteronomy and Joshua." Pages 187–223 in *The Pentateuch as Torah: New Models for Understanding Its Promulgation and Acceptance*. Edited by Gary N. Knoppers and Bernard M. Levinson. Winona Lake: Eisenbrauns, 2007.

–. "The Priestly Covenant, Its Reinterpretations, and the Composition of 'P.'" Pages 87–134 in *The Strata of the Priestly Writings: Contemporary Debate and Future Directions.* ATANT 95. Edited by Sarah Shectman and Joel S. Baden. Zürich: Theologischer Verlag, 2009.

–. "The Literary Relationship between Deuteronomy and Joshua: A Reassessment." Pages 79–114 in *Deuteronomy in the Pentateuch, Hexateuch, and the Deuteronomistic History.* FAT II 56. Edited by Konrad Schmid and Raymond F. Person Jr. Tübingen: Mohr Siebeck, 2012.

NODET, ETIENNE. "Israelites, Samaritans, Temples, Jews." Pages 121–171 in *Samaria, Samarians, Samaritans: Studies on Bible, History and Linguistics.* SS 6. Edited by József Zsengellér. Göttingen: de Gruyter, 2011.

NÖLDEKE, THEODORE. *Untersuchungen zur Kritik des Alten Testaments.* Kiel: Schwers'sche Buchhandlung, 1869.

NOORT, ED. "Bis zur Grenze des Landes? Num 27:12–23 und das Ende der Priesterschrift." Pages 99–119 in *The Books of Leviticus and Numbers.* BETL 215. Edited by Thomas Römer. Leuven: Uitgeveru Peeters, 2008.

NOTH, MARTIN. *Das vierte Buch Mose: Numeri.* ATD 7. Göttingen: Vandenhoeck & Ruprecht, 1966.

–. *Geschichte Israels.* Göttingen: Vandenhoeck & Ruprecht, 1966.

–. *Überlieferungsgeschichtliche Studien I: Die sammelnden und bearbeitenden Geschichtswerke im Alten Testamentum.* ND Darmstadt: Wissenschaftliche Buchgesellschaft, 1967.

–. *Numbers.* Translated by James D. Martin. OTL London: SCM Press, 1968.

ODED, BUSTANAY. "II Kings 17: Between History and Polemic." *Jewish History* 2.2 (1987): 37–50.

OEMING, MANFRED. "Rethinking the Origins of Israel: 1 Chronicles 1–9 in the Light of Archaeology." Pages 303–318 in *Rethinking Israel: Studies in the History and Archaeology of Ancient Israel in Honor of Israel Finkelstein.* Edited by Oded Lipschits et al. Winona Lake: Eisenbrauns, 2017.

OLSON, DENNIS T. *The Death of the Old and the Birth of the New: The Framework of the Book of Numbers and the Pentateuch.* BJS 71. California: Scholars Press, 1985.

–. *Numbers.* Int. Louisville: John Knox Press, 1996.

OSWALD, WOLFGANG. "Die Revision des Edombildes in Numeri XX 14–21." *VT* 50.2 (2000): 218–232.

–. *Staatstheorie im Alten Israel: Der politische Diskurs im Pentateuch und in den Geschichtsbüchern des Alten Testaments.* Stuttgart: Kohlhammer, 2009.

OTTO, ECKART. "Forschungen zur Priesterschrift." *TRu* 62 (1997): 1–50.

–. *Das Deuteronomium: Politische Theologie und Rechtsreform in Juda und Assyrien.* BZAW 284. Berlin: Walter de Gruyter, 1999.

–. *Das Deuteronomium im Pentateuch und Hexateuch: Studien zur Literaturgeschichte von Pentateuch und Hexateuch im Lichte des Deuteronomiumrahmens.* FAT 30. Tübingen: Mohr Siebeck, 2000.

–. "Forschungen zum nachpriesterschriftlichen Pentateuch." *TRu* 67 (2002): 125–155.

–. "The Pentateuch in Synchronical and Diachronical Perspectives: Protorabbinic Scribal Erudition Mediating between Deuteronomy and the Priestly Code." Pages 14–35 in *Das Deuteronomium zwischen Pentateuch und Deuteronomistischem Geschichtswerk.* FRLANT 206. Edited by Eckart Otto and Reinhard Achenbach. Göttingen: Vandenhoeck & Ruprecht, 2004.

–. "Das postdeuteronomistische Deuteronomium als integrierender Schlußstein der Tora." Pages 71–102 in *Die deuteronomistischen Geschichtswerke: Redaktions- und religionsgeschichtliche Perspektiven zur "Deuteronomismus" – Diskussion in Tora und Vorderen Propheten*. BZAW 365. Edited by Jan Christian Gertz et al. Berlin: De Gruyter, 2006.

–. "A Hidden Truth Behind the Text or the Truth of the Text. At a Turning Point of Biblical Scholarship Two Hundred Years after De Wette's Dissertatio Critico-Exegetica." Pages 19–28 in *South African Perspectives on the Pentateuch Between Synchrony and Diachrony*. LHBOTS 463. Edited by Jurie le Roux and Eckart Otto. London: T&T Clark, 2007.

–. "The Pivotal Meaning of Pentateuch Research for a History of Israelite and Jewish Religion and Society." Pages 29–53 in *South African Perspectives on the Pentateuch Between Synchrony and Diachrony*. LHBOTS 463. Edited by Jurie le Roux and Eckart Otto. London: T&T Clark, 2007.

–. "The Holiness Code in Diachrony and Synchrony in the Legal Hermeneutics of the Pentateuch." Pages 135–156 in *The Strata of the Priestly Writings: Contemporary Debate and Future Directions*. ATANT 95. Edited by Sarah Shectman and Joel S. Baden. Zürich: Theologischer Verlag, 2009.

–. *Deuteronomium 1–11: Erster Teilband: 1,1–4,43*. HThKAT. Freiburg: Herder, 2012.

–. *Deuteronomium 1–11: Zweite Teilband: 4,44–11:32*. HThKAT Freiburg: Herder, 2012.

–. "The Integration of the Post-Exilic Book of Deuteronomy into the Post-Priestly Pentateuch." Pages 331–341 in *The Post-Priestly Pentateuch: New Perspectives on its Redactional Development and Theological Profiles*. FAT 101. Edited by Federico Giuntoli and Konrad Schmid. Tübingen: Mohr Siebeck, 2015.

–. *Deuteronomium 12–34: Erster Teilband: 12,1–23,15*. HThKAT. Freiburg: Herder, 2016.

–. *Deuteronomium 12–34: Zweiter Teilband: 23,16–34,12*. HThKAT. Freiburg: Herder, 2017.

PAKKALA, JUHA. *God's Word Omitted: Omissions in the Transmission of the Hebrew Bible*. FRLANT 251. Göttingen: Vandenhoeck & Ruprecht, 2013.

PAMUK, AYSE. "Geography of Immigrant Clusters in Global Cities: A Case Study of San Francisco, 2000*." *International Journal of Urban and Regional Research* 28.2 (2004): 287–307.

PARKER, BRADLEY J. "Garrisoning the Empire: Aspects of the Construction and Maintenance of Forts on the Assyrian Frontier." *Iraq* 59 (1997): 77–87.

PERLITT, LOTHAR. "Priesterschrift im Deuteronomium?" *ZAW* 100 (1988): 65–88.

PETERSON, JOHN L. and RAMI ARAV. "Rehob (Place)." *ABD* (1992): 5:660–661.

PETIT, THIERRY. *Satrapes et satrapies dans l'empire achéménide de Cyrus le Grand à Xerxès Ier*. Bibliothèque de la Faculté de Philosophie et Lettres de l'Université de Liège 254. Paris: Diffusion, 1990.

PITKÄNEN, PEKKA. *A Commentary on Numbers: Narrative, Ritual and Colonialism*. RSBW. Abingdon: Routledge, 2018.

PLÖGER, JOSEF G. *Literarkritische, formgeschichtliche und stilkritische Untersuchungen zum Deuteronomium*. BBB 26. Bonn: Peter Hanstein, 1967.

POLA, THOMAS. *Die ursprüngliche Priesterschrift: Beobachtungen zur Literarkritik und Traditionsgeschichte von Pg*. WMANT 70. Neukirchen-Vlyun: Neukirchener, 1995.

PORTEN, BEZALEL ET AL. *The Elephantine Papyri in English: Three Millennia of Cross-Cultural Continuity and Change*. DMOA 22. Leiden: E. J. Brill, 1996.

PORTER, ANNE. "You Say Potato, I Say … Typology, Chronology and the Origins of the Amorites." Pages 69–115 in *Sociétés humaines et changement climatique à la fin du troisième millénaire: une crise a-t-elle eu lieu en Haute Mésopotamie?* Varia

Anatolica XIX. Edited by Catherine Kuzucuoğlu and Catherine Marro. Istanbul: Institut français d'études anatoliennes, 2007.

PRITCHARD, JAMES B., ed. *Ancient Near Eastern Texts Relating to the Old Testament.* Princeton: Princeton University Press, 1969.

PUMMER, REINHARD. *The Samaritans: A Profile.* Grand Rapids: Eerdmans Publishing, 2016.

PYSCHNY, KATHARINA. *Verhandelte Führung: Eine Analyse von Num 16–17 im Kontext der neueren Pentateuchforschung.* HBS 88. Freiburg: Herder, 2017.

RAINY, ANSON F. *The El-Amarna Correspondence: A New Edition of the Cuneiform Letters from the Site of El-Amarna based on Collations of all Extant Tablets.* Vol. 1. Edited by William M. Schniedewind. Leiden/Boston: Brill, 2015.

REISNER, GEORGE ANDREW ET AL. *Harvard Excavations at Samaria 1908–1910: Volume I. Text.* Harvard Semitic Series. Cambridge: Harvard University Press, 1924.

RENDSBURG, GARY A. "The Internal Consistency and Historical Reliability of the Biblical Genealogies." *VT* 40.2 (1990): 187–206.

RENDTORFF, ROLF. *Das überlieferungsgeschichtliche Problem des Pentateuch.* BZAW 147. Berlin: De Gruyter, 1977.

ROBKER, JONATHAN MILES. "The Balaam Narrative in the Pentateuch/Hexateuch/Enneateuch." Pages 334–366 in *Torah and the Book of Numbers.* FAT II 62. Edited by Christian Frevel et al. Tübingen: Mohr Siebeck, 2013.

–. *Balaam in Text and Tradition.* FAT 131. Tübingen: Mohr Siebeck, 2019.

ROGERSON, J.W. "Protestant Biblical Scholarship on the European Continent and in Great Britain and Ireland." Pages 203–222 in *Hebrew Bible/Old Testament the History of Its Interpretation. III/1.* Edited by Magne Sæbø. Göttingen: Vandenhoeck & Ruprecht, 2013.

RÖLLIG, WOLFGANG. "Eine neue phönizische Inschrift aus Byblos." *Neue Ephemeris für Semitische Epigraphik* 2 (1974): 1–15.

RÖMER, THOMAS. *Israels Väter: Untersuchungen zur Väterthematik im Deuteronomium und in der deuteronomistischen Tradition.* OBO 99. Göttingen: Vandenhoeck & Ruprecht, 1990.

–. "Nombres 11–12 et la question d'une rédaction deutéronomique dans le Pentateuque." Pages 481–498 in *Deuteronomy and Deuteronomic Literature: Festschrift C.H.W. Brekelmans.* BETL 133. Edited by Marc Vervenne and Johan Lust. Leuven: Leuven University Press, 1997.

– ., ed. *The Future of the Deuteronomistic History.* BETL 147. Leuven: Leuven University Press, 2000.

–. "Das Buch Numeri und das Ende des Jahwisten Anfragen zur 'Quellenscheidung' im vierten Buch des Pentateuch." Pages 215–231 in *Abschied vom Jahwisten: Die Komposition des Hexateuch in der jüngsten Diskussion.* BZAW 315. Edited by Jan Christian Gertz et al. Berlin: De Gruyter, 2002.

–. "Nombres." Pages 198–210 in *Introduction à l'Ancien Testament.* Edited by Thomas Römer et al. Genève: Labor et Fides, 2004.

–. "Das doppelte Ende des Josuabuches: einige Anmerkungen zur aktuellen Diskussion um 'deuteronomistisches Geschichtswerk' und 'Hexateuch.'" *ZAW* 118.4 (2006): 523–548.

–. "Entstehungsphasen des 'deuteronomistichen Geschichtswerkes.'" Pages 45–70 in *Die deuteronomistischen Geschichtswerke: Redaktions- und religionsgeschichtliche Perspektiven zur "Deuteronomismus" – Diskussion in Tora und Vorderen Propheten.* BZAW 365. Edited by Jan Christian Gertz et al. Berlin: De Gruyter, 2006.

–. "The Elusive Yahwist: A Short History of Research." Pages 9–27 in *A Farewell to the Yahwist? The Composition of the Pentateuch in Recent European Interpretations.* SBLSymS 34. Edited by Thomas B. Dozeman and Konrad Schmid. Atlanta: Society of Biblical Literature, 2006.

–. "Israel's Sojourn in the Wilderness and the Construction of the Book of Numbers." Pages 419–445 in *Reflection and Refraction: Studies in Biblical Historiography in Honour of A. Graeme Auld.* VTSup 113. Edited by Robert Rezetko et al. Leiden: Brill, 2007.

–. "De la périphérie au centre: Les livres du Lévitique et des Nombres dans le débat actuel sur le Pentateuque." Pages 3–34 in *The Books of Leviticus and Numbers.* BETL 215. Edited by Thomas Römer. Leuven: Uitgeveru Peeters, 2008.

– , ed. *The Books of Leviticus and Numbers.* Vol. 215, BETL. Leuven: Uitgeveru Peeters, 2008.

–. "How Many Books (teuchs): Pentateuch, Hexateuch, Deuteronomistic History, or Enneateuch?" Pages 25–42 in *Pentateuch, Hexateuch, or Enneateuch?* AIL 8. Edited by Thomas B. Dozeman et al. Atlanta: Society of Biblical Literature, 2011.

–. "Tracking Some 'Censored' Moses Traditions Inside and Outside the Hebrew Bible." *HBAI* 1 (2012): 64–76.

–. "'Higher Criticism': The Historical and Literary-critical Approach – with Special Reference to the Pentateuch." Pages 393–423 in *Hebrew Bible/Old Testament the History of Its Interpretation. III/1.* Edited by Magne Sæbø. Göttingen: Vandenhoeck & Ruprecht, 2013.

–. "Deuteronomistic History." *EBR* (2013): 6:648–653.

–. "Egypt Nostalgia in Exodus 14 – Numbers 21." Pages 66–86 in *Torah and the Book of Numbers.* FAT II 62. Edited by Christian Frevel et al. Tübingen: Mohr Siebeck, 2013.

–. "How to Write a Literary History of the Hebrew Bible? A Response to David Carr and Konrad Schmid." *Indian Theological Studies* 50 (2013): 9–20.

–. "Zwischen Urkunden, Fragmenten und Ergänzungen: Zum Stand der Pentateuchforschung." *Zeitschrift für die Alttestamentliche Wissenschaft* 125 (2013): 2–24.

–. "The Problem of the Hexateuch." Pages 813–827 in *The Formation of the Pentateuch: Bridging the Academic Cultures of Europe, Israel and North America.* FAT 111. Edited by Jan C. Gertz et al. Tübingen: Mohr Siebeck, 2016.

–. "How Jeroboam II became Jeroboam I." *HBAI* 6.3 (2017): 372–382.

–. "Eckart Otto's Contributions to Pentateuchal Research." *Verbum et Ecclesia* 40.1 (2019): 1–7.

RÖMER, THOMAS and MARC Z. BRETTLER. "Deuteronomy 34 and the Case for a Persian Hexateuch." *JBL* 119 (2000): 401–420.

RON, ZVI. "The Daughters of Zelophehad." *JBQ* 26 (1998): 260–262.

ROSE, MARTIN. "Deuteronomistic Ideology and Theology of the Old Testament." Pages 424–455 in *Israel Constructs Its History: Deuteronomistic Historiography in Recent Research.* Edited by Albert de Pury et al. Sheffield: Sheffield Academic Press, 2000.

ROSKOP ERISMAN, ANGELA. "Transjordan in Deuteronomy: The Promised Land and the Formation of the Pentateuch." *JBL* 132.4 (2013): 769–789.

–. "For the Border of the Ammonites Was ... Where? Historical Geography and Biblical Interpretation in Numbers 21." Pages 761–776 in *The Formation of the Pentateuch: Bridging the Academic Cultures of Europe, Israel and North America.* FAT 111. Edited by Jan C. Gertz et al. Tübingen: Mohr Siebeck, 2016.

ROSKOP, ANGELA R. *The Wilderness Itineraries: Genre, Geography, and the Growth of Torah.* HACL 3. Winona Lake: Eisenbrauns, 2011.

298 *Bibliography*

Roth, Martha T. *Law Collections from Mesopotamia and Asia Minor.* WAW 6. Atlanta: Scholars Press, 1995.

Rudnig, Thilo Alexander. "Gemeinde (At)." (2014): https://www.bibelwissenschaft. de/stichwort/19220/2020).

Magne Sæbø, ed. *Hebrew Bible and Old Testament: The History of Its Interpretation: The Nineteenth Century.* Vol. 3.1, Göttingen: Vandenhoeck & Ruprecht, 2013.

Sakenfeld, Katharine Doob. "Zelophehad's Daughters." *PRSt* 15 (1988): 37–47.

Samuel, Harald. *Von Priestern zum Patriarchen: Levi und die Leviten im Alten Testament.* BZAW 448. Berlin/Boston: Walter de Gruyter, 2014.

Satlow, Michael L. *Jewish Marriage in Antiquity.* Princeton: Princeton University Press, 2001.

Schenker, Adrian. "What Connects the Incest Prohibitions with the Other Prohibitions Listed in Leviticus 18 and 20?" Pages 162–185 in *The Book of Leviticus: Composition and Reception.* VTSup 93. Edited by Rolf Rendtorff and Robert A. Kugler. Leiden: Brill, 2003.

Schmid, Hans Heinrich. *Der sogennante Jahwist: Beobachtungen und Fragen zur Pentateuchforschung.* Zürich: Theologischer Verlag, 1976.

Schmid, Konrad. "Zurück zu Wellhausen?" *TRu* 69 (2004): 314–328.

–. "Hatte Wellhausen Recht? Das Problem der literarhistorischen Anfänge des Deuteronomismus in den Königebüchern." Pages 19–43 in *Die deuteronomistischen Geschichtswerke: Redaktions- und religionsgeschichtliche Perspektiven zur "Deuteronomismus" – Diskussion in Tora und Vorderen Propheten.* BZAW 365. Edited by Jan Christian Gertz et al. Berlin: De Gruyter, 2006.

–. "The So-Called Yahwist and the Literary Gap Between Genesis and Exodus." Pages 29–50 in *A Farewell to the Yahwist? The Composition of the Pentateuch in Recent European Interpretations.* SymS 34. Edited by Thomas B. Dozeman and Konrad Schmid. Atlanta: Society of Biblical Literature, 2006.

–. "Der Pentateuchredaktor: Beobachtungen zum Theologischen Profil des Toraschlusses in Dtn 34." Pages 183–197 in *Les dernières rédactions du Pentateuque, de l'Hexateuque et de l'Ennéateuque.* BETL 203. Edited by Thomas Römer and Konrad Schmid. Leuven: Leuven University Press, 2007.

–. *Genesis and the Moses Story: Israel's Dual Origins in the Hebrew Bible.* Siphrut 3. Winona Lake: Eisenbrauns, 2010.

–. "Judean Identity and Ecumenicity: The Political Theology of the Priestly Document." Pages 3–26 in *Judah and the Judeans in the Achaemenid Period: Negotiating Identity in an International Context.* Edited by Oded Lipschits et al. Winona Lake: Eisenbrauns, 2011.

–. "The Emergence and Disappearance of the Separation Between the Pentateuch and the Deuteronomistic History in Biblical Studies." Pages 11–24 in *Pentateuch, Hexateuch, or Enneateuch?* AIL 8. Edited by Thomas B. Dozeman et al. Atlanta: Society of Biblical Literature, 2011.

–. "Deuteronomy within the 'Deuteronomistic Histories' in Genesis–2 Kings." Pages 8–30 in *Deuteronomy in the Pentateuch, Hexateuch, and the Deuteronomistic History.* FAT II 56. Edited by Konrad Schmid and Raymond F. Person Jr. Tübingen: Mohr Siebeck, 2012.

–. "Die Samaritaner und die Judäer: Die biblische Diskussion um ihr Verhältnis in Josua 24." Pages 31–49 in *The Samaritans and the Bible: Historical and Literary Interactions between Biblical and Samaritan Traditions.* SJ 70. Edited by Jörg Frey et al. Berlin: De Gruyter, 2012.

–. *The Old Testament: A Literary History.* Minneapolis: Fortress Press, 2012.

–. "Exodus in the Pentateuch." Pages 27–60 in *The Book of Exodus: Composition, Reception, and Interpretation.* VTSup 164. Edited by Thomas B. Dozeman et al. Leiden: Brill, 2014.

–. "Distinguishing the World of the Exodus Narrative from the World of Its Narrators: The Question of the Priestly Exodus Account in Its Historical Setting." Pages 331–344 in *Israel's Exodus in Transdisciplinary Perspective: Text, Archaeology, Culture, and Geoscience.* Quantitative Methods in the Humanities and Social Sciences. Edited by Thomas E. Levy et al. Heidelburg: Springer, 2015.

–. "Von Jakob zu Israel: Das antike Israel auf dem Weg zum Judentum im Spiegel der Fortschreibungsgeschichte der Jakobüberlieferungen der Genesis." Pages 33–67 in *Identität und Schrift: Fortschreibungsprozesse als Mittel religiöser Identitätsbildung.* BThSt 169. Edited by Marianne Grohmann. Neukirchen-Vlyun: Neukirchener, 2017.

–. "Shifting Political Theologies in the Literary Development of the Jacob Cycle." Pages 11–24 in *The History of the Jacob Cycle (Genesis 25–35): Recent Research on the Compilation, the Redaction and the Reception of the Biblical Narrative and Its Historical and Cultural Contexts.* ArchB 4. Edited by Benedikt Hensel. Tübingen: Mohr Siebeck, 2021.

SCHMIDT, LUDWIG. *Studien zur Priesterschrift.* BZAW 214. Berlin: De Gruyter, 1993.

–. "Literatur zum Buch Numeri." *TRu* 63 (1998): 241–266.

–. "Die Ansiedlung von Ruben und Gad im Ostjordanland in Numeri 32,1–38." *ZAW* 114 (2002): 497–510.

–. "Die Kundschaftererzählung in Num 13–14 und Dtn 1,19–46: Eine Kritik neuerer Pentateuchkritik." *ZAW* 114 (2002): 40–58.

–. "Leviten-und Asylstädte in Num. XXXV und Jos. XX; XXI 1–42." *VT* 52 (2002): 103–121.

–. "Bileam: Vom Seher zum Propheten Jahwes: Die literarischen Schichten der Bileam-Perikope (Num 22–24)." Pages 333–351 in *Gott und Mensch im Dialog: Festschrift für Otto Kaiser zum 80. Geburtstag.* BZAW 345/1. Edited by Markus Witte. Berlin: De Gruyter, 2004.

–. *Das vierte Buch Mose: Numeri 10,11–36,13.* ATD 7/2. Göttingen: Vandenhoeck & Ruprecht, 2004.

–. "Neuere Literatur zum Buch Numeri (1996–2003)." *TRu* 70 (2005): 389–407.

–. "Sihon und Og in Num 21,21 ff. und Dtn 2,24 ff. – Ein Beitrag zur Entstehung des Buches Numeri." Pages 314–333 in *Torah and the Book of Numbers.* FAT II 62. Edited by Christian Frevel et al. Tübingen: Mohr Siebeck, 2013.

SCHMITT, HANS-CHRISTOPH. "Das Hesbonlied Num. 21,27aßb–30 und die Geschichte der Stadt Hesbon." *ZDPV* 104 (1988): 26–43.

SCHORCH, STEFAN. "La formation de la communauté samaritaine au 2e siècle avant J.-Chr. et la culture de lecture de Judaïsme." Pages 5–20 in *Un carrefour dans l'histoire de la Bible: Du texte à la théologie au IIe siècle avant J.-C.* OBO 233. Edited by Innocent Himbaza and Adrian Schenker. Göttingen: Vandenhoeck & Ruprecht, 2007.

–. "The Samaritan Version of Deuteronomy and the Origin of Deuteronomy." Pages 23–37 in *Samaria, Samarians, Samaritans: Studies on Bible, History and Linguistics.* SS 6. Edited by József Zsengellér. Göttingen: de Gruyter, 2011.

–. "Der Pentateuch der Samaritaner: Seine Erforschung und seine Bedeutung für das Verständnis des altestamentlichen Bibeltextes." Pages 5–29 in *The Samaritans and the Bible: Historical and Literary Interactions between Biblical and Samaritan Traditions.* SJ 70. Edited by Jörg Frey et al. Berlin: De Gruyter, 2012.

300 Bibliography

–. "Der Samaritanische Pentateuch in der Geschichte des hebräischen Bibeltextes." *VF* 60.1 (2015): 18–28.

SCHORN, ULRIKE. *Ruben und das System der Zwölf Stämme Israels.* BZAW 248. Berlin: Walter de Gruyter, 1997.

SCHWARTZ, BARUCH J. "Introduction: The Strata of the Priestly Writings and the Revised Relative Dating of P and H." Pages 1–12 in *The Strata of the Priestly Writings: Contemporary Debate and Future Directions.* ATANT 95. Edited by Sarah Shectman and Joel S. Baden. Zürich: Theologischer Verlag, 2009.

SEEBASS, HORST. "zu Num. X 33 f." *VT* 14 (1964): 111–113.

–. "Num. XI, XII und die Hypothese des Jahwisten." *VT* 28 (1978): 214–223.

–. "Machir im Ostjordanland." *VT* 32 (1982): 496–503.

–. "Einige Vertrauenswürdige nachrichten zu Israels anfängen: zu den Söhnen Hobabs, Sichon und Bileam im Buch Numeri." *JBL* 113 (1994): 577–585.

–. "Zur literarischen Gestalt der Bileam-Perikope." *ZAW* 107 (1995): 409–419.

–. "Pentateuch." *TRE* 26 (1996): 185–209.

–. "Edom und seine Umgehung nach Numeri XX–XXI: Zu Numeri XXI 10–13." *VT* 47 (1997): 255–262.

–. "Erwägungen zu Numeri 32:1–38." *JBL* 118 (1999): 33–48.

–. *Numeri: 2. Teilband. Numeri 10,11–22,1.* BKAT 4/2. Neukirchen-Vlyun: Neukirchener, 2003.

–. "'Holy' Land in the Old Testament: Numbers and Joshua." *VT* 56 (2006): 92–104.

–. *Numeri: 3. Teilband. Numeri 22,2–36,13.* BKAT 4/3. Neukirchen-Vlyun: Neukirchener, 2007.

–. "Das Buch Numeri in der Heutigen Pentateuchdiskussion." Pages 233–259 in *The Books of Leviticus and Numbers.* BETL 215. Edited by Thomas Römer. Leuven: Uitgeveru Peeters, 2008.

–. "Ein Fall am Rande des Rechts: Das Gottesurteil von Num 5,11–31." Pages 188–199 in *"Gerechtigkeit und Recht zu üben" (Gen 18,19): Studien zur altorientalischen und biblischen Rechtsgeschichte, zur Religionsgeschichte Israels und zur Religionssoziologie; Festschrift für Eckart Otto zum 65. Geburtstag.* Edited by Reinhard Achenbach and Martin Arneth. Wiesbaden: Harrassowitz, 2009.

–. "Old and New, Memory of Failure and Outlook for Renewal in the Book of Numbers." Pages 265–279 in *Geschichte Israels und deuteronomistisches Geschichtsdenken: Festschrift zum 70. Geburtstag von Winfried Thiel.* Edited by Peter Mommer and Andreas Scherer. Münster: Ugarit-Verlag, 2010.

–. "Das Buch Josua als Literarisch nicht zu erwartende Forsetzung des Buch Numeri." Pages 249–257 in *The Book of Joshua.* Edited by Ed Noort. Leuven: Uitgevarij Peeters, 2012.

–. *Numeri: 1. Teilband. Numeri 1,1–10,10.* BKAT 4/1. Göttingen: Neukirchener Theologie, 2012.

–. "Numeri als eigene Komposition." Pages 87–108 in *Torah and the Book of Numbers.* FAT II 62. Edited by Christian Frevel et al. Tübingen: Mohr Siebeck, 2013.

SERGI, OMER. "The Gilead between Aram and Israel: Political Borders, Cultural Interaction and the Question of Jacob and Israelite Identity." Pages 333–354 in *In Search of Aram and Israel: Politics, Culture, and Identity.* ORA 20. Edited by Omer Sergi et al. Tübingen: Mohr Siebeck, 2016.

–. "The United Monarchy and the Kingdom of Jeroboam II in the Story of Absalom and Sheba's Revolts (2 Samuel 15–20)." *HBAI* 6.3 (2017): 329–353.

–. "Jacob and the Aramean Identity of Ancient Israel between the Judges and the Prophets." Pages 283–305 in *The Politics of the Ancestors: Exegetical and Historical Perspectives on Genesis 12–36*. FAT 124. Edited by Mark G. Brett, and Jakob Wöhrle. Tübingen: Mohr Siebeck, 2018.

SHECTMAN, SARAH and JOEL S. BADEN, eds. *The Strata of the Priestly Writings: Contemporary Debate and Future Directions*. ATANT 95. Zürich: Theologischer Verlag, 2009.

SIMONS, J. "Two Connected Problems Relating to the Israelite Settlement in Transjordan." *PEQ* 79.1 (1947): 27–39.

–. "Two Connected Problems Relating to the Israelite Settlement in Transjordan." *PEQ* 79.2 (1947): 87–101.

SINGER-AVITZ, LILY. "On Pottery in Assyrian Style: A Rejoinder." *TA* 34.2 (2007): 182–203.

SKA, JEAN LOUIS. "The Yahwist, a Hero with a Thousand Faces: A Chapter in the History of Modern Exegesis." Pages 1–23 in *Abschied vom Jahwisten: Die Komposition des Hexateuch in der jüngsten Diskussion*. BZAW 315. Edited by Jan Christian Gertz et al. Berlin: De Gruyter, 2002.

–. "Le récit sacerdotal. Une 'histoire sans fin'?" Pages 631–653 in *The Books of Leviticus and Numbers*. BETL 215. Edited by Thomas Römer. Leuven: Uitgeveru Peeters, 2008.

SMELIK, K. A. D. "Moabite Inscriptions: The Inscription of King Mesha." *COS* 2 (2000): 137–138.

SMEND, RUDOLF. "The Work of Abraham Kuenen and Julius Wellhausen." Pages 424–453 in *Hebrew Bible/Old Testament: The History of Its Interpretation. III/1*. Edited by Magne Sæbø. Göttingen: Vandenhoeck & Ruprecht, 2013.

SMOAK, JEREMY. "Arubboth." *EBR* (2009): 2:870–872.

SNAITH, NORMAN H. "The Daughters of Zelophehad." *VT* 16 (1966): 124–127.

SPEIER, SALOMON. "Bemerkungen zu Amos." *VT* 3.3 (1953): 305–310.

STACKERT, JEFFREY. *Rewriting the Torah*. Tübingen: Mohr Siebeck, 2007.

–. "The Holiness Legislation and Its Pentateuchal Sources: Revision, Supplementation, and Replacement." Pages 187–204 in *The Strata of the Priestly Writings: Contemporary Debate and Future Directions*. ATANT 95. Edited by Sarah Shectman and Joel S. Baden. Zürich: Theologischer Verlag, 2009.

STAUBLI, THOMAS. *Die Bücher Levitikus Numeri*. NSKAT 3. Stuttgart: Katholisches Bibelwerk, 1996.

STERN, EPHRAIM. *Archaeology of the Land of the Bible: Volume II: The Assyrian, Babylonian, and Persian Periods 732–332 BCE*. AYBRL. New Haven/London: Yale University Press, 2001.

STORDALEN, TERJE. "Heshbon: The History of a Biblical Memory." Pages 246–263 in *New Perspectives on Old Testament Prophecy and History: Essays in Honour of Hans M. Barstad*. Edited by Rannfrid I. Thelle et al. Leiden: Koninklijke Brill, 2015.

TADMOR, HAYIM. "The Southern Border of Aram." *IEJ* 12.2 (1962): 114–122.

TADMOR, HAYIM and SHIGEO YAMADA. *The Royal Inscriptions of Tiglath-pileser III (744–727 BC), and Shalmaneser V (726–722 BC), Kings of Assyria*. RINP 1. Winona Lake: Eisenbrauns, 2011.

TAMMUZ, ODED. "On Ideology and Lions: A Hypothesis on the Authorship of 2 Kgs 17:7–41." *UF* 49 (2018): 305–317.

TÄUBLER, EUGEN. *Biblische Studien: Die Epoche der Richter*. Edited by Hans-Jürgen Zobel. Tübingen: J. C. B. Mohr, 1958.

302   Bibliography

TAVGER, AHARON. "E.P. 914 East of Beitin and the Location of the Ancient Cult Site of Bethel (Hebrew)." *In the Highland's Depth: Ephraim Range and Binyamin Research Studies* 5 (2015): 49–69.

TAYLOR, MARION ANN. "Hoglah (Person)." *ABD* (1992): 3:237.

TIMM, STEFAN. *Moab zwischen den Mächten: Studien zu historischen Denkmälern und Texten.* ÄAT 17. Wiesbaden: Otto Harrassowitz, 1989.

TOBOLOWSKY, ANDREW. *The Sons of Jacob and the Sons of Herakles: The History of the Tribal System and the Organization of Biblical Identity.* FAT II 96. Tübingen: Mohr Siebeck, 2017.

TOLKIEN, J. R. R. *Tolkien on Fairy-stories.* Edited by Verlyn Flieger and Douglas A. Anderson. London: Harper Collins, 2008.

TOV, EMANUEL. *Textual Criticism of the Hebrew Bible.* Minneapolis: Fortress Press, 1992.

UEHLINGER, CHRISTOPH. "Göttinen in der Welt und Umwelt des antiken Israel." Pages 18–29 in *Die weibliche Seite Gottes.* Edited by Michaela Feurstein-Prasser and Felicitas Heimann-Jelinek. Wien: Bucher, 2017.

ULRICH, DEAN R. "The Framing Function of the Narratives about Zelophehad's Daughters." *JETS* 41.4 (1998): 529–538.

VAN DER TOORN, KAREL. *Family Religion in Babylonia, Syria & Israel: Continuity & Change in the Forms of Religious Life.* Leiden/New York/Köln: Brill, 1996.

VAN SETERS, JOHN. "The Conquest of Sihon's Kingdom: A Literary Examination." *JBL* 91 (1969): 182–197.

–. "Critical notes: Once Again – The Conquest of Sihon's Kingdom." *JBL* 99 (1980): 117–124.

–. *Prologue to History: The Yahwist as Historian in Genesis.* Westminster: John Knox Press, 1992.

–. *The Life of Moses: The Yahwist as Historian in Exodus–Numbers.* Louisville: Westminster/John Knox Press, 1994.

–. "The Deuteronomistic Redaction of the Pentateuch: The Case Against it." Pages 301–319 in *Deuteronomy and Deuteronomic Literature: Festschrift C.H.W. Brekelmans.* BETL 133. Edited by Marc Vervenne and Johan Lust. Leuven: Leuven University Press, 1997.

–. "The Deuteronomistic History: Can it Avoid Death by Redaction?" Pages 213–222 in *The Future of the Deuteronomistic History.* BETL 147. Edited by Thomas C. Römer. Leuven: Leuven University Press, 2000.

–. *The Edited Bible: The Curious History of the "Editor" in Biblical Criticism.* Winona Lake: Eisenbrauns, 2006.

VERVENNE, MARC and JOHAN LUST, eds. *Deuteronomy and Deuteronomic Literature: Festschrift C.H.W. Brekelmans.* BETL 133. Leuven: Leuven University Press, 1997.

VON RAD, GERHARD. *Das 1. Buch Mose: Genesis.* ATD 2–4. Göttingen: Vandenhoeck & Ruprecht, 1987.

WEIMAR, PETER. *Untersuchungen zur Redaktionsgeschichte des Pentateuch.* BZAW 146. Berlin/New York: Walter de Gruyter, 1977.

–. *Studien zur Priesterschrift.* FAT 56. Tübingen: Mohr Siebeck, 2008.

WEINFELD, MOSHE. *Deuteronomy 1–11: A New Translation with Introduction and Commentary.* TAB 5. New York: Doubleday, 1991.

WEINGART, KRISTIN. "'Jakob hatte zwölf Söhne' (Gen 35,22): Die Konstruktion kollektiver Identität im alten Israel." *Wort und Antwort* 60.2 (2019): 53–58.

WEINGREEN, JACOB. "The Case of the Daughters of Zelophchad." *VT* 16 (1966): 518–522.

Weippert, Manfred. "The Israelite 'Conquest' and the Evidence from Transjordan*." Pages 15–34 in *Symposia Celebrating the Seventy-Fifth Anniversary of the Founding of the American Schools of Oriental Research (1900–1975)*. Edited by Frank Moore Cross. Cambridge: American Schools of Oriental Research, 1979.

–. *Historisches Textbuch zum Alten Testament. Grundrisse zum Alten Testament*. Vol. 10. Göttingen: Vandenhoeck & Ruprecht, 2010.

Wellhausen, Julius. *Prolegomena to the History of Israel*. Translated by J. Sutherland Black and Allan Menzies. Evinity Publishing, [1885] 2009.

–. *Die Composition des Hexateuchs und der Historischen Bücher des Alten Testaments*. Berlin: Georg Reimer, 1899.

Wenham, Gordon J. *Numbers: An Introduction and Commentary*. TOTC 4. Leicester: Inter-Varsity Press, 1981.

Wevers, John William. *Notes on the Greek Text of Numbers*. SCS 46. Atlanta: Scholars Press, 1998.

Wise, Michael Owen. *A Critical Study of the Temple Scroll from Qumran Cave 11*. SAOC 49. Chicago: The University of Chicago, 1990.

Witte, Markus. *Die biblische Urgeschichte: Redaktions- und theologiegeschichtliche Beobachtungen zu Genesis 1,1–11,26*. BZAW 265. Berlin: De Gruyter, 1998.

–. "Der Segen Bileams – eine redaktionsgeschichtliche Problemanzeige zum 'Jahwisten' in Num 22–24." Pages 191–213 in *Abschied vom Jahwisten: Die Komposition des Hexateuch in der jüngsten Diskussion*. BZAW 315. Edited by Jan Christian Gertz et al. Berlin: De Gruyter, 2002.

Wöhrle, Jakob. *Fremdlinge im eigenen Land: Zur Entstehung und Intention der priesterlichen Passagen der Vätergeschichte*. FRLANT 246. Göttingen: Vandenhoeck & Ruprecht, 2012.

–. "Koexistenz durch Unterwerfung: Zur Entstehung und politischen Intention der vorpriesterlichen Jakoberzählung." Pages 307–327 in *The Politics of the Ancestors: Exegetical and Historical Perspectives on Genesis 12–36*. FAT 124. Edited by Mark G. Brett and Jakob Wöhrle. Tübingen: Mohr Siebeck, 2018.

Wolff, Hans Walter. "The Elohistic Fragments in the Pentateuch." *Int* 26.2 (1972): 158–173.

Wright, John W. "Remapping Yehud: The Borders of Yehud and the Genealogies of Chronicles." Pages 67–89 in *Judah and the Judeans in the Persian Period*. Edited by Oded Lipschits and Manfred Oeming. Winona Lake: Eisenbrauns, 2006.

Wüst, Manfried. *Untersuchungen zu den siedlungsgeographischen Texten des Altes Testaments: I. Ostjordanland*. BTAVO 9. Wiesbaden: Dr. Ludwig Reichert, 1975.

Yadin, Yigael. "Expedition D – The Cave of the Letters." *IEJ* 12.3/4 (1962): 227–257.

Yoo, Philip Y. "Delegitimizing a Witness: Composition and Revision in Joshua 22." *JHebS* 18 (2018): 1–21.

Zenger, Erich. "Priesterschrift." *TRE* 27 (1997): 435–436.

Zenger, Erich and Christian Frevel. "Die Bücher Levitikus und Numeri als Teile der Pentateuchkomposition." Pages 35–74 in *The Books of Leviticus and Numbers*. BETL 215. Edited by Thomas Römer. Leuven: Uitgeveru Peeters, 2008.

Zenger, Erich et al. *Einleitung in das Alte Testament*. Edited by Christian Frevel. Kohlhammer Studienbücher Theologie 1,1. Stuttgart: Kohlhammer, 2016.

Zertal, Adam. "The Wedge-Shaped Decorated Bowl and the Origin of the Samaritans." *BASOR* 276 (1989): 77–84.

–. "The Pahwah of Samaria (Northern Israel) during the Persian Period. Types of Settlement, Economy, History and New Discoveries." *Transeu* 3 (1990): 9–15.

–. "Arubboth (Place)." *ABD* (1992): 1:465–467.

–. "The Province of Samaria (Assyrian Samerina) in the Late Iron Age (Iron Age III)." Pages 377–412 in *Judah and the Judeans in the Neo-Babylonian Period*. Edited by Oded Lipschits and Joseph Blenkinsopp. Winona Lake: Eisenbrauns, 2003.

–. *The Manasseh Hill Country Survey: Volume I: The Shechem Syncline*. CHANE 21.1. Leiden: Brill, 2004.

–. *The Manasseh Hill Country Survey: Volume II: The Eastern Valleys and the Fringes of the Desert*. CHANE 21.2. Leiden: Brill, 2008.

ZERTAL, ADAM and NIVI MIRKAM. *The Manasseh Hill Country Survey: Volume III: From Nahal 'Iron to Nahal Schechem*. Edited by Shay Bar. CHANE 21.3. Leiden: Brill, 2016.

ZIEMER, BENJAMIN. *Kritik des Wachstumsmodells: Die Grenzen alttestamentlicher Redaktionsgeschichte im Lichte empirische Evidenz*. VTSup 182. Leiden/Boston: Brill, 2020.

ZOBEL, HANS-JÜRGEN. "כְּנַעַן." *TDOT* VII (1995): 211–228.

–. "מִשְׁפָּחָה." *TDOT* IX (1995): 79–85.

Index of Ancient Sources

Genesis

1:28	61, 106
12:6–8	52
12:8	48
13:6	155–156
14:13	138
15:18–19	187
17:8	154–155, 170
28:1	156
31:48	152
32:2	152
36:6	173
36:7	155
36:8	156
38	193, 205–206

Exodus

6:4	157
6:8	158
7:3	120, 166
13:17	67
14	81
16:35b	157
20:24	8
22:15–17	195
30	24
35	24

Leviticus

4	24
10	24
14:34a	157
18:3	157
20:10	203
20:21	203–204
25:8–16	250
25:23	154
25:38	157
27:16–24	250

Numbers

1:1	23
1:3	158
13:17a	157
13:17b–20	157
13:17b	157
13:29	138
16–17	212–213
20:1	97
20:17	130
20:21	125–126, 141
20:22	97
21:4–9	214
21:4	97
21:10–20	97
21:12	97–98
21:13	97–98
21:14	135
21:20	97–98
21:21	125–127
21:22	127–132
21:23	130, 132–133
21:24	129, 133
21:25	129, 133, 142–143, 184
21:26	133
21:27–30	134–136
21:31–35	134
21:32	134, 173–175
21:33–35	126, 175
22–24	174
25:1	96, 98
26–36	74–79
26:3	70, 77
26:5–9	214
26:29–32	150
26:52–56	246, 251
27:1–7a	208–218
27:2	209–211
27–3–4	211–215
27:5–7a	216–218
27:8–11a	199–207
27:21	163, 179
32:1	82–93, 100–101
32:2	161–162, 178–179
32:3	179–180
32:4	161–162, 178–179
32:5	104–106, 162
32:6	104
32:7–15	183–187
32:16–17	181–182
32:16	102–104
32:17a	101–102

32:17b	104, 170–171, 180–182	4:5	114
32:18	169–171	4:45	114
32:19	169–171	7:1	115, 118, 120, 127, 137,
32:20	107, 162		166–167
32:21	162	11:25	166
32:22	107	12:13–14	8
32:23	187	13:1	42
32:24	107	20:10–15	115, 124–125
32:25	161–162	20:10	116
32:26	162	20:15	115, 124, 137
32:27	163	20:16–17	168
32:28	163, 179	20:17	115, 118, 120, 127, 137,
32:29	163		166–167
32:30	163–164	21:15–17	198
32:31–32	182–183	23:3	118
32:33	107, 171	23:4	170
32:34–38	107, 140–148	23:7	118
32:34–36	140	23:8	187
32:36	180–182	25:5–10	199–207
32:39–42	148–153		
32:40	172	*Joshua*	
33:50–56	79	3:15–17	108
33:54	246	4:12–13	102
34:13	246	6–10	58–60
36:1	244–246	10:40–42	59–62
36:2	246–248	11:15–23	61
36:3–4	248–252	13	84–85
36:5	252–254	13:8	183
36:6	254–255	13:18	132, 147
36:7	255–256	13:21	78
36:8–9	256–257	13:25–26	90
36:10–12	257	17:1–12	232–235
		18:1	61, 106
Deuteronomy		21:37	132
1:20–27	139	22:4	183
2:6	117	22:9	162
2:8	119, 130–132	22:19	164–165
2:9	140	22:23	165
2:13	97, 114		
2:19	175	*Judges*	
2:24–25	115–116, 166	1:27–28	235
2:26	116	5:14	151
2:27–29	116–120	5:16	100
2:30	120, 166	5:17	151
2:31	120–121, 166	10:17	152
2:32–35	121, 166	11:19–22	109
2:36–37	121–122		
3:1–11	122, 167–169	*Ruth*	
3:12	123–124	2:1	207
3:13	123–124	4:5	205
3:14	123	4:6	208
3:15	123	4:10	205
3:16–17	123	4:14–17	205

Index of Ancient Sources

1 Samuel
10a:6–9	170
12:8	57

2 Samuel
9:4	151
9:5	151
17:27	151
24:5	85

1 Kings
4:7–19	235–240
11:26–12:25	54

2 Kings
10:33	89
13:17	89
13:25	89
15:29	92
17:6	223
17:24–27	229–230
17:24	223
21:11	138
23:4	47
23:15	47
24:2	142

1 Chronicles
2:21–23	251
2:34–35	205
23:22	205

Ezra
2:61–63	202

Nehemiah
7:63	202
11:1	247

Isaiah
15:4	94
16:8–9	94
16:9	85

Jeremiah
41:5	49
48:2	94
48:32	85
48:34	94
48:45	94

Hosea
6:8	84

Amos
6:13	90

Tobit
6:12	205

Index of Authors

Aaron, David H. 191–192, 211, 250
Achenbach, Reinhard 21, 25–27, 73, 82, 85, 95, 105–107, 109, 117, 119, 132, 149, 155, 158, 170, 172, 199, 209, 243, 247–248
Aharoni, Yohanan 89, 219, 235–238
Albertz, Rainer 16, 27–30, 39, 43, 54, 60, 126, 132, 172, 184
Alt, Albrecht 235–236
Arie, Eran 89
Artus, Olivier 183, 186–187
Ashley, Timothy R. 70
Assis, Elie 165
Astruc, Jean 7

Baden, Joel 10, 19, 27, 43, 213
Baentsch, Bruno 83
Ballhorn, Egbert 233–234
Barkay, Gabriel 239
Bartlett, John R. 126, 133
Bauks, Michaela 154
Ben-Barak, Zafira 195–196
Benjamin, Don C. 195, 206
Berner, Christoph 34
Bieberstein, Klaus 34
Bienkowski, Piotr 92–93
Binns, L. Elliott 2
Blanco Wißmann, Filipe 55
Blenkinsopp, Joseph 47
Blum, Erhard 21, 32–33, 36, 42, 89, 141–142
Boer, Roland 195
Boling, Robert G. 138, 151, 232
Boorer, Suzanne 186
Brett, Mark G. 155, 242
Brettler, Marc 61
Briant, Pierre 231
Budd, Philip J. 11–12, 70, 83, 199
Bunimovitz, Shlomo 228–229
Butler, Trent C. 60

Campbell, Anthony 9
Campbell Jr., Edward F. 207
Carr, David M. 8, 17–18, 21, 33, 43–44, 53, 63, 106–107, 154, 172, 256, 263
Chavel, Simeon 191–192, 201, 206, 253, 256

Cocco, Francesco 69, 204, 212
Cortese, Enzo 235
Crawford, Sidnie 72
Cross, Frank Moore 50, 90

Daviau, Paulette M. M. 147
Davies, Eryl 13, 70, 199, 202, 206, 254
Davies, G. I. 97
Davies, Philip R. 65
de Pury, Albert 19, 155
de Vaulx, J. 83
de Vaux, R. 218
de Wette, Wilhelm M. L. 7–8, 50
Dearman, J. Andrew 101, 146
Douglas, Mary 71

Elliger, Karl 21
Eskenazi, Tamara C. 196

Faust, Avraham 228
Finkelstein, Israel 48, 53, 59, 62–66, 86–88, 142, 228, 251
Fischer, Irmtraud 143
Fishbane, Michael 192, 212
Fistill, Ulrich 69, 83
Fleming, Daniel E. 56–57, 109, 138
Forrer, Emil 92, 239
Forsling, Josef 70
Frankel, David 213
Frevel, Christian 3, 23, 37–40, 45–46, 54, 57–61, 66, 69–71, 74, 78, 93, 118, 142–143, 162, 191, 210, 213, 253–254
Frey, Jörg 50
Frolov, Serge 151

Galil, Gershom 92
Gaß, Erasmus 133, 233, 235
Germany, Stephen 35–36, 43, 59, 61–62, 83, 116, 118, 120–121, 124, 135, 157, 167–168, 174, 247
Gertz, Jan Christian 3
Graf, Karl Heinrich 1
Gray, George B. 82
Guillaume, Phillippe 4, 19, 63–65, 90, 143, 154, 163–164, 250

Index of Authors

Gunkel, Hermann 141
Gunneweg, A.H. 161

Haran, Menahem 18
Hawk, L. Daniel 230, 233–234
Hensel, Benedikt 50–51, 55, 142, 224, 243
Hjelm, Ingrid 52
Hobson, Russell 242
Holzinger, Hermann 230
Homsher, Robert S. 137
Hupfeld, Hermann 8
Hutchens, Kenneth D. 158
Hutzli, Jürg 155, 158

Itach, Gilad 219–223

Japhet, Sara 251
Jeon, Jaeyoung 159
Jericke, Detlef 138, 186
Ji, Chang-Ho C. 130

Kilchör, Benjamin 202–203
Kislev, Itamar 214, 251, 254–255
Kleiman, Assaf 53
Klostermann, August 21
Knauf, Ernst Axel 9, 29, 47–48, 55–56, 60–61, 64–65, 68, 90, 101, 106, 117, 135–136, 139, 142–143, 151, 164–165, 170, 179, 186–187, 210, 217, 232, 235
Knierim, Rolf P. 249
Knohl, Israel 21–22
Knoppers, Gary N. 51–52, 55, 226, 251
Köckert, Matthias 155
Kratz, Reinhard G. 34–37, 40–41, 43, 59, 66
Kuenen, Avraham 18, 53

Lemaire, André 89, 95, 151–152, 218, 238
Levine, Baruch 13–14, 82, 86, 96, 128, 174, 199–200, 212–213, 232, 249
Levy, Daniel 209
Lipschits, Oded 47–48
Litke, John D. 199, 216, 257
Liverani, Mario 226
Lohfink, Norbert 110
London, Gloria 222–223
Lonergan, Bernard 47
Lundbom, Jack R. 206

MacDonald, Burton 130
MacDonald, Nathan 1, 68–69
Magen, Yitzhak 50, 55

Marquis, Liane M. 83, 102, 106, 162–163, 184
Matthews, Victor H. 206
Mazar, Amihai 158
Mendenhall, George E. 137
Milgrom, Jacob 12, 69, 74, 102–103, 105, 129, 157, 192, 199, 209–211, 215, 255, 257
Miller, J. Maxwell 97
Mittmann, Siegfried 83, 122, 129, 144

Na'aman, Nadav 46, 48, 63–64, 225–227, 230, 236, 239
Niditch, Susan 118
Nihan, Christoph 18, 21–22, 24, 34, 52, 61–62, 203–204
Nodet, Etienne 52
Nöldeke, Theodore 18
Noth, Martin 1–2, 8–9, 11, 24, 70, 74, 82, 98, 100, 130, 138, 144, 158, 191, 209, 249, 252

Oded, Bustanay 230
Olson, Dennis T. 68–70
Oswald, Wolfgang 143
Otto, Eckart 7, 26, 72, 96, 116–117, 119, 122–123, 127, 168–169, 206

Pakkala, Juha 42–46
Parker, Bradley J. 226
Perlitt, Lothar 19–20
Pitkänen, Pekka 252
Plöger, Josef G. 120, 122

Rendtorff, Rolf 13, 17–18
Robker, Jonathan M. 174
Röllig, Wolfgang 138
Römer, Thomas 1–2, 9, 19, 22–24, 33, 44, 57, 60–61, 109, 142
Rose, Martin 9
Roskop (Erisman), Angela 42, 93, 173

Samuel, Harald 210
Satlow, Michael L. 195–198
Schenker, Adrian 204
Schmid, Hans Heinrich 31–32
Schmid, Konrad 3, 10, 17–18, 34, 54, 56, 141–142
Schmidt, Ludwig 14–15, 70, 81, 83, 100, 104–105, 107, 122, 125–127, 168, 170, 175, 191, 205, 247
Schmitt, Hans-Christoph 135–136
Schorch, Stefan 52
Schorn, Ulrike 83, 90, 100, 102, 148

Index of Authors

Schwartz, Baruch J. 22
Seebass, Horst 15–16, 83, 106, 133, 158, 174–175, 201–202, 210, 230–231, 245–246, 249, 253
Sergi, Omer 49, 95, 142
Singer-Avitz, Lily 48, 239
Ska, Jean Louis 18–19
Smelik, K.A.D. 146
Snaith, Norman H. 151, 245
Staubli, Thomas 83
Stern, Ephraim 224, 239
Stordalen, Terje 135

Tammuz, Oded 230
Tobolowsky, Andrew 143
Tolkien, J.R.R. 49

Van Der Toorn, Karel 54
Van Seters, John 31–32, 59, 83, 109, 126, 133, 174

Weingreen, Jacob 192
Weippert, Manfred 122, 135
Wellhausen, Julius 11, 18, 236
Wenham, Gordon J. 200
Wevers, John W. 178
Wöhrle, Jakob 20, 141–142, 155–156
Wolff, Hans Walter 53
Wright, John W. 231
Wüst, Manfried 83, 100–102, 231, 247

Yasur-Landau, Asaf 228–229

Zenger, Erich 17, 37–40, 96
Zertal, Adam 218–223, 225–228, 238
Ziemer, Benjamin 43

Subject Index

Aaron/Aaronites 209
Abra(ha)m 20, 48, 52, 61, 155–157, 187, 243, 268
Ammon 87, 93–95, 134, 147, 151
Amorites 115, 137–139, 165–169
Assyria(ns) 62–68, 90–93, 223–228, 239–240

Babylon(ians) 20
– Exiles *see Golah*
Bethel 47–49

Canaan 20–21, 93, 154–159, 164–165
Cisjordan *see Canaan*

Deuteronomistic History 8–10
Documentary Hypothesis 7–16

Edom 117–119
Eleazar 161, 163, 178–179, 209, 245–246
"Empirical" evidence 42–46

Farewell to the Yahwist 17–18

Gad 101, 140–144
Gilead
– Land 84–95, 162–163
– Ancestor 150–152, 218–219
Golah 20–21, 67–68, 156, 250

Hazael 66, 89
Heshbon
– City 95, 134–136, 180
– Sihon, king of 110–125
– Song of 134–136
Holiness Code 21–22

Israel
– Northern Kingdom 53–56, 62–67, 88–93

– Pan/All 141–144
– Pre-Monarchic/United 65–66, 235–236
– 'True' *see Golah*
– Postexilic community *see Samaria*

Jacob 141–144
Jazer 84–95, 134, 174–175
Jeroboam II 53–56
Jordan 56, 67, 81–82, 93
Joshua 56–68
Josiah *see Joshua*
Judah
– Exiled *see Golah*
– Land 56–68

Manasseh 148–153, 218–219, 232–235
Mesha 88–90, 96–97, 101, 140–141, 146–147
Moab 70–72, 81, 88–90, 93–94, 96–98
Moses 161–162, 252–254

Nimshi(des) 53–56, 107–109

Og 115, 121–122, 149, 152–153
Omri(des) 65–66, 88–90, 93

Priestly Writings 20–22, 153–165, 208–218

Refugees 62–65
Reuben 90, 128

Samaria/Samaritans 49–52, 218–244
Sihon 109–139, 165–169

Zelophehad
– Daughters 218–244
– Self 212–216
– Wife 193, 199–200

Archaeology and Bible

Edited by
Israel Finkelstein, Deirdre Fulton, Oded Lipschits,
Christophe Nihan, Thomas Römer, and Konrad Schmid

Since the collapse of traditional "biblical archaeology," biblical studies and the archaeology of ancient Israel have developed largely independently of each other. The series *Archaeology and Bible* aims to build new bridges between these two academic disciplines by providing original, cutting-edge critical studies on the literature and the material culture of ancient Israel in its Levantine context from archaeological, epigraphic, and biblical perspectives. To that effect, the series will especially promote inter- and trans-disciplinary studies, as well as new methodological and theoretical approaches in order to bring archaeological and biblical research into a close conversation.

ISSN: 2698-4520
Suggested citation: ArchB

All available volumes can be found at *www.mohrsiebeck.com/archb*

Mohr Siebeck
www.mohrsiebeck.com